CASH FOR
GRAD SCHOOL™

OTHER BOOKS BY CYNTHIA RUIZ MCKEE AND PHILLIP C. MCKEE JR.

Cash for College™, Revised Edition

Cash for College's™ Write It Right

CASH FOR GRAD SCHOOL™

THE ULTIMATE GUIDE TO GRAD SCHOOL SCHOLARSHIPS

Cynthia Ruiz McKee and Phillip C. McKee

HarperResource
An Imprint of HarperCollins*Publishers*

I dedicate this book to Sheri Schad Townsley, a true friend and kindred spirit. There's Lucy and Ethel, Laverne and Shirley, and you and me. Through every adventure and mishap, you always believed in and supported my endeavors.

—CRM

HarperCollins books may be purchased for educational, business, or sales promotional use. For information please write: Special Markets Department, HarperCollins Publishers Inc., 10 East 53rd Street, New York, NY 10022.

FIRST EDITION

Designed by Richard Oriolo

Library of Congress Cataloging-in-Publication Data

McKee, Cynthia Ruiz.
   Cash for grad school : the ultimate guide to grad school scholarships / Cynthia Ruiz
  McKee and Phillip C. McKee.—1st ed.
    p. cm.—(A HarperResource book)
  Includes index.
  ISBN 0-688-13956-6
   1. Student aid—United States—Handbooks, manuals, etc. 2. Graduate students—Scholarships, fellowships, etc.—United States—Handbooks, manuals, etc. I. McKee, Phillip C. II. Title. III. Series.

LB2337.4.M2855 2003
378.3'3—dc21   2002192230

04 05 06 07 08 WBC/CW 10 9 8 7 6 5 4 3 2 1

CONTENTS

ACKNOWLEDGMENTS

As in most endeavors, it takes the coordination of a lot of people to get a book this size into print and in bookstores. We would like to thank Jessica Chin, production editor, for all her attention to details to make this a better book. Nicholas Darrell, assistant editor, always had a smile in his voice when we talked and an encouraging word in all our e-mails. Though we didn't work as much with Toni Sciarra, senior editor, she's responsible for this book being written and published. Eileen Fallon, our one and only agent, worked out the details for the contract. We are indebted to Shirley Banez, Assistant Director of the University of Texas at San Antonio, Financial Aid Office. Her insight and suggestions made the financial aid chapter so much better.

Dr. Holly Bell, Dr. Matt Kaufmann, and Pat Cathcart, friends and sounding boards, provided listening ears when the little things, and not so little things, started getting the best of me. James L. Thompson III never got tired of hearing my woes, or at least never admitted it. Our son, Phillip C. McKee III, always had a joke to cheer us up when the end seemed so far away. Last, and absolutely as important, are all the students and families whom we've worked with and who need the information in this book. To all of you, we give a great big, heartfelt thanks.

PART I

Please Read This Page Before Using This Book

Every effort has been made to ensure that the information provided in this book is up-to-date and correct. Scholarship foundations, companies, and other organizations create and discontinue scholarships continually, change the criteria, relocate, or go out of business without warning. We have no control over these occurrences. Please notify us of any listings that need to be updated, so that we can locate current information to provide to you and anyone else who contacts us.

Some discrepancies are unavoidable because of the lengthy lead time in producing a book of this type. Our database currently contains over 400,000 listings. Even though we are constantly updating the listings, with your help we can continue to provide quality information to all of our students. If you hear of any new scholarships, we would be glad to add them to our database.

With this book, we have provided you with the most comprehensive, step-by-step guide available for searching for scholarship opportunities. Your success will de-

pend on your qualifications and on your perseverance in applying to as many scholarships and contests as possible. We can't guarantee that you will receive a scholarship or fellowship; anyone who makes that kind of promise is probably a scam artist. You can be assured, however, that this book contains a great deal of relevant information that will help you in the application process.

Please take note that our company name is: College Resource Materials, and not any other derivative of that name.

Thank you for purchasing our book, and we hope to hear from you soon. Contact us at:

College Resource Materials
1633 Babcock Road, PMB 425
San Antonio, TX 78229–4725
Phone and fax: (210) 877–0913
mckee@cashforcollege.com
http://www.cashforcollege.com

ONE

HOW TO USE THIS BOOK

Congratulations, you've decided to go to graduate or professional school. Attending a graduate or professional school is more expensive than attending an undergraduate degree program. At the graduate and professional school level, there is no access to Federal Pell Grants and Federal Supplemental Educational Opportunity Grants (FSEOG). Therefore, once you've decided to pursue a graduate or professional degree, you must next figure out how to pay for it. This book will help you discover different ways of funding a graduate or professional education.

Before we go any further, we would like to explain what we mean when we refer to graduate or professional school. A graduate school is any institution that offers a master's or doctorate degree. For a complete listing of the various degrees, please refer to Chapter 2, Key to Abbreviations. We divide graduate education into four disciplines: arts, humanities, sciences, and social sciences. Each category includes many subdisciplines. Although graduate schools may subdivide their departments differently, we decided to organize the disciplines in this manner to simplify the overall organization of the book.

The **Arts** include: architecture, architecture-landscape, art, art history, cinematography, conservation art, creative writing, dance, drama, drawing, film, fine arts, interior design, museum studies, music, numismatic studies, painting, performance art, photography, playwriting, printmaking, screenwriting, sculpture, studio art, television, theater arts, and any visual art. The **Humanities** include: classics (Latin and Greek), communications and mass communications, comparative literature, history, journalism, languages, linguistics, literature, philosophy, religion, rhetoric and debate, speech, and theology (including theological professions). The **Sciences** include: archeology, audiology, aviation, biology, biochemistry, chemistry, computer science and information science, dietetics, engineering, environmental studies, food service, forensic science, geology, kinesiology, math, medicine and related fields, nutrition, paleontology, physics, speech pathologies, and statistics. The **Social Sciences** include: agribusiness, anthropology, area and ethnic studies, aviation management, banking, business and related fields, economics, education and related fields, family and consumer science, geography, government, health care and administration, hospitality and related fields, law, library science, marketing, political science, psychology, public administration, public relations, real estate, services (cooking, etc.), sports administration, social work, sociology, statistics, travel and tourism, and urban planning.

Professional schools include: law school (L.L.M. and J.D.), medical school (M.D., M.D.-Ph.D., and O.D.), dental school (D.D.S.), nursing school (M.S.N. and Ph.D.), veterinary school (D.V.M.), and pharmacy school (Pharm.D.). Although many other degrees are considered to be professional degrees, such as degrees in architecture, education, engineering, and more, we aren't referring to them when using the term professional school. Masters and doctorate degrees in architecture, business, education, engineering, sciences, and social work all fall into the category of graduate school. In this book, scholarship listings for law school are included in the social science section and scholarship listings for medical, dental, nursing, pharmacy, and veterinary schools are in the science section.

A student shouldn't have to select a degree program solely on a financial basis. Unfortunately, the reality of today's economy makes tuition a major factor in deciding which graduate or professional school to attend—and even whether to obtain an advanced degree at all.

Applying to, and financing, graduate or professional school shouldn't be a frustrating experience for students. Though you may have seen articles in magazines suggesting that parents set aside $125–$240 per month per child in order to save for their child's undergraduate college education, not much is written about financing an advanced degree. To be able to save that kind of money even for undergraduate school would require that most families do without something basic, such as food or shelter. It's for these reasons that we formed College Resource Materials and began writing the *Cash* series of books (*Cash for College* was our first).

While our son, Phillip III, was still in middle school, he decided that he wanted to attend an Ivy League college when he graduated from high school. Since he was an excellent student, we knew he stood a good chance of attending any school he chose. We knew that tuition costs were steadily rising, but we felt that he was bright enough to be offered scholarships from private sources. Besides, high school graduation and college seemed so far away. We thought we had plenty of time before we had to look into scholarships.

In the spring of 1989, when our son was a junior in high school, we began researching college scholarships, thinking we were getting a head start on the process. Much to our dismay, we found there were many scholarship opportunities that Phillip had missed. In fact, students should begin obtaining free cash for college as early as kindergarten!

During the next six months, we spent more than 100 hours reading every reference we could find to locate possible scholarships. While we sifted through information, we saw many students and parents come in, take a book or two off the shelf, stare at the pages as if the book was written in hieroglyphics, and then leave within an hour or two. There was no way these people could have found more than a handful of scholarships. Researching scholarships takes time, even if you're skilled at doing it.

By the time our son graduated from high school, he had been accepted by all the schools to which he applied, approached by four other universities offering full scholarships, and offered over $342,000 in scholarships. Although our son was an extraordinary student, he wasn't the class valedictorian or salutatorian. Nonetheless, he was offered more free scholarship money than any other student in his class.

Our son completed his undergraduate degree at Yale University in May 1994. During his senior undergraduate year, he began the process of applying to graduate school. We learned a great deal in the process. By the time he graduated from Yale, he was actively recruited by several graduate schools. He decided to attend Harvard's Graduate School of History. To date, our son has received over $500,000 in scholarship offers. Phillip is currently working and living in the Washington, DC, area. If and when he decides to further his education, we will start searching for scholarships and fellowships a year before he registers.

We're sharing our story to demonstrate that students don't have to have straight A's or a 4.0 grade point average (GPA) to win scholarships. Some competitions are based solely on submission of an essay. In addition, there are all types of scholarships, fellowships, grants, and writing competitions that can yield much-needed money at all levels of education. Scholarship competitions aren't just for high school seniors.

We founded College Resource Materials (CRM) in August of 1989 and have since helped thousands of students across the country and abroad in obtaining money to pursue vocational/technical, associate, baccalaureate, graduate, and professional degrees. Cynthia assumed the task of organizing all the information we found. We've seen many students who have benefitted from using our methods in their application processes.

College Resource Materials is a family-owned and operated company that knows how difficult and expensive it is to send a student to college and graduate/professional school. We realize that not every student knows how to research scholarships and fellowships for advanced degrees, how to stay organized while applying for them (in order not to miss an application deadline), or has the time and/or the inclination to do either.

Through our products and services we have provided step-by-step advice on how, when, and where to apply for scholarships, grants, fellowships, and loans. Our first book, *Cash for College*™, was published in 1993, with a revised edition released in 1999. *Cash for College*™ offers detailed advice on how to apply for undergraduate college money, as well as having the largest scholarship listing of any book on the market. *Cash for Graduate and Professional School* offers the most advice and guidance on the application process and the largest and most comprehensive listing of scholarships and fellowships of any book or CD on the market. It contains just over 2,500 individual listings, which represent over 1,000,000 scholarships, fellowships, grants, and internships offering over $8.5 billion in financial assistance. In the Appendices, we've included the forms we created to make the chore of applying that much easier.

We've heard many parents and students say that most books on the subject of financing a college education are hard to use, difficult to understand, and simply don't offer enough help when it comes to knowing what to do, how to do it, and when to start. Well, not anymore. Having helped thousands of students of all types and ages obtain scholarships for undergraduate and graduate degrees, in addition to having gone through the process ourselves, we're able to give you the shortcuts and warn you about possible pitfalls.

This book is straightforward, organized, and accessible. We want you to feel confident about applying for scholarships and fellowships. That's why this book doesn't just offer information on where to look for resources. There's more to obtaining financial assistance than just knowing where to look. Early chapters assist you not only in surviving the application process but also in refreshing the organizational skills needed to

stay on track. A missed deadline is money lost. Being neat, orderly, and prompt are essential in giving the best impression possible to a scholarship committee. If you only have one shot, make it your best one! We'll help you do just that.

How We Obtained Our Information

The information in this book about the scholarships, fellowships, and grants offered by organizations, foundations, clubs, or businesses was obtained either by direct contact or by information printed in a magazine or newspaper. We contacted scholarship committees by letter, fax, or phone to get an accurate description of the scholarship and eligibility requirements, address, and (when available) phone, fax number, e-mail, and web sites.

We update our addresses each summer or when we're contacted by an organization, foundation, club, business, college, or university about a change in eligibility requirements or address. The fact that some addresses change is a reality we all must face. Even after we update the addresses each summer, a company or organization may relocate. When there is a change, we update our computer listing, but you might find out about the change before we do. We invite you to notify us of any such changes so we can include them in future editions. You might also want to check our web site (www.cashforcollege.com) for updates and additional information.

If you know of a scholarship or fellowship not listed (whether it's offered by a foundation, organization, business, college, or university), please let us know!

A Taste of What's to Come

The chapters are organized according to the step-by-step process of researching and applying for money. You'll learn how to apply effectively for scholarships, fellowships, and grants and to graduate or professional school (**Getting In**). We give you information on requesting applications and provide examples of what you should list on an extracurricular activities résumé (**Creative Résumés**). You'll also learn what you should be doing to save time (**Organization Made Easy**) and about special scholarship categories (**Getting Down to**

Specifics). Subsequent chapters provide the nuts and bolts of requesting recommendation letters, succeeding in interviews, and writing essays and personal statements (**Writing Persuasive Essays and Personal Statements**).

The **Glossary** provides easy-to-understand explanations of terms students and parents may encounter during the application process. Not only does it explain what FAFSA, GMAT, GRE, MCAT, LSAT, and other acronyms mean, but it also points out the differences between scholarships, fellowships, and grants and loans, and the various types of grants and loans.

The scholarship and fellowship listings in *Cash for Graduate and Professional School* are different from those in *Cash for College*. Scholarships are listed alphabetically, each with a respective number. To make it easier for students perusing the listings to decide whether an entry might be useful, to the right of that number, in parentheses, are letters (A for arts, H for humanities, S for sciences, and SS for social sciences), and/or the word "contest." There is an **At-a-Glance Index** just before the scholarships listings that cross-references the listings by major qualifying characteristics, ethnicity, contests, gender, disabilities, religious affiliation, and more.

Although the **At-a-Glance Index** is a fast way to look for scholarships and fellowships offered by organizations, foundations, clubs, and businesses within each discipline, we strongly suggest that you take the time to read through all the listings. You might find a scholarship, fellowship, grant, or internship for which you unexpectedly qualify.

Not all of the awards in the listings go toward college tuition. Some go directly to the student to use at his/her discretion. Many of these types of competitions do not evaluate academic achievement or extracurricular activities or specify a field of study. The winners are chosen solely on the merits of what they've entered. By winning enough of these types of competitions, the student can easily pay for textbooks, living expenses, or any other incidental expenses.

Colleges, universities, and professional schools also offer a variety of scholarships, fellowships, and grants.

The information on school-based scholarships, grants, loans, and work-study is readily available on the Internet, so we have chosen not to include it in this book.

How Concerned Others Can Help

When searching for financial assistance for graduate or professional school students, we strongly suggest that at least one person (spouse or parent) get actively involved in the process. All possible opportunities must be investigated and tracked. There are letters to write, postcards to mail, and applications to type. The applicant is usually inundated with writing essays and personal statements for scholarships, fellowships, grants, and program applications, as well as pursuing extracurricular activities, going to school, and/or working. Any help another person can provide will be appreciated. Think of it as an investment in your loved one's future.

Our Advice to You

Read all the chapters, then start working. If you follow our suggestions, send out as many inquiries as possible to scholarships and fellowships for which you qualify, and stay on track in your application process, you will significantly improve your chances of getting one or more awards. Good luck and best wishes as you build toward your future and realize your dreams!

Don't think any question is stupid or silly. If you've never applied for scholarships and fellowships, or to graduate and/or professional school, you can't be expected to know all the answers. Remember, we're here for you. If there's anything you don't understand in this book, read it again or contact us.

College Resource Materials
1633 Babcock Rd. PMB 425
San Antonio, TX 78229
(210) 877–0913 (phone and fax)
mckee@cashforcollege.com
http://www.cashforcollege.com

T W O

KEY TO ABBREVIATIONS AND ACRONYMS

GENERAL LIST

AACSB	American Assembly of Collegiate Schools of Business
AADSAS	American Association of Dental Schools Application Service
AALS	Association of American Law Schools
AAMC	Association of American Medical Schools
ABA	American Bar Association
ABD	All But Dissertation
ACT	American College Testing Service
AIE	Association of International Educators (was NAFSA)
ALP	Alternative Loan Program (private loan portion of MedLoan Program)
AMCAS	American Medical College Application Service
AOA	American Optometric Association
BIA	Bureau of Indian Affairs

CGS	Council of Graduate Schools
CM	Congressional Methodology
COE	Cost of Education
COPA	Council of Postsecondary Accreditation
CWSP	College Work-Study Program (Federal)
DAT	Dental Admissions Test
DOE	Department of Energy
ED	Department of Education
EDP	Early Decision Program
EFN	Exceptional Financial Need (Federal Scholarship)
EMSAP	Early Medical School Acceptance Program
ETS	Educational Testing Service
FADHPS	Financial Assistance for Disadvantaged Health Professions Students
FAF	Financial Aid Form (no longer used, now called PROFILE Registration)
FAFSA	Free Application for Federal Student Aid

FAO	Financial Aid Office or Officer
FAT	Financial Aid Transcript
FICA	Federal Insurance Corporation of America (Social Security Tax)
FLAS	Foreign Language and Area Studies
FY	Fiscal Year
GAPSFAS	Graduate and Professional School Financial Aid Service
GEM	Graduate Education for Minorities
GMAC	Graduate Management Admissions Council
GMAT	Graduate Management Admissions Test
GRA	Graduate Research Assistant (also called RA)
GRE	Graduate Record Examinations
GSL	Guaranteed Student Loan (now called Federal Stafford Loan)
GTA	Graduate Teaching Assistant (also called TA or TF—Teaching Fellow)
HACU	Hispanic Association of Colleges and Universities
HBCU	Historically Black Colleges and Universities
HEA	Higher Education Act
HEAL	Health Education Assistance Loan
HPSL	Health Professions Student Loan
IIE	Institute of International Education
IREX	International Research and Exchange Board
LAAB	Landscape Architectural Accreditation Board
LAL	Law Access Loan
LSAT	Law School Admissions Test
LSDAS	Law School Data Assembly Service
MAT	Miller Analogies Test
MCAT	Medical College Admissions Test
MELAB	Michigan English Language Assessment Battery
MMPI	Minnesota Multiphasic Personality Inventory
NAFSA	National Association for Foreign Student Affairs (now Association of International Educators)
NAS	National Academy of Sciences
NASA	National Aeronautics and Space Administration
NASFAA	National Association of Student Financial Aid Administrators
NCATE	National Council for Accreditation of Teacher Education
NDSL	National Direct Student Loan (now called Perkins Loan)
NELLIE MAE	New England Loan Marketing Association
NIH	National Institute of Health
NIJ	National Institute of Justice
NIMH	National Institute of Mental Health
NLNGNE	National League of Nursing Graduate Nursing Examination
NPRM	Notice of Proposed Rule Making
NPSAS	National Postsecondary Student Aid Study
NRC	National Research Council
NRSA	National Research Service Award
NSF	National Science Foundation
NTE	National Teaching Examination
NUCEA	National University Continuing Education Association
OAT	Optometry Admissions Test
ONR	Office of Naval Research
PAEG	Prueba de Admisiones para Estudios Graduados
PCAT	Pharmacy College Admissions Test
PHS	Public Health Service
RA	Research Assistant (also called Graduate Research Assistant)
SALLIE MAE	Student Loan Marketing Association, a secondary loan market
SSRC	Social Science Research Council
SSIG	State Student Incentive Grants
TA	Teaching Assistant (also called Graduate Teaching Assistant)
TERI	The Education Resources Institute
TF	Teaching Fellow (same as TA)
TOEFL	Test of English as a Foreign Language

TSE	Test of Spoken English
TWE	Test of Written English
USAF	United Student Aid Fund
USIA	United States Information Agency
VA	Veterans' Affairs
VMAT	Veterinary Medicine Admissions Test
WICHE	Western Interstate Commission for Higher Education

MASTER'S DEGREES

A.M.	Master of Arts
A.M.B.A.	Accounting Master of Business Administration
E.M.B.A.	Executive Master of Business Administration
LL.C.M.	Master of Comparative Law
LL.M.	Master of Law
M.A.	Master of Arts
M.A.A.	Master of Applied Art, Master of Administrative Arts, Master of Aeronautics and Astronautics
M.A.A.B.S.	Master of Arts in Applied Behavioral Science
M.A.A.E.	Master of Arts in Applied Economics, Master of Aeronautical and Astronautical Engineering
M.A.Am.St.	Master of Arts in American Studies
M.A.A.T.	Master of Arts in Art Therapy
M.A.B.S.	Master of Arts in Behavior Science
M.A.C.	Master of Arts in Communications
M.Ac.	Master of Accounting
M.Acc.	Master of Accounting
M.A.C.A.	Master of Arts in Computer Applications
M.A.C.C.T.	Master of Arts in Community College Teaching
M.A.C.E.	Master of Arts in Church Education
M.A.C.T.	Master of Arts in College Teaching
M.Ad.	Master of Arts Administration
M.Ad.Ed.	Master of Arts in Adult Education

M.A.E.	Master of Agricultural Extension, Master of Agricultural Engineering
M.A.Ed.	Master of Arts in Education
M.Ag.	Master of Agriculture
M.Ag.Ed.	Master of Agricultural Education
M.Ag.Ext.	Master of Agricultural Extension
M.Aq.	Master of Aquacultures
M.A.F.C.	Master of Arts in Family Counseling
M.A.H.	Master of Arts in Humanities
M.A.H.E.	Master of Arts in Human Ecology
M.A.H.E.&F.E.	Master of Arts in Home Economics and Family Ecology
M.A.H.R.M.	Master of Arts in Human Resource Management
M.A.H.S.	Master of Arts in Human Services
M.A.H.S.M.	Master of Arts in Human Services Management
M.A.I.A.	Master of Arts in International Affairs
M.A.I.D.	Master of Arts in International Diplomacy, Master of Arts in Interior Design
M.A.I.R.	Master of Arts in International Relations
M.A.I.S.	Master of Arts in International Studies, Master of Arts in Interdisciplinary Studies
M.A.L.T.	Master of Arts in Language Teaching
M.A.M.	Master of Arts Management, Master of Animal Medicine, Master of Aviation Management
M.A.M.F.C.	Master of Arts in Marriage and Family Counseling
M.A.M.R.D.	Master of Agricultural Management and Resource Development

M.A.O.M.	Master of Aerospace Operations Management	M.C.E.	Master of Chemical Engineering, Master of Civil Engineering
M.A.P.A.	Master of Arts in Public Administration, Master of Arts in Public Affairs	M.C.H.	Master of Community Health
M.A.P.E.	Master of Arts in Physical Education	M.C.I.S.	Master of Computer Information Systems
M.Appl.Lit	Master of Applied Literature	M.C.J.	Master of Comparative Jurisprudence, Master of Criminal Justice
M.Appl.M.	Master of Applied Mathematics	M.C.J.A.	Master of Criminal Justice Administration
M.Ap.Sc.	Master of Applied Science	M.C.L.	Master of Comparative Law, Master of Civil Law
M.A.P.P.	Master of Arts in Public Policy		
M.A.P.R.S.	Master of Arts in Pacific Rim Studies	M.C.M.	Master of Church Music
M.A.Psych.	Master of Arts in Psychology	M.C.P.	Master of City Planning, Master of Community Planning, Master of Counseling Psychology
M.A.R.	Master of Arts in Religion, Master of Arts in Research		
M.Arch.	Master of Architectural Engineering	M.Crim.	Master of Criminology
M.Arch.H.	Master of Architectural History	M.C.R.P.	Master of City and Regional Planning
M.Arch.U.D.	Master of Architecture in Urban Design	M.C.S.	Master of Computer Science
M.A.S.	Master of Actuarial Science, Master of Aeronautical Science, Master of Applied Statistics, Master of Archival Studies	M.C.Sc.	Master of Commercial Science
		M.C.S.E.	Master of Computer Science and Engineering
		M.Des.	Master of Design
M.A.T.	Master of Arts in Teaching	M.Des.S.	Master of Design Studies
M.A.U.A.	Master of Arts in Urban Affairs	M.Div.	Master of Divinity
M.A.U.D.	Master of Arts in Urban Design	M.D.S.	Master of Dental Science, Master of Decision Sciences
M.A.U.R.P.	Master of Arts in Urban and Regional Planning		
		M.E.	Master of Engineering
M.A.W.	Master of Arts in Writing	M.E.A.	Master of Engineering Administration, Master of Engineering Architecture
M.B.A.	Master of Business Administration		
M.B.A.I.B.	Master of Business Administration in International Business	M.Ed.	Master of Education
		M.E.D.	Master of Environmental Design, Master of Education of the Deaf
M.B.E.	Master of Business Education, Master of Business Economics		
		M.E.E.	Master of Electrical Engineering
M.B.I.	Master of Biological Illustration	M.E.M.	Master of Engineering Management
M.Biorad.	Master of Bioradiology	M.E.M.S.	Master of Engineering in Manufacturing Systems
M.B.M.	Master of Brand Management		
M.B.S.	Master of Basic Science, Master of Behavioral Science, Master of Building Science	M.Eng.	Master of Engineering
		M.E.P.C.	Master of Environmental Pollution Control
M.B.T.	Master of Business Taxation	M.E.Sc.	Master of Engineering Science
M.C.	Master of Commerce, Master of Counseling, Master of Communication	M.Env.S.	Master of Environmental Science
		M.Ex.St.	Master of Experimental Statistics
M.C.D.	Master of Communication Disorders	M.Ext.Ed.	Master of Extension Education

M.E.P.	Master of Environmental Planning
M.E.R.	Master of Energy Resources
M.E.T.	Master of Education in Teaching
M.F.	Master of Forestry, Master of Finance
M.F.A.	Master of Fine Arts
M.F.E.	Master of Forest Engineering
M.F.R.	Master of Forest Resources
M.F.S.	Master of Family Studies, Master of Foreign Service, Master of Forest Science, Master of Forensic Science
M.F.T.	Master of Family Therapy
M.G.A.	Master of Government Administration
M.G.E.	Master of Geological Engineering
M.G.S.	Master of General Studies, Master of Gerontological Studies
M.G.T.	Master of Gas Technology
M.H.	Master of Health, Master of Humanities
M.H.A.	Master of Health Administration, Master of Hospital Administration
M.H.A.M.S.	Master of Historical Administration and Museum Studies
M.H.C.A.	Master of Health Care Administration
M.H.E.	Master of Health Education, Master of Higher Education, Master of Home Economics
M.H.E.Ed.	Master of Home Economics Education
M.H.Ed.	Master of Health Education
M.H.K.	Master of Human Kinetics
M.H.P.	Master of Heritage Preservation, Master of Historical Preservation
M.H.R.	Master of Human Resources
M.H.S.	Master of Health Services, Master of Human Services
M.H.S.A.	Master of Health Services Administration
M.I.	Master of Insurance
M.I.A.	Master of International Affairs
M.I.B.	Master of International Business
M.I.B.A.	Master of International Business Administration
M.I.D.	Master of Industrial Design, Master of Interior Design
M.I.E.	Master of Industrial Engineering
M.I.L.R.	Master of Industrial and Labor Relations
M.I.L.S.	Master of Information and Library Science
M.Ind.Adm.	Master of Industrial Administration
M.Ind.Ed.	Master of Industrial Education
M.I.M.	Master of Industrial Management
M.I.P.A.	Master of International Public Administration
M.I.P.P.	Master of International Public Policy
M.I.R.	Master of Industrial Relations
M.I.S.	Master of Individualized Studies, Masters of Information Services, Master of Interdisciplinary Studies
M.J.	Master of Journalism
M.J.N.M.M.	Master of Journalism in New Media Management
M.J.S.	Master of Juridical Science
M.L.	Master of Librarianship
M.L.A.	Master of Landscape Architecture, Master of Liberal Arts
M.L.A.U.D.	Master of Landscape Architecture in Urban Development
M.L.I.R.	Master of Labor and Industrial Relations
M.Lib.	Master of Librarianship
M.L.I.S.	Master of Library and Information Science
M.Lit.M.	Master of Liturgical Music
M.L.L.	Master of Law Librarianship
M.L.S.	Master of Legal Studies, Master of Liberal Studies, Master of Library Science, Master of Life Science
M.L.S.P.	Master of Law and Social Policy
M.L.&T.	Master of Law and Taxation
M.M.	Master of Music, Master of Management, Master of Mathematics
M.M.A.	Master of Marine Affairs, Master of Manpower Administration, Master of Medical Art, Master of Musical Art
M.M.B.	Master of Medical Biochemistry
M.M.C.	Master of Mass Communication

M.M.E.	Master of Material Engineering, Master of Mechanical Engineering, Master of Mineral Engineering
M.M.Ed.	Master of Music Education
M.M.F.C.C.	Master of Marriage, Family, and Child Counseling
M.M.F.T.	Master of Marriage and Family Therapy
M.Mgt.	Master of Management
M.M.I.S.	Master of Management Information Systems
M.M.P.	Master of Marine Policy, Master of Museum Practice
M.M.R.	Master of Marketing Research
M.M.S.	Master of Management Science, Master of Marine Science, Master of Materials Science
M.M.Sc.	Master of Management Science, Master of Marine Science, Master of Medical Science
M.Mu.	Master of Music
M.Mus.	Master of Music
M.M.T.	Master of Movement Therapy, Master of Music Teaching
M.N.	Master of Nursing
M.N.A.	Master of Nursing Administration, Master of Nonprofit Administration
M.Nat.Sci.	Master of Natural Science
M.N.E.	Master of Nuclear Engineering
M.N.Ed.	Master of Nursing Education
M.N.S.	Master of Nursing Science, Master of Nutritional Sciences, Master of Natural Sciences, Master of Nuclear Science
M.Nuc.Sc.	Master of Nuclear Science
M.O.B.	Master of Organizational Behavior
M.Oc.E.	Master of Oceanographic Engineering
M.Opt.	Master of Optometry
M.O.D.	Master of Organizational Development
M.O.E.	Master of Ocean Engineering
M.O.T.	Master of Occupational Therapy
M.P.	Master of Pharmacy, Master of Planning
M.P.A.	Master of Public Administration, Master of Public Affairs, Master of Professional Accounting
M.P.Acc.	Master of Public Accounting
M.P.C.	Master of Personnel Counseling
M.P.D.	Master of Product Design
M.P.E.	Master of Physical Education
M.P.E.R.	Master of Personnel and Employee Relations
M.Pet.E.	Master of Petroleum Engineering
M.P.H.	Master of Public Health
M.P.H.Ed.	Master of Public Health Education
M.Pharm.	Master of Pharmacology
M.Phil.	Master of Philosophy
M.P.H.&.T.M.	Master of Public Health and Tropical Medicine
M.P.I.A.	Master of Public and International Affairs, Master of Pacific International Affairs
M.P.M.	Master of Personnel Management, Master of Public Management
M.P.M.&P.H.	Master of Preventive Medicine and Public Health
M.P.N.	Master of Psychiatric Nursing
M.P.O.T.	Master of Psychiatric Occupational Therapy
M.P.P.	Master of Public Policy
M.P.P.A.	Master of Public Policy Administration
M.Prof.Acc.	Master of Professional Accounting
M.P.P.P.M.	Master of Plant Protection and Pest Management
M.Pr.Met.	Master of Professional Meteorology
M.P.R.T.M.	Master of Park, Recreation, and Tourism Management
M.Ps.Sc.	Master of Psychological Science
M.P.S.	Master of Personnel Service, Master of Political Science, Master of Public Service
M.P.T.	Master of Physical Therapy
M.P.V.M.	Master of Preventive Veterinary Medicine
M.Q.S.	Master of Quantitative Systems
M.R.A.	Master of Recreation Administration, Master of Rehabilitation Administration, Master of Resource Administration
M.R.C.	Master of Rehabilitation Counseling

M.R.C.P.	Master of Regional and Community Planning	M.Sc.D.	Master of Science in Dentistry
M.R.E.	Master of Religious Education	M.S.C.Ed.	Master of Science in Continuing Education
M.R.Ed.	Master of Recreation Education	M.S.Ch.E.	Master of Science in Chemical Engineering
M.Rel.Ed.	Master of Religious Education	M.S.Cer.E.	Master of Science in Ceramic Engineering
M.R.E.C.M.	Master of Real Estate and Construction Management	M.S.C.J.	Master of Science in Criminal Justice
M.R.E.D.	Master of Real Estate Development	M.Sc.T.	Master of Science Teaching, Master of Science in Teaching
M.R.M.	Master of Resource Management	M.S.D.	Master of Science in Dentistry, Master of Science in Dietetics
M.R.P.	Master of Regional Planning		
M.R.P.A.	Master of Recreation and Parks Administration	M.S.E.	Master of Science Education, Master of Science in Education, Master of Science in Engineering, Master of Software Engineering
M.R.T.P.	Master of Rural and Town Planning		
M.S.	Master of Science		
M.S.A.	Master of Science in Accounting, Master of Science in Administration, Master of Sport Administration	M.Sec.Sch.Sci.	Master of Secondary School Science
		M.S.Ed.	Master of Science Education, Master of Science in Education
M.S.A.A.E.	Master of Science in Aeronautical and Astronautical Engineering	M.S.E.E.	Master of Science in Electrical Engineering, Master of Science in Environmental Engineering
M.S.A.E.	Master of Science in Aerospace Engineering	M.S.E.M.	Master of Science in Engineering and Mining
M.S.Ag.	Master of Science in Agriculture		
M.S.A.I.	Master of Science In Artificial Intelligence	M.S.E.Mech.	Master of Science in Engineering Mechanics
M.San.Sc.&.P.H.	Master of Sanitary Science and Public Health	M.S.E.Mgt.	Master of Science in Engineering Management
M.S.Ap.Sc.	Master of Science in Applied Science	M.S.E.R.	Master of Science in Energy Resources
M.S.A.S.	Master of Science in Architectural Studies	M.S.Envr.E.	Master of Science in Environmental Engineering
M.S.B.A.	Master of Science in Business Administration	M.S.E.S.S.	Master of Science in Exercise and Sport Studies
M.S.B.E.	Master of Science in Biomedical Engineering	M.S.F.	Master of Science in Finance, Master of Science in Forestry
M.S.C.	Master of Speech Communication, Master of Science in Counseling	M.S.F.S.	Master of Science in Forensic Science, Master of Science in Foreign Service
M.Sc.A.	Master of Social Administration	M.S.G.	Master of Science in Gerontology
M.S.Ch.E.	Master of Science in Chemical Engineering	M.S.H.S.	Master of Science in Health and Safety, Master of Science in Health Systems
M.S.C.E.	Master of Science in Civil Engineering, Master of Science in Computer Engineering		
		M.S.Hyg.	Master of Science in Hygiene

M.S.I.A.	Master of Institutional Administration, Master of Science in International Affairs
M.S.I.E.	Master of Science in Industrial Engineering
M.S.I.E.O.R.	Master of Science in Industrial Engineering and Operations Research
M.S.I.M.	Master of Science in Information Management
M.S.I.R.	Master of Science in Industrial Relations
M.S.I.S.	Master of Science in Information Science
M.S.J.A.	Master of Science in Judicial Administration
M.S.J.P.S.	Master of Science in Justice and Public Service
M.S.K.	Master of Science in Kinesiology
M.S.L.S.	Master of Science in Library Science
M.S.M.	Master of Sacred Music, Master of Science in Management
M.S.Mat.S.E.	Master of Science in Materials Science Engineering
M.S.M.C.	Master of Science in Mass Communication, Master of Science in Marketing Communication
M.S.M.E.	Master of Science in Mechanical Engineering
M.S.Mgt.	Master of Science in Management
M.S.M.I.	Master of Science in Medical Illustration
M.S.M.S.Ed.	Master of Science in Mathematics and Science Education
M.S.M.T.	Master of Science in Medical Technology
M.S.N.	Master of Science in Nursing
M.S.N.A.	Master of Science in Nursing Administration, Master of Science in Nurse Anesthesia
M.S.N.E.	Master of Science in Nuclear Engineering
M.S.O.	Master of Science in Orthodontics
M.S.O.D.	Master of Science in Organizational Development
M.S.O.R.	Master of Science in Operations Research
M.S.O.T.	Master of Science in Occupational Therapy
M.S.P.A.	Master of Science in Public Administration
M.S.Pet.E.	Master of Petroleum Engineering
M.S.P.Ex.	Master of Science in Physiology and Exercise
M.S.P.H.	Master of Science in Public Health
M.S.Poly.	Master of Science in Polymers
M.S.P.S.	Master of Science in Psychological Services
M.S.P.T.	Master of Science in Physical Therapy
M.S.Rad.Sc.	Master of Science in Radiation Science
M.S.S.	Master of Science in Safety, Master of Social Service, Master of Sport Science
M.S.S.A.	Master of Science in Social Administration
M.S.Stat.	Master of Science in Statistics
M.S.S.T.	Master of Science in Science Teaching
M.S.S.W.	Master of Science in Social Work
M.S.T.	Master of Science in Taxation, Master of Science Teaching, Master of Secondary Teaching, Master of Sacred Theology, Master of Science in Teaching, Master of Science in Speech Therapy, Master of Science in Tourism
M.S.T.E.	Master of Science in Technical Education, Master of Science in Transportation Engineering
M.S.T.Ed.	Master of Science in Technical Education
M.S.Text.	Master of Science in Textiles
M.S.T.M.	Master of Science in Technology Management, Master of Science in Tropical Medicine
M.S.T.S.L.	Master of Science in Teaching a Second Language
M.S.U.D.	Master of Science in Urban Design
M.S.V.C.	Master of Science in Vocational Counseling
M.S.W.	Master of Social Work
M.T.	Master of Taxation, Master of Teaching, Master of Technology

M.T.A.	Master of Tax Accounting, Master of Teaching Arts, Master of Theater Arts
M.Tech.	Master of Technology
M.Th.	Master of Theology
M.T.M.H.	Master of Tropical Medicine and Hygiene
M.Tox.	Master of Toxicology
M.T.P.W.	Master of Technical and Professional Writing
M.T.S.	Master of Teaching of Science
M.T.S.C.	Master of Teaching Speech Communication, Master of Technical and Scientific Communication
M.T.T.	Master of Textile Technology
M.U.A.	Master of Urban Affairs, Master of Urban Architecture
M.U.D.	Master of Urban Design
M.U.P.	Master of Urban Planning
M.U.P.P.	Master of Urban Planning and Policy
M.U.R.P.	Master of Urban and Regional Planning, Master of Urban and Rural Planning
M.U.S.	Master of Urban Studies
M.V.A.	Master of Visual Arts
M.Vet.Sc.	Master of Veterinary Science
M.V.S.	Master of Valuation Sciences
M.V.T.E.	Master of Vocational Technical Education
M.W.P.S.	Master of Wood and Paper Science
M.Z.S.	Master of Zoology Science
Phil.M.	Master of Philosophy
S.T.M.	Master of Sacred Theology
Th.M.	Master of Theology
X.M.B.A.	Executive Master of Business Administration

SIXTH-YEAR DEGREES

A.C.E.	Advanced Certificate in Education
Ad.M.Ed.	Advanced Master of Education
Ad.M.L.S.	Advanced Master of Library Science
A.G.C.	Advanced Graduate Certificate
A.G.S.	Advanced Graduate Specialist

A.S.Ed.Cert.	Advanced Specialist in Education Certificate
C.A.G.S.	Certificate of Advanced Graduate Study
C.A.G.S.B.	Certificate in Advanced Graduate Study in Business
C.A.S.	Certificate of Advanced Standing, Certificate of Advanced Study
Ed.A.	Advanced Degree in Education
Ed.S.	Specialist in Education
Eng.	Engineer
Op.S.	Specialist in Optical Science
P.D.	Professional Diploma
Ph.L.	Licentiate in Philosophy
S.A.S.	School Administrator and Supervisor
S.C.C.T.	Specialist in Community College Teaching
Sc.S.	Specialist in Science
S.Ed.	Specialist in Education
S.G.S.	Specialist in Guidance and Counseling
Sp.A.	Specialist in Art
Sp.App.Biol.	Specialist in Applied Biology
S.P.A.	Specialist in Public Administration
S.C.G.	Specialist Certificate in Gerontology
Sp.E.S.	Special Education Specialist
Sp.S.	Specialist in Science
S.S.A.	Specialist in School Administration
S.S.P.	Specialist in School Psychology
S.S.P.A.	Specialist in Speech Pathology and Audiology
S.T.L.	Licentiate in Sacred Theology

DOCTORAL DEGREES

Au.D.	Doctor of Audiology
A.Mus.D.	Doctor of Musical Arts
D.A.	Doctor of Arts
D.A.I.S.	Doctor of Arts in Information Science
D.Arch.	Doctor of Architecture
D.A.T.L.	Doctor of Arts in Training and Learning

D.B.A.	Doctor of Business Administration
D.C.L.	Doctor of Comparative Law, Doctor of Civil Law
D.Chem.	Doctor of Chemistry
D.Crim.	Doctor of Criminology
D.D.S.	Doctor of Dental Surgery
D.E.	Doctor of Engineering
D.Ed.	Doctor of Education
D.E.D.	Doctor of Environmental Design
D.Eng.	Doctor of Engineering
D.Eng.Sc.	Doctor of Engineering Science
D.Env.Des.	Doctor of Environmental Design
D.E.S.	Doctor of Engineering Science
D.F.	Doctor of Forestry
D.F.A.	Doctor of Fine Arts
D.F.E.S.	Doctor of Forestry and Environmental Systems
D.H.S.	Doctor of Health and Safety, Doctor of Human Services
D.I.B.A.	Doctor of International Business Administration
D.I.T.	Doctor of Industrial Technology
D.L.I.S.	Doctor of Library and Information Science
D.L.S.	Doctor of Library Science
D.M.	Doctor of Music
D.M.A.	Doctor of Musical Arts
D.M.D.	Doctor of Medical Dentistry, Doctor of Dental Medicine
D.M.Ed.	Doctor of Music Education
D.Min.	Doctor of Ministry
D.M.L.	Doctor of Modern Languages
D.M.Sc.	Doctor of Medical Science
D.Mus.	Doctor of Music
D.Mus.Ed.	Doctor of Music Education

D.N.	Doctor of Nursing
D.N.Sc.	Doctor of Nursing Science
D.O.	Doctor of Osteopathy
D.P.A.	Doctor of Public Administration
D.P.E.	Doctor of Physical Education
D.P.H.	Doctor of Public Health
Dr.P.H.	Doctor of Public Health
D.R.E.	Doctor of Recreation Education
D.Rel.Ed.	Doctor of Religious Education
D.Sc.	Doctor of Science
D.Sc.D.	Doctor of Science in Dentistry
D.Sc.V.M.	Doctor of Science in Veterinary Medicine
D.S.M.	Doctor of Sacred Music
D.S.Sc.	Doctor of Social Science
D.S.W.	Doctor of Social Work
D.Th.	Doctor of Theology
D.V.M.	Doctor of Veterinary Medicine
Ed.D.	Doctor of Education
J.D.	Doctor of Jurisprudence
J.S.D.	Doctor of Judicial Science
L.L.D.	Doctor of Laws
M.D.	Doctor of Medicine
Pharm.D.	Doctor of Pharmacy
Ph.D.	Doctor of Philosophy
Psy.D.	Doctor of Psychology
Re.D.	Doctor of Recreation
Rh.D.	Doctor of Rehabilitation
Sc.D.	Doctor of Science
S.D.Hyg.	Doctor of Science in Hygiene
S.J.D.	Doctor of Judicial Science
S.T.D.	Doctor of Sacred Theology
Th.D.	Doctor of Theology
V.M.D.	Doctor of Veterinary Medicine

THREE

GETTING IN (INCLUDING ENTRANCE EXAMS)

The playing field has changed since you first applied to colleges and universities for your undergraduate study. In this chapter we'll provide some basic guidelines you may want to consider if you haven't already chosen a graduate or professional school.

Choosing a Program That's Right for You!

The best place to get information about evaluating and selecting a graduate program is from the schools and programs themselves. Contact them and request catalogs and brochures. Visit their web sites. You can also approach professors who taught you, professionals in your career of interest, and mentors whom you respect. There are books and magazines that provide general program information, but why get secondhand information when you can go directly to the source?

Many books and magazines rank schools and programs, but we consider that a drawback. It doesn't matter if a program is number one in the country, in the South, or in a certain major, if you don't like the school,

you won't do your best. You will get out of a program as much as you put into that program. If it's not the best place for you, the school's ranking doesn't matter. Our son attended graduate school at Harvard and although academically he did well, he just wasn't happy. He stayed only one year. We also know scores of graduate and professional school students who absolutely loved Harvard. Harvard was the best place for them, but not for our son. Only you can determine the best place for yourself.

When you were in high school, you might have asked yourself any or all of the following questions about colleges. How far from home is the school located? Will I be able to come home once a month or only once a semester? In what part of the country is the school located? Do I want to see snow, or would I rather be warm during my nine-month school year? Is the college in a small, mid-size, or large community? Is it in the middle of rural America or in the center of a bustling city? How many students live on campus? How many students commute? Will I be able to live on campus if I so choose? Is dormitory housing at a premium? Does the school offer a strong program in my major or possible major? Will I be challenged academically? Do I want to be a big fish in a little pond, or a little fish in a great big lake? How much is it going to cost?

All these questions are still good ones to consider when evaluating graduate programs. You just need to ask yourself a few more. You must ask professors, other students, and any alumni you know for their opinions on at least two topics: faculty and facilities. You may want to consider the quality of the student body and the quality of the school, but both of these areas are harder to evaluate. Exactly what would be the guidelines for objectively determining the quality of the school? Reputation? Endowment? Admission requirements?

As to the quality of the student body, you won't know who will be in your class until you've started the year. Moreover, the quality of the students who are already enrolled may not have that much effect on the quality of the education you'll receive. It all comes back to the fact that you'll get out of your graduate school experience what you're willing to put into it.

You can get information on a school's professors by requesting the school catalog, which will list the professors and where they received their degrees. You might also check *Who's Who in America* and/or the *The Directory of American Scholars*.

Any graduate student, regardless of discipline, will have to use the library. How large are the holdings and how accessible are these resources to graduate students? There should be study carrels, preferably assigned, to ensure that you will have a quiet place to read while you're using the library. If you'll be doing graduate work in the sciences, you'll want to know what type of labs and other facilities are available in your area of study.

At the graduate level, you no longer declare a major like you did in undergraduate school. You must narrow your field of interest to consider a period or a topic. Are you interested in the women's movement since the Industrial Revolution? Perhaps you want to study the economic impact of the Crusades. You might want to ask professors which schools he/she might recommend in the area of study you've selected. You might be able to find five to ten schools that offer studies in your particular area of interest.

The next step is to find out which professors are conducting research and studies in the general area in which you have an interest. Your undergraduate advisor may suggest possible individuals, you can talk to professors when you visit a school, or you can conduct a search on the Internet, which will provide you with a plethora of information about who is currently studying an area. The field of research need not be identical to your interests but close enough so that the professor can give you guidance. You need to find out if the professors are willing to take on another graduate student. You must have an advisor, someone who will not only agree to be your advisor but who you feel you can work with for the duration of your studies.

If you're seeking to work on a master's degree, the time frame for study will vary. It could take one year of intense class work (36 credit hours) and no requirement to write a thesis. Or it could take two years or more if you must write a thesis.

If you're working on a doctoral degree, you could be working from four to seven years or more. The length of time will depend on the area of study (i.e., business vs. science) and sometimes even on the institution.

Will you be getting both your master's and doctorate at the same school? If so, you could be there for eight years. Ask yourself, can I work and study at this particular school and with this particular person for this length of time?

Once you've answered these questions, along comes an even tougher question to answer. Does this school have a large endowment, or will competition for available scholarship money be fierce? This question may not be as important as some of the other ones you've been asking yourself because you have one thing on your side. You've already opened this book. When it comes to selecting a school, make it easier on yourself by applying for scholarships, fellowships, grants, and internships nine to twelve months before you'll have to decide which school to attend. Apply to as many outside scholarships (also called external scholarships) as possible. Outside scholarships can be used at any school you decide to attend.

You're now several steps into the process of determing where you'll be attending graduate or professional school, as well as how you're going to fund your degree. Now for the next steps. If you never thought of yourself as a juggler, you will before the year is out. You will be researching programs, applying to programs, applying for federal assistance, and applying for scholarships, fellowships, and grants all at one time. We know you can do it. It isn't hard. It just requires patience and organization. If you have any questions along the way, please don't hesitate to contact us.

Admission Requirements

Admission requirements for graduate and professional schools vary, just as they do for undergraduate schools. Every graduate or professional program will require an official undergraduate transcript. If you attended more than one undergraduate institution, you may be required to submit a transcript showing all transferred courses accepted by the school where you received your bachelor's degree or you may be required to submit an official transcript from each undergraduate institution you attended. Graduate school admission is usually a joint procedure conducted between a dean's office, a department, and/or the admissions office, so you may have to submit two or more transcripts from each of the undergraduate institutions you attended. If you have already completed some graduate courses, you will have to submit those records as well.

Letters of recommendation are also required, from one to as many as five different people. More information on the best letters of recommendation can be obtained in Chapter 9.

If your graduate school application isn't viewed as reflecting an area of specialization, some departments may require special departmental applications. Departments that might require such special applications include architecture, art, business administration, and education.

Some graduate departments may have additional requirements for admission. If you're pursuing an advanced degree in music, for example, you may have to audition or submit compositions. Art programs will require a portfolio of photographs or slides of finished work. Some programs may require that you submit proposed plans for research, a thesis, or a project. Some departments may require an interview if your credentials aren't as strong as the guidelines specify but they feel you hold promise for success.

Some graduate programs (approximately 20%) require that a student have fluency in at least one foreign language for completion of a master's degree. Some programs may require competency in more than one foreign language, with some programs even specifying which foreign languages in which you must be competent.

Generally, at the master's level, a student must be able to read and comprehend a modern foreign language (such as French, German, Spanish, or Russian). Departmental requirements may vary within a graduate school. At the doctoral level, a student could be required to have competency in two foreign languages.

If you choose to major in certain time periods in history or theology/divinity, you may be required to have competency in Latin. If you're specializing in the women's movement during and after industrialization, most research papers would probably be written in English, which is why some graduate schools have eliminated the language requirements or have reduced it for students at the doctoral level.

The process of admission to professional schools is different from that for graduate study because there are fewer professional schools than graduate programs, and therefore many more applicants than available slots in a given class. This is especially true for students applying to veterinary schools. There are only twenty-seven veterinary schools in the entire country accredited by the American Veterinary Medical Association. There are approximately four times more medical schools than veterinary schools, so the competition for admission to veterinary school can be fierce. Keep in mind that students are under admission consideration at more than one school yet can only enter one program; this is why some students must apply twice, sometimes three times or more before gaining acceptance into a professional school.

If you truly want to gain admission you may have to be willing to apply to schools regardless of their location or supposed ranking. We can't say often enough that you will only get out of your graduate education what you're willing to put into it. You get what you pay for, not necessarily with money, but with your efforts. In order to maintain accreditation by a professional association, schools must meet certain criteria, so you can be assured that there are few bad schools.

As for areas of undergraduate study, some programs could require intense related undergraduate study, while others may accept students with a vastly different undergraduate course of study. A case in point is law school. Entrance to law school doesn't require a social science major. On the other hand, if you're seeking admission into an advanced degree program in physiology, you must have taken extensive undergraduate preparation in the natural and physical sciences. If you want to attend medical school, you don't have to have majored in the sciences as an undergraduate but you must have taken certain sciences, labs, and math classes for admission. An English major can gain acceptance to medical school with the same ease as a biology major, as long as those sciences, lab, and math requirements have been met.

A bachelor's degree is required by all law schools. It is possible to gain entrance to dental and/or medical school at the end of your junior undergraduate year, but you must indeed be a highly qualified candidate. Some veterinary schools may accept you if you've completed as little as two years of undergraduate study, but once again, only if you're an exemplary student.

Admission Standards

As a rule, graduate programs require a B- or 3.0 grade point average (GPA) based on a 4.0 scale. This rule can be interpreted differently from school to school or even from department to department. The minimum GPA may be computed based on all four years, the last two years, or just on courses in that student's major. Some schools may rigidly adhere to the minimum GPA, while others use it as a guideline and will accept students with a lower GPA, if there are mitigating factors.

Entrance Exams

Required entrance exams vary, just as graduate programs do. Check with the graduate schools to which you are considering applying to determine which tests you must take. You should also check with your selected department in each graduate school. Their requirements might be different from those of the school. Professional schools are much more consistent than graduate schools regarding standard entrance exams.

Graduate schools and individual departments may require different exams, or parts of exams, such as the general or appropriate subject test of the Graduate Record Examination (GRE). Some might accept either the GRE or the Miller Analogies Test; some might require both. Generally, a graduate school will require a minimum test score whereas departments may be more lenient or rigid in their requirements.

Entrance exam scores may or may not be accurate predictors for a student's chances of admission, which is why minimum test scores and required exams vary from school to school. Because graduate and professional school classes are much smaller than undergraduate classes, applicants for these programs are expected to be highly qualified. Entrance exams are used to screen applicants and make the selection process easier.

Graduate School Admission Tests

Graduate Record Examination (GRE)

The most commonly used exams for entrance into graduate programs are the Graduate Record Examination (GRE), the Miller Analogies Test (MAT), and the Graduate Management Admissions Test (GMAT). Some schools may have their own admission tests that they require students to take in addition to the aforementioned standardized tests.

The GRE is a general test that is divided into twenty-five different subject fields. The test has three sections: verbal, quantitative, and analytical. Each section is scored separately and attempts to predict a student's scholastic ability in specific areas. The verbal section tests vocabulary and reading comprehension. The quantitative section tests arithmetic, algebra, geometry, and data interpretation. The analytical section covers logic games (which test ability to use logic) and logical reasoning. Sometimes this section also includes analysis of explanation (which provides a story or situation and asks whether there is enough information to answer certain questions). Some graduate programs may not use the score on the analytical section when considering admission. You should ask the schools you are considering whether they require the analytical section or not.

The GRE is only offered as a Computer Adapted Test (CAT) and is administered by private companies. The main advantage to the CAT is that a student only has to give the company a two-day notice to take the test. The test takes three hours, though a student can finish it in less time. Unfortunately, when a student must take a subject test, the test is still administered on paper. This test also takes three hours.

The GRE begins with a tutorial that provides instruction on how to take the test. If the student answers the current question incorrectly, the computer goes to a question at a lower level of difficulty. If the student answers correctly, the computer may go to a question of equal or higher level of difficulty. The harder questions are weighted, and students are not penalized for incorrect answers.

A student can score from 200 to 800 points on each of the three test sections. Though there isn't a hard-and-fast rule on a possible "minimum score," each school will decide on an adequate score for entrance requirement. Generally, scores below 450 on any section are considered inadequate, but there are exceptions to all rules.

Upon completion of the test, students must decide whether they want their score reported without knowing the outcome of the test. Students CANNOT change their minds after knowing their score. Students must retake the exam to have the score reported. Once they answer, the score is immediately made available to them. Graduate programs receive notification of test results within a two-week period, if students want their scores released.

As time goes on, more and more entrance exams will convert to CAT, especially at the graduate level. If you have any questions about the GRE, contact the Educational Testing Service in Princeton, NJ, (609) 921–9000.

Miller Analogies Test (MAT)

The Miller Analogies Test (MAT) provides insight into measurement of verbal and reasoning ability and only takes fifty minutes to complete. The MAT is accepted by many graduate education programs in lieu of the GRE. If you have any questions about this test you should contact your graduate admissions office or the Psychological Corporation, 19500 Bulverde Road, San Antonio, TX 78259, (800) 622–3231 or (210) 339–8710, http://www.tpcweb.com/mat.

Graduate Management Admission Test (GMAT)

The Graduate Management Admission Test (GMAT) is required by graduate business schools. The GMAT requires that a student think systematically and logically, and tests verbal and reasoning skills that have been developed over a long period of time. If you have questions, write to GMAT, CN 6101, Princeton, NJ, 08541–6106, (609) 771–7330. The GMAT also offers four test dates.

National League of Nursing Graduate Nursing Examination (NLNGNE)

The National League of Nursing Graduate Nursing Examination (NLNGNE) is not always required, so students should contact the graduate programs at the nursing schools in which they have an interest.

Professional School Admission Tests

Professional schools all have different entrance exams. Each school may have differing minimum scores for each exam, just as in graduate exams.

Dental Admissions Test (DAT)

Students wanting to enter dental school are required to take the Dental Admissions Test (DAT). Students can obtain applications from a dental school or from the Division of Educational Measurements, American Dental Association, 211 East Chicago Avenue, Chicago, IL 60611, (312) 440–2686, http://www.ada.org. The DAT is offered twice a year.

Medical College Admission Test (MCAT)

Medical schools will require the Medical College Admission Test (MCAT) which is administered by the ACT Program, P.O. Box 451, Iowa City, IA 52243, (319) 337–1276. The MCAT is offered twice a year and is six and a half hours long. Students may want to order a copy of *The MCAT Student Manual* and/or *The Practice Medical College Admission Test*. These books contain sample problems and an explanation of the various types of questions a student will find on the MCAT and will provide a general outline of what each subject area covers. Both of these books can be ordered from the Association of American Medical Colleges, ATTN: Membership and Publication Orders, One Dupont Circle, N.W., Washington, DC 20036. To find out more about the MCAT, log on to http://www.aamc.org/stuapps/admiss/mcat.

Veterinary College Admission Test (VCAT)

There is such a test as the Veterinary College Admission Test (VCAT), but not all veterinary schools require this exam for entrance. Students should contact the admissions office of each of the veterinary schools they are considering. Applications for this exam are available from the Psychological Corporation, 19500 Bulverde Road, San Antonio. TX 78259, (800) 622–3231 or (210) 339–8710, http://www.tpcweb.com/pse/g-vcatO.htm. To find out more about veterinary schools in general log on to http://www.avma.org.

Law School Admissions Test (LSAT)

The Law School Admissions Test (LSAT) is required by law schools. The minimum test score required on the LSAT for entrance varies from school to school. Questions concerning the LSAT should be addressed to the Educational Testing Service, Box 994, Princeton, NJ, 08541, (609) 921–9000 or to the Law School Admissions Service, Box 2000, Newtown, PA 18940, (215) 968–1001, http://www.lsac.org. There are four test dates for the LSAT every year.

Most professional schools will invite students who are under serious consideration to visit the school and be interviewed. After the initial screening of applica-tions and credentials, medical and dental schools usually use these interviews to make their final selections.

If you're dissatisfied with your scores on any of these standardized tests, there are several ways to try to improve your scores. You may want to check with your undergraduate school library or city library to see if any books or videos on preparing for your specific exam are available. You can also purchase test preparation books at local bookstores. Some bookstores and computer stores may even carry software that can help coach students on how to take entrance exams.

A variety of private companies offer test preparation courses for the GRE, MCAT, LSAT, and GMAT, but these classes can be pricey. There are no test prep courses specifically for the DCAT because it is almost identical to the MCAT, excluding the physics section. Although taking these courses is much more expensive than purchasing books on the subject, only you can determine if it may be worth the investment.

FOUR

DISTANCE LEARNING

With the technological advances that have occurred in the last twenty years, it's not surprising to find out that distance learning programs have become such a viable alternative to the traditional on-campus method of obtaining a degree. More and more campuses are offering undergraduate, graduate, and professional certificate programs via technology that makes it possible for students to participate in programs without leaving their home or office.

Some of the more popular degree plans which are conducive to distance learning include accounting, adult and continuing education, advertising, aeronautics, agriculture and animal sciences, some allied health programs, applied arts and science, business and related courses, communications, computer science, criminal justice, economics, education, many engineering programs (among the most popular), food science, foreign languages, government, health care administration, human resource development, illustration, interdisciplinary studies, international relations, liberal arts, library and information science, management, marketing, production and inventory control, psychology, public ad-

ministration, robotics, social sciences, sociology, special education, teacher education, technical communication, telecommunications, and tourism and hospitality.

Employers at large corporations and small businesses have discovered that by providing tuition reimbursement and access to distance learning programs, their employees are able to continue upgrading their skills and degrees, thus becoming more valuable to the company. Employees are encouraged to continue their education without having to worry whether local or nearby educational institutions offer programs they're seeking. This enables many individuals to continue their climb up corporate ladders without having to relocate, uproot their families, or leave a lucrative position within a company.

Distance learning clearly has many benefits, but you should consider whether or not it's right for you. Here are some questions to consider before enrolling: Are you motivated enough to pace yourself? Do you have good time management skills? Are you willing to sit in front of a television or computer screen and listen to a taped version of a class? Are you able to remind yourself that you have a project or paper due? If you answered yes to these questions, you may be a good candidate for this type of program.

Most students who opt for distance learning are over the age of twenty-five, female, and employed and already have completed some college course work. Whatever your reasons for choosing distance learning, you will easily find many challenging programs. Some of the institutions that provide reputable distance learning programs are Arizona State University, Ball State, Embry-Riddle Aeronautical University, George Washington University, New York University, Pennsylvania State University, Purdue University, Rice University, Rochester Institute of Technology, Southern Methodist University, Stanford University, University of Wisconsin-Madison, Virginia Polytechnic Institute & State University, and Western Michigan University.

To learn more about these programs, your best option is to go to the source. Disregard e-mails about on-line or mail-order diplomas, as reputable schools and programs don't send out spam mail. If getting an advanced degree were as easy as supplying someone with your credit card number, everyone would have a doctorate.

Unfortunately, there aren't many outside scholarship programs that can be used to pay for distance learning degrees. Perhaps as more and more institutions offer the programs, scholarship committees will find that they have to change with the times. Awards from writing competitions can be used to pay for distance learning programs. Writing awards are cash awards, rather than scholarships. What you use the money for is your business. You should also inquire with your employer about the possibility of tuition assistance and even reimbursement for distance learning.

If you decide that distance learning is the right method for you, you will find yourself among approximately 30,000 students who are enrolled in degree programs and over 300,000 students who are taking for-credit courses via their computers and/or cable televisions. If you want to get another degree, sometimes you have to be flexible and innovative to reach your goals.

ORGANIZATION MADE EASY

One of the most important things to remember when applying for scholarships, fellowships, and grants is to stay ORGANIZED! The following ten tips will help you stay on track and on time.

1. An Organizational System Is Important

It will be less likely that you'll lose an important application or other relevant information if all paperwork is kept together. It doesn't matter whether you use a loose-leaf notebook, cardboard file box, file cabinet, desk drawer, or the Cash for College™ Organizer System, as long as you keep all financial aid and college information in one convenient place. Photocopy the Scholarship & Application List Form (from Appendix B) and place it in the front section of your system to help keep track of all scholarships, fellowships, and grants you've requested or plan to request. Remember that you probably have less time now than you did while applying for your undergraduate program, so an organizational system is more important than ever.

2. Dividers/Hanging File Folders Help You Stick to Deadlines

Dividers or hanging file folders can be extremely useful in keeping your applications organized. You should include the following subdivisions:

1. Tracking Charts & Forms
2. Letters & Postcards to Be Mailed
3. Résumés & Transcripts
4. Recommendation Letters
5. Essays/Personal Statements
6. Financial Aid Forms (make this one red)
7. Scholarships, twelve files, labeled by month, starting with September and running through August, the

usual academic year, or use the academic year the program you're applying to follows.

8. One folder for each program that you are applying to.

Using twelve dividers/folders for the twelve months of the year will help you stay organized. If the due date for a completed application is December 1, file it in November. If it's due March 15, file it in February. Obviously, it's better to be a week or even a month early than to miss the deadline.

At this stage of study, there aren't as many scholarships, fellowships, and grants available as there were when you were a high school senior. You can't afford to miss any opportunities. As you receive information, mark application due dates in a calendar, and consult it regularly.

3. Use the Lists in This Book & Stay Ahead of the Game

You should always start looking for scholarships and fellowships a year before you're going to need them. You must apply to graduate or professional schools at the same time you are applying for scholarships. It takes a leap of faith, but you must assume that you will be accepted somewhere and will need the money. If you decide to delay starting graduate or professional study for whatever reason, you need to advise the scholarship committees as soon as you know. There may be times when a scholarship, fellowship, or grant can be held in reserve. Of course there are also times when you must pass up receiving an award because you aren't able to attend a graduate program.

As you send for information from different sources (scholarships, fellowships, grants, foundations, companies, schools, and programs), fill in the Scholarship & Application List Form in Appendix B. This form helps you keep track of what you've done, what you still need to do, and what information has already been received. Use this form only for tracking your requests for information. Use the Scholarship Tracking Form (Appendix C) to keep track of the actual application process.

After using the Quick-Find Scholarship Index on page 87 to locate the scholarships, fellowships, and grants to which you wish to apply, write all the addresses on the Scholarship List Form (Appendix B). Also add any scholarships you may find in other sources such as newspapers, magazines, and your school's financial aid or scholarship office. Send out by e-mail, request letters, or the easy-to-use Information Request Postcards (Appendix G).

It's especially important to note exactly when you request information. If six weeks goes by without a response from a scholarship, write to the committee again. Many times a scholarship committee or foundation may not be able to send out applications before a certain date, or sometimes your request is lost or misplaced. After all, committee members are only human. In some cases, you might want to call, but if a scholarship listing in this book doesn't show a phone number or if the listing specifies that written inquiries are preferred, don't call. But don't give up either—just write again instead.

4. Know Your Accomplishments

Once all the Request Postcards and letters have been sent out, create or update your résumé. Begin working on any writing or scholarship competitions that have deadlines coming up. If you've been out of college for a while, now is a good time to refresh your skills. Stay calm and keep reading; we'll show you how!

Compile a list of all the activities you did during your undergraduate years, as well as those years since you've been out of college. If you aren't sure what should be included in a résumé or activities list, you'll find all the information you need in Chapter 7, Creative Résumés. It's important that you have an accurate list of all school-related and extracurricular activities. Keep this list handy in a journal or notebook. All graduate and professional schools and scholarships will ask for a copy. If you have a current list of all your activities, you're less likely to forget an important event when asked for a résumé or to list the information on a scholarship or college application.

If you're out of college and working, keep a copy of your undergraduate résumé on hand. Some scholarships may ask a student for the activities they've participated in during the last four years, regardless of whether the student has been in college or working. Being able to cite examples for the last four years is a definite plus, because people aren't usually as active in extracurricular activities during their first year of being on the job. This allows you to use the activities accomplished during your time as an undergraduate to show your involvement in school or the community.

If you're an older student returning to college, you'll

still need a résumé. Chapter 7 will help you to create a résumé suited to your circumstances.

5. Don't Lose Those Awards and Certificates!

Save all certificates of achievement or award letters you received while an undergraduate or on the job. A few scholarship applications allow you to send photocopies of awards. Copies of certificates and award letters serve to confirm your achievements. If you don't have time to join organizations because you work or because you have to take care of your children in the afternoon, don't worry. Most applications have a section for a student to explain unusual circumstances that prevent him/her from participating in extracurricular activities.

6. Rely on Timetables and Calendars

Whether you're an undergraduate or working full-time, you need to have a copy of the Graduate/Professional School Timetable provided in Appendix A. You might want to keep a copy in a notebook pocket or taped to the inside of the cover of your notebook, or wherever you can refer to it easily. Check the Timetable at least once a month, though once a week would be better.

Use a calendar to note the due dates for scholarship applications, graduate or professional school applications, financial aid information, and other important dates (such as interviews, for example). Being able to see a month at a glance will remind you about important upcoming deadlines. Be sure to look at the calendar once a week. It's important to not miss a deadline. Most graduate and professional schools and scholarships will not accept applications past their due dates. Even if you were able to get an extension (your chances are slim), it wouldn't put you in the best light with the committee.

7. Use Different Colors to Highlight

Use different color highlighter markers to mark important dates on the calendar. Always use red to indicate financial aid deadlines.

8. Use Postcards and a Checklist to Keep Track of Information

As you mail applications, transcripts, or recommendation letters, include a self-addressed and stamped return receipt postcard. A return receipt postcard is a postcard that is mailed to you after an item is received by a scholarship or college admissions committee. If you still haven't received the postcard a week or two before the application deadline, start asking questions. Call the scholarship or program admissions committee and ask if they've received it and possibly overlooked mailing the postcard. If the return receipt postcard was included in a recommendation letter, you might want to send the letter-writer a thank you card to give a gentle reminder to send the recommendation letter.

Keep each returned postcard with the scholarship or college information. We've provided a master copy of return receipt postcards in Appendix G.

In addition, when you send an application or a recommendation letter form, fill in the date on the Scholarship & Program Application Tracking Chart provided in Appendix C. This lets you see what materials still must be sent for each scholarship or college application.

9. Keep Copies

We strongly suggest that you photocopy everything you mail out. If you can't afford to do this, then hand-write your answers onto another piece of paper and label it (by program, scholarship, financial aid packet, etc.). It isn't unheard of for an application to be lost or never received. If you have an exact duplicate of the application, it won't be difficult for you to photocopy it and resend it quickly.

10. Do a Rough Draft for Each Application

When you begin to fill out applications, first do a rough draft on scrap paper. This allows you to revise or rewrite an answer until you get it just the way you want it. If you're not sure whether all your answers are grammatically correct, ask someone to help you. If you think this suggestion is excessive or entails a lot or work, just remember that scholarship or graduate and professional school applications are some of the most important applications you will ever fill out. It's worth a little extra effort.

If possible, it's best to type applications. If you don't know how to type, ask a friend to do it for you. There are some applications that can't be run through a printer, so you must either fill them out by hand or use a typewriter. You want to make the best impression possible. Make it easy for them to read about you!

If you're unable to have an application typed, print the information using your best penmanship. If you make a mistake, use Liquid Paper to correct it. Don't scratch through a word and leave it that way. This bit of information may be unnecessary for many potential applicants, but if it helps one student win a scholarship or gain entrance to a graduate program, then it was worth saying.

Persistence is your best tool in your search for financial assistance. Take the time to inquire about any grant, foundation, or scholarship for which you might be eligible. You only have a postage stamp to lose.

Just because you can't afford tuition doesn't mean you can't further your education. You just have to be more tenacious, more inventive, and more adventurous in seeking a way to do so. You have to try. You have to be prepared.

You have to dream.

REQUESTING APPLICATIONS AND INFORMATION

Requesting applications isn't a difficult task, but there are certain things you should remember when doing so. These easily done details may lead to some much-needed free money.

Query letters are an important part of the application process; they are your first introduction to scholarship and admission committees. You need to be aware of the impression you want to make. When you write a query letter, don't think that you have to tell the committee your life history. They're not going to care whether Grandma Jones, your mother, and Aunt Harriet all went to Rahrah College. The only time it might be worthwhile to mention a detail such as this is if the college library is named after your grandfather. But chances are if the library is named after your grandfather, the college or university already knows this and you probably don't need financial assistance!

Organization and foundation scholarship committees receive hundreds and even thousands of letters each year. The more you write, the more they have to read. They'll appreciate your brevity.

Scholarship committees will need to know your name, the year in which you're graduating or graduated from an undergraduate program. We've included three examples of query letters in Appendix F to give you some ideas of what you might include in your letter. The first is written for a student who is still an undergraduate but is applying for a graduate or professional school; the second is for a student who wants to begin graduate or professional school studies after having completed an undergraduate degree many years earlier; the third is written for a student already in graduate or professional school.

Items to Include in a Query Letter

1. **GPA** If the scholarship you seek is for academic achievers only, you should let them know what your current GPA is. If you're applying to a scholarship after just starting your graduate studies, you might not have received any grades yet. If that's the case, you can include your undergraduate GPA; after all, that GPA was what earned your acceptance into

graduate school. If you completed your undergraduate studies more than three years before applying for a graduate program, and you haven't had any college courses since, let them know how long you've been away from a classroom and use your undergraduate GPA. If you took some random, general interest courses since you obtained your bachelor's degree, you may or may not choose to mention those grades; it's really up to you. Taking random classes will help you stay in the habit of studying and keep current with changes taking place within a college community.

Don't let a low GPA stop you from applying to a graduate or professional school. If low grades are due to extenuating circumstances, mention it. You might be able to enter provisionally, which allows you to then prove your worth.

2. **Test Scores** If you're an undergraduate and have started taking required entrance exams (DAT, MCAT, VCAT, LSAT, NLNGNE, GMAT, MAT, or GRE) you may want to mention your highest score. If a scholarship requirement clearly states that you must have scored a certain score and you didn't, then don't request an application. You're wasting your time and energy and you're causing the organization or foundation to waste time and money by sending you an application for a scholarship for which you are not qualified.

3. **Eligibility Information** If there is any question about whether you qualify for a given scholarship, write and ask. State in your letter the reason why you think you may qualify. The committee can then decide whether you do or don't and will send you an application if you do. Unfortunately, memberships in high school (such as 4-H, Future Farmers of America, and Boy Scouts) aren't usually considered when a student is applying for graduate-level scholarships. But if these organizations offer graduate scholarships themselves, you might want to inform them of the years in which you participated, even if it was during high school.

4. **Financial Need** Even though, according to federal regulations, graduate students are considered independent students, regardless of age, your family's income may still be assessed. If a scholarship is based on financial need and you aren't sure if you qualify, *briefly* explain your financial situation in the letter. Perhaps your family has had to pay unexpected, cost-ly medical bills due to a family member's illness. Perhaps, by the time you're ready to attend graduate or professional school, your family will have two other children in college. Tell this to the committee, because even one child in college can be expensive, depending on your family's income and the cost of the college involved.

Alternatives to Query Letters

Now that we've explained how to write query letters, we'd like tell you about an easier way to request applications and information: postcards! Not only do postcards cost less to mail, they're easier to write. You can make it even easier if you photocopy the master copy from Appendix G onto a ream (250 sheets) of 8½" x 11" cover stock. Cover stock is available at most office supply stores, and a ream usually costs from $7 to $9.

Purchase white cover stock (basis 110 or 90). Don't buy hot pink or fluorescent green, thinking you'll make an impression. You'll make an impression, just not the kind of impression you want to make to a scholarship committee or college!

Once you've bought the cover stock, take the ream to any photocopy center. We suggest you make a copy of the master copy on regular, 20# bond and keep it in a folder. That way you'll always have a good copy in a safe place and won't have to worry about the master getting wrinkled, torn, or dirty. If the store has self-service machines, try making one copy with the cover stock to see if the machine will handle heavy paper. If the image is being distorted, have someone from the center do it for you. If the photocopy establishment doesn't want to make photocopies of the masters because of copyright infringement, show them the copyright page. At the top of the copyright information, we give individuals permission to photocopy certain pages in this book.

You also have the option to make your own postcard master. Include a brief description of your situation (much as you would in a query letter, but shorter), your level in school, GPA, intended major, the graduate or professional school you wish to attend, the cost of one year's tuition, room, board, and any additional costs. Also mention that you and your family will have financial need and whether you're a member of the organization offering the scholarship. Make sure to make four copies of your postcard to place on one master copy.

NOTE: Some scholarship committees want to see a student take the time to write them an individual letter. The scholarship descriptions in this book will state if this is a requirement. Once again, do what it takes.

Both reproducing the master postcard sheet in Appendix G and creating your own will be inexpensive. Making photocopies can range in price from 4¢ to 10¢ for an 8½" × 11" sheet. A ream of 8½" x 11" cover stock costs approximately $9. Photocopying an entire ream ranges in cost from $10 to $25, which comes to 10¢ to 14¢ per sheet, or 2½¢ to 3½¢ per postcard.

If you're still an undergraduate, one ream of cover stock will probably provide enough postcards to last through all of your graduate or professional school years. You might want to find two or more friends who also want postcards and are willing to share the cost of the ream. Mailing postcards instead of letters saves postage, too.

Request information from a broad range of schools in which you have an interest in order to make an educated choice among the colleges to which you want to apply. The same holds true for scholarship applications. Whether you use postcards, request letters, e-mail—gathering information doesn't have to be a chore. All it takes is a little foresight and persistence.

SEVEN

CREATIVE RÉSUMÉS

The day you started high school, you should have started keeping a résumé. If you didn't, and you're an undergraduate junior or senior, then start today. If you can't remember what you did during your freshman year in college, sit down with a copy of your college yearbook and page through it or sit down with a friend or a member of your family and try to reconstruct your earlier years.

Maybe you jotted down appointments on an old calendar and you still have it. An old calendar may contain valuable information. If you don't know what a résumé should look like, some sample résumés can be found in Appendix E.

School activities

You should keep a record of every membership in a school-related club, organization, honor society, committee, play, band, or athletic activity (as a player, trainer, or manager). Keep an accurate list of every leadership position you held in clubs, organizations, or student government. Leadership positions are impor-

tant because they show you have initiative and can take responsibility. Don't be shy. Try for those positions. Maybe you don't want to be president, vice-president, secretary, or treasurer of a club. But, there are some positions that don't receive as much limelight that are still important, such as historian and parliamentarian.

At one of our workshops a parent gave us an excellent suggestion. If you take part in activities that print a program listing your name and role in the activity, keep copies of the programs. This is especially true if you're involved in musical or theater events. This way you have a record of exactly when the activity took place and how you participated. You can keep this type of information in the same notebook where you keep other college and scholarship information.

Community activities

Just because you do something outside of school doesn't mean it isn't important. It is. Keep a record of any community work you may do, whether as an unpaid volunteer or a paid employee. Volunteer work isn't just for high school students. Undergraduate, graduate, and professional school students should all be involved in volunteer work.

If you've been out of college for a while and have been working, you just need to be a bit more creative. There may be many things you're already doing that you haven't considered. If you read to children at your local library on Saturday mornings, put it on your résumé. Maybe you make crafts, mow lawns, or type research papers for other students. Guess what? You're self-employed! You're an entrepreneur! Self-employment shows that you have the confidence, responsibility, and maturity to run your own business. If you're active in your church, keep a record of it. If you're in the church choir, work in the nursery, or teach a class or Bible school, make a note of it.

Volunteer work is important. More and more high schools are considering requiring that students do a certain amount of volunteer work as part of graduation requirements. Volunteer work not only looks good on a résumé and shows a student is compassionate; a student also learns compassion as a result of doing volunteer work. Remember that no matter where you're at in life, you should continue doing volunteer work.

It will be important to do volunteer work at the graduate level because most scholarships prefer that applicants give back to their community. Graduate and professional schools are also just as concerned that applicants are multifaceted. By the time you've completed your degree, prospective employers, especially large companies, will also want to see that you've been participating in volunteer activities.

Maybe you're not sure what type of volunteer work you want to do, but you know that visiting a nursing home or being a candy-striper isn't your cup of tea. You might want to call the local United Way to get a list of possible volunteer positions in which to participate. The list will have a wide variety of volunteer positions needed within a community.

If you live in a small community without a United Way, ask the local newspaper to run a story about various community groups in need of volunteers. Maybe you can take the initiative to start a volunteer network. Businesses, organizations, hospitals, or individuals can contact you with volunteer positions for other students. You can conduct the network out of your home and still be serving a needed volunteer task. If you have children and don't have much time, you might want to

call organizations and volunteer to address envelopes whenever they're doing a mass mailing, especially invitations—which etiquette stipulates should be hand-written and not computer generated. You're still completing volunteer work, without having to pay for a babysitter or day care.

When our son started high school, we insisted that he begin volunteering one hour per weekend at a local nursing home. As we drove him to the first visit, he complained endlessly. At the end of the hour, the change in our son was unbelievable. He realized the residents needed to talk to someone and to have someone talk to them. Some of the residents received few, if any, visitors. Our son's visits made a difference in their lives, and they certainly made a difference in our son's life. He continued the visits throughout his high school years, and whenever he was home from college, he returned to visit the residents. One of the residents would introduce him as her grandson. While an undergraduate at Yale, he volunteered as a tutor one year, he worked in a soup kitchen one lunchtime a week, and at Yale-New Haven Hospital. By his senior year, he was the volunteer coordinator. During his time at Harvard Graduate School, he volunteered to work for a local politician. Any student, regardless of age, can have wonderfully fulfilling experiences if they do volunteer work. Volunteer work also enhances your résumé and helps attract scholarships, fellowships, grants, internships, and eventually a job.

As you compile your résumé, keep track of when you did each activity. Maybe you were a member of the Environment Club during your undergraduate freshman and sophomore years, but a member of a service group during your junior year. Dates become important because some scholarship applications will ask you for information from all undergraduate years of study, while others may want information only from your current year.

Another important thing to remember is how much time you spent on each activity. Maybe the Environment Club met for only thirty minutes every other week, but once a month you may have worked an entire day cleaning parks, highway medians, or yards for shut-ins. You may have spent thirty minutes twice a week at meetings as Student Government Representative but did not have to spend time preparing for the meeting. Thus, the Environment Club, with nine hours per month, is therefore a much more time-consuming activity than Student Government (four hours per month).

Everything you've done—24 hours a day, seven days a week, 52 weeks a year—during the last four years is important, whether you were in an undergraduate program or working. If you take or conduct dance or karate classes, help coach a Little League team, or are the leader in your child's Boy or Girl Scout troop, write it down on your résumé. In the long run, the special things you do will be what makes you different from the next person and could possibly mean the difference in who wins scholarship money and who doesn't. They could also determine whether or not you get into the graduate program or professional school of your choice.

In Chapter 15, Additional Sources of Information, we've included the names of some good books that show a wide variety of ways to construct a résumé. Use these references to help you create your own résumé format.

In Appendix E, we've included examples of three résumés; the first for an undergraduate student, the second for a student who is currently in a graduate program, the third for a student who has been out of college for several years but is beginning a graduate/professional program. These are just suggestions of what a résumé can look like. If you prefer a different format, then by all means use it. Just don't leave out any information!

Perhaps you haven't had time to join organizations. Perhaps you have one or more jobs, on top of taking college courses. You might be a nontraditional student and work full-time to support a family. Either way, you don't have to worry. Most applications contain a section where a student can explain unusual circumstances.

When in doubt about whether something qualifies as an extracurricular or volunteer activity, list it on your résumé. The college or scholarship committee can decide whether it wants to acknowledge the activity. One thing is certain: If you don't list it, a committee will never know that you did it.

It's much easier to arrive at a destination if you have a map. Your detailed résumé will provide all the information you'll need to show scholarship and admission committees the roads you chose to travel in your life to date and how those choices reflect your goals, ideals, and ambitions for the future.

EIGHT

GETTING DOWN TO SPECIFICS

Outstanding qualities count when applying for scholarships, fellowships, grants, internships, or to a graduate or a professional school. Take time now to evaluate yourself and even your parents to see if you might be overlooking a possible source of FREE MONEY!

Scholarship Resources

Companies

If one of your parents works for a large company, have them find out whether the company offers scholarships to children of employees. The company's Human Resources (Personnel) Department should have this information. Despite being considered an independent student, some companies offer scholarships to employee dependents, whether they're undergraduate *or* graduate students. If your parents are civilian or military federal employees, the Federal Employee Education and Assistance Fund has a scholarship and loan program for employees and their dependents for any level of study.

Keep in mind that if you're working for a large, or even a small, company there might be a tuition assistance or tuition reimbursement program for upgrading your skills. If, on the other hand, you're completely changing careers and your new career choice is completely unrelated to your current job, the company probably won't help.

Unions

Many unions offer scholarships to members' children. A free booklet is available to dependents of AFL-CIO union members (see Chapter 15, Additional Sources of Information). The same information holds true for unions as for companies.

Memberships

Some organizations offer scholarships to students who are, or have been, members. These include Alpha Mu Gamma, America Accounting Association, American Association of Housing Educators, Delta Gamma Foundation, Omega Psi Phi, National Society of Professional Engineers, and many others.

Religious Groups

Various religious groups offer scholarships to members. Baptist Life Association, Aid Association for Lutherans, Council of Jewish Federations, Fellowship of United Methodists, Knights of Columbus, and the Presbyterian Church are a few that do so.

Disabled Students

Handicapped students can also receive assistance. For example, students who are legally blind can contact the National Federation of the Blind for an application to apply to the various scholarships. Gallaudet University offers financial aid to students who are hearing impaired. Physically challenged students can contact their state Rehabilitation Commission. At the Rehabilitation Commission, the student is assigned a counselor who works with the student to find a career, the necessary education and training, and the financial assistance the student may need to further his education within his physical limits. It's possible that assistance for graduate studies may be limited or even nonexistent in your community. If there is a large monetary drain on available resources by undergraduate students, then no money will be available for graduate study. Also, Rehabilitation Commissions may not help unless a student is having to upgrade skills due to his/her physical limitations. Check to see if any local disability groups sponsor scholarships.

You may want to get on the mailing list for the Heath Resource Center, a national clearinghouse for financial aid and educational programs for physically disabled or learning disabled children and students. (See Chapter 15.)

State Agencies

Contact the educational agencies in your state (addresses are in the State Agency listings in Chapter 16) to inquire about special state-sponsored programs. Not all states offer assistance at the graduate or professional school level, but you have nothing to lose by asking.

Ethnic Background

Other organizations provide financial help to students with a particular ethnic ancestry. Many organizations offer financial assistance to several different minorities or to specific minorities.

There are many organizations that offer assistance to African American students, such as the National Associ-ation for the Advancement of Colored People (NAACP), National Association of Black Accountants, and National Association of Black Journalists.

Hispanic American students at the graduate or professional school level can contact the Hispanic Scholarship Fund, the National Hispanic Journalists.

Special programs also exist for students who are Japanese American, Native Alaskans, or Native Americans. These programs vary for students seeking degrees in specific programs such as accounting, business administration, education, engineering, geosciences, journalism, law, psychology, nursing, pharmacy, and other health professions.

Women

Many scholarship opportunities are available to women of all ages. The Business and Professional Women's Foundation helps women through a variety of programs. The American Association of University Women (AAUW) provides assistance to women completing graduate and professional degrees. The AAUW also sponsors PROJECT RENEW, which helps women whose last degree was obtained before a certain date and who wish to update their education and skills or change careers. From AT&T Bell Laboratories to Zonta International, there are programs that assist women in graduate programs in science and engineering fields. These programs are all described in the scholarship listings in Part II of this book.

Athletic

Most people know that sports scholarships in football, baseball, basketball, soccer, swimming, and other types of athletic sports are available for men, but few realize that there are also sports scholarships for women. However, not many schools offer athletic scholarships to graduate students, usually because it is assumed graduate students will not have the time to participate. Professional schools generally don't offer athletic scholarships.

The National Collegiate Athletic Association does offer scholarships to graduate and professional school students who participated in varsity teams while undergraduates. Also, students in kinesiotherapy can contact the American Kinesiotherapy Association. The National Strength & Conditioning Association offers scholarships to graduate students in areas related to strength and conditioning, but they must be members of the National Strength & Conditioning Association.

To see what categories you belong to, flip to the Index in Part II of this book. This index lists many different categories that might apply to you and tells you which scholarship opportunities are available to students in those categories. There are literally thousands of scholarships available in special categories. You just have to know what to ask, when to ask, and where to look for information.

NINE

RECOMMENDATION LETTERS

There are two types of recommendation letters: confidential and open. A confidential letter either must be sent directly to the scholarship or college admissions committee by the person writing it or must be in a sealed envelope with the person's signature written across the sealed flap to show that the envelope hasn't been opened or tampered with. In contrast, an open letter is one that the student may view. Schools will specify which type they require. Scholarship applications that don't specify which type of recommendation letter they want will accept an open letter.

Some people would rather not write a recommendation letter if there's a chance that the student might see it. If the person you ask tells you they will write the letter only if it's kept confidential, then you must decide if you want to give up the right to read it. If you're comfortable in your relationship with that person, chances are you have nothing to fear. If you ever had a disagreement with the person or if you're less than comfortable in your relationship, then thank them politely and look for someone else to write the letter.

What Is a Good Recommendation Letter?

A good recommendation letter is typed on one side only, is grammatically correct, and gives some insight into the student's potential, academic ability, leadership ability, motivation, responsibility, integrity, honesty, diligence, perseverance, cooperativeness, emotional stability, judgement, and common sense. It's also good to keep them at one page only.

Whom to Ask

For the most part, scholarships and graduate and professional schools will require two recommendation letters. At least one, if not both, of these letters should be from a professor in your field of interest. These professors will be able to comment on your promise of success within that field because that is their area of expertise. If a third recommendation letter is requested, it can come from a professor of a favorite class, a department chairman, dean, or mentor.

You also might want to ask a supervisor of a volunteer activity, a pastor, priest, employer, or even a neighbor to write a third letter if it is required. The neighbor might know that you've supervised neighborhood children during the summer or after school or may know that you've done volunteer work of some type. Whomever you ask, remember that they must know you well.

For scholarship applications, you might want to request a recommendation letter written by a professor in your field of interest, but you don't necessarily have to ask for one from your *current* professors. If you're an undergraduate senior or a graduate student, you could ask your freshman, sophomore, or junior year professor in that subject. Again, make sure you have a good relationship with the person whom you're asking to write a recommendation letter. There's no reason to take a chance if you don't have to. Scholarship committees are interested in you as a person and whether you will complete your education. Admission committees are looking to see if you have the necessary educational foundation to complete your goals.

If you're applying for admission to a graduate or professional school, your letters must all be from professors in your field of interest. Letters of recommendation written by upper-level professors are better than those written by lower-level professors because your skills should have developed since you took a lower-level course. Therefore, an upper-level professor can evaluate your current strengths and skills far better than a professor who taught you when you first entered undergraduate study.

You may be asked for a third, fourth, or even fifth optional recommendation letter. When a letter is optional, whether as a third, fourth, or fifth letter, the choice of whom to ask is up to you. If you can, ask any of the previously mentioned people or someone who is a prominent figure in the area where you live (mayor, senator, member of Congress, or prominent businessperson). But if you don't know the mayor, don't worry.

When you ask someone to write a recommendation letter, be sure to ask them if they have time to write one. Be sure they truly want to write the letter and that they can take the time to do so. After all, you are the person who stands to lose if a recommendation letter is written in haste. There are also individuals who want to write a letter but just don't have the time. If they ask if you could write it and they will sign it, say "YES!" That letter could be the best letter you get. There is nothing unethical about that.

Recommendation Letter Forms

If a form is provided, it should be used. Some organizations and institutions want all the applications to be uniform in appearance, so use the supplied form. Sometimes scholarships don't supply forms, so we have supplied a copy of a sample Recommendation Letter Form in Appendix H. This form can be photocopied and used in the event that a form isn't supplied.

Some organizations like to receive a letter that shows it was written especially for them. Therefore, after you make copies of the form we've provided, type the title of the scholarship application over the heading. Whoever is writing the recommendation will then be able to refer to the name of the scholarship in their letter. If the person writing your recommendation would rather use school or business letterhead, that's okay, but if a school or scholarship supplies a form, you must use it.

Just remember to have the letter writer mention your full name, the name of the scholarship or college to which the letter will be submitted, and possibly even your social security number on each page of the letter. Your Social Security number might not be needed if you have a particularly unique full name and/or you're applying for a local scholarship or to a small college. On the other hand, if you're a David, Elizabeth, George, Juan, Mary, Pat, Richard, or Tony and your last name is something like Adams, Garcia, Jones, Sanchez, Smith, Thompson, or Washington, you might be in trouble. There may be more than one applicant with that name, and a recommendation letter might get filed in the wrong application folder. If, in addition, you happen to be applying to a large college or university, then you increase the chances of your paperwork winding up in someone else's folder. Why take the chance? Have your Social Security number on all the pages.

When using a form, be sure to fill in the information at the top of the form that pertains to you before you give it to the person writing the recommendation. It's best to type your part of the information, if possible. Most people will also type the recommendation letter, but it is acceptable for it to be handwritten. Recommendation letters should be written on one side of the page only, with additional sheets added if necessary (this requirement is usually written on the form).

Make It Easy for Them

Once a person has agreed to write a recommendation letter, make it as easy as possible for them to write it. This is especially true if they're professors, department chairpersons, deans, or community leaders, since these people probably are writing a number of recommendation letters for other students as well. When you give them the recommendation form, always provide an envelope in which to mail it. The envelope should be addressed and stamped with sufficient postage to arrive at its destination. You don't have to supply large (9" × 12") envelopes unless you want to. A standard #10 letter-size envelope will do.

You might also want to consider giving the person writing your recommendation letter a copy of your résumé. No matter how close you are to the person, no one knows you better than yourself. If you give them a résumé they'll know exactly what you have accomplished and when you've participated in certain activities or won awards. The person you ask will appreciate this kind of assistance. It also may impress a selection committee to see that your participation in various activities is so consistently noted and praised by professors, chairpersons, deans, or employers writing your letters of recommendation. This little extra effort might make the difference in your getting a scholarship.

Let the professor or whoever is writing the letter know ahead of time how many copies you will need. Sometimes this is impossible, since you may not know what scholarship you'll discover in March when it's only October. Also, if possible try to have an original signature and current date on each letter, even if the letter is a photocopy. A parent who attended one of our workshops gave us an excellent added suggestion: Have the person writing the recommendation letter sign their name in blue ink. Then it's obvious that the signature is an original.

Finally, don't wait until the day before a deadline to ask for a recommendation letter. You want to allow the person enough time to write a well-thought-out, complimentary letter, not a dashed-off note that says nothing. After all, it is your future that hangs in the balance.

How to Send Recommendation Letters

Some scholarships require you to send all the information (application, transcripts, recommendation letters, essays, copies of certificates of merit, résumés, and other information) at one time. Some scholarships may require you to send all the information flat, open, and either stapled together or spiral-bound in a convenient package. If you choose to spiral bind the application package, most photocopy centers will do this for you for a small fee. Spiral binding is an attractive and convenient way to put an application package together.

Return Receipt Postcards

Whenever our son asked someone for a recommendation letter, we would enclose a stamped, self-addressed, return receipt postcard. When the recommendation letter arrived, whoever opened the letter would date and sign the postcard and put it in the mail. This way, we were able to keep track of what had been sent, not sent, received, or not received. We received every return receipt postcard we included with recommendation letters, applications, and financial aid information. A sample return receipt postcard can be found in Appendix G.

How to Give Gentle Reminders

It's always a gracious gesture for you to write a thank you note or card to anyone who writes a recommendation letter. A week or two before the letter is due at the scholarship or college admissions committee, mail or hand deliver the card to the person. The thank you card is serendipitous and serves as a gentle reminder to someone who might be so busy that they've forgotten about writing your recommendation letter.

What Not to Do

Never submit a recommendation letter written for one scholarship or graduate program to a different one. If there is a reference to a different scholarship or program in the body of a recommendation letter, a committee member may assume the student didn't care enough to ask for a second letter. Committee members want to see that a student has taken time to obtain required material. Also, they have no way of knowing if you asked permission of the letter-writer to send copies to several different committees.

A student shouldn't substitute anything for a written recommendation. We can assure you that committee members don't have time to chase down people by telephone to get an oral recommendation. Scholarship and program application instructions are usually simple, reasonable, and straightforward. Not following the directions doesn't make a good impression on the selection committee.

Never ask a relative, guardian, or godparent to write a recommendation letter—even if you work for them. Relatives aren't considered objective sources. Find someone who isn't related to you to write the letter.

We both serve on various scholarship committees, and just when we think we've seen it all, another student makes an unexpected, unthinkable move. This sounds as if we made it up, but we didn't. Though we never would have thought we would need to say this, you should NEVER submit a recommendation letter written by another student. It doesn't matter if your supervisor at an on-campus, work-study job is a student,

there has to be someone in the line of hierarchy who is not a student—ask that person. This may also sound obvious, but it's worth repeating: Never ask for a recommendation from someone who you're not certain will write a positive one. A confidential recommendation letter which is negative or noncommittal will hurt your chances of obtaining scholarships.

Something to Remember

We've started a foundation that administers scholarships that are funded by private organizations or businesses. This service allows businesses and organizations offering scholarships to assure students there's no favoritism in selecting scholarship recipients. We administer several scholarships and see a wide variety of recommendation letters. Although we take into account that a student shouldn't be penalized because the person who wrote the recommendation letter did a poor job of writing it, not all committees are as lenient.

This is the only opportunity a scholarship or graduate/professional school acceptance committee has to hear someone else's opinion of you. Take your time in deciding whom to ask. Make it your best choice!

TEN

IMPRESSIVE INTERVIEWS

You've just been granted an interview by either a scholarship or graduate school representative or committee. Many times a graduate program requires students be interviewed to determine who will receive sought-after fellowships. What should you do? Don't panic—there aren't many do's and don'ts about interviews.

Points to Ponder

1. **Don't be late.** If you're driving and don't know the way, take a practice drive the day before. If you're depending on public transportation, take possible delays into consideration. It's better that you wait in a lobby or spend a few minutes browsing in a nearby shop than for you to show up late.

2. **Dress appropriately.** The important thing is to be clean, neat, and well groomed. You want to give the best impression possible.

   Wear a color that looks good on you. Don't wear something that's distracting. Women shouldn't wear a skirt that makes it difficult to maintain your dignity while sitting down. If you have to continually pull on your hemline to sit appropriately, don't wear it.

   Men can wear bright ties, as long as they're not gaudy. A good rule to adhere to is "If it needs batteries, don't wear it." Don't wear a school tie of the school to which you're applying. You should even think about your shoes. Men should wear shoes, and socks. Of course, cowboy boots are always appropriate in Texas. Women should wear hose with their shoes. If possible, don't wear open-toed shoes, and definitely no spiky, 4-inch heels. Avoid sandals, tennis shoes, clogs, or any shoe that slaps back on your heels.

   Jewelry should be kept to a minimum or it could distract the interviewer. A necklace or a pin/brooch near the collar is acceptable. Etiquette maintains that men should only wear a wristwatch. A class ring or wedding ring is allowable, but nothing else. Women should wear one earring per ear. Men should consider not wearing any earrings. Think conservatively.

Perfume and/or cologne should also be kept at a minimum. Don't take a bath in it. Wash your hands after applying it, so you won't pass the scent on to the interviewer when you shake hands.

3. **Be gracious.** When you walk in, shake the interviewer's hand firmly (not like a dead fish or as if you're in a contest to see if you can bring the interviewer to his/her knees) and state your name clearly. As you leave, thank the interviewer and shake his or her hand again.

4. **Relax.** The interviewer(s) won't ask you anything you don't already know. He or she just wants to get to know you better. Remember: "Don't let them see you sweat." Being granted an interview means the scholarship committee or admissions committee is impressed by your application and wants to know more about you.

5. **Show your enthusiasm and leadership.** Don't look like you're about to have your wisdom teeth pulled. Don't give one-word answers. Elaborate. You want to be likeable, sincere, honest, optimistic, cheerful, and efficient.

6. **Be aware of your body language.** Don't fidget, jiggle your foot, wave your hands, or shift in your seat. These are distracting movements. Don't sit on the edge of your chair as if you're ready to pounce. Don't grip the arms of the chair as if you're undergoing surgery without anesthesia. Don't slump in your chair. Lastly, don't cross your arms across your chest. This is a protective signal and silently implies that you don't want the interviewer to intrude into your personal space or your life.

7. **Look the interviewer(s) in the eye.** You don't want to look evasive, but you don't want to appear threatening either. When asked a question, don't avoid eye contact.

8. **Be prepared.** Take a résumé with you. Have someone ask you practice questions ahead of time and go in with possible answers. You want to be prepared to ask specific questions that demonstrate your interest in the school, program, or scholarship. Your curiosity and interest will only reflect well on you.

9. **Be aware.** If the interviewer(s) stands, the interview is over. Don't keep talking. The interviewer(s) has a time schedule to keep and others to interview.

10. **Remember:** When you get home, write a thank you card or note.

The person or persons who will interview you simply want to get to know you. Remember, no one knows you better than you. Enjoy yourself!

ELEVEN

WRITING PERSUASIVE ESSAYS

Writing essays shouldn't be an agonizing or frustrating experience. It is one of the most important parts of your application and is as crucial as an interview. Be sure to write it thoughtfully. It goes without saying that no one but you should write your essay. An essay is supposed to reveal the type of person you are. If someone else writes it, it can't reveal anything about you.

It is acceptable, however, to ask someone, a professor, your parents, or another student, to *proofread* an essay. (Believe it or not, parents can be objective judges!) It's sometimes easier for someone else to catch a mistake than it would be for you. If you drop a word or make an error, the mind just accounts for it and you might not see it. When someone else reads your essay, carefully consider their opinions, but don't allow them to rewrite your essay. You have total control, and it's your voice that should be clearly communicated.

To write a well-thought-out essay you should allow yourself sufficient time. Don't wait to write it until the night before you have to mail it. One of our son's favorite excuses for putting off writing an essay or per-

sonal statement was, "I work best under pressure." No one works best under pressure. We often compare writing an essay or personal statement to a fermenting process. Your must consider a topic from different aspects or vantage points. You must allow your unconscious mind to remember details your conscious mind might overlook or even forget. One morning you could wake up and remember an essential detail. You certainly don't want to remember it *after* you've submitted your application.

If it's been several years or more since you were an undergraduate and actively doing a great deal of writing, you might want to practice, practice, practice. Writing essays or personal statements isn't hard, it just takes a little bit of work.

If you're not sure whether your essays are grammatically correct, ask someone to help you. If an English professor doesn't have time to do this, find an English tutor. If you think this suggestion seems excessive or like a lot of work, remember that scholarship and college applications are some of the most important applications you will ever fill out. If you know a professional writer, have him/her proofread your essay and give you pointers. Be wary of companies that promise to write your essay for you. Scholarship and graduate and professional school admission committees want to know what *you* are like, not some company that just wants your money. Again, doing something like this is just plain dishonest.

Above all, the most important thing to remember is to be yourself. Regardless of how much assistance you might get from an English professor or friend, *or if you send them to us to critique for a fee,* the final essay or personal statement must be your work and sound like you.

Try to type the essay, as well as the rest of the application. Some applications require forms that cannot be run through a computer printer, so you must use a typewriter or do it by hand, printed in your best penmanship. If you are asked to write the essay on a separate sheet of paper, use white, 20# bond. Don't ever use erasable paper (it smears on handling) or colored paper (it's hard to read and can make a bad impression). You want to make it as easy as possible for the committee to read your essay.

If you are asked to write your essay directly on the application, consider photocopying the blank application. When you have drafted your final essay, practice typing it on the photocopy. If your essay is within the required word count but is too long to fit in the space provided, try using a smaller size type. You might be able to make your essay fit just by using smaller type. Don't go overboard and reduce it too much. It's best to cut words rather than strain someone's eyesight. Anything smaller than size 10 font is too small.

If an essay must have a specific word count and your essay is too long, reread it. Can you take out excess words like "that" and "had"? In our experience these two words seem to give people the most trouble. If a sentence says the same thing without those words, take them out. Don't use the words "very" and "really." Eliminating them cuts the word count without changing what you're trying to say.

If at any time you're in doubt about the meaning of a question, ask someone—your parents, a professor, the organization offering the scholarship, the graduate or professional school—or (if there's time) write to us (our mailing and e-mail addresses are on the last page of Chapter 1). Don't jeopardize your chances of winning a scholarship or gaining admission to a program by failing to understand the question.

Make sure you keep a copy of every essay you write.

This way, if you find another scholarship you want to apply for later in the year, you might be able to reuse an essay or modify one you've already written. Recycling an essay saves you time. Perhaps all you have to do is update it a bit, reslant it toward the question you're answering, or cut out or add some words. When our son was an undergraduate, he used the first essay he wrote for a scholarship during his high school senior year. Each year he just updated the information and avoided having to write an entirely new essay from scratch.

After having seen all types of applications, we were able to make a list of some of the most commonly asked questions and topics covered. Read through this list and consider how you might answer.

- What ten items would you choose to take along on a solo space flight and why?
- Describe a situation in your life in which you challenged the majority or traditional thoughts of a group. What affect did you have on the group?
- What is the world's greatest problem? Why?
- I wish the admissions committee had asked me . . .
- Describe a risk you have taken, adversity you have overcome, or obstacle you have encountered that influenced who you are today.
- How would you characterize the effect of your contributions to the groups or organizations in which you have participated?
- Describe the characteristics of an exceptional manager using an example of someone whom you have observed or with whom you have worked. How has his/her management style influenced you?
- Describe a personal failure: In what ways were you disappointed in yourself, and what did you learn from the experience?
- The year is 2020, and the annual edition of *Who's Who* includes your biography. What does it say, beginning from the time you completed your next degree?
- Why are you and this school well-matched?

Although an essay should express your beliefs, your ideas, and your personality, there are some topics you should consider avoiding when writing an essay, unless the essay specifically asks for you to address them. Although the following topics may be important to you, they don't have any place in a scholarship essay or personal statement.

- Relationships (boyfriend or girlfriend)
- Religious beliefs
- Political beliefs
- Views on or about drugs and/or alcohol
- Opinions about sex or other moral beliefs
- Views on current events (from abortion to disarmament)

Your goal is to inform the reader as to why you should be selected over someone else. Unless an interview is requested, the essay is the only chance you have to tell the committee your thoughts and dreams, to express in your own words those things that make you a unique individual.

Scholarship and admission committees essentially look for five things in an essay: grammar, spelling, syntax and word usage, content, and creativity. Of these, creativity is probably the most important. This is where you can show a committee your distinctiveness. You might try using humor or actual dialogue. If you're a poet, your talent might come in handy for an essay that doesn't require a specific answer. Be sure to remember the topic and sustain the tone of the essay. If the essay is lighthearted, you can be so throughout, but if you've just related a somber incident that greatly influenced your life, you don't want to ruin the moment with inappropriate humor. Don't mistakenly think that adding several quotations to your essay will reflect how well-read you are. Committees don't care what others have said. Committees want to know who you are. One quotation may be acceptable, but *only* if it's a quotation that has greatly affected your life. Avoid repeating information that appears elsewhere on the application, unless the essay allows you to expand on an activity or a leadership position. Most applications will have a section where either you list your activities or you'll be asked to include a résumé. If you choose to discuss some of your activities as a way to make a point in an essay, by all means do so. Finally, don't generalize in your essay. Don't assume that "everybody" thinks or does something. If you have specific examples, cite them.

If you've been given the opportunity to write about any topic, choose something about which you care deeply. It might be an event that changed your life, a teacher, professor, or mentor who introduced you to a subject area you never before had considered interesting, or an activity which revealed a side of yourself you didn't know about.

Getting Their Attention

Scholarship and admission committees read hundreds and even thousands of essays every year. Your first sentence should hook them. Your essay must not only tell them about yourself but must also hold the reader's attention. We wouldn't recommend telling jokes, but try to be lively and upbeat. The idea is to have them remember you. An essay must tell a story— your story. It must be an interesting, and memorable, story.

You might also want to get a copy of our book, *Write It Right: How to Write the Essay They'll Love and Get the Cash You Need*. The book provides exercises and assignments to help you get started, plus invaluable advice on writing and editing your essays. It also includes fourteen sample essays and 114 essay makeovers with editorial remarks. It shows you how to make a good essay stronger and how to edit a long essay down to the required length.

We also strongly recommend *The Elements of Style*, by William Strunk Jr. and E. B. White. This little book is full of explanations of important rules all writers should remember and also lists words that are commonly misused. The book costs less than $10 new, but you can probably find it in most libraries.

Stay focused when writing your essays. If you have worries on your mind, it's probably best to stop writing for a while and try again when you can concentrate. You don't want to sound wishy-washy or indecisive. You want a reader to realize that you know what you want and how to get it. Also, don't worry if your essays sound as if you're giving yourself a pat on the back. They should honestly reflect your talents and achievements. Don't be afraid to mention accomplishments of which you are proud. Remember to take your time, check your spelling, watch your grammar, and most importantly, be yourself. Show a committee that you're a sensitive, humorous, one-of-a-kind type of person, and they'll remember you.

Writing isn't hard; it just takes practice. The first essay you write might seem as difficult as having your wisdom teeth pulled. However, by the time you've written four or five essays you'll find that it gets easier and easier. You might even find yourself enjoying it!

TWELVE

ASSESSING YOURSELF FOR PERSONAL STATEMENTS

This chapter will deal with assessing who you are, your gifts, your talents, and how best to communicate this to others. This assessment is essential when determining the right topics to use for essays and personal statements—topics that will make a connection with the reader to get the attention they deserve. Your statement must reflect who you are and why you are endeavoring to travel the path you've chosen.

Your personal statement must have a balance of who you are and what you want. Your words must join together to form logical, well-organized thought, but they must also be harmonious and almost lyrical. Your words must caress a reader's ear—not attack it.

Tone

There are times when an essay or statement can be playful, almost whimsical. This approach, when used appropriately, can make your writing stand out from a long line of essays that take a pompous and boring approach: 'My goals are . . . .'

Focus

When working toward obtaining a post-secondary education, a bachelor's degree covers a general area of study, such as biology or archeology. When working toward a master's degree, your focus must be more specific. For example, a student who has an undergraduate major in psychology and a minor in social work may go on to obtain a master's degree in social work, with a major paper written on religion in social work. As a doctoral candidate, the student may write a dissertation on "The Affect of Counseling Battered Women on the Mental Health of Counselors." Just as this student's area of study goes from general to specific, you may want to narrow your goals from general to specific.

Preparation

As we mentioned in the previous chapter, choosing a topic and writing an essay or personal statement is much like a fermentation process. Spend some time thinking about your answers. Consider what you hope to convey. The following questions are meant to help you define who you were, who you are, and who you want to be. You can write down the answers to these questions or simply think about them, but take your time and explore your thoughts fully.

What did you love to do as a child? What could you do for hours on end? What did you do better than those around you? What do your parents, siblings, or friends say you do well? What do you enjoy doing now?

Our goals generally change as we age due to our experiences. When you were in elementary school, what did you want to be? By the time you were in middle school, had your goals changed? When you entered high school, had your goals changed? How about when you graduated from high school? What do you see yourself doing, career-wise, in ten years? Twenty years?

As you create and set goals, be realistic. Though everyone should be proud of accomplishments and have dreams, will you be able to accomplish them? Though you should ALWAYS dream and formulate long-term goals, you also need a plan filled with small goals, all bringing you closer to the long-term goals. You will feel great as you accomplish each small goal toward the big payoff.

Assignment 1

Describe yourself in a series of one-word adjectives. You can start with what you look like because it's actual fact, but make sure you include your personality and not just your physical aspects. What you look like isn't as important as who you are. Do you have a logical side, and an emotional side that combine synergistically to form who you are? Describe every facet of who you are, including strengths and weaknesses.

Assignment 2

Go back to those adjectives and explain why you are a reflection of those words. Don't just write down *funny*. Write: *funny*—I have a joke to fit every occasion. *Determined*—I never take no for an answer.

You also want to put a *positive* spin on all your adjectives and explanations, especially those describing your weaknesses. Perhaps you have a lazy streak in you; you can convince anyone to do anything in order to get out of doing it yourself. The adjective changes from lazy to motivational. Has a friend or parent ever told you that you're stubborn or hardheaded? The positive spin changes hardheaded and stubborn to opinionated. Did your list include the word "indecisive" because you're unable to decide which task to do first, so you tend to start several at one time? Then you're not "indecisive," you're multi-task oriented. You're not "nosey," you're inquisitive.

You never want to accentuate a negative. It would be like taking your undergraduate transcript and highlighting your worst grade before sending it to a school or scholarship committee. Think creatively and positively about yourself.

Assignment 3

Many students state that they want to be a success. If you don't know exactly what it will take to be successful, how will you know you've achieved it? Take the time to determine what you picture personal success to be. Make a list of words or phrases. Will your success include a spouse, companion, friends, children? Will you want a house, condo, apartment, or houseboat? Will your success include a stock portfolio or just enough to always meet your financial obligations? What must you accomplish to be successful? Would you like adventure, challenge, respect, influence, fame, power, or intellectual stimulation?

Assignment 4

Before you begin putting any words on paper you need to prepare to look into yourself and who you are. You might want to surround yourself with familiar objects or favorite mementos or listen to soothing or favorite music to get yourself in a creative mood.

To begin with, you might want to start by forming an idea of what it is you want to achieve by obtaining your educational goals. Don't hesitate to be creative in how you form your thoughts. You might want to write down your thoughts, whether words or phrases. Think about all you've done, all you are, and all you want to accomplish. The sky is the limit. It doesn't cost anything to dream.

Assignment 5

You've now made a list of those goals. Beside each entry, write why you want to accomplish that goal. What must you possess internally and externally to reach your goals? How will achieving that goal enhance who you are?

Assignment 6

Review what you've written in Assignments 4 and 5. Is it accurate? Did you forget something? If you've always known what you wanted as a future career, then your statement should not have changed too much as you have aged and acquired more education. If you're like a lot of individuals, you've changed over time. If that's the case, then your personal statement will be more fluid and reflect these changes. If you think of areas you have overlooked, or if your goals have changed, add and delete to the information from Assignments 4 and 5.

Assignment 7

Begin a new file or page with information about relationships; just don't try to discuss ALL the relationships in your life. Relationships reflect who you are. Just remember not to discuss your love life. Who are some people who have influenced or guided you to becoming who you are and what you want? Have these people reinforced who you know you are and what you want?

Assignment 8

On another page or file, make a list of events that have affected your life. Depending on your age or amount of activities in which you participate, your list could be long or short. Experiences also reflect who you are. Now take each event and put each one at the top of a new page. Jot down notes about that event: date, time of day, where it happened, who you were with, etc. Next, write the specifics about the event.

Assignment 9

In the previous assignment, you listed events that happened to you. In this assignment, we want you to make a list of things or events that YOU accomplished. Whether you achieved them last week or when you were five is irrelevant. That you're proud of the achievement is what's important. Don't worry if they're out of chronological order or order of importance; just write them down. The list might include the first time you were able to give an oral book report in class without turning a bright red, quitting smoking, learning to swim, or asking your boss for a raise and getting it. When you feel your list is complete, go back and write how each accomplishment made you feel.

You should never write a personal statement that includes *all* of your accomplishments, but what you do choose to include in your statement will reveal who you are.

Assignment 10

Now we want you to think about your life and what's important to you. We want you to make two different lists. If you were going to be stranded on a deserted, tropical island or snowed in on top of a mountain, what ten items would you want to have with you? Whether you choose a hot or cold climate is your choice. You can begin by just making a list of as many items as you want, but you *must* pare the list down to ten.

Assignment 11

Changing the situation just a bit will allow you to see another aspect of who you are. This time, compile a list of ten things you would want in a time capsule or said about you as a eulogy. The ten items should reflect who you are and, perhaps, what you've accomplished—thus far. The eulogy must be said about you at your present age. Just as in the first list, you can begin with a long list but you *must* pare it down to ten.

Your list doesn't have to be serious. There could be a funny or whimsical item, if that's the kind of person you are. Maybe you'd want to have a unicycle with you on your island to help pass the time. Or you'd like to include a can of peanuts with a fake snake inside so that whoever opened the time capsule would know you had a sense of humor.

Assignment 12

What activity, talent, or hobby best represents who you are? You might choose to consider an activity that led to your selection of a major or career choice. Or it could be a hobby that is totally out of the sphere of your career.

Through the years, we've worked with hundreds of students. Four students, Izaak, Rachel, Kevin, and Michelle, provide good examples of using their self-knowledge to create uniquely individual essays and personal statements. Izaak chose to center his statement around his writing talent. Basketball is the center of Rachel's life. Kevin's father had a career in the military, which meant his family moved a great deal. After one move, he found himself having to take a theater class because nothing else fit in his schedule. Though quite talented, Michelle didn't have a clue what she wanted to do with her life, so she was going to use her first few years in college to explore the possibilities.

Izaak's first draft (386 words):

I'm an artist. My artwork, however, isn't on the canvas, but on paper. I don't use paintbrushes, but rather a pen or a keyboard. I paint a different kind of picture, a picture of a sea of words that floats together to make my expressions visible as they wash ashore on the printed page. While some artists use chalk, clay, or oils, I use satire, humor, and the facts to highlight, mute, and form a cohesiveness in the stories I tell.

Ever since the first grade, I've been expressing my thoughts through poetry and other writings that often left my teachers saying how I was vastly ahead of my peers in writing. In high school, I have taken my writing a step further, from just writing essays in class to being a main news and sports reporter for my school's newspaper. I also cover the ROTC Unit in the paper because the Naval Science Instructor feels that I know the Corps well enough to show others on the campus what we do. This has led to my being appointed the Public Affairs Petty Officer of our unit and has also helped me to showcase my writing abilities. On the newspaper, I'm a lead reporter who covers all types of stories. I enjoy interviewing people for my columns and enjoy helping to put the entire paper together. When my fellow reporters and I are assigning who'll get which stories for the upcoming issue, and the chief editor tells me that I'll need to fill three whole pages, my eyes light up. I can't wait to get started on all of my assignments.

At my KENS-TV internship, I often get the chance to help write the stories that the broadcasters use on the air. During the newscast, I sit in the control room with the directors and producers. It's thrilling and exciting to hear a broadcast reporter saying words I've written for them.

Writing is a way to share news and information with everyone. I plan to take my special talent and use it to become a broadcast and print journalist in college and in my future career as a professional journalist. Being able to use words effectively was God's gift to me. Using my special talent in print and broadcast journalism will be my gift to God.

Izaak's final Personal Statement (110 words):

I'm an artist. My artwork, however, isn't on the canvas, but on paper. I don't use paintbrushes, but rather a pen or a keyboard. I paint a different kind of picture of a sea of words that floats together to make my expressions visible as they wash ashore on the printed page. While some artists use

chalk, clay, or oils, I use satire, humor, and the facts to highlight, mute, and form a cohesiveness in the stories I tell. Writing is a way to share the news with everyone. I hope to take my special talent and use it to become a broadcast and print journalist in college and beyond.

Rachel's first draft (387 words):

Basketball isn't a game, it's a way of life. Malik Rose, Jackie Styles, Cheryl Swoopes, Rachel Estrada. Since the first time my eight-year-old hand touched a basketball I knew I wanted to play. One of my high school's coaches once remarked that he wanted my signature so that *when*, not *if*, I make it to the WNBA, he'll have something to remember me by.

The ability to avoid distraction on and off the court will be what assists me in getting through college on my way to becoming a coach. A career as a coach suits my personality because I'm able to earn a person's trust by making them laugh. Humor can cut through an attitude easier than a hot knife through butter. Though a silent leader, I can be outspoken when standing up for what I believe.

As a player, I've had coaches with a wide variety of teaching styles, ranging from strict and mean to soft and caring. Having played the game for so many years, I want to be a teacher and also strive to be a friend to the girls. They'll know that they can come to me with their problems or just questions. I will help the girls improve in their athletic endeavors and give them tips for living.

I've observed that it's important to pay attention to every player and to give every player a chance. My students will know that I believe in each one of them and am willing to use all my players. Positive criticism is much more effective and helpful than a scolding. My students will see me as strict but caring, always honest, and perhaps at times a bit goofy. Life is too short to get mad over little things or those things that I can't change. A laugh and a hug can accomplish more than angry scowls and mean words.

Whether I make it to the WNBA or not, I will become a teacher and coach. My striving toward being the best also includes helping others in being their best. After all, any job worth doing is worth doing right. I will work hard to reach my goals. I'll always train, encourage, and motivate my students to always do their best.

Rachel's final Personal Statement (104 words):

Basketball isn't a game, it's a way of life. Malik Rose, Jackie Styles, Cheryl Swoopes, Rachel Estrada. Since the first time my eight-year-old hand touched a basketball, I wanted to play. The ability to avoid distraction on and off the court will assist me in getting through college and pursuing a career in coaching. Whether I make it to the WNBA or not, I will become a teacher and coach. As I work to reach my goals, I'll remember that anything worth doing is worth doing right the first time. I'll train, encourage, and motivate my students to always strive to do their best.

Kevin's final Personal Statement (112 words):

Alaska, Arizona, South Dakota, and Texas. The Lone Star and North Star, Grand Canyon, and Mt. Rushmore. Anchorage, Phoenix, Rapid City, and San Antonio. Dreams for some, vacations for others, reality for me, places that I've called home. But I've always found myself most at home on the stage. Over the past eight years, I've entertained people of all ages, with stories of all kinds, from goofy children's plays to works of Shakespeare, from audiences of church members to those of thespians. My travels have taught me to be open to ideas, challenges, and adventures, which suit my strong-willed and good-hearted personality. I will find my own path and not follow others.

Michelle's final Personal Statement (107 words):

I'm an explorer. My imagination has no bounds. Everything is a possibility. Each new experience is attacked with the fervor of a frisky puppy chasing down a new toy. From neuroscience to political science, it's all fascinating. Studying with a Russian professor at MIT, acting as a civil rights attorney at NHI's Legislative Session at Colorado State, and learning to be a leader at the March of Dimes Youth Conference at Georgetown are just a few of my endeavors. More experiences are still to come. I can't wait to rock climb or try my hand at crew. I'm exploring new territories. Vasco de Gama would be proud.

Assignment 13
What metaphor would best represent your answer in Assignment 12? Though Izaak uses words, he chose a metaphor of art. Rachel threaded basketball and her goal of wanting to be a coach through her statement. Kevin used both acting and all his moving in his statement. Michelle compared herself to an explorer.

Assignment 14
What words could you use to further that metaphor or image in an essay? Izaak's list of words included canvas, paintbrush, chalk, clay, oils, highlights, picture, and artwork. Rachel listed athletes and skills: Malik Rose, Jackie Styles, Cheryl Swoopes, ability to avoid distractions, train, encourage, and motivate. Kevin wanted to include the places he'd lived: Alaska, Arizona, South Dakota, and Texas.

Assignment 15
Keeping the answers to the questions in Assignments 12 to 14 in mind, write a personal statement of who you are and what you want from life. Don't worry about word count—just write. As you share more about yourself, weave the words from Assignment 14 through your essay like a thread through a piece of material. After you're content with your statement, you'll need to cut it down to approximately 100 to 150 words.

Always keep in mind that your personal statement must reflect *all* facets of who you are. Graduate and professional school admission committees, as well as scholarship committee members, want a diverse group of individuals. Diversity is what makes a class come alive and achieve. You could be just the catalyst to stir up new ideas or energy into a group or the solid, dedicated individual who *always* makes sure a task is completed on time and within a budget.

Every assignment we've given you has been preparing you for writing your personal statement *and* making sure that whoever reads it *will* remember you. We suggest that you also get a copy of our previous book, *Cash for College's Write It Right*. It contains 114 essay makeovers, which include essays for graduate and professional school admission. Chapter 6 in that book includes fourteen additional essays that are all used for either admission purposes or for scholarship applications, and they all accomplished the task of getting the student into a program and/or scholarship money. Sample Essay 12 in Chapter 6 was written in response to a question as in our Assignment 10. In 961 words, the writer has given a true presentation of who she is, including an account of her obsessive-compulsive tendencies as well as being able to laugh at herself. The following is the long version of her graduate school essay (reprinted from our essay book), followed by her shorter Personal Statement. Another aspect of this student, one that can't be ascertained from her original statement, is that she was an older student returning to graduate school.

I wake to the sound of water lapping nearby. I can feel the warmth of the sun on my back. Where am I? I open my eyes. I'm on a beach. Marks in the sand indicate that I must have dragged myself out of the sea. I can hear birds chirping in the distant trees. What's happened?

In my befuddled state it takes a few minutes to remember the cruise, the sinking ship, the screaming, the pushing. I'd been on a lifeboat, but when another person tried to climb on, I fell out, and no one noticed. I was wearing a life vest and was able to grab a deck chair as it floated by. That chair must have saved my life and brought me here. But where was here?

I stand and make my way farther from the water's edge. Down the beach I can see the deck chair. I snicker as I think that at least I'll have something to sit on. I realize I'm clutching a bag in my left hand, the bag into which I was hurriedly ramming items as the alarm shrilled onboard the sinking cruise ship.

I sink to the warm sand. I open the bag and dump the contents on the ground. The first thing I notice is my reading glasses glittering in the sand. Next to my glasses is my organizer. At least I'll know which appointments I'm missing. There's the novel I'd brought to read on the trip; although it's waterlogged, it's readable. I'd had the presence of mind to bring my newly refilled bottle of prescription sleeping pills. It's comforting to know I'll be able to sleep for at least 90 days. I'd also grabbed my manicure set in its leather zippered case. The case was somewhat the worse for wear, but I'd be able to stay well groomed. I'd thrown in a sample box of the Whitman chocolates I always carry with me. Ripping the cellophane and opening the box, I discover that the chocolates didn't survive the ocean water. Oh well, I'd been wanting to try to cut my chocolate intake for a while. Now's as good a time as any.

My journal is among the jumble, but it, too, is waterlogged and the entries I'd made are unreadable. I'm not sure what I was thinking as I grabbed my valuables but there was also a plastic bag filled with tea bags and Equal. I could make a cup of tea, if I'd only thought to bring a teapot, a stove, and a portable generator with me. Fortunately, my obsession with resealable plastic bags paid off. I'd also included a plastic bag filled with my favorite granola bars. I'll have to eat them sparingly until I find out where I am and determine the odds of being rescued. The last item I'd shoved into my bag was my travel alarm clock. What was I thinking? Of course, now I'll know exactly when I'm missing those appointments listed in my organizer. I put the clock up to my ear but hear no ticking. What I do hear is water sloshing around inside. So much for knowing what time it is.

Though I know there are many pressing matters to attend to, I can't help thinking that my bagful of items reflects who I am. I'm an obsessive, workaholic, chocoholic, insomniac who tries to relax by reading and who tries to counter her sweet tooth by using Equal in her beverages. If there were ever a time to make changes to my personality, this is it. There won't be anyone to offend as I go through chocolate withdrawal.

So much for meandering thoughts. Putting all the items back into the bag, I look left and right. This might be an island, but I haven't had time to walk the coastline. First I have to make some sort of shelter. Though it's warm now, it might be cold at night, and a shelter would also provide some respite from the unrelenting sun. Second, I'll find a source of fresh water. Then I'll look to see if there are any wild fruits, berries, or nuts to eat. Those granola bars will only last so long. I also have to find some large rocks, so I can write HELP in the sand for airplanes that might fly by. I also want to find some dried firewood and kindling to start a fire. The fire could be seen at night by passing boats and planes, while the smoke could be seen during the day. A fire will also keep me warm at night as well as keep any predators at bay. I might even be able to read by firelight. I'll have to get the fire going before the sun goes down, if I'm going to use the glass in my reading glasses to start a fire.

With a plan of action in mind, I go to work. I'd always thought that time was money, but now time means survival. The sun is directly overhead. I have about seven, maybe eight hours in which to do as much as I possibly can. Whatever doesn't get done today, I'll do tomorrow. Maybe I'll be lucky and round the bend to find a resort with all the comforts of home. Unfortunately, there's a greater chance that around the bend will be more of the same: one of the cleanest, whitest beaches I've ever seen.

As I begin walking down the beach, I realize something. Just before I'd left on the cruise, I'd thought I'd give anything to find enough hours in the day to allow me to rest. I guess the saying is true: Be careful what you wish for, because you just may get it.

Personal Statement: (120 words)

"Never, never, never quit." Winston Churchill. That quote sums up my entire life. Whatever situation I face, I take an aggressive, optimistic, and focused stance. I'm a forty-five-year-old female who's an obsessive, workaholic, chocoholic,

insomniac who tries to relax by reading and who tries to counter my sweet tooth by using Equal. Not one to take the easy way out of any predicament, I've chosen a more difficult, meandering path to follow. Life has occasionally provided me with lemons, and I chose to make a lemon meringue pie. Lemonade might have been easier to make, but the pie is tastier and more filling. I'll savor life to its fullest and never, never, never take no for an answer.

By using the fifteen assignments in this chapter, you will be able to find the right information to include in your statement. As you review the additional sample personal statements below, either mentally or literally highlight the words that are the threads weaving the metaphor through each of the statements. Notice how, even when the topic is the same—the first three statements all deal with athletics, sample 4 deals with acting and theater like Kevin's statement earlier, and samples 5 and 6 are both from students who are undecided on a possible major—each statement uniquely reflects interests, hobbies, and their authors' individualities. The students who wrote samples 7 and 8 had the same career goal in mind, yet each statement is distinct.

Sample 1) (135 words)

It's the bottom of the ninth. I'm up to bat. The bases are empty and the pressure is on. The pitcher releases the ball and "crack!" The ball flies over the fence with incredible speed. Rounding first base, I remember the studying and hard work I put into academics. Jogging to second, I remember how much my skills were honed from all the practices and games. Third base is under my feet as I think of all the essays and letters to colleges and scholarships I've written. Striding past the bag, relief and excitement wash over me. Stepping on home plate, I'm eager to find out what lies beyond and what challenges I'll face next. This is what makes me a baseball player who's ready for the biggest game of my life so far: college.

Sample 2) (125 words)

Walking up to the tournament desk, behind me lingers all the practice and preparation that have led up to this moment. I've hit buckets and buckets of serves late into the night and imagine myself in the vital moments of the match. No doubt about it, I'm ready. With a spring in my step, I confidently

walk up to the desk. As the tournament director hands me the balls, I think of my parents who encouraged me and supported me when I first started school. My opponent represents the obstacles that an education brings. During the warm-up, I remind myself of all the work and preparation I've put in toward this moment. About to begin, I take a deep breath and start the match, the match of life.

Sample 3) (115 words)

Golf has influenced and guided my life since I was seven years old. By playing and understanding golf, I've learned to be patient and be aware of my surroundings. Golf has helped prepare me to work on and with computers. Both are similar—in golf, you're either off or on and a computer is either on or off. Being patient, I work on a program or hole until I get it right, regardless of how frustrating it may be. There's as much variety in golf courses as there is in computer systems—but I adapt. Golf is like life, it's what I strive for, and I have to work hard to get to the green.

Sample 4) (117 words)

Heart throbbing. Pitch black. Curtain call. Lights on. Sweat trickles down my face. The show has begun. I emerge onto the stage walking as another, truly experiencing that life. I breathe the dust of the theater as I step into my role—it's been my life-source since my first time on stage as a high school sophomore. I'm truly at home when I'm acting. The road has been long and rocky, and this is just the beginning. I've been rejected, challenged, and handed unwanted parts. Never giving up, I chose to seize each moment. Not only did I endure, I impressed and surprised. Passion is the driving force that will help me arrive at my destination: actress.

Sample 5) (124 words)

"Dos vidanya reebyatha." Russian is just one of my passions. Russia had always been a distant, frightful land, seemingly isolated in time, yet a place I'll journey to one day. The determination to learn such a different and difficult language is truly characteristic of my eagerness to explore new territories. Sometimes I'm as busy as a bumblebee in a field of wild bluebonnets on the first day of spring. From candy-striper to tutor, my exploits keep me on my toes, ready to tackle my latest quest. I envision myself a pioneer out to venture into uncharted territories, pursing my wildest dreams and experiencing new endeavors. I can't wait to climb the highest mountain, journey to distant shores, and travel from sea to shining sea.

Sample 6) (115 words)

So much to discover, so little time. In order to get the most out of my life, I strive to do my best at everything I endeavor. The physical, mental, and spiritual aspects of life each provide unique challenges. From scuba diving to rock climbing, I've taken on formidable tasks in my journey to find myself. I'm willing and ready to try anything. The inner peace I strive to achieve helps me to succeed. Though I live in the moment, I take the time to slow down and appreciate the beauty around me. I will always help others along the road of life. Friend or foe, in their time of need, I'll always be there.

Sample 7) (107 words)

Homes and careers all must start with a strong foundation. The foundation for my future career will be my education. The walls of my career began with an internship with a nationally recognized architectural firm. A roof is last. A well-rounded education, degree, and license will be the roof above me. My skills, knowledge, and talent will provide the security to turn a house into a home, upon which all aspects of my life and career will be built. The internship turned an interest into a passion, and through this experience I know exactly what I want to become in life. I'm going to be an architect!

Sample 8) (117 words)

I'm a dreamer, but an organized, prepared dreamer. My blueprint is to be an architect who'll run his own architectural firm. By taking a co-op course this year, I've prepared for the transition from high school to college. Vocational drafting has exposed me to real-life architectural demands, such as drafting, floor plans, elevations, and model-making. Through determination and the education I've received in high school and will receive in college, my dream will become reality. College will challenge me to stretch my imagination, strengthen my experiences, and enable me to go from blueprint to reality. My dreams will result in aesthetically pleasing structures in which I, my neighbors, and friends will live, work, and play.

Sample 9) (127 words)

My life is a parade of images. The band, much like my education, marches in unison, rhythmically tapping, yet is inspired by my individuality, sending an unexpected rush of bass through my heart. My art, like colored confetti floating through the air, allows me to wordlessly enhance and focus the news of my life. As each dance team passes, I'm able to experience the past memories of old parades. Horses prance confidently down the street, tossing their shining manes to and fro, just as I offer my views in my artwork. A cacophony of words assaults my ears, infusing my mind with the appreciation for our differences. My breath quickens in anticipation, as my eyes revert to the parade and look up the street toward the future.

Sample 10) (109 words) This last statement has a whimsical metaphor—*The Wizard of Oz*, but it was appropriate since the author wanted to become a veterinarian.

Lions, tigers, and bears—Oh my! Well, maybe not lions, but for sure dogs and cats. At seventeen years of age, I'm a young lady who loves animals. My plans for the future are to become a veterinarian and, hopefully, someday open up my own animal hospital. Though I'm unsure whether I'll major in pre-veterinary medicine or biology, I'll be in school for more years than most. Once my life includes a family, I'll balance the two in such a way as to ensure my family comes first while continuing to help families with their pets. Whatever happens, someday I may be able to get my own ruby slippers.

Though most of these statements were written by younger students, the students who wrote samples 4 and 9 wrote them for graduate school applications. The age and level of education aren't critical aspects of each student. They were writing about who they were. Michelle and the students who wrote samples 5 and 6 will have evolved a bit by the time they are ready to apply for graduate school. They will have found their focus and career goals, and their subsequent statements will reflect that. Even if you've decided on a major, your career goals can, and probably will, change. For all you know, you could be preparing for an eventual career that hasn't even been developed yet. Thus, you could write a statement about one career and end up in an entirely different profession. Don't worry about it. Not one admissions officer or scholarship committee member will track you through your education to make sure you adhere to your personal statement. Your task is to just write the best personal statement possible that reflects who you are *right now*.

Good luck and get to writing!

THIRTEEN

UNDERSTANDING FINANCIAL AID

About $28 billion is available annually in the form of grants, fellowships, scholarships, and loans from colleges, the state, and the federal government. At the undergraduate level, most schools maintain that if a student is accepted to their school, there shouldn't be any reason why they can't attend. The financial aid officers at these schools work hard to put together an attractive financial aid packages. Unfortunately, this isn't always the case at the graduate school level. Both students and parents must be aware that they may have to contribute financially to a graduate or professional school education. Sometimes students must decline acceptance into their first-choice schools because the school doesn't offer them sufficient financial aid.

Though it would be great to know how much financial aid you will qualify for *before* you apply to a given school, it doesn't work that way. Colleges and universities have enough work processing financial aid packages for students who have been accepted or who are already attending the school without also having to determine what every student who is applying might receive.

How Much Financial Assistance Will You Need?

Not knowing how much you or your parents will have to contribute doesn't mean that you must blindly pick and choose a graduate or professional school. Expected family contribution (EFC) is still determined by the federal government, but the EFC is calculated on your and your spouse's income (if you have one) and generally not on your parents'. There are cases when a graduate student can still be considered a dependent, which means your parent's EFC is still used; however, this is rare. Unfortunately, as a graduate or professional school student, you no longer qualify for federal aid, such as Federal Pell Grants or Federal Supplemental Education Opportunity Grants (FSEOG), but may qualify for other types of federal aid. NOTE: This allows for both federal and school aid.

Basis for Financial Aid

Just as when you were an undergraduate, the lower your income, the better your chances are for receiving financial aid. But, at the graduate or professional school level, the type of aid you will be receiving has changed. Your financial aid may be provided by school endowment funds or even your home state. Remember you're now an independent student whose income may be much lower than your parents' income. At the same time, if you're working and have no dependents, you may not be eligible for much free money.

How Is a Family's Expected Contribution Determined?

In order to determine a family's expected contribution, all colleges require students to complete the Free Application for Federal Student Aid (FAFSA). The federal methodology and PROFILE evaluation are used to calculate the expected family contribution (EFC). Students may be required to complete additional forms provided by the college in addition to the FAFSA. The information obtained by those methodologies will be analyzed to determine the type of financial assistance (federal, state, and institutional grants) you are qualified to receive.

Remember, you must submit some type of financial aid form as soon as possible after January 1, prior to the fall semester in which you will need the financial assistance. Any student needing financial aid to attend college (during any year in college) must fill out a new form each year.

Expected Family Contribution

A family's expected contribution stays the same, regardless of the varying costs of tuition and room and board from one college to another. Therefore, if Family 1 is expected to contribute $15,000 and college costs (tuition, room, and board) for one year are $25,000, that family's financial need is $10,000. On the other hand, if the student from Family 1 is applying to a state-supported school and the college's costs for one year are $15,000, then Family 1 wouldn't need any extra financial assistance. In contrast, a student from

Family 2 whose expected contribution is $2,000 will need financial assistance at both the $25,000 and the $15,000 school. That student's need varies from $13,000 (for the $15,000 school) to $23,000 (for the $25,000 school).

	PRIVATE COLLEGE		STATE-SUPPORTED COLLEGE	
	FAMILY 1	FAMILY 2	FAMILY 1	FAMILY 2
college cost	$25,000	$25,000	$15,000	$15,000
expected family contribution	$15,000	$2,000	$15,000	$2,000
financial need	$10,000	$23,000	$0	$13,000

Improving Your Financial Aid Profile

There are many ways in which families can change their financial aid profile in order to be eligible for more assistance.

- Shift a student's assets to parental assets.
- Reassess the value of your home and assets.
- If you own or work for a small company, convert income money into a business asset by purchasing equipment or setting up a pension plan.
- Account for all college expenses—including transportation.

The higher a family's income, the more strongly we recommend that the family seek a reputable financial planner as soon as possible. Your financial need will be based on your and/or your family's tax information from the previous year.

How Outside Scholarships Can Change Your Financial Need

Some schools may deduct the first $500 in outside scholarships from any loans the student may have to incur. Each subsequent dollar amount provided by an outside scholarship is then split either 50-50 or 60-40 and deducted from what the student must borrow and, at times, from in-college scholarships. Some colleges may allow outside scholarships to lower the amount a student may have to borrow, which means your hard work in applying for and winning scholarships will really pay off!

	COLLEGE A	COLLEGE B	COLLEGE C
college cost	$25,000	$25,000	$25,000
student's EFC	$10,000	$10,000	$10,000
school award (grants)	$15,000	$15,000	$15,000
TOTAL AWARDS	$25,000	$25,000	$25,000
first outside scholarship	$1,000	$1,000	$1,000
student's EFC	$9,000	$9,000	$10,000
school award (grants)	$15,000	$15,000	$14,000
TOTAL AWARDS	$25,000	$25,000	$25,000
second outside scholarship	$5,000	$5,000	$5,000
student's EFC	$6,500	$4,000	$10,000
school award (grants)	$12,500	$15,000	$10,000
TOTAL AWARDS	$25,000	$25,000	$25,000
third outside scholarship	$5,000	$5,000	$5,000
student's EFC	$4,000	$0	$10,000
school award (grants)	$10,000	$14,000	$5,000
TOTAL AWARDS	$25,000	$25,000	$5,000

You should be aware that there are some colleges (College C above) where it doesn't matter how much outside gift money you bring with you—it won't lower how much you or your family pays. We're not sure how those schools would be attractive to a student, but many times the fact that it's the only local school available means that there will be students to attend the school.

Outside scholarships won't change an EFC unless certain conditions are met. If you've been awarded enough outside scholarships to cover full college costs for a year, or enough outside scholarship money to cover all the amount of free money offered by the college and all of your expected contribution, then your family's expected contribution is only your traveling costs and other incidental expenses.

Becoming a Sought-After Student

Being a sought-after student means you are being wooed to attend a particular graduate or professional school program. Sought-after status is something for which you should strive. GPA, admission test scores, and number of extracurricular activities are the factors that greatly increase the chances of getting gift money, and the awards that are available to students with superior academic records are generally for large amounts.

Independent Student Status

In the past, many parents did not claim their student as a dependent on their taxes, hoping it would make the student independent for scholarship purposes. However, the parents continued to provide the student with room, board, and other living needs. The government has strict guidelines for determining eligibility. If you answer yes to any one of the guidelines, you will be considered independent. The guidelines are:

- Are you an orphan?
- Are you a ward of the court (a foster child)?
- Are you married?
- Do you have a dependent other than a spouse?
- Are you a veteran?
- Are you 24 years of age?
- Are you a graduate or professional school student?

Since you are applying to a graduate or professional school, you are now an independent student—regardless of age or other situations. A Financial Aid Officer (FAO) of an institution can change the dependency status of a student, as well as alter the EFC. If, when you receive your Student Aid Report or Financial Aid Award Letter from the schools, circumstances have occurred changing your financial status since the time you filed the FAFSA, you can appeal. In such cases, students can submit a Special Circumstances Form to their institutions Financial Aid Office. FAOs can then use their professional discretion to determine a new budget for the student and thereby increase their financial aid award package. The FAO may or may not be able to adjust your contribution to a more reasonable amount. So be aware that monetary relief isn't guaranteed. It's always best to prepare yourself.

Financial Aid Forms

The federal government requires that all students requiring financial assistance of some type must now file a

Free Application for Federal Student Aid (FAFSA). Some graduate programs even require the parents to fill out a FAFSA, despite the fact the student is considered independent. The information is not used in evaluating the student's needs, but it must be filed nonetheless.

You can contact the Department of Education to request a hard copy of the current FAFSA form by calling (800) 4-FED-AID / (800) 433–3243 or obtain a copy at your institution. It will take about two weeks to receive it in the mail. If you'd like to expedite your receiving the FAFSA form, you can access it on the Internet. The web site is: http://www.fafsa.ed.gov.

A current hard copy of the FAFSA is generally available around Thanksgiving each year, but you can't file your FAFSA until after January 1 of the year in which you need the aid.

A Students must contact the Financial Aid Office of the individual graduate and professional schools to which they are applying and inquire whether other financial aid forms are required. The PROFILE Registration (formerly known as the Financial Aid Form—FAF) and Graduate and Professional School Financial Aid Service (GAPSFAS) are supplemental forms that may be required. Some schools or states may have their own financial aid forms, and it's good to know ahead of time. Remember, if all necessary forms aren't completed, you will not be eligible for financial aid.

Student Aid Report (SAR)

After you've submitted the FAFSA, you will receive a Student Aid Report (SAR). The SAR contains the information you reported on the FAFSA.

Keep in mind that if you file the actual forms for the FAFSA, it will take up to six weeks to receive your SAR. If you file the FAFSA on-line, the evaluation is prepared within three to seven workdays.

Which Colleges Should Receive the Information

You should indicate all the schools to which you are considering applying on the FAFSA, GAPSFAS, or any other financial aid form you are filing. You can add additional schools at a later date, if you need to. You also want to make sure to keep a copy of the FAFSA and GAPSFAS, because an outside scholarship may require you to send them a copy and it's a good idea to keep a copy for your records.

Sources of Financial Aid

The money needed to fulfill a student's "financial need" can be obtained from a variety of sources, such as federal guaranteed loans, federal unsubsidized loans, state grants, grants, fellowships, scholarships, and loans from within a college, federal work-study jobs, and outside scholarships. Remember, Pell Grants and FSEOG are not available to graduate and professional school students.

For More Federal Grant Information
To find out more about federal grants, send for *The Student Guide*. This free booklet can be requested from: U.S. Department of Education, U.S. Government Printing Office, Washington DC 20402. If you still have questions about student aid, call the Federal Student Aid Information Center at its toll-free number: (800) 4-FED-AID. The office hours are Monday through Friday from 9:00 a.m. until 5:30 p.m. (Eastern Time). You can also access the Department of Education on the Internet. Their web site is http://www.ed.gov.

Other Sources of Financial Aid
Ask the graduate and professional schools to which you're applying if they know of any other scholarships available from outside sources (such as clubs, foundations, and private companies). Make sure the department to which you're applying knows that you will need financial assistance. Many graduate departments offer scholarships in specific areas of interest (engineering, journalism, music, agriculture, etc.).

While waiting for acceptance letters, or after acceptance, check with banks about special low-interest loan programs for students or parents who wish to save or borrow for college expenses. Some low-interest and no-interest loan programs are provided in the list of scholarship opportunities in this book.

You also should check with campus bookstores. It's not uncommon for campus bookstores to be run by an outside company, such as Barnes & Noble, and it's possible that they could offer scholarships. In our experience, few students apply for these scholarships, which means you have a better chance of winning them.

Federal Stafford Loans

In the past, the federal government has offered federally guaranteed student loans to students who have financial need not met by Pell Grants or FSEOGs. Knowing that not all students qualify for a Subsidized Stafford Loan, the federal government now offers an Unsubsidized Stafford Loan. Your income, as well as your parents', must still be within certain limits to qualify for a Subsidized Stafford Loan. But with the Unsubsidized Stafford Loan, *there is no income qualification*. Any student may apply for an Unsubsidized Stafford Loan, regardless of the student's or parents' income.

As a graduate or professional school student, you will be eligible to borrow $8,500 per year (students with extreme financial need may borrow up to $10,000). Once again, if you've been granted any portion up to $8,500 from the Stafford Loan program, you can borrow the remainder from the Unsubsidized Stafford Loan program. If you've been denied a Stafford Loan, you may borrow up to $8,500 from the Unsubsidized Stafford Loan program.

Federal Perkins Loans

A Perkins Loan is a low-interest loan (through a college or university) available to graduate or professional school students. You may borrow up to $5,000 per year for each year of graduate or professional school study. You begin repaying this loan nine months after you graduate or when you enroll for less than full-time status. You have up to ten years to repay the loan. Contact your Financial Aid Officer for more information.

Don't Forget

Be sure to fill out financial aid applications completely. Financial aid may be rejected or delayed for reasons as simple as no signature on the form, no Social Security number on the form, or incorrect information. Make sure the forms are completed and mailed by the due date.

Financial Aid Packages

If, by the end of April, you haven't heard from the Financial Aid Office at the school to which you are applying or you are attending, call their Financial Aid Office. If the office is still working on the awards, it could be a couple of weeks before the award letters are sent. If you haven't received word by the end of May, call again. If the end of June arrives and you haven't been notified, call every two weeks. It's important for you to keep on top of the financial aid situation because once registration starts, you might have to resort to taking out a loan in order to cover tuition and other costs.

Registration dates are slightly different for medical schools and some other professional schools that start their school years in July or August instead of September. You should adjust your expectation of receiving information according to the start of your school program.

Once you've received your financial aid package, take the time to fill in the Financial Assistance Analysis Chart in Appendix D. This chart provides an easy way to compare packages from different schools. If, once the financial aid packages are offered, you know that you or your parents will be unable to contribute as much tuition as is expected by the college, call the Financial Aid Office. Explain your situation to the Financial Aid Officer and see if they will increase federal loans, school grants, and/or loans, student loans, or campus work-study job (teaching assistantships and research assistantships). There are a few things to remember when doing this:

1. Always write down the name of the person with whom you speak so you can ask for them by name the next time you call. This ensures that the person you deal with will know the details of your file. It's not unheard of to talk to ten different people within a Financial Aid Office and receive ten different answers to a question.

2. When you call the Financial Aid Office, have as much documentation on hand as possible. A student might have to provide details proving that he or spouse has lost his or her job, that a divorce has occurred and has altered the family finances, that a spouse has suffered an injury that will diminish how much he or she will earn, or that a spouse has suddenly decided to return to college, causing additional financial strains on the family.

3. You might want to compile a monthly budget of your expenses to indicate how your money is spent. You should include an allowance for clothing and entertainment, but bear in mind that you are or will be in school. Don't have a $10,000 clothing and/or entertainment allowance. The FAO might suggest you get a video rental card and shop at consignment shops or thrift stores. Use your best judgment when assessing your monthly budget. Check our website for a sample of what items a monthly budget can include.

4. Keep in mind that although colleges have some leeway in how much they can change a financial aid package, there isn't an enormous amount of flexibility. If, however, you have been offered a greater amount of money by a comparable school, then a Financial Aid Officer might match that offer, assuming the you are a sought-after student.

When evaluating aid packages, be sure to be thorough, but don't take so long that the deadline for accepting the school's offer slips by. Compare your offers carefully, so you can start school knowing you've made the best choice.

FOURTEEN

GLOSSARY OF TERMS

Academic Year The time in which a full-time student is expected to complete the equivalent of two semesters, two trimesters, or three quarters at an institution.

Accreditation Accreditation is given to schools that have fulfilled certain requirements set by the state or federal government or a recognized accrediting agency. Students who attend a nonaccredited school will not qualify for federal or state aid and sometimes not even for scholarships.

American College Testing Program (ACT) A company in Iowa City, Iowa, that offers national testing and need analysis service. This company evaluates the PROFILE form and also offers the Medical College Admissions Test (MCAT).

Appeal Procedures There are many reasons why students or their families may decide to request that the college Financial Aid Officer (FAO) reevaluate a student's financial aid eligibility or awards. Some of the reasons for an appeal may include loss of a parent's or spouse's job, ill health of a parent or spouse, death of a parent or spouse, a student's or parent's request to change the self-help portion of a financial aid package (the money the student is expected to contribute from savings, summer earnings, student loans, or a work-study job), and any reason the school should reconsider a student's financial aid package because of additional information that hadn't previously been available.

Assets Assets may vary and may include the money in your checking and savings accounts, investments (money market funds, certificates of deposit, stocks, bonds, trust funds), and boats and real estate. Cars usually aren't considered assets by the federal government or by a college. Possessions such as stamp collections, antiques, or musical instruments are not considered assets. Usually only 12% of net assets are considered (in evaluating financial need) after deducting money earmarked for retirement purposes. Some schools may make additional adjustments in their assessment of a family's finances to offset gross income, parent salaries, or other primary income sources. A school may choose not to allow income shelters, tax write-offs, or secondary or passive income sources (second or summer homes, rental property, real estate for sale, alimony, business income, capital gains, pensions, annuities, unemployment, or Social Security) to be deducted from earned income and could possibly consider that income as an asset.

Campus-Based Financial Aid Programs These are financial aid programs (primarily federally funded programs), administered by post-secondary institutions (colleges and universities). Some examples include Perkins Loans and College Work-Study Programs.

Citizen/Eligible Noncitizen In order to receive federal aid, a student must be a U.S. citizen, a U.S. national (natives of American Samoa or Swain's Island), or a U.S. permanent resident with an Alien Registration Receipt Card. If a student doesn't fall into one of these categories, he or she must inquire about his or her eligibility for financial assistance from a college or outside scholarship.

College Work-Study (CWS) The CWS Program is a federal program that provides limited funding to create on- and off-campus jobs for financially disadvantaged students. College work-study is open to both undergraduate and graduate students. The amount a student earns cannot exceed his/her level of financial need as determined by the financial aid forms. Each school sets its own deadlines for applying for CWS. Graduates may be paid by the hour or may receive a salary. All students are paid at least monthly. Many of the on-campus jobs are teaching or research assistants.

Computer Adapted Test (CAT) The CAT version of the GRE is administered by private companies. The CAT version of the GRE begins with a tutorial that provides instruction on how to take the test.

Conditional Awards Any award (grant, fellowship, scholarship, or loan) that is given to a student but requires additional documents (such as a tax statement) be provided to the school before the award goes into effect. Conditional awards may be modified or withdrawn if the information on the documentation varies from information previously provided.

Congressional Methodology (CM) The Federal Congressional Methodology (developed by Congress and revised in 1992) is utilized by most colleges and universities to determine how much the student seeking financial aid must contribute toward his or her college education.

Cost of Education The total amount it will cost a student to go to school (tuition, room, board, books, transportation, miscellaneous fees, and other expenses).

Default Default is a student's failure to repay a student loan and to abide by the rules of the loan contract the student signed. If the loan is a federally funded one, the IRS may withhold the family's or the student's income tax refund until the loan is paid.

Deferment Loan Repayment of loans often can be deferred by a student until he or she has the financial resources to begin repaying. Most loan payments are deferred until the student is no longer a full-time student, with the payment schedule usually beginning six to nine months after the student has stopped his or her education. Student loans sometimes can be canceled if certain requirements set by the lending institution are met. For information on these requirements, contact the lending institution.

Dental Admissions Test (DAT) The DAT is the test required for entrance to dental schools. Students can obtain applications from a dental school or from the Division of Educational Measurements, American Dental Association, 211 East Chicago Avenue, Chicago, IL 60611, (312) 440–2686. The DAT is offered twice a year.

Educational Testing Service A nonprofit organization in Princeton, New Jersey, that administers the Law School Admissions Test (LSAT).

Emergency Loans Emergency loans are short-term loans available to enrolled students. Emergency loans are intended for use by the student to meet an emergency or unexpected expense, such as high book costs or purchase of expensive equipment (architectural or drawing supplies, etc.), or for living expenses until a grant, stipend, or scholarship is paid to the school. The loan cannot be used to pay the student's tuition bill. Loans may range from $50 to $500 and are usually interest-free but must be repaid by a certain date. Overdue loans can accrue interest charges.

Enrollment Status This term describes a student's course/credit hour load at a college. A student must be at least a half-time student in order to qualify for student aid. If a full-time student is awarded $1,000, a three-quarter-time student receives $750 and a half-time student receives $500.

Expected Family Contribution (EFC) The amount that parents and/or the student can reasonably be expected to pay for post-secondary education. The EFC is determined by analyzing the family's financial data.

Expected Student Contribution (ESC) Most colleges and universities expect students to make the maximum effort to contribute toward their own graduate or professional school education. The ESC is independent of the EFC and can come from a student's earnings, savings, assets, and other possible sources such as relatives, friends, agencies, or organizations.

Federal College Work-Study *see* College Work-Study.

Federal Family Education Loans (FFEL) This terminology refers to the Federal Stafford Loan program. FFEL, Federal Stafford Loans, and Stafford Loans are terms that can be used interchangeably. This new terminology was introduced in 1995.

Federal Perkins Loans *see* Perkins Loan.

Federal Stafford Loans *see* Stafford Loan.

Federal Work-Study *see* College Work-Study and Work-Study Job.

Fellowship A fellowship is a type of financial aid that is free money and need not be repaid. A fellowship may be sponsored by a school or by an outside agency (association, organization, business, fraternity, or sorority). A student may obtain an application at an institution or may need to request an application from the organization. A student doesn't have to repay a fellowship but must fulfill all requirements (academic, extracurricular, athletic, or essay) to be awarded the scholarship. If the fellowship is renewable, the student may have to maintain a certain grade point average (GPA) in order to continue to receive it. The term *fellowship* is used interchangeably with scholarship and grant.

Financial Aid Award Package There are many types of financial aid, and most schools combine various types of aid into one program called a financial aid award package. Financial aid award packages may vary from school to school, but most contain student loans, self-help (student's earnings, savings, and assets, other possible sources such as relatives, friends, agencies, or organizations, and work-study job), grants, fellowships, or scholarships.

Financial Aid Officer (FAO) An individual at an educational institution who is responsible for preparing and communicating information pertaining to student loans, grants, fellowships, scholarships, and employment programs, as well as for advising, awarding, reporting, counseling, and performing office functions related to student financial aid.

Financial Need There is no clear-cut number or income for financial need. Each family's situation is unique and therefore must be evaluated individually. Financial need is based on family income, assets, number of dependents in the family, number of dependents in college, medical expenses, and other factors. There is no maximum allowable family income that you must meet in order to qualify as having financial need. That's why it's always worth the effort to apply for federal financial assistance and have your family's circumstances evaluated.

Free Application for Federal Student Aid (FAFSA) The federal form that all undergraduate and even graduate students must file if they need financial assistance to attend a graduate or professional school. This form evaluates the student's and parents' income and assets and determines whether a student is eligible for federal financial assistance. There is no cost in filing this form.

Graduate Management Admissions Test (GMAT) The GMAT requires that a student think systematically and logically. The GMAT tests verbal and reasoning skills that have been developed over a long period of time.

Graduate Record Examination (GRE) This is a general test that tests verbal, quantitative, and analytical areas. Each section is scored separately (from 200 to 800 points) and attempts to predict a student's scholastic ability in each section. The verbal section tests vocabulary and reading comprehension. The quantitative tests arithmetic, algebra, geometry, and data interpretation. The analytical covers logic games (which test ability to use logic) and logical reasoning, and some tests now also include analysis of explanation (which provides a story or situation and asks whether there is enough information to answer certain questions). The analytical portion is much like the analytical portion of the Law School Admissions Test (LSAT). Some graduate programs may not use the score on the analytical section when considering admission.

Grant A type of federal, state, or school financial aid award that is free money, that is, the student doesn't have to repay it. However, students are required to contact the Financial Aid Office of the school they want to attend in order to obtain the forms needed to apply for this money. This term is used interchangeably with scholarship and fellowship.

Guaranteed Student Loans (GSL) The GSL is a federally sponsored loan program administered by private lending institutions (banks, savings & loans, and credit unions). The loan is insured by the federal government or by a state guarantee agency. Repayment of the loan and interest begins six months after the student leaves school or graduates. The student may have from five to ten years to repay the loan, depending on how much was borrowed.

Independent Student Status Independent status is granted if the student is an orphan, a ward of the court, in an adverse parental situation, at least age twenty-four, a veteran of the U.S. Armed Forces, is married, has a child, or is a graduate or professional school student.

Law School Admissions Test (LSAT) The LSAT is required for admission to any law school. The minimum test scores required on the LSAT for entrance vary from school to school. Questions concerning the LSAT should be addressed to the Educational Testing Service, Box 994, Princeton, New Jersey 08541, (609) 921–9000 or to the Law School Admission Service, Box 2000, Newtown, Pennsylvania 18940, (215) 968–1001. There are four test dates for the LSAT every year.

Loan A loan is a type of financial aid award that must be repaid by a student or parent over a specified amount of time, usually after the student has graduated or has left school. Some loans don't start accruing interest until the student graduates or leaves school. A Perkins Loan is borrowed from the university and must be repaid to the university. Stafford and PLUS (Parent Loan for Undergraduate Students) loans are offered through lending institutions and are repaid to the institution.

Medical College Admissions Test (MCAT) Medical schools require the MCAT for admissions. This test is administered by the ACT Program, P.O. Box 451, Iowa City, Iowa 52243, (319) 337–1276. The MCAT is offered twice a year.

Miller Analogies Test (MAT) The Miller Analogies Test provides insight into measurement of verbal and reasoning ability and takes only fifty minutes to complete. The MAT is accepted by many graduate education programs in lieu of the GRE. If you have any questions about this test you should contact your graduate admissions office or the Psychological Corporation, 19500 Bulverde Road, San Antonio, TX 78259, (800) 622–3231 or (210) 339–8710, http://www.tpcweb.com/mat.

National League of Nursing Graduate Nursing Examination (NLNGNE) The NLNGNE is not always required, so students should contact the graduate programs at the nursing schools in which the student has an interest.

Parental Contribution Parental Contribution is the same as Expected Family Contribution (EEC). Using the income of the year prior to the year when financial assistance will be needed (i.e., 2004 if applying for 2005–2006), the Congressional Methodology (CM) determines the available income that can be used by a student or parent for a student's college education based on a parent's income and assets. The CM takes the following items into consideration: federal and FICA taxes, estimated state and local taxes; work expenses of both parents (or of one parent, in the case of a single-parent household); medical expenses not covered by insurance; elementary and secondary private school tuition (usually only up to a certain limit); and basic living expenses (rent/mortgage, food, clothing, transportation, insurance, etc.). The allowable basic living expenses are determined using a federal determined guideline and are based on the size of the family and the number of dependents in college. The parental contribution may be appealed (at the college financial aid office) if special circumstances arise (such as loss of a parent's job, a parent's ill health, or death of a parent).

Parental Leave Deferment This denotes the period of time (usually up to six months) that loan payments can be postponed if a borrower is pregnant or is taking care of a newborn or a newly adopted child and cannot be attending school. During this time of deferment, the student (new parent) must be unemployed. To find out about other types of deferments, contact the lending institution from which the money was borrowed.

Perkins Loan This loan program (formally called the National Direct Student Loan) is open to both undergraduate and graduate students. It is a loan from the federal government that must be repaid directly to the school. It has a 5% interest rate, and repayment must begin nine months after the student stops being a full-time student. This loan can be deferred for up to three years for military service, Peace Corps work, or other such service work or if the student remains a half-time student. Under certain conditions, loan repayment may be waived.

PROFILE Registration The PROFILE is a form that the student and parent might have to fill out if financial aid is being sought from certain institutions. The PROFILE is obtained from the institution's financial aid office. This form was formerly known as the Financial Aid Form (FAF).

Promissory Note This is the contract you sign when you receive a student loan. The student should carefully read this document and save it, because it contains the conditions under which the money was borrowed.

Satisfactory Academic Progress This term describes a student who is making measurable progress toward the completion of a course of study. Without satisfactory progress, financial aid is revoked.

Scholarship A scholarship is a type of financial aid that is free money, i.e., it is not a loan and need not be repaid. A student may be nominated by faculty at an institution or he/she may need to request an application. A student doesn't have to repay a scholarship but must fulfill all requirements (academic, extracurricular, athletic, or essay) to be awarded the scholarship. If the scholarship is renewable, the student may have to maintain a certain grade point average (GPA) in order to continue to receive it.

Self-Help Funds Self-help funds (loans and work-study jobs) refer to monies borrowed or earned by a student; thus they are called self-help. These funds must be used to further his or her education.

Stafford Loans This loan is open to both undergraduate and graduate students. The interest rate is variable. The award for a graduate student varies from $8,500 to $10,000 per year. Various lenders (bank, credit union, etc.) may make this loan. There is no deadline for applying, but students should apply as soon as possible after acceptance into a college and after they have received their financial aid package. Students must sign a promissory note agreeing to repay the loan. The lender, or the federal government, will collect any unpaid loan balance from students who default by garnishing wages or by taking any federal income tax refunds they are due. Under certain conditions, the loan may be deferred. Loan repayment can be canceled only in the event of a student's total and permanent disability or death.

Student Budget The amount of money a typical graduate or professional school student who is unmarried and financially independent of his/her parents, with dorm or off-campus living expenses, and attending college on a full-time basis will need each academic year. Actual costs will vary from school to school, but will include tuition; room and board; books and supplies; personal expenses; travel allowance; and freshman or transfer orientation fees. The transportation allowance is based on two trips per academic year for United States residents and one trip per year for foreign students and will vary depending on the student's place of permanent residence.

Student Certification Also called Statement of Educational Purpose and State of Registration Status. This is a document signed by a student financial aid applicant indicating that all information submitted for aid is true and complete and that the student certifies that he or she has fulfilled registration requirements for the aid program.

Transcript The record kept by a school that lists all classes taken and the grades received by a student. If an official transcript is required by a college or scholarship committee, the transcript must show the school seal on one of its pages and must bear an *original* signature from a school official.

Veterinary College Admission Test (VCAT) The VCAT is available, but not all veterinary medical schools require this exam for entrance. Students should contact the admissions office of each of the veterinary schools they are considering. Applications for this exam are available from the Psychological Corporation, 19500 Bulverde Road, San Antonio, TX 78259, (800) 622–3231 or (210) 339–8710, http://www.tpcweb.com/pse/g-vcatO.htm.

Work-Study Job Most financial aid recipients can expect to have employment offered as part of their financial aid package. Most financial aid recipients should expect to work anywhere from 10 to 20 hours a week. Generally, students are encouraged not to work more than 12 hours per week. Most students work on campus (though some off-campus jobs may be available) in various university departments, offices, cafeterias, or in the school library. A work-study job counts toward the self-help requirement.

FIFTEEN

ADDITIONAL SOURCES OF INFORMATION

We suggest you look for the books at your school or public libraries, nonprofit foundation libraries, or at your local bookstore before ordering it directly. Prices are subject to change.

AAMC Curriculum Directory
Association of American Medical Colleges
ATTN: Membership and Publication Orders
2450 N Street, N.W.
Washington, DC 20037
(202) 828–0400
(202) 828–0416 (to place orders)
http://www.aamc.org

AAMC MEDLOANS Program
Section for Student Services
Association of American Medical Colleges
2450 N Street, N.W.
Washington, DC 20037
(202) 828–0400
http://www.aamc.org

Allied Health Education Directory
American Medical Association
515 North State Street
Chicago, IL 60610
(800) AMA–3211
(312) 464–5000
http://www.ama-assn.org

American Accounting Association (AAA)
5717 Bessie Drive
Sarasota, FL 34233–2399
(941) 921–7747
(941) 923–4093 (Fax)
http://www.aaa-edu.org

American Association for the Advancement of Science
1200 New York Avenue, N.W.
Washington, DC 20005
(202) 326–6400
http://www.aaas.org

American Association of Colleges for Teacher Education
1307 New York Avenue, N.W., Suite 300

Washington, DC 20005–4701
(202) 293–2450
(202) 457–8095
http://www.aacte.org

American Association of University Women
1111 16th Street, N.W.
Washington, DC 20036
(800) 326–AAUW
(202) 785–777 (TDD)
(202) 872–1425 (Fax)
http://www.aauw.org
info@aauw.org

American Business Women's Association (ABWA)
9100 Ward Parkway
P.O. Box 8728
Kansas City, MO 64114
(816) 361–6621
(800) 228–0007
http://www.abwahq.org
pquerra@abwahq.org

American Indian College Fund
8333 Greenwood Blvd
Denver, CO 80221
(303) 426–8900
http://www.collegefund.org

American Indian Graduate Center (AIGC)
4520 Montgomery Boulevard, N.E., Suite 1-B
Albuquerque, NM 87109
(505) 881–4584
(505) 884–0427 (Fax)
http://www.aigc.com

American Institute of Physics (AIP)
One Physics Ellipse
College Park, MD 20740–3843
(301) 209–3100
http://www.aip.org

American Management Association (AMA)
1601 Broadway
New York, NY 10019
(212) 586–8100
http://www.amanet.org

American Marketing Association
311 South Wacker Drive, Suite 5800

Chicago, IL 60606
(312) 542–1150
(800) AMA–1150
(312) 542–9001 (Fax)
http://www.ama.org
info@ama.org

American Mathematical Society
201 Charles Street
Providence, RI 02940–6248
(401) 455–4000
(800) 321–4AMS
(401) 331–3842 (Fax)
http://www.ams.org
ams@ams.org

American Physical Society (APS)
One Physics Ellipse
College Park, MD 20740–3844
(301) 209–3200
(301) 209–0865 (Fax)
http://www.aps.org/edu
tara@aps.org

American Political Science Association
1527 New Hampshire Avenue, N.W.
Washington, DC 20036–1206
(202) 483–2512
http://www.apsanet.org
apsa@apsanet.org

American Psychological Association
750 First Street, N.E.
Washington, DC 20002–4242
(800) 374–2721
(202) 336–5500
http://www.apa.org

American Society for Engineering Education
1818 N Street, N.W., Suite 600
Washington, DC 20036–2479
(202) 331–3500
(202) 265–8504 (Fax)
http://www.asee.org

American Sociological Association
1307 New York Avenue, N.W., #700
Washington, DC 20005
(202) 383–9005
http://www.asanet.org

American Speech-Language-Hearing Association
10801 Rockville Pike
Rockville, MD 20852
(301) 897–5700
(800) 638–8255
http://www.asha.org

American Veterinary Medical Association
1931 N. Meacham Road, Suite 100
Schaumburg, IL 60173–4360
(847) 925–8070
(847) 925–1329 (Fax)
http://www.avma.org
AVMAINFO@avma.org

Association for Canadian Studies in the United States
1317 F Street, N.W., Suite 920
Washington, DC 20004–1105
(202) 393–2580
(202) 393–2582 (Fax)
http://www.acsus.org
info@acsus.org

Association for the Study of Higher Education
Department of Educational Administration
ATTN: Academic Advisor II
Harrington Tower, Room 511
Texas A&M University
College Station, TX 77843–4226
(409) 847–9098
(409) 862–4347 (Fax)
http://www.coe.tamu.edu/~edad
jnelson@tamu.edu

Association of American Law Schools (AALS)
1201 Connecticut Avenue, N.W., Suite 800
Washington, DC 20036–2605
(202) 296–8851
(202) 296–8869 (Fax)
http://www.aals.org
aals@aals.org

Association of American Medical Colleges (AAMC)
2450 N Street, N.W.
Washington, DC 20037–1126
(202) 828–0400
(202) 828–1125 (Fax)
http://www.aamc.org

Careers in Librarianship and
Financial Assistance for Library Education &
Information Studies
Office of Library Personnel Resources
American Library Association
50 East Huron Street
Chicago, IL 60611
(312) 944–7298
http://www.ala.org/olpr

Educational Awards Handbook
The Rotary Foundation of Rotary International
One Rotary Center
1560 Sherman Avenue
Evanston, IL 60201
(847) 866–3000
(847) 328–8554 (Fax)
http://www.rotary.org/index.htm

Federal Benefits for Veterans and Dependents
U.S. Government Printing Office
1000 Liberty Avenue, #501
Pittsburgh, PA 15222
(412) 644–2721
http://www.gpo.gov
wwwadmin@gpo.gov

Fellowships & Grants of Interest to Philosophers
American Philosophical Association
31 Amstel Avenue
University of Delaware
Newark, DE 19716
(302) 831–1112
http://www.apa.udel.edu/apa/index.html

Financial Advice for Minority Students Seeking an
Education in the Health Professions
Office of Statewide Health Planning and Development
Assistant Director of Public Affairs
1600 Ninth Street, Suite 435
Sacramento, CA 95814
(916) 654–1499
http://www.oshpd.cahwnet.gov
dschell@oshpd.cahwnet.gov

Financial Aid for College Students
American Chemical Society
Education Department
1155 16th Street, N.W.
Washington, DC 20036

(800) 227–5558
(202) 872–4600
http://www.acs.org/education

Foundation Grants to Individuals
(ISBN 0–87954–883–5)
The Foundation Center
79 Fifth Avenue, 2nd Floor
New York, NY 10003
(212) 620–4230
(212) 691–1828 (Fax)
http://www.fdncenter.org
feedback@fdncenter.org

Fulbright Grants and Other Grants for Graduate Study
Abroad
Institute of International Education
809 United Nations Plaza
New York NY 10017–3580
(212) 883–8200
http://www.iie.org
info@iie.org

Funding for U.S. Study: A Guide for Foreign
Nationals
Institute of International Education
809 United Nations Plaza
New York NY 10017–3580
(212) 883–8200
http://www.iie.org/
info@iie.org

Grants and Awards Available to American Writers
PEN American Center
568 Broadway, #401
New York, NY 10012
(212) 334–1660
http://www.pen.org

Grants at a Glance: A Directory of Funding and
Financial Aid Resources for Women in Science
Association for Women in Science
1200 New York Avenue, N.W., Suite 650
Washington, DC 20005
(202) 326–8940
(202) 326–8960 (Fax)
http://www.awis.org
awis@awis.org

Grants, Fellowships & Prizes of Interest to Historians
American Historical Association
400 A Street, S.E.
Washington, DC 20003–3889
(202) 544–2422
(202) 544–8307 (Fax)
http://www.theaha.org
aha@theaha.org

Guide to American Graduate Schools
by Harold R. Doughty
(ISBN 0–14–0469869)
Penguin Putnam Inc.
375 Hudson Street
New York, NY 10014
(212) 645–3121

Guide to Doctoral Programs in Business and
Management
American Assembly of Collegiate Schools of Business
600 Emerson Road, Suite 300
St. Louis, MO 63141–6762
(314) 872–8481
(314) 872–8495 (Fax)
http://www.aacsb.edu

Guide to Graduate & Professional Fellowships for
Minority Students
Black Collegian Magazine
140 Carondelet Street
New Orleans, LA 70130
(504) 523–0154
http://www.black-collegian.com

Guide to Grants and Fellowships in Linguistics
Linguistic Society of America
1325 18th Street, N.W., Suite 211
Washington, DC 20036–6501
(202) 835–1717 (Fax)
http://www.lsadc.org

Handbook for Minority Pre-Med Students
American Medical Student Association
1902 Association Drive
Reston, VA 20191
(703) 620–6600
http://www.amsa.org
amsa@www.amsa.org

Helping Hand
American Medical Association
515 N. State Street
Chicago, IL 60610
(312) 464–5000
http://www.ama-assn.org

Higher Education Opportunities for Minorities & Women
Superintendent of Documents
Office of Higher Education Programs
7th and D Streets, S.W.
Washington, DC 20202
(800) USA–LEARN
http://www.ed.gov
CustomerService@inet.ed.gov

Hispanic Financial Resource Handbook
Hispanic Student Programs
Ethnic Student Services
1739 North High Street, #345
340 Ohio Union
Columbus, OH 43210–1392
(614) 688–4988
http://www.osu.edu/units/stuaff/ess.htm

Journalism Career and Scholarship Guide
Dow Jones Newspaper Fund, Inc.
P.O. Box 300
Princeton, NJ 08543–0300
(609) 452–2820
(800) DOW–FUND
(609) 520–5804 (Fax)
http://djnewspaperfund.dowjones.com/fund

Law School Admission Council (LSAC)
661 Penn Street
Newtown, PA 18940
(215) 968–1001
(215) 968–1119 (Fax)
http://www.lsac.org
LSACinfo@LSAC.org

Mathematical Association of America
1529 Eighteenth Street, N.W.
Washington, DC 20036–1385
(202) 387–5200
(800) 741–9415
(202) 265–2384 (Fax)
http://www.maa.org
maahq@maa.org

MCAT Student Manual
Association of American Medical Colleges
Publications and Information Resources
2450 N Street, N.W.
Washington, DC 20037–1126
(202) 828–0400
(202) 828–1125 (Fax)
http://www.aamc.org/findinfo/start.htm

Medical School: Getting In, Staying In, Staying Human
by Keith Russell Ablow, M.D.
Bedford/St. Martin's
175 Fifth Avenue
New York, NY 10010
(212) 674–5151
http://www.stmartins.com

Minority Fellowship Program Aided at Supporting
Education
Opportunities in Psychology
American Psychological Association
750 First Street, N.E., #100
Washington, DC 20002–4242
(202) 336–5510
(800) 374–2721
http://www.apa.org

Minority Student Information Clearinghouse
Association of American Medical Colleges
2450 N Street, N.W.
Washington, DC 20037–1126
(202) 828–0400
(202) 828–1125 (Fax)
http://www.aamc.org/findinfo/start.htm

National Black MBA Association (NBMBAA)
180 N. Michigan Avenue, Suite 1400
Chicago, IL 60601
(312) 236–2622
(312) 236–4131 (Fax)
http://www.nbmbaa.org
mail@nbmbaa.org

National Clearinghouse for Professionals in Special
Education
1110 North Glebe Road, Suite 300
Arlington, VA 22201–5704
(800) 641–7824

http://www.special-ed-careers.org/contact_us/index.html

National Clearinghouse on Post-Secondary Education
for Individuals with Disabilities
The George Washington University
HEATH Resource Center
2121 K Street, N.W., Suite 220
Washington, DC 20037
(800) 544–3284
http://www.heath.gwu.edu.

National Directory of Internships
National Society for Experiential Education
9001 Braddock Road, Suite 380
Springfield, VA 22151
(703) 426–4268
(800) 803–4170
http://www.nsee.org

National Institute of General Medical Sciences
National Institute of Health
45 Center Drive, MSC 6200
Bethesda, MD 20892–6200
(301) 496–7301
http://www.nih.gov.nigms

National Society of Accountants
1010 North Fairfax Street
Alexandria, VA 22314
(703) 549–6400
(800) 966–6679
http://www.nsacct.org

The Practice Medical College Admission Test
Association of American Medical Colleges
ATTN: Membership and Publication Orders
2450 N Street, N.W.
Washington, DC 20037–1126
(202) 828–0400
(202) 828–1125 (Fax)
http://www.aamc.org/findinfo/start.htm

The Résumé Catalog (revised): 200 Damn Good
Examples
by Yana Parker
(ISBN 0–89815–891–5)
Ten Speed Press
P.O. Box 7123

Berkeley, CA 94709
(510) 559–1600
(510) 559–1629 (Fax)
http://www.tenspeed.com

Scholarships and Loans in Nursing Education
National League for Nursing
61 Broadway
New York, NY 10006
(Request Publication #41–2638)
(800) 669–1656
(212) 363–5555
http://www.nln.org

Selected List of Fellowship Opportunities and Aids to
Advanced Education for U.S. Citizens and Foreign
Nationals
Publication Office
The National Science Foundation
4201 Wilson Boulevard
Arlington, VA 22230
(703) 292–5111
(800) 877–8339 (FIRS)
(703) 306–0090 (TDD)
http://www.nsf.gov
info@nsf.gov

United Negro College Fund, Inc.
8260 Willow Oaks
Corporate Drive
Fairfax, VA 22031
(703) 205–3400
(800) 331–2244
http://www.uncf.org

U.S. Public Health Service
4350 East West Highway
Bethesda, MD 20814
(800) 279–1605
(301) 594-3360
http://www.usphs.gov

World Directory of Medical Schools
World Health Organization
2 United Nations Plaza
DC–2 Building, Room 0956–0976
New York, NY 10017
http://www.who.org

SIXTEEN

WHERE TO GO FOR STATE HELP

These agencies should have information about, or have responsibility for, most state student aid programs. State agencies may not have information about health profession programs, minority programs, veterans' assistance, or National Guard programs. When there are alternate addresses for these specific groups, the alternate addresses are provided. For information about the National Guard programs, write to the State Adjutant General; the address is in your local or state capital's telephone directory. One place to start your search is: http://www.ed.gov/offices/OPE/agencies.htm.

Alabama
Alabama Department of Higher Education
50 North Ripley Street
P.O. Box 302101
Montgomery, AL 36104
(334) 242–9700
http://www.alsde.edu
[For scholarship, grant, and loan information]

Alaska
Alaska Post-Secondary Education
3030 Vintage Boulevard
Juneau, AK 99801–7109
(907) 465–2962
http://www.state.ak.us/acpe
[For scholarship, grant, and loan information]

Arizona
Arizona Post-Secondary Education
2020 North Central Avenue, Suite 275
Phoenix, AZ 85004–4503
(602) 229–2500
(602) 229–2599 (Fax)
http://www.abor.asu.edu/
[For scholarship and grant information]

Arkansas
Arkansas Department of Higher Education
114 East Capitol Avenue
Little Rock, AR 72201

(501) 371–2000
(800) 443–6030
http://www.arkansashighered.com

Student Loan Guarantee Foundation of Arkansas
219 South Victory
Little Rock, AR 72201–1884
(501) 372–1491

California
California Student Aid Commission
P.O. Box 419027
Rancho Cordova, CA 95741–9027
(916) 526–7590
(888) 224–7268
http://www.csac.ca.gov/default.asp

Colorado
Colorado Commission on Higher Education
Colorado Heritage Center
1380 Lawrence Street, Suite 1200
Denver, CO 80204
(303) 866–2723
http://www.state.co.us/cche_dir/hecche.html

Connecticut
Connecticut Department of Education
Student Financial Assistance Commission
P.O. Box 2219
Hartford, CT 06145
(860) 713–6523
http://www.state.ct.us/sde/dirmain.htm

Delaware
Delaware Higher Education Commission
State Office Building
820 North French Street
Wilmington, DE 19801
(800) 292–7935
(302) 577–3240
(302) 577–6765 (Fax)
http://www.doe.state.de.us/high-ed/index.htm
mlaffey@state.de.us

District of Columbia
District of Columbia Office of Postsecondary Education
441 4th Street, N.W., Suite 920S
Washington, DC 20001

(202) 727–6436
http://www.ci.washington.dc.us

Florida
Board of Regents
Student Financial Assistance Commission
1940 N. Monroe Street, Suite 70
Tallahassee, FL 32303–4759
(888) 827–2004
(904) 487–0649
http://www.bor.state.fl.us

Georgia
Georgia Student Finance Commission
2082 East Exchange, Suite 245
Tucker, GA 30084
(770) 724–9000
(800) 776–6876 (In-state)
http://www.gsfc.org

Hawaii
Hawaii State Postsecondary Education Commission
2444 Dole Street
Honolulu, HI 96804
(808) 956–8213
http://www.k12.hi.us
http://www.hern.hawaii.edu/hern
http://www.doe.hawaii.edu

Idaho
State Board of Education
650 West State Street
P.O. Box 83720
Boise, ID 83720–0037
(208) 332–6800
http://www.sde.state.id.us/Dept

Illinois
Illinois State Board of Education
State Scholarship Commission
100 North First Street
Springfield, IL 62777
(217) 782–4321
http://www.isbe.state.il.us

Indiana
State Student Assistance Commission of Indiana
150 West Market Street, Suite 500

Indianapolis, IN 46204
(317) 232–2350
http://www.state.in.us/ssaci
grants@ssaci.state.in.us

Iowa
Iowa College Student Aid Commission
200 10th Street, 4th Floor
Des Moines, IA 50309–2824
(800) 383–4222
(515) 242–3344
http://www.state.ia.us/government/icsac

Kansas
Kansas Department of Education
120 S.E. 10th Avenue
Topeka, KS 66612–1182
(785) 296–3201
http://www.ksbe.state.ks.us

Kentucky
Kentucky Higher Education Assistance Authority
Council on Postsecondary Education
1050 U.S. 127 South, Suite 102
Frankfort, KY 40601–4323
(800) 928–8926
(502) 573–1555
http://www.kheaa.com

Louisiana
Louisiana Department of Education
626 North 4th Street
P.O. Box 94064
Baton Rouge, LA 70804–9064
(800) 259–5626
(504) 342–2098
http://www.doe.state.la.us
webteam@mail.doe.state.la.us

Maine
Maine Department of Education
23 State House Station
Augusta, ME 04333–0023
(800) 228–3734
(207) 287–5800
(207) 287–2550 (TDD)
http://www.state.me.us/education

Maryland
Maryland Higher Education Commission
839 Bestgate Road, Suite 400
Annapolis, MD 21401
(410) 260–4500
(800) 974–0203
http://www.mhec.state.md.us

Massachusetts
Board of Higher Education
One Ashburton Place, Room 1401
Boston, MA 02108–1696
(617) 994–6950
http://www.mass.edu
[For scholarship and grant information]

Massachusetts Office of Student Financial Assistance
330 Stuart Street, Suite 304
Boston, MA 02116
(617) 727–9420
(617) 727–0667 (Fax)
http://www.osfa.mass.edu

Michigan
Michigan Department of Education
Scholarships
608 West Allegan Street
Lansing, MI 48909
(517) 373–3394
http://www.michigan.gov/mde

Minnesota
Minnesota Higher Education Services Office
1450 Energy Park Drive, Suite 350
Saint Paul, MN 55108–5227
(800) 657–3866
(651) 642–0567
http://www.mheso.state.mn.us

Mississippi
Office of State Student Financial Aid
301 North Lamar, Suite 508
Jackson, MS 39201
(601) 359–3468
(866) 671–3468
http://www.state.ms.us

Missouri
Missouri Coordinating Board for Higher Education
Student Assistance Resource Services
3515 Amazonas Drive
Jefferson City, MO 65109–5717
(573) 751–2361
(800) 473–6757
(573) 751–3940
http://www.mocbhe.gov

Montana
Montana Commission of Higher Education
P.O. Box 203101
2500 Broadway
Helena, MT 59620–3101
(800) 537–7508
(406) 444–6570
(406) 444–1469 (Fax)
http://www.montana.edu/wwwoche

Nebraska
Nebraska Coordinating Commission for Postsecondary
Education
301 Centennial Mall, South
Lincoln, NE 68509–4987
(402) 471–2295
http://www.nde.state.ne.us

Nevada
Nevada Board of Education
700 East Fifth Street
Carson City, NV 89701
(775) 687–9200
http://www.nde.state.nv.us

New Hampshire
New Hampshire Department of Education
101 Pleasant Street
Concord, NH 03301–3860
(603) 271–3494
http://www.state.nh.us

New Jersey
Department of Higher Education
Office of Student Assistance
20 West State Street
P.O. Box 542
Trenton, NJ 08625–0542

(609) 292–4310
http://www.state.nj.us/highereducation

New Mexico
New Mexico Commission on Higher Education
1068 Cerrillos Road
Santa Fe, NM 87501
(800) 279–9777
(505) 827–7383
http://www.nmche.org

New York
New York State Education Department
Office of Higher Education
Scholarship Unit
89 Washington Avenue
Albany, NY 12234
(518) 474–5313
http://www.nysed.gov

North Carolina
North Carolina State Education Assistance Authority
301 N. Wilmington Street
Raleigh, NC 27601
(919) 807–3300
http://www.dpi.state.nc.us

North Dakota
North Dakota Department of Public Instruction
State Capitol Building, 10th Floor
600 East Boulevard Avenue
Bismarck, ND 58504–0440
(701) 224–2271
(701) 328–2461 (Fax)
http://www.dpi.state.nd.us

Ohio
Ohio Board of Regents
30 East Broad Street, 36th Floor
Columbus, OH 43215–3414
(888) 833–1133
(614) 466–6000
(614) 752–5903 (Fax)
http://www.regents.state.oh.us

Oklahoma
Oklahoma State Regents for Higher Education
655 Research Parkway, Suite 200
Oklahoma City, OK 73101–3000

(800) 247–0420
(405) 225–9100
http://www.okhighered.org

Oregon
Oregon State Scholarship Commission
1500 Valley River Drive, Suite 100
Eugene, OR 97401–2130
(503) 687–7400
http://www.ossc.state.or.us

Pennsylvania
Pennsylvania Higher Education Assistance Agency
(PHEAA)
1200 North 7th Street
Harrisburg, PA 17102
(800) 692–7435 (in PA)
(717) 720–3600
http://www.pheaa.org

Rhode Island
Board of Governors for Higher Education
State House, Room 217
Providence, RI 02903
(401) 222–2357
(401) 222–2311 (TDD)
http://www.state.ri.us

South Carolina
South Carolina Commission on Higher Education
1333 Main Street, Suite 200
Columbia, SC 29201
(803) 737–2260
http://www.che400.state.sc.us

South Dakota
South Dakota Department of Education & Cultural
Affairs
Office of the Secretary
700 Governor's Drive
Pierre, SD 57501–2291
(605) 773–4747
http://www.state.sd.us/deca

Tennessee
Tennessee Higher Education Commission
404 James Robertson Parkway, Suite 1900
Nashville, TN 37243–0820

(615) 741–3605
http://www.state.tn.us/thec

Texas
Texas Higher Education Coordinating Board
P.O. Box 12788, Capitol Station
Austin, TX 78711
(800) 242–3062
(512) 483–6101
(512) 483–6169 (Fax)
http://www.thecb.state.tx.us

Utah
Utah State Office of Education
250 East 500 South
Salt Lake City, UT 84111
(801) 538–7517
http://www.state.ut.us/html/education.htm

Vermont
Vermont Department of Education
120 State Street
Montpelier, VT 05620–2501
(802) 828–3147
(802) 828–3140 (Fax)
http://www.state.vt.us/educ

Virginia
State Council of Higher Education for Virginia
James Monroe Building, 9th Floor
101 North 14th Street
Richmond, VA 23219
(804) 225–2600
http://www.schev.edu

Washington
Washington State Higher Education Coordinating
Board
Old Capitol Building
P.O. Box 47200
Olympia, WA 98504–7200
(360) 725–6000
http://www.k12.wa.us

West Virginia
West Virginia Department of Education
1018 Kanawha Boulevard, East, Suite 700
Charleston, WV 25301

(304) 558–2101
http://www.hepc.wvnet.edu

Wisconsin
Wisconsin Department of Public Instruction
125 South Webster Street
P.O. Box 7841
Madison, WI 53707–7841
(608) 266–3390
(800) 441–4563
http://www.state.wi.us/agencies/dpi

Wyoming
Wyoming State Department of Education
Hathaway Building
2300 Capitol Avenue, 2nd Floor
Cheyenne, WY 82002–0050
(307) 777–6265
(307) 777–6234 (Fax)
http://www.k12.wy.us

American Samoa
American Samoa Community College
Board of Higher Education
P.O. Box 2609
Pago Pago, AS 96799–2609
(684) 699–1141

Guam
Department of Education
Student Financial Assistance
University of Guam, UOG State
303 University Drive

Mangilao, Guam 96923
(671) 734–4469
http://www.doe.edu.gu

Northern Mariana Islands
Northern Marianas College
Olympio T. Borja Memorial Library
As-Terlaje Campus
P.O. Box 501250
Saipan, MP 96950–1250
(670) 234–3690
http://www.nmcnet.edu

Puerto Rico
Puerto Rico Council on Higher Education
P.O. Box 19900
San Juan, PR 00910–1900
(787) 724–7100

Virgin Islands
Virgin Island Joint Boards of Education
Charlotte Amalie
P.O. Box 11900
St Thomas, VI 00801
(340) 774–4546

For Federal Student Aid Information,
call 1 (800) 4–FED AID [1 (800) 433–3243].
To get information explaining the formula used to
calculate Expected Family Contribution, write to:
Federal Student Aid Information Center
P.O. Box 84
Washington, DC 20044

PART II

AT-A-GLANCE INDEX

2100, 2127, 2138–2143, 2155–2157, 2169–2170, 2172, 2174, 2291, 2314–2315, 2322–2328, 2343–2351, 2353–2363, 2365, 2379, 2382, 2397–2398, 2429, 2441, 2466, 2470, 2472, 2479, 2491, 2495, 2498, 2500, 2505

Human Relations 3, 1306, 1328, 1337

Human Resources 3, 634, 915, 998–999, 1190, 1417, 1434, 1545, 1907

Hydrology 398, 400, 513, 516, 1239, 1630, 1875

Ichthyology 11, 855, 1346

Illustration 2216, 2273, 2313

Immigration Studies 2177

Industrial Design 1753, 2214

Industrial Organization 923

Information Management 404, 1368, 1543, 1545, 1935

Information Science 247–248, 476, 660, 819–822, 888–892, 952–955, 971–974, 1332, 1428, 1543, 1577–1578, 2130, 2380, 2393, 2397

Information Technology 3, 225, 484–489, 987, 1324, 1543, 1545, 2002

Institutional Management 196

Insurance 979, 1228, 2002–2003, 2307

Interior Design 434, 685–687, 1292, 1374, 1435, 2114

International Affairs 46, 459–460, 1209, 1278, 1340, 1912, 2308, 2334, 2397, 2402–2403, 2499–2500

International Law 598, 1278, 1415, 2505

International Peace 995, 1415, 2013, 2402–2403

International Relations 598, 781, 924–925, 1262, 1340, 1393, 1404, 2055, 2308, 2334, 2402–2403, 2469

International Security 1208, 992–995, 2308, 2469

International Studies 615, 992–995, 998–999, 2308, 2334, 2402–2403

Islamic Studies 635–636

Italian Art 1791

Italian Literature 118, 230, 1653, 1791

Italian Studies 230

Italian Theater 1791

Jewish Education 1462, 1468–1471

Jewish Professional Services 77, 1462, 1468–1471

Jewish-Related Studies 459–462, 1462, 1468–1471

Journalism 13, 78, 92, 167, 224, 458, 463, 597, 602, 631, 634, 740–743, 780, 790–797, 806–807, 815–816, 822–833, 942–944, 983, 1014, 1035, 1134, 1269, 1279–1280, 1312, 1337, 1381, 1386, 1508, 1593, 1668, 1688–1693, 1829, 1875, 1924, 1965, 2050–2051, 2066, 2100, 2285, 2322–2328, 2336, 2397–2398, 2412, 2437

Journalism, Broadcast 597, 740–743, 795–797, 806–807, 826, 942, 1337, 1508, 1668–1689, 1691–1692, 1924, 2050–2051, 2285, 2322–2328, 2365, 2412, 2437

Journalism, Communications 78, 92, 167, 2398, 2412

Journalism, Editorial 1312

Journalism, Educators 793

Journalism, Geography 2285

Journalism, Graphic Art 1312

Journalism, Magazine 597, 1381, 2365

Journalism, Newspaper 597, 1312, 1381, 2365

Journalism, Photo 795, 1312, 1830–1834

Journalism, Print 597, 794–796, 1156, 1688–1689, 1691–1693, 2365

Journalism, Print and Electronic 794–795, 2365

Journalism, Radio and Television 739–743, 826, 942, 1337, 1508, 1668, 1688–1692, 1835, 2050–2051, 2322–2328, 2365

Journalism, Religious 2365

Kinesiotherapy 464

Labor Relations 372, 1434

Land Economics 755, 1551

Land Management 1875

Landscape Architecture 122, 124, 126, 689–696, 1137, 1231–1232, 1292, 1551–1552, 1880, 1904, 2163–2164, 2214, 2504

Landscape Design 1231–1232, 2163–2164

Land Surveying 320–322, 698, 946–951, 1045–1048, 1054, 1263, 1376, 1582, 1588, 1642, 1925, 2045–2047, 2061, 2331, 2449

Language, Arabic 88–89

Language, Chinese 88–89, 859, 998–999

Language, Eastern European 89, 325, 338–339

Language, Esperanto 89

Language, Finnish 89, 1404

Language, Foreign 89

Language, French 87–89, 2006

Language, German 60, 88–89, 325–326, 428–429, 1271, 1274

Language, Greek 88–89, 652–653, 2006

Language, Indian 88

Language, Italian 88

Language, Japanese 88–89, 861, 999–1000

Language, Latin 88

Language, Portuguese 88–89

Language, Russian 88–89, 998–999

Languages 5, 60, 86–89, 224, 338–339, 428–429, 639, 651–653, 862, 908, 998–999, 1271, 1274, 1404, 1569, 1656, 1856, 2006, 2379

Language Slavic 88

Languages, Modern 1658, 2379

Language, Spanish 88–89

Language, Testing 1155

Language, Turkish 639

Latino Studies 2126–2127

Law 13, 22, 46, 51, 204–208, 210, 213–214, 224, 243, 266–283, 300, 400, 430, 463, 592, 598, 781, 801–802, 849–851, 859, 901–904, 922, 981, 983, 986, 988, 991–992, 993–995, 998–999, 1009, 1114, 1143, 1205–1206, 1269,

Medicine, Osteopathic 8, 75–76, 243, 407, 505, 569, 770–772, 1028, 1032, 1040, 1101, 1123, 1141, 1200, 1266, 1465, 1519, 1579–1580, 1614, 1633, 1644, 1670, 1741, 1763–1766, 1773–1790, 1792, 1807–1825, 1839, 1858, 1894, 1917, 1935, 1996, 2017, 2038, 2041, 2068–2069, 2090–2092, 2107, 2196, 2224, 2330, 2339, 2341, 2389–2394, 2431

Medicine, Podiatry 8, 75, 300, 1227, 1465, 2390

Medicine, Psychiatry 132–133, 508, 604–606, 1465, 1472, 1476, 1591

Medicine, Rehabilitation 309, 316, 319, 1439–1440, 1548, 1935

Medicine, Sports 309, 1548

Mental Health 1591

Mental Health Research 1591

Mental Health Therapy 53, 607–609, 940, 1465, 2390

Meteorology 37, 65, 398, 513–517, 1170, 1630, 1838, 2503

Microbiology 1055

Microelectronics 2102–2104

Micropaleontology 2230

Military Policy 987

Military Professions 767–773, 1637

Mineralogy 1639–1640, 1755

Mineral Science 1639–1640

Ministry 18–22, 77, 253–265, 1001, 1033, 1164, 1441, 2314–2315

Missionary Work 1517, 2470–2484

Museum Studies 224, 799, 1098, 1598–1599, 1607–1608, 2128–2129, 2132, 2136, 2142–2143, 2145, 2149–2150, 2152, 2158–2159, 2161, 2166, 2288–2291, 2453

Music 13, 17, 115, 145, 284–285, 369, 374, 521–526, 645, 679, 719, 799–800, 803, 870, 879, 882, 886, 927, 1037, 1042, 1131–1133, 1197, 1281, 1329, 1416, 1519, 1532–1533, 1539–1542, 1546–1547, 1611–1613, 1632, 1635, 1643, 1727, 1733–1736, 1791, 1805, 1897, 1902, 1905, 1919, 1938, 2014–2016,

2032–2133, 2288, 2294–2295, 2318, 2429, 2432, 2443

Music, Business 886, 2294–2295

Music Composition 115, 145, 679, 870, 930, 1365, 1400, 1477, 1532–1533, 1636, 1727, 1735, 1846, 1938, 2022, 2062, 2088, 2318

Music Education 1632

Music, Instrumental 882, 1329, 1519, 1532–1533, 1727, 1919, 2318–2319, 2432

Music, Instrumental (Stringed) 369, 719, 1532–1533, 1541, 1635, 1727, 1919, 2318–2319, 2432

Musicology 521–526, 799

Music, Performance 17, 803, 882, 1037, 1281, 1329, 1532–1533, 1611–1613, 1727, 1919, 2088, 2318–2319, 2432, 2506

Music, Performance (Piano) 284, 1037, 1281, 1329, 1532–1533, 1541, 1727, 1902, 1919, 2088, 2318–2319, 2421, 2432, 2506

Music, Performance (Stringed) 719, 1037, 1532–1533, 1541, 1635, 1727, 1919, 2088, 2318–2319, 2432

Music, Performance (Vocal) 17, 284, 879, 882, 1037, 1532–1533, 1571, 1611–1613, 1697, 1727, 1894, 1905, 1919, 2088, 2318

Music Theater 897

Music Therapy 1686

Mycology 1673

National Security 5, 987, 1115, 1353, 1726, 1856, 1937, 2377, 2469

Natural History 518, 520, 1152, 1873

Natural Resource Management 1875

Natural Resource-Related 11, 65, 588

Natural Resource Science 65, 588, 753, 988, 1725, 1874, 2381

Natural Resources Conservation 588, 988, 1000, 1148, 1152, 1699, 1725, 1874–1875, 1885, 2381

Natural Sciences 11, 46, 332, 398, 588, 761, 992–993, 995, 1081–1083, 1176, 1377, 1464, 1738, 2118

Nautical Archeology 1346

Naval Science 1346

Neuroscience 66, 1293–1294, 2187–2194

Nuclear Science 528–530

Numismatics 531–533

Nurse Anesthetist 772–773

Nurse Practitioner 53, 851, 1200, 1695

Nursing 37, 53, 139, 183–186, 221–223, 287–292, 302, 423, 466, 527, 534–556, 607–609, 634, 769, 771–772, 838–839, 845, 851, 1005, 1031, 1101, 1110, 1141, 1160, 1178, 1224, 1333, 1440, 1450, 1515, 1520, 1524, 1525, 1535–1536, 1628–1629, 1650, 1695, 1705–1712, 1762, 1806, 1867–1871, 1917, 1935–1936, 1940–1958, 2038, 2074, 2091, 2110, 2390, 2431, 2460, 2491, 2502

Nursing, History 172–176

Nursing, Holistic 423

Nursing, Midwife 302, 1057–1058, 1589

Nursing, Registered 53

Nursing, Research 534–556, 1450, 1762, 1940–1958

Nutrition 40–42, 199–200, 202, 311, 348, 353–362, 365, 646–648, 939, 1395, 1645–1649, 1838, 1863, 2107, 2370

Nutrition, Communication 364, 1649

Nutrition, Education 353, 358

Nutrition-Related 362, 364–365

Nutrition, Research 353

Occupational Therapy 557–558, 1440, 1628–1629, 1686, 2020, 2390

Oceanography 65, 398, 513, 516, 654, 885, 918, 1000, 1148, 1172, 1346, 1755, 1934, 2375

Oceanography, Geological 1346

Operations Management 601

Operations Research 1324, 1577–1578

Optical Science 65, 1443

Optometry 75, 395–396, 559, 771–772, 867, 893

Ornithology 518–520, 563–568, 1484, 2458

Painting 2, 52, 126, 788, 1348, 1400, 1426, 1442, 1451, 1567, 2350, 2443

Paleobiography 1244

Paleobiology 1099–1100

Paleoceanography 1249

Paleogeography 1244

Paleontology 226, 1755, 1992–1994, 2168, 2271–2277

Paleontology, Vertebrate 2271–2277

Paleo-ornithology 568

Palynology 228–229

Paper Science 1411

Performing Arts 73, 372, 799, 884, 1042, 1121, 1342, 1487–1505, 1561–1563, 1892, 1906, 2461

Personnel Administration 634, 998–999, 1190, 1328, 1434

Petrology 1253, 1639–1640, 2195

Pharmaceutical Sciences 3, 379–382, 2205, 2224, 2391

Pharmacology 3, 65, 2002, 2005, 2201, 2247–2268

Pharmacy 300, 379–382, 683, 776, 868, 1101, 1515, 1532–1533, 1696, 2002, 2005, 2390

Philanthropy 1064, 2178

Philology 1103, 1140

Philosophy 332, 570–574, 981, 1023, 1103, 1280, 1348, 1311, 1832, 1917, 2505

Philosophy of Science 1850, 1852

Photogrammetry 698, 2045–2047

Photographic Science 2186

Photography 748, 799, 998–999, 1881, 1915–1916, 2085, 2350, 2429, 2437, 2443

Photo Journalism 795, 1312, 1830–1834

Photo Science 998–999

Physical and Human Geography 1755

Physical Education 635, 941

Physical Sciences 26, 38, 46, 224, 397, 746, 761, 835, 992–993, 995, 1023, 1084–1085, 1170, 1182, 1187, 1419–1420, 1428, 1464, 1699, 1847–1852, 1928, 2367, 2376

Physical Therapy 576, 1440, 1515, 1628–1629, 1686, 2390

Physician's Assistant 1628–1629, 2019, 2390–2391

Physics 26, 37, 46, 65–66, 171, 513, 575, 660, 918, 998–999, 1023, 1136, 1332, 1411, 1417, 1428, 1577–1578, 1634, 1683, 1827, 1836, 2091, 2336, 2371, 2380, 2394, 2450, 2503

Physics, Cosmic 1136

Physics, Health 1931

Physics, Theoretical 1136

Physiology 3, 26, 46, 577–582

Phytopathology 1444

Planetary Geology 398, 1257

Planetary Physics 1396, 2125

Planetary Sciences 2125

Planning 583–595

Plant Biochemistry 2071, 2338

Plant Biology 1873, 2071, 2165, 2168, 2338, 2504

Plant Pathology 1444, 2504

Plant Physiology 65, 662, 1444, 2071, 2338, 2504

Plant Sciences 1097–1098, 1321, 1444, 2165, 2168, 2338, 2504

Police Administration 51, 843

Police Science 51

Political Economics 1307–1308, 1353, 1638

Political Philosophy 598, 1014

Political Science 171, 224, 368, 463, 596–599, 983, 998–999, 1013, 1074, 1105, 1129–1130, 1218–1219, 1262, 1269, 1290, 1306, 1340, 1638, 1839, 1875, 2427, 2469, 2500, 2505

Political Theory 1393

Politics 224, 599, 926, 981, 992–993, 995, 1393, 1404

Pomology 600

Population Studies 1393, 2033, 2054, 2177

Printing 998–999, 1400

Printmaking 2, 1480, 2085, 2443

Production Management 601

Psychology 53, 171, 603–610, 634, 772, 1023, 1306, 1837–1839, 2107, 2371, 2394, 2502

Psychology, Clinical 772, 1837–1839

Public Administration 46, 598, 612, 634, 780, 789, 1288–1291, 2148, 2396–2398

Public Affairs 129, 983, 1058, 1638, 2072

Public Health 1059, 1333, 1450, 1719–1720, 2370, 2390, 2397, 2491, 2502

Public Health Nutrition 939, 2390

Public Policy and Administration 463, 634, 802, 923–924, 977–978, 987, 997, 1014, 1038–1039, 1043, 1215, 1307–1308, 1353, 1386, 1638, 1662–1663, 2040, 2054–2055, 2101, 2396–2398, 2440, 2491

Public Relations 92, 224, 368, 458, 634, 834, 910, 915, 1015, 1018, 1055, 1060–1063, 1113, 1151, 1322, 1327, 1337, 1668, 2066, 2072, 2412, 2437, 2453

Public Safety 744

Public Service 1058–1059, 1309, 1372, 1959, 2452, 2499

Public Works 612

Publishing 224, 1386

Pulp and Paper Technology 1411

Quarternary Geology 1251, 1258–1259

Radiation Sciences 1927, 2390

Range Management 2285

Real Estate 755, 1008, 1551, 1631

Real Estate Appraising 755

Real Estate-Related 755, 1009, 1044

Rehabilitation 1439, 1515, 1686, 1935, 2020

Religion 18–22, 77, 253–265, 654, 1001, 1103, 1140, 1163, 1311, 1441, 1669, 2314–2315, 2343–2351, 2353–2363, 2470–2484

Religion-Related 18–22, 77, 253–265, 1001, 1140, 1163, 1188, 1311, 1441, 1462, 1517, 1519, 1637, 2314–2315, 2343–2351, 2353–2363, 2470–2484

Religious, Cantoral Studies 77, 1462

Religious Careers 77, 253–285, 1163, 1189, 1441, 1517, 1519, 1637, 2314–2315, 2343–2351, 2470–2484

Strength and Conditioning 1863–1866

Surveying and Mapping 320–322, 698, 945–951, 1045–1048, 1054, 1263, 1376, 1582–1583, 1588, 1642, 1925, 2045–2047, 2061, 2331, 2449

Technical Communications 1055

Telecommunications 1055, 1965, 2049, 2199

Teratology 2321

Textile-Related 231–239

Textiles 198, 202, 231–237, 1595, 1601

Theater Arts 13, 70, 224, 799, 884, 927, 1132–1134, 1197, 1342, 1374, 1401–1402, 1487–1505, 1643, 2319, 2461

Theology 18–22, 77, 253–265, 1001, 1140, 1311, 1967, 2353–2363

Therapy, Art 165

Toxicology 1002–1003, 1875, 2241–2268

Translation 6, 1731, 2000–2001

Transportation 1054, 2162, 2055, 2399–2400

Travel and Tourism 700–702, 1287

Travel Business Management 700–702, 1287

Travel Industry Management 700–702, 1287

Turf Management (Golf Course) 1284–1286

Urban Administration 2370

Urban Design 2117

Urban Development 2370

Urban Planning 583, 586, 593, 1353, 1551, 2117

Urban Studies 434, 592, 1551

Vacuum Science 721, 1447, 2269–2270

Veterinary Medicine 1, 75, 407, 566, 749–750, 836, 1134, 1484, 1581, 1719–1720, 1839, 2005, 2246, 2339, 2372

Visual Arts 126, 645, 799, 1194, 1557–1563, 1636, 1643, 1732, 2053, 2062, 2082–2086, 2319, 2492–2494

Visual Arts, Drama 1342, 1400, 1487–1505, 1636, 1643, 2319

Visual Arts, Film and Video 13–16, 224, 645, 674, 799, 804, 1007, 1127–1128, 1145–1147, 1214, 1279–1280, 1296, 1386, 1451, 1480, 1576, 1593, 1636, 1643, 1732, 1906, 1995, 2042–2043, 2082–2086, 2085, 2319, 2414–2419, 2429

Viticulture 662, 2064

Vocational Education 385, 1439

Vocational Rehabilitation 385, 1439

Volcanology 1253

Water Resources 1875, 1926

Welding Technology 723, 1454

Wildlife Biology 1873–1875, 1934, 2065, 2285, 2455

Wildlife Conservation 518, 520, 855, 985, 990, 1000, 1873–1875, 1916, 1934, 2285

Wildlife Ecology 985, 990, 1934, 2285, 2445, 2455

Wildlife Habitat Management 1875, 2065, 2285, 2445, 2455

Wildlife Management 518, 520, 1875, 2065, 2285, 2445, 2455

Wildlife Research 885, 2285, 2445, 2455,

Wildlife Science 2285, 2455

Women's Issues 224, 835, 935, 937, 997, 1192, 1317–1319, 1506, 1660, 1876, 2440

Women's Studies 224, 835, 935, 937, 997, 1192, 1317–1319, 1506, 1660, 1876, 2440

Writing 9, 52, 115–118, 645, 798, 911–913, 930, 965, 1017, 1027, 1065–1067, 1131–1133, 1150, 1164, 1194, 1197, 1282, 1315, 1345, 1348, 1365–1367, 1381–1382, 1386, 1400, 1456, 1587, 1636, 1643, 1728–1729, 1803, 1877, 1898, 1920–1924, 1997–2001, 2034–2037, 2052, 2078, 2081–2082, 2089, 2301–2303, 2306, 2309–2310, 2319, 2428, 2508

Writing, Plays 897–899, 930, 1348,

1365, 1382, 1490–1491, 1496, 1498, 1504, 2023–2025, 2306

Writing, Poetry 6–7, 115, 118, 120, 911–913, 930, 1027, 1164, 1315, 1348, 1367, 1587, 1728–1729, 1922–1923, 2028–2029, 2036, 2078, 2081–2082, 2301–2303, 2309

Writing, Science 1065–1067

Writing, Screenplay 9, 930, 2417

Youth Leadership 1087

Youth or Adolescent Development 1317

Zoology 985, 1222, 1755, 1873

Zoo-Related 915, 1878–1881

Characteristics

Academic Merit 11, 154, 845

Age, Betwen Ages 18 and 30 2070

Age, Over Age 25 1526–1527, 2056

Age, Over Age 50 1559

Age, Over Age 55 2052

Age, Under Age 27 67

Age, Under Age 30 2078

Age, Under Age 33 24

Age, Under Age 35 60, 62

Age, Under Age 40 61, 64

Amateur Licensed Radio Operator 613–633

Athletic 1721–1723

Child Development 2196–2198

Colonial Heritage 1020

Community Action 114, 239

Community Leadership 932

Community Service 744

Contest 21, 33, 69, 72, 145, 751–752, 1019, 1135, 1159, 1162, 1196, 1210, 1216, 1286, 1299, 1326, 1336, 1354, 1378, 1453, 1572, 1574–1575, 1592, 1651, 1797–1804, 1828, 1898–1900, 1960, 2026–2028, 2030, 2048, 2304, 2332, 2335, 2404–2411, 2426, 2441, 2446, 2454, 2456, 2509–2510

Dog-Related 1134

Educational Administrators 1226

Females Between the Ages of 25 and 30 2006

Schools

Portland Public School District #1
1968
Purdue University 1529
Radford University 234
Siena College, NY 1211
Southern University Law School 901
Southwestern University 1573
Stanford Medical School 1808
State University of New York
Maritime College 2221
Synod-Related Schools 2314–2315
Texas Southern University Thurgood
Marshall Law School 901
University of Arizona 585, 762
University of California, Berkeley
2221
University of California, Davis
School of Medicine 1808
University of California, Los Angeles
780, 1590, 1995
University of Cambridge 1233–1234
University of Georgia 236, 1267
University of Hawaii 1149
University of Maryland, College Park
1584, 1586
University of Massachusetts,
Dartmouth 235
University of Michigan 781, 2221
University of Nebraska, Kearney
1886
University of Nebraska, Lincoln
1886
University of Nebraska Medical
Center 1886
University of Nebraska, Omaha 1886
University of Newfoundland 2221
University of New Orleans 1573
University of North Carolina,
Charlotte 1211
University of North Carolina,
Greensboro 234
University of Pennsylvania 586
University of Rhode Island 235
University of San Francisco School
of Medicine 1808
University of Southern California
1995
University of Toledo 833
Vanderbilt University 357, 2423
Western Michigan University 1631

Cities, Residents of

Allentown, PA 1392
Anchorage, AK 1508
Austin, TX 738
Bethlehem, PA 1392
Chicago, IL 739, 2056
Chinook, MT 1570
Cleveland, OH 1936
Columbus, OH 823
Dallas, PA 2296
Dallas, TX 740, 824
Detroit, MI 825
Easton, PA 1392
Fort Worth, TX 826
Grey Forest, TX 1297
Hood River, OR 1969
Houston, TX 741–743
Long Beach, CA 1485
Long Island, NY 1467
Los Angeles, CA 614, 828, 1512
Miami, FL 827
New York, NY 798, 829, 1467
Orange, CA 614
Philadelphia, PA 1557–1563
St. Louis, MO 1107, 2095
San Antonio, TX 830–831
San Diego, CA 614
San Francisco area, CA 2284
Santa Barbara, CA 614
Seattle, WA 832
Toledo, OH 833
Warsaw, IN 1526

Countries

Alameda, CA 946
Barnstable, MA 1158
Bexar, TX 830–831
Bucks, PA 1560–1563
Chester, PA 1560–1563
Clinton, IL 2095
Contra Costa, CA 946
Cook, IL 908, 1464–1466
Cuyahoga, OH 8, 1101, 1936
Delaware, PA 1560–1563
Detroit, MI 1619
Dupage, IL 908, 1141
Erie, OH 1030
Franklin, MO 2095

Grauga, OH 1936
Hampden, MA 1341
Hood, TX 826
Jackson, WV 1295
Jefferson, MO 2095
Jersey, IL 2095
Johnson, TX 826
Kern, CA 1347
Kosciusko, IN 1514–1538
Lake, OH 1936
Lincoln, MO 2095
Lorain, OH 1026–1033, 1936
Madison, IL 2095
McHenry, IL 908
Merced, CA 945
Midland, MI 1627–1635
Monroe, IL 2095
Montgomery, PA 1560–1563
Nassau, NY 1507
Parker, TX 826
Philadelphia, PA 1560–1563
Queens, NY 1507
Riverside, CA 942, 944
San Bernadino, CA 942, 944
San Joaquin, CA 945
Santa Barbara, CA 2088–2090
Stanislaus, CA 945
St. Charles, MO 2095
St. Clair, IL 2095
St. Louis, MO 2095
Suffolk, NY 1507
Tarrant, TX 826
Umatilla, OR 1966
Will, IL 908

States

Alabama 38–45, 613, 726
Alaska 47–51, 626, 1240, 1252
Arizona 466, 614, 763
Arkansas 466, 621, 764–765
California 110, 466, 727–730, 774,
777, 782, 806–807, 828, 941–963,
1283, 1374, 1461, 1485, 1810,
2081–2087
California, Northern 1374, 2081
California, Southern 110
Colorado 2045–2047, 2076–2077,
2283

Countries, Residents of (other than U.S.)

Study in Specific Countries (other than U.S.)

Scholarship Listings

A – Arts
H – Humanities
S – Sciences (including mathematics and
   engineering)
SS – Social Sciences

NOTE: When no physical address is provided, the organization prefers contact via an Internet site. When an organization provides multiple listings, some of the listings may have alternate web site addresses. Alternate web site addresses are provided under the name of the award, internship, or contest. When a web site is provided, we recommend you visit the site to obtain more information before contacting the organization. If a listing requests written inquiries, or if U.S. mail is the only viable way for you to contact a listing, we recommend you supply a self-addressed, stamped envelope.

1. (S, SS)
Abbie Sargent Memorial Scholarship, Inc.
295 Sheep Davis Road
Concord, NH 03301
(603) 224–1934

Scholarships of at least $200 for graduate and undergraduate students who are residents of New Hampshire and majoring in agriculture, veterinary medicine, or home economics. Based on academic achievement and character. Must be legal U.S. resident. Renewable with reapplication. Deadline: March 15.

2. (A)
Abbey Major Scholarship
British School at Rome
10 Carlton House Terrace
London
SW1Y 5AH UK
020 79695202
http://www.bsr.ac.uk

1 scholarship providing a stipend of 3,300 pounds, plus board, lodging, a grant of 500 pounds for working materials, a contribution toward the cost of return travel to Rome, and up to 200 pounds for travel within Italy to doctoral candidates, postdoctoral fellows, and professionals in the areas of architecture, painting, printmaking, and sculpture to spend a year working in a studio at the British School in Rome. Applicants must be citizens of the United States, United Kingdom, or the Commonwealth and should be able to speak, read, and write Italian. Award lasts for one year. Deadline: Mid-January.

3. (S, SS)

Abbott Laboratories
Manager of College Relations
Department 39K, Building AP6D
200 Abbott Park Road
Abbott Park, IL 60064–3500
(708) 937–7000
http://www.abbott.com

150 to 200 12-week internships providing from $340 to $600 per week for undergraduates and from $650 to $1,000 per week for graduate students; includes round-trip travel and housing expenses. Internships are in Lake County, IL. Accepted majors are accounting, business, computer science, engineering (computer engineering, contract administration, energy management, equipment application, facilities design, fermentation development, instrument development, manufacturing support, materials management, new technology research and development, plant maintenance and utilities, process controls design, product development, project engineering, quality, research and development, site engineering software development, start-up engineering, support of production processes and systems, validation), finance, human relations, information technology, sales and marketing/business development, production/operations, and research and development/science (biology, biochemistry, chemistry, pharmacology, physiology, etc.). Preference given to undergraduate juniors and above. For more information, visit their web site. Résumés must be submitted online. Deadline: September 1 through March 1.

4. (A, S, SS)

Academic Study Associates
Internship Coordinator
10 New King Street
White Plains NY, 10604
(800) 752–2250
(914) 686–7730
http://www.asaprograms.com/choose.html

60 summer internships providing $200 per week and free room and board, open to graduate students and junior and senior undergraduate students. International students are also eligible. Internships last from 5 to 8 weeks, with interns working as resident advisors and program teachers. The program provides academic instruction in the areas of art, business, computers, law, physics, psychology, theater, writing, and the SAT. There are also field trips, weekend excursions, sports, and recreation. The program is conducted at Stanford, Colorado at Boulder, Massachusetts at Amherst, and Oxford. Round-trip travel expenses are provided for students selected to participate at Oxford. Deadline: April 15.

5. (H)

Academy for Educational Development
National Security Education Program
1825 Connecticut Avenue, N.W.
Washington, DC 20009–5721
(202) 884–8000
http://www.aed.org

Fellowships of varying amounts to graduate students to enhance their understanding of geographic areas and countries whose languages and cultures are critical to our national security but are less frequently studied by U.S. graduate students. Funded by the Department of Defense. Deadline: none specified.

(A)

Academy of American Poets
177 East 87th Street
New York, NY 10028
(212) 427–5665
http://www.poets.org

6. (A)
Raiziss de Palchi Translation Awards Fund

1 fellowship of $20,000 and a $5,000 book prize are awarded every other year to any citizen of the United States for the translation into English of a significant work of modern Italian poetry. For guidelines and an entry form, visit web site or send a self-addressed, stamped envelope to the Academy in August. The awards include a $20,000 fellowship, given in odd-numbered years for the translation into English of modern Italian poetry.

7. (A)
Walt Whitman Award

1 cash award of $5,000, publication of first book, and a 1-month residency at the Vermont Studio Center to any citizen of the United States who has neither published nor committed to publish a book of poetry 40 pages or more in length in an edition of 500 or more copies. Book-length manuscripts (50 to 100 pages) may be submitted to the Academy between September 15 and November 15 of each year. An entry form and fee are required. For information, visit web site or send a self-addressed, stamped envelope after August 1.

8. (S)
Academy of Medicine of Cleveland Auxiliary Health Careers Committee Scholarships
ATTN: Maurine M. Ruggles
11001 Cedar Avenue
Cleveland, OH 44106
(216) 229–2200
(216) 520–1000
http://www.amcnoma.org

Numerous scholarships ranging from $400 to $600 to residents of Cuyahoga County who have been accepted to an accredited Cuyahoga County professional school. Must be pursuing a medical health profession. Must have financial need and a minimum 2.0 GPA.

(A)
Academy of Motion Picture Arts and Sciences Foundation
8949 Wilshire Boulevard
Beverly Hills, CA 90211
(310) 247–3010
http://www.oscars.org/nicholl/index.html

9. (A)
Nicholl Fellowship in Screenwriting

5 fellowships of $25,000 to any U.S. citizen who is pursuing a career as a screenwriter. Must not have been paid to write a screenplay or teleplay. Screenplays must be written in English in a standard feature-film format. Deadline: May 1.

10. (A)
Student Academy Awards Competition

Awards of $2,000 (Bronze), $3,000 (Silver), and $5,000 (Gold) to graduate or undergraduate film students who submit a film that has been made in a teacher-student relationship within the curricular structure of that institution. Awards are presented in each of the following categories: alternative, animation, documentary, and narrative. Based on resourcefulness, originality, entertainment, and production quality. No entry must be longer than 60 minutes long. Deadline: April 1 (early) and May 1 (final).

(S)
Academy of Natural Sciences of Philadelphia
1900 Benjamin Franklin Parkway
Philadelphia, PA 19103–1195
(215) 299–1000
http://www.acnatsci.org/research/jessupinfo.html

11. (S)
Bölhke Memorial Endowment Fund

Travel awards of less than $500 to graduate students and recent postdoctoral researchers to work with the Ichthyology collection and library at the Academy. Awarded on academic merit and financial need. Deadline: rolling.

12. (S)
Jessup and McHenry Awards

Grants providing $500 (U.S., Mexican, and Caribbean applicants) and $1,000 (for applicants from other parts of the world) for travel expenses and a $250 weekly stipend to predoctoral and new postdoctoral students to support botany research at the Academy. Grants are for a research period ranging from 2–16 weeks. Students from the Philadelphia area are not eligible. Deadline: March 1 and October 1.

(A, H, SS)
Academy of Television Arts & Sciences
Education Department
5220 Lankershim Boulevard
North Hollywood, CA 91601
(818) 754–2800
http://www.emmys.org
collegeaward@emmys.org

13. (A, H, SS)
Internships

31 8-week summer internships providing a $2,500 stipend and a $500 disbursement if living outside of Los Angeles. Open to full-time graduate students, recent college graduates, as long as graduation was before January 1 of the application year, and undergraduate students. Must have in-depth exposure to professional television production, techniques, and practices. Though open to all majors, preference given to the following: art, theater arts, law, business, advertising, marketing, journalism, cinema, music, TV/film, and English. All finalists are required to submit a videotaped interview responding to questions sent by the Academy. Most internships are located in Los Angeles. Deadline: March 15.

14. (H)
Bricker Family College Award

1 award of $4,000 to a first place winner whose work best represents a humanitarian concern. Award recognizes excellence in college student film/video productions. Some years, a similar award is given to the second place winner. Deadline: none specified.

15. (A)
College Television Awards

Cash awards of $500, $1,000, and $2,000 to graduate and undergraduate students in a national competition that provides industry recognition for outstanding student-produced films and videos. Deadline: none specified.

16. (A)
Walter Lantz Foundation Award

2 animation awards of varying amounts, as well as two animation internships to graduate and undergraduate students. Winners are honored at a black-tie gala in Los Angeles each spring. A Festival of Winners takes place the day following the gala. Winners are mentored by television industry professionals. Deadline: none specified.

17. (A)
Academy of Vocal Arts
Scholarships
1920 Spruce Street
Philadelphia, PA 19103
(215) 735–1685
http://www.avaopera.com

Full-tuition scholarships to unusually gifted graduate students with 2 years of college or equivalent voice training. A college degree is preferred. Scholarship is for complete training in voice, operatic acting, and repertoire. Based on competitive audition. Tuition-free scholarships are only to students of the Academy. Student body enrollment is limited to 30. Deadline: 2 weeks prior to auditions in the spring.

(H)
Action Institute
161 Ottawa N.W., Suite 301
Grand Rapids, MI 49503
http://www.acton.org/programs/students/homiletics

18. (H)
Calihan Research Assistance Program

Grants of up to $3,000 to advanced graduate students whose research agenda shows outstanding promise in integrating religious ideas with core principles of the classical liberal tradition.

19. (H)
Calihan Travel Grant Program

Grants of up to $1,000 to graduate students who have been selected to present, at an academic conference, research that is relevant to the integration of religious ideas with the core principles of the classical liberal tradition. Also open to students who need to travel to, and perform research at, archives or libraries.

20. (H)
Homiletics Award

Awards of $500, $1,000, and $2,000 to seminarians and graduate students in degree programs preparing them for preaching and teaching ministries. Selection based on a manuscript and an audiotape of a delivered sermon between 12 and 20 minutes in length. Judged on preparation and presentation, content, structure, and exegetical accuracy, as well as delivery, clarity, and style. Deadline: March 15.

21. (H)
Lord Acton Essay Contest

Awards of $500, $1,000, and $2,000 to graduate students, seminarians, priests, pastors, scholars, and professors interested in the themes of religion, liberty, and their contribution to a free and virtuous society. Must submit a scholarly paper, op-editorial, published or unpublished article, or treatise. Paper should deal with themes of personal or economic liberty, theology, and/or their institutions of support. Deadline: November 15.

22. (H)
Religion and Liberty Fellowship Program

Fellowships of up to $5,000 to graduate students who show outstanding promise in integrating religious ideas with core principles of the classical liberal tradition (such as the recognition of human rights and dignity, protection of rights through the rule of law, and freedom in economic and political life). Deadline: none specified.

23. (A, H, S, SS)
Adelante Educational Foundation
P.O. Box 2267
Ames, IA 50010
(515) 292–7733
(866) 318–1907
http://www.adelante.org

Up to 32 scholarships of $1,000 to male graduate or undergraduate students who are or will be attending Iowa State University and who join Adelante Fraternity.

Based on academic achievement, extracurricular involvement, and leadership. Deadline: rolling.

24. (A, H, S, SS)
Adenauer Foundation
Institute for the Sponsorship of Talented Students
Rathausallee 12
D 53757 Sankt Augustin
Germany
0049–2241–630
http://www1.kas.de/stiftung/englisch/
think_tank.html

Fellowships in all academic areas for talented graduate and doctoral students under age 33 to study at German universities. Write or visit their web site for more information and deadline.

25. (A, H, S, SS)
Adolf Van Pelt Foundation Inc.
Native American Financial Aid Grants
ATTN: Olga Patterson
Fargo Lane
Irvington-on-Hudson, NY 10533
written inquiries only

40 to 50 awards ranging from $500 to $1,500 to Native American undergraduates and graduates who would like to pursue a professional career in any area of study and help other Native American students. Proof of ancestry is required. Based on financial need. Deadline: April 15.

26. (S)
Advanced Light Source
ALS Doctoral Fellowship in Residence
Lawrence Berkeley National Laboratory
1 Cyclotron Road, M/S 90–1140
Berkeley, CA 94720
(510) 486–7793 (Fax)
http://www–als.lbl.gov/als/fellowships/index.html

Fellowships providing a $16,000 annual stipend to doctoral students who have completed all required course work and qualifying verbal and written exams. Must be in a full-time doctoral program in the physical or biological sciences, pursuing thesis research based on the use of synchrotron radiation. Deadline: May 1.

(A, H, S, SS)
Aerospace Education Foundation
1501 Lee Highway
Arlington, VA 22209
(703) 247–5839
(800) 291–8480 ext. 5801
http://www.aef.org

27. (A, H, S, SS)
Air Force Spouses Scholarship

30 awards of $1,000 to spouses of air force active duty, reserve, or National Guard personnel for graduate, postgraduate, or undergraduate studies. Based on academic merit, career goals, and recommendation letters. Nonrenewable. Deadline: January 31.

28. (S)
Christa McAuliffe Memorial Award

2 cash awards of $1,000 to recognize outstanding public, private, or parochial school teachers (kindergarten through twelfth grade) who have brought a fundamental awareness of aerospace activities to their students. Must be nominated by an Air Force Association representative. Must be a U.S. citizen or legal resident. Nominators may send a self-addressed, stamped envelope or visit web site to receive information. Renewable. Deadline: May 30 (postmark).

29. (A, H, S, SS)
Jodi Callahan Memorial Graduate Scholarship

1 scholarship of $1,000 to an air force active duty, full-time Guard or Reserve (officer or enlisted), Air Force Association member pursuing a master's degree in a nontechnical field of study. Selection based on academic merit, career goals, recommendation letters, and AFA membership in good standing. Nonrenewable. Deadline: June 30 (postmark).

(S, SS)
Agency for Healthcare Research and Quality (AHRQ)
Division of Research Education
2101 East Jefferson Street, Suite 400
Rockville, MD 20852–4908
(301) 594–1364
http://www.ahrq.gov/fund/training/rsrchtng.htm
training@AHRQ.gov

30. (S, SS)
Health Services Dissertation Research Grants

Grants providing a salary equivalent to that of other full-time students in a similar status at their educational institution who receive research or teaching assistantships to students for full-time dissertation research undertaken as part of an academic program to earn a research doctoral degree. Proposed project should support, conduct, and disseminate research that improves access to care and the outcomes, quality, cost, and utilization of health care services. Deadline: May 15, September 15, and January 15.

31. (S, SS)
Predoctoral Fellowship Awards for Minority Students

Predoctoral fellowships providing an annual stipend of at least $15,600 to help meet the fellow's living expenses, plus an allowance for tuition, fees, and health insurance in accordance with NIH policy and an annual institutional allowance, to minority graduate students. Designed to enhance racial and ethnic diversity in the health services research sciences, this fellowship provides up to 5 years of support for research training leading to a Ph.D. or equivalent research degree; the combined M.D./Ph.D. degree; or other combined professional and research doctoral degrees. Deadline: May 1 and November 15.

32. (S)
Agronomic Science Foundation
Frank D. Kiem Graduate Fellowship
677 South Segoe Road
Madison, WI 53711
(608) 273–8080
http://www.agronomy.org

Fellowships of varying amounts to graduate students and undergraduate seniors pursuing a career in agronomy or a closely related field. Award recognizes top students in agronomy for outstanding scholarship and leadership. Deadline: none specified.

33. (Contest)
Aim Magazine Short Story Contest
738 South Eberhart Avenue
Chicago, IL 60619
(773) 874–6184

Contest for unpublished short stories (4,000-word maximum) promoting brotherhood among people and cultures. This is a cash award for the winner to use at his/her discretion and not a scholarship. Deadline: August 15.

34. (S, SS)
Air-Conditioning & Refrigeration Wholesalers International
David M. Lawson Memorial Scholarship Fund
ARWI Research & Education Foundation
1650 South Dixie Highway, 5th Floor
Boca Raton, FL 33432
(561) 338–3495
http://www.hardinet.org
mail@arwi.org

12 scholarships of up to $750 each for students who are in their last year of undergraduate study and will be returning for the completion of their HV AC-R or Distribution studies. Minimum 3.0 GPA or better required. Deadline: May 30.

35. (S, SS)
Aircraft Owners of Pilots Association Air Safety Foundation
Koch Corporation Scholarship
Scholarship Coordinator
421 Aviation Way
Frederick, MD 21701–4798
(301) 695–2000
http://www.aopa.org

1 award of $1,500 to a graduate or undergraduate student pursuing a course of study focusing on aviation. Selection based on academic achievement and an essay on an assigned topic. Must be a U.S. citizen, attend an accredited institution, and have at least a 3.25 GPA on a 4.0 scale. Deadline: July 31.

36. (H)
Air Force Historical Foundation (AFHF)
Fellowship
1535 Command Drive, Ste. A122
Andrews AFB, MD 20762–7002
(301) 736–1959
http://www.afhistoricalfoundation.com

1 fellowship of $1,000 to a graduate or postdoctoral student to work on aerospace history. Applicants must show some evidence of scholarly achievement (prefer publications) and must be U.S. citizens. Write a letter briefly detailing proposed research. Deadline: December 1.

37. (A, S)
Air Force ROTC
One Year Scholarships
(866) 423–7682
http://www.afrotc.com/scholarships/enlschol/scholprog/ascp.htm

Scholarships of up to $15,000 toward tuition and fees, $510 for textbooks, and a monthly stipend of $250 to graduate students or students who received an undergraduate degree no more than one year prior to applying and have attended an accredited institution with an AFROTC unit. Open to the following majors: nursing, aeronautical engineering, aerospace engineering, architecture, architectural engineering, chemical engineering, civil engineering, computer engineering, computer science, environmental engineering, industrial engineering, mathematics, mechanical engineering, nuclear engineering, physics, electrical engineering, and meteorology. Must have at least a 2.0 GPA, be medically qualified, have passed the AF Officer Qualifying Test, meet all other requirements for enlistment, be recommended by Air Force ROTC detachment commander, and be under the age of 31. Students must apply on-line. For more information, visit web site or locate a local recruiter. Deadline: September 30.

38. (A, S, SS)
Alabama Commission on Higher Education
Minority Doctoral Scholars Program
P.O. Box 302000
Montgomery, AL 36130–2101
(334) 242–1998
(334) 242–0268
http://www.ache.state.al.us

Grants providing a stipend of $12,000, and up to $5,000 for tuition and fees, to minority students who are planning to enroll in a doctoral program in the arts, business, engineering, or sciences. Education is not area of emphasis, with the exceptions of mathematics education and science education. Must not already be enrolled in a doctoral program. Must be Alabama residents or planning to attend a doctoral program in Alabama. Deadline: none specified.

(S)

Alabama Dietetic Association
P.O. Box 11594
Montgomery, AL 36111
(334) 360–7970
http://www.eatrightalabama.org

39. (S)
Alabama Memorial Scholarship

1 award of $500 to a graduate student in dietetics or a related field. Must be admitted to, or enrolled in, a regionally accredited college or university in Alabama. Selection is based on academic achievement, professional potential, and financial need. Deadline: February 1.

40. (S)
Southeast Alabama Dietetic Association Scholarship

1 award of $750 to a graduate or undergraduate student or dietetic intern majoring in the field of human nutrition, dietetics, foods, nutrition, or food systems management or admitted or enrolled in a dietetic internship. Must have at least a cumulative 2.5 GPA on a 4.0 scale and a 3.0 GPA or above on a 4.0 scale in major courses of study. Visit web site for complete eligibility criteria. Deadline: February 1.

41. (S)
William E. Smith Scholarship Award

1 award of $1,000 to a full-time graduate student in dietetics. Selection based on demonstrated ability and potential in the field of dietetics and nutrition and financial need. Must be an active, associate, or junior member in the ADA. Visit web site for complete eligibility criteria. Deadline: February 1.

42. (S)
Wood Fruitticher Grocery Company

1 scholarship of $500 to a part-time graduate student or a full-time upper-level undergraduate. Must be attending an ADA-accredited Alabama institution. Selection based on demonstrated ability and potential in the field of dietetics and nutrition and financial need. Must be an active, associate, or junior member in the ADA. Visit web site for complete eligibility criteria. Deadline: February 1.

43. (SS)
Alabama Library Association
EBSCO Grant
400 South Union Street, Suite 395
Montgomery, AL 36104
(334) 263–1272
(877) 563–5146
http://www.allanet.org

Scholarships of $1,000 to a graduate student or undergraduate senior majoring in library science. Must be accepted to or attend an ALA-accredited library science program. Some of the scholarships must be used at the University of Alabama. Deadline: none specified.

(S, SS)

Alabama Public Library Service
Assistant Director
6030 Monticello Drive
Montgomery, AL 36130
(334) 213–3900
(800) 723–8459 (within AL only)
http://www.apls.state.al.us

44. (SS)
Continuing Education Scholarships

16 scholarship grants of up to $600 to a current employee of an ALA public library or a trustee of an ALA public library for a continuing education program. Program must be approved prior to attendance. Travel expenses are not included. Only 2 grants per ALA public library per year. Deadline: none specified.

45. (S)
Educational Grant Program

Grants of $6,000 for full-time study and up to $4,000 (cumulative total for part-time) to graduate students pursuing a master's of library science degree at an accredited school of library science. Must be Alabama residents and agree to work in an Alabama public library for 2 years after graduation. Part-time students must be currently employed by an Alabama public library. Deadline: May 1.

46. (S, SS)
Alabama Space Grant Consortium
University of Alabama in Huntsville
MSB 205

Huntsville, AL 35899

(256) 824–6800

http://www.uah.edu/ASGC

Varying number of fellowships of $22,000 ($16,000 student stipend and $6,000 tuition/research/travel allowance) to graduate students in biological, natural, or physical sciences; behavioral sciences; business; communications; computer science; economics; education; engineering; international affairs; law; public administration; or sociology. Selection based on academic excellence, proposed research or field of study, and career interests coincident with NASA's aerospace, science, and technology programs. Award is for a 12-month period and may be renewed up to 36 months following competitive proposal review. Visit web site for detailed information, listing of participating institutions, and an application. Deadline: March 1.

47. (A, H, S, SS)
Alaska Commission on Postsecondary Education
Alaska A.W. "Winn" Brindle Memorial
Scholarship Loan Program
3030 Vintage Boulevard
Juneau, AK 99801–7109
(907) 465–6740
http://www.ache.state.ak.us

Awards covering tuition, fees, books, supplies, room and board, and transportation for up to 2 round trips between recipient's home and school each year. Can be used for 5 years of undergraduate study, 5 years of graduate study, or a combined maximum of 8 years of study. Recipient has up to 10 years to repay the loan with 8% interest. Applicants must be residents of Alaska and full-time undergraduate or graduate students at an accredited institution. Deadline: none specified.

(SS)
Alaska Library Association
P.O. Box 81084
Fairbanks, AK 99708
(907) 465–2458
http://www.akla.org
akla@akla.org

48. (SS)
Graduate Library Studies Scholarship

1 scholarship of $3,000 to a graduate student enrolled in or admitted to a library media specialist certificate program. Award may be used for on-campus and/or distance education programs. Must commit to work in an Alaska library for at least 1 year after graduation. If student fails to fulfill the work commitment, the scholarship reverts to a loan and must be repaid. Must be an Alaska resident. Preference given to students who meet federal definition of Alaska Native ethnicity. Selection based on academic achievement, writing skills, goals, references, and financial need. For more information or an application, visit web site. Deadline: January 15.

49. (SS)
School Library Media Specialist/School Librarian Jo Morse Scholarship

1 scholarship of $3,000 to a graduate student enrolled in or admitted to a library media specialist/school librarian certificate program. Award may be used for on-campus and/or distance education programs. Must commit to work in an Alaska library for at least 1 year after graduation. If student fails to fulfill the work commitment, the scholarship reverts to a loan and must be repaid. Must be an Alaska resident. Preference given to students who meet federal definition of Alaska Native ethnicity. Selection based on academic achievement, writing skills, goals, references, and financial need. For more information or an application, visit web site. Deadline: January 15.

50. (A)
Alaska State Council on the Arts
Individual Artist Fellowships & Grants
411 West Fourth Avenue, Suite 1–E
Anchorage, AK 99501
(907) 269–6610
http://www.aksca.org

Varying numbers of grants of $5,000 to Alaska residents who are experienced professional artists for the creation of new work. Not for academic study. Apprenticeship grants and travel grants are also available. Deadline: October 16.

51. (SS)

Alaska State Troopers

Michael Murphy Memorial Scholarship Loan Fund

ATTN: Lt. Coile

5700 East Tudor Road

Anchorage, AK 99507

http://www.dps.state.ak.us/ast

3 to 6 scholarship/loans of up to $1,000 to full-time graduate or undergraduate students majoring in criminal justice, criminology, law enforcement, police administration, social services, or other law enforcement–related field. Must be attending an accredited 2- or 4-year institution and be a resident of Alaska. 20% of the full loan amount is forgiven for each year employed in law enforcement. Renewable. Deadline: April 1.

52. (A)

Albee Foundation

14 Harrison Street

New York, NY 10013

(212) 226–2020

http://www.pipeline.com/~jtnyc/albeefdtn.html

6 fellowships of varying amounts to writers, painters, and sculptors for paid residency at the Flanagan Memorial Creative Persons Center ("The Barn") in Montauk, New York. Write a letter briefly detailing experience. Deadline: April 1.

53. (S, SS)

Albert Ellis Institute

Internship Coordinator

45 East 65th Street

New York, NY 10021

(800) 323–4758

(212) 525–0822

http://www.rebt.org

4 to 10 internships that last at least 6 months and provide $280 per week to graduate students and $230 per week to undergraduates, plus health insurance, to work in environmental and public policy efforts with grassroots community groups, government leaders, and business entrepreneurs. Interns work conducting research, policy initiatives, coalition building, and technical assistance. Interns work in either Minneapolis, Minnesota, or Washington, DC. Internships are conducted on an ongoing basis. Deadline: rolling.

(A, H, S, SS)

Alexander Graham Bell Association for the Deaf

3417 Volta Place, N.W.

Washington, DC 20007–2778

(202) 337–5220 (Voice or TDD)

written inquiries only

http://www.agbell.org

agbell2@aol.com

54. (A, H, S, SS)

David J. Von Hagen Scholarship Award

Scholarships ranging from $500 to $1,000 to oral deaf students who were born with profound hearing impairment or who lost their hearing before acquiring language. Applicants must be able to use speech and residual hearing and/or speech reading as their preferred form of communication. Applicants must be accepted to or enrolled in a college or university. Open to all majors, though preference is given to students majoring in science or engineering. Request applications between September 1 and January 1. Deadline: April 15.

55. (A, H, S, SS)

Elsie Bell Grosvenor Scholarship Awards

2 scholarships (1 of $500 and 1 of $1,000) to oral deaf students who are from the metropolitan Washington, DC, area or will be attending college in the DC area. Students must have been born with a profound hearing impairment or suffered the loss before acquiring language. Open to all areas of study. Visit web site or send a self-addressed, stamped envelope for more information. Request applications between September 1 and January 1. Deadline: April 1.

56. (A, H, S, SS)

General Scholarship Program

2 scholarships of $500 to $1,000 to oral deaf students who were born with profound hearing impairment or who lost their hearing before acquiring language. Applicants must be able to use speech and residual hearing and/or speech reading as their preferred form of communication. Applicants must be accepted to or enrolled in a college or university. Open to all majors, though some awards give preference to students majoring in science or engineering. Some of the awards are restricted to students who

are accepted to or enrolled in a college or university for hearing students. Visit web site or send a self-addressed, stamped envelope for more information. Request applications between September 1 and January 1. Deadline: April 15.

57. (A, H, S, SS)
Margaret Marsh Memorial Scholarship Award

2 scholarships of $500 for oral deaf students who were born with profound hearing impairment or who lost their hearing before acquiring language. Must use speech and residual hearing and/or speech reading as their preferred form of communication. Must be accepted to, or enrolled in, a college or university for hearing students and pursuing a degree in any major. Visit web site or send a self-addressed, stamped envelope for more information. Request applications between September 1 and January 1. Deadline: April 1.

58. (A, H, S, SS)
National Rural Letter Carrier's Association Ladies' Auxiliary Scholarships

2 scholarships of $500 for oral deaf students who were born with profound hearing impairment or who lost their hearing before acquiring language. Must use speech and residual hearing and/or speech reading as their preferred form of communication. They must be accepted to, or enrolled in, a college or university for hearing students and pursuing a degree. Visit web site or send a self-addressed, stamped envelope for more information. Request applications between September 1 and January 1. Deadline: April 1.

59. (A, H, S, SS)
The Oral Hearing Impaired Section Scholarship

1 scholarship of $1,000 for an oral deaf student who was born with profound hearing impairment or lost their hearing before acquiring language. Must use speech and speech reading as their preferred form of communication. They must be accepted to or enrolled in a college or university for hearing students and pursuing a degree. Visit web site or send a self-addressed, stamped envelope for more information. Request applications between September 1 and January 1. Deadline: April 1.

(A, H, S, SS)
Alexander Von Humboldt Foundation
ATTN: Selection Department
US Liaison Office
1012 14th Street, N.W.
Washington, DC 20005
(202) 783–1907
http://www.humboldt-foundation.de/en

60. (SS)
German Chancellor Scholarships

10 scholarships providing a stipend of a monthly allowance to cover housing and living expenses. The amount ranges from EUR 2,000 to EUR 3,500. In addition to the monthly stipend, the scholarship covers travel expenses to and from Germany. During one-year research stays, scholars are also given an opportunity to gain an insight into the social, cultural, economic, and political situation in Germany. Recipients take part in a 4-week introductory seminar in Bonn and Berlin in September, a fact-finding tour of Germany, and an evaluation seminar in Bonn. The Foundation provides the costs for preparatory German language tuition and an intensive course of several weeks in Bonn. Upon request, the Foundation may add an allowance for support of a spouse and children. Open to prospective leaders from the USA (under 35 years of age) in the academic, economic, and political fields, enabling them to carry out research projects of their own choice in Germany. Deadline: none specified.

61. (A, H, S, SS)
Research Fellowships for Foreign Scholars

500 fellowships of varying amounts to postdoctoral fellows to conduct research in Germany in any field of study. Applicants must be 40 years old or younger. Applicants in the humanities and social sciences must provide a language certificate proving they have a good command of the German language. Fellowships last from 6 to 72 months. Deadline: none specified.

62. (A, H, S, SS)
Roman Herzog Research Fellowship

Fellowships ranging between EUR 1,500 and EUR 2,000 per month to young (35 years old or younger), highly qualified scholars with outstanding leadership qualities in research and teaching from central and southeast Europe (including the Baltic states) to carry out research projects of their own choice in Germany. Deadline: none specified.

63. (A, H, S, SS)
Summer Research Fellowships for U.S. Scientists and Scholars

Fellowships ranging between EUR 2,100 and EUR 3,000 per month for a period ranging from 18 months to 3 years to postdoctoral scholars to work at a research institution elsewhere in Europe (home countries excepted), if this is essential for the execution of their research project. These stays abroad can be used, for example, to visit libraries, use special experimental facilities, or to discuss scientific topics with colleagues. Deadline: none specified.

64. (A, H, S, SS)
2-Year Postdoctoral Fellowships for U.S. Scientists and Scholars

Awards provide monthly research fellowships of between EUR 2,100 and EUR 3,000 to young (under 40 years of age), highly qualified U.S.-American postdoctoral students for a research project of their own choice in Germany. Applications may be submitted for long-term research stays of 24 months. Deadline: none specified.

(S, SS)
Alfred Sloan Foundation
350 Fifth Avenue, Suite 2212
New York, NY 10118–2299
(212) 279–2626
http://www.sloan.org

65. (S)
Sloan Ph.D. Program

Fellowships of varying amounts to minority graduate students pursuing a doctoral degree in animal sciences, biochemistry, biological sciences, biomedical sciences, chemistry, computer science, engineering (aeronautics and astronautics, bioengineering, chemical, civil, computer, electrical, environmental, industrial, systems, and operational, management, materials, mechanical, nuclear, environmental science), geosciences, materials science, mathematics (applied and statistics), meteorology, natural resources sciences, neurosciences, oceanography, optical sciences, pharmacology, physics and applied physics, and plant physiology. Selection is

based on academic achievement, recommendations, goals, and financial need. Awards are tenable at 39 different schools. Visit web site for a list of the schools. Deadline: rolling.

66. (S, SS)
Sloan Research Fellowships

8 fellowships of $25,000 to postdoctoral students in chemistry, economics, physics, or neuroscience. Applicants cannot be over 32 years of age in the nomination year (special circumstances will be considered). Open to faculty members of a college or university in the U.S. or Canada. Write an introductory letter and include a self-addressed, stamped envelope. Deadline: September 15.

67. (A)
Alice Freeman Palmer Fellowship
Graduate Fellowship
c/o Wellesley College, Box GR
Secretary, Graduate Fellowships
Wellesley, MA 02181
(617) 235–0320
http://www.wellesley.edu

Awards of up to $4,000 to unmarried females for graduate study or research at an institution of her choice in U.S. or abroad. Must have bachelor's degree from U.S. institution. Must be under 27 years of age. Applications available up to November 20. Limit of 4 applications per institution and must be filed through the graduate institution. Deadline: December 1.

68. (H)
Alicia Patterson Foundation
Fellowship Program
1730 Pennsylvania Avenue N.W., Suite 850
Washington, DC 20006
(202) 393–5995
http://www.aliciapatterson.org

5 to 7 fellowships of $25,000 to print journalists and editors who have been working as professional journalists for 5 years or longer. Fellowships are for work and travel and not for academic study. For more information, visit web site. Deadline: October 1.

69. (Contest)
Allegheny Review Literary Awards
Allegheny Review
Review Editors
P.O. Box 32, Allegheny College
Meadville, PA 16335
(814) 332–3100
http://webpub.alleg.edu/group/review/submit.html

1 prize of $50 and publication for best entry in each division (Fiction and Poetry). This contest for unpublished short fiction and poetry is only for college students. Fiction submissions aren't to exceed 15 pages, double spaced. Poetry submissions can be 3 to 5 poems. All work must be typed and must be accompanied with name, address, school name, and class year. A cover letter detailing experience is helpful but not necessary. If you want your manuscripts returned, include a self-addressed, stamped envelope. This is a cash award for the student to use at his/her discretion. Deadline: late-September, may vary.

70. (A, H, SS)
Alley Theatre
ATTN: Director of Interns
615 Texas Avenue
Houston, TX 77002
(713) 228–9341
http://www.alleytheatre.org/alley

10 to 30 internships providing $200 per week to graduate students, college graduates, undergraduates, and high school graduates. Interns may work in the following areas: acting, arts administration, casting, company management, costumes, development, dramaturgy, general management, lighting, marketing, props, public relations, sound, stage management, and technical direction. Internships may be part- or full-time with openings in January through May and September through December. Applicants should have basic skills in chosen field. Submit a letter outlining interests, resume, recommendation letters, application form, and interview (in person is preferred, but by phone is acceptable). Deadline: late May (fall interns), otherwise open.

71. (H, S, SS)
Alliance for Health Reform
1444 Eye Street, N.W., Suite 910
Washington, DC 20005–6573

(202) 789–2300
http://www.allhealth.org

4 internships lasting from 3- to 4-months, open to graduate students, upper-level undergraduates, or mid-career persons. Media interns work locating, cataloging, and securing reprint permission for articles, update database of media contacts, and assist with press releases. Policy interns work with the Executive Director in transcribing and compiling notes from high-level meetings and draft policy papers and memorandums. Individuals must have knowledge of the U.S. governmental process and knowledge of health care issues. Strong writing skills are essential. Individuals with experience in policy work, health care course work, or media exposure are preferred. Must submit a letter outlining interests, resume, letters of recommendation, transcript, and a writing sample. Deadline: mid-April (summer internships), midsummer (fall internships), otherwise open.

72. (Contest)
All-Ink.com College Scholarship Program
http://www.all-ink.com/storeinfo/
scholarship/scholarship.html

5 scholarships of $1,000 to graduate and undergraduate students with at least a GPA of 2.5. Students must write a 50- to 200-word essay on the person having the greatest affect on their life and a 50- to 200-word essay on what they hope to achieve in personal and professional life after college. Applicants must be U.S. citizens or permanent residents to be considered for this award. Must apply online. Deadline: July 31.

(A)
Alpha Delta Kappa
1615 West 92nd Street
Kansas City, MO 64114
(816) 363–5525
http://www.alphadeltakappa.org

73. (A)
Fine Arts Grant

Awards ranging from $2,500 to $5,000 to graduate students, professionals, or other individuals to conduct additional study and/or in a project the applicant might have in mind to further his/her artistic skills.

Specific performing art & fine art categories change each biennium. Open to all qualified individuals. Write an introductory letter briefly describing your proposed study or project; include a self-addressed, stamped envelope. Deadline: June 1 of even-numbered years.

74. (A)
Scholarships

Scholarships ranging from $500 to $1,500 to graduate, professional, or undergraduate students who have completed at least 1 full year of undergraduate study. Applicants must submit 3 letters of recommendation and an official transcript. Request applications between December 1 and January 31; include a self-addressed, stamped envelope. Deadline: mid-February.

75. (S)
Alpha Epsilon Delta
National Office
James Madison
MSC 4307
Harrisburg, VA 22807
(540) 568–2594
http://www.jmu.edu/org/nationaled

15 cash awards of $300 to students who are members of AED pursuing careers in medicine, dentistry, osteopathy, optometry, podiatry, or veterinary medicine. Students must be entering the professional school by the fall in the year award is given. Applicants must be nominated by their Chapter Faculty Advisor and two officers of the chapter. Based on academic record, financial need, service to AED and any other preprofessional services in the health fields. Deadline: March 20.

76. (S)
Alpha Epsilon Iota Scholarship Program
1412 N. Jordan Avenue
Bloomington, IN 47406
(812) 336–2504
http://www.iuaepi.com

2 scholarships of $4,000 to female students enrolled in, or accepted to, accredited U.S. allopathic or osteopathic medical schools. Based on academic achievement and financial need. Write an introductory letter. Renewable with requalification. Request applications after January 1. Deadline: May 31.

77. (H)
Alpha Epsilon Pi Foundation
Dunn Scholarship for Jewish Communal Service
8815 Wesleyan Road
Indianapolis, IN 46268–1171
(317) 876–1913
http://www.alphaepsilonpi.org/foundation/index.html

1 scholarship of $1,000 to an outstanding graduating brother who is entering a recognized graduate program in Rabbinical studies, Cantoral studies, or Jewish Communal Service. Scholarship allows recipient to continue his education by attending an accredited school offering such a program in the United States, Canada, or Israel. Must demonstrate financial need, should have served in a leadership capacity in his undergraduate chapters, should have an excellent reputation among his peers, and should exhibit the values and ideals of a brother of Alpha Epsilon Pi. Deadline: none specified.

78. (H)
Alpha Epsilon Rho Scholarships
National Broadcasting Society
ATTN: Scholarships
Box 915,
St. Charles, MO 63302–0915
(866) 272–3746
http://www.onu.edu/org/nbs

Scholarships of $500 to graduate student members of AER. May be used for any area of study in journalism or communications. Must be nominated by their local chapters and attending accredited institutions. Renewable. Deadline: March 1.

(A, H, S, SS)
Alpha Kappa Alpha Educational Advancement Foundation
5656 South Stony Island Avenue
Chicago, IL 60637
(312) 684–1282
(312) 947–0026
http://www.akaeaf.org/scholarshipprogram.html

79. (A, H, S, SS)
Endowment Scholarships

Scholarships ranging from $500 to $1,500 to graduate, professional, or undergraduate students who have completed at least one full year of undergraduate study. Applicants must submit three letters of recommendation and an official transcript. Request applications after January 1; include a self-addressed, stamped envelope or visit web site. Deadline: February 15.

80. (A, H, S, SS)
Financial Need Scholarships

Scholarships ranging from $500 to $1,500 to graduate, professional, or undergraduate students who have completed at least 1 full year of undergraduate study. Applicants must submit 3 letters of recommendation and an official transcript (must have at least a 2.5 GPA) and demonstrate financial need. Request applications after January 1; include a self-addressed, stamped envelope or visit web site. Deadline: February 15.

81. (A, H, S, SS)
Merit Scholarships

Awards of $1,000 to graduate and undergraduate students who have completed at least 1 full year of higher education. Applicants must submit three letters of recommendation and an official transcript. Must have at least a 3.0 GPA, commitment to community service and involvement. Visit web site for more information. Deadline: February 15.

82. (A, H, S, SS)
Mu Rho Omega Chapter

1 scholarship of $1,000 to a minority female graduate or undergraduate student. Must from the Glades area and demonstrate academic achievement, extracurricular activities, positive self-image, and motivation. Visit web site for more information and deadline.

(A, H, S, SS)
Alpha Lambda Delta
P.O. Box 4403
Macon, GA 31208–4403
(478) 744–9595
http://www.mercer.edu/ald/index.html

83. (A, H)
Fellowships for Members

23 graduate fellowships: 1 for $7,500, 7 for $5,000, and 15 for $3,000 to graduate or professional school students who are members of ALD. Must have at least a 3.5 GPA on 4.0 scale. Awards are good for all areas of study. When requesting information, applicants should include membership date and school where they are a member. Deadline: Friday before Martin Luther King Jr. Day (postmark).

84. (A, H, S, SS)
Graduate Fellowships

23 awards ranging from $3,000 to $7,500 to graduate students and undergraduate seniors who intend to pursue graduate study. Must be members of Alpha Lambda Delta. Must have at least a 3.5 GPA on 4.0 scale. Awards are good for all areas of study. When requesting information, applicants should include membership date and school where they are a member. Deadline: January 31.

85. (A, H, S, SS)
Alpha Lambda Tau International Social Fraternity, Inc.
Scholarships
P.O. Box 17550
Indianapolis, IN 46217
(877) 660–8845
http://www.alphalambdatau.org/main.htm

Scholarships of varying amounts to graduate and undergraduate student members for any area of study. Established to provide social, educational, financial, career, and character building opportunities for gay, bisexual, transgender, and alternative lifestyle–friendly male college students through motivational, creative, and meaningful recreational, scholastic, and community service programs. Deadline: none specified.

(H)
Alpha Mu Gamma Scholarships
Los Angeles City College
855 North Vermont Avenue
Los Angeles, CA 90029
(323) 644–9752
http://www.lacc.cc.ca.us/activities/honor/amg/Scholars.htm

86. (H)
Bilingual Award

1 scholarship award of $500 to a bilingual graduate or undergraduate student majoring in language, literature, or linguistics. Must be AMG members to be eligible for the award. Include a self-addressed, stamped envelope with your request for information. Deadline: February 1.

87. (H)
Full-Tuition Summer Scholarship

1 scholarship providing full summer tuition to a student member to study French from July to August at Laval University in Quebec. Applicants must be studying a foreign language. Deadline: December 31, may vary.

88. (H)
Merit Scholarship

1 scholarship providing full tuition for one academic year to an AMG member for study at the Monterey Institute of International Studies. Must be studying either Arabic, Chinese, French, German, Greek, Japanese, Portuguese, Russian, or Spanish. Deadline: December 31, may vary.

89. (H)
National Scholarships

3 scholarships of $500 to graduate or undergraduate student members for use at any accredited institution for continued language study. Applicants must be studying a foreign language. Include a self-addressed, stamped envelope with your request for information. Deadline: December 31, may vary.

(A, H, S, SS)
Alpha Omicron Pi Foundation
Scholarship Committee
P.O. Box 395
Brentwood, TN 37024–0395
(615) 370–0920
http://www.aoiifoundation.org

90. (A, H, S, SS)
Alpha Tau Chapter Scholarship

1 award of varying amount to a graduate student member pursuing any field of study. Selection is based on academic achievement, commitment to chapter, recommendation letter, and financial aid. Preference is given to a legacy. Deadline: March 1.

91. (S)
Angels of Kappa Theta Memorial Scholarship

1 award of varying amount to a graduate student member pursuing any field of study. Selection is based on academic achievement, commitment to chapter, recommendation letter, and financial aid. Preference is given as follows: 1) a member enrolled in a Southern California chapter, 2) a member at any California school, and 3) to any West Coast chapter should there be no active chapter in California. Deadline: March 1.

92. (H)
Carolyn Huey Harris Scholarship

1 scholarship of varying amount to a Lambda Sigma Chapter member who is a graduate student or undergraduate junior or senior. Must be pursuing a career in communication (journalism, public relations, marketing, speech, media) and have at least a 3.0 GPA. Selection based on academic achievement, character, judgment, involvement in chapter, and being a well-rounded individual. If no Lambda Sigma member applies or is qualified, members from other Georgia colleges, and finally sisters from other states, will be considered. Deadline: March 1.

93. (A, H, S, SS)
Diamond Jubilee Scholarship

Numerous scholarships of varying amounts to graduate or undergraduate student members pursuing any field of study. Selection is based on academic achievement, commitment to chapter, recommendation letter, and financial aid. Deadline: March 1.

94. (S)
Edith Huntington Anderson Scholarship

1 award of varying amount to a student member pursuing a career in medicine or a medically related field. Must already have a bachelor of science degree or be receiving one by July 1 of the application period. Selection is based on academic achievement, service to chapter, and personal attributes and attitudes, with financial aid considered last. Deadline: March 1.

95. (A, H, S, SS)

Helen Haller Scholarship

1 scholarship of varying amount to a graduate or undergraduate student member pursuing any field of study. Selection is based on academic achievement, commitment to chapter, recommendation letter, and financial aid. Deadline: March 1.

96. (A, H, S, SS)

Jo Ann Gibbons Scholarship

1 scholarship of varying amount to a Kappa Alpha Chapter member. Must maintain a 2.5 GPA or better and have a proven record of service to the chapter. If a Kappa Alpha doesn't apply, a member of another Indiana Chapter will be eligible for the award. Deadline: March 1.

97. (A, H, S, SS)

Karen Tucker Centennial Scholarship

1 scholarship of varying amount to a graduate or undergraduate student member pursuing any field of study. Selection is based on academic achievement, commitment to chapter, recommendation letter, and financial aid. Deadline: March 1.

98. (A, H, S, SS)

Langston/Purdy Lambda Sigma Scholarship

1 scholarship of varying amount to a graduate or undergraduate student member of Lambda Sigma chapter. Selection is based on academic achievement, commitment to chapter, recommendation letter, and financial aid. Deadline: March 1.

99. (A, H, S, SS)

L. Laura McDowell Scholarship

1 scholarship of varying amount to a graduate or undergraduate student member pursuing any field of study. Selection is based on academic achievement, commitment to chapter, recommendation letter, and financial aid. Deadline: March 1.

100. (A, H, S, SS)

Pi Kappa Scholarship

1 scholarship of varying amount to an alumna or undergraduate member. Must be in good standing and planning to attend a college or university in the state of Texas. Selection is based on financial need. Deadline: March 1.

101. (A, H, S, SS)

Rho Omicron Scholarship

1 scholarship of varying amount to a student member in good standing pursuing any field of study. Selection is based on academic achievement, commitment to chapter, recommendation letter, and financial aid. Preference is given as follows: 1) an alumna graduate student, 2) a member about to finish an undergraduate degree, and 3) any AOP member residing, or attending a university, in Tennessee. Deadline: March 1.

102. (S)

Ruth M. Johnson Memorial Scholarship

1 award of varying amount to a student member attending medical school or participating in a medical research program. Selection is based on academic achievement, service to chapter, and personal attributes and attitudes, with financial aid considered last. Deadline: March 1.

103. (A, H, S, SS)

San Diego Alumnae Chapter Honor Scholarship

1 scholarship of varying amount to a graduate or undergraduate student member for any field of study. Selection is based on academic achievement, commitment to chapter, recommendation letter, and financial aid. Must demonstrate active involvement and loyalty to and participation in AOP activities. Preference given as follows: 1) member of the San Diego Alumnae Chapter, 2) any alumna living in California, and 3) any AOP alumna living on the West Coast. Deadline: March 1.

104. (S)

Alpha-1 Foundation
Postdoctoral Research Fellowships
Director, Research & Grant Programs
2937 S.W. 27th Avenue, Suite 302
Miami, FL 33133
http://www.alphaone.org

Awards of up to $50,000 to postdoctoral fellows with either a Ph.D. or M.D. who are about to enter a fellowship or residency training program in basic science or clinical investigation related to AAT Deficiency. Visit web site for more information and submission guidelines. Deadline: November 1.

(A)
Alpha Phi Delta Fraternity, Inc.
916 62nd Street
Brooklyn, NY 11219
(718) 745–9551
http://www.apd.org
apdoffice@apd.org

105. (A, H, S, SS)
Alpha Phi Delta Award

1 award of $1,000 to a full-time graduate or undergraduate student member for use in any area of study. Based on academic achievement and contribution to their respective organization. Deadline: June 15.

106. (A, H, S, SS)
Ernest Coletti Award

1 award of $1,600 to a full-time graduate or undergraduate student member for use in any area of study. Based on academic achievement and contribution to their respective organization. Deadline: June 15.

107. (A, H, S, SS)
Founders Award

1 award of $2,400 to a full-time graduate or undergraduate student member for use in any area of study. Based on academic achievement and contribution to their respective organization. Deadline: June 15.

108. (A, H, S, SS)
John Pasta Award

1 award of $1,600 to a full-time graduate or undergraduate student member for use in any area of study. Based on academic achievement and contribution to their respective organization. Deadline: June 15.

109. (A. H, S, SS)
Scholarships

15 scholarships of $750 to full-time graduate and undergraduate student members for use in any area of study. Based on academic achievement and contribution to their respective organization. Deadline: June 15.

110. (A, H, S, SS)
Southern California Alumni Club Award

1 scholarship of $750 to a full-time graduate or undergraduate student member for use in any area of study. Based on academic achievement and contribution to their respective organization. Must be a resident of Southern California. Deadline: June 15.

111. (A, H, S, SS)
Alpha Phi Delta Society
Seward Scholarship
6126 Lincoln Avenue
Morton Grove, IL 60053
(847) 581–1992
http://www.adps.org/contact.html

Scholarships of $1,000 to full-time graduate and undergraduate students who are members. Based on academic achievement and contribution to their respective organization. Deadline: June 15.

112. (A)
Alpha Tau Delta
Scholarships
ATTN: National Awards Committee Chairperson
150 Chuickshank Drive
Folsom, CA 95630
(916) 984–9150
http://www.atdnursing.org

Varying numbers of scholarships of $1,000 to graduate students who are members of Alpha Tau Delta. Based on academic achievement, financial need, interest in and support of organization, recommendations, and professional activities. Must have at least a 2.5 GPA. Deadline: March 1.

113. (SS)
Amelia Island Plantation
Internship Coordinator
Resort Operations Building
P.O. Box 3000
Amelia Island, FL 32035–1307
(904) 277–5904
http://www.aipfl.com/ContactUs/contact.htm

70 internships lasting from 12 to 16 weeks during the summer, fall, or spring; provides $100/week housing stipend and one free meal per day to graduate students, recent college graduates, college graduates of any age, and undergraduate students. International students are eligible. The Amelia Island Plantation is a 1,250-acre luxury resort and residential community situated 29 miles northeast of Jacksonville, Florida. The Plantation offers 45 holes of golf, 25 tennis courts, bicycling, paddleboating, horseback riding, fishing, swimming pools, seven dining facilities, and a health and fitness center. Interns work in flora/horticulture, culinary, promotions, recreation, health and fitness center, special events, and public relations. Submit résumé, cover letter, and recommendations. Deadlines: February 15 (summer), May 15 (fall), and November 15 (spring).

114. (SS)
Alston/Bannerman Fellowship Program
1627 Lancaster Street
Baltimore, MD 21231
http://www.bannermanfellowship.org
http://www.AlstonBannerman.org

10 fellowships of $15,000 to minority individuals committed to continuing to work for social change. Must live in the U.S. or its territories and have more than 10 years of community organizing experience. Fellows are encouraged to take at least 3 months and devote time to activities that are substantially different from their normal routine. Fellows must be endorsed by their organization and sabbaticals taken within a year of being awarded the fellowship. Visit web site for more information. Deadline: December 2.

(A)
American Academy and Institute of Arts and Letters
633 West 155th Street
New York, NY 10032
(212) 368–5900
http://www.nyc-arts.org/nyc-arts

115. (A)
Awards

17 awards in excess of $5,000 each to writers, composers, and artists who are not members of the Institute. For more information, write a brief introductory letter and include a self-addressed, stamped envelope. Deadline: none specified.

116. (A)
Award of Merit

An award of varying amount to a graduate student, doctoral candidate, or professional novelist. This award is based on past work. Must be a U.S. citizen. Deadline: varies.

117. (A)
Gold Medal for Poetry

1 award of varying amount to a graduate student, doctoral candidate, or professional for best poetry published in written form. All candidates must be nominated by an Academy-Institute member. No applications are accepted. Possible candidates should contact the Academy and inquire about local members.

118. (A)
Rome Fellowship in Literature

A 1-year residency is awarded to a graduate or doctoral student or a professional to conduct research in Rome in the area of literature. All candidates must be nominated by an Academy-Institute member. No applications are accepted. Possible candidates should contact the Academy and inquire about local members.

119. (A)
Sue Kaufman Prize for First Fiction

1 award of $2,000 is given to the best work of fiction published in the preceding year. All candidates must be nominated by an Academy-Institute member. No applications are accepted. Possible candidates should contact the Academy and inquire about local members.

120. (A)
Witter Bynner Prize for Poetry

1 award of $2,500 is given to a younger poet. All candidates must be nominated by an Academy-Institute member. No applications are accepted. Possible candidates should contact the Academy and inquire about local members.

(A, H, SS)
American Academy in Rome
ATTN: Fellowship Coordinator
7 East 60th Street

New York, NY 10022–1001
(212) 751–7200
http://www.aarome.org

121. (A, H)
Doctoral Fellowships

Approximately 24 fellowships ranging from $7,500 to $17,000 for doctoral candidates for study in architecture, art, history, music, and related fields in Rome. Must have completed all work for Ph.D. and done at least 1 year's work on dissertation. There is a $30 fee for each field of application. Send a self-addressed, stamped envelope. Deadline: varies.

122. (A)
National Endowment for the Arts Fellowships

3 6-month fellowships providing a stipend of $5,000 plus a travel allowance of $800 to graduate students in architecture, design arts, and landscape architecture. Must have had 7 years of professional practice in one of these areas. Award must be used at the Academy in Rome, Italy. Must be U.S. citizens. Deadline: November 15.

123. (A, H)
National Gallery of Art Predoctoral Fellowship in Art History

1 fellowship providing a cash award for travel, expenses, study, and room and board to a doctoral candidate in art history to assist with independent study and research at the American Academy in Rome. Candidates must be sponsored by their graduate schools and be a U.S. citizen. Contact: Professor Henry Millon, National Gallery of Art, 6th and Constitution Avenue, N.W., Washington, DC 20565. Deadline: November 15.

124. (A, H, SS)
Rome Prize Creative Disciplines Fellowships

30 6- to 12-month fellowships providing a stipend ranging from $7,500 to $17,000, plus housing and a studio, to doctoral candidates who wish to conduct independent creative work or research in archeology, architecture, art history, fine arts, landscape design, musical composition, or classical studies at the American Academy in Rome. Applicants must have a bachelor's or master's degree. Must be a U.S. citizen. Deadline: November 15.

125. (A, H)
Rome Prize Fellowships, School of Classical Studies

Varying numbers of 1-year residential fellowships in classical studies, archeology, classical art, history of art, postclassical humanistic studies, and Medieval and Renaissance studies at the American Academy in Rome. Awards provide $5,400 stipend and an $800 travel allowance. Recipient must have completed all course work and 1 year of work on dissertation, may not hold a job, or travel extensively during the fellowship year. Deadline: November 15.

126. (A)
Rome Prize Fellowships, School of Fine Arts

Up to 10 1-year fellowships in architecture, design arts, landscape architecture, painting, sculpture, visual arts, and musical composition at the American Academy in Rome. Awards provide an approximately $4,600 stipend and a dependent's allowance, $800 travel allowance, and $600 supplies allowance for painters, sculptors, and visual artists. Applicants in painting, sculpture, and visual arts need not have a degree but must have at least 3 years of professional experience, ability, and current studio work. Applicants in architecture and landscape architecture must have appropriate degrees. Applicants in other areas must hold a B.A. degree. There is a $30 application fee. Deadline: December 31.

127. (A, H)
Samuel H. Kress Foundation Predoctoral Fellowships

2 fellowships providing a stipend of $7,500, plus a traveling allowance of $800, to doctoral students to conduct independent study and research. 1 of the fellowships is in Classical Art History and 1 is in Italian Art History. Awards must be used at the American Academy in Rome. Recipients must have completed all course work and must be beginning the second year of dissertation work. Selection is based on basis of proposed research. Award lasts 2 years. Must be a U.S. citizen. Deadline: November 15.

128. (S)

American Academy of Allergy, Asthma, and Immunology
Summer Fellowships
611 East Wells Street
Milwaukee, WI 53202
(414) 272–6071
http://www.aaaai.org

10 to 15 fellowships of $1,500 to medical students who have completed at least 8 months of medical school. Award is to encourage students to pursue research in allergy & immunology during summer break. Must be U.S. or Canadian resident. Deadline: March 15.

129. (A, S, SS)

American Academy of Arts and Sciences
Norton's Wood's
136 Irving Street
Cambridge, MA 02138–1996
(617) 567–5000
http://www.amacad.org

Numerous fellowships of varying amounts to graduate or professional students in the arts, sciences, or public affairs. The Academy was founded in 1780 "to cultivate every art and science which may tend to advance the interest, honor, dignity, and happiness of a free, independent, and virtuous people." For more information, send a self-addressed, stamped envelope. Deadline: varies.

(S)

American Academy of Audiology
11730 Plaza America Drive, Suite 300
Reston, VA 20190
(800) AAA–2336
http://www.audiology.org/students/rap

130. (S)

Student Investigator Research Award

Awards of up to $5,000 to graduate students working toward a degree in audiology to complete a research project as part of their course of study. These awards are for students who have not conducted any research before. When possible, awards will be made for both clinical/applied research and basic research. Visit web site for more information and an application. Deadline: November 15.

131. (S)

Student Summer Research Fellowship

Fellowships providing a $2,500 stipend to graduate students and undergraduate seniors pursuing a career in audiology to gain a limited but significant exposure to a research environment. Visit web site for more information and an application. Deadline: November 15.

(S)

American Academy of Child and Adolescent Psychiatry
AACAP Department of Research and Training
3615 Wisconsin Avenue, N.W.
Washington, DC 20016–3007
(202) 966–7300
http://www.aacap.org/research/Spurlck2.htm

132. (S)

Jeanne Spurlock Minority Medical Student Clinical Fellowship

Up to 14 fellowships of up to $2,500 to minority medical students to work with a child and adolescent psychiatrist mentor. Fellows also receive expenses for 5 days at the AACAP Annual Meeting. Must attend an accredited U.S. medical school. Deadline: April 4.

133. (S)

Jeanne Spurlock Research Fellowship in Drug Abuse and Addiction

Up to 5 fellowships of up to $2,500 to minority medical students to work with a child and adolescent psychiatrist research mentor. Fellows also receive expenses for 5 days at the AACAP Annual Meeting. Must attend an accredited U.S. medical school. All applications must relate to substance abuse research. Deadline: April 4.

(S)

American Academy of Neurology
1080 Montreal Avenue
St. Paul, MN 55116
(651) 695–2756
(800) 879–1960
http://www.aan.com

134. (S)
AAN Award for Creative Expression of Human Values in Neurology

1 award of $2,000 ($500 to winner and $1,500 to winner's specified charity) for an original, unpublished poem, short story, essay, memoir, or personal history that expresses human values in the practice of neurology. Entry should promote compassion for persons suffering from neurological disorders and regard for the physicians who devote themselves to bettering the lives of those who are afflicted. Must be an AAN member. Visit web site for more information. Deadline: December 1.

135. (S)
Auxiliary Awards: Founders and S. Weir Mitchell

2 awards of $1,000 (1 each Founders and S. Weir Mitchell) to junior members who are senior authors of submitted research-based manuscripts. Recipient also receives travel reimbursement and $50 per diem to attend the Annual Meeting and present the paper. Selection is based on originality, scientific merit, neurological interest, and clarity of expression. Visit web site for more information and deadline.

136. (S)
Medical Student Essay Awards

3 awards of $350 and 1 award of $1,000 to medical students for an original essay of interest to general neurologists. Award is meant to stimulate interest in the field of neurology and is given for the best essay in 4 areas: historical aspects, neuroscience, clinical, and experimental neurology. Recipients also receive a 1-year subscription to *Neurology* and reimbursement for travel, lodging, and meals to attend the Annual Meeting. Must attend an accredited medical school. Visit web site for more information and deadline.

137. (S)
Michael S. Pessin Stroke Leadership Prize

1 award of $1,500 and registration to the Annual Meeting to medical students, residents, fellows, or junior faculty who are AAN members. Consideration is given to those in clinical research aimed at enhancing the understanding of stroke or improving acute treatment protocols. Visit web site for more information and deadline.

138. (S)
Sleep Science Award

1 award of $1,500 and registration to the Annual Meeting to medical students, residents, fellows, and junior members. Awarded to stimulate and reward individuals in the pursuit of basic and clinical research in sleep. Must have participated in basic or clinical sleep research. Visit web site for more information and deadline.

139. (S)
American Academy of Nursing Fellowships
600 Maryland Avenue, S.W., Suite 100 W
Washington, DC 20024–2571
(202) 651–7238
http://www.nursingworld.org/aan

Fellowships of varying amount to graduate students. Applicants must be in good standing in a state nurses association that holds membership in the American Nurses Association. Must show evidence of outstanding contributions to nursing and evidence of potential to continue contributions to nursing. Deadline: none specified.

140. (S)
American Academy of Pediatrics Residency Scholarships
141 N.W. Point Boulevard
Elk Grove Village, IL 60007–1098
(847) 434–4000
http://www.aap.org

Numerous scholarships ranging from $1,000 to $5,000 to physicians who have completed their internships (PL-0 or PL-1) and have a commitment for a first-year pediatric residency or be a pediatric resident. Applicants must have financial need. Must have a letter of support from chief of service attesting to that need. Applications are available after November 1. Must be a citizen or legal resident of the U.S. or Canada. Deadline: February 1.

(S)
American Academy of Periodontology
737 Michigan Avenue, Suite 800
Chicago, IL 60611–2690

(312) 573–3256

http://www.perio.org

141. (S)
Abram and Sylvia Chasens Teaching and Research Fellowship

2 fellowships of $30,000 to students who have a stated career goal of periodontal education and who are in their third year of an accredited periodontal residence program. Must be citizens of the United States or Canada. Deadline: varies.

142. (S)
AAP Student Scholarships

Up to 5 scholarships of $5,000 as a one-time cash award. Applicants must be U.S. citizens in their final year of dental school and accepted to a postgraduate periodontal program in the United States or Canada. Deadline: March 1.

143. (S)
Bud and Linda Tarrson Fellowship

1 fellowship of $10,000 per year for up to 3 years to either a full-time faculty member at the instructor or assistant level or a part-time faculty member; must be nominated by their periodontal program director. Applications are mailed to all periodontal program directors and deans in March.

144. (S)
Dr. and Mrs. Gerald M. Kramer Scholarship for Excellence

1 award of $10,000 to a third-year full-time periodontal student at an accredited U.S. or Canadian periodontal program. Must be nominated by their periodontal program director. Deadline: varies.

145. (A, Contest)
American Accordion Musicological Society Contest
ATTN: JoAnn Arnold
322 Haddon Avenue
Westmont, NJ 08108–2864
http://www.aamsaccordionfest.com

Awards ranging from $100 to $250 to amateur composers who are graduate, undergraduate, or high school students, or professional music composers. Must write a serious composition for the accordion lasting at least 6 minutes. This is a cash award and may be used at student's discretion. Deadline: February 28.

(SS)
American Accounting Association
5717 Bessie Drive
Sarasota, FL 34233–2399
(941) 921–7747
http://aaahq.org/index.cfm

146. (SS)
Arthur H. Carter Scholarship

40 scholarships of $2,500 to graduate students or undergraduate juniors and seniors for study of accounting at any accredited U.S. institution. Must have completed at least 2 years of undergraduate study and have at least 1 full year of study remaining. Based on merit not need. For more information, visit web site. Deadline: April 1.

147. (SS)
Fellowship Program in Accounting

From 5 to 18 fellowships of $1,000 to doctoral students in programs accredited by the AACSB and pursuing a career in teaching in the U.S. or Canada. Based on merit, not financial need. For more information, visit their web site. Deadline: February 1.

148. (SS)
Outstanding Dissertation Award

1 award of unspecified amount to a doctoral student for an outstanding dissertation. Selection will be based on relevance and originality of the research question(s); development of a theoretical framework; appropriateness of the research method and analysis; quality of writing; potential for publication in a scholarly journal; and potential for the results to have practical implications for accounting practitioners and organizations. For more information, visit web site. Deadline: March 1.

149. (S)
American Airlines
First Officer Candidate Course Scholarship
Commercial Flight Training
P.O. Box 619617

MD 821, GSWFA
DFW Airport, TX 75261–9617
(800) 678–8686
http://www.aa.com

2 scholarships of $8,500 to individuals who have or are about to receive a 4-year degree from a University Aviation Association member institution. Applicants must be within one semester of graduation or no more than 1 year beyond graduation at the time of the deadline. Award is meant to provide a "bridge" between university aviation flight education and the airline cockpit and to promote interest in the First Officer Candidate Course at Eagle Training Center. Applicants must be 21 years of age by the application deadline, have at least a 3.5 overall GPA on a 4.0 scale, hold the FAA commercial certificate with instrument and multiengine ratings, and have 400 total flight hours and at least 40 hours of multiengine time. Applicants must have completed their university's FAA-approved flight training program. Applications are available from UAA member institutions as well as from American Airlines. Deadline: May 1.

(H)

American Antiquarian Society
185 Salisbury Street
Worchester, MA 01609
(508) 755–5221
http://www.americanantiquarian.org/

150. (H)
American Historical Print Collectors Society

Fellowships of varying amounts to support research on American prints of the 18th and 19th centuries or for projects using prints as primary documentation. The award is funded jointly by the American Historical Print Collectors Society and AAS. Visit web site for specific guidelines. Deadline: January 15.

151. (H)
American Society for 18th Century Studies Fellowships

Fellowships of varying amounts to doctoral candidates to conduct research on projects related to the American 18th century. The award is jointly funded by the American Society for 18th-Century Studies and AAS. Visit web site for specific guidelines. Deadline: January 15.

152. (H)
Joyce Tracy Fellowships

Fellowships of $1,000 per month to doctoral candidates to enable them to conduct research for a period from 1 to 3 months. All awards are for a period of residence to use the AAS Library's resources for research and writing on newspapers and magazines or for projects using these resources as primary documentation. Visit web site for specific guidelines. Deadline: January 15.

153. (H)
Kate B. and Hall J. Peterson Fellowships

Varying numbers of 1- to 3-month fellowships providing a stipend of up to $1,000 per month to doctoral candidates to do research on any topic in American history and culture (through 1876). Research must be conducted at the American Antiquarian Society Library. Visit web site for specific guidelines. Deadline: January 15.

154. (H)
Legacy Fellowships

Fellowships providing a monthly stipend of up to $1,000 to doctoral candidates in American history and culture (through 1876). Research may be on any topic supported by the American Antiquarian Society Library. Visit web site for specific guidelines. Deadline: January 15.

155. (H)
Mellon Postdoctoral Research Fellowships

1 fellowship of up to $40,000 to doctoral candidates to enable them to conduct research for a period from 9 to 10 months. All awards are for a period of residence to use the AAS library's resources for research and writing on any topic supported by the Library. Visit web site for specific guidelines. Deadline: January 15.

156. (H)
National Endowment for the Humanities Fellowships

2 or more fellowships of varying amounts to doctoral candidates to enable them to conduct research for a period from 4 to 12 months. All awards are for a period of residence to use the AAS Library's resources for research and writing on any topic supported by

the Library. Funds come from the National Endowment for the Humanities. Visit web site for specific guidelines. Deadline: January 15.

157. (H)
Northeast Modern Language Association Fellowship

Fellowships of varying amounts to doctoral candidates to conduct research in American literary studies through 1876. The award is jointly funded by the Northeast Modern Language Association and AAS. Visit web site for specific guidelines. Deadline: January 15.

158. (H)
Reese Fellowship

Fellowships of $1,000 per month to doctoral candidates to support research in American bibliography and projects in the history of the book in America. Visit web site for specific guidelines. Deadline: January 15.

159. (H)
Stephen Botein Short-Term Fellowship

Numerous fellowships providing a stipend of up to $1,000 to scholars who are conducting research on the study of publishing history in American culture. Award must be used to conduct research and be in regular and continuous residence at the American Antiquarian Society Library. Visit web site for specific guidelines. Deadline: January 15.

(A)
American Architectural Foundation
1799 New York Avenue, N.W.
Washington, DC 20006–5292
(202) 626–7318
http://www.archfoundation.org

160. (A)
AIA/AAF Scholarships for Advanced Degree/Research Candidates

Varying number of scholarship grants ranging from $1,000 to $2,500 to students who have already earned a professional degree in architecture or related fields. Awards are not for tuition assistance for an advanced degree but are based on the merits of a research project proposal. Awards are for one full year. Applicants must be enrolled in an accredited U.S. or Canadian institution. Visit web site or send a self-addressed, stamped envelope for details. Deadline: mid-February.

161. (A)
AIA/AAF Scholarships for First Professional Degree Candidates

1 or more scholarship grants ranging from $500 to $2,500 to students in the final 2 years of a professional degree program. Applicants must write a personal essay, file a financial aid need analysis, and provide a drawing, transcripts and class ranking, and 3 letters of recommendation. Award must be used for full-time study at an accredited U.S. or Canadian institution. Applications are only available from the departments of architecture at NAAB- and RAIC-accredited programs. The dean or a designated scholarship committee selects applicants. Deadline: January 31.

162. (A)
AIA/AHA Graduate Fellowship in Health Facilities Planning and Design

2 or more awards ranging from $1,000 to $2,500 to students who have earned and received a professional degree or are in the final year of academic work leading to such a degree. To be considered for this award, you must submit a proposed study program and demonstrate your potential ability to make a contribution in the field of health care architecture. Open to citizens of the U.S., Canada, or Mexico Deadline: January 31.

163. (A)
RTKL Traveling Fellowship

1 fellowship of $2,500 to a student submitting the winning proposal outlining a foreign itinerary that is directly relevant to his or her education goals. Students must complete travel prior to graduation. Applications available online. Deadline: mid-February.

164. (A)
Richard Morris Hunt Fellowship

A fellowship of varying amount to American and French architects to learn and exchange information about their respective countries' historic preservation process and techniques. Visit web site for contact information. Deadline: none specified.

165. (A, SS)
American Art Therapy Association
Research Assistance Grant
1202 Allanson Road
Mundelein, IL 60060–3808
(888) 290–0878
(847) 949–6064
http://www.arttherapy.org

Scholarships of varying amounts to professional art therapists conducting significant research in the art therapy field. Research may be related to master's thesis or doctoral dissertation. Must be a member of AATA and a U.S. citizen. Send a self-addressed, stamped envelope for more information. Deadline: spring.

(S)
American Association for the Advancement of Science
Education and Human Resources Department
1200 New York Avenue, N.W.
Washington, DC 20005
(202) 326–6400
http://www.aaas.org

166. (S)
Environmental Science and Engineering Fellowship

Places graduate and undergraduate students in a summer-long research program at the Environmental Protection Agency on topics of agency interest. Applicants should be student members of AAAS or applying for membership. Deadline: March 1.

167. (S)
Mass Media, Science, and Engineering Fellowship

Summer-long internships to undergraduate and graduate science and engineering students as science reporters for various media outlets. Applicants should be student members of AAAS or applying for membership. Deadline: February 1.

168. (S)
Newcomb Cleveland Prize

1 award of varying amount to the author(s) of the year's best article, research article, or report published in *Science*. Author(s) should be member(s) of AAAS or applying for membership. Recipient(s) must have exceptional competence in some area of science or engineering or have a broad scientific or technical background. Deadline: varies.

169. (S)
Postdoctoral Awards

Varying numbers of awards of $26,500 for one-year postdoctoral study in engineering; science; and mathematics. Applicants should be members of AAAS or applying for membership. Recipients must have exceptional competence in some area of science or have a broad scientific or technical background. Deadline: December 1.

170. (S)
William D. Carey Science Award

1 award of varying amount to a graduate student for travel and subsistence funds to encourage their attendance at the AAAS Annual Meeting. There is also a special committee on Opportunities in Science that seeks to help women, minorities, and the handicapped advance in the scientific professions. Deadline: December 1.

171. (S)
Women's International Science Collaboration Program (WISC)

Grants of up to $5,000 to graduate, predoctoral, and postdoctoral students or those with equivalent research experience to travel to a partner country to conduct research. Must be U.S. citizens or permanent residents. Predoctoral candidates must be conducting research in an established doctoral program in the U.S. Open to the following research areas: astronomy, biochemistry, biophysics and genetics, biological sciences, chemistry, computer science, earth sciences, economics, engineering, environmental sciences, geography, history and philosophy of science, linguistics, materials science, mathematics, physics, political science, nonclinically oriented psychology, science education and communication, science and technology policy, and sociology. Deadline: January 15.

(H, S)
American Association for the History of Nursing, Inc.
P.O. Box 175
Lanoka Harbor, NJ 06734
(609) 693–7250
http://www.aahn.org/awards.html

172. (H, S)
Cadet Nurse Corps Award

An award of varying amount to a master's graduate student to support scholarly study in the full range of topics related to nursing history. Submissions may include completed thesis and other publishable manuscripts based on a research project. Selection is based on the rigor of the historical research, scholarly discussion, and quality of writing. Deadline: May 15.

173. (H, S)
Competitive Student Research Award

Awards of $1,000 to graduate students to conduct historical research that focuses on a significant question in the history of nursing. Students must be enrolled in an accredited graduate program and a member of AAHN. Visit web site for specific guidelines. Deadline: May 15.

174. (H, S)
Lavinia L. Dock Awards

2 awards of varying amounts to recognize outstanding research and writing. 1 award is for a book-length work, and 1 is for an article-length work. Postdoctoral research manuscripts, articles, or books are acceptable. Manuscript must be based on original historical research related to the history of nursing. Selection based on rigor of the historical research and the quality of the writing. Deadline: May 15.

175. (H, S)
Society of Nursing History Research Award

1 award of $2,000 for postdoctoral research in nursing history. Must be members of AAHN with a doctoral degree. Selection based on scholarly merit and significance to the field of nursing history. Deadline: May 15.

176. (H, S)
Teresa E. Christy Award

1 award of varying amount for doctoral work based on original historical research related to the history of nursing. Given for doctoral work and submissions that are usually dissertations. Selection based on the rigor of the historical research and the quality of writing demonstrated in the manuscript. Deadline: May 15.

177. (SS)
American Association of Advertising Agencies Minority Advertising Internships
405 Lexington Avenue, Suite 18th Floor
New York, NY 10174–1801
(212) 682–2500
http://www.aaaa.org

1 scholarship of $2,000, and a summer internship, to minority graduate students or an undergraduate junior or senior. Internship is in either Chicago, Detroit, Los Angeles, San Francisco, or New York. Transportation and housing costs, plus a salary, are covered by the Association. Write an introductory letter briefly stating educational and career goals and financial situation. Deadline: January 15.

(S)
American Association of Airport Executives (AAAE)
AAAE Foundation Scholarship Program
Scholarship Coordinator
601 Madison Street, Suite 400
Alexandria, VA 22314
(703) 824–0500
http://www.aaae.com

178. (S)
AAAE Scholarships

10 scholarships of $1,000 and 1 scholarship of $5,000 to graduate or upper-level undergraduate students in an aviation program. Must have a cumulative GPA of 2.75 on a 4.0 scale or equivalent. Selection based on academic achievement, financial need, and community activities. Must submit transcripts. Limit of 1 student scholarship application per university. Must apply through your university. Deadline: May 15 (for $1,000 scholarship) and March 31 (for $5,000 scholarship).

179. (S)
Scholarship Program

Varying numbers of scholarships of $1,000 to graduate or undergraduate junior or senior students who will be enrolled in an aviation program. Must have at least a 3.0 GPA on a 4.0 scale. Selection is based on academic achievement, financial need, extracurricular activities, work experience, and personal statement. Membership in AAAE is not required. Write or visit web site for more information. Deadline: not specified.

180. (S)
The Landrum & Brown Scholarship

1 scholarship of $5,000 to a graduate or upper-level undergraduate student in an aviation program. Must be a full-time student, enrolled in an aviation program at an accredited college or university, with a cumulative GPA of 2.75 or higher on a 4.0 scale or equivalent. Must submit an application with necessary documents. Sponsor is an airport planning consulting firm. Deadline: March 31.

181. (S)
American Association of Blood Banks
Fenwal Scholarships
8101 Glenbrook Road
Bethesda, MD 20814–2749
(301) 907–6977
http://www.aabb.org

5 scholarships of $1,500 to graduate, doctoral, or undergraduate students attending an accredited SBB program. Submit original essays to the AABB for review. The 3 categories are scientific, analytical, and educational. Awards must be used for educational endeavors. Deadline: April 1.

182. (S, SS)
American Association of Cereal Chemists
Graduate Fellowships
3340 Pilot Knob Road
St. Paul, MN 55121–2097
(651) 454–7250
http://www.aaccnet.org

Scholarships ranging from $1,000 to $3,000 to graduate students majoring, or interested, in a career in cereal science or technology, including baking or a related area. Based on academic achievement and career goals. AACC membership is helpful but not required. Deadline: April 1.

(S)
American Association of Critical Care Nurses
101 Columbia
Aliso Viejo, CA 92656–4109
(949) 362–2000
(800) 899–2226
http://www.aacn.org
info@aacn.org

183. (S)
Dale Medical Products Scholarships

Up to 3 scholarships of $1,500 to graduate students to be used to offset registration fees, travel, and lodging expenses to attend the National Teaching Institute/ Advanced Practical Institute & Critical Care Exposition (NTI/API & CCE). Must be in an accredited graduate nursing program, have an active RN license, and be an AACN member. Deadline: February 1.

184. (S)
Educational Advancement Scholarship Program

45 awards of $1,500 for full-time graduate or doctoral students. Must be a current AACN member and a registered nurse. RN must have worked critical care for 1 year out of last 3. Must maintain a B average. Based on academic record and 150-word essay. Deadline: April 1.

185. (S)
RN.com

Up to 9 awards of $1,500 to minority graduate nurses to offset registration fees, travel, and lodging expenses to attend the NTI/API & CCE. Must have an active RN license, have financial need, and/or be a member of AACN. Deadline: February 1.

186. (S)
Vision Partner

10 pairs of awards of $500/partner to offset costs to attend NTI/API & CCE. Partner 1 must be an AACN member who selects and accompanies a Vision Partner to the NTI or API and commits to continuing the partnership upon return to the workplace. Partner 2 is

a colleague who can benefit from AACN while also introducing the AACN member to a new perspective. Deadline: February 1.

(SS)

American Association of Family and Consumer Sciences (AAFCS)
ATTN: Fellowships and Awards Committee
1555 King Street
Alexandria, VA 22314–2852
(703) 706–4600
http://www.aafcs.org

187. (SS)
Effie I. Raitt Fellowship

1 fellowship of $3,500 to a graduate student majoring in an area of family and consumer sciences. Must be a U.S. citizen or permanent resident. There is a nonrefundable application fee to apply. Visit web site for more information and an application. Deadline: February 1.

188. (SS)
Ellen H. Richards Fellowship

1 fellowship of $3,500 to a graduate student in family and consumer sciences who is pursuing a degree with an emphasis in administration and has worked in an administrative area such as supervision, college or university administration, cooperative extension, or business. Must be a U.S. citizen or permanent resident. There is a nonrefundable application fee to apply. Visit web site for more information and an application. Deadline: February 1.

189. (SS)
Ethel L. Parker International Fellowship

Fellowships of $5,000 to international graduate students in family and consumer sciences. Must be attending an accredited U.S. institution. There is a nonrefundable application fee to apply. Visit web site for more information and an application. Deadline: February 1.

190. (SS)
Flemmie D. Kittrell Fellowship

1 scholarship of $3,500 to a minority graduate student in an area of family and consumer sciences. Must be a U.S. citizen or permanent resident. There is a nonrefundable application fee to apply. Visit web site for more information and an application. Deadline: February 1.

191. (SS)
Freda A. DeKnight Fellowship

1 fellowship of $3,500 to an African-American graduate student pursuing a career in the area of family and consumer sciences communication or cooperative extension. Must be a U.S. citizen or permanent resident. There is a nonrefundable application fee to apply. Visit web site for more information and an application. Deadline: February 1.

192. (SS)
Hazel Putnam Roach Fellowship

1 scholarship of $3,500 to a graduate student pursuing a master's degree in any area of family and consumer sciences. Must be a U.S. citizen or permanent resident. There is a nonrefundable application fee to apply. Visit web site for more information and an application. Deadline: February 1.

193. (SS)
Inez Eleanor Radell Fellowship

1 fellowship of $3,500 to a graduate student in the design, construction, and/or marketing of clothing for aged and/or handicapped adults. Recipient must have earned a bachelor's degree in family and consumer sciences with an undergraduate major in clothing, art, merchandising, business, or a related field. Must be a U.S. citizen or permanent resident. There is a nonrefundable application fee to apply. Visit web site for more information and an application. Deadline: February 1.

194. (SS)
Jeannette H. Crum Fellowship

1 fellowship of $3,500 to a graduate student in family and consumer sciences. Must be a U.S. citizen or permanent resident. There is a nonrefundable application fee to apply. Visit web site for more information and an application. Deadline: February 1.

195. (SS)
Jewell L. Taylor Fellowships

8 fellowships of $5,000 to graduate students in family and consumer sciences. Must be a U.S. citizen or

permanent resident. There is a nonrefundable application fee to apply. Visit web site for more information and an application. Deadline: February 1.

196. (SS)
Margaret E. Terrell Fellowship

Fellowships of $3,500 to a graduate student in the area of institutional management or food service systems administration. Must be a U.S. citizen or permanent resident. There is a nonrefundable application fee to apply. Visit web site for more information and an application. Deadline: February 1.

197. (SS)
Marie Dye Fellowship

1 fellowship of $3,500 to a doctoral candidate studying any area of family and consumer sciences. Must be an active member of AAFCS. Must be a U.S. citizen or permanent resident. There is a nonrefundable application fee to apply. Visit web site for more information and an application. Deadline: February 1.

198. (SS)
Mary Josephine Cochran Fellowships

4 fellowships of $3,500 to full-time graduate students pursuing a degree in textiles and clothing. Must be a U.S. citizen or permanent resident. There is a nonrefundable application fee to apply. Visit web site for more information and an application. Deadline: February 1.

199. (SS)
Mildred B. Davis Fellowship

1 fellowship of $3,500 to a student who plans to major in nutrition upon completing a bachelor's degree. Must be an active student member of AAFCS. Must be a U.S. citizen or permanent resident. There is a nonrefundable application fee to apply. Visit web site for more information and an application. Deadline: February 1.

200. (SS)
Naomi R. and Freeman A. Koehler Fellowship

1 fellowship of $3,500 to a graduate student working toward a degree in nutrition or family and consumer sciences education. Preference is given to a student whose goal is to teach at the college level. Must be a U.S. citizen or permanent resident. There is a nonre-

fundable application fee to apply. Visit web site for more information and an application. Deadline: February 1.

201. (SS)
Project 1000

Fellowships ranging from $1,000 to $3,000 to master's and doctoral minority students in home economics. Preference is given to topics in administration, aging, nutrition, and communications. Selection based on academic achievement, proposed research or study, and personal, professional, and educational goals. Must have at least 1 year of professional home economics experience or traineeship. Must be U.S. citizen or permanent resident. There is an application fee of $15 for AHEA members or $30 for nonmembers. Fee must accompany request for application forms. Deadline: January 15.

202. (SS)
Virginia F. Cutler Fellowship

1 fellowship of $3,500 to a minority graduate student in the area of consumer studies that are related to home economics, such as administration, aging, clothing, textiles, or home economics communication. Must either be a member of a minority group or a non-U.S. citizen (international student). Visit web site for more information and an application. Deadline: February 1.

203. (A, S, SS)
American Association of Housing Educators (AAHE)
Executive Director
Jean A. Memken, Ph.D., CFCS, Editor
5060 FCS Department
Illinois State University
Normal, IL 61790–5060
(309) 438–5802
http://www.exnet.iastate.edu/pages/housing/aahelinks.html

Awards to graduate students of $300 or reasonable travel costs to conference to present a paper at the Annual Conference of the AAHE. Students must write and submit an original paper on research or position about some aspect or current issue in housing. Papers must not be over 15 typed pages, including title page, abstract, references, tables, and figures. Submit papers and applications to: Chairperson, AAHE Awards Committee, 6953 Campbell Drive, Salem, VA 24153. Deadline: mid-June.

(SS)
American Association of Law Libraries
53 W. Jackson, Suite 940S
Chicago, IL 60604
(312) 939–4764
http://www.aallnet.org/database/contact_aall.asp

204. (SS)
AALL & West—George A. Strait
Minority Scholarship Endowment Application

1 scholarship grant of $3,500 to a minority graduate student or undergraduate senior with library experience. Must be a degree candidate in an ALA-accredited library school or an ABA-accredited law school who intends to have a career in law librarianship. Must have at least one quarter/semester remaining after the scholarship is awarded. Deadline: April 1.

205. (SS)
Arizona Association of Law Libraries (AzALL) Grant

http://www.aallnet.org/chapter/azll/dgrants.htm

Grants of varying amounts to graduate student members to 1) attend an AALL Annual Meeting, institute, or workshop registration, 2) cover AALL Annual Meeting, institute, or workshop travel expenses, 3) AALL membership, 4) AzALL-sponsored or other relevant Library Association seminars or meetings, or 5) law library scholarship or internship program. Must be members of AzALL. Deadline: varies.

206. (SS)
Association of Law Libraries of Upstate New York (ALLUNY) Grant
Library Studies Student Grant

1 or more grants of up to $150 to a graduate or undergraduate student in library science/studies to attend the AALUNY Annual Meeting.

207. (SS)
Colorado Association of Law Libraries

2 scholarships of $170 to graduate or undergraduate students enrolled in library school to attend an Annual Meeting of library associations, conferences, workshops, specials, or institutes. Preference is given to member of CoALL of 5 years or less. Selection based on proved or potential ability, promise of future usefulness and permanence in the law library field, financial need, contribution of the applicant to CoALL and/or the profession, and need for representation by a member of CoALL at the institute or meeting.

208. (SS)
Final Year of Law School for Library School Graduate

1 fellowship of $2,000 to a student with a degree in library science who has completed 2 years in an accredited law school. Upon obtaining a law degree, recipients must work 2 years in a law library or the fellowship must be repaid. Send a self-addressed, stamped envelope with request for information. Deadline: April 1.

209. (SS)
Institute for Court Management (ICM) Scholarship

1 scholarship to cover tuition registration for the 6 required courses that comprise Phase I of CEDP to a graduate student or individual wanting to pursue continuing education with ICM. Must be a current member of AALL and a current member of the State, Court, & County Law Libraries Special Interest Section. Visit web site for more information. Deadline: April 1.

210. (SS)
James F. Connolly/LexisNexis Academic and Library Solutions Scholarship

1 scholarship of $3,000 to a library school graduate who is a law school student who intends to pursue a career in law librarianship. Must be attending an ABA-accredited law school. Deadline: April 1.

211. (SS)
Law Librarians Association of Wisconsin
http://www.aallnet.org/chapter/llaw/grants/index.htm

Grants of varying amounts to members to attend a professional development activity. Selection is based on lack of financial assistance from employer, commitment to law librarians as demonstrated by employment record and professional activities, participation in LLAW and potential benefit to the chapter, potential benefit to the applicant for enhancing skills and professional development, and whether the applicant has been awarded a LLAW grant previously. Deadline: none specified.

212. (SS)
Law Librarians of New England
http://aallnet.org/chapter/llne/policies/scholarships.htm

2 or 3 scholarships of $150 and 1 award of $500 to members to further their continuing education. Must be a current member of LLNE. Selection based on lack of financial assistance from employer, individuals new to law librarianship and/or LLNE, demonstrated commitment to LLNE or law librarianship, relevance or expressed interest in particular of the meeting, and long-standing members of LLNE who have been unable to attend meetings due to financial constraints. Deadline: none specified.

213. (SS)
Library Degree for Law School Graduate—Type I Scholarship

Scholarships of varying amounts to a law school graduate working toward a degree in an accredited library school with the intention of having a career as a law librarian. Preference is given to AALL members, but awards are not restricted to members. Preference is also given to persons with meaningful law library experience. Must demonstrate financial need. Deadline: April 1.

214. (SS)
Library School Graduates Attending Law School—Type II Scholarship

Scholarships of varying amounts to a library school graduate working toward a degree in an accredited law school with the intention of having a career as a law librarian. Must have had meaningful law library experience and no more than 36 semester (54 quarter) credit hours remaining before qualifying for the law degree. Preference is given to AALL members, but awards are not restricted to members. Must demonstrate financial need. Deadline: April 1.

215. (SS)
Library Degree for Non-Law School Graduates—Type III Scholarship

Scholarships of varying amounts to a graduate student in an accredited library school who intends on pursuing a career as a law librarian. Preference is given to members of AALL and to applicants working for degrees with emphasis on courses in law librarianship. Must have meaningful law library experience and demonstrate financial need. Deadline: April 1.

216. (SS)
Library School Graduate Seeking a Non-Law Degree—Type IV Scholarship

Scholarships of varying amounts to graduate students in an area other than law, who are library school graduates, whose degree will be beneficial to the development of a professional career in law librarianship and who intend to pursue a career as a law librarian. Must be members of AALL and demonstrate financial need. Deadline: April 1.

217. (SS)
Law Librarians in Continuing Education Courses—Type V Scholarship

Scholarships of varying amounts to law librarians with a degree from an accredited library or law school who are registrants in continuing education courses related to law librarianship. Deadline: April 1.

218. (SS)
Minority Leadership Development Award

1 scholarship covering travel, lodging, and registration expenses to attend the Annual Meeting of AALL to a member of AALL to ensure that AALL's leadership remains vital, relevant, and representative of the Association's diverse membership. Recipient must be a member of a minority group, have earned a master's degree in library or information science, have no more than 5 years of professional library or information service work experience, have either been a member of AALL for at least 2 years or have 2 years of law library work experience, and demonstrate leadership potential. Recipient is paired with an experienced AALL leader who serves as a mentor for at least one year, and serves on an AALL committee during the year following the award. Deadline: April 1.

219. (SS)
State Chapters

Various state chapters offer scholarships and grants for their members to further their professional development by attending annual meetings, workshops, and seminars. Visit web site for listing of chapters and contact links. Deadline: varies by chapter.

220. (S)

American Association of Medical Colleges
Minority Medical Education Program
2450 N Street, N.W.
Washington, DC 20037
ATTN: MMEP
(877) 312–MMEP
http://www.aamc.org/students/minorities/mmep
mmep@aamc.org

A 6-week summer program providing full tuition, housing, and meals to upper-level minority undergraduate students who are planning to apply to medical school. Program is conducted at eleven medical school sites around the country. Some of the locations provide a stipend and travel allowance, but not all. Program offers an intensive and personalized medical school preparation. Students must have at least a 3.0 GPA, with at least a 2.75 in the sciences. Each site makes its own student selection. Visit web site for more information. Some sites stop accepting applications when they reach capacity. Deadline: March 1.

(S)

American Association of Occupational Health
Nurses
2920 Brandywine Road, Suite 100
Atlanta, GA 30341
(770) 455–7757
http://www.aaohn.org

221. (S)

Charles J. Turcotte Academic Scholarship
Award

Awards of up to $2,000 to graduate or doctoral students with emphasis on occupational health. For more information on application guidelines, write to above address. Deadline: none specified.

222. (S)
Mary Louis Brown Award

Awards of up to $3,000 to graduate or doctoral students to conduct research that will benefit occupational health nurse knowledge. For more information on application guidelines, write to above address. Deadline: none specified.

223. (S)
Otis Clap Award

Awards of up to $2,000 to graduate or doctoral students to conduct research on issues relating to occupational health. For more information on application guidelines, write to above address. Deadline: none specified.

224. (A, H, S, SS)
American Association of Overseas Studies
158 West 81st Street, #112
New York, NY 10024
(800) EDU–BRIT
(212) 724–0804
http://www.worldwide.edu/uk/aaos/aboutaaos.html

100 internships lasting at least 4 weeks during the summer, fall, or spring providing a stipend of $1,000 plus room and board ranging from $600 to $1,000 per month to graduates, undergraduates, recent college graduates, high school graduates, and high school students. Internships are tailored to the requirements of the intern and may be arranged in the following areas: architecture, art, banking, business, community service, computer science, economics, engineering, fashion, film, geology, government, journalism, languages, law, marketing, museum, music, physical and life sciences, politics, public relations, publishing, sports, stock market trading, theater, and women's studies. Internship sites include: New York, NY, London, England, and Israel. Deadline: rolling.

225. (S)
American Association of People with Disabilities
Microsoft-AAPD Federal Internship Program
1629 K Street, N.W. Suite 503
Washington, DC 20006
(202) 457–0046
(800) 840–8844
http://www.aapd-dc.org

10 paid internships to disabled graduate and undergraduate students interested in information technology (IT). Designed to enable students to gain real-world work experience and further enhance employment opportunities, increase skills and interest in IT careers, increase placement in IT careers, and introduce students to national disability leaders through a series of seminars and special events such as the anniversary observance of passage of the Americans with Disabilities Act. The internship takes place in Washington, DC. Visit web site for information and application. Deadline: March 17.

226. (S)
American Association of Petroleum Geologists Grants-In-Aid
AAPG Headquarters
P.O. Box 979
Tulsa, OK 74101–0979
(918) 560–2664
http://www.aapg.org

75 grants ranging from $500 to $2,000 to graduate students working on research projects related to the search for hydrocarbons and economic sedimentary minerals or to environmental geology. Projects can be in the areas of sedimentology, stratigraphy, paleontology, mineralogy, structural geology, geochemistry, or geophysics. Request applications after October 1. Deadline: January 15.

227. (SS)
American Association of School Administrators Scholarship
1801 North Moore Street
Arlington VA 22209–9988
(703) 528–0700
http://www.aasa.org

5 awards of $5,000 to graduate students majoring in education or educational administration. Applicant should inquire with the dean of education at his/her college. Applicant must be nominated for the award. Deadline: June 1.

(S)
American Association of Stratographic Palynologists
Dr. Thomas Demchuk
ConocoPhillips
Staff Biostratigraphic Specialist

Stratigraphic Prediction and Analysis
P.O. Box 2197
Houston, TX 77252–2197
(281) 293–3189
http://www.palynology.org/default.html

228. (S)
AASP Student Scholarships
2 scholarships of $1,000 to graduate and advanced undergraduate students majoring in the branch of science dealing with pollen and spores. Selection based on originality and imagination evident in the proposed project and the likelihood of significant contributions to the science of palynology. Visit web site for more information. Deadline: March 31.

229. (S)
Cranwall Award
1 award ranging from $1,000 to $1,500 to a graduate student, based on originality and imagination evident in the proposed project. Open to students in all countries. Need not be members of GSA. Deadline: March 31.

230. (H)
American Association of Teachers of Italian College Essay in Italian
c/o Indiana University
Language Department
Bloomington, IN 47401
(812) 337–2508
http://www.italianstudies.org/aati

Awards of $100 and $250 to graduate and undergraduate students based on an essay. Essay topic must relate to literature or literary figures. Applicants must be U.S. citizens and attending an accredited institution in the U.S. Deadline: June 30.

(S)
American Association of Textile Chemists and Colorists
P.O. Box 12215
Research Triangle Park, NC 27709–2215
(919) 549–3549
http://www.aatcc.org

231. (S)

Delaware Valley Section Scholarships

2 scholarships of $500 to graduate and undergraduate students who are pursuing careers in a textile- or technology-related field. Must be members of the Delaware Valley Section of the AATCC or their dependent sons and daughters. Must have at least a 3.0 GPA on a 4.0 scale. Visit web site for specific information and an application. Deadline: July 30.

232. (S)

Herman and Myrtle Goldstein Student Paper Competition

Awards of $500 and $1,000 to the 2 top papers of graduate students to encourage independent or group student research. A project and appropriate results may be submitted by any student (or group of students) who is a member of AATCC. Visit web site for specific submission guidelines. Deadline: May 30.

233. (S)

Metropolitan Section Scholarships

2 scholarships of $500 to graduate and undergraduate students who are pursuing careers in a textile-related field. Selection will be based on academic achievement, extracurricular activities, and goals. Must attend the Fashion Institute of Technology in New York. Visit web site for specific submission guidelines and contact person. Deadline: none specified.

234. (S)

Northern Piedmont Section Scholarships

2 scholarships of $1,200 to graduate and undergraduate students who are pursuing careers in a textile-related field. Selection will be based on academic achievement, extracurricular activities, commitment to textile industry, and goals. Must be an active member of the AATCC Student Chapter on their campus. Must attend University of North Carolina at Greensboro, North Carolina State University, or Radford University. Visit web site for specific submission guidelines and contact person. Deadline: none specified.

235. (S)

Rhode Island Section Scholarships

http://ww.aatcc.org/membership/students/scholarships.htm

Scholarships of varying amounts to graduate and undergraduate students who are pursuing careers as textile chemists. Selection will be based on academic achievement, extracurricular activities, and goals. Must attend the University of Rhode Island or the University of Massachusetts at Dartmouth. Visit web site for specific submission guidelines and contact person. Deadline: none specified.

236. (S)

Southeastern Section Scholarships

3 scholarships of $1,500 to graduate and undergraduate students who are pursuing careers as textile chemists. Selection will be based on academic achievement, extracurricular activities, and goals. Must attend Auburn University, Georgia Institute of Technology, or the University of Georgia. Visit web site for specific submission guidelines and contact person. Deadline: none specified.

237. (S)

Student Research Support

Awards ranging from $250 to $2,000 to graduate and undergraduate students with research on textile-related projects. Selection will be based on originality of the proposed research, importance and practical value to textile science, relevancy to current activities, issues, and/or needs of textile processing, scientific contributions, experimental design, and other specific matters. Visit web site for more information, possible topic suggestions, and an application. Deadline: September 15.

(A, H, S, SS)

American Association of University Women
1111 Sixteenth Street, N.W.
Washington, DC 20036
(800) 821–4364
(202) 728–7602
http://www.aauw.org

238. (A, H, S, SS)

Career Development Grants

Varying numbers of grants ranging from $1,000 to $5,000 to women who are in the early stages of master's or doctoral studies in order to reenter the workforce, change careers, or advance their current careers. Funds may be used for tuition, fees, books, supplies, local transportation, or dependent care. Women must be U.S. citizens or permanent residents, have earned a bachelor's degree, and have received their last degree before July 30 5 years prior to the year in which fellowships will be in effect. Applicants must also enroll in courses that are prerequisites for professional employment plans. Doctoral candidates may seek funding for course work only and not for researching or writing their dissertations. Applicants who are eligible for another AAUW fellowship or grant are not eligible for Career Development Grants. Special consideration is given to qualified AAUW members, women of color, women pursuing their first terminal degree, or those pursuing degrees in nontraditional fields. Grant year runs from July 1 through June 30. Request applications between August 1 and December 20. Deadline: January 3 (postmark).

239. (S, SS)
Community Action Grants

Grants ranging from $500 to $5,000 to women or AAUW branches and states for programs or nondegree research projects to promote education and equity for women and girls. Applicants must be women who are U.S. citizens or permanent residents and hold a bachelor's degree. Applicants may apply up to 2 times for the same proposed grant project. Funds may cover project-related costs such as office and mailing expenses, promotional materials, honoraria, and transportation. Visit web site for detailed information. Request applications from August 1 of one year through August 15 of the following year. Deadline: early September (fall), early February (spring).

240. (A, H, S, SS)
Dissertation Fellowships

Fellowships of $14,500 to doctoral students in all fields of study (except engineering) who will complete the writing of their dissertation during the fellowship year. Applicants are expected to receive a doctoral degree by the end of the fellowship year. Applicants must have completed all their course work, passed all preliminary exams, and had their dissertation research proposal approved by November 15 of the application year. Students who received a fellowship for the writing of a dissertation in the year prior

to the AAUW fellowship year are not eligible to apply. Must be U.S. citizens or legal residents. Fellowships may not be used to fund extensive research. Scholars may apply up to 2 times for a dissertation fellowship on the same topic. Fellowship year runs from July 1 through June 30 of the following year. Request applications between August 1 and November 1. Deadline: November 15 (postmark).

241. (S)
Eleanor Roosevelt Teacher Fellowships

Varying numbers of fellowships ranging from $1,000 to $10,000 to females who work as full-time teachers at U.S. public schools in grades K through 12 to implement programs that will increase girls' participation in mathematics and sciences. Recipients must have had at least 3 years of consecutive full-time teaching prior to award and must intend to return to the classroom for 5 years after the fellowship. Must be U.S. citizens or legal residents. Fellowship year runs from July 1 through August 30 of the following year. Request applications from August 1 through December 18. Deadline: early January (postmark).

242. (S)
Engineering Dissertation Fellowships

Fellowships of $14,500 to female doctoral candidates in engineering. Must complete all required course work and have passed all preliminary exams by November 15 of the application year. Fellows must devote full time to writing their dissertations and receive their degrees at the end of the fellowship year. Students holding any fellowship for the writing of a dissertation in the year prior to the AAUW fellowship year are not eligible. These fellowships cannot cover tuition for additional course work. Must be U.S. citizens or legal residents. Fellowship year runs from July 1 through June 30. Request applications between August 1 and November 1. Deadline: mid-November.

243. (S, SS)
Focus Professions Group Fellowships

Fellowships ranging from $5,000 to $9,500 to female master's and doctoral students for completion of graduate and professional degrees. Applicants should be women from historically underrepresented ethnic minorities in business administration (MBA,

2-year and executive programs only), law (J.D.), and medicine (M.D. or D.O.). Applicants must enter their final year of study during the fellowship year. Special consideration is given to applicants who show professional promise in innovative or neglected areas of research and/or practice in public interest concerns. Must be U.S. citizens or legal residents. Fellowship year runs from September 1 through June 30. Request applications from August 1 through December 2 for law and medicine, and from August 1 through January 21 for business. Deadline: mid-December (law and medicine) and early February (business).

244. (A, H, S, SS)
Founders Distinguished Senior Scholar Award

An honorarium award of $1,000 is presented to a scholar in any field who is at the pinnacle of her career. Scholar may self-nominate or be nominated by a colleague or an AAUW member. Must be U.S. citizens or legal residents. Request applications between August 1 and November 1. Deadline: November 15 (postmark).

245. (A, H, S, SS)
International Fellowships

43 fellowships of up to $15,160 to full-time graduate or postgraduate students for study or research in the U.S. Applicants must not be U.S. citizens or permanent residents. Must have earned the equivalent of a U.S. bachelor's degree before December 1 of the application year and show outstanding academic ability. Selection is based on professional potential and the importance of their studies to women and girls in their country of origin. Preference given to women who have demonstrated prior commitment to the advancement of women and girls through civic, community, or professional work. Fellowship year runs from July 1 through June 30 of the following year. Request applications from August 1 through November 15. Deadline: early December (postmark).

246. (H, S, SS)
One-Year Research/Postdoctoral Fellowships

10 fellowships ranging from $20,000 to $25,000 to females who earned a doctorate by a specified date (inquire with AAUW for that date). 3 fellowships each in the arts and humanities, social sciences, and natural sciences, and 1 specifically for a woman from an underrepresented minority group. Must be U.S. citizens or legal residents. Fellowship year runs from July 1 through June 30 of the following year. Request applications between August 1 and November 1. Deadline: November 15 (postmark).

247. (S)
Science and Technology Fellowships

Fellowships ranging from $5,000 to $9,500 to females who will enter their final year of master's degree (including 1-year) programs in architecture, computer/information science, and mathematics/statistics. Special consideration is given to applicants who show professional promise in innovative or neglected areas of research and/or practice in public interest concerns. Must be U.S. citizens or legal residents. Fellowship year runs from September 1 through June 30. Request applications from August 1 through December 2. Deadline: mid-December.

248. (A, S)
Selected Professions Fellowships

Fellowships ranging from $5,000 to $9,500 to females who will enter their final year of master's degree (including 1-year) programs in architecture, computer/information science, and mathematics/statistics. Special consideration is given to applicants who show professional promise in innovative or neglected areas of research and/or practice in public interest concerns. Fellowship year runs from September 1 through June 30. Request applications from August 1 through December 2. Deadline: mid-December.

249. (A, H, S, SS)
Summer Fellowships

6 summer fellowships providing a stipend of $5,000 to women faculty at colleges and universities whose teaching loads limit active research. Fellowships allow recipients to conduct 8 weeks of summer research. Scholars with strong publishing records should seek other funding or apply for the 1-year research leave or postdoctoral fellowships. Must be U.S. citizens or legal residents. Fellowship year runs from July 1 through June 30 of the following year. Request applications between August 1 and November 1. Deadline: November 15 (postmark).

(A, H, S, SS)

American Association of University Women, Delaware Branch

1800 Fairfax Boulevard

Wilmington, DE 19803–3199

(302) 428–0939

http://www.udel.edu/educ/aauw

250. (A, H, S, SS)

Scholarships

Scholarships ranging from $800 to $2,500 to graduate female students who are residents of Delaware and attending an accredited institution. Based on academic record, test scores, extracurricular and community activities, and financial need. Deadline: February.

251. (A, H, S, SS)

Upperclassmen Scholarships

2 scholarship grants of $1,000 to female graduate or upper-level undergraduate students who are residents of Delaware and attending an accredited institution in Delaware. Based on academic record, extracurricular and community activities, and financial need. Deadline: January.

252. (S)

American Association of Women Dentists (AAWD) Colgate-Palmolive Awards

645 North Michigan, Suite 800

Chicago, IL 60611

(312) 644–6610

(800) 920–2293

http://www.womendentists.org

5 to 10 awards ranging from $500 to $1,000 to female dental students in their third or fourth year. Must be a member of the AAWD. Selection based on academic achievement and contribution to dental school. Must be enrolled at an accredited 4-year institution. Deadline: February 1.

253. (H)

American Baptist Churches of Wisconsin

15330 Watertown Plank Road

Elm Grove, WI 53122–2391

(262) 782–3140

http://www.abcofwi.org/TheWisconsinBaptist/2000-02/04.htm

Awards of $2,000 to graduate students pursuing a master's of divinity or equivalent degree. Must be used for full-time study in an accredited seminary. Visit web site for more information. Deadline: January 1.

(A, H)

American Baptist Financial Aid Program

Educational Ministries ABC/USA

P. O. Box 851

Valley Forge, PA 19482–0851

(800) ABC–3USA

http://www.abc-em.org

254. (A, H)

Asian American Summer Intern Grants

Grants of $500 to graduate Asian-American students to gain ministerial experience, including minister of music, in a church during the summer. Must be American Baptist. The employing church is expected to contribute matching funds. Church pastors may nominate a seminarian. The church provides supervision during the internship. Letters of nomination must be received by May 31.

255. (A, H)

Continuing Education Grants

Varying numbers of grants of $250 to enable students to attend an educational event not covered by "Cultivating NEW LIFE." Applicants must be listed in the current ABC Professional Registry. Applications must be submitted before attending the event/program. (D.Min. students are eligible for these awards in each of their first two years of study.) Available every two years.

256. (A, H)

Continuing Education Grants for Seminarians

One-time grants of $100 to graduate seminarian students to attend a nondegree educational program. Must be American Baptist members, attending an American Baptist–related seminary, and interested in pursuing a church-related career, such as ministers of music. Applications must be submitted before attending the event or program.

257. (A, H)
Cultivating NEW LIFE

Grants of $300 to ministerial leaders, including ministers of music, to attend conferences, workshops, and seminars focused on personal and congregational renewal. Ministerial leaders who are listed in the current ABC Professional Registry may apply and are encouraged to attend a minimum of 3 events related to NEW LIFE 2010 goals during this decade. Cultivating NEW LIFE grants may not be combined with other continuing education funding provided by Educational Ministries. Applications must be submitted before attending the event/program.

258. (H)
The Daniel E. Weiss Fund for Excellence

Scholarships of varying amounts to graduate students who might not otherwise undertake theological study, to provide them with substantial financial assistance for the first year of seminary. Selection is based on academic success and membership as an American Baptist. Scholarships are awarded to nominated candidates who can bring qualities of theological thinking and leadership that will strengthen American Baptist congregations and their witness in the world. Please call for a nomination form. Deadline: November 1.

259. (A, H)
Doctoral Study Grants

1-time grants of $3,000 to doctoral students who have completed at least 1 year of studies. Students must plan to teach in a college or seminary, in a field of study directly related to preparing American Baptist ministerial leaders, such as ministers of music. Must demonstrate academic achievement in the first year(s) of doctoral studies. D.Min. students are not eligible. Deadline: May 31.

260. (A, H)
Ellen Cushing Scholarships

Scholarships of varying amounts to female graduate students preparing for a church-related vocation (such as minister of music) or a human service may apply. Preference is given to students active in their school, church, or region. Seminarian Support Program recipients are not usually considered for this scholarship. Must be American Baptist members, attending an American Baptist–related seminary, and interested in pursuing a church-related career, such as ministers of music. Deadline: May 31.

261. (A, H)
Hispanic Scholarship Funds

Grants of $500 to Hispanic students who are undergraduates or pursuing their first professional degree. Must be American Baptist members, attending an American Baptist–related seminary, and be interested in pursuing a career as ministers of music. Must demonstrate financial need. These grants may not be combined with other Educational Ministries aid but are renewable. Deadline: May 31.

262. (A, H)
Individual Seminarian Grants

Scholarships of up to $750 to graduate students who are not American Baptist members and are interested in pursuing a church-related career, such as ministers of music. Seminarians must be enrolled at least two-thirds time in one of the following first professional degree programs: M.Div., M.C.E., M.A.C.E., M.R.E. (D.Min. students are not eligible). Recipients must be resident students of the American Baptist–related seminary that will award the degree. May reapply for up to 3 years of assistance. Deadline: May 31.

263. (A, H)
Sabbatical Grants

Sabbatical/study leave grants of varying amounts to ministerial leaders, including ministers of music. Applications must be received by November 1.

264. (A, H)
Seminarian Support Program (SSP)

Scholarships of up to $1,000 to graduate students who are American Baptist members and attending American Baptist–related seminaries and interested in pursuing a church-related career, such as ministers of music. Seminarians must be enrolled at least two-thirds time in one of the following first professional degree programs: M.Div., M.C.E., M.A.C.E., M.R.E. (D.Min. students are not eligible). Recipients must be resident students of the American Baptist–related seminary that will award the degree. Deadline: May 31.

265. (H)
Upper-Level Undergraduate Scholarship

Scholarships of $1,000 to $2,000 to full-time, upper-level undergraduate students attending an American Baptist–related college or university who plan to continue their education. Preference will be given to persons preparing for careers in church leadership or human services. Must maintain satisfactory academic standing to be considered for the award. Applicants must also be a member of an American Baptist church for at least 1 year before applying for aid, enroll at an accredited educational institution in the U.S. or Puerto Rico and be a U.S. citizen. Deadline: May 31.

(H, SS)
American Bar Association
750 N Lake Shore Drive
Chicago, IL 60611
(312) 988–5000
http://www.abanet.org/

266. (SS)
ABA Journal of Affordable Housing and Community Development Law Writing Competition

1 award of $1,000, plus airfare and lodging, to attend the Forum's Annual Conference and publication in the Forum's journal. Open to all students currently enrolled in an accredited law school. Papers should address any legal issue regarding affordable housing and/or community development law. Visit web site for specific guidelines. Deadline: March 15.

267. (SS)
Antitrust Law Section

1 award of $1,000 plus travel, lodging, and registration to the Spring Meeting. Open to currently enrolled law students. Each law review or legal journal sponsored by an ABA-accredited law school is invited to nominate an article addressing antitrust law or competition policy issues. Students need not be members of the Section of Antitrust Law to participate. Visit web site for specific guidelines. Deadline: March 15.

268. (SS)
Entertainment Law Initiative National Writing Contest

1 award of $5,000 and an all-expense-paid trip to the Grammy Awards for an outstanding essay written on a compelling legal issue facing the music industry. Open to all law students enrolled in an ABA-accredited law school. Students are challenged to research an issue and propose a resolution. Visit web site for specific guidelines. Deadline: December 15.

269. (SS)
Environmental Justice Essay Competition

1 prize of $1,000 and 2 awards of $500, for an essay on the environment and the law. Open to law students enrolled in ABA-accredited law schools. The first-prize essay is published in the *Boston College Environmental Affairs Law Review,* the second- and third-prize essays are published on-line through the ABA. Visit web site for specific guidelines. Deadline: February 1 (filing intent to enter) and March 15 (postmark).

270. (SS)
Health Law Writing Competition

1 award of $500 and airfare, hotel for 2 nights, and $50 per diem for 2 days to attend the Emerging Issues conference. Open to any law student enrolled in an ABA-accredited law school. Papers should be on a topic that will be addressed at the Section's Emerging Issues Conference. Topics vary every year. Committee wishes to promote the study of health law and to provide an incentive to law students to learn about the Section and to consider membership in the Section. Deadline: November 30.

271. (SS)
Higginbotham Student Award for Excellence in an Essay

1 travel subsidy award of $300 to travel to the ABA Annual Meeting. Open to members of the Law Student Division of the ABA. The essay must deal with any aspect of an unmet legal need of children. Essays will be judged on clarity of theme or thesis, significance of the selected topic, manner in which topic is presented, organization, analysis quality, quality of research and authority, and grammar, syntax, and form. Visit web site for specific guidelines. Deadline: May 15.

272. (SS)
Howard C. Schwab Essay Contest

1 award each of $500, $1,000, and $1,500 and possible publication for an essay focusing on any aspect of family law. Open to all second- and third-year full-time law students (and second- through fourth-year part-time students) and first-year students in school with family law in the first-year curriculum. Essay subject may be any aspect of family law and focus should be an issue of law, although some interdisciplinary material may be useful in addressing a legal issue. Visit web site for specific guidelines. Deadline: April 15.

273. (SS)
Jacques T. Schlenges Student Writing Contest

1 award of $2,000, 1-year free Section membership, and round trip and accommodations to attend the Sections Fall Meeting and possible publication in the Section's magazine. Second- and third-place winners receive $500 and $250, respectively. Open to any law student enrolled in an ABA-accredited law school within the U.S. and its possessions. Essay must be on a current topic dealing with real property, probate, or trust law. Visit web site for specific guidelines. Deadline: June 15.

274. (SS)
James B. Boskey Law Student Essay Contest on Dispute Resolution

2 awards of $1,000 for an essay about any aspect of dispute resolution. 1 award is to a law student and the other to a non-law graduate student. Open to all second- and third-year full-time law students (and second- through fourth-year part-time students) as well as master's and doctoral candidates enrolled in graduate schools at accredited colleges and universities and master's and doctoral candidates enrolled in graduate schools and universities located outside of the U.S. and recognized as schools of graduate study in their respective countries. Visit web site for specific guidelines. Deadline: May 30.

275. (SS)
Law and Aging Student Essay Competition

Cash awards of $1,000, $3,000, and $5,000, plus up to 10 honorable mentions of up to $100. Given to current law students in an ABA-accredited law school and to those who graduated within the last year. Essays should address any public policy or practice issue in serving socially, economically, or physically vulnerable older persons. Judging criteria will be based on level of scholarliness, insight, and helpfulness to understanding and addressing important policy and practice issues. Visit web site for specific guidelines. Deadline: April 1.

276. (SS)
Legal Assistance to Military Personnel

1 award of $1,000 to an essay that challenges conventional wisdom by proposing modifications to current directives, policies, customs, or practices relating to military legal assistance and preventative law. Open to law students, paralegals, and military and civilian lawyers. Entries should identify the greatest challenge facing legal assistance and develop a resolution to the problem. Visit web site for specific guidelines. Deadline: July 1.

277. (SS)
Legal Opportunity Scholarship

20 awards of $5,000 to entering law students. Award is renewable for 2 years. Selection is based on academic achievement. Deadline: March 28.

278. (SS)
Mendes Hershman Student Writing Contest

1 award each of $500, $1,000, and $2,500, with the top award–winner also receiving all expenses to attend the Annual Meeting to collect the prize. Each ABA-accredited school must nominate a paper considering aspects of business law written during the current academic year by a student enrolled in the law school. The paper may be written specifically for the competition, for a class, seminar, or independent study, or a proposed law review/journal note, comment, or article. Papers will be judged on research and analysis, choice of topic, writing style, originality, and contribution to the literature available on the subject. Visit web site for specific guidelines. Deadline: February 3.

279. (H, SS)
Program in Legal History

5 to 10 awards of up to $6,000 to graduate or post-graduate students. Awards are research grants for

younger scholars conducting research in legal history. Write an introductory letter detailing proposed research and your credentials. Deadline: none specified.

280. (SS)
Ross Student Writing Contest

1 award of $7,500, plus travel and lodging to the Annual Meeting. Article must appear in a law review sponsored by an ABA-accredited school. Open to enrolled students or recent graduates who were in good standing at ABA-accredited law schools when articles were published. Selection will be based on legal thought, including advancing new legal concepts and influencing the law, writing style and readability, and usefulness to practice of law by ABA members. Visit web site for specific guidelines. Deadline: March 15.

281. (SS)
Theodore Tannenwald Jr. Foundation for Excellence in Tax Scholarship

1 award each of $1,000, $2,000, and $3,000 to full- or part-time law school students (J.D., LL.M., or S.J.D.) for an essay on any tax-related topic involving any type of tax or the law of any taxing jurisdiction. Papers based on research or other work done in connection with law firm or other employment are eligible for the competition, as are papers evolving from moot court or legal clinic involvement. Visit web site for specific guidelines. Deadline: June 30.

282. (SS)
Tort Trial and Insurance Practice Section (TIPS)

1 award of $1,500 plus travel and lodging to TIPS fall meeting, and possible publication in Section's magazine, and 1 second-place award of $500. Open to all students enrolled in an accredited law school. Papers should address an essay on a current topic in a legal area covered by one of the Section's substantive committees. Visit web site for specific guidelines and suggested essay topics. Deadline: March 1.

283. (SS)
William W. Greenhalgh Student Writing Contest

1 award of $2,000 plus all-expense-paid trip to the Annual Meeting to attend the Criminal Justice Section's Annual Meeting Luncheon. Open to all students in good standing who attend an ABA-accredited law school within the U.S. and who are members of the ABA. All entrants receive a 1-year complimentary membership in the section. Purpose is to judge the ability to apply scholastic knowledge to practical issues facing criminal justice system and to suggest solutions. Visit web site for specific guidelines. Deadline: March 1.

(A)
American Berlin Opera Foundation, Inc.
Scholarship Competition
6 East 87th Street
New York, NY 10128
(212) 534–5383
http://www.operafoundation.org/applic.htm

284. (A)
Awards for Piano

Awards range from $1,000 to $3,500 in cash, tuition payment, or a combination and may be used anywhere. Pianists must be between 20 and 30 years of age with proven training and experience. Must be U.S. citizen or permanent resident. Deadline: February 1.

285. (A)
Awards for Voice

At least $25,000 in prizes in cash, tuition payment, or a combination. Tuition payment may be used anywhere. Singers must be between 20 and 35 years of age with proven vocal training and experience. Must be U.S. citizen or permanent resident. Deadline: February 1.

286. (SS)
American Business Women's Association
P.O. Box 8728
9100 Ward Parkway
Kansas City, MO 64114–0728
(800) 228–0007
http://www.abwahq.org

Financial assistance of varying amounts to graduate and undergraduate female students to continue their education. Interested students must contact and apply through local chapter. DO NOT contact national association. The national association will not provide information on local chapters. Need not be members of the national association. Deadline: varies by chapter.

(S)
American Cancer Society (ACS), Inc.
1599 Clifton Road, N.E.
Atlanta, GA 30329
(404) 320–3333
(800) ACS–2345
http://www.cancer.org

287. (S)
Clinical Oncology Social Work Training Grants

Training grants of varying amounts to graduate students pursuing careers in social work to conduct research in clinical oncology. Must be a U.S. citizen or permanent resident. Deadline: varies.

288. (S)
Doctoral Degree Scholarships in Cancer Nursing

Scholarships of $8,000 to master's and doctoral degree students who are pursuing careers as educators, clinical experts, administrators, and/or researchers in cancer nursing. Applicants must be enrolled in, or applying to, doctoral degree programs in nursing science or a science relevant to nursing. Applicants must project a course of study that integrates oncology nursing and provide evidence for faculty support. Applicants must provide evidence of their commitment to cancer nursing through experience, education, and/or research in the specialty area. Students must be in an NLN-accredited master's or doctoral program that offers specific educational experience in oncology nursing. Applicants must have a current RN license and be a U.S. citizen or legal permanent resident. Preference is given to full-time students. Renewable for up to 4 years with satisfactory progress. Request applications after September 1. Deadline: February 15.

289. (S)
Faculty Research Awards

Numerous awards for postdoctoral fellows for proposed cancer research and teaching activities. Amount of award is based on applicant's experience and accomplishments and salary schedule of the institution. Travel funds may be provided when moving to a different institution. Must be U.S. citizen or permanent resident and be recommended by head of department and dean of college. Institution must be within the U.S. or its territories. Contact institution concerning joint application. Deadline: March 1 and October 1.

290. (S)
Master's Degree Scholarships in Cancer Nursing

Scholarships of $8,000 to master's degree students who are pursuing careers as researchers in cancer nursing. Applicants must be enrolled in, or applying to, a master's degree program in nursing science or a science relevant to nursing. Applicants must project a program of study that integrates oncology nursing and provide evidence for faculty support. Applicants must provide evidence of their commitment to cancer nursing through experience, education, and/or research in the specialty area. Students must be in an NLN-accredited master's program that offers specific educational experience in oncology nursing. Applicants must have a current RN license and be a U.S. citizen or legal permanent resident. Preference is given to full-time students. Renewable for up to 4 years with satisfactory progress. Request applications after September 1. Deadline: February 15.

291. (S)
Physician's Research Training Fellowship

Awards providing stipends of $22,000 the first year, $24,000 the second year, and $26,000 the third year to individuals with a doctoral degree or those who will have attained a doctoral degree prior to activation of the grant. Applicants must be endorsed by a mentor and head of department where training will be received. Must be a U.S. citizen or permanent resident. Training can be in either basic or clinical research. Research must be on a full-time basis; applicant cannot have significant clinical responsibilities during the grant period. Contact above address for information and application. Deadline: March 1 and October 1.

292. (S)
Postdoctoral Fellowships

Grants providing $22,000 in first year, $24,000 in second year, and $26,000 in third year for postdoctoral fellows to conduct cancer research. A $2,000 institutional allowance may be included. Must be U.S. citizen or permanent resident. Must be recommended by mentor and head of department in which training will be received. May be used in any country. Must submit annual progress report. Contact above address for more information. Deadline: March 1 and October 1.

(H)
American Catholic Historical Association
Mullen Library, Room 318
The Catholic University of America
Washington, DC 20064
(202) 635–5079
http://www.research.cua.edu/acha

293. (H)
Howard R. Marraro Prize

1 prize of $750 to the most distinguished work dealing with Italian history or Italo-American history or relations published in a preceding 12-month period. Any author who is a citizen or permanent resident of the United States or Canada is eligible. Deadline: May 15.

294. (H)
John Gilmary Shea Prize

1 prize of $300 for best book published within last year, judged to have made the most significant contribution to the history of the Catholic Church. Authors must be U.S. or Canadian citizens or permanent residents. Publishers or authors must send 3 copies of the work to the judges. Deadline: October 1.

295. (H)
John Tracy Ellis Dissertation Award

An award of $1,200 to a graduate student working on some aspect of the history of the Catholic Church. Those wishing to enter the competition for the award must be citizens or authorized residents (i.e., permanent residents or on student visas) of the United States or Canada and must be enrolled in a doctoral program at a reception at a recognized institution of higher education. Deadline: September 30.

296. (H)
Peter Guilday Prize

1 prize of $100 for the best article of 30 pages or less on the history of the Catholic Church. Authors must not have had previous work published. Parts of doc-

toral dissertations are accepted. Applicants must be U.S. or Canadian citizens or legal residents. Judges are the editors of the *Catholic History Review*. Deadline: October 1.

297. (S)
American Chemical Society
Women Chemists Committee
1155 16th Street, N.W.
Washington, DC 20036
(800) 227–5588 ext. 6123
http://membership.acs.org/W/WCC/travflyer2001.htm
help@acs.org

Limited number of travel grants to pay for registration, travel, and accommodations to female postdoctoral and graduate students to assist them in presenting research results at scientific meetings. Must be U.S. citizens or permanent residents. Visit web site for specific application guidelines. Travel is restricted to meetings within the U.S. Deadline: September 15.

(S, SS)
American College of Healthcare Executives
ATTN: Scholarship Coordinator
1 North Franklin Street, Suite 1700
Chicago, IL 60606
(312) 424–2800
http://ww.ache.org

298. (S, SS)
Albert Dent Scholarship

3 awards of $3,000 to minority or handicapped graduate students and 1 award of $3,000 to a full-time graduate student in health care management. Must be enrolled in or accepted to a health administration program accredited by the Accrediting Commission on Education for Health Services Administration. Must be an associate member in good standing. Must be a U.S. or Canadian citizen. Must have financial need. For more information, visit web site or send a self-addressed, stamped envelope after January 1. Deadline: March 31.

299. (S, SS)
Foster G. McGaw Scholarship

1 award of $3,000 to a full-time graduate student in health care management. Must be an associate mem-

ber in good standing. Must be a U.S. or Canadian citizen. Must have financial need. For more information, visit web site or send a self-addressed, stamped envelope after January 1. Deadline: March 31.

300. (S, SS)
American College of Legal Medicine
Student Writing Competition
Executive Director
611 East Wells Street
Milwaukee, WI 53202
(414) 276–1881
http://www.aclm.org

3 awards of $1,000 to students enrolled in schools of law, medicine, dentistry, podiatry, nursing, pharmacy, health science, or health care administration. Must be attending an accredited school in the U.S. or Canada. Based on best paper on any aspect of legal medicine. Deadline: February 1.

301. (S, SS)
American College of Medical Practice Executives
ACMPE Scholarships
Administrative Director
104 Inverness Terrace East
Englewood, CO 80112–5306
(888) 608–5601
(303) 799–1111
http://www.mgma.com/acmpe/scholars.html

Scholarships ranging from $500 to $2,000 to full-time graduate or undergraduate students majoring in ambulatory care or medical group management. Must be pursuing a clinically related degree in the health care field or a business administrative or health care administrative degree in the health care field. Must be attending an accredited institution. Based on academic record, recommendations, and career goals. Write a letter briefly detailing your educational and financial situation. Students who are pre-med, physical therapy, nursing, or other clinically related degrees or attending medical school are ineligible. Some scholarships are restricted to specific states, majors, or schools. Deadline: June 1.

302. (S)
American College of Nurse-Midwives Foundation
Scholarship Program
818 Connecticut Avenue, N.W., Suite 900
Washington, DC 20006
(202) 728–9860
http://www.acnm.org

5 to 10 awards of up to $1,500 to students enrolled in ACNM-accredited certificate or graduate nurse-midwifery programs. Must be a student member of ACNM and have completed 1 clinical module or semester. Obtain applications from director of nurse-midwifery program at accredited school. Deadline: February 15.

(S)
American College of Physicians—American Society
of Internal Medicine
Manager, Associate Programs Section
190 North Independence Mall West
Philadelphia, PA 19106–1572
(800) 523–1547, ext. 2697
http://www.acponline.org/srf/med_scho.htm

303. (S)
Associates Leadership and Recognition Award
http://www.acponline.org/srf/lead_award.pdf

1 award of an expense-paid trip to Annual Session to ACP-ASIM associate member in good standing. Selection is based on demonstrated leadership qualities. For more information visit web site. Deadline: December 6.

304. (S)
Student Scholarship Program
http://www.sctweb.org/student_scholarship_
program.cfm

3 awards of up to $1,750 to graduate students enrolled in accredited institutions, doctoral fellows, or physicians enrolled in an accredited residency program. Based on submitted manuscripts related to original work that has not yet been published. Papers should describe a completed study, one in progress, or a proposal for carrying out a clinical trial. Sponsored by Society for Clinical Trials Student Scholarship Program. For more information, visit web site. Deadline: December 1.

American College of Prosthodontics Educational Foundation

211 E. Chicago Avenue, Suite 1000
Chicago, IL 60611
(312) 573–1260
http://www.prosthodontics.org

305. (S)
EM ESPE/American College of Prosthodontics Research Fellowship

3 grants of $6,000 to dental students, residents, fellows, and graduate students in dental-related fields. Research should advance basic scientific and applied clinical knowledge in the area of geriatric prosthodontics. Must be enrolled in an accredited U.S. institution. Visit web site for specific guidelines. Deadline: October 15.

306. (S)
John J Sharry Prosthodontic Research Competition

1 award each of $500, $750, and $1,250, plus travel and per diem, to postdoctoral students in a prosthodontic program or who completed it within the last 3 years. Selection is based on writing competition held to stimulate and acknowledge original research. Visit web site for specific submission guidelines and deadline.

307. (S)
Procter & Gamble/American College Prosthodontics Research Fellowship

6 grants of $6,000 to dental students, residents, fellows, and graduate students in dental-related fields. Awarded to support research proposals that seek to advance basic science and applied clinical knowledge in the area of complete denture prosthodontics. Must be enrolled in an accredited U.S. institution. Visit web site for specific guidelines. Deadline: October 15.

308. (S)
Scholarships

Scholarships of varying amounts to a full-time graduate student entering their first year in prosthodontic training. Must be accepted into an accredited advanced dental education program. Visit web site for specific guidelines. Deadline: October 1.

American College of Sports Medicine

P.O. Box 1440
Indianapolis, IN 46206–1440
(317) 637–9200
http://www.acsm.org

309. (S)
Active Aging Partnership's Behavioral Research Initiative

Awards of up to $10,000 to graduate doctoral students to conduct research on the barriers to physical activity for older adults. Priority is given to research addressing a plan to overcome barriers identified in the Robert Wood Johnson Foundation's *National Blueprint*. Applications are available after October 1. Visit web site for more information and an application. Deadline: January 31.

310. (S)
Doctoral Student Research Grants

Grants of up to $5,000 to full-time graduate students. Awards may be used for experimental subjects, supplies, and small equipment needs. Applications are available after October 1. Visit web site for more information and an application. Deadline: January 31.

311. (S)
EAS Research Grants on Sports Medicine and Human Performance

Grants of up to $5,000 to graduate students to conduct research in nutrition and human performance. Of particular interest are new and innovative approaches to nutrition and the aspects of human performance. Applications are available after October 1. Visit web site for more information and an application. Deadline: January 31.

312. (S)
Fellowship Fund for Epidemiological Research on Physical Activity

1 grant of $10,000 to postdoctoral fellows and researchers early in their career to conduct research dealing with physical activity epidemiology. Applicants must have received their doctoral degrees within the previous 2 years or have completed their clinical training. Applications are available after

October 1. Visit web site for more information and an application. Deadline: January 31.

313. (S)
Graduate Scholarships for Minorities and Women

Scholarships of up to $1,500 to minority full-time graduate and/or professional students in exercise science, sports medicine, or a related field. Selection is based on outstanding promise and strong interest in research and scholarly activities within the fields of sports medicine and exercise science. Recipients also receive free student membership in ACSM, but students do not have to be members to apply. Applications are available after October 1. Visit web site for more information and an application. Deadline: early April.

314. (S)
NASA Space Physiology Research Grants

4 grants of up to $2,500 to full-time graduate doctoral students to conduct research in the area of exercise, weightlessness, and musculoskeletal physiology. Must be U.S. citizens or legal residents. Applications are available after October 1. Visit web site for more information and an application. Deadline: January 31.

315. (S)
National Student Research Award

Awards providing complimentary registration to the annual meeting, hotel accommodations for 3 nights, meals for 4 days, airfare from home city to conference, and 2 tickets for the banquet to graduate or professional students in the areas of clinical and basic exercise science and sports medicine. Must be enrolled in, or accepted at, an accredited university. Must submit an abstract of a research project conducted the previous year. The abstract must be original research in exercise science. Must be a member of the American College of Sports Medicine or one of its regional chapters. Applications are available after October 1. Visit web site for more information and an application. Deadline: February 28.

316. (S)
NFL Charities Pediatric Research Award

1 or 2 awards of up to $5,000 to graduate doctoral students to conduct pediatric research in exercise science with a focus on human performance and injury prevention in youth. Of particular interest is research pertaining to youth sports programs, especially community football programs. Applications are available after October 1. Visit web site for more information and an application. Deadline: January 31.

317. (S)
Ray and Rosalee Weiss Research Endowment

1 award of $1,500 to graduate students studying the health benefits—physical, mental, and emotional—of physical activity and sports. The research should be for applied, rather than basic research, with the intent of applying the results to programs involving physical activity and sports. Applications are available after October 1. Visit web site for more information and an application. Deadline: January 31.

318. (S)
Research Endowment

1 grant of $10,000 to investigators within 5 years of attaining a doctoral degree or equivalent. Award provides seed money support while further funding is being sought from other sources. Applications are available after October 1. Visit web site for more information and an application. Deadline: January 31.

319. (S)
American Congress of Rehabilitation Medicine Awards
5700 Old Orchard Road, First Floor
Skokie, IL 60077–1057
(708) 966–0095
http://www.acrm.org

Cash awards ranging from $50 to $200 to graduate and undergraduate students. Based on best essays, papers, and articles on subjects relating to physical medicine and rehabilitation. Word count varies. Visit web site or send a self-addressed, stamped envelope for guidelines. Deadline: March 1.

(S)
American Congress on Surveying and Mapping (ACSM)
ACSM Awards Director
6 Montgomery Village Avenue, Suite #403
Gaithersburg, MD 20879

(240) 632–9716, ext. 108
http://www.acsm.net

320. (S)
American Association for Geodetic Surveying Fellowship

1 fellowship of $2,000 to a graduate student, who must be nominated by a member of ACSM or ASPRS. Students must be working in the area of surveying. Write an introductory letter detailing your professional goals, educational situation, and financial situation. Deadline: January 1.

321. (S)
Graduate Fellowship Award

1 fellowship of $2,000 to a graduate student enrolled in or accepted to a program in mapping and surveying. Applicants must have at least 2 years of work experience in the area of surveying. Write an introductory letter detailing your professional goals, educational situation, and financial situation. Deadline: varies.

322. (S)
Joseph F. Dracup Scholarship

1 scholarship of $2,000 to graduate students in a geodetic surveying program. Must be nominated by a member of ACSM or ASPRS. Students must be working in the area of surveying. Based on academic record, recommendation, career goals, and at least 2 years of employment experience. Visit web site for more information. Deadline: varies.

(A, H, S, SS)
American Council of Learned Societies (ACLS)
Fellowships & Grants
633 Third Avenue
New York, NY 10017–6795
(212) 697–1505
http://www.acls.org

323. (H, SS)
Chinese Fellowships for Scholarly Development

8 fellowships providing a living allowance, health insurance, and international airfare to individuals with a master's or doctoral degree or equivalent to Chinese scholars who currently reside in China. Individuals conduct research in the social sciences or humanities. Visit web site for more information and deadline.

324. (SS)
Dissertation & Area Studies Fellowships

Awards ranging from $10,000 to $25,000 to doctoral candidates and for Ph.D. holders. Research and dissertation must be in either Chinese studies or East European studies. Write an introductory letter detailing proposed research. Visit web site for more information or send a self-addressed, stamped envelope. Deadline: December 1.

325. (H)
Eastern European Dissertation Fellowships

10 to 12 fellowships providing stipends of up to $15,000 to graduate students who have completed all requirements, except the dissertation, to conduct dissertation research related to Eastern Europe, for research-related study at a university abroad. Studies must be in the area of the humanities and social sciences. Selection based on academic achievement, financial need, and proposed research. Must be a U.S. citizen or legal resident. Renewable for second year. Deadline: November 15.

326. (H)
East European Language Training Grants

Numerous grants providing $2,000 for language training in the U.S., $2,500 for language training in Eastern Europe, and $7,500 for training in least commonly taught languages to undergraduate, graduate, and doctoral students and postdoctoral scholars for academic study the first or second year of an Eastern European language (excluding Russian) during a summer program in the U.S. Applicants must be U.S. citizens or legal residents. Women and minority students are particularly invited to apply. Individuals must request applications in writing and provide the following information: highest academic degree and date received, citizenship or residence, academic standing, field of specialization, proposed subject of research or study, proposed date of tenure, and which program for which requesting application. Visit web site for more information. Deadline: March 1.

327. (H, SS)
Fellowships for Dissertation Research Abroad Related to China

Numerous fellowships providing stipends of up to $20,000 to doctoral candidates in the humanities and social sciences for dissertation research in Chinese studies, which must be conducted in any country except the People's Republic of China or the U.S. The dissertation must be related to China but may be comparative in nature. Foreign nationals must be full-time doctoral students in U.S. institutions. Selection based on academic achievement, financial need, and proposed research. Must be a U.S. citizen or legal resident. Visit web site for more information. Deadline: November 15.

328. (SS)
Fellowships for Postdoctoral Research in Chinese Studies

Awards of up to $25,000 to postdoctoral fellows to conduct research or writing on Chinese culture or society, including research to synthesize their past research and develop a scholarly overview of a topic important to the study of China. This award does not support research within the People's Republic of China. Visit web site for more information. Deadline: December 1.

329. (H, SS)
Fellowships for Postdoctoral Research in East European Study

Awards of up to $30,000 to postdoctoral fellows to conduct research in the social sciences or humanities relating to Albania, Bulgaria, the former Czechoslovakia, Germany, Hungary, Poland, Romania, and the former Yugoslavia. Must conduct full-time research for up to 6 months. Not intended to support research within East Europe. Must be a U.S. citizen or legal resident. Visit web site for more information. Deadline: December 1.

330. (A, H)
Henry Luce Foundation—Dissertation Fellowship Program in American Art

Fellowships of $20,000 for a 1-year nonrenewable term beginning in the summer to graduate students who have completed all course work and are at any stage of doctoral dissertation research or writing focused on a topic in the history of the visual arts of the U.S. Open to U.S. citizens or permanent residents. Fellowship funds may not be used to defray tuition costs. Applicants must be doctoral candidates in a department of art history with a dissertation focused on the above topic. Applicants should have completed all requirements for their doctorate except for the dissertation before beginning tenure. Deadline: November 15.

331. (H, SS)
International Dissertation Field Research Fellowships

Fellowships of varying amounts to full-time graduate students in the humanities or social sciences. Award helps fund dissertation field research in all areas and regions of the world. U.S. citizenship is not required, but applicants must be enrolled in a doctoral program in the U.S. Deadline: none specified.

332. (H, S, SS)
Post-Doctoral Research Fellowships

Awards of up to $15,000 to scholars with a doctorate or equivalent. Research fellowships are for 6 to 12 months of study in humanities, philosophy, anthropology, economics, certain social and natural sciences. Grants-in-aid for personal expenses while doing research are also available. Applicants must show evidence of highest academic degree; field of specialization; proposed research topic; time needed; etc. Applicant must be a U.S. citizen or legal resident. Visit web site for more information. Deadline: September 30 (fellowships), December 15 (grants).

(A, H, S, SS)
American Council of the Blind
1155 15th Street, N.W., Suite 1004
Washington, DC 20005
(800) 424–8666
(202) 467–5081
http://www.acb.org

333. (A, H, S, SS)
ACB Scholarships/Vteck Scholarships

7 scholarships ranging from $1,000 to $1,500 to legally blind graduate, professional, or undergraduate students, for use in any major. Students must be accepted to, or enrolled in, an accredited institute.

Applicants must be U.S. citizens or legal residents. For more information, send a self-addressed, stamped envelope or visit web site. Deadline: April 1.

334. (A, H, S, SS)
Floyd Qualls Scholars

4 scholarships ranging from $1,000 to $2,000 to legally blind students who are graduate or undergraduate students or students in vocational/technical schools. Based on academic record, recommendation, and biographical sketch. Must be U.S. citizens or legal residents. For more information, send a self-addressed, stamped envelope or visit web site. Deadline: April 1.

335. (A, H, S, SS)
Melva T. Owen Scholarships

Scholarships ranging from $500 to $4,000 to legally blind outstanding graduate, undergraduate, or vocational/technical students accepted to or enrolled in an accredited 2- or 4-year institution. Based on academic record, recommendation, and biographical sketch. Must be U.S. citizens or legal residents. Open to any area of study. For more information, send a self-addressed, stamped envelope or visit web site. Deadline: March 1.

336. (SS)
American Council on Education
ACE Fellows Program
One Dupont Circle
Washington, DC 20036–1193
(202) 939–9300
http://www.acenet.edu

7 fellowships providing stipends and relocation and travel allowance to doctoral candidates with 5 years of experience. Must be nominated by their institution's president. ACE identifies and prepares future leaders in higher education to become faculty members and administrators. Recipients have demonstrated leadership abilities. Minorities and women are encouraged to apply. Nominating institution continues to pay the fellow's salary and benefits during the fellowship year. Hosting institution is responsible to provide fellow's travel and meeting attendance costs. The institution providing the internship experience is also responsible for the $2,500 program fee payable to ACE. Deadline: November 1.

337. (SS)
American Council on Rural Special Education (ACRES)
ACRES Scholarship
Kansas State University
2323 Anderson Avenue, Suite 226
Manhattan, KS 66502–2912
(785) 532–2737
http://extension.usu.edu/acres

1 award of $1,000 to a teacher who is currently (or has been) employed by a rural school district as a certified teacher in regular or special education. You must be working with students with disabilities or planning to make a career change to special education from regular education. Must submit an essay and 2 letters of recommendation. Applicants must be pursuing a goal of increasing skills in special education or "retooling" from a regular education to a special education career and be a citizen of the United States. Deadline: December 1.

(A, H, S, SS)
American Councils
1776 Massachusetts Avenue, N.W., Suite 700
Washington, DC 20036
(202) 833–7522
http://www.americancouncils.net

338. (A, H, S, SS)
Title VIII Central, Eastern & Southern European Language Program

Fellowships providing full tuition at a major university in east-central Europe, international round-trip airfare from the fellow's home city to host city, living stipends, housing stipends or direct payment for housing in university dormitories, insurance, visa support as necessary, and graduate-level academic credit through Bryn Mawr College for programs providing 7 weeks or more of full-time instruction. Open to graduate students at the M.A. level or higher who have at least elementary language skills to spend the summer, a semester, or an academic year abroad at one of 140 participating institutions. All applicants must be U.S. citizens or permanent residents. Applicants should explain how their plans for language study support their overall research goals. While students with a wide range of interests and research goals have received Title VIII support in the past, all applicants should specify how their studies will contribute to a body of knowledge that enables U.S. policy makers to better understand the region. Funded by the U.S. Department of State. Deadline: October 1 (spring) and January 15 (summer, fall, academic year).

339. (A, H, S, SS)

Title VIII Central, Eastern & Southern European Research Scholar Program

Fellowships providing full support, including international travel, housing, insurance, living stipend, academic affiliation(s), and visa(s) to doctoral students, postdoctoral researchers, and faculty to spend at least 3 months in the field; language program participants must spend at least 1 month in the region. Research trips for periods of 4 to 9 months are particularly encouraged. Provides fellowship support for research or a combination of research and language study in any of the following countries: Albania, Bulgaria, the Czech Republic, Estonia, Hungary, Latvia, Lithuania, Poland, Romania, Slovakia, and the former Yugoslavia. Must be U.S. citizens or permanent residents. Funded by the U.S. Department of State and American Councils. Must be used at any one of the 140 participating institutions. Deadline: October 1 (spring) and January 15 (summer, fall, academic year).

340. (S, SS)

American Criminal Justice Association
Lambda Alpha Epsilon National Scholarship
P.O. Box 601047
Sacramento CA 95860–1047
(916) 484–6553
http://www.acjalae.org

9 scholarships ranging from $100 to $400 to graduate and undergraduate students majoring in criminal justice, criminology, legal services, or social sciences. Open to members and nonmembers. Selection is based on a paper written on an assigned theme of the upcoming national conference. Must be enrolled in a 2- or 4-year institution. Must submit an application, transcript, essay, and recommendation letters. Deadline: December 31.

341. (S)

American Dental Association
211 East Chicago Avenue, Suite 820
Chicago, IL 60611

(312) 440–2567
http://www.ada.org/ada/resources/endow/
minority.html

Scholarships ranging from $1,000 to $2,500 to minority students in dental school. Awards are based on financial need, academic achievement, and recommendation letters. Must be enrolled in an accredited U.S. dental school. Deadline: July 1.

(S)

American Dental Hygienists' Association
444 North Michigan Avenue, Suite 3400
Chicago, IL 60611
(312) 440–8900
http://www.adha.org

342. (S)

Dr. Alfred C. Fones Scholarships

Varying numbers of scholarships of up to $1,500 to part-time and full-time students with a dental hygiene certificate who are graduate students, doctoral degree candidates, or about to enter their undergraduate senior year. Must have at least a 3.0 GPA (B average) on a 4.0 scale. Applicants must intend on becoming a dental hygiene teacher or educator and be a member of ADHA. Based on academic record and financial need. Visit web site or send a self-addressed, stamped envelope for an application. Deadline: May 1.

343. (S)

Graduate Fellowship Program

Numerous of scholarships of up to $1,500 to full-time students within a dental hygiene education program. Must have at least a 3.0 GPA (B average) on a 4.0 scale and be a member of ADHA. Based on academic record and financial need. Visit web site or send a self-addressed, stamped envelope for an application. Deadline: May 1.

344. (S)

John C. Thiel Faculty Research Fellowship

2 fellowships of up to $5,000 to faculty members or graduate students pursuing a master's of science in dental hygiene educator or doctoral work. Must be members of the U.S. interested in research complimenting the ADHA national research agenda. Must have a 3.5 GPA on a 4.0 scale, be a faculty member of

an accredited dental hygiene program, hold a license to practice dental hygiene, and an active member of ADHA. Visit web site for more information. Deadline: June 30.

345. (S)
Part-Time Scholarship

1 scholarship of up to $1,500 to a part-time student pursuing a graduate, bachelor's or associate degree or certificate in dental health/services. May be used at either a 2- or 4-year accredited U.S. institution. Must have at least a 3.0 GPA (B average) on a 4.0 scale and be a member of ADHA. Selection based on academic achievement, application, and financial need. Visit web site or send a self-addressed, stamped envelope for an application. Entering freshmen are ineligible. Deadline: May 1.

346. (S)
Research Grant

Research grants of $5,000 to graduate students to conduct research that will promote the oral health of the public by improving dental hygiene education and practice. The principal investigator must be a licensed dental hygienist or a student pursuing a dental hygiene degree or a current member of ADHA or SADAH. Visit web site for more information. Deadline: January 30.

347. (S)
Rosie Wall RDH Community Spirit Grant

2 scholarships of $1,000 to graduate students involved in a specific community health or research project. One recipient must be from Hawaii and the other may be from any of the 50 states. Proposed research or project should offer a creative approach to increasing the public's oral and general health. Visit web site for more information. Deadline: February 28.

(S)
American Dietetic Association Foundation
216 West Jackson Boulevard, Suite 800
Chicago, IL 60606–6995
(800) 877–1600
(312) 899–0040
http://www.adaf.org

348. (S)
Diabetes Care and Education Dietetic Practice Group Medical Nutrition Therapy Outcomes Research Award

1 award of $10,000 to a Diabetes Care and Education DPG member to conduct outcomes research in diabetes medical nutrition therapy. Proposed project must be completed within 2 years after receipt of award. Deadline: February 29.

349. (S)
Dietetic Internships

Unspecified number of internships ranging from $500 to $1,000 to graduate or undergraduate students accepted into an ADA-accredited dietetic internship program. Must have financial need, be a U.S. citizen or a permanent resident, and be an ADA member. Visit web site for more information. Deadline: February 15.

350. (S)
First International Nutritionist Dietitian Fellowship

1 award of $2,000 to a professional foreign dietitian/nutritionist, preferably from a developing country, to enable him/her to attend a workshop or seminar or to participate in a continuing education program or orientation project in the U.S. For specific guidelines, visit web site. Deadline: May 1.

351. (S)
Foundation Practice Awards

3 scholarships of $1,000 to students who are ADA members or dietetic interns accepted to, or involved in, graduate study in administrative dietetics or a related area. Must have financial need. Some awards require specific areas of study (e.g., public health nutrition, food service administration). Some awards are limited to U.S. citizens, whereas others are open to citizens of U.S., Mexico, or Canada. Request applications after September 15. For more information, visit web site or send a self-addressed, stamped envelope. Deadline: February 15.

352. (S)
Gaynold Jensen Scholarship Fund for Short-Term Education

An unspecified number of scholarships of $250 for short-term educational programs at the graduate, undergraduate, or certification level. Must be a member of the Consultants Dietitians in Health Care Facilities Dietetic Practice Group. For more information and deadline date, visit web site or send a self-addressed, stamped envelope.

353. (S)
Graduate Scholarships

Scholarships ranging from $500 to $5,000 to graduate students or undergraduate seniors pursuing a career related to nutrition research, nutrition education, or consumer awareness. Undergraduate seniors must be planning to attend an accredited graduate school program. Must be a U.S. citizen or permanent resident and a member of ADA. For specific information, visit web site. Deadline: varies by category.

354. (S)
Gwendolyn Rossell Memorial Fund

1 award of up to $250 to a member of the Public Health Nutrition Dietetic Practice Group to attend a short-term educational program. Must be a U.S. citizen or permanent resident and a member of ADA. For specific information, visit web site. Deadline: rolling.

355. (S)
Karen Lechowich Continuing Education Fund

2 awards of $500 to new members to attend the annual Food and Nutrition Conference & Exhibition (FNCE). Selection is based on an essay competition. The essay may be no more than 250 words in length explaining why they would like to attend FNCE and the benefits they hope to gain from attending. Must be an ADA member of less than 5 years. Deadline: August 30.

356. (S)
Leadership Development Award

1 award of up to $1,000 to an ADA member to attend a state or national meeting. Selection is based on demonstrated leadership abilities and commitment to ADA. For more information, visit web site. Deadline: May 1.

357. (S)
Lois P. Hampton Scholarship Fund for Short-Term Education

1 scholarship of $200, or 2 scholarships of $100, for short-term education programs at the graduate, undergraduate, or certification level. Must be a Vanderbilt University Dietetic Internship graduate. Request applications after September 15. For more information, visit web site or send a self-addressed, stamped envelope. Deadline: February 15.

358. (S)
Lulu G. Graves Award

Awards of varying amounts to an individual or group to conduct a program in nutrition education. For specific guidelines, visit web site. Deadline: March 1.

359. (S)
Marie and August LoPresti Sr. Endowment Fund

1 award of varying amount to graduate students and faculty members wanting to participate in a faculty development project. Applicants must be residents of northeast Ohio and U.S. citizens. Selection is based on academic qualifications, professional potential, and financial need. Deadline: February 28.

360. (S)
Mary Abbott Hess Award

1 award of $1,000 to a dietetic professional for an innovative effort in food/culinary education. Must be a member of ADA who is either a registered dietitian or a registered dietetic technician. Selection is based on specific criteria, such as demonstrating an original concept, meeting a food/culinary need of the intended market, and creativity and professionalism in the execution of the effort. For more information, visit web site. Deadline: March 1.

361. (S)
Mary C. Zahasky Scholarship Fund for Short-Term Education

Unspecified numbers of scholarships of $250 for short-term education programs at the graduate, undergraduate, or certification level. Must be a registered dietician. Request applications after September 15. For more information, visit web site or send a self-addressed, stamped envelope. Deadline: February 15.

362. (S)
Mary Swartz Rose Fellowship

1 fellowship of $1,000 to a graduate or doctoral student who is an ADA member. Undergraduate major must have been nutrition or an allied field. Students must have been in the upper quarter of their class and have professional promise. For more information, visit web site or send a self-addressed, stamped envelope. Deadline: February 15.

363. (S)
Preprofessional Practice Program—AP4

Awards ranging from $250 to $2,500 to students enrolled in or who have applied to an ADA-approved preprofessional practice program. Based on academic achievement, promise of being a contributing member of the profession and financial need. Must be a U.S. citizen. Request applications before January 15. For more information, visit web site or send a self-addressed, stamped envelope. Deadline: February 15.

364. (S)
Susan T. Borra Fellowship

1 award of $5,000 to individuals to fund an internship that will enhance their capabilities in the area of nutrition communication in leading universities, health organizations, professional societies, and industry. Deadline: February 28.

365. (S)
Winpfheimer-Guggenheim Fund for International Exchange in Nutrition, Dietetics, and Management

1 award of $1,000 for an essay by a professional dietitian/nutritionist describing an innovative international team approach to solve a nutritional problem in neighboring countries. The project must be effective, practical and attainable and should serve as a model for further collaborations. For specific guidelines, visit web site. Deadline: May 1.

(SS)
American Economics Association
2014 Broadway, Suite 305
Nashville, TN 37203
(615) 322–2595
(615) 343–7590
http://www.vanderbilt.edu/AEA

366. (SS)
Awards

Numerous awards of a stipend of $1,000 to minority students majoring in economics or related majors. Program goal is to increase the number of professional economists from minority groups. The 8-week institute recruits undergraduate minority students who have shown promise in economics and who might be interested in studying for a doctorate. It gives them a chance to test their abilities in graduate-level economics and at the same time reveals to them professional options they may not have considered before. The program is held on the campus of Temple University in Philadelphia. Deadline: March 1.

367. (SS)
Federal Reserve Minority Fellowship Program

Numerous fellowships providing $900 monthly stipends to minority doctoral students. Must be beginning dissertation research. Must be U.S. citizens enrolled in an accredited economics program. Deadline: March 1.

368. (SS)
American Enterprise Institute for Public Policy Research
Internship
1150 Seventeenth Street, N.W.
Washington, DC 20036
(202) 862–5800
http://www.aei.org

45 internships to graduate and undergraduate students and postgraduates in the areas of economic policy, foreign and defense studies, social and political studies, public relations, *The American Enterprise Magazine*, communications, seminars and conferences, publications, publications marketing, information systems, marketing, and accounting. Internships are unpaid. Deadline: April 1 (summer), September 15 (fall), and December 1 (winter/spring).

369. (A)
American Federation of Musicians (AFM)
Congress of Strings Summer Scholarship Program
1501 Broadway #600
New York, NY 10036
(212) 869–1330
http://www.amf.org

Summer scholarships of varying amounts to young string instrumentalists who are between 16 and 23 years of age. Applicants do not need to be children of AFM members to compete. Audition required. Audition winners go on to study and perform for 6 weeks during the summer. Deadline: early February.

(A, H, S, SS)
American Federation of Television and Radio Artists (AFTRA)
Memorial Foundation, Inc.
260 Madison Avenue, 7th Floor
New York, NY 10016–2402
(212) 532–0800
http://www.aftra.org

370. (A, H)
Bud Collyer Memorial Scholarships

Scholarships of varying amounts to members in good standing for at least 5 years, or their children. Members may use the award for graduate or undergraduate study. Children of members may use the award for undergraduate study. To be used for study in the academic and performing arts fields. Deadline: none specified.

371. (A, H, S, SS)
Bud Jacoby Memorial Scholarships/Jerry Walter Fund

Scholarships of varying amounts to members in good standing for at least 5 years, or their children. Members may use the award for graduate or undergraduate study. Children of members may use the award for undergraduate study. May be used for any course of study. Deadline: none specified.

372. (A, SS)
George Heller Memorial Scholarships

Scholarships of varying amounts to AFTRA members in good standing for at least 5 years, or their children.

Members may use the award for graduate or undergraduate study. Children of members may use the award for undergraduate study. Intended for college enrollment, general study, study in the performing arts fields, or study of labor relations. Deadline: none specified.

373. (A, H, S, SS)
Ken Harvey Scholarship Fund

1 scholarship of varying amount to a member in good standing for at least 5 years, or to a member's child. Members may use the award for graduate or undergraduate study. Children of members may use the award for undergraduate study. Offers financial aid for vocal coaching. Deadline: none specified.

374. (A)
Travis Johnson Memorial Scholarships

Scholarships of varying amounts to members in good standing for at least 5 years, or their children. Members may use the award for graduate or undergraduate study. Children of members may use the award for undergraduate study. To be used for the study of any branch of music. Deadline: none specified.

375. (H, S, SS)
American Forests
Education Coordinator
P.O. Box 2000
Washington, DC 20013
(202) 667–3300
http://www.americanforests.org

20 to 25 internships open to graduate students, recent college graduates, and undergraduate sophomores, juniors, or seniors to work in a national citizens conservation organization. Students work as either interns or fellows in the areas of advertising and marketing, communications, education, Global ReLeaf International, management, policy, publications, research, and urban forestry. International applicants are eligible. Internships last from 3 to 6 months on an ongoing basis in Jacksonville, FL, and Washington, DC. Deadline: rolling.

(S)

American Foundation for Aging Research Fellowship

70 West 40th Street
New York, NY 10018
(212) 703–9977
http://www.afar.org

376. (S)
AFAR Scholarships

Scholarships ranging from $500 to $2,000 to graduate, predoctoral, or undergraduate students who are involved in research related to aging. Research cannot be sociological or psychological. Based on student's personal qualifications and project proposal. Must have at least a 3.0 GPA. Based on academic record, research proposal, and recommendations. Students who have already completed an M.D. or Ph.D. degree are ineligible. Deadline: none.

377. (S)
Cecille Gould Memorial Fund Cancer Fellowship

5 scholarships ranging from $500 to $2,000 to graduate and professional school students who are involved in research related to aging. Based on student's personal qualifications and project proposal. Must have at least a 3.0 GPA. Based on academic record, research proposal, and recommendations. Students who have already completed an M.D. or Ph.D. degree are ineligible. Deadline: none.

378. (S)
American Foundation for AIDS Research

Intern Coordinator
120 Wall Street, 13th Floor
New York, NY 10005–3902
(212) 806–1600
http://www.amfar.org

4 10-week summer internships providing a $2,500 stipend to graduate students and upper-level undergraduates. Internships are conducted at the DC office only. Interns monitor, research, and evaluate HIV/AIDS policy issues at AmFAR, the nation's leading organization that supports AIDS research. Interns work on public policy, research, and development. Deadline: February 15.

(S)

American Foundation for Pharmaceutical Education

One Church Street, #202
Rockville, MD 20850
(301) 738–2160
http://www.afpenet.org

379. (S)
AASP-AFPE Gateway Scholarships

4 scholarships of up to $10,000 to students in a Pharm.D. program or in the last year of a bachelor's degree program who are planning on seeking a doctorate in a pharmacy graduate project. The awards are divided into certain percentages and applied to undergraduate research projects and graduate school expenses. Students must be U.S. citizens or legal residents. Contact: American Association of Pharmaceutical Scientists, 601 King Street, Alexandria, VA 22314–3105. Deadline: October 1 and March 1.

380. (S)
Fellowship Program

Fellowships of $6,000, $7,000, and $10,000 to graduate students who have completed at least one semester of work toward a doctorate in pharmacy. Students must be U.S. citizens or legal residents. Contact: American Association of Pharmaceutical Scientists, 601 King Street, Alexandria, VA 22314–3105. Deadline: October 1 and March 1.

381. (S)
MERCK-AFPE Gateway Scholarships

4 scholarships of up to $10,000 to students in a Pharm.D. program or in the last year of a bachelor's degree program who are planning on seeking a doctorate in a pharmacy graduate project. The awards are divided into certain percentages and used for undergraduate research projects and graduate school expenses. Based on academic record, recommendations, awards, and reason for applying for the scholarship. Students must be U.S. citizens or legal residents. Contact: American Association of Pharmaceutical Scientists, 601 King Street, Alexandria, VA 22314–3105. Deadline: October 1 and March 1.

382. (S)
Springboard to Teaching Fellowship Program

1 award of $7,500 to a doctoral student in their last year of study to encourage pharmacy graduate students to consider pursuing a career in teaching in a college of pharmacy. An additional $15,000 over 2 years is awarded for the student to conduct a research project while completing a teaching appointment in a pharmacy college. Must be a U.S. citizen or legal resident. Visit web site or send a self-addressed, stamped envelope for information. Deadline: March 1.

(A, H, S, SS)
American Foundation for the Blind
11 Penn Plaza, Suite 300
New York, NY 10001
(800) 232–5463
(212) 502–7600 (TDD)
http://www.afb.org/afb
afbinfo@afb.org

383. (SS)
Delta Gamma Foundation Florence Margaret Harvey Memorial Scholarship

1 scholarship of $1,000 to a legally blind graduate or undergraduate student majoring in a field of education for visually impaired and blind persons. Based on evidence of legal blindness, academic record, essay, and recommendations. Must be U.S. citizens. May be used for any area of study. Deadline: April 1.

384. (SS)
Dissertation Support Awards

Varying numbers of dissertation research grants of $4,000 to doctoral candidates in social and behavioral sciences as related to blindness and severe visual impairment. Preference is given to topics relating to literacy, service access, quality of life, and socioeconomics. Selection based on proposed research. Must be a U.S. citizen. Deadline: April 12.

385. (SS)
Florence Margaret Harvey Memorial Scholarship

1 scholarship of $1,000 to a legally blind graduate or undergraduate student majoring in a field of rehabilitation and/or education of visually impaired and blind persons. Based on evidence of legal blindness, academic record, essay, and recommendations. Must be a U.S. citizen. Deadline: April 1.

386. (A, H)
Gladys C. Anderson Scholarship Fund

2 scholarships of $1,000 to legally blind females enrolled in either religious or classical music study at a recognized institution. Sample performance tape of voice or instrumental selection is required. Must be U.S. citizens. Based on evidence of legal blindness, academic record, recommendations, talent, and essay. Deadline: June 1.

387. (A, H, S, SS)
Karen D. Carsel Memorial Scholarship

1 scholarship of $500 to a legally blind full-time graduate student. May be used for any area of study at an accredited institution. Must be U.S. citizen. Based on financial need. Must provide proof of legal blindness, graduate school acceptance, financial need, a personal statement, and letters of recommendation. Visit web site or send a self-addressed, stamped envelope for an application. Deadline: June 1.

388. (A, H, S, SS)
Dr. Katherine Michalowski Memorial Scholarship Fund

1 award of $500 to a legally blind female graduate or undergraduate student at an accredited institution. Must be a California resident. May be used for any area of study. Must be U.S. citizen. Visit web site or send a self-addressed, stamped envelope. Written inquiries only. Deadline: June 1.

389. (A, H, SS)
National Chinese-American Scholarship Fund

Varying numbers of scholarships of up to $2,000 to Chinese-American graduate or undergraduate students who are legally blind. May be used at any accredited college or university for use in habilitation, rehabilitation, and/or vocational training. Preference given to students who are ineligible to receive federal or state assistance. Must be U.S. citizens. Deadline: June 1.

390. (A)
R. L. Gillette Scholarship Fund

2 scholarships of $1,000 to legally blind women enrolled in either creative writing or music performance in a 4-year bachelor's degree program at a recognized institution. A writing sample or music performance tape is required. Must be a U.S. citizen. Based on evidence of blindness, academic record, recommendations, talent, and essay. Deadline: June 1.

391. (A, H, SS)
Rudolph Dillman Scholarship

3 scholarships of $2,500 to legally blind graduate students majoring in a field that deals with the education of visually impaired and blind persons. Applicants must submit proof of visual impairment in a statement from an optometrist. Based on evidence of legal blindness, academic record, recommendations, career goals, and essay. Must be a U.S. citizen. Deadline: April 1.

392. (A, H, SS)
TeleSensory Scholarship

1 scholarship of $1,000 to a legally blind graduate or undergraduate student majoring in a field that will deal with the education of visually impaired and blind persons. Applicants must submit proof of visual impairment in a statement from an optometrist. Based on evidence of blindness, academic record, recommendations, and essay. Must be a U.S. citizen. Deadline: April 1.

393. (A, H, SS)
Vtek Scholarship Fund

1 scholarship of $1,000 to a legally blind undergraduate or graduate student accepted to, or enrolled in, an accredited program within the broad areas of education of the blind and visually impaired. Applicants must submit proof of visual impairment in a statement from an optometrist. Based on evidence of blindness, academic record, essay, and recommendations. Must be a U.S. citizen. Deadline: June 1.

394. (S)
American Foundation for Urologic Disease & National Kidney Foundation
Resident Research Fellowship
1128 North Charles Street
Baltimore, MD 21201
(410) 468–1800
http://www.afud.org

Fellowships providing a $25,000 stipend to urology residents and $46,000 to postdoctoral scientists to conduct urology research into urologic or related dysfunctions. Fellows must have no more than 1 year of research experience above the doctorate level. Individuals must have a strong interest in clinical or lab research within the broad field of urology. Recipients must agree to dedicate 2 years in the AFUD/Ph.D. program as a full-time researcher. For more information, visit web site or send a self-addressed, stamped envelope. Deadline: September 1.

(S)
American Foundation for Vision Awareness
243 North Lindbergh Boulevard
St. Louis, MO 63141
(800) 927–2382
http://www.mioptassn.org/page8.html

395. (S)
Education/Research Grants

Scholarships of $1,000 to optometry students and research grants ranging from $5,000 to $10,000 to scientists to conduct research in the field of vision. For more information and an application, send a self-addressed, stamped envelope or visit web site. Deadline: February 1.

396. (S)
Scholarships

Scholarships ranging from $700 to $1,000 to students accepted to, or enrolled in, a school of optometry. Must be Washington State residents. Renewable. For more information, visit web site or send a self-addressed, stamped envelope. Deadline: December 15.

American Geological Institute
4220 King Street
Alexandria, VA 22302–1502
(703) 379–2480
http://www.agiweb.org

397. (S)
Congressional Science Fellowship

Fellowships providing a stipend of $49,000 (plus $2,000 travel relocation allowance, a $2,000 allowance for travel during the year, $1,000 allowance to travel to AGU meetings, and health care benefits) to postdoctoral students (who have completed all course and dissertation work prior to commencing program), scientists, engineers, or other professionals. Must be AGI members to work on the staff of one of the members of the United States Congress or Congressional Committee. Prospective applicants should have a broad geoscience background and excellent written and oral communication skills. Should have an interest in applying science to the solution of public problems. Preference given to U.S. citizens or legal residents. Deadline: February 1.

398. (S)
Minority Participation Program Scholarships

Varying number of scholarships ranging from $250 to $1,000 to minority graduate and upper-level undergraduate students who are African-American, Hispanic-American, or Native American (American Indian, Eskimo, Hawaiian, Samoan). Must be U.S. citizens and majoring in geosciences (geology, geochemistry, geophysics, hydrology, meteorology, oceanography, planetary geology, marine sciences and earth science education). Based on academic achievements, maturity, background, financial need, and likelihood of becoming a successful geoscientist. Must submit financial profile, résumé, and 3 letters of recommendation. Students must have at least a 3.0 GPA in science and mathematics. Award can only be used at a 4-year institution. Renewable with satisfactory academic progress. Deadline: March 1.

(S)
American Geophysical Union
2000 Florida Avenue, N.W.
Washington, DC 20009–1277
(800) 966–2481
http://www.agu.org

399. (S)
Congressional Science Fellowship Program

Fellowships providing a stipend of $49,000 (plus $2,000 travel relocation allowance, a $2,000 allowance for travel during the year, $1,000 allowance to travel to AGU meetings, and health care benefits) to postdoctoral students (who have completed all course and dissertation work prior to commencing program), scientists, engineers, or other professionals. Must be AGU members to work on the staff of one of the members of the United States Congress or congressional committee. Must be U.S. citizens or legal residents. Deadline: February 1.

400. (S)
Horton Research Grants

1 or more research grants ranging from $4,500 to $9,500, plus a travel allowance, to doctoral students who are conducting research in hydrology and/or water resources. Research proposals may be in hydrology or in water resources policy sciences (economy, sociology, and law). Must be a member of AGU. For more information, visit web site or send a self-addressed, stamped envelope for an application. Deadline: March 1.

401. (S)
June Bacon-Bercey Scholarships

Numerous scholarships of $500 to female graduate or undergraduate students pursuing a career in atmospheric sciences. For more information, visit web site or send a self-addressed, stamped envelope for an application. Deadline: May 1.

402. (S)
Student Travel Grants

Awards of up to $250, plus meeting registration, to graduate and undergraduate student members of AGU who are presenting papers at the fall or spring meeting. For more information, visit web site or send a self-addressed, stamped envelope for guidelines. Deadline: 6 to 8 weeks prior to meeting.

403. (S)
American Geriatrics Society
Henderson Memorial Student Award
350 Fifth Avenue, Suite 801
New York, NY 10118
(212) 308–1414
http://www.americangeriatrics.org

1 award of $1,000, plus an honorarium to medical students. Preference is given to students who have conducted research or clinical investigation in geriatrics or are participating in an ongoing clinical project in gerontology or aging. Formal papers are not required but are welcomed. The recipient attends as an invited guest. Deadline: April 10.

404. (SS)
American Health Information Management Association
Foundation of Research and Education
233 N. Michigan Avenue, Suite 2150
Chicago, IL 60611–5800
(312) 233–1100
http://www.ahima.org/

Scholarships ranging from $1,000 to $5,000 to graduate and doctoral students who are pursuing careers in information management, medical records administration, or related areas. Must be active AHIMA members, credentialed medical record professionals, and hold a baccalaureate degree. Awards may be used at any accredited U.S. institutions. Must be U.S. citizens or legal residents. Deadline: August 1.

(S)
American Heart Association (AHA)
7272 Greenville Avenue
Dallas, TX 75231
(800) AHA–USA1
http://www.americanheart.org

405. (S)
British-American Research Fellowships

Fellowships of varying amounts to postdoctoral individuals who may not yet be clearly qualified to conduct independent research. Open to U.S. citizens who seek research training in British institutions and who have either an M.D. or Ph.D.

406. (S)
Clinician-Scientist Award

Numerous awards of up to $40,000 per year for 3 years to postdoctoral fellows to conduct research projects. Award includes fringe benefits of up to $9,600, an initiation grant of $33,000 per year, and travel and moving expenses of up to $7,000. Total 5-year commitment is $301,300. Recipients must devote virtually 100% of their time to research and related activities. While the postdoctoral fellow is in a researcher's lab, the researcher receives a small grant to offset research expenses. Must be a U.S. citizen or permanent resident. Must already have a medical or doctoral degree and have at least 3 years of postdoctoral clinical training. Deadline: June 1.

407. (S)
Grants-in-Aid

Varying number of grants of approximately $40,000 per year for a period ranging from 1 to 3 years to advanced professionals and postdoctoral students who hold an M.D., Ph.D., D.Sc., D.O., D.D.S., D.V.M., or equivalent, to conduct independent cardiovascular research. The award may cover cost of supplies, animals, limited travel, special equipment, and other related expenses. Award is not for salary. Grants for research conducted outside the U.S. are limited to U.S. citizens. Deadline: July 1.

408. (S)
International Research Fellowships

Varying number of grants of $25,000 for 1 year to postdoctoral students or advanced professionals. Award is for short-term cardiovascular research training in the U.S. or a foreign research center. Recipients also receive $6,000 in fringe benefits and $4,000 for travel expenses. Deadline: June 1.

409. (S)
Medical Student Research Fellowship

Up to 6 fellowships of $12,000 per medical school to provide medical students the opportunity to undertake a 1-year full-time research endeavor. Students take a year off to work on a research project with a faculty mentor at their own, or other, institution. Fellowship provides a stipend and an institutional allowance to cover travel to meetings, publishing/printing research papers, and health insurance. No tuition funds are provided. Institutions, not the students, apply to AHA. Deadline: June 1.

410. (S)
Summer Internships

250 to 300 10- to 12-week summer internships providing stipends ranging from $600 to $3,000 to medical, graduate, undergraduate, or high school students. No research experience is required, though some programs require students to have completed organic chemistry, biology, and physics or calculus. Internships are conducted at state AHA affiliates. Contact the Research Division of the AHA state affiliate in which the student wishes to work. The 800 number connects students to appropriate office. Deadline: varies according to state affiliate.

(S)
American Heart Association, Minnesota Affiliate
4701 West 77th Street
Minneapolis, MN 55435
(952) 835–3300
http://www.americanheart.org/presenter.
jhtml?
identifier=3012442

411. (S)
Helen N. and Harold B. Shapiro Scholarship Awards

1 scholarship of $1,000 to a medical student working in a course of study with possible application to patients with diseases of the heart and cardiovascular system. Must be attending an accredited Minnesota medical school. Based on academic record. Deadline: April 1.

412. (S)
Howard B. Burcell Heart and Nelson Heart Scholarships

2 scholarships, 1 of $1,200 and 1 of $1,500, to medical students to conduct cardiovascular research and teaching. Award is for up to 3 months of full-time research. Must submit an abstract of proposed project, résumé, sponsor's curriculum vitae, and 2 letters of recommendation. Must be registered students at an accredited Minnesota medical teaching institution. Deadline: April 1.

(S)
American Heart Association, Western States Affiliate
1710 Gilbreth Road
Burlingame, CA 94010–1317
(650) 259–6700
http://www.heartsource.org/research/med_student.
html

413. (S)
Medical Student Research Program

8 10- or 12-week research awards providing $480 per week to full-time medical school students to carry out cardiovascular-related research. Provides medical students who are potentially interested in a research career with an opportunity to explore a research career that is related to the cardiovascular area or stroke. Students may propose a preceptor/project at any nonprofit research institution within the Western States Affiliate (California, Nevada, or Utah). Visit web site for more information and an application. Deadline: March 3.

414. (S)
Predoctoral Fellowship

Fellowships providing an $18,500 stipend, plus $3,000 annual departmental allowance, to doctoral students in any of the basic or clinical biomedical sciences, the social or behavioral sciences, the epidemiology or related area. Must be enrolled in an accredited institution in California, Nevada, or Utah, show evidence of potential for a research career, and show an interest in pursuing a career in cardiovascular research. Medical students with little or no prior research training are strongly encouraged to apply for 2 years of support. Visit web site for specific guidelines and deadline. Deadline: January.

415. (S)
American Helicopter Society
217 N. Washington Street
Alexandria, VA 22314
(703) 684–6777
http://www.vtol.org

Awards ranging from $1,000 to $2,000 to graduate and undergraduate students pursuing studies in vertical flight engineering. Visit web site for more information. Deadline: none specified.

(H)
American Historical Association
400 A Street, S.E.
Washington, DC 20003
(202) 544–2422
http://www.theaha.org

416. (H)
Albert Beveridge Grants

20 to 25 awards of up to $1,000 to graduate or postgraduate students to support research on the history of the Americas Hemisphere. Only AHA members are eligible. Visit web site or send a self-addressed, stamped envelope for an application. Deadline: February 1.

417. (H)
Bernadette E. Schmitt Grants for Research in European, African, or Asian History

Awards of $1,000 to advanced doctoral students, nontenured faculty, or unaffiliated scholars to further research in progress. May be used for travel to a library or archive, and for microfilms, photographs, photocopying, etc. Must be AHA members. Deadline: September 15.

418. (H)
Fellowships in Aerospace History

Awards of $25,000 for individuals with a doctorate and $12,000 for doctoral students, plus travel expenses, to conduct research projects in American History–Aerospace. Must have completed all but their dissertation. Recipients must spend 6 months to a year as part of the history office at NASA while doing their research project. Applicants must be U.S. citizens. Visit web site or send a self-addressed, stamped envelope for an application. Deadline: February 1.

419. (H)
J. Franklin Jameson Fellowship

Awards of $9,000 to graduate students and postdoctoral fellows to support significant scholarly research in American history in the collections of the Library of Congress for 1 semester or longer. Visit web site or send a self-addressed, stamped envelope for an application. Deadline: March 15.

420. (H)
Littleton-Griswold Grants

5 to 7 awards of $1,000 to graduate students or postgraduate students to support research project on American legal history and the field of law and society. Applicant should join AHA before applying. Visit web site or send a self-addressed, stamped envelope for an application. Deadline: February 1.

421. (H)
Michael Kraus Research Award Grant

1 award of $800 to a graduate or postgraduate student. This is a cash award for most deserving research proposal relating to work in progress on American colonial history with reference to intercultural aspects of American and European relations. Applicants should join AHA before applying. Visit web site or send a self-addressed, stamped envelope for an application. Deadline: February 1.

422. (H)
Published Book Awards

Awards ranging from $500 to $1,000 to individuals who have already published books on historical subjects ranging from 17th-century European history to the history of the feminist movement. This is not a contest and not for high school students. The award is given to books that have already been published. Deadline: May 15.

423. (S)
American Holistic Nurses Association
Charlotte McGuire Scholarship
P.O. Box 2130
Flagstaff, AZ 86003–2130
(800) 278–2462
http://www.ahna.org

1 award of $500 to a graduate student in an accredited nursing program in holistic health or alternative modalities. Preference is given to students with experience in holistic health care or alternative health practices. Applicants must be members of AHNA, with

nursing prerequisites completed, and have at least a 3.0 GPA on a 4.0 scale. Request applications after January 1. Deadline: March 15.

424. (SS)

American Hotel & Lodging Educational Foundation Rama Scholarship for the American Dream

1201 New York Avenue, N.W., Suite 600
Washington, DC 20005–3931
(202) 289–3100
http://www.ahlef.org

Scholarships of varying amounts to graduate and undergraduate students in hospitality management. Money is distributed through 15 participating schools that select the recipients. Preference is given to students of Asian-Indian descent, members of minority groups, and JHM Hotel employees. Applications must be obtained in the dean's office of participating schools. Information regarding the program and a list of participating schools can be found on the web site. Deadline: varies by school.

425. (A, H, S, SS)

American Indian Graduate Center

4520 Montgomery Boulevard, N.E., Suite 1-B
Albuquerque, NM 87109
(505) 881–4584
(800) 628–1920
http://www.aigc.com

From 250 to 300 scholarships of up to $10,000 to graduate and doctoral students who are ¼ or more American Indian or Alaska native for any area of study. Based on career statement, scholastic ability, and leadership qualities. Those students whose intent is to return to the Indian communities upon degree completion are given preferential consideration. Visit web site or send a self-addressed, stamped envelope for an application. Deadline: none specified.

426. (A, H, S, SS)

American Indian Graduate Fellowship Program Graduate Fellowships

Office of Indian Education
U.S. Department of Education
400 Maryland Avenue, S.W.
Room 3W111, FOB-6

Washington, DC 20202–6335
(202) 260–3774
http://www.ed.gov/offices/OESE/oie

Approximately 600 fellowship awards of up to $5,500 to graduate and professional school students in all areas of study. Must be Native Americans enrolled in a federally recognized tribe or Alaska native group. Must be accepted to or enrolled in a master's or doctoral program in an accredited U.S. institution. Send a self-addressed, stamped envelope for more information and an application to above address or to: American Indian Graduate Center, 4520 Montgomery Boulevard, N.E., Suite 1-B, Albuquerque, NM 87109. Deadline: April 30.

427. (S, SS)

American Indian Science & Engineering Society (AISES)

5661 Airport Boulevard
Boulder, CO 80301–2339
(303) 939–0023, ext. 29
http://www.colorado.edu/AISES/intern

Summer internships providing salaries, benefits, and round-trip travel expenses to American Indian full-time graduate or undergraduate (sophomore, junior, and senior) students who are preparing for careers in science, technology, engineering, business, and other academic areas. Though AISES arranges the housing for interns working in Washington, DC, interns are responsible for their lodging costs. Internships are conducted nationwide. Applicants must have at least a 2.5 GPA on a 4.0 scale, be enrolled in an accredited college or university, and be a U.S. citizen. Deadline: mid-February.

(H, SS)

American Institute for Contemporary German Studies

1400 16th Street, Suite 420,
Washington, DC 20036–9312
(202) 332–9312
http://www.aicgs.org

428. (H, SS)

DAAD-AICGS Summer Grant

Varying numbers of grants providing full tuition, room, partial board, and excursions to doctoral candidates and recent doctoral graduates (within 2 previous years) to participate in a 6-week summer research/study program in the German language, or historical, cultural, and economic aspects of contemporary Germany, at the University of Regensburg in Germany. Must be between the ages of 18 and 32, have taken at least 2 years of college-level German, and be either U.S. or Canadian citizens. Students with previous study experience in Germany are ineligible. Selection based on academic achievement. For information and application visit web site. Deadline: April 15.

429. (H, SS)
Research Fellowship Program

Varying numbers of research grants of varying amounts providing monthly stipends, a monthly research budget, and 1 round-trip airfare to graduate students, doctoral candidates, and recent doctoral recipients to conduct research in postwar Germany. Fellowships fund stays ranging from 1 to 4 months. Project proposals should address one or more of the Institute's 5 research and programming areas. For information and application visit web site. Deadline: none specified.

430. (SS)
American Institute for Economic Research
AIER Summer Fellowship
P.O. Box 100
Great Barrington, MA 01230
(413) 528–1216
http://www.aier.org

Fellowships providing a $450-per-month stipend for an 8-week summer program, plus room and board, are open to graduate students and undergraduate seniors in economics or an affiliated program (e.g., law and economics, economic history). Preference given to graduate students and U.S. citizens. Based on academic record, recent paper, and recommendations. Visit web site or send a self-addressed, stamped envelope for an application. Deadline: March 31.

(H, SS)
American Institute for Sri Lanka Studies
5/22 Suleiman Terrace
Colombo 5, Sri Lanka
074–513706, 508512
http://www.bostonwebco.com/aisls/fellowship.html

431. (H, SS)
AISLS Travel Stipends

Travel grants of $200 to graduate students who present a paper concerning Sri Lanka at the Annual Conference on South Asia. Must be members of AISLS or enrolled in an institution that is a member of AISLS. Visit web site for more information and deadline.

432. (H, SS)
Council of American Overseas Research Centers Fellowship Program

Fellowships providing a stipend of $6,000 and $3,000 for travel expenses to graduate students and scholars to conduct research in Sri Lanka and at least one other country. Must be U.S. citizens. Funded by CAORC. Visit web site for more information and deadline.

433. (H, SS)
International Dissertation Research Fellowships

Fellowships of varying amounts to graduate students to conduct research for a period ranging from 6 to 12 months. There are no citizenship requirements. Administered by the Social Science Research Council. Visit web site for more information and deadline.

(A)
American Institute of Architects, New York Chapter
200 Lexington Avenue, 6th Floor
New York, NY 10016
(212) 683–0023
http://www.aiany.org

434. (A)
Arnold W. Brunner Grant

Research grants of $15,000 to professional architects for advanced study that will contribute to the practice, teaching, or knowledge or the art and science of architecture. Must be U.S. citizens. Traveling fellowships for research are also available. Visit web site or send a self-addressed, stamped envelope for an application. Deadline: November 1.

435. (A)
Douglas Haskell Award

Awards of varying amounts to graduate and undergraduate students enrolled in a professional architecture or related program, such as art history, interior design, or urban studies. Qualified students submit an article, essay, or journal that has been or will soon be published. Deadline: late May.

436. (A)
Stewardson Keefe LeBrun Travel Grants

3 to 5 grants of up to an overall total of $6,000 to individuals who have already obtained a professional degree. The amount of the award is based upon the applicant's travel program and is at the discretion of the jury. This grant is to encourage travel within North America and overseas in furtherance of the architectural education and professional development of the recipients. Must be a member of the AIA New York Chapter. Deadline: late May.

(SS)
American Institute of Certified Public Accountants Scholarships
1211 Avenue of the Americas
New York, NY 10036–8775
(212) 575–7641
http://www.aicpa.org/index.htm

437. (SS)
AICPA/Accountemps Student Scholarship

2 scholarships of $2,500 to graduate and undergraduate students in accounting and business. Must be used for full-time study at an accredited U.S. institution. Must be U.S. citizens. Visit web site for more information. Deadline: April 1.

438. (SS)
Financial Assistance to Minority Beginning Doctoral Candidates

Numerous awards of $5,000 per year for up to 3 years to beginning doctoral minority students who have applied to, or been accepted into, an AACSB-accredited program. Preference is given to high academic performance, CPA holders or candidates, applicants with professional experience, and U.S. citizens. Applicants must be fluent in English. Active doctoral students are not eligible. Deadline: April 1 (U.S. citizens) and March 1 (noncitizens).

439. (SS)
Grants-in-Aid for Doctoral Dissertations in Accounting

5 to 7 awards of $800 per month for a maximum of 12 months to doctoral students at an accredited school that is a member of the American Assembly of Collegiate Schools of Business. Applicant must have approved dissertation topic. Deadline: March 1 (U.S. citizens) and January 15 (noncitizens).

440. (SS)
John L. Carey Scholarships in Accounting

Up to 7 scholarships of $5,000 to undergraduate seniors planning to attend a graduate program in accounting. Must be liberal arts undergraduate majors in an accredited U.S. institution. Renewable for second year. Deadline: April 1.

441. (SS)
Scholarship for Minority Students in Business

1 scholarship of $5,000 to a minority graduate student who is enrolled in a 5-year program in accounting, business administration, finance, or taxation. Must be attending an accredited school that is a member of the American Assembly of Collegiate Schools of Business. Deadline: July 1 and December 1.

(S)
American Institute of Chemical Engineers
3 Park Avenue
New York, NY 10016–5901
(212) 705–7478
http://www.aiche.org

442. (S)
Donald F. & Mildred Topp Othmer National Scholarship Awards

15 scholarships of $1,000 to graduate and undergraduate students majoring in chemical engineering and who are members of AIChE. Selected based on academic achievement and student chapter activities. Each chapter can only nominate 1 member. Deadline: May 7.

443. (S)

Environmental Division Graduate Student Paper Award

Awards of $150, $300, and $450 to graduate students in chemical engineering to recognize outstanding contributions to environmental protection through chemical engineering. Selection is based on student AIChE membership at the time of submission; work must be carried out while a graduate student is enrolled in a university with an accredited chemical engineering program; student must be the primary author; paper must describe original research or design; paper must be suitable for publication and must represent a contribution to environmental protection through the application of chemical engineering. Paper will be judged on quality, technical content, writing, and organization. Deadline: early September.

444. (S)

Minority Affairs Committee Award for Outstanding Scholastic Achievement

1 award of $1,500 to a graduate or undergraduate student in chemical engineering who serves as a model for minority students. Selection based on academic achievement (at least a 3.0 GPA on a 4.0 scale), research contributions, technical presentations, outreach activities, and recommendations. Deadline: April 15.

445. (S)

Process Development Division Student Paper Award

1 award of $200, plus assistance to cover expenses associated with attending the Annual AIChE Meeting, to a graduate or undergraduate student who prepares the best technical paper to describe the results of process development related studies within chemical engineering. Must be a student member of AIChE. Deadline: June 15.

446. (S)

SACHE Student Design Competition for Safety in Design

1 award of $200 for an individual and 1 award of $300 for team design to graduate and undergraduate students. The contest typifies a real working, chemical engineering design situation that requires a wide range of skills in calculation and evaluation of both technical data and economic factors that apply appropriate principles of chemical process safety. Deadline: June 1.

447. (S)

Separations Division Graduate Student Research Award

6 awards of $300 to graduate students in each of the following areas: adsorption and ion exchange, crystallization and evaporation, distillation and absorption, extraction, fluid-particle separations, and membrane-based separations. Papers must contribute to separation fundamentals or applications in the specific area, and report on research, investigation, or design, and be part of the student's work for a graduate degree, and student must be the primary author. Judged on technical content, quality of writing, and organization. Must be student members of AIChE. Deadline: August 1.

448. (S)

Ted Peterson Student Paper Award

1 award of $1,500 to a graduate or undergraduate student in chemical engineering. Award recognizes a published work on the application of computing and systems technology to chemical engineering. The work must have been done by the individual while pursuing a graduate or undergraduate degree in chemical engineering. Deadline: April 15.

449. (S)

American Institute of Professional Geologists

ATTN: Education Committee Chair
8703 Yates Drive, Suite 200
Westminster, CO 80031–3681
(303) 412–6205
http://www.aipg.org
aipg@aipg.org

Varying numbers of scholarships of $1,000 to graduate and undergraduate students majoring in geology or earth science. Must attend an accredited U.S. institute and be a student member of AIPG. Recipients must prepare a 600- to 800-word article for publication in *The Professional Geologist* related to a timely professional issue. Visit web site for more information. Deadline: February 15.

American Institute of Indian Studies
c/o University of Chicago
1130 East 59th Street
Chicago, IL 60637
(773) 702–8638
http://www.indiastudies.org
aiis@uchicago.edu

450. (SS)
AIIS Junior Fellowships

Doctoral fellowships of up to $7,000 to foreign nationals in residence at U.S. colleges. Awards are open to specialists in Indian studies who wish to study in India to complete their doctoral degree requirements. Visit web site or send a self-addressed, stamped envelope for an application. Deadline: July 1.

451. (SS)
AIIS 9-Month Language Program

12 fellowships of $3,000, plus travel expenses to India, to graduate students with a minimum of 2 years (240 classroom hours) in a language of India. Visit web site or send a self-addressed, stamped envelope for an application. Deadline: January.

452. (SS)
Professional Development Awards

Varying numbers of fellowships of $11,000, plus travel, to doctoral students to conduct professional study in India. Open to U.S. citizens or foreign nationals in residence at U.S. institutions. Deadline: July 1.

453. (SS)
Senior Performing and Creative Arts Fellowships

Awards of varying amounts to accomplished practitioners of the performing arts of India and creative artists who demonstrate that study in India would enhance their skills, develop their capabilities to teach or perform in the U.S., enhance American involvement with India's artistic traditions, and strengthen links with peers in India. Fellowships are for periods of 6 to 9 months. Visit web site for more information. Deadline: July 1.

454. (SS)
Senior Research Fellowships

40 short-term and 50 long-term awards ranging from $6,000 to $11,000, plus travel expenses, to postdoctoral fellows. Open to U.S. citizens or foreign nationals in residence at U.S. institutions. Fellows must have Ph.D. and must agree to be formally affiliated with an Indian university while in India. Deadline: July 1.

(H, SS)

American Institute of Pakistan Studies
Wake Forest University
P.O. Box 7568
Winston-Salem, NC 27109
(910) 758–5453
aips@wfu.edu

455. (H, SS)
Graduate Student Fellowships

4 or more 2- to 4-month fellowships of up to $2,500 for travel expenses, plus a monthly stipend of $1,750, to graduate students who have yet to complete doctoral course work. Students must have completed one or more years of graduate study toward a master's or doctoral degree and demonstrate interest in topics related to Pakistan studies. Must be a U.S. citizen. Deadline: February 1.

456. (H, SS)
Postdoctoral Fellowships

2 or more 2- to 9-month fellowships of up to $2,500 for travel expenses, and a monthly stipend of $3,550, to postdoctoral scholars. Topics should contribute to scholarship in Pakistan studies. Must be a U.S. citizen. Deadline: February 1.

457. (H, SS)
Predoctoral Fellowships

4 or more 4- to 9-month fellowships of up to $2,500 for travel expenses, and a monthly stipend of $2,450, to predoctoral students (ABD). Topics should contribute to the completion of a dissertation on a topic related to Pakistan studies. Must be U.S. citizens. Deadline: February 1.

458. (H, SS)

American Institute of Polish Culture, Inc.
Scholarships
ATTN: Chairman Scholarship Committee
1440 79th Street Causeway, Suite 117
Miami, FL 33141
(305) 864–2349
http://www.ampolinstitute.org/

12 to 15 scholarships of $1,000 to full-time graduate or undergraduate students majoring in journalism, communications, or public relations at any accredited U.S. institute. Preference given to Polish-American students. Selection is based on achievement, talent, and involvement in public life. Awards renewable with satisfactory academic progress. Visit web site or send a self-addressed, stamped envelope for an application. Deadline: March 14.

(H, SS)

American Jewish Archives
3101 Clifton Avenue
Cincinnati, OH 45220
(513) 221–1875
http://www.americanjewisharchives.org

459. (H, SS)

Dissertation & Postdoctoral Research Fellowships

Fellowships ranging from $1,000 to $3,000 to postdoctoral candidates or persons at the dissertation stage for up to 3 months of research or writing at the American Jewish Archives during the stipend year. Must be studying American Jewish aspects of folklore, history, languages, literatures and linguistics, liberal studies, philosophy, religion, political science, public policy, sociology, anthropology, archeology, women's studies, and interdisciplinary topics in the humanities and social sciences, education, and international affairs. Visit web site or send a self-addressed, stamped envelope for an application. Deadline: April 1.

460. (H, SS)

Lowenstein-Wiener Summer Fellowship Awards in American Jewish Studies

5 to 8 fellowships providing a stipend of $1,000 to doctoral candidates and stipends of $2,000 to post-doctoral candidates studying American Jewish aspects of folklore, history, languages, literatures and linguistics, liberal studies, philosophy, religion, political science, public policy, sociology, anthropology, archeology, women's studies, and interdisciplinary topics in the humanities and social sciences, education, and international affairs. Doctoral candidates must be at the dissertation stage. Award is for 1 month of research or writing at the American Jewish Archives during the stipend year. Selection based on proposed research. Visit web site for more information. Deadline: April 1.

461. (H)

Marcus Center Fellowships

11 awards of varying amounts to doctoral candidates, postdoctoral fellows, and senior or independent scholars. Fellowships are for month-long stays to do research and writing at the Jacob Rader Marcus Center. Must be conducting serious research in some area relating to the history of North American Jewry. For specific submission guidelines, visit web site. Deadline: March 18.

462. (H)

American Jewish Historical Society
Fellowships
2 Thornton Road
Waltham, MA 02154
(781) 891–8110
http://www.ajhs.org

Fellowships of varying amounts to full-time graduate students. Must be used for study on American Jewish history at an accredited institution. No religious affiliation is required. Research fellowships are also available at Brandeis University. Visit web site or send a self-addressed, stamped envelope for information and an application. Deadline: none.

463. (SS)

American Judicative Society
Internship Program
ATTN: Personnel Coordinator
180 North Michigan Avenue, Suite 600
Chicago, IL 60601
(312) 558–6900
http://www.ajs.org

6 internships lasting 3 months to graduate and undergraduate students, mid-career persons, persons with career work experience, and persons reentering the work force. Open to areas of English, journalism, justice studies, political science, pre-law, law, or public policy majors. Applicants should have excellent written and oral communication skills and should have an interest in research and the courts. Interns work on a variety of projects, such as producing instructional videotapes, programs on judicial selection, conduct and ethics in the courts and policy making based on knowledge and judicial reform, as well as conduct research, write, and analyze data. Programs would be suitable for young lawyers, judges, and citizens. The positions can be part- or full-time, with openings year-round. Applicants should submit a letter detailing interests, a resume, references, and writing sample. Deadline: open.

464. (S)
American Kinesiotherapy Association Scholarships
Scholarship and Grant-in-Aid Committee
Time Werner, RKT
15312 142nd Court, S.W.
Miami, FL 33177
(800) 296–2582
written queries only
http://www.akta.org

Grants-in-aid of up to $100 to registered kinesiologists working in some area of rehabilitation service. Must be a member of AKTA. Send a self-addressed, stamped envelope for an application. Deadline: May 1.

465. (A, H, S, SS)
American Legion Auxiliary, Illinois
Attn: Adjutant
P.O. Box 2910
Bloomington, IL 61702
(309) 663–0361
http://www.legion-aux.org/contact_us

1 scholarship of $800 and 1 scholarship of $1,200 for graduate or undergraduate students who are veterans (WWI, WWII, Korea, Vietnam, or Desert Storm) or dependent children of veterans who must have financial assistance to continue their education. May be used for any area of study. Must have resided in Illinois for at least 3 years. For more information, visit web site. Deadline: March 15.

466. (S)
American Legion Education Program
George B. Boland Nurses Scholarship Committee
ATTN: Eight and Forty Scholarships
Box 1055
Indianapolis, IN 46204
http://www.legion.org/content-site-map

Scholarships of $2,500 to help registered nurses obtain their master's or doctorate in nursing sciences. Applicants must have interest in pursuing a full-time career in lung and respiratory disease prevention and treatment. The American Legion also provides assistance to nursing students in Arizona, Arkansas, California, Georgia, Idaho, Illinois, Iowa, Kansas, Michigan, Minnesota, Nebraska, Nevada, New Hampshire, New Jersey, New York, Ohio, Oregon, South Dakota, Texas, Washington, Wisconsin, and Wyoming. For more information, visit web site or contact local post. Deadline: May 15.

(SS)
American Library Association
ATTN: Staff Liaison
50 East Huron Street
Chicago, IL 60611
(800) 545–2433, ext. 4277
(312) 944–6780
http://www.ala.org

467. (SS)
AASL Collaborative School Library Media Award

1 award of $2,500 to a school library media specialist to work or execute a project, event, or program to further information literacy, independent learning, and social responsibility using resources of the school library media center. Award is funded by the American Association of School Librarians and Sagebrush Corporation. For specific guidelines, visit web site. Deadline: February 3.

468. (SS)
AASL/Highsmith Research Grant

1 grant of up to $5,000 or 2 grants of $2,500 to one or more school library media specialists, library educators or library information science or education professors to conduct innovative research aimed at measuring and evaluating the effect of school library

media programs on learning and education. Visit web site for specific guidelines or contact aaas@ala.org. Deadline: February 3.

469. (SS)
Association for Library Science to Children of the American Library Association Melcher Scholarships

Scholarships of up to $5,000 to graduate students accepted to a program in children's librarianship. Must attend an ALA-accredited library education program. Must be a U.S. or Canadian citizen. Deadline: March 1.

470. (SS)
Baker and Taylor Scholarship Grants

2 scholarships of $1,000 to attend the ALA Annual Conference. Open to members of the Young Adult Library Services Association (YALSA) who have between 1 and 10 years experience working with teenagers. Visit web site for specific guidelines and an application. Deadline: December 1.

471. (SS)
Bound to Stay Bound Books Scholarship

4 scholarships of up to $6,000 to graduate students in library science who plan to work in the area of library service to children. The work may be serving children, up to and including age 14, in any type of library. Must be a U.S. or Canadian citizen or legal permanent resident and enrolled in an ALA-accredited graduate program. Selection based on academic achievement, leadership, commitment to library science. A personal statement and 3 letters of recommendation are required. Visit web site for more information. Deadline: March 1.

472. (SS)
BRASS Thomson Financial Student Travel Award

1 cash award of $1,000 to a graduate student enrolled in an ALA-accredited master's degree program to attend the ALA Annual Conference. Applicant should have demonstrated an interest in a career as a business reference librarian. Must submit a statement stating their academic and professional achievements and reasons for choosing business librarianship as a profession, a transcript, and 3 letters of reference. Deadline: none specified.

473. (SS)
Century Scholarship

1 award of $2,500 to a student enrolled in, or admitted to, an ALA-accredited program. The award will fund services or accommodations that are either not provided by law or otherwise by the university, enabling the student to successfully complete the course of study for a master's or doctorate in library or information studies profession. Visit web site for more information and application. Deadline: March 1.

474. (SS)
Christopher Hoy/ERT Scholarship

1 scholarship of $3,000 to graduate students in library science. Must not have completed more than 12 hours toward a master's degree; must be a U.S. or Canadian citizen or legal permanent resident and enrolled in an ALA-accredited graduate program. Selection based on academic achievement, leadership, commitment to library science, and a personal statement. Deadline: March 1.

475. (SS)
Coutts Nijhoff International

1 grant of up to 4,500 Euros (or U.S. equivalent) to a librarian employed in a university, college, community college, or research library to conduct research pertaining to Western European studies, librarianship, or the book trade. Selection will be based on the proposed project as a contribution to the study of the acquisition, organization, or use of library materials from or relating to Western Europe. Visit web site for more information.

476. (SS)
Dain Library History Dissertation Award

Awards of $500 to doctoral students in library and information science for an outstanding dissertation in the general area of library history. The work should embody original research on a significant topic relating to the history of books, libraries, librarianship, or information science. Awarded only on odd-numbered years. Selection based on clear definition of the research questions and/or hypothesis, use of appropriate source materials, depth of research, superior quality of writing, ability to place the subject within its broader historical context, and significance of the conclusions. Deadline: January 31.

477. (SS)
David H. Clift Scholarship Program

Scholarships of $3,000 to graduate students enrolled in, or accepted to, an ALA-accredited graduate library education program. Selection based on academic achievement, leadership abilities, and commitment to library career. Must be a U.S. or Canadian citizen or legal resident. For more information, visit web site or send a self-addressed, stamped envelope for details. Deadline: March 1.

478. (SS)
Doctoral Dissertation Fellowship

1 award of $1,500 to a doctoral student in the academic librarianship area. Must have completed all course work and had a dissertation proposal accepted by the institution. Student doesn't need to be a member of ACLR. Selection is judged on the potential significance of the research to the field of academic librarianship, validity of the methodology and proposed method of analysis, originality and creativity, clarity and completeness of the proposal, presentation of a convincing plan for completion, and evidence of a continuing interest in scholarship. Deadline: early December.

479. (SS)
Frances Henne Award

1 award of $1,250 to a school library media specialist to attend an AASL conference or an ALA Annual Conference for the first time. Applicants must be an AASL member. Selection based on demonstrated leadership qualities with students, teachers, and administrators. Deadline: February 3.

480. (SS)
Frederic G. Melcher Scholarship

2 scholarships of $6,000 to graduate students who are pursuing an M.L.S. degree and who plan to work in children's librarianship. This work may be serving children, up to and including age 14, in any type of library. Must be a U.S. or Canadian citizen or legal permanent resident and enrolled in an ALA-accredited graduate program. Selection based on academic achievement, leadership, commitment to library science, 3 letters of recommendation, and a personal statement. Visit web site for more information. Deadline: March 1.

481. (SS)
Hewins Scholarship Program
http://www.hartfordpl.lib.ct.us/

Scholarships of $4,000 to students accepted to, or enrolled in, a graduate program in a library school accredited by the ALA. Must intend to specialize in children's librarianship. Must be a U.S. citizen or legal resident. Preference given to students pursuing a career in public library service. Deadline: March 1.

482. (SS)
Jesse H. Shera Award for Excellence in Doctoral Research

2 awards of $500 to doctoral students for dissertation research. Papers must represent completed research not previously published and that relates in at least a general way to library and information studies. For submission guidelines, visit web site. Deadline: mid-February.

483. (SS)
Justin Winsor Prize for Library History Essay

1 cash award of $500 for a previously unpublished manuscript that embodies original historical research on a significant topic in library history. For specific submission guidelines, visit web site. Deadline: January 31.

484. (SS)
Information Technology Pathfinder Award

1 award each of $1,000 to a school library media specialist and $500 to the library in 2 categories (elementary and secondary). Awarded based on demonstrated vision and leadership through the use of information technology to build lifelong learners. Applicants must be AASL members. For information and application, visit web site. Deadline: February 3.

485. (SS)
LITA/Christian Larew Memorial Scholarship in Library and Information Technology

1 award of $3,000 to a qualified individual to enter graduate work in the library and information technology field. Selection will be based on a statement indicating the nature of library experience and their

view on what he/she can bring to the profession, emphasizing experience indicating a potential for leadership and commitment to library automation, and letters of reference. Must not have completed more than 12 hours toward a master's degree and be a U.S. or Canadian citizen or legal permanent resident enrolled in an ALA-accredited graduate program. Economic need is considered when all other criteria are equal. Deadline: March 1.

486. (SS)
LITA/Endeavor Student Writing Award

1 award of $1,000 and a certificate to a graduate student in a library and information studies program based on the best unpublished manuscript on a topic in the area of libraries and information studies. Recognizes superior student writing and seeks to enhance the professional development of students through publication of the winning article in LITA's referred journal. Deadline: February 28.

487. (SS)
LITA/LSSI Minority Scholarship in Library and Information Technology

1 award of $2,500 to a minority student for work toward a master's degree in library science. Must be employed in the library or automation field, plan to follow a career in that field, and demonstrate leadership and potential in, and a strong commitment to, the use of automated systems in libraries. Selection will be based on a statement indicating the nature of library experience and their view on what he/she can bring to the profession. Must not have completed more than 12 hours toward a master's degree and be a U.S. or Canadian citizen or legal permanent resident enrolled in an ALA-accredited graduate program. Economic need is considered when all other criteria are equal. Deadline: March 1.

488. (SS)
LITA/OCLC Minority Scholarship in Library and Information Technology

1 award of $3,000 to a minority student for work toward a master's degree in library science. Must be employed in the library or automation field, plan to follow a career in that field, and demonstrate potential in, and a strong commitment to, the use of auto-

mated systems in libraries. Must be a U.S. or Canadian citizen or legal permanent resident enrolled in an ALA-accredited graduate program. Deadline: March 1.

489. (SS)
LITA/SIRSI Scholarship in Library and Information Technology

1 award of $2,500 to a student for work toward a master's degree in library science. Must be employed in the library or automation field, plan to follow a career in that field, and demonstrate potential in, and a strong commitment to, the use of automated systems in libraries. Selection will be based on a statement indicating the nature of library experience and their view on what he/she can bring to the profession, emphasizing experience that indicates a potential for leadership and commitment to library automation, and letters of reference. Must not have completed more than 12 hours toward a master's degree and be a U.S. or Canadian citizen or legal permanent resident enrolled in an ALA-accredited graduate program. Economic need is considered when all other criteria are equal. Deadline: March 1.

490. (SS)
Marshall Cavendish Scholarship

1 scholarship of $3,000 to a graduate student in library science. Must not have completed more than 12 hours toward a master's degree and be a U.S. or Canadian citizen or legal permanent resident enrolled in an ALA-accredited graduate program. Selection based on academic achievement, leadership, commitment to library science, and a personal statement. Deadline: March 1.

491. (SS)
Mary V. Gaver Scholarship

1 scholarship of $3,000 to a graduate student who plans to specialize in the field of library youth services. Must not have completed more than 12 hours toward a master's degree and be a U.S. or Canadian citizen or legal permanent resident enrolled in an ALA-accredited graduate program. Selection based on academic achievement, leadership, commitment to library science, 3 letters of recommendation, and a personal statement. Visit web site for more information. Deadline: March 1.

492. (SS)
Miriam L. Hornback Scholarship

1 scholarship of $3,000 to a graduate student who is library support staff currently working in a library. Must not have completed more than 12 hours toward a master's degree and be a U.S. or Canadian citizen or legal permanent resident enrolled in an ALA-accredited graduate program. Selection based on academic achievement, leadership, commitment to library science, 3 letters of recommendation, and a personal statement. Visit web site for more information. Deadline: March 1.

493. (SS)
New Members Round Table (NMRT) EBSCO Scholarship

1 scholarship of $1,000 to a graduate student in library science. Must not have completed more than 12 hours toward a master's degree and be a U.S. or Canadian citizen or legal permanent resident enrolled in an ALA-accredited graduate program. Selection based on academic achievement, leadership, commitment to library science, and a personal statement. Deadline: March 1.

494. (SS)
Shirley Olofson Memorial Award

1 award of $1,000 to help defray costs to attend the ALA Annual Conference, open to members of ALA and NMRT. Must be active within the library profession, show promise or activity in the area of professional development, have valid financial need, and have attended no more than 5 ALA Annual Conferences. Visit web site for more information.

495. (SS)
Spectrum Initiative Awards

50 scholarships of $5,000 to minority graduate students in library and information studies. Applicants must not have completed more than 12 hours toward a master's degree and be a U.S. or Canadian citizen or legal permanent resident enrolled in an ALA-accredited graduate program. Selection based on academic achievement, leadership, commitment to library science, and a personal statement. Deadline: March 1.

496. (SS)
3M/NMRT Professional Development Grant

1 grant providing round-trip airfare, lodging, conference registration fees, and incidental expenses to an ALA member within the first 10 years of his/her membership. Selection is based on potential for future involvement within NMRT. Must be a member of ALA and NMRT. Visit web site for more information and contact information. Deadline: none specified.

497. (SS)
Tom & Roberta Drewers Scholarship

1 scholarship of $3,000 to a graduate student in library science. Must not have completed more than 12 hours toward a master's degree and be a U.S. or Canadian citizen or legal permanent resident enrolled in an ALA-accredited graduate program. Selection based on academic achievement, leadership, commitment to library science, and a personal statement. Deadline: March 1.

498. (SS)
Tony B. Leisner Scholarship

1 scholarship of $3,000 to a graduate student who is library support staff and currently working in a library. Must not have completed more than 12 hours toward a master's degree and be a U.S. or Canadian citizen or legal permanent resident enrolled in an ALA-accredited graduate program. Selection based on academic achievement, leadership, commitment to library science, 3 letters of recommendation, and a personal statement. Visit web site for more information. Deadline: March 1.

499. (SS)
WNBA-Ann Heidreder Eastman Grant

1 award ranging from $500 to $750 to a librarian with a master's in library science or its equivalent to participate in an intensive institute devoted to aspects of publishing as a profession or to provide reimbursement for study completed within the past year. Applicant must provide a personal statement of no more than 300 words concerning the ongoing interest in the publishing process and how a better understanding of this process would enhance the applicant's library career. For specific guidelines, visit web site. Deadline: November 3.

500. (S)

American Liver Foundation

Student Research Fellowships

75 Maiden Lane, Suite 603

New York, NY 10038

(800) 465–4837

http://www.liverfoundation.org

Varying numbers of 3-month awards of $2,500 to medical or veterinary students or doctoral candidates to conduct medical research. The award is given to encourage and expose students to research and encourage them to consider liver research as a career option. Deadline: December 15.

(S)

American Lung Association

Medical Affairs Division

1740 Broadway

New York, NY 10019–4374

(212) 315–8700

http://www.lungusa.org

501. (S)

Career Investigator Awards

Awards of $35,000 to physician investigators who are making the transition from junior to mid-level faculty. Must be conducting research in areas related to lung disease. Pulmonary-related applications from other scientists and postdoctoral students may be considered. Must be U.S. or Canadian citizens or permanent U.S. residents at an U.S. institution. Renewable for up to 2 years. For more information, visit web site or send a self-addressed, stamped envelope. Deadline: October 1.

502. (S)

Dalsemer Research Scholar Award

Awards of up to $25,000 to physicians who have completed graduate training in pulmonary disease and are beginning a faculty track in a U.S. school of medicine. Must be a U.S. or Canadian citizen or a permanent U.S. resident training at a U.S. institution. Renewable for 1 year. For more information, visit web site or send a self-addressed, stamped envelope. Deadline: November 1.

503. (S)

Nursing Research Training Award

Awards of up to $11,000 to professional nurses with a master's degree who are enrolled in a full-time doctoral program related to lung disease. Priority given to individuals pursuing a career in teaching. Must be a U.S. or Canadian citizen or permanent resident of the U.S. who is training in a U.S. institution. Renewable for 1 year. For more information, visit web site or send a self-addressed, stamped envelope. Deadline: October 1.

504. (S)

Research Grants

Awards of up to $25,000 to postdoctoral students who are new or not already established investigators. Targeted for instructors or assistant professors who have completed at least 2 years of research training in lung disease. Open to U.S. or Canadian citizens or permanent residents training in a U.S. institution. Research grants may be for laboratory, clinical, epidemiological, social, or other areas of investigation relevant to lung disease. For more information, visit web site or send a self-addressed, stamped envelope. Deadline: November 1.

505. (S)

Research Training Fellowships

Awards of up to $32,500 to individuals with either an M.D., D.O., Ph.D., Sc.D., or comparable qualifications who are seeking further training as scientific investigators in lung biology and disease. May be renewed with annual review. For more information, visit web site or send a self-addressed, stamped envelope. Deadline: October 1.

506. (SS)

American Management Association

Internships

ATTN: Coordinator

1601 Broadway

New York, NY 10019

(212) 586–8100

http://www.amanet.org/index.htm

60 12-week internships providing $170 per week to graduate students, recent college graduates, undergraduates, high school graduates, and high school students. International students may also apply. The Association

provides seminars on management issues, creates videos on subjects such as negotiating skills and communications, and publishes a variety of periodicals covering management subjects. Interns work in training and development, human resources, publishing, general management, marketing, international management market research, and sales and marketing. Applicants must submit a résumé, cover letter, and recommendations (1 academic and 1 employment). Deadline: rolling.

507. (S)
American Mathematical Society
Centennial Fellowships
201 Charles Street
Providence, RI 02940–6248
(800) 321–4AMS
http://www.ams.org

Fellowships of $43,900 to established mathematicians to conduct research. Applicants must be 7 to 12 years past the doctoral degree and have not had extensive postdoctoral research support. Must be a citizen or legal resident of a North American country. For more information, visit web site or send a self-addressed, stamped envelope. Deadline: December 1.

508. (S)
American Medical Association
Rock Sleyster Memorial Scholarship Program
Department of Undergraduate Evaluation
515 N State Street
Chicago, IL 60610
(800) AMA–3211
(312) 464–5000
http://www.ama-assn.org

Scholarships of varying amounts to fourth-year medical students who are planning to specialize in psychiatry. Awards based on academic achievement, financial need, and interest in psychiatry. For more information, visit web site or send a self-addressed, stamped envelope. Deadline: none specified.

509. (S)
American Medical Student Association
Health Promotion and Disease Prevention Program (HPDP)
1902 Association Drive
Reston, VA 20191–1502

(800) 767–2266
(713) 620–6600
http://www.amsa.org

Numerous 6- to 8-week health care projects provide a stipend and relocation travel allowance to first- and second-year medical students. Students are placed in federally funded community and migrant health centers and in health care projects for the homeless. School credit might be provided for the preclinical experience. Contact above address or visit web site for an application. Deadline: none specified.

(A, H, S, SS)
American Mensa Education and Research Foundation
contact local chapter
http://www.usmensa.org

510. (A)
Ashley Zanca Honorary Scholarship

1 scholarship of $500 to graduate and undergraduate students for study in the arts. Award based on essay. For an application, visit web site to obtain local chapter. Please include a self-addressed, stamped envelope. Request application after October 1. Deadline: mid- to late January.

511. (A, H, S, SS)
Rita Levine Memorial Scholarship

1 scholarship of $500 to a female returning to school after an absence of 7 or more years who is enrolled, for the academic year following the award, in a graduate or undergraduate degree program in an accredited U.S. college or university. It is also available to women who are already in college but who had at least 7 years between their last time in school and returning to college. Based on a 550-word essay that describes the applicant's career, vocational, or academic goal toward which the scholarship is to provide aid. You only have to request and submit one Mensa application. You will be considered for all scholarships to which you qualify. You do not need to be a member or qualify to be a member of Mensa to apply. For more information on local chapters, visit web site. When requesting an application, please include a self-addressed, stamped envelope. Request application after October 1. Deadline: mid- to late January, may vary.

512. (A, H, S, SS)
Scholarship Program

Numerous scholarships of varying amounts ranging from $200 to $1,000 to graduate or professional school students, undergraduates, or high school seniors. Award is based on a 550-word essay. Request and submit 1 Mensa application. You will be considered for all scholarships for which you qualify. You do not need to be a member or qualify to be a member of Mensa to apply to their scholarships. When requesting an application, please include a self-addressed, stamped envelope. Request application after October 1. Deadline: mid- to late January, may vary.

(S)
American Meteorological Society Awards

45 Beacon Street   1120 G Street, N.W., Suite 800
Boston, MA 02108–3693   Washington, DC 2005–3826
(617) 227–2425   (202) 737–9000
http://www.ametsoc.org/AMS/

513. (S)
AMS/Industry/Government Graduate Fellowships

Fellowships of $15,000 for a 9-month period to graduate students entering first year of study in chemistry, computer sciences, engineering, environmental sciences, mathematics, or physics and who intend to pursue a career in the atmospheric, oceanic, or hydrologic sciences. Selection based on undergraduate work. Visit web site for more information, application, and deadline. Deadline: none specified.

514. (S)
Congressional Science Fellowship

Up to 35 fellowships providing a stipend of $50,000 and up to $10,000 for moving, travel, and other expenses to doctoral candidates and postdoctoral fellows or individuals with equivalent in atmospheric or related sciences. Must be U.S. citizen. Recipients spend a year working for a member of Congress or a congressional committee on science policy issues. Deadline: February 1.

515. (S)
Father James B. Macelwane Annual Awards

Awards of $300, $200, and $100 are provided by the Weather Corp. of America to honor the world-renowned geophysicist this competition is named for. Awards are given to stimulate interest in meteorology. Based on an original paper concerning some aspect of atmospheric science. Open to all graduate and undergraduate students who are attending college in North, Central or South America. For more information, visit web site or send a self-addressed, stamped envelope. Deadline: June 15.

516. (S)
Graduate Fellowship in the History of Science

1 award of $15,000 to a graduate student to complete a dissertation on the history of the atmospheric, or related oceanic or hydrologic, sciences. Award must be used at a location away from the student's institution with approval of thesis advisor. The goal of the fellowship is to generate a dissertation topic and to foster close working relations between historians and scientists. Visit web site for submission guidelines and application. Deadline: late February.

517. (S)
Student Travel Opportunities

Awards of varying amounts to graduate students to attend the AMS Annual Meeting. Information and application available on web site.

(S)
American Museum of Natural History

Central Park West at 79th Street
New York, NY 10024–5192
(212) 769–5000
http://www.amnh.org

518. (S)
Frank M. Chapman Fund

Grants of varying amounts up to $2,000 to graduate and postdoctoral students to conduct ornithological, marine biology, natural history, or wildlife conservation research. The research may be conducted anywhere on the North American continent, including trips to study the collections at the American Museum of Natural History, or for work at any of the Museum's field stations. Awards are not meant to cover academic study. Send a self-addressed, stamped envelope for an application. Deadline: February 15.

519. (S)
Lerner Fund for Marine Research

Grants of varying amounts to graduate and postdoctoral students to conduct marine biology research. The research may be conducted anywhere on the North American continent, including trips to study the collections at the American Museum of Natural History, or for work at any of the Museum's field stations. Awards are not meant to cover academic study. Send a self-addressed, stamped envelope for an application. Deadline: February 15.

520. (S)
Theodore Roosevelt Memorial Fund Grant

Grants ranging from $200 to $2,000 to graduate students to conduct natural history research or wildlife conservation. The research may be conducted anywhere on the North American continent, including trips to study the collections at the American Museum of Natural History, or for work at any of the Museum's field stations. Awards are not meant to cover academic study. Send a self-addressed, stamped envelope for an application. Deadline: February 15.

(A, H)
American Musicological Society
201 South 34th Street
Philadelphia, PA 19104–6313
(215) 898–8698
http://www.ams–net.org

521. (A)
Alfred Einstein Award

1 cash award to a doctoral fellow or scholar in the early stages of his/her career. Nominations and self-nominations may include eligible authors. Visit web site for specific guidelines and contact information. Deadline: June 1.

522. (A, H)
Dissertation Fellowships

Varying numbers of fellowships of $14,000 to doctoral candidates who have completed all course work and will use the award to fund dissertation writing in musicology. Award is for 1 year. Visit web site for specific submission guidelines. Deadline: January 15.

523. (A, H)
Howard Mayer Brown Fellowship

1 fellowship providing a one-time, 12-month stipend of $14,000 to a minority full-time graduate student who intends on pursuing a doctoral degree. Award is based on merit only and not limited to just dissertation work. Visit web site for specific application guidelines. Deadline: January 15.

524. (A)
Noah Greenberg Award

1 cash award as a grant-in-aid to graduate students, scholars, and performers. Award may subsidize the publication costs of articles, monographs, or editions, as well as public performance, recordings, or other projects. Visit web site for specific guidelines. Deadline: August 15.

525. (A)
Otto Kinkeldey Award

1 cash award of varying amount to a graduate student or other individual in musicological scholarship. Selection based on the most distinguished of those published during the previous year in any language and in any country, but scholar must be a citizen or permanent resident of the U.S. or Canada. To be considered, individual must be nominated or self-nominated. Visit web site for more information. Deadline: none specified.

526. (A)
Paul A. Pisk Prize

1 award of varying amount to a graduate music student for a scholarly paper. Paper will be read at the Annual Meeting of the Society. Abstract must be submitted to the program committee, and it must be accepted for inclusion in the meeting. Visit web site for specific submission guidelines. Deadline: October 1.

527. (S)
American Nephrology Nurses' Association
National Office
East Holly Avenue, Box 56
Pitman, NJ 08071–0056

(888) 600–ANNA
(856) 256–2320
http://www.annanurse.org

Scholarships and fellowships of varying amounts to students pursuing undergraduate and graduate degree programs in nursing. Applicants must be interested and dedicated to contributing to information advancement in nephrology. Deadline: varies.

(S)
American Nuclear Society
555 North Kensington Avenue
La Grange Park, IL 60526
(708) 352–6611
http://www.ans.org

528. (S)
Graduate Scholarships

Scholarships ranging from $500 to $4,000 to full-time graduate and undergraduate students pursuing advanced degrees in nuclear science or engineering program. Must be a U.S. citizen or legal resident. Based on academic record and financial need. Deadline: March 1.

529. (S)
John and Muriel Landis Scholarships

7 scholarships of $3,000 to full-time graduate, undergraduate, or high school students pursuing advanced degrees in nuclear engineering or a related field at a U.S. institution. Must be a U.S. citizen or legal resident. Must have financial need or be disadvantaged (poor high school or undergraduate preparation due to family poverty). Must be a U.S. citizen or legal resident. Based on academic record and financial need. Deadline: March 1.

530. (S)
Student Design Competition

Cash awards, certificates, and travel costs to the Winter Meeting in a design competition open to graduate and undergraduate students in nuclear science or engineering. Contact the nuclear engineering department at your institution for information. Deadline: varies.

(A)
American Numismatic Society
ATTN: Chief Curator
Broadway at 155th Street
New York, NY 10032
(212) 234–3130
http://www.amnumsoc.org

531. (A)
Dissertation Fellowships

Fellowships of $3,500 to graduate students who are at the dissertation level and grants of $2,000 to students who have completed 1 year of graduate study. Graduate work must make significant use of numismatic evidence. Recipient must have attended 1 ANS seminar. Must attend a U.S. or Canadian institution. Deadline: March 1.

532. (A)
Frances M. Schwartz Fellowship

1 fellowship of $2,000 to master's and doctoral candidates in numismatics and museum practices. Selection based on academic achievement. Award includes employment at the American Numismatic Society. Must attend a U.S. institution. Deadline: March 1.

533. (A)
Summer Seminar Grants

Varying numbers of grants of $1,200 to master's and doctoral candidates in archaeology. Must have completed 1 year of graduate study in the classics, archaeology, history, art history, or related field. Selection based on academic achievement. Must attend a U.S. or Canadian institution. Deadline: March 1.

(S)
American Nurses Foundation
600 Maryland Avenue, S.W., Suite 100 West
Washington, DC 20024–2571
(800) 274–4ANA
(202) 651–7000
http://www.nursingworld.org

534. (S)
Ada Sue Hinshaw, RN Research Award

1 award of $7,500 open to graduate nursing students with at least a master's degree who are either begin-

ning or experienced researchers. No restrictions on research area. Visit web site for more information and specific guidelines. Deadline: May 1.

535. (S)
ANA Presidential Scholar

1 award of $3,500 open to graduate nursing students who are beginning researchers. Research areas are unrestricted, but preference is given to health disparities. Visit web site for more information and specific guidelines. Deadline: May 1.

536. (S)
Ann Zimmerman, RN Research Award

2 awards of $5,000 to graduate nursing students who are either beginning or experienced researchers. Research must be related to nursing practice or social policy issues that will advance the profession. Visit web site for more information and specific guidelines. Deadline: May 1.

537. (S)
Aventis Pasteur Award

1 award of $7,500 to a graduate student conducting nursing research. Awarded to expand knowledge in the area of immunization. Restricted to pediatric or lifespan immunization issues in the U.S. The researcher is expected to make research available to nurses through either monograph, abstract published and presented at a conference, or periodical. Awarded by Aventis Pharmaceuticals, Inc. Deadline: none specified.

538. (S)
Bobbie K. Young Award

1 award of $3,500 to a graduate nursing student who is either a beginning or experienced researcher. Award supports cancer pain management or patient outcomes research. Visit web site for more information and specific guidelines. Deadline: May 1.

539. (S)
Clinical Research Predoctoral Fellowship

Fellowships of $5,000 in tuition assistance and a $16,500 stipend to graduate students to pursue doctoral study on minority psychiatric–mental health and substance abuse issues. Program addresses the need for rigorously educated underrepresented mi-

nority nurse scientists to conduct research in various aspects of mental health areas, such as child abuse, school violence, psycho-gerontology or substance abuse with minority, underserved and underrepresented populations. Deadline: February 25.

540. (S)
Commission on Graduates of Foreign Nursing Schools

1 award of $5,000 to a graduate nursing student who is either a beginning or experienced researcher. Award must address international nursing issues or issues related to internationally educated nurses in the U.S. workforce only. Visit web site for more information and specific guidelines. Deadline: May 1.

541. (S)
Fellowships

Approximately 25 fellowships of $2,700 to graduate, professional, and postdoctoral students for a nursing research project. Must be U.S. registered nurses who hold at least a bachelor's degree. Selection is based on the scientific merit of the proposal, with consideration given to the investigator's ability to conduct the study. For more information on criteria required for eligibility, visit web site or send a self-addressed, stamped envelope to above address. Deadline: May 1.

542. (S)
Germaine S. Krysan Research Grant

1 award of $5,000 to a graduate nursing student who is either a beginning or experienced researcher. Research areas of special interest are diabetes and chronic pulmonary disease. There are no citizenship restrictions for principal investigators. Visit web site for specific guidelines to determine researcher qualifications. Deadline: May 1.

543. (S)
GlaxoSmithKline Research Grant

1 research grant of $7,500 open to graduate nursing students who are either beginning or experienced researchers. Research must be conducted in the area of smoking cessation. There are no citizenship restrictions for principal investigators. Visit web site for specific guidelines to determine researcher qualifications. Deadline: May 1.

544. (S)
Gloria Smith, RN Research Grant

1 award of $5,000 and 1 award for $15,000 to graduate nursing students who are either beginning or experienced researchers. Research must be related to accessibility or quality of health care delivery to socioeconomic and ethnic minority populations. There are no citizenship restrictions for principal investigators. Visit web site for specific guidelines to determine researcher qualifications. Deadline: May 1.

545. (S)
Hyundai Motor America Nursing Research Grant

1 award of $5,000 to a graduate nursing student who is either a beginning or experienced researcher. Award must be used for clinical nursing research. Visit web site for specific guidelines to determine researcher qualifications. Deadline: May 1.

546. (S)
ICN/3M Nursing Fellowship Program

Fellowships of up to $8,000 to doctoral students in accredited doctoral nursing programs. Must be members in good standing of their state Nurse's Association for at least 2 years. For an application, contact above address or state association, include a self-addressed, stamped envelope. Deadline: August 30.

547. (S)
Julie Hardy, RN Research Grant

2 awards of $5,000 to graduate nursing students who are experienced researchers. Award supports health care systems research only. There are no citizenship restrictions for principal investigators. Visit web site for specific guidelines to determine researcher qualifications. Deadline: May 1.

548. (S)
Leninger Transcultural Nursing Grant Award

1 award of $5,000 to a graduate nursing student who is either a beginning or experienced researcher. Applicant must have had graduate study in transcultural nursing and be eager to discover research-based knowledge using Leninger's Theory of Culture Care or a similar theory. Visit web site for specific guidelines to determine researcher qualifications. Deadline: May 1.

549. (S)
Merck Company Foundation Grants

2 awards of $7,500 to graduate nursing students who are either beginning or experienced researchers. No restrictions on research topics, though preference is given to immunization research. There are no citizenship restrictions for principal investigators. Visit web site for specific guidelines to determine researcher qualifications. Deadline: May 1.

550. (S)
Minority Fellowship Program

Fellowships ranging from $2,000 to $8,000 to graduate and doctoral minority students majoring in nursing in the mental health professions. Must be nominated by a nurses' association. For an application, contact above address or state association, include a self-addressed, stamped envelope. Deadline: January 31.

551. (S)
Nurses Charitable Trust, District V FNA

1 award of $10,000 to a graduate nursing student who is either a beginning or experienced researcher. No restrictions on research areas. Visit web site for specific guidelines to determine researcher qualifications. Deadline: May 1.

552. (S)
Sayer Memorial Fund

1 award of $3,500 to a graduate nursing student who is a beginning researcher. Research should be in the area of interaction between clinical practice and the role of those occupying leadership/management positions. Preferential consideration will be given to studies examining this relationship in a community or managed care setting as opposed to acute care. Visit web site for specific guidelines to determine researcher qualifications. Deadline: May 1.

553. (S)
Sigma Theta Tau International/ANF Scholar

1 award of $7,500 to a graduate nursing student, with at least a master's degree, who is a beginning or experienced researcher. Award must be used for clinical nursing research. Funding can be used to support salaries for principal co-investigators, and non-U.S. nurses are eligible. There are no citizenship restric-

tions for principal investigators. Visit web site for specific guidelines to determine researcher qualifications. Deadline: May 1.

554. (S)
Southern Nursing Research Society Grants

1 award of $4,000 to a graduate nursing student who is either a beginning or experienced researcher. Applicants must be current SNRS members. There are no citizenship restrictions for principal investigators. Visit web site for specific guidelines to determine researcher qualifications. Deadline: May 1.

555. (S)
Virginia Stone Research Grants

1 award of $10,000 and 1 award for $20,000 to graduate nursing students who are experienced researchers. Award supports clinical gerontological nursing research only. There are no citizenship restrictions for principal investigators. Visit web site for specific guidelines to determine researcher qualifications. Deadline: May 1.

556. (S)
Wyeth Vaccines Research Grant

1 award of $6,500 open to graduate nursing students who are either beginning or experienced researchers. Research supported only for vaccine-related topics. There are no citizenship restrictions for principal investigators. Visit web site for specific guidelines to determine researcher qualifications. Deadline: May 1.

(S)
American Occupational Therapy Foundation, Inc.
ATTN: Office of Professional Research Services
P.O. Box 31220
Bethesda, MD 20824–1220
(301) 652–2682
http://www.aota.org

557. (S)
Doctoral Fellowship

1 fellowship of $20,000 for 3 years to a doctoral candidate in biological or social sciences as related to occupational therapy. Applicants must have a master's degree, must be a registered occupational therapist, and must be a member of OATA with at least 5 years of experience. Deadline: February 1.

558. (S)
Scholarships

25 scholarships ranging from $150 to $1,500 to graduate and undergraduate students (preference given to juniors and seniors) majoring in occupational therapy. Based on academic achievement and financial need. Must have at least a 3.2 GPA. For more information, visit web site or send a self-addressed, stamped envelope for an application. There is a $1 application fee. Deadline: December 15.

559. (S)
American Optometric Foundation
William Ezell OD Fellowship
6110 Executive Boulevard, Suite 506
Rockville, MD 20852
(301) 652–0905
http://www.aaopt.org

Fellowships of up to $6,000 to students pursuing a doctorate in optometry who want to teach and/or conduct research. Send a self-addressed, stamped envelope for information. Deadline: April 15.

560. (S)
American Orchid Society
Grants for Orchid Research
16700 AOS Lane
Delray Beach, FL 33446–4351
(561) 404–2000
http://www.theaos.org

Awards ranging from $500 to $12,000 per year for up to 3 years to postdoctoral fellows to conduct experimental projects and fundamental and applied research on orchids. Graduate students may apply for assistance with research if research involves or applies to orchids. Postgraduates may only apply on behalf of the institution where they are employed. Deadline: January 1 and August 1.

(A, H)
American Oriental Society
Hatcher Graduate Library
University of Michigan
Ann Arbor, MI 48109–1205
http://www.umich.edu/~aos/

561. (H)
Fellowship Program

Varying numbers of scholarships of $7,000 to doctoral candidates who have completed 3 years of Chinese language study. One program requires U.S. citizenship and one doesn't. Deadline: February 1.

562. (A, H)
Louise Wallace Hackney Fellowship for the Study of Chinese Art

Fellowships of $8,000 to predoctoral or postdoctoral students of Chinese art and history of Chinese art, who have studied Chinese for 3 years or equivalent, to permit the study of Chinese art and the translation into English of works on the subject. Must be U.S. citizens. Deadline: February 1.

(S)
American Ornithologists' Union
1313 Dolley Madison Boulevard, Suite 402
McLean, VA 22101
http://www.aou.org/aou/Member.html

563. (S)
Betty Carnes Fund

Awards of up to $1,800 to female graduate students to conduct ornithological research. Recipients must be nonsmokers (have not smoked for at least the previous 6 months). Applicants are limited to 1 award per degree or project. Must be student members of AOU. Visit web site for more information. Deadline: January 31.

564. (S)
Margaret Morse Nice Fund

Awards of up to $1,800 to female graduate students to conduct ornithological research. Applicants are limited to 1 award per degree or project. Must be student members of AOU. Visit web site for more information. Deadline: January 31.

565. (S)
Membership Grants

Several hundred grants of 3-year AOU memberships to graduate and undergraduate students interested in pursuing a career in ornithology. Must have no current or prior membership in the AOU. Visit web site for specific application guidelines. Deadline: January 31.

566. (S)
Student Research and Travel Awards

5 to 15 research awards ranging from $500 to $1,500 and 1 to 5 travel awards ranging from $500 to $1,000 to veterinary students or graduate or undergraduate students majoring in animal or veterinary science. Research awards are meant to assist students who have no access to regular funding for research on any aspect of avian biology. The travel award is provided to assist in defraying travel expenses to attend a meeting at which they present a paper in the area of ornithology. Award is not renewable. Individuals who already have their doctorate degrees are ineligible. Selection based on application and references. Deadline: May 1.

567. (S)
Van Tyne, Bleitz, and Research Awards

Awards of up to $1,800 to graduate and doctoral students to conduct research in all areas of avian biology. Applicants are limited to 1 award per degree or project. Must be student members of AOU. Visit web site for more information. Deadline: January 31.

568. (S)
Wetmore Memorial Fund

Awards of up to $1,800 to graduate and doctoral students to conduct research in avian systematics, paleo-ornithology, biogeography, and netropical biology. Applicants are limited to 1 award per degree or project. Must be student members of AOU. Visit web site for more information.

569. (S)
American Osteopathic Foundation
Scholarship Program
Scholarship Chairperson
142 East Ontario Street
Chicago, IL 60611
(800) 621–1773
http://www.osteopathic.org

Scholarships ranging from $2,000 to $4,000 to second-year osteopathic medical school students. Must be in the top 20% of their class or have honors from their first year, be attending an approved college of osteopathy, have financial need, and be pursuing a career in osteopathic medicine. Must be a U.S. or Canadian citizen. For more information, visit web site or send a self-addressed, stamped envelope for an application. Deadline: June 1.

(H)
American Philosophical Society
ATTN: Assistant Librarian for Research Programs
104 South Fifth Street
Philadelphia, PA 19106–3387
(215) 440–3400
http://www.amphilsoc.org

570. (H)
Franklin Research Grants

Grants of $1,000 up to $6,000 to postdoctoral scholars, or individuals who have published work of doctoral character and quality. American citizens and residents of the United States may use their Franklin awards at home or abroad. Foreign nationals must use their Franklin awards for research in the United States. The Franklin program is particularly designed to help meet the cost of travel to libraries and archives for research purposes, the purchase of microfilm, photocopies, or equivalent research materials, the costs associated with fieldwork, or laboratory research expenses. Deadline: October 1 and December 1.

571. (H)
Library Resident Research Fellowships

Fellowships of $2,000 per month to doctoral scholars and doctoral candidates who have passed their preliminary exams and independent scholars. Open to both U.S. citizens and foreign nationals. Term of the fellowship is a minimum of 1 month and a maximum of 3, with fellows expected to be in residence for 4 consecutive weeks during the period of their award. There is no special application form, and the notice on their web site provides all the essential information needed to apply. Deadline: March 1.

572. (H)
Phillips Fund Grants

Grants ranging from $2,200; grants do not exceed $3,000. To graduate students for research on master's or doctoral dissertations and doctoral scholars for projects in archaeology, ethnography, psycholinguistics, or for the preparation of pedagogical materials. Grants are intended for such extra costs as travel, tapes, films, and consultants' fees, but not for general maintenance or the purchase of books or permanent equipment. Deadline: March 1.

573. (H)
Research Grant Award

300 research grants averaging $2,000 to postdoctoral students. Grants are rarely awarded to people who have had their doctorate for less than a year and never for predoctoral study and research. Applicants may be U.S. residents; American citizens on the staff of foreign institutions; or foreign nationals whose research can only or best be carried out in the U.S. Open to all areas of research. Deadline: varies.

574. (H)
Sabbatical Fellowships

Fellowships providing a stipend of $40,000 to mid-career faculty of universities and 4-year colleges in the United States who have been granted a sabbatical/research leave but for whom financial support from the parent institution is available for only part of the year. Must submit a statement of the project, must include how the work will increase or modify current knowledge of the subject; explain precisely why a full year of leave will represent a major scholarly advantage. For specific guidelines, visit web site. Deadline: November 1.

575. (S)
American Physical Society & American Institute of Physics
Congressional Science Fellowship Program
One Physics Ellipse
College Park, MD 20740–3843
(301) 209–3100
http://www.aip.org/pubinfo/index.html

25 fellowships providing a stipend of $49,000 (plus $2,000 travel relocation allowance, a $2,000 allowance for travel during the year, $1,000 allowance to travel to AGU meetings, and health care benefits) to postdoctoral students (who have completed all course and dissertation work prior to commencing program), scientists, engineers, other professionals in physics or a closely related field. AIP fellows must be members of one or more AIP member societies. APS fellows must be members of APS,

and in exceptional cases, the Ph.D. requirement may be waived on an application with compensating experience. Fellows work on the staff of one of the members of the United States Congress or Congressional Committee. Must be U.S. citizens or legal residents. Visit web site for more information. Deadline: January 15.

576. (S)
American Physical Therapy Association
Mary McMillan Scholarship
Director, Department of Education
1111 North Fairfax Street
Alexandria, VA 22314–1488
(800) 999–2782
(703) 684–APTA
http://www.apta.org

Scholarships of varying amounts to students who are in their final year of study in a physical therapy program. Faculty members nominate individuals. For more information, visit web site or send a self-addressed, stamped envelope. Deadline: varies.

(S)
American Physiological Society
9650 Rockville Pike
Bethesda, MD 20814–3991
(301) 634–7132
http://www.the-aps.org

577. (S)
APS Travel Fellowships for Minority Students

Awards of varying amounts to minority graduate students to attend the APS conferences and/or meetings. Meetings range in length from 3 to 5 days. Fellowship allows students the opportunity to attend symposia, workshops, tutorials, and slide/poster sessions and interact with leading scientists in the field of physiology. Visit web site for more information and deadline.

578. (S)
Curriculum Development Fellowships

Fellowships providing stipends and travel expense reimbursements to middle school and high school science teachers. Recipients serve as mentors and instructors at the Instructors for Summer Workshop Retreat, develop on-line, interactive, inquiry-based science activities for upper elementary, middle, or high school classrooms. Visit web site for more information and deadline.

579. (S)
Explorations in Biomedicine

A program for science teachers and tribal college science faculty who are Native American or teachers of Native American students to promote the participation of Native American students in physiological/biomedical careers. Visit web site for more information and deadline.

580. (S)
Fellowships for Genomic Research and Analysis

3 types of fellowships: 1) to predoctoral graduate students with disabilities or who are members of an underrepresented minority, 2) to postdoctoral fellows who received their doctoral degree within the last 7 years, and 3) to senior postdoctoral fellows who received their doctoral degrees more than 7 years ago. Award enables recipients to engage in research relevant to the Human Genome Project. Training of scholars in examining the ethical, legal, and social implications of human genome research is encouraged. Visit web site for more information. Deadline: November 15 and May 1 (predoctoral students); April 5 and August 5 (postdoctoral fellows); and December 5, April 5, and August 5 (senior postdoctoral fellows).

581. (S)
Frontiers in Physiology Professional
Development Fellowship

Fellowships of varying amounts to middle school and high school science teachers to participate in an intensive exploration of effective teaching methods. The fellowship includes 7 to 8 weeks working fulltime in a research project in a physiology research lab close to home. Visit web site for more information. Deadline: January 10.

582. (S)
Porter Physiology Fellowship Program

Fellowships of $18,000 to minority full-time graduate students in the physiological sciences. Must be U.S. citizens or permanent residents and accepted into a doctoral program at an accredited U.S. institution. Fellowships are for 1 year, renewal for a second year is considered, and in exceptional cases a third year may be awarded. Award does not provide tuition, fees, or a dependent allowance. Deadline: January 15 and June 15.

(SS)
American Planning Associates
1776 Massachusetts Avenue, N.W., Suite 400
Washington, DC 20036
(202) 872–0611
http://www.planning.org

583. (SS)
APA Congressional Fellowship Program

2 fellowships of $1,000 and $2,000 to graduate students studying urban planning to participate in a 6-month-long internship. Fellows gain direct and substantial experience in the legislative process. Deadline: May 15.

584. (SS)
APA Planning Fellowships

Awards ranging from $1,000 to $5,000 for African-American, Hispanic, or Native American first- or second-year graduate students. Must be U.S. citizens and enrolled in an approved Planning Accreditation Board (PAB) graduate planning program. Deadline: April 30.

585. (SS)
Arizona APA Chapter

3 scholarships of $2,000 to graduate students majoring in planning at Arizona State University, University of Arizona, or Northern Arizona University. Visit web site for contact information. Deadline: none specified.

586. (SS)
Charles Abrams Scholarship

Scholarships of $1,000 and $2,000 to a graduate student studying urban planning. Must be attending Columbia University, Harvard University, New School for Social Research in New York City, University of Pennsylvania, or MIT. Must be nominated by their school. Must have financial need. Some awards are limited to minority students. Contact head of department or above address. Deadline: April 30.

587. (S)
Economic Development Division Student Scholarship

1 award of $1,000 to a graduate student (master's level). Awarded to encourage graduate students who exhibit a commitment to planning in general and economic development in particular. Awarded based on a letter of recommendation from a full-time faculty member and an original paper or work having to do with a substantive and relevant topic related to economic development. For more information, visit web site. Deadline: January 15.

588. (SS)
Environment, Natural Resources, and Energy Division Student Fellowship Program

1 scholarship of $1,000 (for each of 2 semesters, contingent upon maintaining eligibility) to a full- or part-time, second-year graduate student. Must be enrolled in an accredited graduate school planning program focusing on issues related to the environment, natural resources, or energy and be an APA member, with Environment, Natural Resources, and Energy Division membership strongly preferred. Must have a 3.0 GPA or better (on a 4.0 scale) and submit a recommendation from major advisor. Major must promote sound environment, natural resources and energy planning, and resource use policies among individual members of APA and the general public, and within the planning profession and communities of all scales. Visit web site for more information. Deadline: January 15.

589. (SS)
FEMA Community Planning Fellowships

Several fellowships to master's degree candidates, providing a stipend of independent research study, tuition and fees for 6 credit hours, reimbursement of travel costs and expenses, housing for 8 weeks spent at FEMA. For more information, visit their web site. Deadline: January 21.

590. (SS)
Judith McManus Price Scholarship Fund

Scholarships of varying amounts to graduate and undergraduate students pursuing planning degrees and who have demonstrated a genuine financial need. The scholarship fund is awarded to encourage women and minorities to enter the field of planning.

591. (SS)
Mildred Colodny Scholarship for the Study of Historic Preservation

1 scholarship of $15,000 to an undergraduate senior about to begin graduate study in a preservation-related program, a paid ($5,000) summer internship with the National Trust or one of their partners, and $1,500 assistance to attend the National Preservation Conference. For more information, visit the web site. Deadline: January 31.

592. (SS)
Native American Economic Development Scholarship

6 scholarships of $5,000 to Native American graduate students who are studying in the areas of law, business, or planning, and who are committed to economic development in Native American communities. For more information, visit the web site. Deadline: none specified.

593. (SS)
Planning & the Black Community Division Fellowships

Awards of $30,000 for 2 years of study to graduate students for study at the Milano Graduate School at the New School for Social Research in New York City. This fellowship is geared toward advance study in urban planning or urban policy analysis. Deadline: rolling.

594. (SS)
Population-Environment Fellows Program

Fellowships place graduate students in 2-year positions at overseas agencies. Qualified applicants must hold a graduate degree in a relevant area, have course work or experience demonstrating both population and environmental expertise, and be U.S. citizens or permanent residents. Visit web site for information on applying. Deadline: rolling.

595. (SS)
State APA Awards

Scholarships of varying amounts to graduate students majoring in planning or related fields. Awards are provided by various states. Each state has different guidelines. For specific information, visit the APA web site. Deadlines: vary.

(SS)
American Political Science Association
1527 New Hampshire Avenue, N.W.
Washington, DC 20036
(202) 483–2512
http://www.apsanet.org

596. (SS)
Congressional Fellowships for Political Scientists

3 or 4 fellowships providing a stipend of $28,000 plus travel allowance to postdoctoral fellows with a scholarly interest in Congress and the policy making process. Must have completed (or be near completion of) their Ph.D. within the last 15 years. Fellowship stipend may be supplemented at fellow's initiative with university support. Deadline: December 1.

597. (SS)
Congressional Fellowships for Print & Broadcast Journalists

1 fellowship providing a stipend of $28,000 plus travel allowance to journalists for the opportunity to work as congressional aids for 9 months and to strengthen understanding of Congress and national politics. Applicant must have a bachelor's degree and at least 2 to 10 years of full-time professional experience. Deadline: December 1.

598. (SS)
Doctoral Dissertation Awards

8 prizes of $250 to outstanding dissertations written by doctoral candidates in fields related to political science: comparative politics, general state and local politics, public law and judicial process, policy studies, international relations/law/politics, government and politics, political philosophy, or public administration. Send a copy of the dissertation and a letter of recommendation from the department chair must be sent to each member of the award committee. Dissertation must have been completed within the last 2 calendar years. Deadline: January 15.

599. (SS)
Graduate Minority Fellowships

Fellowships of at least $6,000 to Native American (1), Hispanic-American (1), and African-American (3) students who are pursuing doctoral degrees in political science. May have mixed social science undergraduate majors, but must be majoring in political science at the doctoral level. Must attend an accredited U.S. institution. Must be U.S. citizens. Deadline: November 30.

600. (S)
American Pomological Society
Hendrick Awards
R. M. Crassweller, Treasurer
103 Tyson Building
University Park, PA 16802–4200
http://hortweb.cas.psu.edu/aps

A writing competition with prizes of $50 and $150 (plus 1-year subscription), open to graduate and undergraduate students who author or coauthor a paper with an advisor. Papers must be acceptable for publication by *Fruit Varieties Journal* and be on some area of fruit cultivation (deciduous, tropical, or subtropical with relation to climate, soil, experiments, history, etc.). It may be a literature review, a thesis paper, or personal experience. Deadline: no later than 60 days before the APS meeting.

601. (SS)
American Production and Inventory Control Society, Inc.
Graduate Student Awards Program
Educational Society for Resource Management
5301 Shawnee Road
Alexandria, VA 22312–2317
(800) 444–2742
(703) 354–8851
http://www.apics.org

Awards of varying amounts to full-time graduate students. Prize is for best paper dealing with operations management, production management, industrial management, or business administration. May attend a U.S. or Canadian institute. Write for complete details. Deadline: June 1.

602. (H)
American Prospect, Inc.
Writing Fellows Program
2000 L Street, N.W., Suite 717
Washington, DC 20036
(202) 776–0730
http://www.prospect.org/fellows

Fellowships providing an annual stipend of $20,000, plus travel expenses for conferences and reporting, to young journalists to spend a full year at the magazine's office in Boston, developing, practicing, and honing their journalistic skills. Fellows write 3 or 4 full-length, in-depth articles, contribute short pieces, and assist with general editorial work. Deadline: mid-February.

(SS)
American Psychiatric Association
1000 Wilson Boulevard, Suite 1825
Arlington, VA 22209-3901
(888) 35–PSYCH
(703) 907–7300
http://www.psych.org

603. (SS)
Burroughs Wellcome Fellowship

Awards of varying amounts to graduate and professional school students in a 2-year fellowship program to acquaint residents with APA work and national issues affecting psychiatry and to give APA the benefit of the ideas and perspective of future leaders in psychiatry. Deadline: April 1.

604. (SS)
Doctoral Awards

Up to 30 awards of up to $7,084 for 10 months to doctoral minority students in neuroscience or psychology for minority students. There are 2 programs: 1 is for physicians to obtain clinical training, and 1 is to support M.D.s and Ph.D.s in obtaining research training. Must be U.S. citizens or legal residents. Awards are renewable for up to 3 years. Deadline: January 15.

605. (S)
Fellowships

Awards of varying amounts to graduate and medical school students in a 2-year fellowship program to acquaint residents with APA work and national issues affecting psychiatry and to give APA the benefit of the ideas and perspective of future leaders in psychiatry. Up to 30 awards of up to $7,084 for 10 months to doctoral minority students in neuroscience or psychology to conduct research in areas identified as important by the National Institute of Mental Health. There are 2 programs: 1 is for physicians to obtain clinical training, and 1 is to support M.D.s and Ph.D.s in obtaining research training. Must be U.S. citizens or legal residents. Awards are renewable for up to 3 years. Deadline: January 15 and April 1.

606. (S)
Minority Fellowship Program in Psychology

Up to 30 awards of up to $7,000 for 10 months to minority doctoral students in neuroscience or psychology to conduct research in areas identified as important by the National Institute of Mental Health. There are 2 programs: 1 is for physicians to obtain clinical training, and 1 is to support M.D.s and Ph.D.s in obtaining research training. Must be U.S. citizens or legal residents. Awards are renewable for up to 3 years. Deadline: January 15.

(S)
American Psychiatric Nurses Association
1555 Wilson Boulevard, Suite 515
Arlington, VA 22209
(703) 243–2443
http://www.apna.org/foundation/scholarships.html

607. (S)
APNF Lego Research Grant

1 scholarship grant of $1,000 to a master's or doctoral student or a registered nurse with a master's degree in psychiatric mental health. Award supports research investigating psychotherapeutic interventions. Minorities are encouraged to apply. Visit web site for specific guidelines and an application. Deadline: January 10.

608. (S)
APNF Peplau Scholarship

1 award of $1,000 open to a graduate student or registered nurse to continue his/her studies. Selection is based on a personal statement, community involvement, professional references, and career goals. Visit web site for more information. Deadline: January 10.

609. (S)
Janssen Student Scholar Program

Scholarships ranging from $1,000 to $2,500 to senior undergraduate nursing students to learn more about a career in psychiatric mental health nursing leadership. Award covers travel expenses, hotel, conference fees, and meals. Each student is provided with a year's membership in the American Psychiatric Nurses Association. Deadline: January 30.

610. (SS)
American Psychological Association
Congressional Fellowship Program
750 First Street, N.E.
Washington, DC 20002–4242
http://www.apa.org/ppo/funding/congfell.html

Up to 5 fellowships with a stipend ranging from $48,500 to $64,400, depending on experience, and a relocation allowance of up to $3,000 to postdoctoral students with 2 years of postdoctoral experience. Fellows spend 1 year working as a legislative assistant on the staff of a member of Congress or congressional committee. Awarded to provide psychologists with an invaluable public policy learning experience, to contribute to the more effective use of psychological knowledge in government, and to broaden awareness about the value of psychology-government interaction among psychologists and within the federal government. Deadline: January 1.

611. (S)
American Public Power Association
DEED Scholarships
Washington, DC 20037–1484
(202) 467–2900
http://www.appanet.org

10 scholarships of $3,000 to graduate or undergraduate students in energy-related majors at 4-year accredited institutions. For information on qualifying criteria, visit web site or send self-addressed, stamped envelope to above address. Deadline: varies, usually February and August.

612. (S, SS)
American Public Works Association Foundation
Matching Scholarship Program
2345 Grand Avenue, Suite 500   1401 K Street, N.W.,
Kansas City, MO 64108–2641   11th Floor

(816) 472–6100   Washington, DC 20005
http://www.pubworks.org   (202) 408–9541

Numerous scholarships of $2,500 to graduate students studying in public works management within master's degree in public administration or civil engineering from institutions officially recognized by the APWA. Deadline: varies.

(A, H, S, SS)
American Radio Relay League Foundation
225 Main Street
Newington, CT 06111
(800) 594–0200
http://www.arrl.org/arrlf/

613. (A, H, S, SS)
Charles Clarke Cordle Memorial Scholarship

1 scholarship of $1,000 to a graduate or undergraduate student in any area of study. Must be resident of Georgia or Alabama and attend an accredited institution in Georgia or Alabama. Must have at least a 2.5 GPA or higher. Must be an ARRL member and have any class of amateur radio license. Deadline: February 1.

614. (H, S)
Charles N. Fisher Memorial Scholarship

1 scholarship of $1,000 to a graduate or undergraduate student in electronics, communications, or a related field. Must be a resident of an ARRL Southwestern Division (Arizona, Los Angeles, Orange, San Diego, or Santa Barbara, CA). Must be an ARRL member and hold any class of amateur radio license. Deadline: February 1.

615. (SS)
Donald Riebhoff Memorial Scholarship

1 scholarship of $1,000 to a graduate or undergraduate student in international studies. Must be an ARRL member and have a Technician Class amateur radio license. Deadline: February 1.

616. (H, S)
Dr. James L. Lawson Memorial Scholarship

1 scholarship of $500 to a graduate or undergraduate student in communications, electronics, or a related field. Must attend an accredited institution in New England or New York State. Must be an ARRL member, a resident of a New England state (ME, NH, VT, MA, CT, RI) or New York, and hold at least a general amateur radio license.

617. (S)
Earl I. Anderson Scholarship

3 scholarships of $1,250 to graduate or undergraduate students in an electronic engineering major or a related technical field. Must be attending an accredited U.S. institution in IL, IN, MI, or FL, be an ARRL member, and hold any class of amateur radio license. Deadline: February 1.

618. (S)
Edmond A. Metzger Scholarship

1 scholarship of $500 to a graduate or undergraduate student in electrical engineering. Must be a member of ARRL, a resident of the ARRL Central Division (IL, IN, WI), and be attending an accredited U.S. institution in the ARRL Central Division. Must hold at least a novice amateur radio license. Deadline: February 1.

619. (A, H, S, SS)
Eugene "Gene" Sallee, W4YFR Memorial Scholarship

1 scholarship of $500 to a graduate or undergraduate student in any area of study. Must be a resident of Georgia, a member of ARRL, and have a technician plus amateur radio license. Must have at least a 3.0 GPA or higher. Deadline: February 1.

620. (A, H, S, SS)
Francis Walton Memorial Scholarship

1 or more scholarships of $500 to graduate or undergraduate students in any area of study. Must be a resident of the ARRL Central Division (IL, IN, WI), have a 5 WPM certification, and attend an accredited U.S. institution. Deadline February 1.

621. (H, S)
Fred R. McDaniel Memorial Scholarship

1 scholarship of $500 to a graduate or undergraduate student in communications, electronics, or a related field. Must be a resident of FCC's Fifth Call District (TX, OK, AR, LA, MS, NM), be a member of ARRL, and hold at least a general amateur radio license.

Preference given to students with a 3.0 GPA or higher. Deadline: February 1.

622. (A, H, S, SS)

General Fund Scholarships

Multiple scholarships of $1,000 to a graduate or undergraduate student in any area of study. Must be a member of ARRL and hold any class of amateur radio license. Deadline: February 1.

623. (H, S)

Irving W. Cook WA0CGS Scholarship

1 scholarship of $1,000 to a graduate or undergraduate student majoring in electronics, communications, or a related field. Must be a Kansas resident who holds a general amateur license and is an ARRL member. May be used at any accredited U.S. college or university. Deadline: February 1.

624. (A, H, S, SS)

K2TEO Martin J. Green, Sr. Memorial Scholarship

1 scholarship of $1,000 to a graduate or undergraduate student majoring in any major. Must hold a general amateur license and be an ARRL member. May be used at any accredited U.S. college or university. Preference given to a student ham from a ham family. Deadline: February 1.

625. (H, S)

L. Phil Wicker Scholarship

1 scholarship of $1,000 to a graduate or undergraduate student. Preference given to a student studying communications, electronics, or related fields. Must be a resident of the Roanoke Division (NC, SC, VA, WV) and attend an institution in that area. Must hold a general amateur license and be an ARRL member. Deadline: February 1.

626. (H, S)

Mary Lou Brown Scholarship

1 or more scholarships of $2,500 to full-time graduate or undergraduate students majoring in a field related to communications. Must be a resident of the ARRL Northwest Division (AK, ID, MT, OR, WA). Must attend an accredited institution. Must be a licensed radio amateur and an ARRL member and maintain a 3.0 GPA or better. Must demonstrate an interest in promoting the Amateur Radio Service. Deadline: February 1.

627. (H, S)

Mississippi Scholarship

1 scholarship of $500 to a graduate or undergraduate student majoring in electronics, communications, or a related field. Must be a resident of Mississippi, attending an accredited institution in Mississippi, and under the age of 30. Must be an ARRL member and have any class of amateur radio license. Deadline: February 1.

628. (A, H, S, SS)

New England FEMARA Scholarships

Multiple scholarships of $600 to graduate or undergraduate students in any field of study. Must be residents of the New England states (ME, NH, VT, MA, CT, RI), be an ARRL member, and hold a technician amateur radio license. Deadline: February 1.

629. (H, S)

Paul and Helen L. Grauer Scholarship

1 scholarship of $1,000 to a graduate or undergraduate student majoring in electronics, communications, or a related career. Must be residents of the AARL Midwest Division (IA, KS, MO, NB). Must be attending an institution in that area. Must be an ARRL member. Preference given to students majoring in communications, electronics, or related areas. Deadline: February 1.

630. (S)

Perry F. Hadlock Memorial Scholarship

1 scholarship of $2,000 to a graduate or undergraduate student in technology-related studies, with preference given to electrical and electronics engineering majors. Must be attending Clarkson University; if there are no applicants, the award is open to all Atlantic and Hudson Divisions. Must be an ARRL member with a technician license. Deadline: February 1.

631. (H, S)

PHD ARA Scholarship

1 scholarship of $1,000 to a graduate or undergraduate student in journalism, computer science, or electronic engineering. Must be a resident of the ARRL Midwest Division (IA, KS, MO, NE), hold any class of amateur radio license, and be the child of a deceased radio amateur. Deadline: February 1.

632. (H)

Senator Barry Goldwater (#K7UGA) Scholarship Fund

1 scholarship of $5,000 to a full-time graduate or undergraduate student majoring in a field related to communications. Must attend an accredited institution. Must be a licensed radio amateur and an ARRL member. Deadline: February 1.

633. (A, H, S, SS)

"You've Got a Friend in Pennsylvania" Scholarship

1 award of $1,000 to a graduate or undergraduate student in any major. Must be a resident of Pennsylvania, be a member of ARRL, and hold a general radio amateur license. Deadline: February 1.

634. (S)

American Red Cross
ATTN: Volunteer Personnel
8111 Gatehouse Road, 6th Floor
Falls Church, VA 22042
http://www.redcross.org

Varying number of internships of varying length to anyone interested in helping prevent, prepare for, and cope with emergencies. Interns help develop public relations campaigns for Red Cross service departments, provide crisis counseling for military families, provide emergency assistance to disaster victims, assist in planning for response to disasters, assist with health and safety courses and programs, assist with all aspects of blood services department, help with fundraising, including special events, and work in the volunteer personnel service department. No compensation is provided. Open to individuals with backgrounds in the following areas: advertising, business, education, English, fundraising, health, journalism, marketing, nursing, personnel management, physical education, psychology, public administration, public policy, public relations, social services, sociology, and speech communications. Deadline: open.

(A, H)

American Research Center in Egypt
ATTN: U.S. Director
Emory Briarcliff Campus
1256 Briarcliff Road, N.E.

Building A, Suite 423W
Atlanta, GA 30306
(404) 712–9854
http://www.arce.org/

635. (A, H, SS)

Egyptian Graduate Student Fellowships

1 to 5 6- to 12-month fellowships providing a monthly stipend of $600 to doctoral candidates to conduct research. Must be Egyptian citizens enrolled in an accredited U.S. institution. Applicants must be engaged in research relating to Egyptian development, archaeology, architecture, art, Egyptology, history, humanities, Islamic studies, and social sciences. Award is for maintenance support of research conducted in Egypt during the fellowship period. Must be proficient in Arabic. Send a self-addressed, stamped envelope for details. Deadline: November 30.

636. (A, H, SS)

Fellowships for Graduate Study in Egypt

Up to 20 3- to 12-month fellowships providing a monthly stipend commensurate with academic status and number of accompanying dependents, plus round-trip air transportation for recipients only. Open to students who have completed all requirements for the doctoral degree except their dissertation. Must be currently enrolled in a graduate program in U.S. or Canada. Egyptian candidates must have J1 student visa status. Applicants must be engaged in research relating to Egyptian development, archaeology, architecture, art, Egyptology, history, humanities, Islamic studies, and social sciences. The Egyptian Development Fellowships are made to support Egyptian students' dissertation research relating to Egyptian development. Deadline: November 1.

637. (A, H)

Kress Predoctoral Fellowship in Egyptian Art and Architecture

Up to 20 3- to 12-month fellowships providing a monthly stipend of $1,000 plus round-trip airfare, and, if needed, a dependent's stipend to doctoral candidates and postdoctoral scholars in architecture, art, and art history. Selection is based on proposed research. Doctoral candidates must have completed all course work and only need to conduct dissertation research. Award is meant to be used as maintenance support for research conducted in Egypt during fellowship period. Recipients may not hold outside employment during fellowship period and must be proficient in Arabic. For more information, visit web site or send a self-addressed, stamped envelope for details. Deadline: November 30.

(A, H, SS)
American Research Institute in Turkey
c/o The University Museum
33rd and Spruce Streets
Philadelphia, PA 19104–6324
(215) 898–4001
(215) 898-0657
http://www.museum.upenn.edu

638. (H, SS)
AFIT Fellowships

10 1- to 12-month fellowships ranging from $1,000 to $4,000 to doctoral candidates to conduct research related to Turkey in the areas of ancient, medieval, and modern times in any field of the humanities or social sciences. Candidates must have completed all required course work, only need to conduct dissertation research, must obtain research permission from the Turkish government, and be affiliated with a U.S. or Canadian institution. Award is meant to be used for maintenance support for dissertation research in Turkey during the fellowship period. For more information, visit web site or send a self-addressed, stamped envelope. Deadline: November 15.

639. (H)
Bosporus University Summer Turkish Language Program

Varying number of grants, which will cover tuition, a maintenance stipend, and round-trip travel, to college graduates, graduate students, and doctoral candidates to participate in an 8-week summer program for the study of Turkish language. Must have at least a 3.0 GPA, have taken 2 years of college-level Turkish language courses or equivalent, and take a written and oral exams. Must be a U.S. citizen or legal resident. Nonrenewable. For more information, visit web site or send a self-addressed, stamped envelope. Deadline: February 15.

640. (H, SS)
Doctoral Dissertation Research Fellowships

8 to 10 fellowships ranging from $1,000 to $4,000 to doctoral students to support doctoral dissertation research in Turkey on ancient, medieval, or modern times in the areas of the humanities or social sciences. Selection awarded on the basis of individual proposals. Must be attending institutions in the U.S. or Canada. Must have completed all their course work. Deadline: November 15.

641. (A, H)
NEH Fellowships for Research in Turkey

Fellowships can be held for periods of 4 to 12 months. Stipends ranging from $10,000 to $30,000 to advanced graduate students or degree recipients engaged in research on Turkey in ancient, medieval, or modern times in the areas of the humanities (including prehistory, history, art, archaeology, literature, and linguistics, as well as interdisciplinary aspects of cultural history). Award is given to support up to 1 year of postdoctoral research in Turkey. Selection awarded on the basis of individual proposals. Deadline: November 15.

642. (H, SS)
Studies at Athens Fellowships

Varying number of fellowships providing $6,000 plus room and board to master's and doctoral candidates to conduct study and/or research in Greece in the areas of archaeology, classical studies, and ancient Greece. Selection based on academic achievement, examination results, and recommendations. Applicants must be enrolled in a U.S. or Canadian institution. For more information, visit web site or send a self-addressed, stamped envelope. Deadline: January 5.

643. (A, H, S, SS)
American Samoa Government
Financial Aid Program
Department of Education
Office of Student Services
Pago Pago, American Samoa 96799
(684) 633–4255
http://www.doe.as/programs

Approximately 50 scholarships of $5,000 to graduate or undergraduate students majoring in any area. Must attend an accredited institution. Off-Island applicants may also be eligible if parents are citizens of American Samoa. Renewable. Deadline: April 30.

(A)
American-Scandinavian Foundation
58 Park Avenue
(between 37th and 38th Streets)
New York, NY 10016
(212) 879–9779
http://www.amscan.org

644. (A)
Fellowships for Study/Research in Scandinavia in the Arts

Varying numbers of fellowships and grants from $2,000 to $15,000 for graduate, professional, advanced professional, and postdoctoral students for study in Scandinavian countries (Denmark, Finland, Iceland, Norway, and Sweden). Must be citizens or permanent U.S. residents. Based on academic merit, proposed plan of study, and applicant's qualifications. Must have some ability in the language of the country of intended study. Request applications in the fall. Visit web site for detailed information and an application. Deadline: November 1.

645. (A)
Fellowships for Study/Research in Scandinavia in the Creative Arts

Varying numbers of fellowships and grants from $2,000 to $15,000 for graduate, professional, advanced professional, and postdoctoral students in the creative arts (creative writing and translation, dance, film, music, and visual arts). Awards are for study in Scandinavian countries (Denmark, Finland, Iceland, Norway, and Sweden). Must be citizens or permanent U.S. residents. Based on academic merit, proposed plan of study, and applicant's qualifications. Must have some ability in the language of the country of intended study. Request applications in the fall. Visit web site for detailed information and an application. Deadline: November 1.

(SS)
American School Food Service Association
700 South Washington Street, Suite 300
Alexandria, VA 22314–3436

(800) 877–8822
(703) 739–3900
http://www.asfsa.org

646. (SS)
Professional Growth Scholarship

Varying number of scholarships of $500 to students who are members of the American Food Service Association. Applicant must be updating their education for a career in food service (food science technology, nutrition, or food service) and have at least a 2.7 GPA. Deadline: April 15.

647. (SS)
Research Grant

Research grants of at least $2,500 to graduate students to conduct, or supervise the conduct of, research that will advance the knowledge base of school food service and nutrition programs. Must be an active member of ASFSA or be supervised on the grant by an active member of ASFSA. Must have at least a 3.0 GPA on a 4.0 scale, with a major in foods and nutrition, nutrition education, food service management, or a related field at an accredited institution. Research must be applicable to school food service and child nutrition. Deadline: April 30.

648. (SS)
Tony's Food Service Scholarship

75 scholarships of $500 to graduate students who are members or whose parent is a member of the American School Food Service Association. Applicants must be planning on pursuing a career in food service (food science technology, nutrition, or food service) and have at least a 2.7 GPA. Deadline: April 15.

(A)
American School of Classical Studies at Athens
6–8 Charlton Street
Princeton, NJ 08540–5232
(609) 683–0800
http://www.ascsa.org

649. (SS)
Fellowships

Fellowships providing up to $4,000, plus room and board, to graduate students at U.S. and Canadian institutions for study in Greece in the area of archaeology, classical studies, or ancient Greece. Recent graduates are also eligible. Study is conducted at ASCSA in Greece. Open to U.S. and Canadian graduate students. Deadline: January 5.

650. (SS)
Gennadeion Fellowship

Awards of up to $4,000, plus room and board, to graduate students, postdoctoral fellows, and junior academics to support work and study in the area of Byzantine and Greek studies at the Gennadeion in Athens, Greece. Study is conducted at ASCSA in Greece. Open to U.S. and Canadian graduate students. Deadline: January 15.

651. (A, H, SS)
Jacob Hirsch Fellowship

1 fellowship of $4,000, plus room and board, open to doctoral candidates majoring in art, art history, culture, history, language, literature, or linguistics to conduct study or research in Greece. Selection based on academic achievement and proposed research. Applicants must be at dissertation level. Must be either U.S. or Israeli citizen. Deadline: January 31.

652. (A, H, SS)
NEH Fellowship in Classical and Byzantine Studies

Fellowships of up to $30,000 to U.S. residents or U.S. citizens who wish to undertake postdoctoral work. Scholars at all levels, from assistant through full professors, are encouraged to apply. Award is given to assist studies by American scholars in the fields of art history, architecture, archaeology, and history in the areas of Classical and Byzantine studies including language, history, archaeology, art, and postclassical Greek studies. Deadline: November 15.

(A, H, S, SS)
American Schools of Oriental Research
ATTN: Administrative Director
Boston University
656 Beacon Street, 5th Floor
Boston, MA 02215
(617) 353–6570
http://www.asor.org

653. (H)
Endowment for Biblical Research, Summer Research & Travel Grants

2 stipends of $1,500 to seminarian graduate students or recent postdoctoral scholars from outside the Middle East or the eastern Mediterranean. 16 Summer Travel Grants of $1,000 to undergraduate, graduate, seminary, or recent postdoctoral students. Must be or become members of ASOR or be attending an institution that is a corporate member. Deadline: February 1.

654. (H, S, SS)
George A. Barton Fellowship

Varying number of fellowships providing $2,000, plus room and half board, to doctoral candidates in the humanities, social sciences, marine science, or oceanography to conduct from 1 to 5 months of study or research at the Albright Institute for Archaeological Research in Jerusalem. Selection is based on proposed research. Fellowship may not be used for summer study. Deadline: September 15 and October 15.

655. (SS)
Jennifer C. Groot Fellowship

2 scholarships providing stipends of $1,000 to graduate or undergraduate students to assist them in participating in an archaeological excavation or survey in Jordan for 1 to 3 months. Must be or become members of ASOR or be attending an institution that is a corporate member. Deadline: February 1.

656. (H, SS)
Mesopotamian Fellowship

1 fellowship of $5,000 to doctoral candidates and postdoctoral scholars to study and research on ancient Mesopotamian civilization and culture. Selection based on proposed research. Must be an ASOR member. Preference given to projects affiliated with ASOR. Deadline: February 1.

657. (A, H, SS)
Samuel H. Kress Foundation Fellowships

Varying number of fellowships providing a stipend of $4,500 plus room and half board to doctoral candidates in art history, archaeology, or architecture to conduct from 9 to 10 months of dissertation research at the Albright Institute in Jerusalem. Selection based on proposed research. Deadline: September 30.

658. (H)
William Foxwell Albright Fellowships

Varying number of fellowships of $5,000 to doctoral candidates and postdoctoral scholars in Middle Eastern studies to conduct 4 to 9 months of study or research at ASOR institutes in Jerusalem, Amman, or Cyprus. Selection based on proposed research. Applicants must either be students at an ASOR-affiliated institution or have been members of ASOR for at least 2 years. Fellows cannot conduct extended travel during the award period. Renewable. Deadline: September 30.

(S, SS)
American Society for Engineering Education
1818 N Street, N.W., Suite 600
Washington, DC 20036
(202) 331–3516
http://www.asee.org
ndseg@asee.org

659. (S)
National Defense Science & Engineering Graduate Fellowships

Approximately 120 fellowships to doctoral students in aeroscience, chemistry, engineering, or mathematics. Awarded to encourage students to train in fields of military importance. Renewable for 3 years. Must be U.S. citizens or nationals. Permanent residents are ineligible to apply. Deadline: early January.

660. (S)
Office of Naval Research Graduate Fellowships

50 fellowships of varying amounts to doctoral students in biological sciences, computer science, engineering, information science, mathematics, or physics. Must be attending an institution that offers doctoral degrees in designated sciences and engineering. Awards are for 36 months. Fellows are encouraged to continue their studies and research during the summer sessions. GRE scores (general test only) are required. Deadline: varies.

661. (S, SS)
Washington Internships for Students of Engineering

A 10-week summer program in Washington, DC, for third-year engineering students. Program teaches how engineers contribute to public policy decisions on complex technological matters. 15 internships are also available. Students receive $2,400, travel allowance, and 5 quarter credits from the University of Washington. Based on academic achievement. Deadline: December 31.

662. (S)
American Society for Enology and Viticulture Scholarships
Scholarship Committee
P.O. Box 1855
Davis, CA 95617–1855
http://www.asev.org

20 scholarships ranging from $1,000 to $3,000 for graduate or upper-level undergraduate students for the study of enology (winemaking), viticulture (grape growing), and related subjects. Renewable. Applicant must submit a written statement of career goals in the area of winemaking, grape growing, food science, horticulture, or plant physiology. Must be attending an accredited North American institution and be a resident of North America. Graduates must have at least a 3.2 GPA or better. Undergraduates must have at least a 3.0 GPA. Selection is based on academic achievement and financial need. Deadline: March 1.

663. (S)
American Society for Metals Foundation for Education and Research
N. J. Grant
ATTN: ASM International
Materials Park, OH 44073–0002
(800) 336–5152
(440) 338–5151
http://www.asm-intl.org

1 full tuition scholarship providing full tuition to a graduate and upper-level undergraduate student enrolled in the department of materials science or materials engineering in metallurgy. Based on interest in metallurgy, academic achievement, letters of recommendation,

potential for success in metallurgy, and financial need. Must be citizens of U.S., Canada, or Mexico and attending an institution in any of these countries. Renewable for 1 year. Deadline: June 15.

(S)
American Society of Agronomy
677 South Segoe Road
Madison, WI 53711
(608) 273–8080
http://www.agronomy.org

664. (S)
Congressional Science Fellowship

Fellowships providing stipends of $52,067, plus relocation expenses of up to $1,500, to highly qualified individuals in early or mid-career who have exceptional competence in some area of the agronomic, crop, soil, or related fields of science and education. Provides a public policy learning experience. Fellows spend one year in Washington, DC. Must be members of ASA, CSSA, and/or SSSA and be a U.S. citizen. Deadline: March 1.

665. (S)
Deere & Company Graduate Fellowship

1 scholarship of $2,500 to a graduate student working on a master's degree in agronomy, crop science, or soil science. Must not have begun graduate work and must be student's final degree. Visit web site for more information. Deadline: February 28.

666. (S)
Harry J. Larsen/Hydro Memorial Scholarship

Scholarships of $5,000 to graduate (master's or doctoral) students in practical soil fertility and crop production. Must have completed 1 year of graduate school in a field of emphasis on practical soil fertility and crop production within either the A, C, or S Division of ASA. Visit web site for more information. Deadline: February 28.

667. (S)
Science Policy Internship

3- to 6-month internships providing a stipend of up to $1,000 per month, plus living expenses of up to $500 per month, based on experience, time frame, and need, to graduate and undergraduate students in agronomy, crop or soil science, or a closely related field. Undergraduates must have completed the first semester of sophomore year to be eligible to apply. Selection based on academic achievement, letter of interest, letters of recommendation, a 300-word essay on qualifications and goals, and a résumé showing education and experience. Must be a U.S. citizen, a member of ASA or SSSA, and have a strong interest in the science policy area. Visit web site for more information. Deadline: March 31.

668. (H)
American Society of Arms Collectors
Antique Weapons Research Fellowships
Col. Dean S. Hartley Jr.
520 Erin Avenue
Monroe, LA 71201
(318) 325–3624

Fellowships of $5,000 to graduate students to conduct research into the origin, manufacture, or use and history of rare or historical weapons. Must be working on a master's or doctoral degree that is consistent with the Society's aims and purposes. Research should result in a scholarly paper that can be published in the Society's bulletin. Renewable. Deadline: March 15.

(H)
American Society of Church History
P.O. Box 8517
Red Bank, NJ 07701
(732) 345–1787
http://www.churchhistory.org

669. (H)
Albert C. Outler Prize

Awards of $1,000 to the author of a book-length manuscript dealing with ecumenical church history and a possible grant of $3,000 for publication. Work should deal with the problems of Christian unity and disunity in any period. Selection is based on creative writing and theology. Deadline: June 1.

670. (H)
Frank S. and Elizabeth D. Brewer Prize

Award of $1,000 to the best unpublished book-length manuscript or essay written on topics dealing with church history. Prize is for assistance in publishing the work. Work must not have been previously submitted. Deadline: November 1.

671. (H)
Jane Dempsey Douglass Prize

1 award of $250 for the author of the best essay published during the previous calendar year on any aspect of the role of women in the history of Christianity. Deadline: August 1.

672. (H)
Philip Schaff Prize

1 award of $2,000 to the author of the best book published in the previous calendar years, originating in the North American scholarly community, that presents original research on any period in the history of Christianity. Deadline: March 1.

673. (H)
Sidney E. Mead Prize

1 prize of $250 given to the best essay in any field of church history written by a doctoral candidate or recent Ph.D. whose essay comes directly from their doctoral research. Winners will be published in *Church History*. Deadline: March 1.

674. (A)
**American Society of Cinematographers
Seitz Heritage Award**
P.O. Box 2230
Hollywood, CA 90078
(800) 448–0145
(323) 969–4333
http://www.theasc.com

1 or more cash awards of varying amount to a graduate, undergraduate, or recent graduate who majored in film. Selection is based on how effectively the students used visual grammar to tell stories in ways generally transparent to viewers.

(S)
American Society of Civil Engineers
1801 Alexander Bell Drive
Reston, VA 20191
(800) 548–2723
http://www.asce.org/inside/stud_scholar.cfm

675. (S)
Arthur S. Tuttle Memorial National Scholarship

1 or more scholarships, ranging from $1,000 to $2,000, to graduate students majoring in civil engineering. Must be a student member of ASCE in good standing and attending an accredited U.S. institution. Selection based on academic achievement, recommendation letters, extracurricular activities, demonstrated leadership, potential for development, ASCE activities, and financial need. Visit web site for more information and an application. Deadline: February 10.

676. (S)
Jack E. Leisch Memorial National Graduate Fellowship

1 or more scholarships of up to $2,500 to graduate (master or doctoral) students in a transportation/traffic engineering degree program in civil engineering. Must be a member of ASCE in good standing and attending an accredited U.S. institution. Selection is based on academic achievement, educational goals, potential for development, leadership capacity, and financial need. Visit web site for more information and an application. Deadline: May 15.

677. (S)
J. Waldo Smith Hydraulic Fellowship

1 scholarship of varying amount and fellowships of $4,000, plus up to $1,000 for physical equipment, to a graduate student in civil engineering to conduct research in experimental hydraulics as distinguished from purely theoretical hydraulics. Must be attending an accredited educational institution. Must be a member of ASCE in good standing. Membership application can be submitted along with scholarship application. Fellowship is made to encourage research in the field of experimental hydraulics. Preference given to associate members. The fellowship is offered every 3 years. Selection based on academic achievement, essay, extracurricular activities, ASCE activities, and financial need. Visit web site for more information and an application. Deadline: February 15.

678. (S)

O.H. Ammann Research Fellowship in Structural Engineering

1 fellowship of $5,000 to a graduate student to conduct research in structural design and construction. Must be a member of ASCE in good standing and attending an accredited institution. Renewable for an additional year, though amount of the additional stipend will be determined based on funds available. Visit web site for more information and an application. Deadline: February 25.

679. (A)

American Society of Composers, Authors and Publishers Foundation
Music Composition Awards Program
ASCAP Building
1 Lincoln Plaza
New York, NY 10023
(212) 621–6000
http://www.ascap.com

15 awards of $800 to young composers under the age of 30 as of March 15 of the year of application. Awards help young composers continue their studies and develop their skills. Write for complete information. Deadline: March 15.

680. (S)

American Society of Crime Laboratory Directors Scholarship Award
15200 Shady Grove Road
Rockville, MD 20850
(702) 229–3932
http://www.ascld-lab.org

Up to 2 scholarships of $500 to graduate and undergraduate students majoring in forensic science at an accredited institution. Based on academic record, internships, and goals. For more information, visit web site or send a self-addressed, stamped envelope for information. Deadline: none specified.

681. (S, SS)

American Society of Criminology
ASC Gene Carte Student Paper Competition
1314 Kinnear Road
Columbus, OH 43212–1156

(614) 292–9207
http://www.asc41.com

Awards of $300, $150, and $100 to graduate and undergraduate students who submit empirical and/or theoretical papers related to criminology. For information on how to submit papers, visit web site or send a self-addressed, stamped envelope. Deadline: April 15.

682. (S)

American Society of Heating, Refrigeration, and Air-Conditioning Engineers
ASHRAE Graduate Grants-in-Aid
Staff Liaison, Scholarship Fund Trustees
1791 Tullie Circle, N.E.
Atlanta, GA 30329
(404) 636–8400
http://www.ashrae.org

Scholarships of up to $7,500 to full-time graduate students majoring in heating, refrigeration, and air-conditioning. Awards are good at any U.S. or Canadian accredited institutions. Deadline: December 15.

683. (A)

American Society of Health Systems Pharmacists Research and Education Foundation
Executive Vice President
7272 Wisconsin Avenue
Bethesda, MD 20814
(301) 657–3000
http://www.ashp.org

1 honorarium award of $500, plus a $500 expense allowance, to attend the Midyear Meeting to a graduate and undergraduate student (B.S., M.S., and Pharm.D.) who submits an unpublished paper on a subject related to hospital pharmacy written during the preceding academic year. Request information after January 1. Deadline: May 15.

(A)

American Society of Interior Designers
Educational Foundation Scholarships
608 Massachusetts Avenue, N.E.
Washington, DC 20002
(202) 546–3480
http://www.asid.org

684. (A)
Dora Brahms Award

1 award of $1,500 to an educational institution on behalf of their students in historic preservation and/or restoration studies. Institute must illustrate how this award will best assist the student of historic preservation/restoration. Deadline: February 15.

685. (A)
Educational Foundation/Steelcase Contract Design Scholarship

2 awards of $3,000 for students enrolled in 3-, 4-, or 5-year FIDER-accredited design programs that offer course work in contract design. Based on academic record, grade point average, creativity, and potential. Request information after December 1. Deadline: March 15.

686. (A)
Environmental Design Award

1 award of $4,000 to individuals, organizations, institutions, or project groups. Award encourages the interaction of the design profession using a holistic approach to the design process when solving environmental problems. Design proposal must illustrate the problem-solving process resulting from research as well as design ability. Deadline: February 15.

687. (A)
Joel Polsky Prize

1 award of $2,000 to recognize outstanding academic contributions to interior design. Entries are judged on bibliography, references, content, breadth of material, coverage of topic, and subject matter. Deadline: December 15.

(A)
American Society of Landscape Architecture
818 18th Street, N.W.
Washington, DC 20006
(202) 331–7070
http://www.asla.org

688. (A)
The Coxe Group Scholarship

1 scholarship of $1,000 to a graduate or undergraduate student who is in the fourth, fifth, or sixth year of a landscape architectural degree program. Selection based on ability and financial need. Send a self-addressed, stamped envelope for information. Deadline: early May.

689. (A)
Edith H. Henderson Scholarship

1 scholarship of $1,000 open to graduate students in any year of study and undergraduate students who are in their beginning or final year of undergraduate study in a landscape architectural degree program. Selection based on ability and financial need. For more information, visit web site or send a self-addressed, stamped envelope for information. Deadline: early May.

690. (A)
Grace & Robert Fraser Landscape Award

1 award of $500 to a graduate or undergraduate student to recognize innovative horticultural research or design relating to landscape architecture. Selection based on ability and financial need. Deadline: early May.

691. (A)
LANDCADD Inc. Scholarship Fund

Scholarships of $500 to graduate or undergraduate students who wish to use computer-aided design, video imaging, and/or telecommunications in their career. Selection based on ability and financial need. For more information, visit web site or send a self-addressed, stamped envelope for information. Deadline: early May.

692. (A)
Lester Walls III Endowment Scholarship

1 scholarship of $500 to a disabled graduate or undergraduate student pursuing a career in landscape architecture, or for research on barrier-free design for the disabled. Selection based on ability and financial need. For more information, visit web site or send a self-addressed, stamped envelope for information. Deadline: early May.

693. (A)
Raymond E. Page Scholarship Fund

Varying numbers of scholarships of $500 to graduate and undergraduate students pursuing a degree in landscape architecture. Selection is based on financial need. Student must submit a 2-page explanation describing financial need and how money will be used. 3 letters of recommendation from previous or current professors or employers are required. For more information, visit web site or send a self-addressed, stamped envelope for information. Deadline: early May.

694. (A)
Student Research Grants

Grants of $1,000 for graduate and undergraduate students to encourage practical educational research that will benefit the profession and the general public. Also allows students to expand their field of interest and propose creative, innovative projects. For more information, visit web site or send a self-addressed, stamped envelope for information. Deadline: mid-April to mid-May.

695. (A)
William Locklin Scholarship

1 scholarship of $500 to a graduate or undergraduate student in a landscape architectural degree with emphasis in lighting design. Purpose is to stress the importance of 24-hour lighting in landscape design. For more information, visit web site or send a self-addressed, stamped envelope for information. Deadline: early May.

696. (S)
American Society of Mechanical Engineers Scholarships
Three Park Avenue
New York, NY 10016–5990
(800) 843–2763
(212) 705–7375
http://www.asme.org

Scholarships of $1,500 to graduate students in the area of mechanical engineering. Based on character, academic achievement, and financial need. For more information, visit web site or send a self-addressed, stamped envelope or contact local ASME faculty advisor. Deadline: February 15.

697. (S)
American Society of Naval Engineers Scholarship
Overseer of Scholarships
1452 Duke Street
Alexandria, VA 22314–3458
(703) 836–6727
http://www.navalengineers.org

16 scholarships of $3,500 for graduate students, or $2,500 to upper-level undergraduates, seeking a degree in engineering with a career in naval engineering. Based on interest in naval engineering, academic achievement, competence, and financial need. Renewable if not a graduate student. Must be U.S. citizens and members of ASNE or SNAME. Deadline: February 15.

698. (S)
American Society of Photogrammetry and Remote Sensing (ASPRS) Scholarships
ASPRS Awards Program Director
5410 Grosvenor Lane, Suite 210
Bethesda, MD 20814–2160
(301) 493–0290
http://www.asprs.org

Scholarships ranging from $500 to $4,000 to graduate and undergraduate students, and 1 fellowship of $4,000 to a master's or doctoral student in photogrammetry. Must be members of the ASPRS or the American Congress of Surveying and Mapping. Applicants must have completed at least 1 course in surveying or photogrammetry. Deadline: December 1.

699. (S)
American Society of Safety Engineers Student of the Year Award and Scholarships
1800 East Oakton
Des Plaines, IL 60018–2187
(847) 699–2929
http://www.asse.org

1 award of $1,000 and a plaque (Student of the Year Award) and 2 scholarships of $2,500 to full-time graduate or undergraduate students. Must be preparing for a career in safety, health, or related specialities. Applicants must be ASSE student members attending an accredited institution. Based on academic record, activities, and

recommendation by faculty advisor, chapter officer, or other faculty member. Deadline: January 31.

(SS)

American Society of Travel Agents (ASTA)
1101 King Street
Alexandria, VA 22314
(703) 739–2782
http://www.astanet.com

700. (SS)
Avis Rent A Car Scholarship

1 scholarship of $1,000 to a graduate or undergraduate sophomore, junior, or senior student learning automation and communication skills for use in a travel and tourism career. Must have worked part-time in a travel career. May be attending 2-year or 4-year program. Must have at least a 2.5 GPA on a 4.0 scale. Must be a U.S. or Canadian citizen or legal resident. Deadline: June 10.

701. (SS)
David Hallissey Memorial Fund

1 scholarship of $1,200 to a graduate or undergraduate student to do research in a travel field. Student must be a travel or tour educator at a postsecondary institution or preparatory school. May be attending 2-year or 4-year program. Must have at least a 2.5 GPA on a 4.0 scale. Must be a U.S. or Canadian citizen or legal resident.

702. (SS)
Scholarship Foundation Scholarship Funds

27 scholarships ranging from $250 to $3,000 to graduate and undergraduate students enrolled in an accredited proprietary school and majoring in travel & tourism. May be attending 2-year or 4-year program. Must have at least a 2.5 GPA on a 4.0 scale. Must be a U.S. or Canadian citizen or legal resident. Deadline: June 10.

703. (SS)
American Society of Women Accountants Scholarships
8405 Greensboro Drive, Suite 800
McLean, VA 22102
(800) 326–2163
(703) 506–3265
http://www.aswa.org

1 scholarship from $1,000 to $4,000 to a female graduate or undergraduate student majoring in accounting at an accredited institution. Student must be nominated through local chapters. For chapter contacts, visit the national web site. Deadline: varies by chapter.

(SS)

American Sociological Association
1307 New York Avene, N.W., Suite 700
Washington, DC 20005
(202) 383-9005
http://www.asanet.org

704. (SS)
Community Action Research Initiative Fellowships

Fellowships ranging from $1,000 to $2,500 to graduate students who are eligible to apply, but the funding cannot be used to support doctoral dissertation research, as well as sociologists in academic settings, research institutions, private and nonprofit organizations, and government. Awarded to encourage sociologists to undertake community action projects that bring social science knowledge, methods, and expertise to bear in addressing community-identified issues and concerns. For specific details, visit web site. Deadline: February 1.

705. (SS)
Minority Fellowship Program

25 to 30 fellowships providing tuition plus stipends of $16,500 to minority students beginning or doing doctoral work with an emphasis on research in sociology with an emphasis on mental health issues of special concern to minorities. For more information and deadline, visit web site.

706. (SS)
Teaching Enhancement Fund Grant

1 or 2 grants of $1,000 to individuals, department, program, or committee of a state/regional association. Awarded to support projects that extend the quality of teaching in the United States and Canada. Applicants must submit a proposal describing the project. For specific information, visit web site. Deadline: February 1.

(H)

American Speech-Language-Hearing Association
10801 Rockville Pike
Rockville, MD 20852
(800) 638–8255
http://www.asha.org

707. (H)
Achievement for Schools-Related Professionals

A recognition award of varying amount to a person who has made significant contributions to the delivery of audiology and/or speech language pathology services in schools. Must be nominated by a colleague. Nomination forms available in January. Deadline: April 19.

708. (H)
Graduate Student Scholarships

Awards of $4,000 to full-time graduate students in communication sciences and disorders programs. Selection based on academic achievement. Request applications after April 1. For more information, visit web site or send a self-addressed, stamped envelope for information. Deadline: June 15.

709. (H)
International/Minority Student

Awards of $2,000 to full-time international/minority graduate students in communication sciences and disorders programs in the United States. Selection based on academic achievement. Request applications after April 1. For more information, visit web site or send a self-addressed, stamped envelope. Deadline: June 14.

710. (H)
New Investigator Research

Awards of $4,000 to new scientists who received their latest degree in communication sciences within the last 5 years. Grants are for research in audiology or speech-language pathology. Request applications after March 1. For more information, visit web site or send a self-addressed, stamped envelope. Deadline: July 12.

711. (H)
Outstanding Lifetime Achievement

1 award of varying amount to a person who has made significant contributions to clinical science and practice over a 20-year period or longer. Must be nominated by a colleague. Nomination forms available in January. For more information, visit web site or send a self-addressed, stamped envelope for information. Deadline: April 19.

712. (H)
Outstanding Recent Achievement

A Recognition Award of varying amount to a person who has made significant contributions to clinical science and practice within the past 3 years. Must be nominated by a colleague. Nomination forms available in January. For more information, visit web site or send a self-addressed, stamped envelope. Deadline: April 19.

713. (H)
Research Grant in Speech Science

Awards of $4,000 to new scientists who received their doctorate within the last 5 years. Field of doctorate is not limited. Grants are for research in audiology or speech-language pathology. Request applications after March 1. For more information, visit web site or send a self-addressed, stamped envelope. Deadline: July 19.

714. (H)
Student Research in Clinical or Rehabilitative Audiology

Research grants of $2,000 to graduate and postgraduate students in communication sciences and disorders to conduct 1-year study. Grants are for research projects in audiology or speech-language pathology. Request applications after March 1. For more information, visit web site or send a self-addressed, stamped envelope. Deadline: July 1.

715. (H)
Student Research in Early Childhood Language

Research grants of $2,000 to graduate and postgraduate students in communication sciences and disorders to conduct a 1-year study. Grants are for research projects in early childhood language development. Request applications after March 1. For more information, visit web site or send a self-addressed, stamped envelope. Deadline: July 1.

716. (H)
Student with Disability Scholarships

Awards of $2,000 to full-time graduate students with disabilities who are enrolled in a communication sciences and disorders program. Selection based on academic achievement. Request applications after April 1. For more information, visit web site or send a self-addressed, stamped envelope. Deadline: June 14.

717. (H)
Young Scholars Award for Minority Student

Awards of $2,000 to minority undergraduate seniors who have been accepted to a graduate program in speech-language pathology or audiology. Must be U.S. citizens. Selection based on academic achievement. Request applications after April 1. Deadline: June 14.

718. (SS)
American Statistical Association
ASA/NSF/BLS Senior Research Fellow and Associate Program
ATTN: Executive Director
1429 Duke Street
Alexandria, VA 22314–3415
(703) 684–1221
(888) 231–3473
http://www.amstat.org

Varying numbers of fellowships and associateships providing a stipend, fringe benefits, and travel allowance (total ranging from $20,000 to $30,000) to doctoral candidates and recent doctorate recipients in business, economics, labor studies, or population studies to participate in research at the Bureau of Labor Statistics. Based on academic achievement and proposed research project. Deadline: varies by program.

(A, H, S, SS)
American Swedish Institute
Education Coordinator
2600 Park Avenue
Minneapolis, MN 55407
(612) 870–3374
(612) 871–4907
http://www.americanswedishinst.org/Scholarship_Info2.htm

719. (A)
ASI Youth Fiddler's Scholarship

1 scholarship of $2,500 to a graduate or undergraduate student who is a fiddler. Award is meant to supplement travel plans to visit Sweden and allow recipient to be immersed in traditional Swedish folk music through firsthand experience of the culture around the music and contact with the tradition-bearers of this music in Sweden today.

720. (A, H, S, SS)
Lilly Lorénzen Scholarship

1 scholarship of $2,500 to a graduate or undergraduate student who plans to carry out scholarly and/or creative studies in Sweden. Must be a Minnesota resident. Applicants must have a working knowledge of the Swedish language, a serious desire to make a contribution to American-Swedish cultural exchange and demonstrable achievement in the selected field of study. A personal interview with the committee may be required. Deadline: May 1.

721. (S)
American Vacuum Society
Graduate Student Prize
120 Wall Street, 32nd Floor
New York, NY 10005
(212) 248–0200
http://www.avs.org

10 awards of $500 and 1 award of $1,500 to graduate students in electrical engineering vacuum science, sciences, engineering, and technologies of interest to the society. Selection based on academic achievement and research excellence. Recipients also receive reasonable travel expenses to attend the National Symposium. $1,500 award is for experimental or theoretical research in any of the technical and scientific areas of interest to the society. Recipients are normally expected to graduate after September 30 of the year following the award. Deadline: March 31.

722. (S)
American Water Works Association
Scholarships and Fellowships
6666 West Quincy Avenue   1401 New York Avenue,
Denver, CO 80235   N.W., Suite 640

(303) 794–7711   Washington, DC 20005
http://www.awwa.org   (202) 628–8303

Varying number of fellowships of up to $10,000 to graduate (master's or doctorate) engineering students and 1 scholarship of $5,000 to a female or minority student. Based on leadership potential. Must be completing degree within 2 years of the award. Must be citizen or permanent resident of U.S., Canada, or Mexico. Deadline: January 15.

723. (S)

American Welding Society
Scholarship Program
550 N.W. Lejeune Road
Miami, FL 33135
(800) 443–9353
(305) 443–9353
http://www.aws.org

Scholarships of varying amounts to graduate or undergraduate students pursuing careers in welding technology who are enrolled in an accredited material joining or similar program. May be used at a 2- or 4-year accredited U.S. college or university. Open to U.S. citizens who reside in the U.S. Deadline: June 1.

724. (S)

American Wind Energy Association
Internship Coordinator
122 C Street, N.W., 4th Floor
Washington, DC 20001
(202) 383–2500
http://www.awea.org

10 12-week internships, providing a salary ranging from $240 to $320 per week, to graduate students, recent college graduates, and undergraduates to work at AWEA to advance the development of wind energy as an economically and technically viable energy alternative. Interns work in administration, finance, legislative, international, membership, and meetings at the Washington, DC, office. Internships are conducted during the summer, fall, and spring. Deadline: rolling.

725. (SS)

American Wholesale Marketers Association
Ray Foley Memorial Scholarship Program
1128 16th Street, N.W.
Washington, DC 20036
(202) 463–2124
http://www.awmanet.org/edu/edu-schol.html

2 scholarships of $5,000 to full-time graduate or undergraduate students pursuing a career in business. Must be an AWMA wholesaler distributor member or an immediate family member of an employee of an AWMA wholesaler distributor member and demonstrate an interest in a career in candy/tobacco/convenience products wholesale distribution. Award may be used to pay for tuition, room and board, books, or other school-related expenses. Deadline: early May.

(SS)

American Woman's Society of CPAs
136 South Keowee Street
Dayton, OH 45402
(937) 222–1872
http://www.awscpa.org
info@awscpa.org

726. (SS)
Alabama Chapter

Scholarships of varying amounts to graduate students or undergraduate seniors who are accounting majors. Must have at least a 3.5 GPA on a 4.0 scale and be a student member of AWSCPA. Visit web site for more information and contact person. Deadline: second Wednesday in April.

727. (SS)
California, Bay Area

10 to 15 scholarships of $1,500 and $2,000 to graduate and upper-level undergraduate students. Must have at least a B average or better and have completed 6 semesters or 9 quarter hours of accounting by fall of the application year. Must continue study in accounting during the award year. Visit web site for more information and contact person. Deadline: May 31.

728. (SS)
California, Los Angeles Chapter

1 to 5 scholarships ranging from $500 to $1,000 and student memberships to AWSCPA to graduate students or undergraduate seniors who are accounting majors. Must have at least a 3.0 GPA on a 4.0 scale and be residents of or attending an accredited institution in the Los Angeles area. Preference given to student members of AWSCPA. Visit web site for more information and contact person. Deadline: May 1.

729. (SS)
California, San Diego Chapter

Scholarships of varying amounts to graduate students or undergraduate seniors who are accounting majors. Must be a student member of AWSCPA and write an essay. Must attend University of San Diego, San Diego State University, or California State University in San Marcos. Visit web site for more information and contact person. Deadline: none specified.

730. (SS)
California, San Francisco

10 to 15 scholarships ranging between $1,500 and $2,000 to graduate or upper-level undergraduates who are accounting majors. Must have at least a B average and have completed 6 semester hours or 9 quarter hours by the start of the scholarship year. Deadline: May 31.

731. (SS)
Georgia Chapter

Scholarships of varying amounts to graduate and undergraduate students who have completed or are enrolled in Intermediate Accounting II. Visit web site for complete guidelines and contact information. Deadline: none specified.

732. (SS)
Massachusetts, Boston Chapter

Scholarships of varying amounts to graduate and undergraduate students in accounting. Must attend an accredited college or university in New York. Must have completed 12 hours of accounting or tax courses by fall of the current year and must be continuing studies in accounting during the current year.

Must expect to graduate between May of the next year and following year or, for the 15-month graduate program, before September of the current year. Visit web site for more information and contact person. Deadline: none specified.

733. (SS)
National Awards

Up to 3 awards of $500 each for unpublished papers dealing with the effects of gender on auditing and accounting, especially research on the effect of gender on professional issues and lifestyle concerns. Papers can be presented at the AWSCPA annual/regional meetings. Visit web site for submission guidelines. Deadline: May 31.

734. (SS)
New York Chapter

Scholarships of varying amounts to graduate or undergraduate students who are accounting majors. Must have at least a 3.5 GPA on a 4.0 scale, have completed at least 1 semester of intermediate accounting course by June 30 of the application year, be a permanent resident or attend college within commuting distance of New York City, and continue taking classes through spring semester. Visit web site for more information and contact person. Deadline: last Friday in February.

735. (SS)
Texas, Houston Chapter

2 scholarships of $1,000 to female graduate (master's only) and undergraduate students who are accounting majors. Must have already completed 20 hours toward their degree, have completed at least 12 hours in accounting, and be present at the June meeting to accept the scholarship. Selection based on academic achievement, financial need, extracurricular activities, and community involvement. Must be attending one of the following schools: University of Houston (Main, Downtown, or Clear Lake campuses), University of St. Thomas, Sam Houston State University, Prairie View A&M University, Texas Southern University, or Houston Baptist University. Must be a U.S. citizen. Visit web site for more information and contact. Deadline: May 15.

736. (SS)
Texas, Lubbock Chapter

Scholarships of varying amounts to graduate or upper-level undergraduate students who are accounting majors. Must have at least a 3.0 GPA on a 4.0 scale, have completed at least 1 semester of intermediate accounting course by December of the previous year, continue working toward an accounting degree, and not expect to graduate prior to December of the current year. Must be attending Texas Tech University, Lubbock Christian University, or Wayland Baptist University. Visit web site for more information and contact person. Deadline: February 15 (postmark).

737. (SS)
Texas, San Antonio Chapter

Scholarships of varying amounts to graduate or undergraduate students who are accounting majors. Must have completed 60 credit hours. Visit web site for more information and contact person. Deadline: October 31.

738. (H)
American Women in Radio & Television
Austin Chapter
Scholarship
KVUE-TV
3201 Steck Avenue
Austin, TX 78757
(512) 459–2010
http://www.awrtaustin.org

1 scholarship of $500 to a graduate or undergraduate student majoring in communications. For more information and deadline, visit web site or send a self-addressed, stamped envelope.

739. (H)
American Women in Radio & Television
Chicago Chapter
Scholarship Chair
P.O. Box 43255
Chicago, IL 60643–0255
http://www.awrtchicago.org

Up to 2 scholarships of $500 to graduate and upper-level undergraduate students majoring in radio, electronic media, and/or a related field. Do not need to be members of Chicago AWRT, but must attend an accred-ited college or university in the Chicago area. Selection based on academic achievement, goals, recommendations, and essay. Though not automatically renewable, recipients may receive the award for up to 2 years with reapplication. Deadline: March 1.

740. (H)
American Women in Radio & Television
Dallas Chapter
Scholarship
KDAF/WB33
8001 John Carpenter Freeway
Dallas, TX 75247
(214) 252–3411
http://www.awrt-dfw.org

1 scholarship of $2,500 to a full-time graduate or upper-level undergraduate student pursuing a major in broadcasting, broadcast journalism, or advertising. Must have at least a 3.25 GPA overall or 3.0 GPA on a 4.0 scale in declared major. May be either female or male. Must attend an accredited college or university in North Texas. Deadline: February 14.

(H)
American Women in Radio & Television
Houston Chapter
Pamm Dudley
LCI
1360 Post Oak Boulevard, #1900
Houston, TX 77056
(713) 439–9359
http://www.awrthouston.org/scholarships.php

741. (H)
Edith Baker Scholarship

1 scholarship of $1,500 to a female graduate or undergraduate student who is pursuing a career in radio or television. Selection is based on academic achievement, goals, and financial need. Recipients also receive an internship. For more information and deadline, visit web site.

742. (H)
Internships

4 or more internships to female graduate and undergraduate students who are pursuing careers in radio

or television. Selection is based on academic achievement, goals, and financial need. For more information and deadline, visit web site.

743. (H)
Scholarships

7 or more scholarships ranging from $1,000 to $1,500 to female graduate and undergraduate students who are pursuing careers in radio or television. Selection is based on academic achievement, goals, and financial need. Recipients also receive an internship. For more information and deadline, visit web site.

744. (A, H, S, SS)
AmeriCorps* NCCC
Office of Recruitment
9th Floor
1201 New York Avenue, N.W.
Washington, DC 20525
(800) 942–2677
http://www.americorps.org/nccc/index.html

A program that provides $4,725 a year for up to 2 years of community service in 1 of 4 priority areas: education, human services, the environment, or public safety. Open to anyone of any age interested in earning assistance to cover educational costs by completing community service. A person must complete 1,700 hours of service work per year. Work can be completed before or after the person has attended a vocational or trade school, an undergraduate college or university, graduate, or professional school. Funds are used to pay current educational expenses or to repay federal student loans. The program provides a living allowance of at least $7,400 per year and, if necessary, health care and child care allowances.

745. (A, H, S, SS)
Amethyst Scholarship Foundation
Scholarships and Awards Committee
P.O. Box 101138
San Antonio, TX 78228
http://www.amethystscholarship.org

2 or more scholarships of at least $1,000 to full-time graduate and undergraduate students. Must be self-identified gay, lesbian, bisexual, or transgendered students who are accepted for enrollment, or currently enrolled, in an accredited program beyond the secondary education level. Must be a U.S. citizen and a resident of Texas for at least 1 year prior to attending post-secondary education and submitting an application. You must demonstrate financial need and maintain a minimum 3.0 GPA to be eligible for this award. Deadline: May: 15.

746. (S)
Amoco Foundation, Inc.
Doctoral Fellowship Program
200 East Randolph Drive
Mail Code 2308
Chicago, IL 60601
http://www.voiceinternational.org/fd/amoco.htm

Financial assistance to students pursuing doctoral degrees in engineering. Awards are renewable for up to 3 years. 1-year doctoral fellowships in earth and physical science are also available. Visit web site for more information or send a self-addressed, stamped envelope. Deadline: none specified.

747. (S)
Amyotrophic Lateral Sclerosis Association
Research Grant Program
27001 Agoura Road, Suite 150
Calabasas Hills, CA 91301–5104
(800) 782–4747
(818) 340–7500
http://www.als.org

Research grants of varying amounts to qualified post-doctoral researchers to conduct research relevant to amyotrophic lateral sclerosis. The association does not offer assistance for education. Scientists researching ALS should write for more information. Deadline: September 15.

748. (A)
Anderson Ranch Arts Center
Box 5598
Snowmass, CO 81615
(970) 923–3181
http://www.artistcommunities.org/andranch.html
artranch@rof.net

12 to 15 8-month studio art internships to college graduates, graduate students, and artists. Interns create a body of work in the resident's media of interest. Interns

receive $100 per month, plus housing and meals. Interns are assigned their own studio space and are able to receive informal training through various visiting lecturers. The Arts Center offers workshops in painting and drawing, ceramics, sculpture, woodworking and furniture design, photography, interdisciplinary studies, and children's studies. Applicants must send a résumé, statement of career goals, and 3 reference letters. Deadline: May 1.

(S)

Animal Health Trust
Head of Finances
Ladwades Park, Kentford
Newmarket, Suffolk CB8 7UU
08700 50 2426
http://www.aht.org/uk

749. (S)
AHT Research Training Scholarship

Numerous scholarships of up to 5,000 pounds sterling for graduate study (English equivalent is a second class honors degree) in the United Kingdom in veterinary science and allied sciences. To be used for training in veterinary research at an approved institution in the United Kingdom. Deadline: March 31.

750. (S)
Blount Memorial Fund Scholarships

Scholarships of 5,000 pounds sterling for graduate students in the United Kingdom in all areas of animal health. To be used for training in veterinary research at an approved institution in the United Kingdom. Renewable for up to 3 years. For more information, visit web site. Deadline: March 31.

751. (Contest)
Annual Poetry Contest
National Federation of State Poetry Societies
http://www.nfsps.com

Varying number of cash awards of varying amounts in a contest for previously unpublished poetry. There are 50 categories. Send self-addressed, stamped envelope for guidelines. Check web site for address to send request to, which varies by category. Entry fees charged. Deadline: varies by category.

752. (A)
Annual Poetry Contest
Rambunctious Review
1221 West Pratt Boulevard
Chicago IL 60626
(312) 338–2439
http://www.sfo.com/~sarapeyton/rambunctious.html

A writing contest with cash prizes of varying amounts for unpublished short stories and poems. Entry fee: $3 per story or $2 per poem. For guidelines, visit web site or send self-addressed, stamped envelope. Deadline: varies.

753. (S)
The Antarctic Project
Internship Coordinator
1630 Connecticut Avenue, NW, 3rd Floor
Washington, DC 20009
(202) 234–2480
http://www.asoc.org

20 internships open to graduate students, recent college graduates, and upper-level undergraduate students to work from 12- to 15-week internships at the TAP office in Washington, DC. Interns conduct research, write fact sheets, and attend conferences that are geared to protecting the natural resources of Antarctica and the southern ocean. No compensation is provided. Internships are conducted during the summer, fall, and spring. Deadline: rolling.

754. (A, H, S, SS)
Apple Computers, Inc.
Internship Program
College Relations
20525 Mariani Avenue
MS:75–2J
Cupertino, CA 95014
(408) 996–1010
http://www.apple.com

12-week summer internships providing salaries ranging from $600 to $1,100 per week (depending on education and work experience) plus round-trip travel expenses to undergraduate and graduate students. Though the majority of interns are majoring in computer science, electrical engineering, and computer engineering, the program is open to all majors. Students must submit a cover letter describing their academic background and how it applies to their area of interest. Include a résumé. The information is placed into a database that is used by managers of various departments. Candidates are interviewed by phone. Deadline: February 28.

755. (SS)
Appraisal Institute Education Trust Scholarship
Romanita Rencher Education Trust
550 West Van Buren Street, Suite 1000
Chicago, IL 60607
(312) 335–4100
http://www.appraisalinstitute.org

Varying number of scholarships of $3,000 to graduate students who are majoring in real estate, land economics, real estate appraising, or an allied field (related to real estate) at an accredited 4-year institution. Based on academic achievement, essay, and recommendations. Deadline: March 15.

(A, H, S, SS)
Archaeological Institute of America
Boston University
656 Beacon Street
Boston, MA 02215–2010
(617) 353–9361
(617) 353–6000 (Fax)
http://www.bu.edu/archaeology/centers/aia.html

756. (H, S, SS)
Anna C. and Oliver C. Colburn Fellowship

1 fellowship of up to $6,000 to an applicant who is at the predoctoral level or postdoctoral (received Ph.D. within last 5 years) in the area of classical archeology. Must be accepted as an incoming associate member or student associate member of the American School of Classical Studies at Athens. Deadline: February 1.

757. (A, H, S, SS)
Kenan T. Erim Award

Awards of $4,000 to American or international research scholars in the areas of archaeology, art history, and related fields. If the project involves work at Aphrodisias, candidates must submit written approval from the Field Director with their applications. Established by the American Friends of Aphrodisias to support a research scholar working on Aphrodisias material. Write to above address or contact by e-mail: aia@bu.edu. Deadline: November 15.

758. (A, H, S, SS)
Olivia James Traveling Fellowship

Fellowships providing a $11,500 stipend are available to graduate and postgraduate students in archaeology, classics, sculpture, history, or architecture. Study must be done in Greece, Aegean Islands, Sicily, Southern Italy, Asia Minor, or Mesopotamia. Preference given for dissertation or postdoctoral research. Cannot be used to support field excavation. Applicants must be U.S. citizens or legal residents. Deadline: November 15.

759. (A, SS)
Archive Films
Internship Coordinator
75 Varick Street
New York, NY 10001
(646) 613–4100
(800) 876–5115
http://www.filmarchive.com

10 internships lasting from 6 to 12 weeks and providing a daily transportation stipend. Open to graduate and undergraduate students, recent college graduates, and high school graduates. Students work in film and photo research, film sales, marketing, or acquisitions/duplications. Archive Films has a collection dating back to 1890 and includes news footage on virtually every 20th-century famous event, personalities, documentaries, and over 10,000 films. Deadline: rolling.

760. (S, SS)
Arctic Institute of North America
Grant-in-Aid Program
ATTN: Executive Director
University of Calgary
2500 University Drive, N.W.
Calgary, Alberta T2N 1N4
Canada
(403) 220–7515
http://www.ucalgary.ca/aina

Varying number of grants of up to $5,000 Canadian to master's and doctoral candidates in natural or social sciences to conduct field work in the northern regions.

Selection based on academic achievement and proposed research. Deadline: January 15.

761. (S)
Argonne National Laboratory
Student Research Participation Program; Thesis Research
Division of Educational Programs
9700 South Cass Avenue
Argonne, IL 60439
(630) 252–2000
http://www.anl.gov

Stipends ranging from $175 to $200 per week for 1-semester accredited internship program to provide students majoring in physical sciences, life sciences, earth sciences, mathematics, computer sciences, engineering, fusion and fission energy an opportunity to work in relation to energy development. Open to full-time graduate students or upper-level undergraduate students. Must be U.S. citizens and legal residents. Thesis research awards available to doctoral candidates working on their dissertation. Deadline: February 1, May 15, and October 15.

762. (S)
Arizona/NASA Space Grant Graduate Fellowship
Lunar & Planetary Laboratory
The University of Arizona
Tucson, AZ 85721
(520) 621–8556
http://www.seds.org/spacegrant.htm

Fellowships of $16,000 plus tuition, fees, and $1,500 for travel to part- or full-time graduate students pursuing degrees in space, related sciences, and engineering. Must be a U.S. citizen and attending either the University of Arizona (outreach program requirement) or Arizona State University. Award is for 2 years. Visit web site for more information or changes. Deadline: early spring.

763. (SS)
Arizona State Library Association
Library Technicians and Paraprofessionals
1700 West Washington, Suite 200
Phoenix, AZ 85007
(602) 542–4035
http://www.lib.az.us/index.html

1 scholarship of $150 to a second-year library technician student. Must be a resident of Arizona and studying in Arizona. Must have at least a 3.0 GPA. For more information, visit web site. Deadline: March 15.

764. (SS)
Arkansas Library Association
Executive Director
9 Shackleford Plaza
Little Rock, AR 72211
(501) 228–0775
http://www.arlib.org
arlassociation@aol.com

1 scholarship grant of $1,500 to a graduate student admitted to an ALA-accredited library program. Must be an Arkansas resident and commit to work 1 year in an Arkansas library after completing master's degree. Deadline: April 15.

765. (SS)
Arkansas School Counselor Association
Hugh Lovett Memorial Scholarship
Chairperson
3915 West 8th
Pine Bluff, AR 71603
(501) 536–4118
Written inquiry

Awards of $1,000 to graduate students pursuing careers in student counseling. Must be enrolled in an approved Arkansas institution. Must work in education for 3 years after completing the program. Deadline: March 1.

(S)
Armed Forces General Practice Residency Program
contact local recruiter

766. (S)
Commander, Air Force Recruiting Command

General practice residency offered by the Air Force designed to broaden the techniques and skills of recent graduates to practice general dentistry. Required to serve on active duty for a specific period of time. Students apply during third year of dental school. Contact school's Financial Aid Director, academic dean, or local recruiter.

767. (S)
Commander, Army Recruiting Command

General practice residency offered by the Army designed to broaden the techniques and skills of recent graduates to practice general dentistry. Required to serve on active duty for a specific period of time. Students apply during third year of dental school. Contact school's Financial Aid Director, academic dean, or local recruiter.

768. (S)
Commander, Navy Recruiting Command

General practice residency offered by the Navy designed to broaden the techniques and skills of recent graduates to practice general dentistry. Required to serve on active duty for a specific period of time. Students apply during third year of dental school. Contact school's Financial Aid Director, academic dean, or local recruiter.

769. (S)
Armed Forces Graduate Education Opportunities
contact local recruiter
http://www.rotc.monroe.army.mil/nurse/Nurse.asp#geo/

2-year ROTC nursing scholarships are available to registered nurses to obtain a master's degree in specific nursing subspecialities and for second-degree students, with no nursing background, in an entry-level program that awards a master of science in nursing.

(S)
Armed Forces Health Professions Scholarship Program
contact local recruiter

770. (S)
Commander, Air Force Recruiting Command

Program provides full tuition, fees, books, expenses, and a monthly stipend of $843 to students enrolled in/or accepted to accredited school of medicine or osteopathy in U.S. or Puerto Rico. Will be appointed as a commissioned officer in air force reserve. Must serve 1 year active duty for each year of support (3 years minimum). Must be U.S. citizen.

771. (S)
Commander, Navy Recruiting Command

The program provides full tuition, fees, expenses, and a monthly stipend of up to $843 to students enrolled in, or accepted to, an accredited school of dentistry, optometry, or nurse anesthesia (master's degree) in U.S. or Puerto Rico. Will be appointed as a commissioned officer in Navy Reserve. Must serve 1 year active duty for each year of support (3 years minimum). Must be U.S. citizens.

772. (S)
United States Air Force Opportunity Center

Scholarships providing tuition, fees, books, educational expenses, and a monthly stipend of at least $843 to students accepted to, or enrolled in, accredited programs of medicine, dentistry, optometry, nurse anesthesia (master's), or clinical psychology (doctorate) in the U.S. or Puerto Rico. Must be U.S. citizens. Must qualify for appointment as an air force officer and sign a contractual agreement. Deadline: none specified.

773. (A)
Armenian Allied Arts Association Scholarship
3063 Dona Marta Drive
Studio City, CA 91604
(323) 962–5878
http://www.armenianalliedarts.org

Awards ranging from $50 to $1,000 to individuals in an art competition, with senior, junior, and child categories. At least one parent must be of Armenian descent, and participants do not have to be U.S. citizens. Selection based on merit of work. Deadline: prior to April.

774. (A, H, S, SS)
Armenian-American Citizens' League Educational & Scholarship Fund, Inc.
P.O. Box 14
Moorpark, CA 93020–0014

Scholarships ranging from $500 to $1,500 to full-time graduate and undergraduate students in any area of study. Must be students of Armenian descent. Must have been living in California for at least 2 years and be citizens of the U.S., though students from Armenia are eligible, if they have been living in California for 2 years. Selection based on grades, need, and involvement in school and community activities. Deadline: varies annually.

775. (S)
Armenian-American Medical Association Scholarship
423 Common Street
Watertown, MA 02172–4940
http://www.armenianmed.com

2 or 3 scholarships ranging from $1,500 to $2,000 to medical school students. Must be Armenian students residing and studying in a private New England medical school. Other students should not apply. Selection is based on academic achievement, financial need, and involvement in Armenian cultural affairs. Deadline: October 15.

776. (S)
Armenian-American Pharmacists' Association Scholarship
Chairman, Ara Demirjian
15 Sumner Street
Burlington, MA 01803
(781) 273–5727

1 scholarship of varying amount to a graduate or undergraduate student pursuing a bachelor's, master's, or doctoral degree in pharmacy. Must be a student of Armenian descent. Must be attending a college of pharmacy in New England (MA, CT, RI). Selection based on academic excellence and/or financial need. Deadline: September 15.

777. (S)
Armenian Dental Society of Southern California
ADSC Scholarship Committee
P.O. Box 2074
Glendale, CA 91209–2074
(818) 956–7137

Varying number of scholarships of $1,000 to third- and fourth-year dental school students. Must be students of Armenian descent, enrolled in an accredited California dental school. Selection based on academic achievement, financial need, and involvement in the Armenian community. Deadline: December 31.

(A, H, S, SS)
Armenian Educational Foundation
600 W. Broadway, Suite 130
Glendale, CA 91204
(818) 242–4150
http://www.aefweb.org

778. (SS)
Hurad Van Der Bedrosian Memorial Scholarship

2 scholarships of $3,000 to graduate students in Armenian studies. Must be of Armenian descent, U.S. citizens, and attending an accredited institution. Selection based on academic achievement, extracurricular activities, financial need, and recommendations. Deadline: April 15.

779. (A, H, S, SS)
Jorjorian Memorial Scholarship

Scholarships of $2,000 to graduate and undergraduate students in any area of study. Must be of Armenian descent and attending either Haigazian University in Beirut or any university in Armenia. Contact for more information and deadline.

(H, S, SS)
Armenian General Benevolent Union
ATTN: Administrator
55 East 59th Street
New York, NY 10022
(212) 319–6383
http://www.agbu.org

780. (H, SS)
Excellence Grant

1 grant of $5,000 to a graduate student in Armenian studies, international affairs, education, journalism, or public administration. Selection based on academic achievement, competence in subject area. Must be of Armenian descent. Must be enrolled in either Columbia University, Harvard University, University of Michigan, or UCLA. Deadline: April 30.

781. (S)
Graduate Scholarship Program

70 grants of $1,000 to graduate students in law, medicine, international relations, or Armenian studies. Selections based on academic achievement, financial need, involvement in Armenian community,

and Armenian descent. Must be enrolled in an accredited U.S. institution. Deadline: April 30.

782. (A, H, S, SS)
Armenian Professional Society
1535 Virginia Avenue
Glendale, CA 91202
(818) 766–1338
hkeyrib@aol.com

1 scholarship of $1,000 to a full-time graduate or undergraduate student in any area of study. Must be a California resident who is of Armenian descent and enrolled in an accredited college or university. Must have at least a 3.2 GPA. Selection based on academic achievement, financial need, and an interview. Deadline: March.

783. (A, H, S, SS)
Armenian Relief Society
Eremian Scholarship
80 Bigelow Avenue
Hairenik Building, 2nd Floor
Watertown, MA 02472
(617) 926–5892

Scholarships of varying amounts to graduate students, undergraduate sophomores, juniors, or seniors in any area of study. Selection based on academic achievement, financial need, and involvement in the Armenian community. Deadline: April 1.

784. (A, H, S, SS)
Armenian Students' Association of America, Inc.
395 Concord Avenue
Belmont, MA 02178
(401) 461–6114
http://www.asainc.org/scholarships.html

50 scholarships and 10 fellowships ranging from $500 to $1,500 to full-time graduate or undergraduate students of Armenian descent who have completed at least 1 year of college. Scholarships are good for all areas of study. Students must have at least a C average (2.5 GPA). Renewable. Number of awards each year may vary with availability of funds. There is an application fee. Deadline: mid-March.

785. (A, H, S, SS)
Army Aviation Association of America Scholarship Foundation, Inc.
AAAA Scholarships
755 Main Street, Suite 4D
Monroe, CT 06468–2830
(203) 268–2450
http://www.quad-a.org

Numerous scholarships totaling $100,000 to graduate and undergraduate students who are members of AAAA, or a spouse, sibling, or dependent of a member. May be used for all areas of study. When requesting an application, list the name of the AAAA member. Deadline: May 1.

786. (S)
Arthritis Foundation
Medical Student Arthritis Research Award
P.O. Box 7669
Atlanta, GA 30357–0669
(800) 283–7800
http://www.arthritis.org

Various research awards of $11,000 to students enrolled in M.D. or M.D./Ph.D. programs at an accredited U.S. medical school. The award provides the opportunity for a student to work conducting research related to arthritis for 1 year prior to obtaining their M.D. Based on an outline proposing a research project. Award begins on July 1. Deadline: September 1.

787. (A)
Art of the Northeast USA Exhibition
Silvermine Guild Arts Center
1037 Silvermine Road
New Canaan, CT 06840
(203) 966–6668
http://www.silvermineart.org

Awards ranging from $4,000 to $8,000 to artists for paintings, drawings, mixed media, and sculptures. Artists must reside in the Northeast (CT, ME, MA, NH, NJ, NY, PA, RI, VT). There is an entry fee of $20/slide. The exhibition run varies, generally during May and early June. For prospectus send a self-addressed, stamped envelope to above address. Deadline: March 22.

788. (A)
Art Renewal Center
ARC Salon and Scholarship Competition
Fred Ross, Chairman
100 Markley Street
Port Reading, NJ 07064
http://www.artrenewal.org/articles/Salon/salon2.
html#salon

7 scholarships ranging from $1,000 to $2,500 to full-time students who are pursuing a degree or the completion of an ARC-approved program. Applicants must submit an original artwork that reflects the principles espoused by the classical methods of drawing, painting, and sculpture, centering on the importance of the techniques developed and evolved from the Renaissance through the late 19th century. This competition is not open to abstract, conceptualist, neo-conceptual or nontraditional constructions. Commercial design art is also excluded. Illustrative works will be judged on a case-by-case basis. Applicants must submit 3 letters of recommendation, a résumé detailing education, honors received, and/or exhibitions, and a 250-word essay entitled "My Long-Term Educational and Career Goals." Please include a stamped, self-addressed envelope if you wish your materials returned. Deadline: March 31.

789. (SS)
Asia Foundation
465 California Street, 14th Floor
San Francisco, CA 94104
(415) 982–4640
http://www.asiafoundation.com

Provides grants of varying amounts to graduate or law school students in a public administration program. Awards supports study in government and law to students of Asian descent. Write an introductory letter detailing your ancestry and your educational and financial situation. Deadline: varies.

(H)
Asian American Journalists Association
1182 Market Street, Suite 320
San Francisco, CA 94102
(415) 346–2051
http://www.aaja.org/
national@aaja.org

790. (H)
AAJA Fellowships

Fellowships of up to $1,000 to members to help attend short-term professional training and skills development programs. Awards are made to provide assistance with tuition, travel, food, lodging, and other program-related expenses. Applicants must be full or associate members with at least 3 years of professional experience. Applications are accepted year-round. Deadline: rolling.

791. (H)
AAJA Local Competitions

Many AAJA chapters offer local scholarships or internship competitions. Students residing near or attending school in an area served by an AAJA chapter may be eligible to apply. Visit the web site for Asian American Journalists Association's national office for information on local chapters. Deadline: varies by chapter.

792. (H)
AAJA/Newspaper Association of America Minority Fellowship

2 fellowships cover seminar registration fees, travel, meals, and hotel expenses to newspaper journalists to attend the annual Executive Leadership Program, which takes place in March. Applicants should be full-time employees of a newspaper organization. For more information, visit web site for the name of the contact person. Deadline: mid-January.

793. (H)
AAJA/Poynter Institute of Media Studies Fellowships

2 fellowships of tuition and hotel costs (covered by Poynter) and transportation costs (covered by AAJA) to mid-career members to attend selected management training courses held at the Poynter Institute, St. Petersburg, FL. Applicants should be full-time employees of a print, broadcast, or online news organization or journalism educators. Deadline: mid-July and late August.

794. (H)
AAJA S.I. Newhouse National Scholarship and Internship Awards

Scholarships of up to $5,000 to graduate and undergraduate students pursuing careers in print journalism. Though open to all students, applicants from historically underrepresented Asian Pacific American groups, including Vietnamese, Cambodians, Hmong and other Southeast Asians, South Asians, and Pacific Islanders are encouraged to apply. S.I. Newhouse Scholarship winners will be eligible for summer internships with a Newhouse publication. Deadline: none specified.

795. (H)
Associated Press Internship Program

22 paid, 12-week internships to full-time graduate or undergraduate juniors and seniors attending an accredited U.S. college or university. The internship is an individually tailored training program for students who are aspiring print, photo, graphics, broadcast, and multimedia journalists. 22 interns will be chosen for the entire program, but only 1 application is chosen as the AAJA nomination. Deadline: November 1.

796. (H)
Minoru Yasui Memorial Scholarship Award

$1,500 scholarship to a promising Asian-American male broadcaster. A civil rights advocate and attorney, Minoru Yasui was one of 3 Nisei who challenged the internment of Japanese-Americans during World War II. Deadline: none specified.

797. (H)
Scholarship Awards

Scholarships of $2,000 to graduate or undergraduate students pursuing careers in broadcast or print journalism or mass communications. Based on academic achievement, financial need, community involvement, demonstrated journalistic ability, and a desire to pursue a news media career. Deadline: early April.

798. (A, H)
Asian American Writers Workshop
Van Lier Fellowship
16 West 32nd Street, Suite 10A
New York, NY 10001–3808
(212) 494–0061
http://www.aaww.org/fellowships/index.html

Awards consisting of a scholarship of $2,000 for writing workshops, a $2,500 stipend for living expenses, and a commission of $3,000 for a manuscript to emerging writers of Asian descent who reside in New York City. Must be under age 30, have not published a book or collection, demonstrate financial need, and exhibit a strong commitment to the literary arts and the Asian-American community. Award also includes professional guidance from a team of mentors (editor, literary agent, English professor, and published writer), inclusion in the Workshop's reading series and Literary Caravan, and publication consideration in *The Asian Pacific American Journal*. Fellows will be chosen on the basis of the quality of their submitted work, financial need, identifiable and achievable goals, and recommendations. Visit web site for specific guidelines.

(A, H, SS)
Asian Cultural Council
437 Madison Avenue, 37th Floor
New York, NY 10022–7001
(212) 812–4300
http://www.asianculturalcouncil.org

799. (A, H)
Fellowship Grants

90 fellowships ranging from $500 to $24,000, and 10 grants ranging from $500 to $10,000, to graduate and postdoctoral students majoring in visual or performing arts. Fellowships are to be used for round-trip travel, per diem, housing, maintenance, medical insurance allowances, and some educational expenses for periods ranging from 1 to 12 months. Open to Asian or American scholars, curators, conservators, specialists, artists, and doctoral students for visual and performing arts and humanities including architecture, art history, conservation, museology, art, dance, design, film, music, photography, and theater. The ACC's aim is to provide training or experience to assist Asian artists, scholars, students, and specialists for study, research, and travel in the U.S. A few grants are given to Americans for similar activities in Asia. Foreign recipients are obligated to return to their country of origin when the fellowship period is completed. Deadline: February 1 and August 1.

800. (H, SS)
Ford Foundation Fellowship Program

9 fellowships providing support for training, travel, and research to predoctoral and postdoctoral students and specialists in archaeology, art history,

conservation, dance ethnology, enthnomusicology, museology, and other disciplines involving traditional Asian culture. Only Asian citizens may apply. Deadline: open.

801. (SS)
Asian Law Caucus
939 Market St., Suite 201
San Francisco, CA 94103
(415) 896–170
http://www.asianlawcaucus.org
alc@asianlawcaucus.org

The Caucus provides legal assistance to individuals and undertakes general projects on behalf of Asian-Americans. It also provides information on legal rights, provides supportive services for prospective law students, and has a series of booklets on legal rights.

802. (SS)
Asian Pacific American Institute for Congressional Studies
Summer Internship Program
209 Pennsylvania Avenue S.E., Suite 100
Washington, DC 20003
(202) 547–9100
http://www.capaci.org

Varying numbers of internships providing a $2,500 stipend to graduate or undergraduate students with an interest in public policy issues and Asian Pacific American community affairs. Interns are expected to make their own travel and housing arrangements. There is no cost to congressional offices and federal departments and agencies participating in the Institute's Summer Internship Program. Must be U.S. citizens or legal permanent residents, able to demonstrate leadership abilities and excellent oral and written communication skills, and have a minimum grade point average of 3.0 on a 4.0 scale. All internships are in the Washington, DC, area. Visit web site for more information. Deadline: first week of February (summer).

803. (A)
Aspen Music School
Music Association of Aspen Scholarships
2 Music School Road
P. O. Box AA
Aspen, CO 81611

(970) 925–3254
http://www.aspenmusicfestival.com

800 partial- to full-tuition scholarships and fellowships to aspiring young and professional musicians. Must enroll in the 9-week summer session at the Aspen Music School for graduate or undergraduate credit. Between June and August, write to the above address. Between September and May, write to Aspen Music School, Office of Student Service, 250 W. 25th Street, 10th Floor East, New York, NY 10019. Deadline: varies.

804. (A)
Assistant Directors Training Program
ATTN: Administrator
14724 Ventura Blvd., Suite 775
Sherman Oaks, CA 91403
(818) 556–6853
http://www.dgptp.org
trainingprogram@dgptp.org

8 to 20 internships lasting 400 working days and providing a salary ranging from $400 to $500 per week to recent college graduates and students receiving an associate's or bachelor's degree by June 30. Interns work with cast and crew members and learn about set operations and the collective bargaining agreements of over 20 entertainment guilds and unions. Interns who complete the program are then placed on the Southern California Area Qualification List for employment as assistant directors. Relevant work experience may be used in place of college work. International applicants are eligible. Deadline: mid-December.

805. (S)
Associated General Contractors Education and Research Foundation
Saul Horowitz Jr. Memorial Graduate Award
Director of Programs
333 John Carlyle Street, Suite 200
Alexander, VA 22314
(703) 548–3118
http://www.agc.org

1 scholarship of $7,500 to a college senior enrolled in undergraduate construction or civil engineering or to a person possessing such a degree. Applicant must be enrolled, or planning to enroll, in a full-time graduate-level construction degree program. Deadline: November 15.

(H)
Associated Press Television-Radio Association of California/Nevada
Associated Press
221 South Figueroa Street, #300
Los Angeles, CA 90012
(213) 626–1200
http://www.aptra.org

806. (H)
APTRA-CLETE Roberts Memorial Journalism Scholarship Awards

2 scholarships of $1,500 to graduate or undergraduate students pursuing careers in broadcast journalism. Selection based on a combination of academic achievement, financial need, and broadcast career goals. Must be attending an accredited institution in California or Nevada. For more information, visit web site or send a self-addressed, stamped envelope. Deadline: mid-December.

807. (H)
Kathryn Dettman Memorial Journalism Scholarship

1 scholarship of $1,500 open to a graduate or undergraduate student pursuing a career in broadcast journalism. Selection based on a combination of academic achievement, financial need, and broadcast career goals. Must be attending an accredited institution in California or Nevada. For more information, visit web site or send a self-addressed, stamped envelope. Deadline: mid-December.

808. (S)
Associated Western Universities, Inc.
AWU-DOE Student Research Fellowships
4190 South Highland Drive, Suite 211
Salt Lake City, UT 84124
(801) 273–8900
http://www.awu.org

Various research fellowships throughout the country for qualified graduate (to work on non-thesis research) and upper-level undergraduate students to work during the summer in an energy-related science or engineering project. Students must have at least a 3.0 GPA on a 4.0 scale. The program encourages and promotes students to attend graduate school and pursue careers in science

or engineering. Contact above address to obtain a list of the participating laboratories. Deadline: March 1; February 1 (for laboratories requiring security clearance).

(A, H, SS)
Association for Asian Studies
1021 East Huron Street
Ann Arbor, MI 48104
(734) 665–2490
http://www.aasianst.org/grants/grants.htm

809. (A, H, SS)
AAS CIAC Small Grants

Grants of up to $1,500 to dissertation-level graduate students and junior and independent scholars at non-research institutions. Awards can be used to travel to major libraries and collections in North America and Taiwan. Award can also be used to fund dissertation-level graduate students to attend colloquia, workshops, and seminars related to their fields. Visit web site for more information. Deadline: February 1.

810. (A, H, SS)
AAS NEAC Japan Studies Grant

Grants of up to $1,500, plus a maximum of $100 for daily expenses, to doctoral candidates and postdoctoral fellows for research travel within the U.S. to conduct dissertation research at appropriate collections at museums, libraries, or archival materials. Must be U.S. citizens or permanent residents. Visit web site for more information. Deadline: February 1.

811. (A, H, SS)
AAS NEAC Korean Studies Grant

Grants of up to $1,500, plus a maximum of $100 for daily expenses, to doctoral candidates and postdoctoral fellows for research travel within the U.S. to conduct dissertation research at appropriate collections at museums, libraries, or archival materials. Must be U.S. citizens or permanent residents. Though primarily for postdoctoral work, predissertation doctoral research will be considered. Visit web site for more information. Deadline: February 1.

812. (A, H, SS)
Korean Studies Scholarship Program

Scholarships of $15,000 to graduate students majoring in Korean studies in any university in North

America. Major may be in any Korean-related course work and/or research in the humanities, social sciences, arts and culture, or comparative research related to Korea. Natural sciences, medical sciences, and engineering are not eligible. Applicants must have sufficient ability to use Korean-language sources in their study and research. Must be attending an accredited U.S. or Canadian university. Korean nationals are eligible if they have permanent residency status in the U.S. or Canada. Visit web site for more information. Deadline: February 28.

(A, H, S, SS)

Association for Education and Rehabilitation of the Blind and Visually Impaired
4600 Duke Street #430
P.O. Box 22397
Alexandria, VA 22304
(703) 823–9690
http://www.aerbvi.org

813. (H, S, SS)
Scholarships

Numerous scholarships of approximately $1,000 to legally blind graduate and professional school students, as well as undergraduates, who are pursuing a career that will service blind and visually impaired individuals. Based on application, certificate of visual status, and career goals. Deadline: April 15 of even-numbered years.

814. (A, H, S, SS)
William and Dorothy Ferrell Scholarship

Numerous scholarships of varying amounts to legally blind college graduate, postgraduate, and undergraduate students who are pursuing a career that will service blind and visually impaired individuals. Based on application, certificate of visual status, and career goals. Deadline: April 15 of even-numbered years.

(H)

Association for Education in Journalism & Mass Communication
234 Outlet Pointe Boulevard
Columbia, SC 29210–5667
(803) 798–0271
http://www.aejmc.org

815. (H)
Correspondence Fund Scholarships

8 to 15 scholarships of up to $2,000 to applicants who are children of print or broadcast journalists who are foreign correspondents for the U.S. media. For graduate, postgraduate, or undergraduate study at any accredited U.S. institution in journalism. Must submit 2 letters of recommendation, a résumé, and a brief letter outlining research interests and career plans. Inquire at above address for details of where to send the application materials. Renewable. Deadline: April 30.

816. (H)
Foreign Correspondents Scholarship

1 scholarship for up to $2,000 to a son or daughter of a present or former foreign correspondent who wishes to study journalism in a U.S. college or university. Applicants must be children of U.S. citizens who are working, or who have worked, for a bona fide news organization in the print or broadcast media as a foreign correspondent, including both American and non-American news organizations. Children of non-U.S. citizens working as foreign correspondents for American news organizations will also be considered. Deadline: April 15.

817. (SS)
Association for International Practical Training
AIPT Hospitality/Tourism Exchange
10400 Little Patuxent Parkway, Suite 250
Columbia, MD 21044–3510
(410) 997–2200
(410) 997–5186
http://www.aipt.org
aipt@aipt.org

610 12-week to 18-month internships providing living expenses of approximately $300 per week to recent college graduates (under age 35), upper-level undergraduates, and international students. The program arranges for students to work abroad in the hospitality and tourism industries. U.S. students are placed in organizations abroad, from Taj International Hotels and Japan Airlines to Queen's Flores Corporation and Pastries of Denmark. Though locations vary each year, the most common destinations for U.S. students have been Switzerland and Germany. Deadline: rolling.

(SS)

Association for Library & Information Science Education
11250 Roger Bacon Drive, Suite 8
Reston, VA 20190–5202
(703) 234–4146
http://www.alise.org
alise@drohanmgmt.com

818. (SS)
Alise Research Grants Program

2 grants of $2,500 to graduate students to conduct research in library science. Must be a member of ALISE. Send a self-addressed, stamped envelope for membership information. Deadline: October 1.

819. (SS)
Doctoral Students' Dissertation Competition Awards

2 awards of $400 for doctoral dissertations having to do with library and information sciences. Selection is based on academic achievement and quality of dissertation. Completed dissertation and a summary must be presented within the current calendar year. Winners also receive conference registration and a 1-year membership to ALISE. Deadline: October 1.

820. (SS)
Research Grants

Varying number of grants totaling $2,500 to graduate, doctoral, and undergraduate students in library and information science. Must not be used for doctoral dissertation research. Selection based on previous work and quality of proposed research. Deadline: October 1.

821. (SS)
Research Paper Competition Awards

2 awards of $500 to master's and doctoral candidates in library and information sciences for research papers, but cannot submit papers written for degree requirements. Must be members of ALISE. Write for details and include a self-addressed, stamped envelope. Deadline: October 1.

822. (H)
Association for Women in Communications, National Offices (AWIC)
780 Ritchie Highway, Suite 28S
Severna Park, MD 21146
(410) 544–7442
http://www.womcom.org

Varying number of scholarships of varying amounts (generally from $200 to $1,000) to female graduate and undergraduate students who are majoring in communications or journalism. There are 70 chapters throughout the United States, and most chapters offer scholarships. For more information, visit web site or send a self-addressed, stamped envelope. Deadline: varies by chapter.

823. (H)
Association for Women in Communications, Inc.—Columbus Chapter
Scholarships
P.O. Box 1332
Hilliard, OH 43026
(614) 523–8222
http://www.columbusawc.org

3 scholarships of $1,000 and 1 scholarship of $500 to graduate or upper-level undergraduate students majoring in journalism or communications. 2 of the scholarships may be used only at Ohio State University, Otterbein, or Ohio University. Must be a resident of central Ohio and a U.S. citizen. The $500 scholarship is for a nontraditional student only. Based on academic record, ability, and financial need. For more information, visit web site or send a self-addressed, stamped envelope. Deadline: varies.

824. (H)
Association for Women in Communications, Inc.—Dallas Chapter
Members' Scholarship
Dallas Morning News
508 Young Street
Dallas, TX 75202
(817) 267–8643
(214) 670–4678
(817) 977–8565
http://www.awcdallas.com

Reimbursement assistance of up to one-half of tuition to graduate and undergraduate students in communications. Award is meant to assist members of WICI, Dallas Chapter, in furthering their education. Must be Texas residents and attend a Texas institution. Must be U.S. citizens. For more information, visit web site or send a self-addressed, stamped envelope. Deadline: none.

825. (H)
Association for Women in Communications, Inc.— Detroit Chapter
Scholarships
Scholarship Chair
1659 Dennett Lane
Rochester Hills, MI 48307
http://www.smartgroups.com/groups/wicofdetroit

2 scholarships of $500 and 1 scholarship ranging from $500 to $1,000 to a female graduate or upper-level undergraduate student in communications, journalism, or TV/radio broadcasting. Must be a resident of Michigan and attend a 4-year accredited Michigan institution. 2 awards are restricted to students in Southeast Michigan only. Must be at least 25 years of age, and be either a nontraditional student or resuming education. Must submit a work sample. Must be recommended by a faculty member or department chairperson. Based on academic record, communication skills, and financial need. Must be a U.S. citizen. Nonrenewable. For more information, visit web site or send a self-addressed, stamped envelope. Deadline: April 1.

826. (H)
Association for Women in Communications, Inc.— Fort Worth Chapter
P.O. Box 9858
Fort Worth, TX 76107
(214) 792–4127

25 scholarships from $300 to $1,500 to graduate or undergraduate students in communications or journalism. Must be residents of Tarrant, Hood, Johnson, or Parker Counties, Texas. Based on academic achievement, writing sample, and financial need. Must be a U.S. citizen. For more information, contact national headquarters. Deadline: January 1.

827. (H)

Association for Women in Communications, Inc.— Greater Miami Chapter
P.O. Box 43–2641
South Miami, FL 33243

Numerous scholarships of varying amounts to female graduate or upper-level undergraduate students with journalism or communications majors. Must be U.S. citizens and Florida residents attending specific Florida institutions. Based on academic achievement, career goals, writing sample, and financial need. Contact national headquarters for more information. Deadline: varies.

828. (H)
Association for Women in Communications, Inc.— Los Angeles Chapter
5200 Caballeros Way
Los Angeles, CA 90027
(410) 544–7442
web site under construction

Scholarships from $100 to $2,500 to graduate or undergraduate students in journalism or communications. Must be attending a 4-year accredited Los Angeles institution. Must be residents of Los Angeles and U.S. citizens. Based on academic achievement, career goals, writing sample, and financial need. For more information, visit national web site or send a self-addressed, stamped envelope.

829. (H)
Association for Women in Communications, Inc.— New York Chapter
355 Lexington Avenue, 17th Floor
New York, NY 10017–6003
(212) 297–2133
http://www.nywici.org

Scholarships of $10,000 to graduate and undergraduate students in communications. Must be attend an accredited institution. Must be U.S. citizens and New York residents. Based on academic record, writing sample, involvement in communication-related activities, recommendations, and financial need. For guidelines and an application, visit web site or send a self-addressed, stamped envelope. Deadline: January 31.

(H)

**Association for Women in Communications, Inc.—
San Antonio Chapter**

P.O. Box 780382

San Antonio, Texas 78278

http://www.wicsa.org

830. (H)

Scholarships

Scholarships of $200 and up to graduate or undergraduate sophomores, juniors, and seniors in communications or journalism. Must be Bexar County residents and U.S. citizens. Based on academic achievement, need, and dedication to the profession of journalism or communications. For more information, visit web site or send a self-addressed, stamped envelope. Deadline: varies.

831. (H)

**Michelle Lima Professional Journalist
Scholarship**

2 scholarships of $1,000 to female graduate or undergraduate students. Must be a citizen of the U.S. and a resident of Bexar County, have graduated from any high school in San Antonio or the surrounding region or have a GED, be currently enrolled, full-time, at an accredited 2- or 4-year Texas college or university, and working toward a degree in journalism or communications. For more information, visit web site or send a self-addressed, stamped envelope. Deadline: March 25.

832. (H)

**Association for Women in Communications, Inc.—
Seattle/Western Washington Chapter
Georgina Davis Scholarships**

AWC Scholarship Chair

1412 SW 102nd Street, PMB 224

Seattle, WA 98146

http://www.seattleawc.org

awcseattle@attbi.com

2 scholarships of $1,500 to graduate or upper-level undergraduate students who are declared communications majors. Must be Washington residents attending an accredited Washington institution. Must be U.S. citizens. Based on financial need, academic achievement, demonstrated excellence in communications, and work samples.

For more information, visit web site or send a self-addressed, stamped envelope. Deadline: February 15.

833. (H)

**Association for Women in Communications, Inc.—
Toledo Chapter**

Attn: Scholarship Chairperson

P.O. Box 1395

Toledo, OH 43603

http://www.awctoledo.org

2 scholarships of $750 to graduate and undergraduate students who are pursuing careers in communications, such as marketing, public relations, journalism, and graphic design. One is awarded to a student attending, or accepted to, Bowling Green University and the other to a student attending, or accepted to, University of Toledo. Selection is based on grade point average, cooperative education/internship participation, community involvement, and stated goals after graduation. Must be an Ohio resident and resident of the Toledo area. Visit web site for more information. Deadline: early March.

834. (S)

**Association for Women in Science
Internships**

1200 New York Avenue, NW, Suite 650

Washington, DC 20005

(202) 326–8940

http://www.awis.org

10 3-month internships per year providing a stipend. Internships are part-time and full-time year-round. Promotes participation of women in science through programs, publications, seminars, lobbying, and coordination of 50 local chapters nationwide. Interns assist with national and chapter-based programs, write articles for magazines, develop and monitor chapter activities, provide services for national members, participate in press and public relations activities, conduct research on status of women in sciences, and develop original projects to aid women and girls in the sciences. Open to graduate and undergraduate students, high school graduates, persons reentering the work force, and retired persons. Interest in science, science education, and women's issues required. Office experience and strong writing skills preferred. Submit letter outlining interests and résumé. Interviews are conducted by phone. For

more information, visit web site or send a self-addressed, stamped envelope. Deadline: open.

835. (S)

Association for Women in Science Educational Foundation
AWIS Predoctoral Awards
ATTN: Director
1200 New York Avenue, NW, Suite 650
Washington, DC 20005
(202) 326–8940
http://www.awis.org

5 to 10 scholarships of $1,000 to female doctoral students majoring in engineering, life sciences, mathematics, physical sciences, behavioral sciences, or social sciences. Must be U.S. citizens and study in the U.S. or abroad. Noncitizens must be attending a U.S. institution. Request applications between October 1 and December 15. For more information, visit web site or send a self-addressed, stamped envelope. Deadline: January 15.

836. (S)

Association for Women Veterinarians
Student Scholarships
Magnolia Association Management Affiliates
310 North Indian Hill Blvd, Box 337
Clavemont, CA 91711–4611
(662) 312–0893
http://www.awv-women-veterinarians.org

4 scholarships of $1,500 to female, second- or third-year veterinary medicine students in the U.S. or Canadian schools. Must be U.S. or Canadian citizen. Essay is required. Contact the Dean of Veterinary School or send a self–addressed, stamped envelope to above address. Deadline: February 15.

837. (SS)

Association of American Geographers
Grants
1710 Sixteenth Street, N.W.
Washington, DC 20009–3198
(202) 234–1450
http://www.aag.org

Varying numbers of grants of $500 to doctoral candidates in the areas of geography, especially those related to international cooperation. Applicants must have completed their course work and must be at the dissertation stage. Selection based on proposed research. Must have been members of AAG for at least 1 year. Award must be used for direct research expenses only. Write for an application form. Deadline: mid-December.

(S)

Association of Black Nursing Faculty, Inc.
5823 Queens Cove
Lisle, IL 60532
(630) 969–3809
http://www.abnfinc.org/awards.shtml

838. (S)
Dissertation Award

Scholarships of varying amounts to minority doctoral students who have made significant progress toward a doctoral degree or equivalent in nursing. Preference is given to students at the dissertation writing stage. Deadline: none specified.

839. (S)
Graduate Nursing Student Scholarship

Scholarships of varying amounts to minority graduate students. Must be currently licensed to practice as a registered nurse, enrolled in an accredited school of nursing, and a member of ABNF. Awarded to increase the number of minority graduate nursing students. Deadline: none specified.

840. (SS)

Association of Certified Fraud Examiners
Ritchie-Jennings Memorial Scholarship
ATTN: Scholarships Program Coordinator
The Gregor Building
716 West Avenue
Austin, TX 78701–2727
(512) 478–9000
http://www.cfenet.com/home.asp

15 scholarships of $1,000 to graduate and undergraduate students who are majoring in accounting or criminal justice. Based on academic achievement, recommendation letters, and a 250-word essay. If student doesn't know a Certified Fraud Examiner, the association will refer the student to a representative of the nearest CFE Chapter. For more information, visit web site. Deadline: April 1.

841. (SS)

Association of College and Research Libraries
Doctoral Dissertation Fellowship
ATTN: Program Assistant
American Library Association
50 East Huron Street
Chicago, IL 60611
(312) 280–2510
http://www.ala.org/acrl

1 fellowship award of $1,000 open to a doctoral candidate in library science who has completed his/her course work and is at the dissertation stage to conduct research. Selection based on proposed research. Also awards travel grants of varying amounts to cover air travel, surface travel, expenses, room and board to scholars in library science to travel for 10 days to study West European professional librarianship. Selection based on proposed research. Must be members of ALA. Deadline: December 1.

842. (A, H, S, SS)

Association of Commonwealth Universities
British Marshall Scholarships
36 Gordon Square
London WC1H OPF
England
+44 (0) 20 7380 6700
http://www.acu.ac.uk

Up to 40 scholarships covering the cost of university fees, cost of living expenses, annual book grant, thesis grant, research and daily travel grants, fares to and from the United States and, where applicable, a contribution toward the support of a dependent spouse. Open to graduate students in all areas of study. Must have at least a 3.7 GPA. Must be U.S. citizens and under age 26. Award is for 2 to 3 academic years of study at a university in the U.K. Contact: British Consulates at embassies in Washington, DC, Chicago, Boston, San Francisco, or Atlanta. Deadline: early to mid-October.

843. (SS)

Association of Former Agents of the U.S. Secret Service
Hanley Scholarships
P.O. Box 848
Annandale, VA 22003–0848

(703) 256–0188
http://www.oldstar.org/Foundation.html

Scholarships ranging from $500 to $1,500 to graduate students or undergraduate sophomores, juniors, and seniors majoring in law enforcement or police administration. Must be a U.S. citizen. Must be enrolled at an accredited 4-year institution and have an interest in leadership. Selection is based on academic achievement, demonstrated leadership abilities, transcript, autobiography, recommendation letters, essay, and financial need. Send a brief, signed letter requesting applications after September 1. Requests for applications between May 1 and September 1 will not be answered. Deadline: May 1.

844. (SS)

Association of Latino Professionals in Finance and Accounting
510 W. Sixth St., Suite 400
Los Angeles, CA 90014
(213) 243–0004
http://www.alpfa.org

Numerous scholarships of at least $1,250 to Hispanic graduate and undergraduate students pursuing a degree in accounting or finance-related field. Selection based on academic achievement, recommendations, essay, and financial need. Must be a U.S. citizen or a legal, permanent resident. Awarded in conjunction with the Hispanic Scholarship Fund. Deadline: April 15.

845. (S)

Association of Operating Room Nurses, Inc.
AORN Scholarship Program
2170 South Parker Road, Suite 300
Denver, CO 80231–5711
(800) 755–2676
http://www.aorn.org

Awards of tuition and fees are open to full- or part-time graduate or undergraduate nursing students attending NLN-accredited programs. Must be currently in, or accepted to, the program. Must be active or associate AORN members for at least 1 consecutive year prior to deadline date. Selection based on academic merit, not financial need. For more information, visit web site or send a self-addressed, stamped envelope. Deadline: March 1.

846. (SS)
Association of School Business Officials International
Exhibitors Scholarships
11401 North Shore Drive
Reston, VA 22090
(703) 478–0405
http://www.asbointl.org

1 scholarship of $1,200 to a graduate student in school business management or educational administration. Must have been a member of ASBO for at least 3 years and employed on a full-time basis in a school business management position for 3 years. Deadline: August 31.

847. (S)
Association of State Dam Safety Officials
ASDSO Scholarship
P.O. Box 55270
Lexington, KY 40555
(859) 257–5140
http://www.damsafety.org

1 scholarship of $2,500 per semester to graduate or undergraduate students who excel in engineering and are planning on pursuing a career in dam safety engineering. Must attend an accredited institution. For more information, visit web site or send a self-addressed, stamped envelope. Deadline: none specified.

848. (SS)
Association of the Bar of the City of New York Fund
42 West 44th Street
New York, NY 10036
(212) 382–6700
http://www.abcny.org

Partial support for a program to aid minorities and disadvantaged law school graduates prepare to take the New York bar exam. C. Bainbridge Smith Fund: The Association administers a trust under which limited financial assistance is provided to "culturally disadvantaged law students from the New York metro area" while they are attending law schools in the New York metro area. Deadline: rolling.

(SS)
Association of Trial Lawyers of America
ATTN: Membership and Education Coordinator
1050 31st Street, N.W.
Washington, DC 20007
(800) 424–2725
http://www.atla.org

849. (SS)
Elaine Osborne Jacobson Award

1 award of $3,000 plus an all-expense-paid trip to national conference and dinner to a female part- or full-time law student. Selection based on academic achievement, clinical work, related activities, and long-term commitment to a legal career and advocacy on behalf of the health care needs of children, women, the elderly, or the disabled. Visit web site for detailed information. Deadline: late January.

850. (SS)
Roscoe Hogan Environmental Law Essay Contest

1 award of $5,000 plus an all-expense-paid trip to national conference and dinner to any student enrolled in an accredited American law school. Selection based on essay. Each entry must be submitted through a faculty adviser. Visit web site for detailed information. Deadline: early February.

851. (S)
Association of Women's Health, Obstetric, and Neonatal Nurses
Professional Development Division
2000 L Street, NW, Suite 740
Washington, DC 20036
(800) 673–8499
http://www.awhonn.org

AWHONN (formerly NAACOG) provides fellowships ranging from $1,500 to $3,000 to graduate or undergraduate students in nursing or a related field or a nurse practitioner or midwifery certificate. Must be a full or associate member for at least 1 year prior to applying. Contact after January 1 and include your membership number. For more information, visit web site or send a self-addressed, stamped envelope. Deadline: April 5.

(A, H, S, SS)

Association on American Indian Affairs, Inc.
245 5th Avenue, Suite 1801
New York, NY 10016–7877
(212) 689–8270
http://www.indian-affairs.org

852. (S)

Emergency Aid and Health Professions Scholarship

Grants ranging from $50 to $300 to students who are Native American Indian or Alaska native students pursing a career in a health profession and who have an emergency need for financial assistance. Applicants must have already registered for college and be a member of a federally recognized tribe. Write a letter covering biographical information, tribal affiliation, educational and career goals, major, year in school, amount of assistance needed, budget of expenditures, name and address of financial aid officer, and social security number. There is no application form. Send a self-addressed, stamped envelope for information. Awards are made on a first-come, first-serve basis. Deadline: mid-September.

853. (A, H, S, SS)

Sequoyah Fellowship Program

Grants ranging from $50 to $300 to graduate students who are Native American Indian or Native Alaskan students. Must be a U.S. citizen with one-quarter or more American Indian or Native Alaskan blood. Must be a member of a federally recognized tribe in the U.S. Proof of tribal affiliation is necessary. Students need to write a letter covering biographical data, tribal affiliation, educational and career goals, major, year in school, amount of assistance needed, budget of expenditures, name and address of Financial Aid Officer, and Social Security number. For more information, visit web site or send a self-addressed, stamped envelope. Applications are accepted starting July 1. Deadline: mid-September.

854. (S)

Asthma and Allergy Foundation of America Fellowship Grants
1233 20th Street, NW, Suite 402
Washington, DC 20036

(202) 466–7643
http://www.aafa.org

4 fellowships ranging from $5,000 to $15,000 to post-doctoral fellows with an M.D. degree. Must be U.S. or Canadian citizens or legal residents. Award is given to conduct research in immunology, allergy, or asthma. For more information, visit web site or send a self-addressed, stamped envelope. Deadline: varies.

855. (S)

AT&T Bell Laboratories
Summer Research Program for Minorities & Women
Crawfords Corner Road, Room 1E–209
Holmdel, NJ 07733–1988
written inquiries only
(908) 949–2940
http://www.research.att.com

60 to 100 summer research positions that pay a salary ranging from $550 to $620 per week, plus travel and living expenses, to African-American, Hispanic-American, Native American, or female graduate students who are majoring in mathematics, engineering, or computer science. The 10- to 12-week summer research program offers technical employment experience to graduate students at an accredited U.S. institution. Based on academic achievement and motivation. Must be a U.S. citizen or legal resident. For more information, visit web site or send a self-addressed, stamped envelope. Deadline: December 1.

856. (S)

Atlantic Salmon Federation
ASF Olin Fellowships

P.O. Box 5200	P.O. Box 807
St Andrews, NB E5B 3S8	Calais, ME 04619-0807
Canada	

(506) 529-1033
http://www.asf.ca

Fellowships ranging from $1,000 to $3,000 to graduate students or individuals who are not enrolled in a degree program but who are seeking to improve their knowledge or skills in advanced fields while looking for solutions to current problems in Atlantic salmon biology, management, and conservation. The fellowships may be applied toward a wide range of endeavors, including salmon management, graduate study, and research. May be used at any accredited university or research laboratory or in an active management program. Must be legal residents of the U.S. or Canada. Deadline: March 15 (received).

857. (SS)
Athersys.Inc
Business Development Internship
3201 Carnegie Avenue
Cleveland, OH 44115–2634
(216) 431–9900
http://www.athersys.com/employment/jobs.php?group_id=32

Internships to graduate MBA students to be a member of the business development team. Intern is responsible for aiding in the analysis, planning, and implementation of business development and strategic planning activities. Works closely with other members to plan and evaluate projects by coordinating market research, determining projects' financial viability, and planning business models to maximize value. Preference is given to students with an undergraduate or graduate degree in biology or other life sciences. Visit web site for more information. Deadline: none specified.

858. (SS)
Attorney-CPA Foundation
Foundation Scholarships
24196 Alicia Parkway, Suite K
Mission Viejo, CA 92691–3926
(800) 272–2889
http://www.attorney–cpa.com

10 scholarships, 2 for $1,000, 4 for $500, and 4 for $250, to second-year law students. Selection based on academic achievement and commitment to the profession of accounting as evidenced by a CPA certificate. Deadline: April 30 (postmark).

859. (SS)
AUCC
Awards Division
Canada China Scholars Exchange Program
ATTN: Enquiries Clerk
151 Slater Street
Ottawa, Ontario K1P 5N1
Canada

(613) 563–1236
http://www.aucc.ca

Scholarships providing tuition, accommodations, and medical service to master's and doctoral students to conduct research in the field of Chinese studies in China. Open to Canadian citizens who obtained their bachelor's degree (or equivalent) from a recognized institution. Preference given to individuals who have a knowledge of the Chinese language. Deadline: October 31.

860. (A, H, S, SS)
Audria M. Edwards Scholarship Fund
P.O. Box 8854
Portland, OR 97207–8854
http://www.peacockinthepark.com/scholarship.shtm

Scholarships of varying amounts to graduate or undergraduate students or graduating high school seniors pursuing a career in academic, trade, vocational, or the arts. Must be gay, lesbian, bisexual, transgender or a child of gay, lesbian, bisexual, or transgender parent(s). Must be a resident of Oregon or Southwest Washington for at least 1 year. Must demonstrate financial need. Deadline: May 1.

(A, H, S, SS)
Aurora Foundation
6630 Sunset Boulevard
Hollywood, CA 90028
(323) 466–1237
http://www.jlsf-aurora.org

861. (A, H, S, SS)
Aurora Challenge Grant

1 award of $3,000 to any individual in any field of endeavor that is related to Japanese culture. There is no age limit and no GPA or scholastic achievement requirement. The award goes to an individual with a creative dream or challenge that, if fulfilled, would contribute to global goodwill and intercultural appreciation. Must be a resident of California. Awarded to enhance their pursuit of their truest, most heartfelt dream by providing them with the opportunity for a once-in-a-lifetime experience. Visit web site for more information. Deadline: May 15.

862. (SS)
Japanese Language Scholarship Foundation

1 scholarship of $3,000 plus round-trip air fare to Japan to a graduate student of Japanese language education, a current Japanese language teacher, or a Japanese language teacher currently studying to obtain a teaching credential for teaching Japanese. Awarded to allow the individual to experience living in Japan and have the opportunity to further their understanding of the Japanese language, improve their teaching abilities, and enrich their appreciation of Japanese culture. Must be U.S. citizen, nonnative Japanese speaker, and be available for either an oral or phone interview. Visit web site for more information. Deadline: September 15.

(H, SS)
Australian National University
Research School of Pacific & Asian Studies
ANU Fellowship Scholarship Committee
Canberra ACT 0200
Australia
http://rspas.anu.edu.au

863. (H, SS)
Doctoral Fellowships

2 awards of up to 1,200 euros for research and up to 900 euros per month and round-trip airfare between west coast USA and Australia to graduate students in Southeast Asia studies. Must be enrolled in an accredited U.S. institution, have completed all work but dissertation, be knowledgeable of pertinent language/languages for doing the proposed project, be able to define/accomplish a research agenda, be able to develop and maintain effective relations with colleagues and others in a university setting, and have an appropriate advisor at the ANU. Visit web site for more information. Deadline: January 15.

864. (H, SS)
Postdoctoral Fellowships

2 awards of up to $A3,000 for research and up to $A4,000 per month and round-trip airfare between west coast USA and Australia to postdoctoral fellows in a social science, or humanities that was completed within the last 5 years. Must be based in the U.S., be knowledgeable of pertinent language/languages for doing the proposed project, be able to define/accomplish a research agenda, be able to develop and maintain effective relations with colleagues and others in a university setting, have field work experience in one or more Southeast Asian countries, professional publications, and not be based at a university with a major center for the study of Southeast Asia. Visit web site for more information. Deadline: January 15.

(A, H, S, SS)
Austrian Cultural Forum
11 East 52nd Street
New York, NY 10022
(212) 319–5300
http://www.acfny.org
desk@acfny.org

865. (A, H, S, SS)
Fellowships for Study in Austria

Graduate fellowships of $300 per month to graduate students for 9 months of study in Austria. Must have demonstrated academic ability and capacity for independent study. Requires fluency in German. Students with master's degree or doctoral candidates are preferred. Must be U.S. citizens. For more information, visit web site or send a self-addressed, stamped envelope. Deadline: January 15.

866. (A, H, S, SS)
Grants for American Graduate Students

Grants of 500 euros or $566 U.S. per month for graduate students and 550 euros or $625 U.S. per month for doctoral students conducting work in Austrian studies. Applicants must be between the ages of 20 and 35 and be U.S. citizens who are proficient in German. Award is to assist in research or study projects in Austria in modern Austrian literature, history, economics, etc. Send a self-addressed, stamped envelope for information. Deadline: January 31.

867. (S)
Auxiliary to the Michigan Optometric Association Scholarship Program
530 West Ionia Street
Lansing, MI 48933–1062
(517) 482–0616
http://www.mioptassn.org

2 to 5 scholarships ranging from $400 to $1,000 to third-year students at any recognized school of optometry. Must be a student member of Michigan Optometric Association, a Michigan resident, and maintain a B average. Must be a U.S. citizen. For more information, visit web site or send a self-addressed, stamped envelope. Deadline: March 1.

868. (S)
Aventis Pharmaceuticals, Inc.
Global Drug Information Residency
200 Crossing Boulevard
P.O. Box 6890
Mail Stop: BX2—506A, Office: 5-304
Bridgewater, NJ 08807–2861
(908) 231–4824
http://www.aventispharma-us.com

1-year residency providing a competitive stipend, health benefits, 4 weeks of paid vacation, and 2 paid trips to clinical meetings in the U.S. to individuals with either a doctoral pharmacy degree or a bachelor of science in pharmacy with a general pharmacy practice residency or 2 years of clinical working experience. The resident is part of the Global Scientific and Drug Information group that provides medical and drug information on Aventis' products and disease areas such as anti-infectives, cardiovascular, metabolism, and oncology to Aventis associates. Visit web site for more information. Deadline: January 15.

869. (S)
Aviation Distributors and Manufacturers Association (ADMA)
ADMA Scholarship Program
1900 Arch Street
Philadelphia, PA 19103–1498
(215) 564–3484
http://www.adma.org

2 scholarships of $750, 1 to an individual working toward a flight major and 1 to an individual working toward an aviation management career. Applicants must contact an ADMA member company for an application. For more information, visit web site or send a self-addressed, stamped envelope. Deadline: April 1.

870. (A)
Awards to Student Composers
Broadcast Music, Inc.
320 West 57th Street
New York, NY 10019
(212) 586–2000
http://www.bmi.com

Awards ranging from $500 to $2,500 to young composers. Must be citizens or permanent residents of the Western Hemisphere (North, Central, and South American and Caribbean nations) who are under 26 years old on December 31 of the application year. Awarded to encourage young composers in the creation of concert music. For more information, visit web site or send a self-addressed, stamped envelope. Deadline: February 10.

(H)
Balch Institute for Ethnic Studies of the Historical Society of Pennsylvania
1300 Locust Street
Philadelphia, PA 19107
http://www.balchinstitute.org

871. (H)
American Society for 18-Century Studies Fellowship

1 fellowship of varying amount to a graduate student or advanced researcher to conduct research on projects related to the American 18th century. Jointly sponsored by the American Society and the HSP. Visit web site for specific submission guidelines. Deadline: March 1.

872. (H)
Balch Fellowships

Fellowships of varying amounts to graduate students and advanced researchers to conduct research on the ethnic and immigrant experience in the United States. Visit web site for specific submission guidelines. Deadline: March 1.

873. (H)
Barra Foundation International Fellowships

2 fellowships of $2,000, plus travel expenses, for foreign national scholars to conduct research in residence at the library. Visit web site for specific submission guidelines. Deadline: March 1.

874. (H)

Library Company's Program in Early American Economy and Society (PEAES)

4 fellowships of varying amounts to graduate doctoral students and advanced researchers to conduct research in Early American economy and society. Length of fellowship is 1 month for researchers and long-term residence for dissertation research. Visit web site for specific submission guidelines. Deadline: March 1.

875. (H)

Library Company's Program in Early American Medicine, Science, and Society Fellowship

1 fellowship of varying amount to a graduate student or advanced researcher to conduct research in Early American medicine and science. Visit web site for specific submission guidelines. Deadline: March 1.

876. (H)

Richard P. Morgan Fellowship

1 fellowship of varying amount to a graduate student or advanced researcher to conduct research in Ohio history and the history of books and reading. Visit web site for specific submission guidelines. Deadline: March 1.

877. (H)

Visiting Research Fellowships in Early American History & Culture

30 fellowships providing a stipend of $1,600 to doctoral and postdoctoral students and advanced researchers to spend 1 month in residence to conduct research. Visit web site for specific submission guidelines. Deadline: March 1.

878. (H)

William Reese Company Fellowships

Fellowships of varying amounts to graduate students and advanced researchers to conduct research in American bibliography and the history of the book in the Americas. Visit web site for specific submission guidelines. Deadline: March 1.

879. (A)

Baltimore Opera Annual Vocal Competition
110 W. Mt. Royal Avenue, Suite 306
Baltimore, MD 21201–5732
(410) 625–1600
http://www.baltimoreopera.com

A vocal competition with prizes from $1,000 to $10,000. The top 3 finalists also receive contract support for an engagement with the Baltimore Opera Company. Students must be between the ages of 20 and 35. Awards must be used to further voice training, to learn operatic roles, develop dramatic ability, and/or to perfect foreign languages. For more information, visit web site or send a self-addressed, stamped envelope. Deadline: May 1.

880. (A, S, SS)

Bechtel Corporation
College Recruiting
P.O. Box 193965
San Francisco, CA 94119–3965
(415) 768–1234
http://www.bechtel.com

30 to 60 internships, providing a salary ranging from $300 to $500 per week, to graduate students and undergraduate sophomores, juniors, and seniors who are majoring in architecture, architectural engineering, construction, or related areas. Student interns are accepted into the areas of civil engineering, automation technology/CADD production, engineering technologies, mechanical engineering, research and development, financing services, accounting, and human resources. Internships range from 4 to 12 weeks. For more information, visit web site or send a self-addressed, stamped envelope. Deadline: rolling.

881. (S)

Bedding Plants Foundation, Inc.
Scholarship Program
Scholarship Coordinator
P.O. Box 280
East Lansing, MI 48826
(517) 333–4617
http://www.firstinfloriculture.org/bpfi

1 scholarship each of $1,000 and $1,500, and 1 travel scholarship of $2,000, to graduate or undergraduate students planning to work and study in a floriculture or horticulture area in another country. Preference is given

to students planning to work/study in another country for 6 months or longer. 80% of the award is paid before departure, and remaining 20% is paid upon Foundation's receipt of written report. Based on recommendations, academic record, and goals. 1 award is only for a Canadian student but may be used in the U.S. or Canada. Deadline: April 1.

882. (A)

BEEM Foundation for the Advancement of Music Scholarships
309 East Hillcrest Boulevard, Suite 350
Inglewood, CA 90301
(310) 677–6793
http://www.beemfoundation.org

Scholarships ranging from $2,000 to $5,000 to winners of the performance of vocal or instrumental music competition. Selection based on the most capable and gifted students in Southern California, both academically and musically. Must be residents of Southern California. Visit web site for more information. Deadline: May 2.

883. (A, H, S, SS)

Belgian American Educational Foundation Graduate Fellowships
195 Church Street
New Haven, CT 06510
(203) 777–5765
http://www.baef.be

Up to 10 fellowships providing a stipend of $17,000, plus round-trip travel, lodging, living expenses, tuition, and fees to doctoral students to study in Belgium. Must have a master's degree. Preference is give to students who have a speaking & reading knowledge of French, German, or Dutch and are under the age of 30. Must be U.S. citizens. For specific information and an application, visit web site. Deadline: January 31.

884. (A, H, SS)

Berkeley Repertory Theater
Internship Coordinator
2025 Addison Street
Berkeley, CA 94704
http://www.berkeleyrep.org/internships.htm

6 to 12 10-month internships providing a salary of $75 per week, plus housing, open to graduates, recent college graduates, and undergraduate students. Interns live in an apartment building within a mile of the Theater. Interns work in artistic administration and company management, costumes, development and marketing/PR, lighting, literary/dramaturgy, properties, scenic construction, scenic painting, sound, or stage management. Interns attend seminars on press and public relations, costuming, casting, and personnel management. Deadline: March 15 (stage management) and April 15 (all other departments).

885. (S)

Bermuda Biological Station for Research
17 Biological Lane
Ferry Reach
St. George's GE01
Bermuda
(441) 297–1880
http://www.bbsr.edu
hlitz@bbsr.edu (WSP)
fred@bbsr.edu (GIP)

10 to 20 summer Work-Study Programs (WSP) providing free room and board and 6 Graduate Intern Programs (GIP), which provide free room and board and $50 per week. The programs allow students to conduct research in the areas of the atmosphere and marine life, from coral reef ecology to oceanography. Research topics have included global climate change, use of optics for sea study, ocean carbon, nitrogen cycling, coral symbiosis, effects of oil spills and smokestack emissions on tropical environments, and larval marine animals. WSP are open to recent college graduates and upper-level undergraduates. GIP are open to graduate students in marine biology, marine chemistry, carbonate geology, and oceanography. Students obtain free scuba diving lessons and access to a 16-foot boat for marine data collection. Open to both U.S. citizens and international students. WSP 16-week programs offered in the summer, fall, and winter. GIP last for 6 months to a year in length and are ongoing. Deadline: WSP: February 1 (summer), June 1 (fall), October 1 (winter); GIP: rolling.

886. (A, H, SS)

Bertelsmann Music Group
MBA Internship
Manager of Training and Development
1540 Broadway, 38th Floor

New York, NY 10036
(212) 930–4000
http://www.myfuture.bertelsmann.com

30 ongoing internships running from 6 months up to 2½ years and averaging 20 hours per week with a salary of $6 per hour and $220 per month for field expenses to graduate students. Interns are chosen on basis of creativity, intellectual abilities, social abilities, passion for music, and experience in the music business. Deadline: none.

887. (A, H, S, SS)

Best Book Buys Scholarship

http://www.bestwebbuys.com/books/scholarship.html

6 awards of $300 and a grand prize of $1,500 to graduate and undergraduate students in all fields of study. Must be attending an accredited institution. Applicants submit a 500-word-maximum essay answering the following question: What book should our political leaders read and why? Applicant must be a legal U.S. resident or international student with valid visa. Must submit entries via e-mail. Deadline: December 15.

(SS)

Beta Phi Mu International Library and Information Science Honor Society
ATTN: Executive Secretary
School of Library and Information Science
University of Pittsburgh
Pittsburgh, PA 15260
(412) 624–9435
http://www.beta-phi-mu.org

888. (SS)

Beta Phi Mu Student Award for Scholarship Chi Chapter, Indiana University

http://www.monroe.lib.in.us/~bpmchi/scholarship.html

1 award of $100 to a graduate student in library and information science based on nominated papers or projects. Selection based on clarity of problem, significance of research problem, appropriateness of methods, findings and conclusions, grammar, spelling, organization, and overall contribution to scholarship. Deadline: mid-February.

889. (SS)

Beta Psi Chapter Student Research Competition

http:/www.org.usm.edu/-bpm

2 awards of $1,000, and the waiving of the basic MLA conference fee, to graduate or undergraduate library and information science students for student research including papers completed for course work, master's projects, and specialist's thesis or projects. Must be enrolled in University of Southern Mississippi, University of Alabama, or Louisiana State University. Papers will be judged on relevance of topic to the profession, quality of research, and suitability for public presentation. Contact: USM Libraries, Box 5053, Hattiesburg, MS 30406–5053. Deadline: September 15.

890. (SS)

Frank B. Sessa Scholarship for Continuing Education

1 scholarship of $750 to an individual to conduct study and research in an area of librarianship. Must be a member of Beta Phi Mu. Submit a résumé, plans for course of continuing education (graduate study or professional development), and a statement of proposed study or research. Deadline: March 15.

891. (SS)

Harold Lancour Scholarship for Foreign Study

Varying number of scholarships of $1,000 to professional librarians and graduate students in library science for foreign study and research. Student applicants must be enrolled in a graduate library school accredited by the ALA. Selection based on proposed research. Write for more information. Deadline: March 1.

892. (SS)

Sarah Rebecca Reed Scholarship

1 scholarship of $1,500 to a graduate student in library science. Must be admitted to, or enrolled in, a graduate library school accredited by the ALA. Selection based on academic achievement. Applicants must submit an application form, transcripts, and references. Write for an application. Deadline: March 1.

893. (S)

Beta Sigma Kappa Student Research Grant
BSK Executive Office
4500 Beechwood Road
College Park, MD 20740

(301) 927–0508

http://www.betasigmakappa.org

1 scholarship of up to $600 to any graduate student of optometry, preferably past the first year, for use in a research project in the field of optometry. Applicant must attend a college with a BSK Chapter in good standing. Student must have a faculty advisor overseeing the project who will see that the student submits a final report to BSK. Deadline: April 1.

894. (A, H, S, SS)

Beta Sigma Phi

Scholarship

1800 W. 91st Place

Kansas City, MO 64114

(816) 444–6800

http://www.betasigmaphi.org

Scholarships of $1,000 to students in graduate or undergraduate school who are members. Must request an application by sending a self-addressed, stamped envelope. Applications are not available on-line. Deadline: February 1.

895. (A, H, S, SS)

Beta Theta Pi General Fraternity

Scholarships and Fellowships

Scholarship Committee Chairman

5134 Bonham Road

P.O. Box 6277

Oxford, OH 45056

(800) 800–BETA

(513) 523–7591

http://www.betathetapi.org

60 or more awards ranging from $500 to $1,500 to graduate or undergraduate student members of Beta Theta Pi Fraternity. May be used for any major or field of study. Based on service to Beta Theta Pi, academic achievement, potential for success, character, and financial need. Award can only be used at a 4-year institution. Request applications after February 1. For more information, visit web site. Deadline: April 15.

(A)

Beverly Hills Theatre Guild

P.O. Box 148

Beverly Hills, CA 90213

(213) 465–2703

http://www.beverlyhillstheatreguild.org

896. (A)

California Musical Theatre Award Competition

1 award of $2,000 to writers to create a play for the musical theater. Award is presented to discover new musical theater works and to encourage established or emerging writers. Visit the web site for guidelines and address for entries. Deadline: none specified.

897. (A)

Competition for Children's Theatre

Awards of $200, $300, and $500 to established or emerging writers to create quality works for children's theater. Plays should be representative of grades 6–8 and grades 9–12. Visit the web site for guidelines and address for entries. When requesting an application, please include a self-addressed, stamped envelope. Deadline: none specified.

898. (A)

Julie Harris Playwright Award Competition

1 third prize of $500, 1 second prize of $1,000, and 1 first prize of $5,000 are offered in an annual competition for full-length (90 minutes), unpublished, unproduced plays written for the theater. Musicals, one-act plays, adaptations, translations, and plays entered in other competitions are not eligible. Plays may be cowritten. Open to U.S. citizens only. For guidelines and address to send entry, please visit their web site. Deadline: November 1.

899. (A, H)

Bibliographical Society of America

Fellowships

ATTN: Executive Secretary

P.O. Box 397, Grand Central Station

New York, NY 10163

(212) 647–9171

http://www.bibsocamer.org

8 to 10 graduate research fellowships of up to $1,000 per month for up to 2 months. Topics may concentrate on books and documents in any field but should focus on the physical book or manuscript as historical evidence, history of book production, publication, distribution, or

establishing text. Selection based on proposed research. Deadline: January 31.

(SS)
Black Entertainment and Sports Lawyers Association (BESLA)
P.O. Box 441485
Fort Washington, MD 20749–1485
(301) 248–1818
http://www.besla.org

900. (SS)
BESLA-Budweiser Urban Scholarship

Scholarships of $1,500 to African-American law students attending any accredited law school in the U.S. Must be leaders of local and regional NBLSA chapters, executive committee members, or heads of entertainment and/or sports law societies. Must have at least a 2.5 GPA on a 4.0 scale. Visit web site for more information. Deadline: none specified.

901. (SS)
BESLA General Scholarship Fund

4 scholarships of $1,500 to African-American law students. Must have taken entertainment law– or sports law–related courses, or actively participated in the entertainment or sports law field through internship or job, or attended an entertainment law or sports law seminar or conference since commencing law school. Must have at least a 2.5 GPA on a 4.0 scale. Must be attending one of the following historically Black law schools: Howard University Law School, North Carolina Central Law School, Southern University Law School, or Texas Southern University Thurgood Marshall Law School. The deans of each school select eligible candidates. Visit web site for more information. Deadline: none specified.

902. (SS)
Jack & Sayde B. Gibson Scholarship Fund

Scholarships of $1,500 to African-American law student volunteers assisting BESLA (e.g., at conferences, events, in the BESLA offices). Must have taken entertainment law– or sports law–related courses, or actively participated in the entertainment or sports law field through internship or job, or attended an entertainment law or sports law seminar or conference since commencing law school. Must have at least a 2.5 GPA on a 4.0 scale. Visit web site for more information. Deadline: none specified.

903. (SS)
LeBaron & Yvonne Taylor Scholarship Fund

Awards of varying amounts through an essay writing competition open to National Black Law Students Association members. Candidates are selected from a pool of students affiliated with local NBLSA chapters. Winners are chosen by the Scholarship Committees of BESLA and NBLSA. Visit web site for more information. Deadline: none specified.

904. (SS)
Malena Rance Award

Scholarships of varying amounts to African-American female law students. Must have taken entertainment law– or sports law–related courses, or actively participated in the entertainment or sports law field through internship or job, or attended an entertainment law or sports law seminar or conference since commencing law school. Must have at least a 2.5 GPA on a 4.0 scale. Visit web site for more information. Deadline: none specified.

905. (A, H, S, SS)
Blackfeet Tribal Education Grant
Blackfeet Tribal Education Department
P.O. Box 850
Browning, MT 59417
(406) 338–7539
http://www.blackfeetnation.com

Financial assistance of varying amounts for graduate or undergraduate students who are members of the Blackfeet Tribe. Open to all majors of study at any accredited 2- or 4-year college, university, or vocational or technical school. Selection is based on academic record and financial need. Deadline: none specified.

906. (A, H, S, SS)
Blacknews.com Scholarship Fund
A.S.J. Media, LLC.
7740 W. Manchester Avenue, Suite 210
Playa Del Rey, CA 90293
scholarship@blacknews.com
http://www.blacknews.com/scholarship.html

Scholarships of at least $1,000 to African-American graduate or undergraduate students in any field of study. Students must submit an essay on an assigned topic. Must be African, African-American, or Caribbean and enrolled in a college or university. All submissions must be sent via postal mail. Visit web site for specific submission guidelines. Deadline: July 15.

907. (H)
Blakemore Foundation
Blakemore Freeman Fellowships for Advanced Asian Language Study Grants
1201 Third Avenue, Suite 4800
Seattle, WA 98101–3266
(206) 583–8778
http://www.blakemorefoundation.org

Grants of varying amounts to graduate students to conduct 1 year of advanced language study in East or Southeast Asia in structured language programs or private tutorial programs where the primary focus is on study of the modern language. Visit web site for a list of eligible languages. Must have taken at least 3 academic years of regular language study at the college level or 1 full-time intensive language study. Visit web site for more information. Deadline: January 15.

908. (SS)
Blind Service Association
Scholarship Awards
22 West Monroe, 11th Floor
Chicago, IL 60603–2501
(312) 236–0808

Numerous scholarships ranging from $50 to $2,500 to graduate or undergraduate students or high school seniors. Must be legally blind residents of 1 of 5 counties (Cook, Dupage, Kane, McHenry, or Will) and enrolled in, or accepted to, a college or university. Award is to promote the independence of blind and visually impaired individuals. Based on certification of visual status, academic record, and recommendations. Deadline: April 1.

909. (A)
Boston Society of Architects
Rotch Traveling Scholarship
ATTN: Secretary
52 Broad Street

Boston, MA 02190–4301
(617) 951–1433, ext. 227
http://www.architects.org

1 scholarship providing a stipend of $30,000 for first prize and $15,000 for second prize in a design competition. Open to Massachusetts residents who have a degree in architecture plus 1 full year of professional experience in an architectural office in Massachusetts or who have received a degree from a Massachusetts school of architecture and had 1 full year of experience in architecture. Open to U.S. citizens who are 35 years or younger. Deadline: January 4.

910. (SS)
Bozell Worldwide Public Relations
Internship Coordinator
800 Blackstone Centre
302 South 36th Street
Omaha, NE 68131–2453
(402) 345–3400
knickels@omaha.bozell.com

30 internships, providing a salary ranging from $150 to $200 per week, to graduate students, recent college graduates, and undergraduate students. Interns are designated "public relations interns" and are involved in writing, researching, and interacting with the media. Internships take place in Costa Mesa, CA, Detroit, MI, Minneapolis, MN, Omaha, NE, New York, NY, London, England, or Milan, Italy. Deadline: rolling.

(A, H)
Bread Loaf Writer's Conference
Middlebury College
Middlebury, VT 05753
(802) 443–5286
http://www.middlebury.edu/~blwc

911. (A, H)
Fellowships

Varying number of fellowships providing tuition, room, and board for a 12-day conference open to writers to provide an exchange of ideas and information. Writers attend lectures, discussion groups, workshops, panels, and readings in both poetry and prose. Attendees must have published 1 original book. Book, galley, or manuscript must be supplied. Self-published books are not accepted. Must be nominated by an editor, publisher, literary agent, creative writing teacher, or well-known writer. Deadline: March 15 (nomination), April 15 (application).

912. (A, H)
Tuition Scholarships

Varying number of fellowships providing tuition, room, and board for a 12-day conference open to writers who have published in a national periodical or university journal but have not had a book published. The Summer Conference works in poetry, fiction, and nonfiction to provide an exchange of ideas and information. Writers attend lectures, discussion groups, workshops, panels, and readings in both poetry and prose. Must be nominated by an editor, publisher, literary agent, creative writing teacher, or well-known writer. Deadline: March 15 (nomination), April 15 (application).

913. (A, H)
Working Scholarships

Varying number of fellowships providing room, board, and partial tuition for a 12-day conference open to writers to provide an exchange of ideas and information. Writers attend lectures, discussion groups, workshops, panels, and readings in both poetry and prose. Must submit a manuscript showing special promise in support of application. Deadline: May 1.

914. (A, H, S, SS)
British Embassy
Marshall Scholarship Program
3100 Massachusetts Avenue, N.W.
Washington, DC 20001–2694
(202) 371–8880
http://www.cwlthuniversitiesassoc.org.uk
info@cwlthuniversitiesassoc.org.uk

Approximately 40 scholarships of 14,000 pounds sterling to graduate students in all areas of study. Must have at least a 3.7 GPA. Must be U.S. citizens and under age 26. Award is for 2 to 3 academic years of study at a university in the U.K. Contact: British Consulates at embassies in Washington, DC, Chicago, Boston, San Francisco, or Atlanta. Deadline: mid-October.

915. (A, H, S, SS)
Brookfield Zoo
Intern Program
Coordinator
8400 31st Street
Brooksfield, IL 60513
(708) 485–0263
http://www.brookfieldzoo.org

20 summer and 5 fall and spring internships providing no compensation and open to graduate students, recent college graduates of any age, and undergraduate juniors and seniors. Must have at least a 2.0 GPA. Interns are assigned to the Small Mammal House, Seven Seas Panarama, Australia House, Animal Hospital, Children's Zoo, Conservation Biology, Birds, Hoofed Stock, Primates, Animal Commissary, or Fragile Kingdom. There are also openings in non-animal departments, such as education, graphic arts, human resources, marketing, and public relations. Interns learn how to maintain an animal's health and well-being, assist visitors by directing them to exhibits and answering their questions on animals, or helping people find demonstrations, or explaining zoo services like the Parent's Program. Applicants must have completed at least 2 years of college before starting the internship. Zoo experience or a science background isn't required but is helpful. Deadline: February 1 (summer), August 1 (fall), and December 1 (spring).

(S)
Brookhaven National Laboratory
ATTN: Office of Scientific Personnel
P.O. Box 5000
Association Universities, Inc.
Upton Long Island, NY 11973–5000
(631) 344–8000
http://www.bnl.gov/HR

916. (S)
BNL/BSA Doctoral Student Awards

2 awards of $3,000 to doctoral students working on research with a BNL-affiliated scientist. Students shouldn't be more than 1 year from the projected completion or more than 1 year after the completion of their degree program. A brief synopsis of the research and why this student deserves the award should be included. For more information, visit web site. Deadline: none specified.

917. (S)
BNL/BSA Postdoctoral Research Awards

3 awards of $5,000 to postdoctoral students working on research with a scientist affiliated with BNL. Students should be at least 1 year, and no more than 3, from the initiation of their postdoctoral appointment. For more information, visit web site. Deadline: none specified.

918. (S)
Postdoctoral Research Associateships

Varying numbers of associateships providing at least $29,000 to postdoctoral fellows in biology, biomedical sciences, chemistry, physics, materials science, or oceanography. Fundamental and applied research must be conducted at the Brookhaven National Laboratory. Fellows must have recently received their doctorates. Contact: Human Resources Division, Bldg. 185, P.O. Box 5000, Upton, NY 11973–5000. Deadline: none.

919. (S)
Brookhaven Women in Science
Renate W. Chasman Scholarship
P.O. Box 183
Upton, NY 11973
(516) 282–7226
http://www.bnl.gov/bnlweb/pubaf/pr/1999/bnlpr110499.html

1 scholarship of $2,000 to a woman reentering graduate or undergraduate studies and pursuing a career in science, engineering, or mathematics whose education was interrupted through family, financial, or other problems. Awarded to encourage women to pursue careers in science, engineering, or mathematics. Must be a U.S. citizen or permanent resident alien who is a resident of Nassau or Suffolk Counties of Long Island, New York. Deadline: April 1.

(SS)
The Brookings Institution
(Name of Program)
1775 Massachusetts Avenue, N.W.
Washington, DC 20036–2188
(202) 797–6050
http://brook.edu/admin/fellowships.htm

920. (SS)
Foreign Policy Studies Predoctoral Fellowship Program

Limited number of fellowships providing a stipend of $19,500, up to $750 for research-related travel, and reimbursement for transportation, to graduate students for policy-oriented predoctoral research in foreign policy. Candidates may be at any stage of their dissertation research. Dissertation topics are directly related to public policy issues and in the interest of the Institution. Must have completed the preliminary examinations. Deadline: December 15.

921. (SS)
Governance Studies Predoctoral Fellowship Program

Limited number of fellowships providing a stipend of $19,500, up to $750 for research-related travel, and reimbursement for transportation, to graduate students for policy-oriented predoctoral research in governance studies. Dissertation topics are directly related to public policy issues and in the interest of the Institution. Must have completed the preliminary examinations. Deadline: February 15.

922. (SS)
Internships

6 12-week summer, fall, and winter/spring internships for graduate students or upper-level undergraduate students majoring in political science, history, public policy, and law. Unpaid internships are in governmental studies in this think tank, which researches public policies facing America in areas such as health care and the budget deficit. Though the Institute is predominantly liberal, it does publish middle-of-the-road books. Deadline: February 15 (summer); June 1 (fall); and October 15 (spring).

923. (SS)
Predoctoral Research Fellowships in Economic Studies

3 to 5 fellowships providing a stipend of $12,500, plus up to $500 for expenses, to doctoral candidates conducting policy-related dissertation research in economics as related to public policy, with emphasis on economic growth, international economics, industrial organization, regulation, human resources, pub-

lic finance, or economic stabilization. Selection based on academic achievement, proposed research, and relevance of research topic to Brookings Institution interests. Recipients have access to Brookings Institution data and staff. Women and minorities are encouraged to apply. Applicants must be nominated by their university graduate departments. Deadline: December 15 (departmental nomination) and February 15 (individual application).

924. (SS)
Predoctoral Research Fellowships in Foreign Policy Studies

Varying number of fellowships providing a stipend of $12,500, plus up to $500 for expenses, to doctoral candidates conducting policy-related dissertation research in U.S. foreign policy and international relations, with emphasis on security policy and economic issues. Selection based on academic achievement, relevance of proposed research to U.S. foreign policy, and relevance of research topic to Brookings Institution interests. Recipients have access to Brookings Institution data and staff. Women and minorities are encouraged to apply. Applicants must be nominated by their university graduate departments. Deadline: December 15 (departmental nomination) and February 15 (individual application).

925. (SS)
Predoctoral Research Fellowships in Governmental Studies

Varying number of fellowships, providing a stipend of $12,500 plus up to $500 for expenses, to doctoral candidates conducting policy-related dissertation research in governmental studies, with emphasis on American political institutions, politics, economic and social policy, and government regulation. Selection based on academic achievement, proposed research, and relevance of research topic to Brookings Institution interests. Recipients have access to Brookings Institution data and staff. Women and minorities are encouraged to apply. Applicants must be nominated by their university graduate departments. Deadline: December 15 (departmental nomination) and February 15 (individual application).

926. (SS)
Research Fellowships

12 fellowships providing a stipend of $15,000 to doctoral candidates. Must be nominated by their graduate departments. Must have completed all their course work in foreign policy, government, or economics. Must be at the research stage. Nomination forms must be obtained by the department head. Deadline: December 15.

(A, H, S)
Bunting Institute of Radcliff College
Radcliffe Institute Fellowships Office
34 Concord Avenue
Cambridge, MA, 02138
(617) 496–1324
http://www.radcliffe.edu/fellowships/apply/index.html
fellowships@radcliffe.edu

927. (A, H)
Bunting Fellowship Program

Fellowships of $50,000 for a 1-year appointment to women scholars, researchers, creative writers, visual and performing artists in the areas of art, classics, music, theater arts, English language, and literature. Artists and writers need not have a Ph.D. or an M.F.A. to apply. Applications from creative writers and visual artists in successive years are not accepted; those applicants may apply after waiting 2 application cycles. Scholars must hold Ph.D. or appropriate terminal degree for at least 2 years prior to appointment. Need to have record of significant accomplishment. Artists must have had solo or group shows; writers, published works. Awarded to support women of exceptional promise and demonstrated accomplishment. Deadline: mid-October (postmark).

928. (S)
Postdoctoral Fellowship Program

Fellowships of $50,000 with additional funds for project expenses to postdoctoral scientists at any level in their careers in the fields of science. Must have received their doctoral degree at least 2 years prior to the award. Both women and men are eligible to apply. Residence in the Boston area and participation in the Institute community are required during the fellowship year. Deadline: October 1 (postmark).

929. (A, H, S, SS)
Bureau of Indian Affairs' Higher Education Grant Programs
Grants
Office of Indian Education Programs
Code 522-Room 3512
19th and C Streets, N.W.
Washington, DC 20240
(202) 208–4871
http://www.doi.gov/bureau-indian-affairs.html

Grants of varying amounts to graduate and undergraduate students in any field of study. Must be attending a 2- or 4-year accredited college or university in the U.S. Must be enrolled members of an Indian Tribe or Native Alaskan descendants. Students eligible for grants from the BIA (Bureau of Indian Affairs) must have a Certificate of Degree of Indian Blood and tribal enrollment. The student doesn't have to live on a reservation but must have a tribal affiliation. Grant amounts vary according to the student's financial need. Deadline: April 1.

(A, SS)
Bush Foundation
E900 First National Bank Building
332 Minnesota Street, East 900
St. Paul, MN 55101
(651) 227–0891
http://www.bushfoundation.org

930. (A, SS)
Artist Fellows Program

12- to 18-month fellowships providing up to $44,000 to artists to further their work, explore new directions, continue work already in progress, or accomplish work not financially feasible otherwise. Categories vary each year, but may include literature (poetry, fiction, and creative nonfiction), music composition, scriptworks (playwriting and screenwriting), and film/video; visual arts: two-dimensional, three-dimensional, and choreography, multimedia, performance art/storytelling. Must have been residents of Minnesota, North Dakota, South Dakota, or western Wisconsin for at least 12 of the 36 months before the application deadline. Applicants must be at least 25 years old. Award isn't for academic study but rather for completion of work. Deadline: varies by category.

931. (SS)
Leadership Fellows Program

Fellowships providing monthly stipends for living expenses, and reimbursement for travel expenses, plus 50% of the first $8,000 in instructional expenses and 80% of expenses after $8,000 up to the amount of the grant, to graduate or undergraduate students preparing for greater leadership responsibilities within their communities and professions. Applicants must be at least 28 years of age. Selection based on personal qualities, work and community service record, and fellowship plans. Must have been residents of Minnesota, North Dakota, South Dakota, or western Wisconsin for at least 12 of the 36 months before the application deadline. Applicants must be at least 25 years old. Award isn't for academic study but rather for completion of work. Deadline: none specified

(A, H, S, SS)
Business and Professional Women's Foundation
ATTN: Assistant Director, Education and Training
Scholarship Department
1900 M Street, NW, Suite 310
Washington, DC 20036
(202) 293–1100
http://www.bpwusa.org

932. (SS)
Avon Products Foundation Scholarship for Women in Business Studies

Scholarships of $1,000 to female undergraduate or graduate students in business. Must be within 24 months of completing an undergraduate or graduate program in the U.S. Selection based on financial need. Award may not be used for doctoral studies, study abroad, or correspondence courses. Must be U.S. citizens. Applications must be requested between October 1 and April 1. Deadline: April 15.

933. (A, H, S, SS)
Career Advancement Scholarships

400 scholarships of $1,000 to female graduate or undergraduate students in all areas of study, with emphasis on computer science, education science, and paralegal training. Must be within 24 months of completing an undergraduate or graduate program

in the U.S. Selection based on financial need. Must be at least 30 years of age. Award may not be used for doctoral studies, study abroad, or correspondence courses. Must be U.S. citizens. Applications must be requested between October 1 and April 1. Deadline: April 15.

934. (A, H, S, SS)
Clairol Loving Care Scholarship Program

Scholarships of up to $1,000 to women over the age of 30 who need financial assistance to upgrade their skills, finish their education or for career advancement. Training must be completed within 24 months. Must furnish information and costs of specific course of study at an accredited school and must be officially accepted into the program. Request preapplication screening form between September 1 and November 30. If you fulfill requirements, you will be sent an application, which is due by February 28. Please send a self-addressed, stamped envelope for preapplication information. Deadline: February 28.

935. (SS)
Lena Lake Forest Fund Research Grants

Research grants ranging from $500 to $3,000 to both men and women who are doctoral candidates or postdoctoral scholars whose research proposal is on issues of importance to today's working women. Predoctoral candidates must have completed all course work and passed qualifying exams. Applicants must be U.S. citizens. Deadline: January 1.

936. (S)
New York Life Foundation Scholarship for Women in Health Professions

Provides funds of varying amounts for tuition, fees, and related expenses to women preparing to enter a health profession. Whether reentry women, women with years of work experience, or women presently in undergraduate programs, the majority of these women face a common problem—the need for financial assistance. Eligibility requirements, program deadlines, and career information are listed in program literature. Student must write a detailed letter outlining educational and financial situation. If you qualify to apply for assistance, they will then mail an application. Deadline: May 1.

937. (SS)
Sally Butler Memorial Fund for Latina Research

Varying numbers of grants ranging from $500 to $3,000 to female doctoral candidates and postdoctoral scholars in all fields of women's studies, with emphasis on economic and employment issues. Must be of Latin American descent; citizens of the U.S. or a Latin American country. Must have completed all course work and qualifying examinations and be conducting dissertation research. Write for more information. Deadline: January 1.

938. (A, H, SS)
Butterfield & Butterfield
Internship Program
220 San Bruno Avenue
San Francisco, CA 94103
(415) 861–7500
http://www.butterfields.com/about/employment/internships.html

12 10-week internships providing a $10 daily stipend to graduate students, college graduates of any age, or undergraduate students. Interns are assigned to Painting, Asian Art, Prints, Fine Photographs, Furniture and Decorative Arts, American Indian/Ethnographic, Oriental Rugs, Rare Books, Public Relations, and Marketing. Students work at least 16 hours per week. Applicants must have taken at least 2 semesters of art history, though some with less are accepted for positions in less art-oriented areas, such as marketing and public relations. Interns are able to learn in general about the auction business and in particular about a type of art or antique. Interns working with Butterfield are able to handle pieces that would be inaccessible in a museum environment. Deadline: March 15 (summer), July 15 (fall), and October 15 (spring).

939. (S, SS)
California Adolescent Nutrition & Fitness Program (CANFit)
Scholarships
2140 Shattuck Avenue, Suite 610
Berkeley, CA 94704–1227
(510) 644–1533
(800) 200–3131
http://www.canfit.org

Scholarships ranging from $500 to $1,000 to graduate and undergraduate students majoring in nutrition, public health nutrition, physical education, or culinary arts or who are in the ADA-approved Preprofessional Practice Program in California. Must be residents of California who are considering careers that will improve adolescent nutrition and fitness. Visit web site for more information and an application. Deadline: March 31.

940. (SS)
California Association of Marriage & Family Therapists
CAMFT Education Foundation Scholarships
7901 Raytheon Road
San Diego, CA 92111–1606
(858) 292–2638
http://www.camft.org

Varying number of scholarships of $1,000 to graduate students and licensed professionals to support research in marriage and family therapy. Research must be done at a recognized institution. Preference is given to (but not limited to) CAMFT members. Deadline: February 28.

941. (H)
California Broadcasters Foundation
Intern Scholarship
915 L Street, Suite 1150
Sacramento, CA 95814
(916) 444–2237
http://www.cabroadcasters.org/scholarship.html

2 scholarships of $500 to radio interns and 2 scholarships of $500 to television interns each semester. Must be a full-time graduate or undergraduate student who is interning at any California Broadcasters Foundation or Association member radio or television station. For specific guidelines and an application, please visit web site. Deadline: December 12 (spring) and June 13 (fall).

(H)
California Chicano News Media Association
USC Annenberg School of Journalism
3800 S. Figueroa Street
Los Angeles, CA 90037–1206
(213) 743–4960
http://www.ccnma.org
ccnmainfo@ccnma.org

942. (H)
Inland Chapter Scholarship

From 3 to 5 scholarships ranging from $250 to $2,000 to Hispanic/Latino graduate or undergraduate students and graduating high school seniors who are committed to pursuing a career in journalism. Must be residents of Riverside or San Bernadino County. Selection is based on academic achievement, community awareness, financial need, and journalistic skills. For specific guidelines and contact address for this specific scholarship, visit web site. Deadline: April 11.

943. (H)
Joel Garcia Memorial Scholarship

Varying number of scholarships ranging from $500 to $2,000 to Hispanic/Latino full-time graduate or undergraduate students or graduating high school seniors. Must either attend a college or university in California, or if a California resident, may attend a college or university outside of California. Open to any field of study, but must be able to prove a sincere interest in pursuing a career in journalism. Selection based on academic achievement, recommendation letters, work samples, and essay. For specific guidelines and contact address for this specific scholarship, visit web site. Deadline: first Friday in April.

944. (H)
Lawrence E. Young Memorial Scholarship

1 scholarship of varying amount to a minority graduate or undergraduate student or a graduating high school senior with an interest in pursuing a journalism or communication career. Must be a resident of Riverside or San Bernadino County. Selection is based on academic achievement, recommendation letters, essay, and journalism-related samples. For guidelines and contact address for this specific scholarship, visit web site. Deadline: April 11.

(S)
California Land Surveyors Association
Education Foundation
P.O. Box 9098
Santa Rosa, CA 95405
(707) 578–6016
http://www.californiasurveyors.org

945. (S)
Central Valley Chapter

1 scholarship of varying amount to a graduate or undergraduate student who is pursuing a career in land surveying or survey engineering. Must be a California resident in a program originating from the area of San Joaquin, Stanislaus, or Merced County. Selection is based on career goals, academic achievements (cumulative 2.5 GPA on a 4.0 scale and 3.0 GPA in their major), extracurricular activities, demonstrated leadership abilities, and an emphasis on educating and helping others. Financial need will only be used to break ties. Visit web site for more information, contact person, and an application. Deadline: December 15.

946. (S)
East Bay Chapter Scholarship

1 scholarship of $1,500 to a graduate or undergraduate student who is pursuing a career in land surveying or survey engineering. Must be a California resident from Alameda or Contra Costa County. Selection is based on career goals, academic achievements (cumulative 2.5 GPA on a 4.0 scale and 3.0 GPA in their major), extracurricular activities, demonstrated leadership abilities, and recommendation letters. Financial need will only be used to break ties. Visit web site for more information, contact person, and an application. Deadline: December 15.

947. (S)
Ed Griffin Memorial Scholarship

1 scholarship of $1,000 to a graduate or undergraduate student who is pursuing a career in land surveying or survey engineering. Must be a California resident. Selection is based on career goals, academic achievements (cumulative 2.5 GPA on a 4.0 scale and 3.0 GPA in their major), extracurricular activities, demonstrated leadership abilities, their interest in pursuing boundary surveying, and their history in the profession. Financial need will only be used to break ties. Visit web site for more information, contact person, and an application. Deadline: December 15.

948. (S)
James E. Adams Memorial Scholarship

1 scholarship of $1,000 to a graduate or undergraduate student who is pursuing a career in land surveying or survey engineering. Must be a California resident. Selection is based on career goals, academic achievements (cumulative 2.5 GPA on a 4.0 scale and 3.0 GPA in their major), extracurricular activities, demonstrated leadership abilities, and an emphasis on educating and helping others. Financial need will only be used to break ties. Visit web site for more information, contact person, and an application. Deadline: December 15.

949. (S)
Ongoing Scholarships

Varying number of scholarships of varying amounts to graduate and undergraduate students who are pursuing careers in surveying or a closely related field. Must be California residents. Selection is based on career goals, academic achievements (cumulative 2.5 GPA on a 4.0 scale and 3.0 GPA in their major), extracurricular activities, demonstrated leadership abilities, and recommendation letters. Financial need will only be used to break ties. Visit web site for more information, contact person, and an application. Deadline: December 15.

950. (S)
President's Scholarship

1 scholarship of $500 to a graduate or undergraduate student who is pursuing a career in land surveying or survey engineering. Must be a California resident. Selection is based on career goals, academic achievements (cumulative 2.5 GPA on a 4.0 scale and 3.0 GPA in their major), extracurricular activities, demonstrated leadership abilities, activities within professional organizations, and activities to promote the career to young students. Financial need will only be used to break ties. Visit web site for more information, contact person, and an application. Deadline: December 15.

951. (S)
W.O. Gentry Scholarship

1 scholarship of $1,000 to a graduate or undergraduate student who is pursuing a career in land surveying or survey engineering. Must be a California resident. Selection is based on career goals, academic achievements (cumulative 2.5 GPA on a 4.0 scale and 3.0 GPA in their major), extracurricular activities, demonstrated leadership abilities, and recommendation

letters. Financial need will only be used to break ties. Visit web site for more information, contact person, and an application. Deadline: December 15.

(SS)
California Library Association
717 20th Street, Suite 200
Sacramento, CA 95814
(916) 447–8541
http://www.cla-net.org

952. (SS)
Edna Yelland Memorial Scholarship

Scholarships of $2,000 to minority graduate students in library science. Must be enrolled in an ALA-accredited master's of library or information science program at a college or university in California. Must be a U.S. citizen. Deadline: spring.

953. (SS)
Multiethnic Recruitment Scholarship Program

Scholarships of $5,000 to minority graduate students in library science. Must be enrolled in an ALA-accredited master's of library or information science program at a college or university in California. Must be a U.S. citizen. Applications can be obtained at participating California libraries and library schools. Contact the school's Financial Aid Office. Deadline: May 1.

954. (SS)
Project 1000

Scholarships of $2,500 to minority students pursuing a graduate degree in library science. Must be enrolled in, or accepted to, an accredited library school in California. Must be a U.S. citizen. Applications can be obtained at participating California libraries and library schools. Contact the school's Financial Aid Office. Deadline: April 15.

955. (SS)
Reference Service Press Fellowship

Scholarships of $2,000 to graduate students or undergraduate seniors enrolled in, or accepted to, a program in library science. May be a California resident enrolled in an ALA-accredited master's of library or information science program at any college or university or a resident of any state attending a library school in California. Must be a U.S. citizen. Deadline: spring.

956. (SS)
California Psychological Association
California Graduate Psychology Scholarships
1022 G Street
Sacramento, CA 95814–0817
(916) 325–9786
http://www.calpsychlink.org

2 scholarships of $2,500 to minority graduate students in doctoral programs in psychology. Scholarships are for full-time study. Deadline: October 15.

(SS)
California State PTA
930 Georgia Street
Los Angeles, CA 90015–1322
(213) 620–1100
http://www.capta.org

957. (SS)
Counseling and Guidance Summer Session Scholarship

40 scholarships of $200 to graduate students for advanced summer study in school counseling and guidance. Must attend a college or university in California for study in this field. Must be a U.S. citizen, California resident, and employed at least half-time in counseling. Apply directly through school. Deadline: March 31.

958. (SS)
Early Childhood/Elementary/Secondary Teacher Education Scholarships

Scholarships of $750 to full-time graduate or upper-level undergraduate students preparing to teach in field of early childhood education in California public schools. Must be resident of California. Must also be attending an accredited California college where the scholarships are available. List available upon request. Deadline: none specified.

959. (SS)
Enforcement Personnel Dependents Grant Program

Grants of up to $1,500 to graduate or undergraduate students who are natural or adopted children of a California law enforcement officer killed or 100% disabled in the performance of duty. Must attend eligible

California institutions and be residents of California and the U.S. Award may be used for tuition, fees, books, supplies, and living expenses. Deadline: none.

960. (SS)
Minority Recruitment Scholarship

20 to 40 scholarship grants ranging from $1,500 to $5,000 to minority graduate students who are pursuing a master's degree in library science. Must attend one of 3 Schools of Library Science in California. Deadline: May 15.

(A, H, S, SS)
California Student Aid Commission
P.O. Box 419026
Rancho Cordova, CA 95741–9027
(916) 526–7590
http://www.csac.ca.gov/about.html

961. (A, H, S, SS)
Enforcement Personnel Dependents Grant Program

Grants of up to $1,500 to graduate or undergraduate students who are natural or adopted children of a California law enforcement officer killed or 100% disabled in the performance of duty. Must attend eligible California institutions and be residents of California and the U.S. Award may be used for tuition, fees, books, supplies, and living expenses. Deadline: none.

962. (A, H, S, SS)
Graduate Fellowship Program

300 fellowships of varying amounts to graduate students in all fields of study at an eligible California graduate school. Must intend to pursue a career as a college or university faculty member. Must be a U.S. citizen, legal resident, or in the process of establishing residency. Renewable. Contact Financial Aid Office or above address. Deadline: March 2.

963. (SS)
California Teachers Association (CTA)
Martin Luther King Jr. Memorial Scholarship Fund
ATTN: Human Rights Department
1705 Murchison Drive
P.O. Box 921
Burlingame, CA 94011–1400

(650) 697–1400
http://www.cta.org

Awards ranging from $250 to $2,000 to minority graduate students in education. Must be a California resident, U.S. citizen, member, or student member. Open to African-American, Hispanic-American, Native American, Native Alaskan, or Pacific Islander. May be used for graduate degree or credentialing. Deadline: March 15.

964. (A, H, S, SS)
Calouste Gulbenkian Foundation
Department of Armenian Communities
Avenida de Berna 45-A
P-1067 Lisboa Codes, Portugal
http://www.gulbenkian.pt

Scholarships of varying amounts to full-time graduate and undergraduate sophomore, junior, or senior students in any area of study. Must be of Armenian descent and enrolled in an accredited institution. Selection based on academic achievement and financial need. Preference is given to students whose immediate family has not previously received a scholarship. Deadline: varies by county of origin.

965. (A, H)
Camargo Foundation
Fellowships
ATTN: Fellowships Office
U.S. Secretariat
400 Sibley Street, Suite 125
St. Paul, MN 55101–1928
(202) 302–7303
http://www.camargofoundation.org

12 residential fellowships providing a furnished apartment in France for 3 to 5 months and a $3,500 stipend to graduate students, teaching faculty, artists, and writers to conduct research. Research may be in the humanities, creative writing, and the fine arts; all areas must be related to the French culture. Selection based on proposed research work and expected benefit of residence in France. Knowledge of French recommended. Graduate students must have completed academic residence and general requirements and must demonstrate the benefit of a stay in France to complete their dissertation. Deadline: February 1.

966. (SS)
Canadian Embassy
Canadian Studies Graduate Student Fellowship
Program
Academic Relations
501 Pennsylvania Avenue, N.W.
Washington, DC 20001
(202) 682–1740
http://canadianembassy.org/offices/index-e.asp

Fellowship grants of $850 per month for 10 months to full-time doctoral students at accredited U.S. institutions whose dissertations are related to the study of Canada. Must be U.S. citizen or legal resident. Grants are also available for U.S. college and university faculty and postdoctoral scholars. Deadline: October 31.

(A, H, S, SS)
Canadian Federation of University Women
ATTN: Fellowships Committee
251 Bank Street
Suite 600
Ottawa, Ontario K2P 1X3
(613) 234–8252
http://www.cfuw.org

967. (A, H, S, SS)
La Bourse Georgette LeMoyne Award

1 award of $1,000 Canadian to females taking refresher studies at the graduate level in any field. Must attend a university where instruction is in French. Applicants must hold either a B.A. or B.S. degree and have been accepted to a graduate program of study. Must be Canadian citizen or have at least 1-year landed immigrant status. Deadline: November 30.

968. (A, H, S, SS)
Polytechnique Commemorative Awards

Varying number of awards of varying amounts to graduate students in any field, with preference given to studies related to women's issues. Must have a bachelor's degree (B.S. or B.A.) and be accepted to a graduate program at an accredited institution. Must be a Canadian citizen or have at least a minimum 1-year landed immigrant status. Write for more information. Deadline: November 30.

969. (SS)
Vibert Douglas Fellowship

Varying number of awards of varying amounts to graduate students in any field, with preference given to studies related to women's issues. Must have a bachelor's degree (B.S. or B.A.) and be accepted to a graduate program at an accredited institution. Must be a Canadian citizen or have at least a minimum 1-year landed immigrant status. Write for more information. Deadline: November 30.

970. (SS)
Canadian Institute of Ukrainian Studies
Doctoral Thesis Fellowships
352 Athabasca Hall
University of Alberta
Edmonton, Alberta T6G 2E8
Canada
(403) 492–2972
http://www.ualberta.ca

Varying number of master's fellowships of $4,500, 1 doctoral fellowship of $8,000, and 1 doctoral dissertation fellowship of $10,000 to graduate students in education, law, history, humanities, social sciences, women's studies, or library science that are related to Ukrainian or Ukrainian-Canadian topics. Must have completed all course work and be at the dissertation stage. Selection based on academic achievement and dissertation topic. Award may be used in Canada or elsewhere. Must be a Canadian citizen or have landed immigrant status. Deadline: May 1.

(SS)
Canadian Library Association
ATTN: Scholarships and Awards Committee
328 Frank Street
Ottawa, Ontario K2P 0X8
Canada
(613) 232–9625
http://www.cla.ca

971. (SS)
CLA Dafoe Scholarship

1 scholarship grant of $3,000 Canadian to a graduate student accepted *to a master's degree program in library and information studies. Selection based on academic achievement, leadership potential, and

demonstrated interest in the profession. Must be a Canadian citizen or have landed immigrant status. Deadline: May 1.

972. (SS)
CLA Library Research and Development Grants

1 or more grants of $1,000 to graduate students to conduct theoretical and applied research in the field of library and information services, to encourage and support research undertaken by practitioners in the field of library and information services, and to promote research in the field of library and information services by and/or about Canadians. Visit web site for submission guidelines. Deadline: March 15.

973. (SS)
H.W. Wilson Scholarship

1 scholarship of $2,500 to a graduate student accepted to a master's degree program in library and information studies. Selection based on academic achievement, leadership potential, and demonstrated interest in the profession. Must be a Canadian citizen or have landed immigrant status. Deadline: May 1.

974. (SS)
World Book Graduate Scholarship in Library and Information Science

1 scholarship grant of $2,500 Canadian to a graduate or doctoral student in library science to continue study. Applicants should hold either a B.L.S. or his/her M.L.S. degree. Must be a Canadian citizen or have landed immigrant status. Selection based on academic achievement and financial need. Program may be in Canada or the United States. Deadline: May 1.

975. (S)
Cancer Research Fund of the Damon Runyon-Walter Winchell Foundation
Postdoctoral Research Fellowships
675 Third Avenue
New York, NY 10017
(212) 697–9550
http://cancerresearchfund.org/apFellowship.html

Approximately 60 awards ranging from $35,000 to $55,000 to individuals with an M.D., Ph.D., D.D.S.,

D.V.M., or equivalent degree. Award is given to basic and physician scientists to advance cancer research. Covers all areas of theoretical and experimental research relevant to the study of cancer and the search for its causes, therapies, and preventions. Awards are for 3 years. Visit web site for more information. Deadline: December 15.

976. (A, H, S, SS)
Carpe Diem Foundation of Illinois
Grants to Teachers for Continuing Education or Special Projects
Gordon Levine, Executive Director
208 S. LaSalle, Suite 1400
Chicago, IL 60604
http://www.carpediemfoundation.org

Awards of varying amounts to teachers to help defray the cost of continuing education or special projects designed to improve the applicants' skills as a teacher and to develop better educational experiences for their students. The grant application for teachers should include the teacher's background and credentials, purpose for which the grant is sought, measurable milestones that must be met and reported to the Foundation to ensure that the purposes of the grant are being satisfied, procedure for independent, third-party monitoring of compliance with the terms of the grant, and an independent certification of successful completion of the grant. The award isn't always granted every year.

(SS)
The Carter Center
1762 Clifon Road
Atlanta, GA 30322
(404) 727–7611
http://www.cartercenter.org

977. (SS)
Graduate Assistantship Program

A limited number of stipends of $3,500 to currently enrolled graduate and professional students who have completed at least 1 year of graduate study. The stipend is for a 10-week, 40-hour-per-week summer term. Programs available: Conflict Resolution, Global Development Initiative, democracy program, Americas Program, China Villages Election Project, Human Rights, and Mental Health. Application available at their web site. Deadline: March 15.

978. (SS)
Internship Program

25 internships with no compensation to graduate, professional, or upper-level undergraduate students. Internships last for 10 weeks during summer, fall, and spring, with a 6-week Winter Break Internship also available. The Carter Center, founded by former President Jimmy Carter in 1982, is a think tank established to improve the quality of life for people around the world. Interns are assigned to any one of a variety of programs: Latin American and Caribbean Studies, African Governance, Human Rights, Global 2000 (a large-scale project to improve health care and agriculture in developing countries), Domestic and International Health Policy, the Atlanta Project (a local program working on social problems associated with poverty in urban areas), Task Force for Child Survival and Development, and Conflict Resolution. There are also positions in administrative offices, such as public information, development, and conferencing. Interns research specific issues, monitor daily events, and write articles for in-house publications. Deadline: July 15 (fall), October 15 (spring), and March 15 (summer).

979. (SS)
Casualty Actuarial Society
CAS Trust Scholarships
1100 North Glebe Road, Suite 600
Arlington, VA 22201–4798
(703) 276–3100
http://www.casat.org/academ/scholarship.htm

Up to 3 scholarships of $1,500 to full-time graduate and undergraduate students who are interested in the property/casualty actuarial profession. Award is to encourage pursuit of the CAS designations. Must demonstrate high scholastic achievement and a strong interest in mathematics or a mathematics-related field. Must be admitted or enrolled in an accredited U.S. institution that either offers a program in actuarial sciences or courses that will serve to prepare the student for an actuarial career. Open to U.S. and Canadian citizens or permanent residents. Preference given to applicants who have passed an actuarial exam and who have not yet won either this scholarship or another Society of Actuary or Casualty Actuary Society scholarship. Visit web site for more information and an application. Deadline: May 1.

980. (SS)
Catholic Library Association
World Book Grant
100 North Street, Suite 224
Pittsfield, MA 01201–5109
(215) 649–5251
http://www.cathla.org

An award of $1,500 to a graduate student or librarian to obtain further certification. Must be a member of the National Catholic Library Association. The grant is awarded to add expertise in the field of children's or school librarianship. Deadline: March 15.

981. (SS)
Cato Institute
Internships
1000 Massachusetts Avenue, N.W.
Washington, DC 20001–5403
(202) 842–0200
http://www.cato.org

Internships providing a monthly stipend of $700 to graduate or undergraduate students or recent graduates. Interns assist professional staff in general research and/or office duties and take part in regular seminars on politics, economics, law, and philosophy. Must share a strong commitment to the values of the Institute. Law students receive specific legal work, as well as a different stipend. Deadline: July 1 (fall), November 1 (spring), and March 1 (summer).

982. (S)
Cave Research Foundation
KARST Research Fellowship Program
1244 South Brook
Louisville, KY 40203–2718
http://www.cave-research.org

2 or 3 fellowships of up to $3,500 to graduate (master's or doctoral) students majoring in any KARST-related area and who will be conducting cave research. Research may be conducted anywhere in the world. Those proposals that do not receive a research fellowship might be awarded small grants. Deadline: March 31.

983. (SS)
CDS International. Inc.
Robert Bosch Foundation Fellowship Program
871 United Nations Plaza
New York, NY 10017–1814
(212) 497–3500
http://www.cdsintl.org
info@cdsintl.org

15 9-month fellowship programs providing a monthly stipend of 1,500 euros, program-related travel, and minimal insurance to graduate students and young professionals in the areas of business administration, economics, journalism, mass communications, law, political science, or public affairs. The internship is in Germany in federal government and then in regional government or private industry. Special seminars are conducted in Berlin, Paris, and Brussels. Program runs from September to May. Open to U.S. citizens. Deadline: October 15.

984. (S, SS)
Center for Advanced Study In the Behavioral Sciences
75 Alta Road
Stanford, CA 94305
(650) 321–2052
https://casbs.stanford.edu
secretary@casbs.stanford.edu

Provides graduate, doctoral, and postdoctoral scholars of exceptional achievement with free time to devote to their own study and to associate with colleagues in the same discipline or related fields in behavioral and biomedical sciences, humanities, certain specialties in statistics and computer science. Fellows must spend the fellowship year at the Center.

985. (S)
Center for Coastal Studies
Internship Review Committee
59 Commercial Studies
P.O. Box 1036
Provincetown, MA 02657
(508) 487–3622
http://www.coastalstudies.org

4 internships providing $75 per week, plus free housing, to graduate students, upper-level undergraduates and recent college graduates with backgrounds in biology, zoology, or wildlife ecology. Interns conduct research projects, education, and conservation programs on coastal and marine environments, field trips, offshore research cruises, free T-shirts, and discounts at the CCS shop. Internships last for 12 weeks in the summer. Open to U.S. citizens and non-U.S. citizens who are legal residents. Deadline: January 31.

986. (H, SS)
Center for Comparative Immigration
Visiting Research Fellows Program
University of California-San Diego
La Jolla, CA 92093–0510
(858) 822–4447
http://www.ccis-ucsd.org/Programs/fellowships.htm

A limited number of awards ranging between $3,000 and $4,000 to doctoral students and postdoctoral fellows to support advanced research and writing on any aspect of international migration and refugee flows, in any of the social sciences, law, history, and comparative literature. Predoctoral students are expected to finish writing their dissertations during their fellowship. Fellowship periods last from 9 to 10 months. Visit web site for more information. Deadline: January 15.

987. (SS)
Center for Defense Information
Information Internships
ATTN: Program Coordinator
1779 Massachusetts Avenue, N.W.
Washington, DC 20036–2109
(202) 332–0600
http://www.cdi.org

Varying number of internships paying $1,000 per month to graduate and undergraduate students interested in military policy, national security, foreign affairs, and related public policy issues and/or an interest in broadcast communications and information technology. Internships last at least 4 months for full-time work as research and outreach assistants at CDI. Selection based on academic achievement and interest in U.S. military policy and related public policy. Applicants should have good writing skills. Deadline: March 1, July 1, and November 1.

(S, SS)

**Center for Free Market Environmentalism
Political Economy Research Center (PERC)**
502 S. 19th Avenue, Suite 211
Bozeman, MT 59718
(406) 587–9591
http://www.perc.org/education/fellowships.html

988. (S, SS)
Graduate and Law Student Fellowship Program

Fellowships providing a monthly stipend of $1,300 and reasonable domestic round-trip travel expenses to Montana to graduate and law students with an interest in natural resources and the environment. Must show potential for research and writing in these areas, preferably by working on a research paper, thesis, or dissertation. Deadline: February 21 (summer) and January 15 (early decision).

989. (S, SS)
Kinship Conservation Institute

Up to 20 awards of $4,500 to graduate students and conservation leaders in the early stages of their careers to take an intense look at how to use market approaches to solve environmental problems. Meals and housing are provided at Montana State University. Deadline: February 1.

990. (S)
Center for Health Services
Station 17, Vanderbilt University
Nashville, TN 37232
(615) 322–4773
http://www.mc.vanderbilt.edu/chs/matcur2.htm

Varying number of internships providing stipends and housing for summer interns. Open to individuals with a background in liberal arts, science, medical, or environmental areas. Interns organize summer and year-round programs, provide community follow-up and technical assistance to community groups, conduct fundraising, and administer budgets. Programs sponsored by the Center include Service Training for Environmental Progress, Student Health Coalition, and Action Research. Interns can work part- or full-time. Submit letter detailing interests, resume, and an application. An interview must be conducted. Deadline: March 21 (summer).

991. (SS)
Center for Human Rights and Constitutional Law
256 S. Occidental Boulevard
Los Angeles, CA 90057
(213) 388–8693
http://www.centerforhumanrights.org

The Center helps recent law school graduates gain experience in public interest law, through a legal fellowship program. Write an introductory letter briefly detailing your educational situation and goals.

(SS)

**Center for International Security and Cooperation
Institute for International Studies**
CISAC
Encina Hall
Stanford, CA 94305–6165
(650) 723–9625
http://cisac.stanford.edu/global/contact.html
chena@stanford.edu

992. (S, SS)
Hamburg Fellowships

Fellowships providing $20,000 to graduate doctoral students in anthropology, economics, history, law, political science, sociology, medicine, and the natural and physical sciences. Students should be studying the prevention of deadline conflict, both in the pre-conflict stage and during the implementation of peace agreements. Deadline: February 1.

993. (S, SS)
Pre/Postdoctoral Fellowships

Fellowships of varying amounts to predoctoral and postdoctoral students working within a broad range of topics related to peace and international security. Areas of interest are anthropology, economics, history, law, political science, sociology, medicine, and the natural and physical sciences. Students should be studying the prevention of deadline conflict, both in the preconflict stage and during the implementation of peace agreements. Deadline: February 1.

994. (S)
Science Policy and International Security Fellowship Program

Fellowships providing stipends of varying amounts based on experience to postdoctoral students, mid-career professionals, scientists, and engineers. Awarded to explore the policy dimensions of a research topic of their choosing in an interdisciplinary environment. Health insurance and subsidies for travel and other research-related expenses are available. Deadline: February 15.

995. (S, SS)
Stanford MacAurthur Consortium Fellowships in International Peace and Cooperation

Fellowships providing a stipend or salary of approximately $4,440 per quarter to doctoral candidates who have achieved TGR status and are writing a dissertation related to one or more of the dimensions in anthropology, economics, history, law, political science, sociology, medicine, and the natural and physical sciences. Students should be studying the prevention of deadline conflict, both in the pre-conflict stage and during the implementation of peace agreements. Deadline: February 1.

996. (A, H, S, SS)
Center for Strategic and International Studies
Internship Coordinator
1800 K Street, N.W., Suite 400
Washington, DC 20006
(202) 887–0200
http://www.csis.org

7 internships providing a stipend ranging from $500 to $1,000, plus free room and board, to graduate students, recent college graduates, undergraduates, high school graduates, or high school students. International students are eligible. The Academy is a think tank that focuses on issues that are vital for social and personal progress. It is helpful if applicants have experience in architecture, design, computer programming, engineering, expository writing, productions, project management, publishing, science and statistics, or research. Interns are assigned research counselors where interns conduct research on 1 or more projects. Internships last 15 weeks to 1 year during the summer, fall, or spring. Deadline: rolling.

997. (SS)
Center for Women in Government
Fellowships on Women and Public Policy
Room 302, Draper Hall
University of Albany, State University of New York
135 Western Avenue
Albany, NY 12222
(518) 442–3900
http://www.cwig.albany.edu

10 fellowships of $9,000 and tuition assistance to female graduate students who are enrolled in, or accepted to, programs in colleges and universities within New York State. Fellows work with state legislators. Recipients work 30 hours a week on issues such as health, economic development, child welfare, and insurance and on other areas of concern to women. Deadline: May 15.

(A, H, S, SS)
Central Intelligence Agency
Recruitment Center
P.O. Box 12727-STU-I
Arlington, VA 22209-8727
(703) 613–8388
http://www.odci.gov/cia/employment/postframe.htm

998. (A, H, S, SS)
Career Trainee Internship Program

Scholarships covering tuition for 1 year, and summer programs providing a salary, to graduate and undergraduate students interested in a career with the Agency in overseas intelligence operations. Program is during the summer between first and second years of graduate school or between junior and senior undergraduate years. Must be majoring in accounting, architecture, business administration, cartography, chemistry, computer science, economics, engineering, finance, geography, graphic design, international studies, languages (Russian, Chinese, or Japanese), law, mathematics, personnel administration, photo sciences, physics, political science, or printing/photography. Based on academic achievement, leadership, character, goals, and recommendations. Contact after August 1. Deadline: varies, usually early in the fall semester.

999. (A, H, S, SS)
Graduate Studies Program

Scholarships covering tuition for 1 year and summer programs providing a salary to graduate and undergraduate students interested in a career with the Agency in overseas intelligence operations. Program is during the summer between the first and second years of graduate school or an undergraduate student's junior and senior years. Must be majoring in accounting, architecture, business administration, cartography, chemistry, computer science, economics, engineering, finance, geography, graphic design, international studies, languages (Russian, Chinese, or Japanese), law, mathematics, personnel administration, photo sciences, physics, political science, or printing/photography. Based on academic achievement, leadership, character, goals, and recommendations. Contact after August 1. Deadline: varies, usually early in the fall semester.

1000. (H, S)
Charles A. and Anne Morrow Lindbergh Foundation
Grants for Research Projects
Research Grant Administration
2150 Third Avenue North, Suite 310
Anoka, MN 55303–1596
(763) 576–1596
http://www.lindberghfoundation.org

Graduate research grants of up to $10,580 to individuals proposing projects representing a significant contribution toward the achievement of balance between technological progress and the preservation of our natural environment. Studies may be in the areas of conservation, natural resource preservation, wildlife preservation, aviation writing, and oceanography. Deadline: June 15.

1001. (H)
Chattanooga Christian Foundation
Dora Maclellan Brown Scholarships
736 Market Street, Suite 1706
Chattanooga, TN 37402–4503
http://www.cccfdn.org

Scholarships of unspecified amounts to graduate students who are pursuing a master's degree in either divinity or theology at a theological seminary approved by the Foundation. Must be Christians who are theo-logically and biblically conservative. Preference given to Chattanooga area residents who are candidates for pulpit ministry or the mission field. Deadline: February 15.

(S)
Chemical Industry Institute of Toxicology
P.O. Box 12137
Research Triangle Park, NC 27709
(919) 558–1200
http://www.ciit.org

1002. (S)
Postdoctoral Fellowships

10 to 15 awards of varying amounts providing a stipend and support to postdoctoral fellows to conduct research in chemical toxicity and/or pathology. Award can only be used at CIT's laboratory. The award is renewable for up to 2 years. Visit web site or send a self-addressed, stamped envelope for an application. Deadline: none.

1003. (S)
Predoctoral Fellowships

10 to 15 awards of varying amounts providing a stipend and support to doctoral students to conduct research in chemical toxicity and/or pathology. Award can only be used at CIT's laboratory. The award is renewable for up to 2 years. Visit web site or send a self-addressed, stamped envelope for an application. Deadline: none specified.

1004. (A, H, S, SS)
Cherokee Nation of Oklahoma
P.O. Box 948
Tahlequah, OK 74465
(800) 256–0671
(918) 456–0671
http://www.cherokee.org

500 scholarships of varying amounts to high school seniors and undergraduate and graduate college students in any area of study. Must be ¼ or more Cherokee Indian. Amount awarded dependent upon educational requirements and financial needs of recipient. May be used at any U.S. institution. Deadline: April 1.

1005. (S)

Chi Eta Phi Sorority

Mabel Keaton Staupers National Scholarship Award

3029 13th Street, N.W.

Washington, DC 20009

(202) 232–3858

http://www.chietaphi.com

chietaphi@erols.com

Varying number of scholarships ranging from $1,000 to $2,000 to female graduate and undergraduate student members pursuing a career in nursing. Selection is based on academic achievement, recommendation, leadership experience and potential, career goals, and financial need. Visit web site for an application and deadline date.

1006. (A, H, S, SS)

Chi Psi Educational Trust

Clifford H. Williams Scholarship

1705 Washtenaw Avenue

P.O. Box 1344

Ann Arbor, MI 48106

(313) 663–9302

http://www.chipsi.org

1 scholarship of $300 in each of the 5 Chi Psi regions to a graduate or undergraduate student. May be used for any field of study. Must be a member of the fraternity. Visit web site for more information. Deadline: May 1.

1007. (A)

CINE

Non-Professional CINE Award of Excellence

1112 16th Street, N.W., Suite 510

Washington, DC 20036

(202) 785–1136

http://www.cine.org

info@cine.org

1 award each of $500 and $1,000 in product grants, plus certificates and trophy, to graduate and undergraduate students and amateurs for an entry in either documentary, entertainment—comedy and animation; or entertainment—drama. For more information, visit web site. Deadline: February 1 (spring early bird) and February 15 (final), or August 1 (fall early bird) and August 15 (final).

1008. (SS)

Citibank

Summer Associate Programs

575 Lexington Avenue

12th Floor/Zone 3

New York, NY 10043

(212) 559–1000

http://oncampus.citigroup.com/cg/cgbus_ccmktg_sa

10- to 13- week summer internships providing salaries ranging from $800 to $1,000 per week for graduate students and from $500 to $700 per week for undergraduate juniors and seniors. Internships are available in New York, NY, Chicago, IL, Los Angeles, CA, Atlanta, GA, and Houston and Dallas, TX. Undergraduates must have completed their junior year to be considered for the program, and graduate students must be 1 year from graduation. All majors are welcome, with internships in corporate finance, sales and trading, financial institutions and transaction services, consumer banking, corporate audit, corporate financial control, private banking, and real estate. Request applications from above address or your college's career center. Deadline: April 1.

1009. (SS)

Citizens Communications Center

600 New Jersey Avenue, N.W., #312

Washington, DC 20001

(202) 662–9535

http://www.georgetown.edu/home/service.html

Second- and third-year law students intern at Citizens Communications Center, a public interest law firm, for 4 to 6 months. Students use their legal skill and training to participate in all legal activities of the firm on behalf of the Citizen group clients. Students receive academic credit from their law schools for their internships. Stipends are $200 a month during the academic semester and $700 a month during the summer months. Visit web site for more information and deadline.

1010. (H, S, SS)

Civil Air Patrol (CAP) Scholarships

CAP Graduate Scholarships

ATTN: National Headquarters/TT

105 South Hansell Street

Building 714

Maxwell AFB, AL 36112–6332

(205) 293–5332

http://www.cap.gov

60 scholarships of $750 to graduate students majoring in aerospace education, science, humanities, or education. Must be a CAP member who has completed requirements for the senior rating in Level II of the senior training program. Must have a bachelor's degree. Deadline: October 1.

(SS)

Civitan International Foundation
P.O. Box 130744
Birmingham, AL 35213–0744
(205) 591–8910
http://www.civitan.org

1011. (SS)
Dr. Courtney W. Shropshire Scholarship

40 scholarships ranging from $500 to $1,000 to graduate and undergraduate students. Must be enrolled in an accredited college or university, planning a career in education, and agree to uphold ideals of Civitan creed. Must be a Civitan or have an immediate family member who is a Civitan member for at least 2 years. Deadline: January 31.

1012. (SS)
Roy M. Abagnale Memorial Fellowship Award

1 fellowship grant of $3,000 to a graduate student majoring in business, economics, marketing, or political science in an accredited university or internship. Must submit outline for an original research or position paper that, in final form, will be suitable for publication in a magazine or scholastic journal. Only the outline is submitted at time of application. Must submit 2 recommendation letters and a copy of a previously completed paper. Deadline: March 1.

(H, SS)

The Claremont Institute
937 West Foothill Boulevard, Suite F
Claremont, CA 91711
(909) 621–6825
http://www.claremont.org

1013. (SS)
Abraham Lincoln Fellowship

Fellowships of varying amounts to young professionals serving elected officials or appointed policy makers in the federal government, as well as staff members of national political parties and nonprofit institutions that research and publish on public policy and constitutional issues. Deadline: none specified.

1014. (H, SS)
Publius Fellows Program

Fellowships of varying amounts to graduate and upper-level undergraduate students and recent graduates in journalism or political philosophy. Applicants should be interested in writing for the public prints. Deadline: none specified.

1015. (SS)
Clarke & Company
ATTN: Internship Manager
535 Boylston Street
Boston, MA 02116
no phone calls
http://www.clarkeco.com/
job-opportunities.htm#internship

9 or 10 internships ranging from 12 to 20 weeks providing a salary of $240 per week to first-year graduate students and upper-level undergraduate students in public relations. Interns assist account coordinators by writing press releases, generating media lists, conducting research for specific clients, setting up for events, archiving client files, and delivering packages to the media. Applicants must submit a résumé and cover letter. Deadline: rolling.

1016. (S)
Clinical Directors Network of Region II, Inc.
54 West 39th Street, 11th Floor
New York, NY 10018
(212) 382–0699
http://www.cdnetwork.org

2 or 3 internships lasting from 3 to 6 months providing local transportation expenses to graduate students, college graduates, undergraduate students, persons reentering the work force, or retired persons. Positions are available in New York and New Jersey. Interns must be computer literate and have an interest in, and commitment to, public and community health. Preference given

to bilingual applicants. Interns assist community health centers in launching outreach activities, help design and pretest research instruments for cancer control project and HIV/AIDS clinical trials projects, help develop a comprehensive resource guide for community health centers, assist with general administrative duties, and help develop a nutrition-oriented therapy for patients with HIV/AIDS. Submit a letter detailing interests, résumé, and references. An interview is conducted in person or by telephone. Deadline: open.

1017. (A, H)
C. L. Sonnichsen Book Award
University of Texas at El Paso
Texas Western Press
500 W. University Avenue
El Paso, TX 79968–0633
(915) 747–5688
http://www.utep.edu/twp/call.htm

1 award of varying amount for a previously unpublished nonfiction manuscript dealing with the history, literature, or cultures of the Southwest. Include self-addressed, stamped envelope for rules. Deadline: March 1.

1018. (SS)
College Connections
Internship Coordinator
329 East 82nd Street
New York, NY
(212) 734–2190
http://www.halsteadpr.com

2 internships providing a salary ranging from $240 to $400 per week to graduate and undergraduate students in public relations. International students may apply. Internship takes place in New York City. Interns assist the staff in writing press releases, pitching stories to various media, and conducting mass mailings. Some of the clients for College Connections are: Baylor University, College Board, Council for Undergraduate Research, Duke University, Monmouth College, *Rolling Stone*, Summerbridge National, and UNICEF. Applicants must submit a résumé and a cover letter. Deadline: rolling.

1019. (A, H, S, SS)
Collegiate Inventors Competition
http://www.invent.org/collegiate

6 awards of $20,000 to full-time graduate and undergraduate students in any area of study. Each winning student or 4-student team receives 1 $20,000 cash prize and a $2,000 gift certificate to www.hpshopping.com. Advisors each receive a $10,000 cash prize. A maximum of 6 awards will be presented. Applicants must submit an original idea and work product that has not been made available to the public as a commercial product or process or been patented or published more than 1 year prior to the date of submission to the competition. The invention will be judged on the originality and inventiveness of the new idea, process, or technology. It must be complete, workable, and well articulated. It will also be judged on its potential value to society (socially, environmentally, and economically) and on its range or scope of use. There are no limits on the number of entries a student or team may submit in a given year; however, only 1 prize per student or team will be awarded. Deadline: June 1.

1020. (A, H, S, SS)
Colonial Dames of America Scholarship
421 East 61st Street
New York, NY 10021
(212) 838–5489
http://www.colonialdames17c.net

Numerous scholarships of $1,000 to graduate and undergraduate students who are of qualified colonial descent. Student may attend any 2- or 4-year U.S. institution. Based on academic record, goals, recommendations, and financial need. May be used for any area of study. Visit web site for more information. Deadline: April 1.

1021. (A, H, S, SS)
Commission Franco-Americaine D'Echanges Universitaires et Culturels
Graduate Fellowships
9 Rue Chardin
Paris 75016
France
33 (1) 44 14 53 60
33 (1) 42 88 04 79
http://international.polytechnique.fr

20 fellowships of varying amounts to graduate students for all fields of study. Open to U.S. students for study and research in France and for French students to study in the U.S. under the Fulbright scholarship program; also for U.S. teachers of French and French teachers of

English to exchange posts. Deadline: August 1 and October 31 (U.S. research scholars and students); December 1 and December 15 (French research scholars and students); October 15 (U.S. exchange teachers); and January 15 (French exchange teachers).

1022. (SS)
Committee of Vice-Chancellors & Principals of the Universities of the UK
Overseas Research Student Awards Scheme
ATTN: Nathalie Bonvalot
CVCP
ORS Award Scheme
Woburn House
20 Tavistock Square
London WC1H 9HQ
England
44-171-383-4573 (Fax)
http://www.columbia.edu/cu/ces/fellowships/april/cvcp.htm

Awards of varying amounts to foreign postdoctoral students who wish to conduct research at a university or higher education college in the U.K. Open to all fields of study. Deadline: April 30.

1023. (A, H, S, SS)
Committee on Institutional Cooperation
Graduate Fellowship for Minorities
302 East John Street, Suite 1705
Champaign, IL 61820–5698
(217) 333–8475
http://www.cic.uiuc.edu

40 to 45 scholarships of tuition, plus a $6,000 stipend, to minority students enrolled in or planning to enroll in a graduate program. Provides the financial assistance to help them receive a Ph.D. degree in a wide variety of fields (agriculture, arts, biology, economics, engineering, government, history, mathematics, philosophy, physical sciences, physics, or psychology). Must attend 1 of 11 participating Midwestern universities (IL, IN, IA, MI, MN, OH, PA, or WI). Deadline: January 31.

1024. (A, H, S, SS)
Commonwealth Universities Association
British Marshall Scholarships
36 Gordon Square
London WC1H OPF

UK
071/387-8572
http://www.cwlthuniversitiesassoc.org.uk
info@cwlthuniversitiesassoc.org.uk

Approximately 40 scholarships of 14,000 pounds sterling to graduate students in all areas of study. Must have at least a 3.7 GPA. Must be U.S. citizens and under age 26. Award is for 2 to 3 academic years of study at a university in the U.K. Contact: British Consulates at embassies in Washington, DC, Chicago, Boston, San Francisco, or Atlanta. Deadline: October 17.

(A, H, S, SS)
Community Foundation of Greater Lorain County
1865 North Ridge Road East, Suite A
Lorain, OH 44055
(440) 277–0142
http://www.cfglc.org

1025. (S, SS)
A.C. Siddall Educational Trust Fund Scholarship

Scholarships of varying amounts to graduate, undergraduate, and postgraduate students pursuing or furthering their education in health care. Award can also be used for short-term refresher courses. Students wanting to become doctors are ineligible. Must be residents of Lorain County. Must have financial need. Applications can be obtained online and submitted starting on January 1. Deadline: February 10.

1026. (S)
Gabriel A. Sabga, M.D., Memorial Scholarship

Scholarships averaging $1,000 to students enrolled in medical school. Must be residents of Lorain County. Must have financial need. Renewable with reapplication. Applications can be obtained on-line and submitted starting on January 1. Deadline: February 10.

1027. (A, H)
Helen Steiner Rice Scholarship in Creative Writing

Scholarships averaging $1,000 to graduate and undergraduate students who are interested in the writing of poetry, prose of an inspirational or devotional nature, articles, or short stories with a Christian/moral theme. Must be residents of Lorain County. Must have financial need. Applications can be obtained on-line and submitted starting on January 1. Deadline: February 10.

1028. (S)
Mary J. and Paul J. Kopsch Fund

Awards of $2,000 to students who have completed at least 1 year in an accredited osteopathic or allopathic medical school. Must be residents of Lorain County. Must have financial need and show promise of satisfactory performance. Renewable with reapplication. Send a self-addressed, stamped envelope for an application. Applications can be submitted starting on January 30. Deadline: February 10.

1029. (A, H, S, SS)
Phillipine American Association of Lorain County Scholarship

Scholarships of varying amounts to students of Filipino descent. Selection is based on academic achievement, extracurricular activities, and financial need. Must be residents of Lorain County. Applications can be obtained on web site and submitted starting on January 1. Deadline: February 10.

1030. (S)
Richard and Roberta Aros Scholarship

1 award of $500 to a dental student enrolled in an accredited dental school who is a resident of Lorain or Erie County. Must have financial need and show promise of satisfactory performance. Renewable with reapplication. Send a self-addressed, stamped envelope for an application. Applications can be submitted starting on January 30. Deadline: February 10.

1031. (S, SS)
Robert E. Bass Scholarship Fund

Awards of varying amounts to nontraditional students who are pursuing medical, nursing, or business degrees. Must be residents of Lorain County. Must have financial need and show promise of satisfactory performance. Applications can be obtained on web site and submitted starting on January 30. Deadline: February 10.

1032. (S)
Roy E. Hayes M.D. Memorial Fund

Awards of $1,000 to students who have been accepted to or enrolled in an accredited osteopathic or allopathic medical school. Must be residents of Lorain County. Must have financial need. Renewable with reapplication. Send a self-addressed, stamped envelope for an application. Applications can be submitted starting on January 1. Deadline: February 10.

1033. (H)
Vera C. Mast Scholarship

Scholarships of $500 to graduate and undergraduate students who are pursuing a career in the ministry. Must be residents of Lorain County. Must have financial need. Applications can be obtained on web site and submitted starting January 1. Deadline: February 10.

1034. (A, H, S, SS)
Community-Technical Colleges of Connecticut Minority Administrative or Teaching Fellowships
Affirmative Action Officer
61 Woodland Street
Hartford, CT 06105
http://www.commnet.edu

Fellowships of $3,000 per semester to minority graduate students interested in pursuing a teaching career at community-technical college sector. Recipient gains professional experience, serves as a role model for students, develops professional relationships, and enhances the ethnic, racial, and intellectual diversity. Open to all areas of study. Deadline: none specified.

1035. (H, SS)
Competitive Enterprise Institute
Warren T. Brookes Journalism Fellowship
1001 Connecticut Avenue, N.W., Suite 1250
Washington, DC 20036
(202) 331–0640 (Fax)
http://www.cei.org/pages/jobs.cfm

1 fellowship of varying amount to a graduate student in journalism with an interest in economic, environmental, and technology issues. Selection based on application, extracurricular activities, writing samples, and cover letter. Deadline: May 30.

1036. (A, H, S, SS)
Compton Fellowships
234 West Galena Street
Milwaukee, WI 53212

(414) 227–2551
http://www.comptonfellowship.com
info@comptonfellowship.com

Fellowships to support master's work in any area to students who have completed their bachelor's degrees. Recipients work for a year, during which they receive $27,948 salary, plus benefits. Though open to all majors, students must have a solid foundation in math, English, and science. Visit web site for more information and an application. Deadline: March 31.

1037. (A)
Concert Artists Guild
Annual Awards Competition
850 Seventh Avenue, #1003
New York, NY 10019
(212) 333–5200
http://www.concertartists.org/html/f_main.html

Awards of $2,500, management services, and other awards in the area of a professional music performance competition. The Annual Professional Level Music Performance Competition is open to singers, pianists, other instrumentalists, and chamber ensembles. The goal is professional career advancement for the winners. Write for complete details. Deadline: mid-January.

(A, S, SS)
Congressional Black Caucus (CBC) Foundation
1720 Massachusetts Avenue, N.W.
Washington, DC 20036
(800) 784–2577
http://cbcfinc.org/index2.html

1038. (SS)
CBC Congressional Fellows

Fellowships providing a stipend of $25,000 over 9 months to students completing graduate work, professionals with at least 5 years' experience and who are pursuing graduate work, and college faculty members. Applicants should have an interest in the legislative policy making process and show evidence of and commitment to Black political empowerment. Selection based on academic achievement, writing sample, essay, and 3 letters of recommendation. Fellows gain insight into how such agencies interact with Congress. Fellowships last from 9 to 12 months and are open to students completing graduate degree requirements.

The appointments are in Washington, DC. Visit web site for more information. Deadline: April 1.

1039. (S, SS)
CBC Internship Program

An internship is available to recipients of the Cheerios Brand Health Initiative Scholarship. Internship is through General Mills. Applications must be sent to local scholarship selection committee. Visit web site for more information and address of local scholarship selection committee. Deadline: rolling.

1040. (S, SS)
CBC Spouses Cheerios Brand Health Initiative Scholarship

Scholarships of varying amounts to full-time graduate, doctoral, and undergraduate students and graduating high school seniors. Students must be pursuing a career in the medical, food services, or any other health-related field. Must attend an accredited school or reside in a congressional district represented by a Congressional Black Caucus member and have at least a 2.5 GPA on a 4.0 scale. Selection based on academic achievement, essay, and letters of recommendation. Applications must be sent to local scholarship selection committee. Visit web site for more information and address of local scholarship selection committee. Deadline: rolling.

1041. (SS)
CBC Spouses Education Scholarship

Scholarships of varying amounts to full-time graduate, doctoral, and undergraduate students and graduating high school seniors. Must attend an accredited school or reside in a congressional district represented by a Congressional Black Caucus member and have at least a 2.5 GPA on a 4.0 scale. Selection based on academic achievement, essay, and letters of recommendation. Applications must be sent to local scholarship selection committee. Visit web site for more information and address of local scholarship selection committee. Deadline: rolling.

1042. (A)
CBC Spouses Performing Arts Scholarship

5 scholarships of varying amounts to full-time graduate, doctoral, and undergraduate students and graduating high school seniors. Students must be pursuing

a career in the performing arts, music, and/or a related field. Must attend an accredited school or reside in a congressional district represented by a Congressional Black Caucus member and have at least a 2.5 GPA on a 4.0 scale. Selection is based on academic achievement, essay, and letters of recommendation, exceptional potential, and videotape. Applications must be sent to local scholarship selection committee. Visit web site for more information and address of local scholarship selection committee. Deadline: rolling.

(SS)
Congressional Hispanic Caucus Institute
504 C Street, N.E.
Washington, DC 20002
(800) 367–5273
(202) 392–3532
http://www.chci.org

1043. (SS)
CHCI National Housing Initiative Fellowships

Fellowships providing an annual stipend of $65,000, round-trip transportation to Washington, DC, health insurance, and other benefits to Hispanic/Latino mid-career-level leaders, with 8 to 10 years of housing experience, to create and implement Latino housing initiatives to increase home ownership opportunities for Hispanic/Latinos in the U.S. Must relocate to Washington, DC, where fellows work in partnership with Fannie Mae to develop needs assessment work for their assigned regions and evaluate and measure the affect of the housing initiative. Must be a U.S. citizen or legal permanent resident, have strong organizational skills and superior communication skills, have extensive travel experience, experience working with media, strong coalition-building skills, and be fully bilingual (English/Spanish). Contact CHCI to see whether program is funded after 2005. Deadline: June 6.

1044. (SS)
CHCI Public Policy Fellowship

30 fellowships lasting 9 months to Hispanic graduate students. Fellowship provides a monthly stipend, housing, and travel expenses to allow students to work in a position involving public policy. Applicants must have recently received their bachelor's degree or be current graduate students. Deadline: April 10.

(S)
Connecticut Association of Land Surveyors, Inc.
78 Beaver Road
Wetherford, CT 06109
(860) 563–1990
http://www.ctsurveyor.com

1045. (S)
Harry E. Cole Memorial Scholarship Award

1 scholarship of varying amount to a graduate or upper-level undergraduate student enrolled in a program leading to a degree in surveying. Must have completed at least half of such degree and be a resident of Connecticut. Selection is based on academic achievements, extracurricular activities, and goals. Visit web site for more information, contact person, and an application. Deadline: June 1.

1046. (S)
Oliver Paquette Memorial Scholarship Award

1 scholarship of varying amount to a graduate or upper-level undergraduate student enrolled in a program leading to a degree in surveying. Must have completed at least half of such degree and be a resident of Connecticut. Selection is based on academic achievements, extracurricular activities, and goals. Visit web site for more information, contact person, and an application. Deadline: June 1.

1047. (S)
William Berglund Memorial Scholarship Award

1 scholarship of varying amount to a graduate or upper-level undergraduate student enrolled in a program leading to a degree in surveying. Must have completed at least half of such degree and be a resident of Connecticut. Selection is based on academic achievements, extracurricular activities, and goals. Visit web site for more information, contact person, and an application. Deadline: June 1.

1048. (S)
William W. Seymour Memorial Scholarship Award

1 scholarship of varying amount to a graduate or upper-level undergraduate student enrolled in a program leading to a degree in surveying. Must have completed at least half of such degree and be a resident of Connecticut. Selection is based on academic

achievements, extracurricular activities, and goals. Visit web site for more information, contact person, and an application. Deadline: June 1.

(SS)
Connecticut Library Association
P.O. Box 85
Willimantic, CT 06226–0085
(860) 465–5006
http://cla.uconn.edu

1049. (SS)
Adeline Mix Award

1 grant of $250 to a full- or part-time graduate or undergraduate student in library science. Must be enrolled in an accredited library program. Award enables student to attend the CLA Annual Convention. Deadline: none specified.

1050. (SS)
Program from Education Grants

4 or 5 educational grants of varying amounts for graduate study or to upgrade their status. Must be library employees, volunteer trustees, or friends of the library in the state of Connecticut. Applicants must be members of CLA to be eligible. Deadline: none.

1051. (SS)
Scholarship Program

Scholarships of $1,000 to a graduate student in library science at Southern Connecticut State University. Must be a Connecticut resident. Selection will be based on academic achievement. Renewable with reapplication. Deadline: late March.

1052. (SS)
Consortium for Graduate Study in Management
Fellowships for Minorities
5585 Pershing Avenue, Suite 240
St. Louis, MO 63112–4621
(314) 877–5500
http://www.cgsm.org

225 fellowships of full tuition, plus $2,500 stipend over 2 years, to minority graduate students studying for the M.B.A. at any one of 11 Consortium institutions. Open to African-Americans, Hispanic-Americans, and Native Americans who have received their bachelor's degree from an accredited institution. Must be U.S. citizens. Deadline: February 1.

1053. (A)
Consortium of College and University Media
Centers
Research Awards
1200 Communications Building
Iowa State University
Ames, IA 50011–3243
(515) 294–1811
http://www.indiana.edu/~ccumc
ccumc@ccumc.org

Awards of up to $2,000 to graduate or undergraduate students, and to faculty or staff person, in a member organization of the Consortium. Research must be conducted within 18 months of submission of proposal. Based on proposed study and how it relates to the needs or opportunities in the production, selection, cataloging, distribution, and/or utilization of educational sound motion picture/video. Application must include a 1- to 2-page description of the study, proposed budget, and a résumé of the investigator. Deadline: May 15.

1054. (S)
Consulting Engineers and Land Surveyors of
California
Graduate Scholarships
1303 J Street, Suite 450
Sacramento, CA 95814
(916) 441–7991
http://www.celsoc.org/Scholarships.asp

Scholarships of $5,000 to graduate or upper-level undergraduate students pursuing careers in consulting engineering or land surveying. Must be enrolled in an accredited, state board–approved program encompassing the specialty graduate degree, such as civil engineering encompassing environmental, geotechnical, structural, transportation, etc. Must have at least a 3.2 GPA in completed engineering and land surveying courses and at least a 3.0 GPA overall on a 4.0 scale. Must be a U.S. citizen and a California resident. Visit web site for additional requirements, application, and specific deadline date. Deadline: early January.

1055. (H, S, SS)
Coors Brewing Company
311 Tenth Street
Mail No. NH210
c/o College Recruiting Representative
Golden, CO 80401
(303) 279–6565
http://www.coors.com

40 to 75 9- to 12-week fall, spring, and summer internships, providing salaries ranging from $390 to $580 per week for graduates and from $390 to $430 per week for undergraduates. Open to graduate students or undergraduate sophomores, juniors, seniors. Internships are in accounting, biology, microbiology, chemistry, distributor development, engineering, journalism, public relations, purchasing, sensory analysis, project management, telecommunications, and the Wellness Center/Recreation. Eligibility requirements vary with the department offering the internship. Internships take place in Golden, CO. Send a self-addressed, stamped envelope for specific application guidelines. Deadline: March 1.

(S)
Corbin Assistance Fund
Maternity Center Association
281 Park Avenue, South, 5th Floor
New York, NY 10010
(212) 777–5000
http://www.maternitywise.org/mca/contact/

1056. (S)
Hazel Corbin Grant

1 grant of $5,000 to a graduate student enrolled in a midwifery education program that is accredited or pre-accredited by the American College of Nurse-Midwives Division of Accreditation. Grant may be used for expenses associated with the planned research. Deadline: August 1.

1057. (S)
Scholarships

20 to 24 scholarships from $500 to $1,500 to students for use in advanced post-RN, nurse-midwifery, and master's degree in midwifery. Applicants must be registered nurses and have financial need. Deadline: none.

(S, SS)
The CORO Foundation
Midwestern Center
1730 South 11th Street
St. Louis, MO 63104
(213) 623–1234
http://www.coro.org/programs/fellows_program/fellows_program.html

1058. (SS)
Fellows Program in Public Affairs

48 9-month internships paying $3,500 in tuition, grants of $10,000 for living expenses, scholarships, installment plans, and tuition loans to graduate students of any age who are interested in public service. The fellowships are open to all majors, disciplines, careers, racial and ethnic groups, and socioeconomic backgrounds. Candidates may apply to only 1 CORO Center, in San Francisco, Los Angeles, St. Louis, or New York. Each center selects 12 graduate students and provides a series of internships, interviews, public service projects, and seminar meetings. Deadline: January 3.

1059. (S)
Health Sciences Fellowship

A program that brings together graduate students in health science to work with people and issues that embody the realities of practice, policy, and discovery in today's entrepreneurial and technological environment. Fellows experience an interdisciplinary team approach to practicing health care, discover a wide array of career paths in health care, and develop a network of professional connections. Candidates may apply to only 1 CORO Center, in San Francisco, Los Angeles, St. Louis, or New York. Deadline: March 3.

(SS)
Council for Advancement and Support of Education
1307 New York Avenue, N.W., Suite 1000
Washington, DC 20005-4701
(202) 328–2273
http://www.case.org/

1060. (SS)
Alice L. Beeman Research Awards

Awards of varying amounts to graduate students in communication for education, including marketing, public relations, government relations, issues management, and institutional enhancement. Theses and dissertation must be helpful to educational advancement practitioners in devising strategies and tactics for accomplishing their work in communications. Deadline: January 31.

1061. (H)
CASE Media Fellowship Program

Fellowship of varying amounts to professional reporters to focus on a subject, meet with the experts, and gain understanding of an issue in a learning environment. Deadline: January 31.

1062. (SS)
Clarence J. Jupiter Fellowship Program

Up to 8 fellowships of at least $17,500 to minority professionals with at least 3 years of professional experience in fields other than educational advancement. Fellows receive training in the 3 professional areas of advancement: alumni relations, communications, and fundraising. Deadline: January 31.

1063. (SS)
H.S. Warwick Research Awards

Awards of varying amounts to graduate students for outstanding master's thesis or doctoral dissertation. Awarded to encourage research in alumni relations, alumni giving, advocacy, student alumni membership, and marketing. Theses and dissertations should be helpful for accomplishing work in alumni relations. Deadline: January 31.

1064. (SS)
John Grenzebach Outstanding Doctoral Dissertation Award

1 award of $2,000, plus travel and lodging, to a doctoral candidate and a faculty member to attend the CASE Annual Assembly. Selection is based on an outstanding doctoral dissertation addressing philanthropy for education. Write for more information. Deadline: January 31.

(H)

Council for the Advancement of Science Writing
P.O. Box 910
Hedgesville, WV 25427

(304) 754–5077
http://www.casw.org

1065. (H)
McGrady/Allard Travel Grants

Grants of varying amounts to graduate students who are aspiring science journalists, including those in graduate science writing programs. Award helps underwrite the cost of travel to major science meetings.

1066. (H)
New Horizons Traveling Fellowships

Fellowships of up to $1,000 for journalists from publications and broadcast outlets that don't usually cover major science meetings or employ a full-time science writer. Award covers the cost of attending the New Horizons in Science Briefing. For specific guidelines, visit web site. Deadline: September 15.

1067. (H)
Rennie Taylor/Alton Blakeslee Fellowships

Scholarships of up to $2,000 to graduate students who are pursuing a career in science writing. Must attend an accredited U.S. institution. For more information, visit web site. Deadline: July 1.

(H, SS)

Council for European Studies
Columbia University
1203 International Affairs Building
MC 3310
420 118th Street
New York, NY 10027
(212) 854–4172
http://www.europanet.org/frames/overall.html

1068. (SS)
Andrew W. Mellon Foundation Fellowships

3 fellowships of up to $4,000 to graduate students to test the research design of their dissertation, determine the availability of archival materials, and contact European scholars in the relevant field. Home institutions must be members of the Council. Doctoral candidates must have completed the majority of their course work but not have passed their dissertation prospectus or begun substantial dissertation research. Must be a U.S. citizen or permanent resident. Deadline: February 1.

1069. (SS)
Florence Gould Foundation Predissertation Fellowships for Research in France

6 fellowships of $4,000 to graduate students in modern history and the social sciences. Award is for research in France to determine the viability of a projected doctoral dissertation. Fellows will test the research design of their dissertation, determine the availability of archival materials, and contact French scholars in the relevant field. Must be U.S. citizen or legal permanent resident. Must have completed at least 2, but no more than 3, years of full-time graduate study by June of application year. Deadline: February 1.

1070. (SS)
German Marshall Fund Summer Predissertation Fellowships

4 fellowships of up to $4,000 to graduate students to test the research design of their dissertation, determine the availability of archival materials, and contact European scholars in the relevant field. Home institutions must be members of the Council. Doctoral candidates must have completed the majority of their course work but not have passed their dissertation prospectus or begun substantial dissertation research. Must be a U.S. citizen or permanent resident. Deadline: February 1.

1071. (H, SS)
Luso-American Development Foundation Fellowships for Research in Portugal

2 fellowships of $4,000 to graduate students to conduct research in Portugal. Institutional membership in the Council is a prerequisite for application. Open to: cultural anthropology, history (post-1750), political science, sociology, geography, and urban and regional planning. Must be U.S. citizen or legal permanent resident. Must have completed at least 2, but no more than 3, years of full-time graduate study by June of application year. Deadline: February 1.

1072. (H, SS)
Max Planck Institute for the Study of Societies Doctoral Fellowships

2 fellowships of varying amounts to graduate students engaged in dissertation projects relating to the Institute's research program and to the ongoing work of its researchers. Residents may spend between 6 and 12 months in residence at the Max Planck Institute in Cologne, Germany. Research may be in political science, sociology, economics, political economy, and some aspects of modern history. Deadline: February 1.

1073. (SS)
Predissertation Fellowship Program

12 research grant fellowships of $2,500 in Western Europe to graduate students who have completed 2 years of study and intend to pursue a Ph.D. Open to U.S. or Canadian citizens or legal residents. Applicant should have at least 1 year of study of an appropriate foreign language. Student may be studying European history, sociology, political science, anthropology, or economics. Deadline: February 1.

1074. (SS)
Society for the Anthropology of Europe Council for European Studies

1 fellowship of $4,000 to a graduate student for short-term (2 to 3 months) independent research in Europe for the purpose of testing the feasibility and research design of a projected doctoral dissertation in the social/cultural anthropology of contemporary Europe. Typically, the fellow is a second- or third-year graduate student who has completed, or is close to completing, course work and/or doctoral qualifying exam but has neither fully formulated nor defended a dissertation prospectus. Deadline: February 1.

(A, H, S, SS)
Council for International Exchange of Scholars
3007 Tilden Street, N.W., Suite 5L
Washington, DC 20008–3009
(202) 686–4000
(202) 362–3442
http://www.cies.org/

1075. (A, H, S, SS)
American Scholars Program

Awards of varying amounts to postdoctoral fellows, faculty, scholars, researchers, and professionals to conduct research and lecture abroad in more than 135 countries in all areas of study. The program is designed to increase mutual understanding between people of the U.S. and people from other countries.

Award duration ranges from 2 to 12 months. Deadline: August 1.

1076. (A, H, S, SS)
Fulbright Scholar Grant Program

Over 1,000 awards of varying amounts to postdoctoral fellows, faculty, scholars, researchers, and professionals to conduct research and lecture abroad in more than 135 countries in all areas of study. The program is designed to increase mutual understanding between people of the U.S. and people from other countries. Award duration ranges from 2 to 12 months. Deadline: August 1.

1077. (A, H, S, SS)
Indo-American Fellowship Program

Awards of varying amounts to postdoctoral fellows, faculty, scholars, researchers, and professionals to conduct research and lecture abroad in more than 135 countries in all areas of study. The program is designed to increase mutual understanding between people of the U.S. and people from other countries. Award duration ranges from 2 to 12 months. Deadline: August 1.

1078. (A, H, S, SS)
NATO Advanced Research Fellowships

Awards of varying amounts to postdoctoral fellows, faculty, scholars, researchers, and professionals to conduct research and lecture abroad in more than 135 countries in all areas of study. The program is designed to increase mutual understanding between people of the U.S. and people from other countries. Award duration ranges from 2 to 12 months. Deadline: August 1.

1079. (A, H, S, SS)
Postdoctorate Research Fellowships

Awards of varying amounts to postdoctoral fellows, faculty, scholars, researchers, and professionals to conduct research and lecture abroad in more than 135 countries in all areas of study. The program is designed to increase mutual understanding between people of the U.S. and people from other countries. Award duration ranges from 2 to 12 months. Deadline: August 1.

(H, S, SS)
Council of American Overseas Research Centers
Smithsonian Institution
P.O. Box 37012

NHB Room CE-123, MRC 178
(202) 842–8636
http://www.caorc.org

1080. (H, S, SS)
Fellowship Program

Up to 9 awards of $9,000 to doctoral candidates and postdoctoral fellows in humanities, social sciences, or allied natural sciences to conduct research of regional or transregional significance. Fellowship requires research be conducted in more than 1 country, at least one of which hosts a participating American overseas research center. Doctoral students must have completed all requirements except for dissertation. Preference given to candidates examining comparative and/or cross-regional questions requiring research in 2 or more countries. Must be U.S. citizens. Visit web site for more information. December 31.

1081. (H, S, SS)
Fellowships for Advanced Multi-Country Research

8 awards providing a stipend of up to $6,000, and a travel stipend of $3,000, to doctoral students in the humanities, social sciences, and related natural sciences. Must have completed all doctoral requirements with the exception of the dissertation. Established postdoctoral scholars are also eligible to apply. Preference given to candidates examining comparative and/or cross-cultural questions requiring research in 2 or more countries. Fellowship tenures must last at least 3 months. Deadline: December 31.

1082. (H, S, SS)
Multi-Country Research Fellowship

9 grants not exceeding $9,000 to doctoral students and doctoral fellows to support study and research in the humanities, social sciences, and allied natural sciences. Doctoral candidates must have completed all requirements except for dissertation. Must be U.S. citizens. Must propose field research in at least 2 countries, with fellowship tenure lasting at least 90 days. Visit web site for more information. Deadline: December 31.

1083. (S, SS)
Council of Energy Resource Tribes (CERT)
Internship Coordinator
6955 S. Colorado Boulevard, Suite 10
Denver, CO 80246
(303) 282-7576
http://www.certredearth.com

10 to 14 10-week summer internships providing $400 per week, free housing, and round-trip travel to graduate students, undergraduate sophomores, juniors, seniors, and recent graduates to work on projects that can focus on tribal water quality studies, tribal/state and local government cooperative planning on environmental issues, hazardous waste operations training, and biodiversity. Interns work with senior CERT staff, tribal leaders, and host companies on technical and scientific issues, policies, and projects. Interested students must submit a résumé, cover letter, writing samples, college transcript, recommendations (from tribal officials, employers, or professors), and, if applicable, tribal affiliation documentation (this last item is not a requirement). Deadline: March 15.

(A, H, S, SS)
Council of Graduate Schools
One Dupont Circle, N.S., Suite 430
Washington, DC 20036–1173
(202) 223–3791
http://www.cgsnet.org

1084. (S, SS)
CGS/UMI International Distinguished Awards

Awards of varying amounts to graduate students in the social sciences, mathematics, physical sciences, or engineering. Nominees must prepare an abstract of his/her dissertation and letters from 3 references. Only one nomination from each regular member institution. Must complete their dissertation within a specified period. Visit web site for more information. Deadline: late July.

1085. (A, H, S, SS)
Distinguished Dissertation Award

2 awards of $1,000 to graduate students for their dissertations in any of the following areas: biological sciences, social sciences, mathematical and physical sciences, humanities, or fine arts. Award includes reasonable travel expenses to attend the Annual Meeting. Dissertations should represent original work making an unusually significant contribution to the disciplines. Both methodological and substantive quality will be judged. Deadline: late July.

(A, H, S, SS)
Council of International Programs
1700 East 13th Street, Suite 4ME
Cleveland, OH 44115–3213
(216) 566–1088
http://www.cipusa.org

1086. (A, H, S, SS)
Higher Education Partners Program

Internships for graduate or upper-level undergraduate students to receive professional training for field placement or degree completion. Program helps students meet new people, broaden their perspective, and learn a different way of thinking. Must be at least 21 years old and have relevant experience in the field in which they plan to train.

1087. (SS)
Youth Worker & Social Worker Exchange Program

Grants of varying amounts to graduate students (with 1 year or more of professional experience), professional social workers, or youth workers. Grants are for participation in a summer exchange program in Germany or France. Applicants must be under 40 years of age. Deadline: none.

(SS)
Council on Social Work Education
1725 Duke Street, Suite 3457
Alexandria, VA 22314–3421
(703) 683–8080
http://www.cswe.org

1088. (SS)
Carl A. Scott Book Scholarships

2 scholarships of $500 to minority graduate or undergraduate students majoring in social work. Must be in their last year of study. Selection based on demonstrated commitment to work for equity and social justice in social work. Deadline: early May.

1089. (SS)
CSWE Doctoral Fellowships in Social Work

Varying number of fellowships providing a monthly stipend of at least $708, plus tuition support, to minority students who have a master's degree in social work, or who will begin full-time study leading to a doctoral degree in social work, or who are currently enrolled full-time in a doctoral social work program. Based on demonstrated potential, interest in research, financial need, commitment to a career in mental health research on ethnic minority clients and communities, and quality of proposed research. Applicants must be U.S. citizens or legal residents. Renewable up to 3 years. Deadline: February 28.

1090. (SS)
Fellowships

11 fellowships of $8,800 to students who have a master's degree in social work, or who will begin full-time study leading to a doctoral degree in social work, or who are currently enrolled full-time in a doctoral social work program. Not limited to minority students. Based on demonstrated potential for leadership roles, financial need, commitment to a career in mental health services for ethnic minority clients and communities. Applicants must be U.S. citizens or legal residents. Renewable up to 3 years. Tuition of up to $1,800 may also be available. Deadline: February 28.

1091. (SS)
Hartford Doctoral Fellows Program

4 fellowships providing a $40,000 dissertation research grant, plus academic career development and leadership training, to graduate students who have an approved doctoral dissertation studying aspects of the health and well-being of older persons and their families. Deadline: February 1 and August 1.

1092. (SS)
Minority Fellowship Program

Fellowships providing a monthly stipend of at least $836 to minority graduate students who already have an M.S.W. and are pursuing a doctorate in social work. Must have an interest in mental health research or mental health services to minorities. Must be U.S. citizen or legal resident. Deadline: February 28.

(S)
Crohn's & Colitis Foundation of America Inc.
386 Park Avenue South, 17th Floor
New York, NY 10016
(800) 932–2423
(212) 685–3440
http://www.ccfa.org

1093. (S)
Career Development Award

Awards providing a salary of $40,000 for 2 years, plus $20,000 per year for supplies, to postdoctoral (M.D. or Ph.D.) fellows to conduct research projects in the field of inflammatory bowel disease. M.D.s must have 5 years of postdoctoral experience, and Ph.D.s must have 2 years of experience. Candidates must be employed by public or private nonprofit institutes or government agencies engaged in health care or health-related research in the U.S. Deadline: January 1 and July 1.

1094. (S)
Research Fellowship Award

Varying numbers of research fellowships of $30,000 per year for 2 years to postdoctoral (M.D. or Ph.D.) fellows who are employed by public or private nonprofit institutes or government agencies. Grants are awarded to encourage research and develop the potential of young basic and/or clinical scientists. Research must be in an area related to inflammatory bowel disease. Deadline: January 1 and July 1.

1095. (S)
Research Grants

Approximately 20 research grants of $80,000 per year for 2 years to postdoctoral (M.D. or Ph.D.) fellows who are employed by public or private nonprofit institutes or government agencies. The grants provide assistance to conduct research on inflammatory bowel disease. Selection will include scientific merit of the proposed research. Recipients must disclose all other funding sources. Deadline: January 1 and July 1.

(S)
Crop Science Society of America
677 South Segoe Road
Madison, WI 53711

(608) 273–8080

http://www.crops.org

1096. (S)
Gerald O. Mott Scholarship

Scholarships of $2,500 to graduate students in crop science. Selection is based on leadership skills, achievements in student associations, committees, scientific and professional groups, and community organizations, personal qualities (integrity, reliability, commitment to excellence, critical skills, and communication skills). Must have completed 1 year toward a master's or doctoral degree in a field of emphasis within any of the divisional areas of CSSA and display potential for leadership. Must be a student member of CSSA and be enrolled in an accredited U.S. institution. Visit web site for more information. Deadline: February 28.

1097. (S)
Pioneer Fellowship in Plant Sciences

1 fellowship of $2,500 plus a year's membership in CSSA to a doctoral candidate in plant science. Must be a full-time student, with a 3.5 GPA on a 4.0 scale. Selection will be based on academic excellence, leadership, experience, and proposed study program, including future plans. Must be enrolled in an accredited U.S. institution. Renewable with satisfactory academic progress. Visit web site for more information. Deadline: February 28.

1098. (A, S, SS)
Crow Canyon Archeological Center
Internship Program
23390 County Road K
Cortez, CO 81321
(907) 565–8975
http://www.crowcanyon.org

4 to 6 11-week internships providing room, board, and a small stipend of $350 to graduate and upper-level undergraduate students. Internships are conducted 4 times a year, from mid-May to early August, early August to mid-October, mid-October to mid-December, and from early January to mid-March. Students interested in a field internship must have prior field experience. Lab and environmental archeology positions require no field experience but do require some course

work in archeology, anthropology, ethnobotany, botany, or museum studies. Deadline: March 15.

(S)
Cushman Foundation for Foraminiferal Research, Inc.
MRC-121, Department of Paleobiology
Smithsonian Institution
Washington, DC 20560–0121
http://cushforams.niu.edu./awards.html

1099. (S)
Joseph A. Cushman Awards for Student Research

Awards of $1,000 to graduate (master's and doctoral) students to support research dealing with foraminifera or allied groups. Judged on scientific merit and financial need. Awarded to support research not funded by other grants. Visit web site for more information. Deadline: September 15.

1100. (S)
William V. Sliter Research Award

Awards of $1,000 to graduate (master's and doctoral) students to support research dealing with foraminifera or allied groups. Judged on scientific merit and financial need. Awarded to support research not funded by other grants. Visit web site for more information. Deadline: September 15.

1101. (S)
Cuyahoga County Medical Foundation Scholarship Grant Program
Academy of Medicine
6000 Rockside Woods Boulevard, Suite 150
Independence, OH 44131–2352
(216) 520–1000

40 scholarships, ranging from $500 to $1,500, to students accepted to, or enrolled in, a school of medicine, dentistry, pharmacy, nursing, or osteopathy. Must be residents of Cuyahoga County. Must be attending an accredited professional school. Interested students may call or send a self-addressed, stamped envelope for an application. Deadline: June 1.

(H, SS)

Cyprus American Archaeological Research Institute
Boston University
656 Beacon Street, Fifth Floor
Boston, MA 02215
http://www.caari.org

1102. (H, SS)
Anita Cecil O'Donovan Grant

1 grant of $750 to a graduate student to pursue research on a project relevant to the archeology of Cyprus. Must be used to fund a period of research in residence at CAARI and to help defray costs of travel. Deadline: February 1.

1103. (H, SS)
National Endowment for the Humanities Postdoctoral Fellowships

Research grants ranging from $20,000 to $30,000 to postdoctoral students in archaeology, anthropology, ancient history and classics, philology, epigraphy, religion, art history, geography, folklore, literature, philosophy, or related disciplines. Open to U.S. citizens or aliens residing in the United States continuously for 3 years immediately preceding the application deadline, holding a Ph.D. degree as of January 1st of the application year. Research should contribute to the understanding of the cultures and peoples of the Eastern Mediterranean and may include humanistic topics, ancient or modern. Cyprus should be the principal focus of the project. Deadline: January 15.

1104. (S)
Cystic Fibrosis Foundation
Student Traineeship Research Grants
6931 Arlington Road
Bethesda, MD 20814
(301) 951–4422
http://www.cff.org

Varying number of research grants of $1,500 to doctoral (M.D. or Ph.D.) students who are planning careers in research and have a lab project that can be completed in less than 1 year. The award is made to encourage students to conduct research in cystic fibrosis research and offset costs of the project. Deadline: none.

1105. (SS)
Dafoe Fellowships
University of Manitoba
Dept. of History, Room 423
University Centre Building
Winnipeg, MB R3T 2N2 Canada
http://www.umanitoba.ca/faculties/graduate_studies/forms

Fellowships of $5,000 a year for graduate students worldwide to study history, economics, or political science at certain Canadian universities. Write a letter briefly detailing your educational and financial situation. Deadline: none specified.

1106. (A, H, S, SS)
Danforth Foundation
Dorothy Danforth Compton Fellowship
1 Metropolitan Square
211 N. Broadway Street
St. Louis, MO 63102
(314) 588–1900
http://www.fs.fed.us/people/gf/gf4.htm

Fellowships providing tuition and an annual stipend of $10,000 to minority doctoral students at 1 of 10 member universities. Must be a U.S. citizen and pursuing a doctoral degree in order to teach at the college or university level. Renewable up to 4 years with continued academic progress. Applicants must contact and apply through the university. Deadline: set by individual institutions.

1107. (A, H, S, SS)
Danforth Foundation
222 South Central Avenue
St. Louis, MO 63105
(314) 588–1900
http://www.orgs.muohio.edu/forumscp/INDEX.html

Over $1 million for several programs for graduate students who plan to teach at the college level and/or who seek to improve the quality of life in St. Louis. Write a letter briefly detailing your educational and financial situation. May be in any area of study. Deadline: none specified.

(A, H, S, SS)

Danish Sisterhood of America Scholarships Scholarship Program
National Scholarship Chairperson
5113 Epping Lane
Zephyrhills, FL 33541–2607
http://www.danishsisterhood.org

1108. (H, SS)

Betty Hansen Continuing Education Grant or a Danish Culture/Heritage Grant

Up to 10 scholarships of $500 to a less than full-time graduate or undergraduate student. May be used in a course, workshop, seminar, and/or language class relating to Danish culture/heritage. Must be a member in good standing for at least 1 year or the dependent of a member in good standing or who was in good standing at the time of her death. 1 award granted per household per year. Deadline: January 31 and August 31.

1109. (A, H, S, SS)

Betty Hansen National Scholarship

Up to 8 scholarships of $1,000 to a full-time graduate or undergraduate student in any field of study. Must be a member in good standing for at least 1 year or the dependent of a member in good standing or who was in good standing at the time of her death. Preference given to first-time applicants. Must have at least a 2.5 GPA on a 4.0 scale. May be used to study in Denmark. Deadline: January 31 and August 31.

1110. (S)

Elizabeth Garde National Scholarship

1 scholarship of $850 to a full-time graduate or undergraduate student pursuing a degree in nursing or other medical profession. Must be a member in good standing for at least 1 year or the dependent of a member in good standing or who was in good standing at the time of her death. Preference given to first-time applicants. Deadline: January 31 and August 31.

1111. (A, H, S, SS)

Past National Officer's Scholarship

1 scholarship of $500 to a graduate or undergraduate student in any field of study. Must be a member in good standing for at least 1 year or the dependent of a member in good standing or who was in good stand-

ing at the time of her death. Preference given to first-time applicants. Must have at least a 3.8 GPA on a 4.0 scale and be selected as a concurrent National Scholarship winner. Deadline: January 31 and August 31.

1112. (A, H, S, SS)

Datatel Scholars Foundation Scholarships
Public Relations Representative
(703) 227–1010
http://www.datatel.com

Scholarships ranging from $700 to $2,000 to graduate and undergraduate students in any field of study. Must plan to attend or be currently attending a Datatel client college or university or work at a Datatel non-education client site and attend any college or university during the upcoming academic year. You must write an essay that summarizes your educational goals and objectives and indicate the difference that a Datatel Scholars Foundation Scholarship would make in your life and to those around you. Request an application by January 31. A list of eligible institutions is available at the web site provided. Please visit the sponsor's web site for additional information.

1113. (SS)

Davis & Company, Inc.
Internship Coordinator
11 Harristown Road
Glen Rock, NJ 07452
(201) 445–5100
(877) 399–5100
http://www.davishays.com

1 to 2 internships lasting 6 weeks, providing a salary of $240 per week, to graduate students, college graduates, and undergraduate students. Interns work in all areas of public relations, from preparing press releases to writing short articles to coordinating special events. Must submit a résumé and cover letter. Deadline: rolling.

1114. (SS)

Defenders of Property Rights
1350 Connecticut Avenue, N.W., Suite 410
Washington, DC 20036
(202) 822–6770
http://www.defendersproprights.org/member/
reporter/employment.htm

Fellowships of varying amounts to law students and undergraduate students to provide an opportunity to work side-by-side with attorneys and other members of the staff, allowing them to gain practical work experience in a public interest legal foundation. Deadline: none specified.

1115. (SS)
Defense Intelligence Agency
Intelligence Community Scholarship Program (ICSP)
ATTN: DIAC, DAH2A
Building 6000
Washington, DC 20340–5100
(202) 231–4713
http://www.dia.mil/Careers/Programs/icsp.html

Up to 4 scholarships to entry-level professionals with a bachelor's degree to enroll in the master's of science of strategic intelligence degree program. Upon completion of the thesis, IC Scholars are placed in a permanent assignment in one of DIA's major directorates. Must score at least 500 on verbal and analytical portions of the GRE, have at least a 3.0 GPA in their undergraduate work, hold a bachelor's degree from a regionally accredited institution, and be a U.S. citizen. Deadline: November 1.

1116. (S)
Delaware State Dental Society
G. Layton Grier Scholarship
1925 Lovering Avenue
Wilmington, DE 19806
(302) 654–4335
http://jeffline.tju.edu

Scholarships of $1,000 to full-time students who have completed at least 1 year of dental school. Must be Delaware residents and have financial need. Awards are also available for postdoctoral training. Send a self-addressed, stamped envelope for more information. Deadline: February 1.

1117. (SS)
Deloitte & Touche Foundation
Doctoral Fellowship Program
10 Westport Road
P.O. Box 820
Wilton, CT 06897–0820

(203) 761–3000
http://www.deloitte.com

10 fellowships of $20,000 to doctoral students enrolled in, or pursuing, a doctoral program in accounting. Must have completed 2 semesters or the equivalent in a doctoral program. Deadline: October 15.

1118. (A, H, S, SS)
Delta Gamma Foundation
Delta Gamma Foundation Fellowships
3250 Riverside Drive
P.O. Box 21397
Columbus, OH 43221–0397 (614) 481–8169
http://www.deltagamma.org

Fellowships of $2,500 to graduate members for use in any area of study. Undergraduate seniors and alumnae may apply. Based on academic record, potential, and financial need. For more information or an application, visit web site. Deadline: April 1.

1119. (A, H, S, SS)
Delta Kappa Gamma Society
A. Margaret Boyd Scholarship
P.O. Box 1589
Austin, TX 78767
(888) 762–4685
http://www.deltakappagamma.org

27 scholarships of $5,000 to graduate students who have completed their master's degree and been accepted into a doctoral program. Must be members for at least 2 years and show promise of distinction. Visit web site for more information and application. Deadline: February 1.

1120. (A)
Delta Omicron International Music Fraternity
Composition Competition—Triennial
Dr. Kay C. Wideman, President
Delta Omicron Foundation, Inc.
503 Greystone Lane
Douglasville, GA 30134
http://www.people.virginia.edu/~hla5f/do/infofrat.html

Awards of $500 and premiere in this music composition competition open to Delta Omicron members. Contest is open to music composers of college age and over for a work of 10 to 15 minutes in duration in the category selected for the particular competition. Deadline: August 1 of every second year at the triennium.

(A, H, S, SS)
Delta Sigma Theta Sorority
1707 New Hampshire Avenue, N.W.
Washington, DC 20009
(202) 986–2400
http://www.deltasigmatheta.org

1121. (A)
Myra Davis Hemmings Scholarship

Awards are given for tuition and school expenses for 1 school year only, in the area of art and performing art. Open to financial members of Delta Sigma Theta. Submit transcripts of all college records. Based on academic achievement. Deadline: March 1.

1122. (A, H, S, SS)
Nonmember Scholarships

Numerous scholarships of varying amounts for either female or male graduate students in any area of study. May apply and receive financial assistance for no more than 2 years. Visit web site for more information. Deadline: March 1.

1123. (S)
Demolay
Grotto Scholarships
10200 NW Ambassador Drive
Kansas City, MO 64153
(800) DEMOLAY
http://www.demolay.org/resources/scholarships

3 scholarships of $1,500 to graduate and undergraduate students who are pursuing careers in medicine or dentistry. Students need not be active members to apply for the awards. Deadline: April 1.

1124. (A, H, S, SS)
Deo B. Colburn Educational Foundation
63 Saranac Avenue
Lake Placid, NY 12946
written inquiries only

29 scholarship grants of varying amounts totaling $46,500 to graduate and undergraduate students and high school seniors. Must be residents of northern New York State. Write an introductory letter briefly detailing

your educational and financial situation. Deadline: none specified.

1125. (S)
Dermatology Foundation
Postdoctoral Fellowship Award Program
ATTN: Executive Director
1560 Sherman Avenue
Evanston, IL 60201–4808
(708) 328–2256
http://www.dermatologyfoundation.org

Awards ranging from $10,000 to $25,000 to postdoctoral (M.D., Ph.D., or equivalent) fellows with a commitment to a career in academic dermatology who want research training. Individuals with more than 2 years of training in skin research are ineligible. Award cannot be used for payment of indirect costs. Selection is competitive. Funding is for 1 year only. Research must be conducted in the U.S. or Canada. Deadline: October 1.

1126. (S)
Diabetes Education and Research Center
Hoechst-Roussel Grants
ATTN: Executive Director
829 Spruce Street, Suite 302
Philadelphia, PA 19107
(215) 829–3426
http://www.diabeteseducationandresearchcenter.org

Awards of up to $20,000 to M.D.s, Ph.D.s, pharmacists, nurses, educators, and other health care professionals to encourage unique initiatives in basic research, clinical research, and education. Open to U.S. citizens or legal residents to conduct research in the U.S. Deadline: March 30 and September 30.

(A)
Directors Guild of America

7920 Sunset Boulevard	110 West 57th Street, #2
Los Angeles, CA 90046	New York, NY 10019
(310) 289–2021	(212) 581–0370
http://www.dga.org	

1127. (A)
Assistant Directors Training Program

10 to 20 400-day internships open to graduate students, undergraduate seniors, or persons with an

associate's degree, a bachelor's degree, or 2 years paid employment in film/television production. Interns have on-the-job training for the position of Second Assistant Director in motion pictures or television. Graduates of the internships are eligible for membership in the Directors Guild of America. The internships are based in Los Angeles County, though some of the work may be out of town or out of state. Must submit application form and transcript (or work equivalency forms). Request applications after September 1. Visit web site for application and contact information. Deadline: mid-November.

1128. (A)
Student Film Award

1 award of $1,000 to a graduate or undergraduate film student. Entry must have been made in the school year and must have been produced for a course credit or under the supervision of a faculty member. Dramas, documentaries, and experimental films are eligible, but animated films are not. All major crew positions must have been held by a student. Awarded to support and encourage filmmakers without prior professional experience who are enrolled in accredited colleges and universities. Award can be used at student's discretion. For more information visit web site. Deadline: April 1.

(SS)
Dirksen Congressional Center
ATTN: Administrative Assistant
301 South 4th Street, Suite A
Pekin, IL 61554
(309) 347–7113
http://www.dirksencenter.org

1129. (SS)
Congressional Research Grants Program

Varying number of grants of up to $3,500 and possibly a salary of $1,500 per month to graduate students who have successfully defended their dissertation, political scientists, historians, biographers, journalists, and others. Must have a serious interest in studying the U.S. Congress. Proposed research must be original and provide new knowledge, new interpretation, or both. Deadline: February 1.

1130. (SS)
Robert H. Michel Civic Education Grants

Grants of up to $5,000 to teachers (grades 4 through 12), community, junior, and 4-year colleges and university faculty, as well as teacher-led student teams and individuals who develop curriculum. Preference is given in the areas of history, government, social studies, political science, and education. Areas of interest include designing lesson plans, creating student activities, and applying instructional technology in the classroom. Must apply on-line. Deadline: October 1 and May 1.

(A, H)
District of Columbia Commission on the Arts & Humanities
410 8th Street, N.W., Fifth Floor
Washington, DC 20004
(202) 724–5613
http://dcarts.dc.gov/services/grants/grants.shtm

1131. (A)
Artist Fellowship Program

2 grants of varying amounts to individuals in a broad range of artistic endeavors. Provides support to artists who make significant contributions to the arts and who promote the arts in DC through artistic excellence. Artistic disciplines rotate on a biannual basis: dance, interdisciplinary/performance art, literature, music, and theater on even years and media, visual arts, and crafts on odd years. Deadline: late May.

1132. (A)
Arts Education Teacher Mini-Grant Program

Grants of varying amounts to art teachers in DC public and public charter schools to support the development and implementation of innovative teaching strategies. Open to teachers in visual arts, dance, creative writing, and theater in grades pre-K to 12. Deadline: December 3.

1133. (A)
Young Artists Program

Grants of $2,500 to artists for support of innovative art projects. Must be between the ages of 18 and 30 and residents of DC. Awarded to recognize up and coming DC artists. Deadline: December 3.

1134. (H, S, SS)

Dog Writers' Educational Trust Scholarship
ATTN: DWET Executive Secretary
P.O. Box 22322
St. Petersburg, FL 33742–2333
http://www.dwet.org

From 4 to 10 scholarships of $2,500 to graduate or undergraduate students with close relatives who have a present or past interest in the world of dogs or have participated as exhibitors, breeders, handlers, judges, club officers, or other activities in the U.S. or Canada. Must be interested in animal/agricultural competition. Preference given to students planning on a career in veterinary medicine, animal behavior, or journalism. Based on academics (must be upper 1/3 of class), potential, leadership, and financial need. Equal importance is given to character, humane attitudes, and high marks in school records. Include a self-addressed, stamped envelope for application. Deadline: December 31.

1135. (Contest)

Drue Heinz Literature Prize
University of Pittsburgh Press
Eureka Building, Fifth Floor
3400 Forbes Avenue
Pittsburgh, PA 15260
http://www.pitt.edu/~press/series/DrueHeinz.html

1 first prize of $10,000 and publication awarded to best collection of novellas or short stories (150 to 300 pages). For rules send a self-addressed, stamped envelope. Deadline: August 31.

1136. (SS)

Dublin Institute for Advanced Studies
School of Theoretical Physics
Research Scholarships
10 Burlington Road
Dublin 4
Ireland
353-1-614 0561
http://www.dias.ie
physics@stp.dias.ie

Limited numbers of scholarships of 13,000 euros (postdoctoral) and 20,000 euros to senior researchers to conduct research in astronomy, cosmic physics, theoretical physics, or Celtic studies at the Dublin Institute.

Good at the Dublin Institute, not a university. Deadline: February 10.

(A, H, SS)

Dumbarton Oaks
1703 32nd Street, N.W.
Washington, DC 20007
(202) 339–6401
http://www.doaks.org
DumbartonOaks@doaks.org

1137. (A)

Awards in Byzantine Studies, Pre-Columbian Studies, and the History of Landscape Architecture

Fellowship awards of up to $34,700 per academic year to doctoral candidates and postdoctoral and junior researchers. Summer fellowships support study and/or research in Byzantine studies, Pre-Columbian studies, or the history of landscape architecture. Deadline: November 1.

1138. (SS)

Bliss Prize Fellowships in Byzantine Studies

Varying numbers of fellowships providing tuition and living expenses of up to $25,000 per year for 2 years and summer travel of up to $5,000 to graduate students and undergraduate seniors about to begin a graduate program in Byzantine studies. Must be accepted to, or enrolled in, an accredited U.S. or Canadian institution and have undertaken at least 1 year of Greek. The travel portion of the award is to assist in improved understanding of Byzantine civilization and culture. Must be nominated by advisor. Deadline: November 1 (advisor nomination) and November 15 (student application).

1139. (A)

Junior Fellowships

Varying numbers of fellowships providing $10,000, plus an $800 research allowance, up to $1,300 travel expense allowance, and (if needed) a $1,500 dependents' allowance to doctoral candidates to conduct independent research. Must have completed all course work, passed preliminary exams, and be at the dissertation level. Selection based on academic achievement and proposed research. Open to all nationalities; must have a working knowledge of relevant language. Write for more information. Deadline: November 15.

1140. (A, H, SS)
Summer Fellowships for Byzantine Studies

10 awards of $1,251 per week for up to 10 weeks for summer fellowships. Open to advanced graduate students of history, archaeology, history of art, philology, theology, and other disciplines. Postdoctoral fellowships are also available. Deadline: November 15.

1141. (S)
Dupage Medical Society Foundation Scholarship Program
498 Hillside Avenue
Glen Ellyn, IL 60137
(630) 858–9603
http://www.dcmsdocs.org

10 scholarships of $1,000 to students who are enrolled or about to enroll in a health professions program (dental hygiene, medical transcription, nursing, medical school, dental school, etc.) Must be registered voters and residents of Dupage County, Illinois. Must be pursuing a health-related career in an accredited health professions program. Pre-med and pre-dental students are not eligible. Students must already be enrolled or accepted to the professional program. Renewable. Deadline: December and March.

1142. (S)
e7 Fellowship/Scholarship for Sustainable Energy Development
e7 Secretariat
1155 Metcalfe Street, Suite 1120
Montreal QC H3B 2V6
Canada
(514) 392–8876
http://www.e7.org

Unspecified number of fellowship/scholarships of US $20,000 per year for students pursuing a master's degree and US $25,000 per year for postdoctoral fellows. Each award is for a 2-year period. Applicants must be students who are citizens of developing countries and countries whose economies are in transition, who are interested in continuing their studies and contributing to the body of knowledge in sustainable energy development. Awards can be used for tuition, books, and living expenses. Deadline: None specified.

1143. (SS)
The Earl Warren Legal Training Program, Inc. Scholarships
99 Hudson Street, 16th Floor
New York, NY 10013
(212) 219–1900
http://www.naacpldf.org/scholarships/e_w_l_training.html

Scholarships of $13,500 to entering African-American law students. Preference given to applicants wishing to enter law schools in the South. Award includes a $1,500 allowance to meet the costs of attending the LDF's yearly Civil Rights Institute. Must show proof of acceptance to an accredited law school. Must be U.S. citizen or legal resident. Renewable with satisfactory academic progress. Applicants under 35 years of age are preferred. Deadline: March 15.

1144. (S)
Earthwatch Institute
Earthwatch Education Awards
3 Clock Tower Place, Suite 100, Box 75
Maynard, MA 01754–0075
http://www.earthwatch.org

Approximately 200 awards ranging from $100 to $2,000 to science teachers in a national competition. Winners aren't given cash awards, but rather varying amounts of expenses are paid to allow the teacher to work in the field for 2 to 3 weeks with a professional scientist on a research expedition in the areas of archeology, anthropology, environmental studies, biology, and marine science. A similar competition is available to their students. Deadline: March 31.

(A)
Eastman Kodak Co.
Entertainment Imaging
8600 N.W. 17th Street, Suite 200
Miami, FL 33126–1006

(305) 507–5146
http://www.kodak.com

1145. (A)
Eastman Product Grants

Awards of up to $1,000 and $2,000 to graduate and undergraduate students majoring in film, film production, or cinematography at the undergraduate and graduate levels. Colleges and universities may nominate 2 students for awards every academic year, and portfolio reviews should be part of the selection process. Selection based on academic achievement, creative and technical ability, initiative, communications ability, and range of filmmaking experience. A blue-ribbon jury evaluates all work and makes final selections. The jury consists of an ASC and/or International Cinematographers Guild Director of Photography, an academic of distinction, an independent filmmaker, and an industry or trade association executive. Film-originated work and creative skill count 50%; the other criteria counts 50%. Deadline: None specified.

1146. (A)
Kodak Faculty Scholars Program

Up to $5,000 to cover costs related to film and/or media to a faculty production work. Selection is based on creativity and technical challenges, growth of development of film and/or production skill, and evidence it will enhance student learning and/or classroom experience. Deadline: May 31.

1147. (A)
Kodak Filmschool Competition

1 award of a round-trip travel and accommodations at the Cannes Film Festival to a full-time graduate or undergraduate student or recent graduate (within 12 months of closing date) who is majoring in film or related production training program. The cinematographer and crew members must also be students or recent graduates. For specific guidelines, visit web site. Deadline: December 31.

(A, S, SS)
East-West Center
EWC-UHM Scholarship Office
Burns Hall 2066

1601 East-West Road
Honolulu, HI 96848–1601
(808) 944–7111
written inquiries only
http://www.eastwestcenter.org/res-ph.asp

1148. (A, S, SS)
Asian Development Bank (ADB) Scholarships

Scholarships providing tuition, fees, housing, living stipend, health insurance, and round-trip airfare to graduate students in architecture, business administration, economics, geography, natural resources & environmental management, ocean & resources engineering, oceanography, Pacific Islands studies, public administration, sociology, tropical plant & soil science, and urban & regional planning. Renewable for up to 2 years for master's and 3 years for doctoral students. Must be a citizen of a developing member country of the Asian Development Bank. Deadline: November 1.

1149. (SS)
Graduate Degree Fellowships

Fellowships providing housing of approximately $4,745, a yearly stipend of $7,200, $5,250 for tuition and fees, and a book allowance of $660 to graduate and doctoral students in the areas of politics, governance, security; economics; environmental change, vulnerability, and governance; population and health; education; and Pacific Islands development. Fellows must be in residence at the University of Hawaii. Must be citizens or permanent residents of the U.S. or of countries in Asia and the Pacific, including Russia. Priority is given to applicants seeking degrees in study related to themes of the Center's research program, focusing on topics in international economics, politics and security studies, the environment, and population and health. Deadline: November 1.

1150. (A)
Eaton Literary Agency
ATTN: Awards Program
P.O. Box 49795
Sarasota, FL 34230–6795
(941) 366–6589
http://www.eatonliterary.com/awards.htm

1 award each of $500 for short stories and articles and $3,000 for published novels and nonfiction books. No reading fee. Send a self-addressed, stamped envelope for guidelines. Deadline: August 31 (book length award) and March 31 (short stories and articles).

1151. (A, S, SS)
Edelman Worldwide Public Relations
Internship Coordinator
211 East Ontario
Chicago, IL 60611
(312) 280–7000
http://www.edelman.com

135 12-week internships providing approximately $250 per week to undergraduate students, college graduates, and graduate students. International students may also apply. Internships are conducted during the summer, fall, and spring. Interns might be assigned to their offices in Chicago, New York, or 25 other offices worldwide. Interns work in media/video production, consumer marketing (food and nutrition), medical/health care, business and industrial, technology, travel, event marketing, investor and financial relations, public affairs, or corporate counsel. Interns must submit a résumé, cover letter, and (optional) writing samples. Deadline: rolling.

1152. (S, SS)
Edmund Niles Huyck Preserve
Graduate and Postgraduate Research Grants
Main Street
Rensselaerville, NY 12147
(518) 797–3440
http://www.huyckpreserve.org

Research grants of $2,500 to graduate fellowships and postgraduate fellows in ecology, behavior, evolution, or natural history. Must be conducting research on the natural resources of the Huyck Preserve. Awards cannot be used to defray academic course work costs. Housing and lab spaces are provided at the preserve. Send a self-addressed, stamped envelope for information. Deadline: February 1.

1153. (A, H, S, SS)
Educational Communications, Inc.
National Dean's List Scholarship
721 North McKinley Road
Lake Forest, IL 60045

(847) 295–6650
http://www.honoring.com

25 scholarships of $1,000 to graduate and undergraduate students who are nominated by their college dean or a faculty member. Based on academic record, extracurricular activities, essay, recommendation, and financial need. Applications available in June, July, and August. There is a $2.50 processing fee. Deadline: mid-December.

1154. (SS)
Educational Foundation for Women in Accounting
Laurel Fund
P.O. Box 1925
Southeastern, PA 19399–1925
(610) 644–3713 (Fax)
http://www.efwa.org/witwin2002.htm

Scholarships ranging from $1,000 to $5,000 to women doctoral students. Must be majoring in accounting. Must present clear evidence that the candidate has established goals and a plan for achieving those goals, both personal and professional, and have financial need. Recipient should prepare for the possibility of making a presentation at regional and/or national conferences. Visit web site for more information. Deadline: none specified.

1155. (SS)
Educational Testing Service
Test of English as a Foreign Language Dissertation Research Grants
ATTN: Director, TOEFL Research Program
MS59-L
P.O. Box 6155
Princeton, NJ 08541–6155
(609) 921–9000
http://www.toefl.org/educators/edraward.html

Varying numbers of grants of $2,500 to doctoral candidates to conduct research on second/foreign language testing conducted as part of dissertation work for doctoral degree. Dissertation must have been accepted by applicant's graduate institution after a specified date. Write for more information. Deadline: none specified.

1156. (SS)
Education Writers Association
Fellowships in National Education Reporting
2122 P Street, N.W., Suite 201
Washington, DC 20037

(202) 452–9830

http://www.ewa.org

ewa@ewa.org

Fellowships providing half-salary for 2 months, travel expenses, access to expert sources, and editing assistance to full-time print or broadcast journalists who have covered education for at least 2 years. Freelance writers may apply if they show they write about education for a substantial portion of their time. Deadline: May 23.

1157. (A, H, S, SS)

Edward Arthur Mellinger Educational Foundation, Inc.

Scholarship Committee

1025 East Broadway

P.O. Box 770

Monmouth, IL 61462

(309) 734–2419

http://www.mellinger.org

Approximately 300 grants totaling over $391,000 to graduate and undergraduate students residing in, or attending college in, the Midwest (western Illinois and eastern Iowa). May be used for any area of study. Write a brief letter detailing your educational and financial situation, and include a self-addressed, stamped envelope. Deadline: June 1.

1158. (S)

Edward Bangs and Elza Kelley Foundation Scholarship Program

243 South Street, Box M

Hyannis, MA 02601

(508) 775–3117

http://www.kelleyfoundation.org

35 to 40 scholarships ranging from $500 to $2,000 to graduate or professional school students, undergraduates, and graduating high school seniors. Must be residents of Barnstable County, MA. Awards support study at recognized, accredited institution. Applicants must be pursuing health, human services, education, or related areas if the acquired skills will help them contribute to the health and welfare of inhabitants of Barnstable County, Massachusetts. Selection is based on academic achievement, recommendations, and financial need. Visit web site or send a self-addressed, stamped envelope for an application. Deadline: April 30.

1159. (Contest)

Eighth Mountain Press

Poetry Prize

624 SE 28 Avenue

Portland, OR 97214–3026

(503) 233–3936

http://www.cbsd.com/pubs.cfm?Search=E

A prize of $1,000 to recognize the importance of the feminist movement. Manuscripts of 50 to 120 pages by a woman writer may be submitted during January. Send a self-addressed, stamped envelope for guidelines and further information. Deadline: January 31.

1160. (A, H, S, SS)

Eleanor Brackenridge Scholarship Committee

ATTN: Scholarship Chairperson

c/o Women's Club

1717 San Pedro

San Antonio, TX 78212

1 scholarship of $500 to a graduate or undergraduate woman who is continuing her education in nursing, teaching, or other such professions. Must be a resident of San Antonio, TX. Either request a scholarship or include a short biographical sketch with financial need included. Send 3 letters of recommendation, name and address of school, and an official transcript. Deadline: February 1.

1161. (S)

Electrochemical Society

Summer Research Fellowships

65 South Main Street, Building D

Pennington, NJ 08534–2839

(609) 737–1902

http://www.electrochem.org

3 fellowships of $2,000 to graduate students majoring in chemistry, chemical engineering, electrical engineering, or energy. Must be attending an institution in the U.S. or Canada. Award is given to support research of interest to the Society and research aimed at reducing energy consumption. Deadline: January 1.

1162. (Contest)

Elf: Eclectic Literary Forum

Ruth Cable Memorial Prize for Poetry

P.O. Box 392

Tonawanda, NY 14150
http://www.econet.net/elf

1 first prize of $500 and publication to an unpublished poem of 60 lines or less. Entry fee includes a free copy of ELF. Charges: $8 for first 3 poems and $3 for each additional poem. Send a self-addressed, stamped envelope for guidelines. Deadline: March 31.

1163. (A, H)
Elmer O. and Ida Preston Educational Trust
801 Grand Avenue, Suite 3700
Des Moines, IA 50309
(515) 243–4191

Varying numbers of grants of varying amounts to graduate, undergraduate, and seminarian students. Must be Christian and preparing for a full-time career in Christian service, including minister of music. Must be residents of Iowa and attending an accredited institution in Iowa. Must provide a recommendation from a minister commenting on the student's potential in his chosen church vocation. Awards both grants and a combination of grant and loan. Deadline: generally, June 30.

1164. (A)
Emily Clark Balch Award
Virginia Quarterly Review
1 West Range Box 400223
Charlottesville, VA 22904–4223
(804) 924–3124
http://www.virginia.edu/vqr

Best short story and poetry accepted and published by the *Virginia Quarterly Review*. Send a self-addressed, stamped envelope for guidelines or visit web site. Deadline: none.

1165. (A, H, S, SS)
Endowment Fund of Phi Kappa Psi Fraternity, Inc.
510 Lokerbie Street
Indianapolis, IN 46202
(317) 632–1852
http://www.phikappapsi.com

Scholarships from $100 to $3,000 to graduate and undergraduate students in any area of study. Preference given to Phi Kappa Psi Fraternity members. Write a brief letter detailing your educational and financial situation, include a self-addressed, stamped envelope. Deadline: none specified.

1166. (S)
Engineering Foundation
Engineering Research Initiation Grants
345 East 47th Street
New York, NY 10017
(212) 705–7835
http://www.engfnd.org

Varying numbers of grants of up to $23,000 to graduate and postgraduate students to conduct a research project in engineering of general interest to ASCE, AIME, ASME, IEEE, or AIChE. Qualified individuals, organizations, or technical societies may apply. Deadline: November 15.

(S)
Engineering Geology Foundation
Association of Engineering Geologist
P.O. Box 4060518
Denver, CO 80246
(303) 757–2926
http://www.aegweb.org

1167. (S)
Marliave Scholarship Fund

1 or 2 scholarships of $2,000 to graduate students in the area of engineering geology. Based on character, academic achievement, ability, student activities, and potential for contributing to the profession. For more information, visit web site or send a self-addressed, stamped envelope and request your letter be forwarded to the current Scholarship Chairperson. Deadline: February 1.

1168. (S)
Norman R. Tilford Field Studies Scholarship

1 scholarship each to a graduate and undergraduate in geology or a related field. Award is to fund field research for the graduate student and a field camp course or senior thesis field research for an undergraduate. Selection is based on academic achievement, recommendation letters, and an essay. Visit web site for more information. Deadline: January 31.

1169. (S, SS)
Enrico Mattei Institute
Fondazione ENI Enrico Mattei
Corso Magenta, 63
20123 Milano
Milan, Italy
+39-2-52036934
http://www.freem.it

55 grants and scholarships of varying amounts to graduate students in science, social science, and other fields, for 1 year of study in Italy. Must be under 33 years of age. Write a brief letter detailing your educational and financial situation, and include a self-addressed, stamped envelope.

(S)

The Environmental Careers Organization (ECO)
179 South Street
Boston, MA 02111
(617) 426–4375
http://www.eco.org

1170. (S)
Environmental Protection Agency

12-week internships providing $500 per week to graduate or upper-level undergraduate students majoring in environmental/earth science, atmospheric science (including meteorology/climatology), geography, or related physical sciences. Candidates should have an interest in climate change science and policy, as well as science communication. Internship takes place in Washington, DC.

1171. (S)
EPS Internship Program

325 internships in the Environmental Placement Services (EPS), providing a salary ranging from $200 to $800 per week. Open to graduate students and upper-level undergraduate students of any age. Students can be assigned to individuals from a variety of corporations, such as IBM, Ford, Boeing, Polaroid, Pacific Gas & Electric. Interns might work in department such as environmental health and safety, where they compile reports or evaluate power produced by alternative energy sources. Deadline: rolling.

1172. (S)
Mitretek Systems, Inc.
http://www.mitretek.org

1 internship providing a salary dependent on education to graduate or upper-level undergraduate students in atmospheric or ocean science, with a balance of quantitative and qualitative skills. Visit web site for more information. Deadline: March 31.

(S, SS)
Environmental Protection Agency
Office of Grants & Debarment
1200 Pennsylvania Avenue, N.W.
Mail Code 3213A
Washington, DC 20460
(202) 272–0167
http://www.epa.gov

1173. (S)
Historically Black College Program

Varying numbers of grants ranging from $3,000 to $6,000 to graduate students majoring in science or engineering. Must have received their bachelor's degree from a historically Black college. Deadline: none specified.

1174. (S)
National Network for Environmental Management Studies Fellowships

Up to 50 awards providing a stipend of varying amounts to graduate and undergraduate students pursuing a program directly related to pollution control or environmental protection. Graduate students must be enrolled or admitted for enrollment in an accredited graduate program. Undergraduate students must have at least a 3.0 GPA on a 4.0 scale and have completed at least 4 courses related to the field of environmental studies. All applicants must be U.S. citizens or legal permanent residents and enrolled in an accredited U.S. institution. Deadline: February 24.

1175. (S, SS)
National Network for Environmental Management Studies Internships

75 to 100 internships providing a grant ranging from $4,000 to $6,000 to graduate or undergraduate

students. Interns work in the following areas: environmental policy, regulations, and law; environmental management and administration; environmental science; public relations and media; and computer programming and development. Internships are available at the headquarters in Washington, DC, Atlanta, Boston, Chicago, Dallas, Denver, Kansas City, New York, Philadelphia, San Francisco, and Seattle. Deadline: early February.

(S)
Environmental Protection Agency
179 South Street
Boston, MA 02111
(617) 426–4783
http://www.epa.gov

1176. (S)
Science to Achieve Results (STAR) Graduate Fellowships

http://es.epa.gov/ncer/fellow

Fellowships of up to $34,000 to graduate students in a field of study related to the environment (mathematics, natural sciences, engineering, social sciences, and multidisciplinary studies related to environmental sciences and technology). Must be U.S. citizens or permanent residents. Deadline: generally, November.

1177. (S)
Student Environmental Associate Program and Diversity Initiative

EPA's Office of Environmental Justice is sponsoring the Student Environmental Associate Program and Diversity Initiative, a cooperative venture between EPA and the Environmental Careers Organization. Last year, EPA sponsored 114 students from a wide variety of communities and tribes across the country. Each student completed a paid, full-time, on-site training opportunity of 3 to 6 months. These talented associates were drawn from a culturally diverse pool of over 2,000 students based on academic achievement, extracurricular activities, and stated interest in pursuing an environmental career. Deadline: None specified.

(S, SS)
Epilepsy Foundation of America
Research Administration
4351 Garden City Drive, Suite 406
Landover, MD 20785–7223
(800) 332–1000
(301) 459–3700
http://www.efa.org

1178. (S)
Behavioral Sciences Student Fellowships

Numerous grants of $1,500 to graduate and undergraduate students in nursing, psychology, and related areas to conduct epilepsy-related study or training projects. Must propose a 3-month epilepsy-related project to be carried out in a U.S. institution at which there is ongoing epilepsy research, service, or training programs. Project must be conducted during a free period in the student's year. Deadline: March 2.

1179. (S, SS)
Graduate Student Fellowships

Research grants of $30,000 to graduate students who are majoring in a biological, behavioral, or social science to conduct an epilepsy-related research project that will advance the understanding, treatment, and prevention of epilepsy. Award is for a 1-year period and renewable for a second year. Selection is competitive. Research must be conducted in a U.S. institution. Deadline: September 1.

1180. (S, SS)
Medical Student Fellowships

6 fellowships of $1,500 or $2,000 each to medical, graduate, and undergraduate students to conduct a 3-month research project in an area of epilepsy. The project must be conducted during a student's free period and can be conducted at a U.S. institution of the student's choice that has an ongoing program of research, training, or service in epilepsy. Students should be interested in epilepsy research or practice in the areas of sociology, social work, psychology, anthropology, nursing, or political science. Send a self-addressed, stamped envelope for information. Deadline: March 1.

1181. (S, SS)
Postdoctoral Research Grants & Fellowships

Varying numbers of research grants and fellowships of varying amounts to postdoctoral fellows to support research projects, clinical training, and clinical research that will advance the understanding, treatment, and prevention of epilepsy. Deadline: September 1.

1182. (S)
Eppley Foundation for Research
Postdoctoral Research Grants
575 Lexington Avenue
New York, NY 10022
written inquiries only
http://www.fundingopps2.cos.com

Postdoctoral grants of up to $25,000 for original advanced research in either physical sciences or biological sciences. Grants are open to established research scientists who are attached to a recognized institution. Deadline: February 1, May 1, August 1, and November 1.

1183. (A, H, S, SS)
Ethel Louise Armstrong Foundation, Inc.
ELA Scholarships
2460 North Lake Avenue, PMB #128
Altadena, CA 91001
(626) 398–8840
http://www.ela.org

Scholarships ranging from $1,000 to $2,000 to women graduate students with physical disabilities. Must be applying to, or enrolled in, an accredited U.S. institution, be active in local, state, or national disability organization, be willing to network with ELA board of directors and alumni, and be willing to update ELA with an annual letter on her academic and professional career. Must write an essay of 1,000 words or less on "How I Will Change the Face of Disability on the Planet," along with an application, transcript, recommendation letters, and verification of disability. Visit web site for specific information and an application. Deadline: June 1.

1184. (A, H, S, SS)
Evrytanian Association of America
121 Greenwich Road
Charlotte, NC 28211

(704) 366–6571
http://www.uch.gr

8 scholarships of $1,200 to graduate and undergraduate students of Evrytanian ancestry (with origins in Evrytania, Greece). 10 scholarships providing room and board to students from Greece to study in Greece. May be used for any field of study. Greek students wanting to study in Greece must contact the Velouchi Association in Greece. Students from Greece wanting to study in the U.S. must contact the U.S. Association. Deadline: June 1 (for U.S. and Greek students to study in U.S.).

(S)
Experimental Aircraft Association (EAA)
Foundation, Inc.
P.O. Box 3086
Oshkosh, WI 54903–3065
(920) 426–4800
http://www.eaa.org

1185. (S)
David Alan Quick Scholarship

1 scholarship of $1,000 to an entering first-year graduate student or undergraduate junior or senior who is pursuing a career in aerospace or aeronautical engineering. Renewable. Must have demonstrated a continuing quality in personal, academic, and aviation pursuits and may be applied toward the achievement of any aviation-related formal education or training. Deadline: March 30.

1186. (S)
Hansen Scholarship

1 scholarship of $1,000 to a graduate or undergraduate student in aerospace engineering or aeronautical engineering. Financial need is considered. Must have demonstrated a continuing quality in personal, academic, and aviation pursuits and may be applied toward the achievement of any aviation-related formal education or training. Deadline: March 30.

1187. (S)
Payzer Scholarship

1 scholarship of $5,000 to a graduate or undergraduate student in technical information who is seeking a major and declares an intention to pursue a professional career in biological or physical sciences, engi-

neering, or mathematics. Must have demonstrated continuing quality in personal, academic, and aviation pursuits and may be applied toward the achievement of any aviation-related formal education or training. Deadline: March 30.

1188. (H, SS)
Family Research Council
Witherspoon Fellowship
801 G Street, N.W.
Washington, DC 20001
(800) 225–4008
http://www.witherspoonfellowship.org/

Fellowships of varying amounts to graduate and undergraduate students to train young Christians to take their religiously inspired convictions and well-reasoned arguments into the public square and contend for the allegiance of their fellow citizens on important matters of public policy. Deadline: November 1 (spring), early March (summer), and April 2 (fall).

1189. (S)
Fannie and John Hertz Foundation
Doctoral Fellowship Program
2456 Research Drive
Livermore, CA 94550–3850
(925) 373–1642
http://www.hertzfoundation.org

25 fellowships providing a cost-of-education allowance and a personal stipend of $25,000 to doctoral students and undergraduate seniors wishing to pursue a doctoral degree. Must have at least a 3.75 GPA during last 2 years of undergraduate study and be a U.S. citizen. Students pursuing a joint Ph.D./M.D. and Ph.D./M.B.A. are ineligible. Must be a U.S. citizen. Renewable up to 5 years. Deadline: November 1.

1190. (SS)
Federal Bureau of Investigation (FBI)
Honors Internship Program
FBI HQ
Room 6329
10th and Pennsylvania Avenue, N.W.
Washington, DC 20535
(202) 324–4991
http://www.fbi.gov

50 to 70 10-week summer internships to graduate students and undergraduate seniors in the area of domestic intelligence and criminal investigation. Internships are conducted at Washington, DC, and Quantico, Virginia. Interns work on projects related to ongoing investigations. Interns work in Personnel Resources, Behavioral Science Services, Criminal Informant, Accounting and Budget Analysis, Legal Forfeiture, European/Asian/Money Laundering, Undercover and Sensitive Operations, and Audit. They have access to Special Agents, tour field offices, DNA labs, and the Quantico Academy. Upon completion of the internship, interns are highly recruited. Must have at least a 3.0 GPA and must be U.S. citizens. Deadline: November 1.

1191. (A, H, S, SS)
Federal Employee Education and Assistance Fund
FEEA Scholarship Program
8441 West Bowles Avenue, Suite 200
Littleton, CO 80123–9501
(800) 323–4140
(303) 933–7580
http://www.feea.org

100 to 250 scholarships ranging from $500 to $2,500 per year to all active civilian federal employees (with at least 3 years service) and their dependents. For graduate, postgraduate, and undergraduate study at a 2- or 4-year institution for any field of study. Minimum 2.5 GPA. Send self-addressed, stamped envelope for details. Deadline: June 5.

1192. (SS)
The Feminist Majority
8105 West Third Street, Suite 1
Los Angeles, CA 90048
(213) 651–0495
http://www.feminist.org

20 internships providing only limited stipends to graduate, undergraduate, and high school students. Students can work either part- or full-time for at least 2 months in either Los Angeles or Washington, DC. The Feminist Majority strives to place feminists in public office or college campus leadership positions and encourages women to seek top positions in their professions. Interns monitor press conferences and congressional hearings, analyze policy, write position papers, and conduct research on women's issues. Deadline: rolling.

1193. (S)
Fight for Sight, Inc.
Research Fellowships and Grants-in-Aid
ATTN: Research Awards Coordinator
500 East Remington Road
Schaumburg, IL 60173–4557
(800) 331–2021
http://www.preventblindness.org

Varying numbers of postdoctoral fellowships of $14,000 and grants ranging from $1,000 to $12,000 to postdoctoral fellows to conduct research projects in ophthalmology, with emphasis on pilot programs. The program is administered by Prevent Blindness America. Obtain application forms and brochures from above address. Deadline: varies.

1194. (A)
Fine Arts Work Center in Provincetown
Fellowship Program
P.O. Box 565
24 Pearl Street
Provincetown, MA 02657
(617) 487–9960
http://www.fawc.org

Fellowships providing a monthly stipend for lodging and/or studio space at the Center are available to emerging writers and visual artists. Applicants must have created a body of work that can be presented by slides; photographs; or manuscripts. The Fine Arts Work Center is not a school but a community providing fellows with an environment to suit their needs. Deadline: December 2 (writing), February 3 (visual art).

1195. (A, H, S, SS)
First Catholic Slovak Ladies Association
Fraternal Scholarship Award
Director of Fraternal Scholarship Aid
24950 Chagrin Boulevard
Beachwood, OH 44122
(216) 464–8015
http://www.fcsla.com

7 scholarships of $1,750 to graduate students in all areas of study. Must be children of members of the Association who have been beneficial members of the Association for at least 3 years prior to the date of application on a $1,000 legal research certificate or a $5,000

participating estate certificate. Based on academic record and essay. Deadline: March 1.

1196. (Contest)
The Flannery O'Connor Award for Short Fiction
The University of Georgia Press
330 Research Drive
Athens, GA 30602–4901
(404) 542–0601
http://www.ugapress.uga.edu/pressinfo/subguide_flan.html

Submission period is June to July 31. Charges: $10 fee. Manuscripts will not be returned. Send self-addressed, stamped envelope for rules and information. Deadline: July 31.

1197. (A)
Florida Arts Council
Individual Artists Fellowships
Florida Department of State
1001 DeSoto Park Drive
Tallahassee, FL 32301
(850) 487–2980, ext. 117
http://www.dos.state.fl.us/dca/Fellowship.html

30 fellowship awards of up to $5,000 to artists to further their work (not their studies) in the following areas: music, theater, dance, literature, media, folk and unusual arts. Fellowship awards support the general artistic and career advancement of the individual artist. Applicants must be Florida residents, over 18 years old, and a U.S. citizen. Deadline: April 1.

(A, H, S, SS)
Florida Department of Education
Student Financial Assistance
255 Collins Building
Tallahassee, FL 32399–0400
(850) 488–4095
(888) 827–2004 (Hotline)
http://www.fldoe.org

1198. (A, H, S, SS)
Jose Marti Scholarship Challenge Grant Fund

Scholarships of $2,000 per year for up to 4 semesters to graduate students in any area of study. Must be either Hispanic or a person of Spanish culture with origins in Mexico, South America, Central America, or the Caribbean (regardless of race). Student must maintain a 3.0 GPA on a 4.0 scale during college study and be a full-time student. Based on academic record and financial need.

1199. (SS)
Teacher Tuition Reimbursement

Tuition reimbursement payments of up to $78 per credit hour for up to 9 hours per academic year, for up to a total of 36 credit hours for graduate study. Awards are made to encourage public school teachers to become certified to teach or to gain a graduate degree in a department of education critical teacher shortage area. Must maintain at least a 3.0 GPA in all courses. Deadline: Specified on application.

1200. (S)
Florida Department of Health & Rehabilitative Services
Florida Health Service Corps
Recruitment/Retention Program
1317 Wine Wood Boulevard
Tallahassee, FL 32399–0700
(904) 488–6811
http://medschool.slu.edu/sfp/housestaff/
repay/flahealthservice.shtml

Awards of up to $25,000 per year for 2 years to board-eligible/board-certified primary care physicians, nurse practitioners, podiatrists, and chiropractors. Award is given to medical personnel to practice in underserved areas (as identified by the Department of Health). Repayment credits outstanding medical school loans. Send a self-addressed, stamped envelope for information. Deadline: none.

1201. (A, H, S, SS)
Florida Endowment Fund for Higher Education
McKnight Black Doctoral Fellowship Program
201 E. Kennedy Boulevard, Suite 1525
Tampa, FL 33602
(813) 221–2772
http://www.fl-educ-fd.org/mdf.pdf

25 awards include an $11,000 stipend, plus $5,000 tuition and fees per year, to African-American students with at least a bachelor's degree from an accredited institution in any area (except law, medicine, or education) and who wish to pursue a doctoral degree. Recipients must attend a Florida institution but do not have to be Florida residents. Renewable for 3 years. Deadline: January 15.

1202. (SS)
Florida House of Representatives
Speaker's Legislative Fellowship Program
826 The Capitol
402 South Monroe Street
Tallahassee, FL 32399–1300
(850) 487–2390
http://www.leg.state.fl.us/house/fellowship/
index.html

Internships paying $13 per hour, plus payment of up to 24 hours of in-state tuition to graduate students or recent college graduates. Must be Florida residents or enrolled in a Florida institution. Selection is based on academic achievement, test scores, recommendation letters, and writing sample. Visit web site for an application and more information. Deadline: May 9.

1203. (SS)
Florida State Board of Administration
Internship Program
P.O. Box 13300
Tallahassee, FL 32317–3300
(850) 488–4406
http://www.fsba.state.fl.us

Internships to graduate students and rising undergraduate seniors, with preference given to students majoring in accounting, business, economics, finance, or management information systems. Must have at least a 3.0 GPA on a 4.0 scale, advanced computer skills, excellent written and oral communication skills, ability to work in a team project–oriented environment, and the ability to manage multiple priorities. Internships are available in: accounting, investment research, management information systems, and real estate. Internships last from 3 months to 1 year and are located in Tallahassee. Deadline: none specified.

(SS)
Food and Drug Law Institute
1000 Vermont Avenue, N.W., Suite 1200
Washington, DC 20005
(202) 371–1420
(800) 956–6293
http://www.fdli.org

1204. (SS)

H. Thomas Austern Memorial Writing Competition

1 award each of $1,000 and $1,500 in each category to full-time students enrolled in any U.S. law school. 2 categories for submissions: papers with up to a maximum of 40 pages and papers of 41 pages and over. Visit web site for specific submission guidelines, deadline date, and address to send submission. Deadline: mid-May.

1205. (SS)

Summer Internship Program

An intensive 1-week program open to full-time law students, graduate or undergraduate students pursuing a scientific or technical degree addressing an area related to the food and drug field, or individuals participating in a summer internship sponsored by a government agency. Selection based on application, essay, academic achievement, recommendations, and resume. There is no fee for full-time students, but a nominal fee is charged to part-time students and government employees/interns. Visit web site for specific guidelines, deadline, and application address.

(SS)

Food Distribution Research Society, Inc.
c/o Dale L. Anderson
P.O. Box 441110
Ft. Washington, MD 20749
(301) 292–1970
http://fdrs.ag.utk.edu/applebaum.html

1206. (SS)

Case Study Competition

Awards of varying amounts to graduate and undergraduate students majoring in food distribution or a closely related field. Competition allows students who work in teams of 3 or 5 to demonstrate their knowledge of agribusiness, in particular food distribution, and agricultural economics to real-world situations. Case study analysis and presentation to promote increased study of the food industry and boost student and industry awareness and involvement in FDRS. Deadline: mid-September.

1207. (SS)

William Applebaum Memorial Scholarship Award

Cash awards of $750 (master's level) and $1,250 (doctoral level) to graduate students for a thesis and $500 (master's level) for a non-thesis paper dealing with a broad range of food and marketing issues. Visit web site for specific guidelines and deadlines.

(A, H, S, SS)

The Ford Foundation
320 East 43rd Street
New York, NY 10017
(212) 573–5000
http://www.fordfound.org

1208. (SS)

Fellowship in Combined Soviet/East European & International Security Study

Varying numbers of training fellowships of varying amounts to doctoral candidates and postdoctoral scholars who have competence in one of these areas: Soviet studies, East European studies, or international security and are seeking training in the other. Open to advanced graduate students and postdoctoral students from all countries and in all disciplines. This is a training fellowship, not a research award. Deadline: March 1.

1209. (A, H, S, SS)

Graduate Fellowships

A limited number of awards to graduate students to conduct research and other activities related to program interests. Most Foundation grants to individuals are awarded through publicly announced competitions or on the basis of nominations from an institution. Selection is based on the merits of their proposals and on their potential contribution to advancing the Foundation's program objectives. Deadline: varies.

1210. (Contest)

Foster City Annual Writers Contest
Foster City Committee for the Arts
650 Shell Boulevard
Foster City, CA 94404
http://www.fostercity.org/Services/recreation/
History-of-Writers-Contest.cfm

Awards of varying amounts, totaling $1,500 in prizes. Contest for unpublished fiction, poetry, humor, and children's stories. Include a self-addressed, stamped envelope for rules. Deadline: April 1 and August 31.

1211. (H, SS)
Foundation for Biblical Archaeology
Student Funds for Archaeology
P.O. Box 1553
Goldsboro, NC 27522–1553
(919) 734–7578
http://www.tfba.org
tfba@tfba.org

Awards of varying amounts to graduate students in programs related to the archaeological aspects of biblical studies. Must attend University of North Carolina at Charlotte, Siena College in New York, Center College in Kentucky, or the American Schools of Oriental Research at Boston University. Visit web site for contacts, more information, and deadline.

(S)
Foundation for Chiropractic Education and Research
1701 Clarendon Boulevard
Arlington, VA 22209
(703) 276–7445
http://www.fcer.org

1212. (S)
FCER Research Fellowship

Varying numbers of awards of up to $10,000 per year, or $30,000 over 5 years, as fellowships for chiropractors pursuing research training leading to a doctorate in a basic science or nonclinical area. Renewable with satisfactory academic progress. Write an introductory letter briefly explaining your educational goals and situation. Please include a self-addressed, stamped envelope for an application. Deadline: October 1 and March 1.

1213. (S)
Fellowships and Scholarships

Varying number of scholarships of varying amounts to students who have had at least 2 years of preprofessional work at the college level before enrollment in a chiropractic program. Must have at least a B average. Deadline: March 1.

1214. (A)
Fox Inc.
(Insert Name of Fox Company)
Personnel Department
P.O. Box 900
Beverly Hills, CA 90213
(310) FOX–1000
http://www.fox.com/home.htm

60 to 90 internships ranging from 8 to 16 weeks during the summer, spring, and fall and providing a salary of $450 per week to graduate students and $300 per week to undergraduates. International students studying in the U.S. may apply. Internships are conducted in Dallas, TX, Los Angeles, CA, and New York, NY, during the summer, fall, and spring. There are 19 separate entertainment companies: Fox Broadcasting, Fox Television Network, Cable Channels fX and fXM, Twentieth Television (syndicates Fox television shows), Morning Studies, Fox Sports, Fox Children's Network, Fox Latin America Channel, Twentieth Century Fox, Twentieth Century Fox TV, Twentieth Century Fox Licensing and Merchandising, and Fox Searchlight Pictures. Interns may work in any of the companies in the following departments: accounting, finance, legal, production, programming, research, and sales & marketing. Interns must receive academic credit for unpaid positions. Must submit a résumé and cover letter. Deadline: rolling.

(SS)
Fraser Institute
1770 Burrand Street, 4th Floor
Vancouver, BC V6J 3G7
Canada
(604) 688–0221
http://www.fraserinstitute.ca

1215. (SS)
Internships

Internships providing $1,500 per month, and reasonable domestic travel will be reimbursed, to graduate and undergraduate students to train as junior policy analysts. Must be proficient in English (written and verbal), word processing, spreadsheet programs, and Internet research. The Fraser Institute is an independent nonprofit organization whose ideas contribute to the economic well-being of individual Canadians. Deadline: January 31 (summer) and May 30 (fall).

1216. (SS)
Student Essay Contest

Awards of $500 and $1,000 to graduate and undergraduate students in any discipline. Students must write an essay on an assigned topic and will be judged based on originality, expression of ideas, presentation, and understanding of competitive markets. Deadline: June 2.

1217. (SS)
Freedoms Foundation
Leavey Awards for Excellence in Private Enterprise Education

Awards Department
P.O. Box 706
Valley Forge, PA 19482–0706
(610) 933–8825
http://www.ffvf.org

Cash grants of $7,500 to high school teachers and college professors who create and teach a free enterprise course. For eligibility information about the Leavey Awards, contact: Mrs. Katherine Wood-Jacobs, Vice-President of Awards and Programs. Deadline: none specified.

(SS)
Friedrich Ebert Foundation

823 United Nations Plaza, Suite 711
New York, NY 10017
(212) 687–0208
http://www.fesny.org

1218. (SS)
Doctoral Research Fellowships

Varying numbers of fellowships providing a monthly stipend of 600 euros plus airfare, domestic travel allowance, tuition and fees, luggage and books allowance, and dependent's allowance (if needed) to doctoral candidates in political science, sociology, history, or economics as related to German/European affairs or German-American relations. Must have completed all course work and be at the dissertation level. Award provides from 5- to 12-month residential study and research in Germany. Must be U.S. citizens, be affiliated with a U.S. institution, and know German. Deadline: February 15.

1219. (SS)
Predissertation/Advanced Graduate Fellowships

Varying numbers of fellowships providing a monthly stipend of 500 euros plus airfare, domestic travel allowance, tuition and fees, luggage and books allowance, and dependent's allowance (if needed) to doctoral candidates in political science, sociology, history, or economics as related to German/European affairs or German-American relations. Must have completed at least 2 years of graduate study. Award provides from 5- to 12-month residential study and research in Germany. Must be U.S. citizens, be affiliated with a U.S. institution, and know German. Deadline: February 15.

1220. (SS)
Friends of the Library of Hawaii
Grants Program

690 Pohukaina Street
Honolulu, HI 96813
(808) 536–4174
http://www.hcc.hawaii.edu/hspls/friends.html

5 to 10 grants ranging from $1,000 to $2,000 to graduate students in library science. Must be Hawaii residents. Deadline: varies.

(S)
Friends of the National Zoo

National Zoological Park
3001 Connecticut Avenue
Washington, DC 20008
(202) 673–4950
http://www.fonz.org

1221. (S)
Graphics & Horticulture Traineeships

12-week summer or fall internships that provide a $2,400 stipend to recent graduates and upper-level undergraduates whose major was either graphic arts or horticulture. Based on interest, academic achievement, relevant experience, and recommendations. All internships are at the National Zoological Park in Washington, DC. Deadline: mid-February.

1222. (S)

Research Traineeship Program

Awards of up to $2,400 to graduate and undergraduate students in zoology to participate in a 12-week summer or fall internship. Selection based on academic achievement, statement of interest, relevant experience, and recommendation letters. Deadline: February 17.

1223. (A, S, SS)

Frito-Lay, Inc.
Minority Internship Program
Staffing
7701 Legacy Drive
Plano, TX 75024–4099
(214) 334–7000
http://www.frito.com

25 12-week summer internships providing a salary ranging from $460 to $600 per week for undergraduates, $540 to $820 per week for graduates, plus a $500 relocation stipend, and a $1,000 bonus, open to minority undergraduate sophomores, juniors, seniors, and graduate students. Interns work in graphic design, engineering, computer science, and some business-related areas at the corporate headquarters in Plano, TX, or at the divisional headquarters in Texas, Georgia, or California. Some interns take field assignments in sales, operations, manufacturing, and distributions in Phoenix, AZ, Los Angeles, CA, Chicago, IL, or Beloit or Milwaukee, WI. Interns working in technical positions develop packaging graphics, install new seasoning systems, develop hardware and software, and track seasoning-usage fluctuations. Interns in nontechnical positions evaluate competitor products, sell and produce chips and dips, write articles, and even interview employees. Deadline: April 15.

1224. (S, SS)

Frontier Nursing Service (FNS), Inc.
Courier Program
132 FNS Drive
Wendover, KY 41775
(800) 394–4881
http://www.frontiernursing.org/courier_program.htm

Numerous 8-week internships that are conducted year-round are open to anyone at least 18 years of age. Any major is accepted, but experience in CPR, first aid, and on Macintosh computers is helpful. Couriers must hold valid driver's licenses. Couriers experience rural life in Kentucky working in FNS, an organization founded in 1925 by Mary Breckinridge following the deaths of her children. FNS provides quality health care to many of Leslie County's poor, rural residents. This internship program is an excellent opportunity for anyone interested in teaching and/or health care. Couriers selected to participate in the program receive no monetary compensation but do receive free room and board. Couriers may visit hospitals to pick up mail, medicine, supplies, and prenatal equipment. They take medical histories of patients, take vital signs, and even participate in various surgical procedures. Applicants must submit a $100 application fee, an application form, cover letter explaining interest in program, and a résumé. Deadline: rolling.

1225. (A)

Fulbright Association
Selma Jeanne Cohen Fund International School on Dance
Executive Director
666 11th Street, N.W., Suite 525
Washington, DC 20001
(202) 333–1590
http://www.fulbright.org/cohen/appcall.htm

Scholarships providing an honorarium, round-trip travel funds, and expenses for dance scholars to present a major paper on dance scholarship at the Fulbright Association's annual conference. There are no requirements regarding academic degree, area of dance scholarship, age, or residency. Deadline: late August.

1226. (A, H, S, SS)

Fulbright Teacher and Administrator Exchange
Graduate School, USDA
600 Maryland Avenue, S.W., Suite 320
Washington, DC 20024–2520
(202) 314–3520
http://grad.usda.gov/info_for/fulbright.cfm
fulbright@grad.usda.gov

An exchange program for teachers and administrators to participate in direct exchanges of positions with colleagues from other countries for 6 weeks, a semester, or a full academic year. Maintenance allowance, when provided, is normally paid in the currency of the host country and based on the cost of living in that country.

Purpose of the program is to promote mutual understanding between the people of the United States and the peoples of other countries. Once selected, participants must attend an orientation program, with the Department of State covering orientation costs, one-way travel to orientation (teacher only), and 2–3 days of food and lodging at the orientation site. Visit web site for a list of the countries and categories of applicants available. Teachers must hold at least a bachelor's degree, be currently employed in a full-time teaching assignment, and have taught for at least 3 years. Must be U.S. citizens and fluent in English. Deadline: October 15.

1227. (S)
Fund for Podiatric Medical Education (FPME) Scholarships
9312 Old Georgetown Road
Bethesda, MD 20814
(301) 571–9200
http://www.apma.org

Scholarships ranging from $1,000 to $7,500 to graduate and third- and fourth-year podiatry students wanting to continue their education in basic and clinical science, public health, and education. Recipient must take at least 12 credit hours per semester at an accredited podiatry school of medicine. Selection based on financial need, academic achievement, and community service. Contact financial aid office of podiatry school, not above address. Renewable for up to 3 years. Deadline: June 1.

1228. (SS)
Gamma Iota Sigma Scholarships
Griffith Foundation for Insurance Education
2586 Oakstone Drive
Columbus, OH 43231
(614) 891–4242
http://www.gammaiotasigma.org

Scholarships from $500 to $6,000 for graduate students or upper-level undergraduate students. May be majoring in insurance/risk management or actuarial science. Support is provided at schools with Gamma Iota Sigma Fraternity Chapters. Renewable. Deadline: none.

(SS)
Gamma Theta Upsilon—International Geographic Honor Society
Towson State University
Dept. of Geography
Towson, MD 21204
(301) 321–2973
http://www.gtuhonors.org

1229. (SS)
Buzzard Undergraduate & Graduate Scholarships

2 scholarships of $500 to graduate students or undergraduate seniors enrolled in, or accepted to, an accredited graduate program in geography. Selection based on academic achievement, must have at least 3.0 GPA. Must be a member of Gamma Theta Upsilon. Obtain application from GTU. Deadline: March 1.

1230. (SS)
Rechardson Scholarship

Varying numbers of scholarships of $500 to graduate students and undergraduate seniors enrolled in, or accepted to, an accredited graduate program in geography. Selection based on academic achievement; must have at least 3.0 GPA. Must be a member of Gamma Theta Upsilon. Obtain application from GTU. Deadline: March 1.

(A, S)
Garden Club of America
GCA Scholarship Committee
14 East 60th Street
New York, NY 10022–1002
(212) 753–8287
http://www.gcamerica.org

1231. (S)
Awards for Summer Environmental Studies

Scholarship awards of $1,500 to graduate or undergraduate students majoring in ecology or related fields. The award is meant for use to cover a summer course in environmental studies. Preference given to undergraduates. Send a self-addressed, stamped envelope to M. Freeman at above address for an application. Deadline: February 15.

1232. (A, S)

GCA Internship in Garden History and Design

Internships providing a weekly stipend of $360 and $420 to graduate and undergraduate students in horticulture, ornamental horticulture, landscape design, and related fields. Internships last from 10 to 16 weeks. Deadline: December 31.

(A, H, S, SS)

Gates Cambridge Trust

P.O. Box 252
Cambridge CB2 ITZ
England
http://www.gates.scholarships.cam.ac.uk/index.html

1233. (A, H, S, SS)

Continuing One-Year Postgraduate Fellowships

Scholarships covering university and college fees, a maintenance allowance, a discretionary allowance, and 1 return economy airfare to graduate students already in residence at the University of Cambridge. Must be intending to undertake a course of research leading to a doctoral degree. Open to all areas of study. Must still independently apply and be accepted to the University of Cambridge. Deadline: varies.

1234. (A, H, S, SS)

New One-Year Postgraduate Fellowships

Scholarships covering university and college fees, a maintenance allowance, a discretionary allowance, and 1 return economy airfare to graduate and undergraduate seniors who will be attending graduate school. Open to all areas of study. Deadline: varies.

1235. (H, SS)

Gay & Lesbian Alliance Against Defamation

GLAAD Dissertation Fellowship Program
248 West 35th Street, 8th Floor
New York, NY 10001
(212) 629-3322
http://www.glaad.org/org/projects/center
fellowship@glaad.org

2 awards of $5,000 to graduate students to conduct original dissertation research on the cultural, economic, and political dimensions of gay, lesbian, bisexual, and transgender representation in the media. Open to the fields of humanities, social sciences, public health, public policy, and education. Must have completed all predissertation requirements at the time of application. Deadline: late June.

(H, S, SS)

Genentech

Genentech Foundation for Biomedical Sciences
Summer Internship Program
1 DNA Way, MS#16 A
South San Francisco, CA 94080–4990
(650) 225–1000
http://www.gene.com

1236. (S)

Genentech Foundation for Biomedical Sciences

Fellowships of varying amounts for postdoctoral students in biotechnology area. Interested students should visit school's career center for details and eligibility criteria.

1237. (H, S, SS)

Internships

85 10- to 12-week summer internships providing $475 per week to graduate students and $400 per week to undergraduate sophomores, juniors, and seniors. Internships are available in business, corporate communications, manufacturing, marketing, medical affairs, quality control, and research. Applicants for biotechnology research must have a science background (biology, chemistry, chemical engineering, etc.). Finalists are interviewed in person or by telephone. Deadline: January 4 (for M.B.A. students) and February 15 (all others).

1238. (A, SS)

Gensler and Associates/Architects

Intern Coordinator
2 Harrison Street
San Francisco, CA 94105
(415) 433–3700
http://www.gensler.com

12 or more internships lasting from 2 months to a year, providing a salary of $9 per hour and possible scholarship, open to graduate students and undergraduate sophomores, juniors, and seniors. Students work in New York, Washington, DC, San Francisco, Los Angeles, Denver, or Houston. Most positions are in architecture,

though a few are available in support departments, such as marketing or the library. Interns are assigned to an architect or a team of architects and are exposed to a variety of educational and cultural programs. Most interns have taken at least 1 or 2 architectural courses, but there are no academic prerequisites. Deadline: February 1 (summer) and rolling (fall and spring).

(S)
Geological Society of America
3300 Penrose Place
P.O. Box 9140
Boulder, CO 80301–9140
(303) 357–1037
http://www.geosociety.org

1239. (S)
Alexander and Geraldine Wanek Fund

Awarded to graduate students to support research projects dealing with coal and petroleum resources, mapping, engineering geology, marine resources, petroleum, economics, appraisal, and evaluation, and the geology of phosphate resources. Must be a student member of GSA. Deadline: February 1.

1240. (S)
Alexander Sisson Award

Award supports research for graduate students pursuing studies in Alaska and the Caribbean. Must be a student member of GSA. Visit web site for more information. Deadline: February 1.

1241. (S)
Allan V. Cox. Award

1 award of varying amount to a graduate student for outstanding student research. Awarded by the Geophysics, Hydrology, Sedimentary Geology, and Structural Geology, and Tectonics Divisions. Must be a student member of GSA. Visit web site for more information and deadline. Deadline: none specified.

1242. (S)
Archeological Geology Division
Claude C. Albritton Jr. Scholarships

Scholarships for graduate students in the earth sciences and archeology. Must be a student member of GSA. Visit web site for more information. Deadline: March 1.

1243. (S)
Bruce L. "Biff" Reed Award

Awarded to promote and support graduate research pursuing studies in the tectonic and magmatic evolution of Alaska, and it also can fund other geologic research. Must be a student member of GSA. Visit web site for more information. Deadline: March 1.

1244. (S)
Charles A. and June R. P. Ross Research Fund

Awarded to support research projects for graduate students, postgraduate students, and postdoctoral researchers in the fields of biostratigraphy (including, but not limited to, fossil age dating and the study of evolutionary faunal successions), stratigraphy and stratigraphic correlation, paleogeography and paleobiography, and interpreting past environments of deposition and their biological significance and the integration of these research areas into better global understanding of (1) past plate motions (plate tectonics and sea-floor spreading), (2) past sea-level events, including their identification and ages, and/or (3) climate changes and effects of those climate changes on the earth's inhabitants through geologic time. Must be a student member of GSA. Visit web site for more information. Deadline: February 1.

1245. (S)
Coal Geology Division
A. L. Medlin Scholarship Award

2 scholarships of $1,000 and 2 scholarships of $500 to full-time graduate students involved in research in coal geology (origin, occurrence, geologic characteristics, or economic implications of coal and associated rocks). Can be used for field or laboratory expenses, sample analysis, instrumentation, supplies, and other expenses essential to successful completion of research project. Must be a student member of GSA. Visit web site for more information. Deadline: February 15.

1246. (S)
Coal Geology Division
Field Research Award

1 award of $1,500 to a graduate student for field study and eligibility for up to $1,000 in travel funds to present results at Annual Meeting. This award is not always offered. Must be a student member of

GSA. Visit web site for more information. Deadline: February 15.

1247. (S)
Engineering Geology Division
Roy J. Shlemon Scholastic Awards

2 scholarships of $1,000 (1 to a master's student and 1 to a doctoral student) with the best research proposals within the broad field of engineering geology. Must be a student member of GSA. Visit web site for more information. Deadline: March 1.

1248. (S)
Graduate Student Research Grants

224 research grants ranging from $200 to $1,600 to graduate, professional, advanced professional, and postdoctoral applicants. Must be proposing investigations that will contribute to the promotion of the science of geology. Provides partial support for master's and doctoral thesis research in geological sciences. Must be citizens of the U.S., Canada, Mexico, or Central America and GSA members. Must be a student member of GSA. Visit web site for more information. Deadline: February 1.

1249. (S)
Gretchen L. Bechschmidt Award

1 award of varying amount to a doctoral student in geological sciences who is pursuing a career in fields of biostratigraphy and/or paleoceanography, and has an interest in sequence stratigraphy analysis, particularly in conjunction with research in deep-sea sedimentology. Must be a student member of GSA. Visit web site for more information. Deadline: February 1.

1250. (S)
Harold T. Stearns Fellowship Award

Awarded annually in support of research on one or more aspects of the geology of Pacific islands and of the circum-Pacific region. Must be a student member of GSA. Visit web site for more information. Deadline: February 1.

1251. (S)
John Montagne Fund

Awarded annually in support of research in the field of quarternary/geomorphology. Must be a student member of GSA. Visit web site for more information. Deadline: February 1.

1252. (S)
John T. Dillon Alaska Award

Award of varying amount to graduate students to support research that addresses earth science problems particular to Alaska, especially field-based studies dealing with structural and tectonic development and those that include some aspect of geochronology (either paleontologic or radiometric) to provide new age control for significant rock units in Alaska. Must be a student member of GSA. Visit web site for more information. Deadline: February 1.

1253. (S)
Lipman Research Award

1 award to a graduate student to conduct research in volcanology and petrology. Must be a student member of GSA. Visit web site for more information. Deadline: February 1.

1254. (S)
North-Central Region
Outstanding Poster and Paper Awards

Awards of varying amounts to graduate and undergraduate students for posters and papers presented at the combined Southeast/North-Central Sections Meeting. Must be student member or student associate. Visit web site for more information and deadline.

1255. (S)
North-Central Region
Section Meeting Student Travel Awards

Travel awards of up to $200, exclusive of field trip fees, to graduate students to attend the North-Central Section Meeting. Priority given to students presenting oral or poster papers, if funds are limited. Students must be currently enrolled in an academic department and certify their student membership. The Section may reduce the amount awarded to provide support to as many eligible students as possible. Must be a student member of GSA. Visit web site for more information. Deadline: February 3.

1256. (S)
North-Central Section
Annual Meeting Student Travel Grants

Travel awards of up to $200 to graduate students to attend the Annual Meeting of the Society. Priority given to students presenting oral or poster papers, if funds are limited. Students must be currently enrolled in an academic department and certify their student membership. The Section may reduce the amount awarded to provide support to as many eligible students as possible. Any Student Member or Student Associate of GSA currently enrolled as a student in an academic department in the North-Central Section is eligible to apply. Deadline: late September.

1257. (S)
Planetary Geology Division
S. E. Dvonic Student Paper Awards

2 awards of varying amounts to graduate students in the field of planetary geology. Must be a student member of GSA. Visit web site for more information and deadline. Deadline: none specified.

1258. (S)
Quarternary Geology & Geomorphology Division
Arthur D. Howard Research Grants

Grants of varying amounts to graduate student research on quarternary geology or geomorphology. Must be a student member of GSA. Visit web site for more information and deadline. Deadline: none specified.

1259. (S)
Quarternary Geology & Geomorphology Division
J. Hoover Mackin Award

Grants of varying amounts to graduate student research on quarternary geology or geomorphology. Must be a student member of GSA. Visit web site for more information and deadline. Deadline: none specified.

1260. (S)
Robert K. Fahnestock Memorial Award

1 award of varying amount made to the applicant with the best application in the field of sediment transport or related aspects of fluvial geomorphology. Must be a student member of GSA. Visit web site for more information. Deadline: February 1.

1261. (S)
Southeastern Section
Research Grants

Grants ranging from $100 to $150 to graduate and undergraduate students in some field of geology. Must be student members or associates of GSA and be enrolled in an accredited institution within the geographical boundaries of the section. Must personally present a paper or poster at either the Section Meeting or Annual Meeting. Must be a student member of GSA. Visit web site for more information. Deadline: February 1 (Section) and October 2 (Annual).

1262. (SS)
George and Carol Olmsted Foundation
Scholarships
103 West Broad Street, Suite 330
Falls Church, VA 22046
(703) 536–3500
http://www.olmstedfoundation.org/public/origin.html

Varying numbers of scholarships of $5,500 to career officers in one of the U.S. Armed Forces who will attend graduate school for study in international relations or political science. Must have attended one of the 3 service academies. Selection based on academic achievement, literary and linguistic ability, success in outdoor sports, and leadership qualities. Interested individuals must apply through military service. Must be nominated by the Department of Defense. Do not contact the Foundation. Deadline: none specified.

1263. (S)
George F. Walker Scholarship Fund
P.O. Box 58143
Seattle, WA 98138–1143
http://www.gfwscholarship.org

1 scholarship of at least $1,500 to a full-time graduate or undergraduate student pursuing a career in surveying and mapping sciences. Must be a resident of Washington State and attending an accredited college or

university. Selection is based on academic achievement, extracurricular activities, references, and career goals. Visit web site for more information and application. Deadline: January 30.

1264. (SS)
Georgia Library Association
Hubbard Scholarship Fund
P.O. Box 793
Rex, GA 30273–0793
written inquiries only
http://www.library.gsu.edu/gla/committees/
scholarship/index.htm

Scholarships of $3,000 to graduate students and undergraduate seniors who have been accepted into an ALA-accredited degree program in library science. Must complete degree requirements within 2 years. Recipient must agree to work in a library or library-related capacity in Georgia or pay back a prorated amount of the award with interest within 2 years. Deadline: May 1.

1265. (SS)
Georgia Police Corps
Scholarships
1000 Indian Springs Drive
Forsythe, GA 31029
(877) 267–4360
http://www.gapolicecorps.org

Scholarships of up to $3,000 to graduate or undergraduate students in any area of study. When accepting the award, student must agree to work for a Georgia state or local law enforcement agency for at least 4 years. If student is a dependent child of an officer killed in the line of duty, there is no repayment or service obligation. Must possess the necessary mental and physical capabilities and moral character to be an effective officer. Deadline: none specified.

1266. (S)
Georgia State Medical Education Board
"Country Doctor" Scholarship Program
State Medical Education Board
Two Northside 75, N.W.
Suite 220
Atlanta, GA 30318–7701
(404) 352–6476
http://www.mcg.edu/students/finaid/smcb.pdf

30 to 35 scholarships of $10,000 per year for 4 years to students accepted to allopathic or osteopathic medical schools. Must be legal residents of Georgia and planning to attend an accredited medical school in the U.S. Must be willing to practice in a rural community with a population of less than 15,000 in Georgia, Those students within the primary care fields who wish to work in severely underserved rural Georgia towns of 15,000 or less are eligible for up to $25,000 per year for up to 4 years for the repayment of medical education debt. Priority is given to students interested in obstetrics or family practice with obstetrics. Must be Georgia residents. Must have financial need. Renewable for up to 4 years. Send a self-addressed, stamped envelope for an application. Deadline: May 15.

1267. (A, H, S, SS)
Georgia Student Finance Commission
Georgia State Regents Scholarship Program
2082 East Exchange Place, Suite 200
Tucker, GA 30084
(770) 414–3200
(800) 776–6878 (In-state)
http://www.gsfc.org

Scholarships of $1,000 for graduate students. Awards are repaid by working in the state of Georgia for 1 year for each $1,000 received or in cash with 3% interest. Must be Georgia resident and a full-time student in a university system of Georgia institution. Based on academic achievement and financial need. Deadline: May 1.

1268. (SS)
Geoscience Information Society
Fellowship for Geoscience Librarians
http://www.geoinfo.org

4-week fellowship providing travel to and from the United States, registration fees, housing, and a small per diem to a geoscience librarian from a developing country. Must be a full-time employee in an academic or governmental geoscience library in a developing country and continue working for at least 1 year past the fellowship. Visit web site for contact information.

(A, H, SS)
German Academic Exchange Service (DAAD)
ATTN: Deutscher Akademischer Austauschdienst
871 United Nations Plaza

New York, NY 10017
(212) 758–3223
http://www.daad.org/

1269. (A, H, SS)
German Chancellor Scholarship Program

Up to 10 scholarships of varying amounts to graduate students or individuals who have completed a bachelor's degree in the arts and humanities, social and political studies, law, business, architecture, journalism, or economics. Program provides for 1 year in Germany for professional development, study, or research. Must be U.S. citizens and under the age of 34 at the time they enter the program. Applicants may come from prospective leaders in professions spanning all sectors of American society—public, private, not-for-profit, cultural, and academic and exhibit outstanding potential for future leadership. Visit web site for more information and contact information. Deadline: October 31.

1270. (SS)
German Studies Research Grants

Awards of varying amounts (see web site for current amounts) to graduate and upper-level undergraduate students to conduct short-term research in either North America or Germany. Awarded to encourage research and promote the study of cultural, political, historical, economic, and social aspects of modern and contemporary German affairs from an inter- and multidisciplinary perspective. Visit web site for more detailed information. Deadline: November 15.

1271. (H, SS)
Goethe Institutes—Inter Nations Summer Language Grants

Grants of varying amounts to full-time graduate or professional school students in any field of study except for those in the areas of English, German, or any other modern language or literature. Must be U.S. or Canadian citizens enrolled in an accredited U.S. or Canadian institution. Must have completed 3 semesters of college German or the equivalent. Selection based on academic achievement, potential, and demonstrated need for acquiring a better proficiency in the German language for their future studies or research. Visit web site for more information. Deadline: January 31.

1272. (H, SS)
Graduate Scholarship for Study/Research in Germany

Scholarships of varying amounts to graduate and doctoral students and postdoctoral candidates for study and/or research at universities or institutes in Germany. Award is for stays ranging from 1 to 10 months in length. For a full degree course in Germany, the study scholarship can be extended up to 24 months. Must be U.S. or Canadian citizens in an accredited U.S. or Canadian university. Visit web site for more information and deadline.

1273. (SS)
"Hochschulsommerhurse" at German Universities Scholarships

Varying number of grants of varying amounts to graduate students and upper-level undergraduates to take a broad range of 3- to 4-week summer language courses with an integrated thematic focus on literary, cultural, political, and economic aspects of modern and contemporary Germany. Must be U.S. or Canadian citizens or permanent residents attending an accredited U.S. or Canadian institution. No restrictions as to field. Must be under age 32, and have at least 2 years of college-level German with adequate reading and speaking knowledge. Deadline: January 31.

1274. (SS)
Language Study Grants at Goethe Institutes for Faculty and Ph.D. Candidates

Varying number of grants providing course fees, room, and partial board to doctoral candidates and faculty members to participate in either 4- or 8-week intensive German language courses at the Goethe Institutes in Germany. Award must be used April through December. Selection based on academic achievement. Must have a basic knowledge of German, with 3 semesters of college-level German preferred, be affiliated with an accredited U.S. institution, and be U.S. citizens. Individuals who have previous study experience in Germany, are previous language scholarship recipients, or are doctoral candidates in modern language and literature are ineligible. Write for more details. Deadline: January 31.

1275. (SS)
Munich University Summer Training (MUST) in German and European Law

Scholarships of varying amounts to law students to participate in a summer program at the Munich University Law School. Must have completed at least 1 year of law school. Must be a U.S. or Canadian citizen or permanent resident enrolled in an accredited U.S. or Canadian law school. Visit web site for more information. Deadline: March 15.

1276. (SS)
Program for International Lawyers

Fellowships of varying amounts to lawyers who have, or will have, passed the bar examination by the beginning of the scholarship period. The importance of gaining a knowledge of German law should be evident from the applicant's stated professional or research goals. Must have a strong command of German, to enable them to actively participate in all lectures and discussions. Must be younger than 30 years of age. Visit web site for more information. Deadline: March 1.

1277. (SS)
Special "DAAD-Leibniz-Scholarships" Program for Doctoral Candidates and Postdocs

Scholarships of varying amounts to doctoral candidates and postdoctoral fellows to complete research with the aim of gaining a doctorate, continuing education, and training programs for postdoctoral fellows. Support can be provided for a period between 1 and 3 years. Support for doctoral programs is limited to 36 months. Visit web site for more information and deadline.

1278. (SS)
German Marshal Fund of the United States Postdoctoral Fellowship Program
11 Dupont Circle, N.W.
Washington, DC 20036
(202) 745–3950
http://www.gmfus.org

11 fellowships providing a $30,000 stipend and a $2,000 travel allowance to postdoctoral fellowships to outstanding scientists to conduct research on U.S.-European issues. Must be U.S. citizen or legal resident. Deadline: November 15.

(A, H, SS)
Getty Center for the History of Art and the Humanities
401 Wilshire Boulevard, Suite 700
Santa Monica, CA 90401–1455
(310) 458–9811
http://www.getty.edu

1279. (A, H)
Postdoctoral Fellowships

Fellowships of $22,000 for a 9-month period, plus funds for some additional expenses such as travel. Funding up to $4,000 is provided for relocation and housing to postdoctoral students in the humanities or social sciences. Must have received doctorate and be rewriting dissertation for publication. Research must relate to the subject or nature of collecting. Residency at the Getty Center is required during the award year. Open to the humanities and social sciences (especially anthropology; cultural, intellectual, and social history; the history of art, architecture, and music; literary criticism and theory; and philosophy). Areas of study include the fine arts, journalism, film, and urban studies in relationship to ecology and historical conditions. Write to above address. Deadline: December 1.

1280. (A. H, SS)
Predoctoral Fellowships

Fellowships of $18,000 for a 9-month period, and up to $4,000 for relocation costs if necessary, plus funds for some additional expenses such as travel. Open to candidates for a doctorate in the humanities or social sciences who expect to complete their dissertations during the fellowship year and whose research relates to the subject of the nature and idea of collecting. Residency at the Getty Center is required during the award year. Humanities and social sciences fields include anthropology; cultural, intellectual, and social history; the history of art, architecture, and music; film and literary criticism and theory; and philosophy. Areas of study include the fine arts, journalism, film, and urban studies in relationship to ecology and historical conditions. Write to above address. Deadline: December 1.

1281. (A)
Gina Bachauer International Piano Competition Award
Bachauer International Piano Foundation
P.O. Box 11664
Salt Lake City, UT 84147
(801) 521–9200
http://www.bachauer.com

Award of up to $5,000 for graduate or undergraduate students or young professionals. Must be between 19 and 33 years old. May be of any nationality. Must submit an audition tape. Send a self-addressed, stamped envelope for information. Deadline: March 1.

1282. (A)
Glimmer Train Press
Northwest Short Story Award for New Writers
710 Southwest Madison Street, Suite 504
Portland, OR 97205
(503) 221–0836
http://www.glimmertrain.com

1 first prize of $1,200 and publication to first-place winner, and an award of $500 to the first runner-up, for a short story written by a writer whose fiction hasn't been published in a nationally distributed publication. May enter up to 2 short stories between 1,200 and 6,000 words. Charges a $10 reading fee per entry. Submit manuscripts between February 1 and March 31. Send a Self-addressed, stamped envelope for guidelines. Deadline: March 31.

1283. (SS)
Golden State Minority Foundation
Minority Foundation Scholarship
1055 Wilshire B1, Suite 1115
Los Angeles, CA 90017
(213) 482–6300
http://www.gsmf.org

75 scholarships of up to $2,000 for minority graduate students and upper-level undergraduate students majoring in business administration. Must be California residents who attend California colleges and universities. Must maintain a 3.0 GPA or better. May not work for more than 25 hours a week. Income must be insufficient to cover expenses. Include a self-addressed, stamped envelope with request for information. Dead-line: August 1 (for Northern California) and February 1 (Southern California).

(A, S, SS)
Golf Course Superintendents Association of America
1421 Research Park Drive
Lawrence, KS 66049–3859
(800) 472–7878
(913) 841–2240
http://www.gcsaa.org

1284. (A)
General Scholarships

5 to 10 scholarships from $1,000 to $5,000 for graduate students and researchers in the U.S. and Canada interested in golf course turf. Must be enrolled in a graduate program or have completed the first year of a 2-year undergraduate program or the second year of a 4-year undergraduate program. Based on career goals, academic record, character, and financial need. Deadline: October 1.

1285. (A, S, SS)
O.M. Scott Scholarship/Internship Program

A scholarship/internship program offers work experience and an opportunity to compete for financial aid awards to graduate and undergraduate students. Students are paid from $1,000 to $5,000 for summer internships. Selection is based on academic achievement and interest in being golf course superintendents and a "green industry" career. Deadline: March 15.

1286. (S)
Student Essay Contest

Awards of varying amounts to graduate and undergraduate students in an essay writing competition. Selection is based on an essay ranging from 7 to 12 pages on assigned topic. Deadline: mid- to late March.

1287. (A, SS)
Gould Farm
Internship Coordinator
Box 157
Monterey, MA 01245–0157
(413) 528–1084
http://www.gouldfarm.org

10 to 12 internships lasting from 6 months to a year on an ongoing basis. Provides a weekly salary, free room and board, and medical benefits to graduate students, recent college graduates of any age, and undergraduates. International applicants are eligible. Interns work in the kitchen, recreation, gardens/grounds, clinical, farm (dairy and other livestock care), and business office. Interns are able to participate in extensive recreational opportunities (maple syrup production, woodcutting, pottery, weaving, furniture making), use of art room and weaving studio. Farm is close to skiing and Tanglewood and other music festivals. The farm owns and operates The Roadside Store & Café, featuring vegetables, bread, and dairy products produced on the farm. Interns must submit a résumé, cover letter, and 3 references. Deadline: rolling.

(SS)
Government Finance Officers Association
203 N. LaSalle Street, Suite 2700
Chicago, IL 60601–1210
(312) 977–9700
http://www.gfoa.org

1288. (SS)
Daniel B. Goldberg Scholarship

1 scholarship of $5,000 to a graduate student in a full-time master's study preparing for a career in state and local finance. Recipient attends an all-expense-paid trip to attend the GFOA Annual Conference. Must be enrolled in the spring semester during the scholarship year, be a U.S. or Canadian citizen or permanent resident, and have a recommendation from academic advisor or dean of the graduate program. Visit web site for more information and deadline.

1289. (SS)
George A. Nielsen Public Investor Scholarship

1 award of $5,000 or 2 awards of $2,500 to graduate or undergraduate students in public administration, finance, business administration, or a related field. Award supports full- or part-time students with career interests in the efficient and productive investment of public funds. Must be employed at least 1 year by a state or local government, or other public entity, be a U.S. or Canadian citizen or permanent resident, and be recommended by employer. Visit web site for more information and deadline.

1290. (SS)
Minorities in Government Finance Scholarship

1 scholarship of $5,000 to a minority graduate student in public administration, governmental accounting, finance, political science, economics, or business administration (with a specific focus on government or nonprofit management). Awarded to recognize outstanding performance by minority students preparing for careers in state and local government finance. Open to full- or part-time students. Must be a U.S. or Canadian citizen or permanent resident and obtain a recommendation from the student's academic advisor or dean of the graduate program (graduate students) or department chair (undergraduate students). Visit web site for more information and deadline.

1291. (SS)
Public Employee Retirement Research and Administration Scholarship

1 scholarship of $4,000 to a graduate student in public administration, finance, business administration, or social sciences. Awarded to support full- or part-time students preparing for a career in the field of public-sector retirement benefits. Must be pursuing a career in state or local government with a focus on public-sector retirement benefits. Must be a U.S. or Canadian citizen or permanent resident and obtain a recommendation from the student's academic advisor or dean of the graduate program (graduate students). Visit web site for more information and deadline.

1292. (A)
Graham Foundation for Advanced Studies in the Fine Arts
Carter Manny Award
4 West Burton Place
Chicago, IL 60610–1416
(312) 787–4071
http://www.grahamfoundation.org
info@grahamfoundation.org

Grants of up to $15,000 to doctoral candidates whose dissertations focus on architecture, landscape architecture, interior design, architectural technologies, architectural research, architectural history and theory, urban design and planning, and in some circumstances, the fine arts in relation to architectural topics. Must have completed their course work, have been advanced to candidacy, and had their dissertation proposals approved. Must be enrolled in accredited institutions in the U.S. or Canada. Deadline: March 15.

(S)
Grass Foundation
400 Franklin Street, Suite 302
Braintree, MA 02184
(781) 843–0219
http://www.grassfoundation.org
grassfdn@aol.com

1293. (S)
Grass Fellowships in Neurophysiology

10 to 12 fellowships providing travel, research, and living expenses to predoctoral (M.D. and Ph.D.) and early postdoctoral (usually no more than 3 years) researchers. Fellowships support neurophysiological research during the summer (10 to 14 weeks) at the Marine Biological Laboratory in Woods Hole, MA. Request Bulletin FA-296, which contains an application and appropriate forms. Deadline: December 1.

1294. (S)
Robert S. Morison Fellowship

Awards providing a stipend of $30,000 per year, plus $700 per dependent, and $3,000 for research expenses to physicians who have been accepted into, or just completed, residencies in neurology, neurosurgery, or neuroscience. Must wish to begin a 2-year program of basic research training at an accredited institution in North America. The 2-year program begins in July of odd-numbered years. Send a self-addressed, stamped envelope for information. Deadline: November 1 of even-numbered years.

1295. (S, SS)
**Greater Kanawha Valley Foundation
Scholarship Program**
Executive Director
P.O. Box 3041
Charleston, WV 25301
(800) 467–5909
http://www.tgkvf.org

506 scholarships of varying amounts totaling over $772,875 for graduate students in science, medical students, and first-year law students. Must be West Virginia residents. Preference given to Jackson County residents. May apply for only 1 award from the Foundation. Based on academic achievement, test scores, financial need, essay, and recommendation letters. Deadline: March 1, may vary.

1296. (A, SS)
**Great Projects Film Company
Internship Program**
594 Ninth Avenue
New York, NY 10036
(212) 581–1700
http://www.greatprojects.com
internship@greatprojects.com

2 to 4 internships running from 10 to 20 weeks providing a salary ranging from $50 to $200 per week to graduate students, college graduates, and undergraduate students. International students may apply. Interns work in New York, NY, in all aspects of the company, including answering phones, typing, logging tapes, writing proposals, editing films, and bookkeeping. Interns are able to see how documentaries are produced, from research and fundraising to production and promotion. Internships are conducted throughout the year. Deadline: rolling.

1297. (A, H, S, SS)
Grey Forest Utilities
P. O. Box 258
Helotes, TX 78023
(210) 695–8781

3 scholarships of $1,000 to Grey Forest Utilities customers and their dependents, 1 scholarship of $1,000 to a Grey Forest community resident or dependent, and scholarship of $1,000 to a Grey Forest Utilities employees or employee dependents. Students may be graduate or professional school students, undergraduate or nontraditional students, or graduating high school seniors. Open to all majors. Based on academic achievement, potential, extracurricular activities, essay, and financial need. Deadline: varies.

1298. (A)
Guggenheim Museum
Internship Program
1071 Fifth Avenue
New York, NY 10128
(212) 423–3500
http://www.guggenheim.org

Museum stipend of varying amounts to graduate students enrolled in graduate programs in art history. Knowledge of a foreign language is required. Award is given to graduate students to supplement their course work with practical museum training in the areas of art history an opportunity to work at Guggenheim Museum on specific projects relating to field of interest. Deadline: August 15.

1299. (A)
Hackney Literary Awards
Birmingham-Southern College
Box A-3
Birmingham, AL 35254
(205) 226–4921
http://www.bsc.edu/events/specialevents/
hackneyguidelines.htm

1 award of $5,000 for an original, unpublished novel and awards of $250, $400, $600, and $2,500 for poetry and short fiction. Visit web site for more information. Charges an entry fee. Deadline: September 30 (novel) and December 31 (poetry and short story).

(SS)
Hagley Museum and Library
Center for the History of Business, Technology, and Society
P.O. Box 3630
Wilmington, DE 19807
(302) 658–2400, ext. 244
http://www.hagley.lib.de.us/center.html

1300. (SS)
Grants-in-Aid

Varying numbers of grants of up to $1,000 per month to doctoral candidates, advanced scholars, independent scholars, and professionals in the areas of business and economic/technological/social history, especially of the Mid-Atlantic region, to conduct re-

search at the Hagley Museum and Library. Research study periods range from 2 to 8 weeks, and individuals are able to use the imprint, manuscript, pictorial, and artifact collections. Selection based on proposed research. Deadline: rolling.

1301. (SS)
Hagley-Winterthur Research Fellowships in Arts and Industries

Varying numbers of 1- to 3-month short-term research fellowships providing $1,000 monthly stipend, plus seminar participation, and use of both research collections. Open to master's and doctoral candidates studying the historical and cultural relationships of economic life and the arts, including design, architecture, crafts, and the fine arts. Recipients selected based on research abilities and relevance to both libraries' holdings. Deadline: December 1.

1302. (SS)
Residential Dissertation Fellowship

1 fellowship of $13,500 to doctoral candidates to conduct research using the Hagley collections in the areas of business, economic, and technological history in social contexts. Applicants must have completed all course work, be conducting dissertation research, and prove the relevance of the Hagley materials to their dissertation topics. Deadline: November 15.

1303. (A, H, S, SS)
Hai Guin Scholarship Association
Scholarship Chairman
P.O. Box 509
Belmon, MA 02178

Scholarships of $1,000 to graduate and undergraduate students (must have completed first semester of freshman year) in any area of study. Must be of Armenian descent and residing and attending an accredited institution in Massachusetts. Selection based on academic achievement and financial need. Deadline: October 25.

1304. (S, SS)
Hallmark Cards
College Relations/Internship Program
Mail Drop #112
P.O. Box 41980
Kansas City, MO 64141–6580

(800) HALLMARK

http://www.hallmark.com

30 to 35 summer internships providing a salary ranging from $1,300 to $2,300 for undergraduate seniors and from $2,400 to $3,400 for graduate students. Interns may choose from a variety of positions in engineering and business-related areas. Applicants must demonstrate academic achievement, leadership abilities, excellent communication skills, and the ability to relate to a wide variety of people and disciplines. Deadline: February 1.

1305. (A, H, S, SS)

Harriet A. Shaw Fellowship

c/o Wellesley College

Box GR

Secretary Graduate Fellowships

Wellesley, MA 02181

(617) 235–0320

http://www.wellesley.edu/CWS/alumnae/wellfs.html

Fellowships of up to $11,000 to female graduate students for any area of study or research. Must have received a bachelor's degree from an accredited U.S. institution and be planning to study or conduct research at any accredited institution in the U.S. or abroad. Applications available up to November 20. Deadline: December 1.

1306. (S, SS)

Harry Frank Guggenheim Foundation Dissertation Fellowships

ATTN: Program Officer

527 Madison Avenue

New York, NY 10022–5304

(212) 644–4907

http://www.hfg.org

Varying numbers of grants of $10,000 to doctoral candidates to conduct research on human dominance, violence, and aggression. Applicants must have completed their course work and be conducting research on their dissertations and may be studying in areas of anthropology, biology, history, political science, psychology, and sociology. Selection based on academic achievement and proposed research. Open to all nationalities. Deadline: February 1.

(H)

Harry S Truman Library Institute

ATTN: Secretary

500 W US Hwy 24

Independence, MO 64050

(816) 833–1400

(800) 833–1225

http://www.trumanlibrary.org

1307. (H)

Dissertation Year Fellowships

1 or 2 grants of $16,000 to graduate students working on some aspect of the life and career of Harry S Truman or the public and foreign policy issues prominent during the Truman years. Students should have substantially completed their research and be prepared to devote full time to writing dissertation. Preference given to projects based on extensive research. Deadline: February 1.

1308. (H)

Research Grants

Grants of up to $2,500 to graduate students, post-doctoral scholars, and other researchers to spend from 1 to 3 weeks to use its collections. Recipients must submit a copy of any thesis, dissertation, and/or published work based in part on grant-funded research and a statement of approximately 750 words that describes the project and contribution toward its development made by research conducted at the library. Research should be on some aspect of the political, economic, and social development of the U.S. between April 26, 1945, and January 20, 1953, or the public career of President Harry S Truman. Deadline: April 1 and October 1.

1309. (S, SS)

Harry S Truman Scholarship Program

712 Jackson Place, N.W.

Washington, DC 20006

(202) 395–4831

http://www.truman.gov

75 to 80 scholarships of $30,000 ($27,000 for graduate school and $3,000 for undergraduate senior year) to rising undergraduate seniors to attend graduate or professional schools to prepare for a career in government. A merit-based award to U.S. citizens, and U.S. nationals

from Pacific islands. Award recognizes outstanding potential as a leader in public service. Award may be used in the U.S. or abroad in a wide variety of fields. Must be in the upper quarter of their junior class, complete an application, and write a policy recommendation. Deadline: late January.

(S, SS)
Hastings Center
21 Malcolm Gordon Road
Garrison, NY 10524–5558
(845) 424–4040
http://www.thehastingscenter.org

1310. (S, SS)
International Fellowship Program

Fellowship stipends ranging from $500 to $1,000 to advanced scholars from foreign countries who have made significant contributions to bioethics in their own countries. Fellowships are for 2- to 6-week stay at the Center. Stipends are limited to those with financial need. Deadline: none specified.

1311. (S, SS)
Internship Program

4 full-time, 4-week internships open to graduate and professional school students, undergraduate students, and college graduates. Must be majoring in, or have majored in, philosophy, theology, law, or medicine. Must be able to work independently. Interns conduct a self-designed research project that examines ethical issues in medicine, the life sciences, or the environment. Submit an application form, resume, letters of recommendation, transcript, writing sample, and a 3- to 5-page project proposal. Deadline: open.

1312. (H)
Hearst Newspapers
Journalism Fellowship Program
801 Texas Avenue
Houston, TX 77002
(713) 665–4230
http://www.chron.com

4 fellowships of varying amounts to graduate or undergraduate students or professionals who are aspiring and talented writers, reporters, editors, photographers, designers, and graphic artists. Each fellowship is 2 years in length. Recipients will receive pay and benefits and experience 3 8-month job rotations, 1 each in a small, medium, and large market. Selection based on brief biography, goals essay, academic achievement, work samples, recommendations, and résumé. Program begins with a 2-week orientation in late August, with the first rotation starting on September 1. Deadline: none specified.

1313. (S)
Heart and Stroke Foundation of Canada
Research Fellowship
Suite 200
160 George Street
Ottawa, Ontario
K1N 9M2
(613) 241–4361
http://www.hsfpe.org

Limited number of fellowships of varying amounts to postgraduate students undertaking full-time training research in cardiovascular or cerebrovascular fields. Awards must be used at Canadian universities. Deadline: November 15.

1314. (A, H, S, SS)
H. E. Butt Foundation
P.O. Box 670
Kerrville, TX 78029
(210) 896–2505
http://www.heb.com

Numerous scholarships of varying amounts for graduate or undergraduate students, and for graduating high school seniors who work for the H.E.B. grocery store chain throughout south Texas. May be used for any field of study. Must meet certain criteria and work at least 300 hours per year for the company. Contact store manager or the company's main headquarters in San Antonio. Deadline: varies.

1315. (A)
Helicon Nine Editions
Literary Prizes
P.O. Box 22412
Kansas City, MO 64113
(816) 753–1095
http://www.heliconnine.com/index.html

1 prize of $1,000 in the Marianne Moore Poetry Competition and publication for a book of unpublished poetry. 1 prize of $1,000 in the Willa Cather Fiction Competition to writers of fiction who live in the U.S. and its territories. For more information either write and include a self-addressed, stamped envelope or visit web site.

1316. (A)
Hemophilia Health Services Inc.
Memorial Scholarship Program
HHS Memorial Scholarship Committee
6820 Charlotte Pike
Nashville, TN 37209
(800) 800–6606, ext. 5175
(615) 850–5175
http://www.hemophiliahealth.com

Scholarships of $1,000 to graduate and undergraduate students and graduating high school seniors who have hemophilia or von Willebrand disease. May be used for any field of study. Selection based on academic achievement, extracurricular activities, and financial need. Must be U.S. citizens. Deadline: May 1.

(SS)
Henry A. Murray Research Center at Radcliffe College
10 Garden Street
Cambridge, MA 02138
(617) 495–8601
http://www.radcliffe.edu/murray

1317. (SS)
Adolescent and Youth Dissertation Award

Grants of up to $5,000 to female doctoral students who have completed their course work on women's issues. Award assists in dissertation research on youth or adolescent development. Projects drawing on the center's data will be given priority, although that is not a requirement. Deadline: April 1.

1318. (SS)
Henry A. Murray Dissertation Award

Grants of up to $5,000 to female doctoral students who have completed their course work on women's issues. Award assists in dissertation research on some aspect of "the study of lives," concentrating on issues in human development or personality. Projects draw-

ing on the center's data will be given priority. Deadline: April 1.

1319. (SS)
Jeanne Humphrey Block Dissertation Grants

Grants of up to $5,000 to female doctoral candidates who have completed their course work on women's issues. Award assists in dissertation research on girls' and women's psychological development. Preference given to projects that use the resources at the Murray Research Center. Deadline: April 1.

1320. (SS)
Herbert Hoover Presidential Library Association
Herbert Hoover Travel Grants
ATTN: Executive Director
P.O. Box 696
West Branch, IA 52358
(319) 643–5327
http://www.hooverassoc.org/
info@hooverassoc.org

Several travel grants ranging from $500 to $1,000 to graduate students, postdoctoral scholars, and independent researchers. Funds must be used for travel and research expenses. The Association will consider requests for extended research at the library. Deadline: March 1.

1321. (S)
Herb Society of America
Research and Education Grant
9019 Kirtland Chardon Road
Kirtland, OH 44060
(440) 256–0514
http://www.herbsociety.org

1 to 3 grants of $5,000 for graduate or undergraduate students or persons with a proposed program of scientific, academic, or artistic investigation of herbal plants in the sciences, humanities, and social sciences. Must submit a 500-word outline for an herbal research project. Proposed budget must be included. Projects must be supervised by the Chairman of the Grants Committee, consultants, or designers. Request applications after February 1. Deadline: January 31.

1322. (H, SS)
Heritage Foundation
ATTN: Intern Coordinator
214 Massachusetts Avenue, N.E.
Washington, DC 20002–4999
http://www.heritage.org

20 to 25 internships to graduate or upper-level undergraduate students and recent college graduates. Interns must demonstrate strong research and writing talents, excellent communication skills, and the inquisitiveness to undertake various research, writing, administrative, and computer projects. Students can apply to intern in Asian Studies, Coalition Relations, Domestic Policy, Educational Affairs, the Executive Offices, Foreign Policy, Government Relations, Lectures and Seminars, or Public Relations. Deadline: March 1.

1323. (S)
The Hermitage
Internship Program
4580 Rachel's Lane
Hermitage, TN 37076–1344
(615) 889–2941
http://www.thehermitage.com

10 internships providing $1,000 per session, housing, and $50 per week food stipend to graduate students, recent graduates, and upper-level undergraduate students. Interns must have academic background in historical archaeology. A field course in archaeology is good but not required. The internship is conducted in Hermitage, TN, at the home of Andrew Jackson. Interns conduct diggings to find artifacts, which help reconstruct life at the Hermitage during Jackson's days. Deadline: April 10.

1324. (S, SS)
Hewlett-Packard
SEED Program
3000 Hanover Street
Mail Stop 20-AC
Palo Alto, CA 94303–1181
(415) 857–2092
http://www.jobs.hp.com

300 to 500 10- to 14-week summer internships providing round-trip travel, relocation allowance, and salaries ranging from $700 to $950 per week for graduate students and from $450 to $625 per week for undergraduates. Open to graduate students and undergraduate sophomores, juniors, or seniors. Internships are in CA, CO, DE, GA, ID, MA, NH, NJ, OR, and WA. Internships are open to the following majors: computer science, engineering (computer, electrical, industrial, mechanical, etc.), accounting, business administration, finance, information technology, and operations research. Deadline: April 30.

1325. (S, SS)
H. Fletcher Brown Fund Scholarships
PNC Bank
222 Delaware Avenue, 16th Floor
Wilmington, DE 19801
(302) 429–1186

1 scholarship of up to $6,600 to a first-year graduate student or graduating high school senior. Must have been born in Delaware, graduated from a Delaware high school, and still be a resident of Delaware. Must be pursuing a career in law, chemistry, dentistry, engineering, or medicine. Based on scholastic achievement, moral character, and financial need. Renewable with satisfactory academic progress. College graduates who have been out of school for a year or two but will be entering their first year of graduate school may also apply. Deadline: March 22.

1326. (Contest)
Highlights for Children Fiction Contest
Highlights for Children
803 Church Street
Honesdale, PA 18431
(570) 253–1080
http://www.highlights.com

Prizes of varying amounts for fictional children's stories that appeal to children ages 2 to 12. Stories should be limited to 900 words for older readers and 600 words for younger readers. Category topics vary. Specify on envelope that manuscript is a contest entry. All entries must be postmarked between January 1 and February 28. Send a self-addressed, stamped envelope for category information and rules. Deadline: February 28.

1327. (SS)
Hill and Knowlton, Inc.
Internship Coordinator
466 Lexington Avenue, #3
New York, NY 10017
(212) 885–0300
http://www.hillandknowlton.com

10 to 15 internships providing $6 per hour to graduate or upper-level undergraduate students. Internships introduce students to day-to-day work in a public relations agency and assist them in developing written and oral communication skills. Interns are assigned to accounts where they write media lists, prepare press releases, and compose pitch letters. Though applications are accepted year-round, preference is given to applications submitted before April 1. Deadline: rolling.

1328. (A, H, SS)
Hill, Holliday, Conners, Cosmopulos Advertising, Inc.
Internship Coordinator
200 Clarendon Street
Boston, MA 02116
(617) 572–3418
http://www.clarendon.hhcc.com

25 to 35 internships providing $250 per week to students participating during summer internships but no compensation during fall, winter, or spring internships. Open to graduate students or undergraduate sophomores, juniors, seniors. Interns work in virtually all departments: art, design, mechanical art, accounting, account service, administration, broadcast, community relations, copy, corporate, direct marketing, human resources, market research, media, management information systems, new accounts, and traffic. Interns work full-time for 8 weeks during the summer, full-time for 4 weeks during the winter, or part-time for 15 to 20 weeks during the fall or spring. Deadline: rolling (at least 2 weeks before beginning the internship).

1329. (A)
Hilton Head Jazz Society
Scholarship and Awards Committee
P.O. Box 22193
Hilton Head Island, SC 29925–2193
http://www.hhjs.org

Scholarships ranging from $1,200 to $2,000 to full-time graduate and undergraduate junior and senior students committed to the performance of jazz. To be eligible for this award, you must be enrolled and actively pursuing a music degree with a declared major and primary emphasis in a jazz music studies program at a college or university in the U.S. The recipient will be selected on the basis of jazz performance proficiency and interest in and commitment to a career in jazz music. Must be proficient in jazz. Application period: January 15 to April 15. Deadline: April 30.

(S)
Hispanic Engineer National Achievement Awards Conference
3900 Whiteside Street
Los Angeles, CA 90063
(323) 262–0997
http://www.henaac.org/scholarships.htm

1330. (S)
Ford/HENAAC Scholars Program

5 scholarships of $5,000 to graduate or undergraduate students in computer science, aeronautical, electrical, industrial, and mechanical engineering majors who competed for the HENAAC Student Leadership Award. Deadline: late-April.

1331. (S)
HENAAC Student Leadership Award

1 award each of $5,000 to a graduate or undergraduate student in engineering, math, computer science, or materials science. Must have at least a 3.0 GPA on a 4.0 scale and enroll in the fall semester following receipt of the award. Selection is based on academic achievement, campus community activities, essay, and recommendation letters. Award includes airfare, hotel accommodations, and registration to HENAAC, speaking role in the HENAAC high school program, and participation in the HENAAC Awards show. Deadline: late April.

1332. (S)
Northrop Grumman/HENAAC Scholars Program

5 scholarships of $5,000 to graduate and undergraduate students in computer science, information science,

math, naval architecture, physics, or aerospace, chemical, civil or structural, electrical, industrial/computer, manufacturing, marine, mechanical, or ocean engineering majors who competed for the HENAAC Student Leadership Award. Deadline: late April.

1333. (S, SS)
Hispanic Health Council, Inc.
Internship Program
175 Main Street
Hartford, CT 06106
(860) 724–0437
http://www.hispanichealth.com

Internships to graduate and undergraduate students pursuing careers in anthropology, medicine, nursing, public health, and social work. Students in other fields are still encouraged to apply. Interns work 10 hours per week during long semesters and full-time during the summer. Internships provide them with experience in applied research through special projects and programs. Specific activities vary depending on areas of interest and level of training. Deadline: none specified.

1334. (SS)
Hispanic National Bar Association (HNBA)
Hispanic Lawyers Scholarship Fund
815 Connecticut Avenue, Suite 500
Washington, DC 20006
(202) 223–4777
http://www.hnba.com

4 to 5 scholarships of $2,500 to Hispanic first-year law students. Must either be residents of Illinois or attending an Illinois law school. Selection based on academic achievement, financial need, contributions to the Hispanic community, and an interview. The HNBA provides scholarships to Hispanic students through the Hispanic Scholarship Fund. Visit web site for contact information and an application. Deadline: March 10.

1335. (A, H, S, SS)
Hispanic Scholarship Fund
Selection Committee
55 Second Street, Suite 1500
San Francisco, CA 94105
(415) 445–9930
http://www.hsf.net

2,262 scholarships of $1,000 to Hispanic-American graduate or professional school students, as well as undergraduates who have completed at least 15 college hours. Must be enrolled and attending college on a full-time basis in a college or university in the U.S. or Puerto Rico. Open to all majors. Selection based on character, leadership, seriousness of purpose, academic achievement, volunteer activities, and financial need. At least 1 parent must be of Hispanic heritage. Request applications after June 1. For information, send a self-addressed, stamped envelope. Deadline: October 1.

1336. (A)
Hollis Summers Poetry Prize
Ohio University Press
Scott Quadrangle
Athens, OH 45701
http://www.ohio.edu/oupress/poetryprize.htm

1 cash prize of $500 and publication by Ohio University Press the following year to published and nonpublished poets. The competition is open to both those who have not published a book-length collection and those who have. There is a submission fee of $15 payable to Ohio University Press to help defray administrative costs. For specific guidelines, visit web site. Deadline: October 31 (postmark).

1337. (A, SS)
Home Box Office
Internship Program
Room 3-14A
1100 Sixth Avenue
New York, NY 10036
written inquiries only
(212) 512–1000
http://www.hbo.com

100 internships lasting from 12 to 16 weeks during the summer, fall, and spring provide a $500 stipend at the end of the internship, which is open to graduate and undergraduate students in the area of television and film. International students may apply but will only work in the finance or international departments. U.S. interns work in Film Programming, Original Programming, Accounting, Advertising, Finance, Human Resources, International Marketing, Production, Public Relations, or Sports. All students must receive academic credit for the internship. Submit a résumé, cover letter, and writing

samples. Deadline: March 31 (summer), August 31 (fall), and November 30 (spring).

(A, H, S, SS)

Honor Society of Phi Kappa Phi
Louisiana State University
Box 16000
Baton Rouge, LA 70893–6000
(800) 804–9880
(225) 388–4917
http://www.phikappaphi.org

1338. (A, H, S, SS)
Graduate Fellowships

52 fellowships of $8,000 and 30 awards of $1,500 to first-year graduate or professional school students in all fields of study. Must be nominated by a PKP Chapter and must be or about to become a member of the nominating chapter. Must have high academic achievement. Obtain applications from local chapters. Deadline: February 1.

1339. (H, S, SS)
Kathleen Grey Fellowship

Fellowships of varying amounts to graduate students. Preference, if given, to students whose undergraduate degree was in a field other than basic sciences. Must be nominated by a PKP Chapter and must be or about to become a member of the nominating chapter. Must have high academic achievement. Deadline: February 1.

1340. (H, SS)
Hoover Institution on War, Revolution, and Peace
National Fellows Program
Stanford University
Stanford, CA 94305
(650) 723–1754
http://www-hoover.stanford.edu

12 to 14 fellowships providing $32,000 to postdoctoral students to spend 1 year on unrestricted creative research and writing at the Hoover Institution. Must have expertise in sociology, modern history, political science, economics, international relations, education, or law. Must be U.S. or Canadian citizen. Deadline: January 13.

1341. (A, H, S, SS)
Horace Smith Fund
Walter S. Barr Scholarship Fellowships
P.O. Box 3034
1441 Main Street
Springfield, MA 01101
(413) 739–4222
http://www.horacesmithfund.com/fellowship.html

Fellowships for graduate or undergraduate students and high school seniors in all areas of study. Applicants must be residents of Hampden County, MA. Scholarship and fellowship applications are available after September 1. Loan applications are available after April 1. Renewable. Financial need is primary concern. Deadline: February 1 (fellowships) and July 1 (loans).

1342. (A)
Horse Cave Theatre
Internships
Box 215
Horse Cave, KY 42749
(502) 786–1200
http://www.horsecavetheatre.org

4 full-time internships providing a small stipend to graduate and undergraduate students, and persons with career work experience in a professional theater that produces comedy, drama, classics, and new works by Kentucky playwrights. Interns are able to work with professional artists and managers, attend classes taught by directors, and perform supporting and understudy roles. Openings are from June through December. If an intern is cast in a play, the intern is enrolled as a membership candidate in Actors Equity Association. Applicants should have extensive knowledge in their area of interest, including acting, scenery, costumes, props, lighting, stage management, public relations and marketing, development, administration, box office, or house management. Applicants should at least have college-level theater experience. Submit application, résumé, references, photograph, and audition (if applicable). Deadline: April 1.

(SS)

Hospitality Sales and Marketing Association
International (HSMAI)
8201 Greensboro Drive, Suite 300
McLean, VA 22102

(703) 610–9024

http://www.hsmai.org/Events/scholarship.cfm

1343. (SS)

Merit Scholarships for Full-Time Students

2 scholarships of $2,000 to full-time graduate or undergraduate students pursuing degrees in hospitality management or a related field. Selection is based on enrollment, demonstrated hospitality work experience, interest in career in hospitality sales and marketing, and academic achievement. Deadline: April 1.

1344. (SS)

Merit Scholarships for Part-Time Students

2 scholarships of $500 to part-time graduate or undergraduate students pursuing degrees in hospitality management or a related field. Selection is based on enrollment, demonstrated hospitality work experience, interest in career in hospitality sales and marketing, and academic achievement. Deadline: April 1.

1345. (A)

Houghton Mifflin
Houghton Mifflin Literary Fellowship
222 Berkeley Streeet
Boston, MA 02116
(617) 351–5000
http://www.hmco.com

1 award of $10,000 ($2,500 outright to author and $7,500 advance against royalties) to first work of fiction or nonfiction that is an outstanding work in creative writing. Selection based on quality of writing and publishability. No support is available for poetry, drama, or juvenile literature. Must be a U.S. citizen. Deadline: rolling.

1346. (S)

Houston Underwater Club
Seaspace Scholarships
P.O. Box 3753
Houston, TX 77253–3753
(713) 467–6675
http://www.seaspace.org

15 to 25 awards ranging from $1,000 to $4,000 to graduate or upper-level undergraduate students majoring in marine or aquatic sciences, marine biology or geology, nautical archeology, biological oceanography, ocean and

fishery sciences, naval/marine engineering, or naval science. Must be pursuing a career in marine science and attend an accredited institution in the U.S. Graduate students must have at least a 3.0 GPA and undergraduates must have at least a 3.5 GPA on a 4.0 scale. Selection is based on career goals, academic achievement, and financial need. Send a self-addressed, stamped envelope for an application. Deadline: February 1.

1347. (A, H, S, SS)

Howard and Mamie Nichols Scholarship Trust Scholarships
Wells Fargo Private Client Services
8405 N Fresno Street, Suite 210
Fresno, CA 93720
written inquiries only
(559) 437–3056
(800) 311–5500
http://www.csubak.edu/FinAid/pdf/fah20010110c.
pdf

Approximately 100 scholarships of varying amounts to graduate and undergraduate students for use for full-time study in all areas of study. Must be graduates of Kern County, CA, high schools, have financial need, and have at least a 2.0 GPA or better. Renewable with reapplication. Deadline: February 28.

1348. (A, H, S, SS)

Howard Foundation
Project Awards
Brown University
42 Charlesfield Street
4th Floor—Graduate School
Providence, RI 02912
(401) 863–2640
http://www.brown.edu/Divisions/Graduate_
School/howard

10 grants of up to $20,000 to individuals engaged in independent projects. Should be assistant or associate professors or their nonacademic equivalents, between 25 and 45 years of age, in middle stages of their career. Applicants must be nominated by one's institution or by a person prominent in one's field. Areas supported rotate in cycles: novels, short stories, poetry, playwriting, essays, and creative nonfiction; literary criticism, film criticism, and translation; sociology, anthropology, and philosophy; and painting, sculpture, and art history.

Deadline: mid-October (nominations), early December (applications).

(S)
Howard Hughes Medical Institute
4000 Jones Bridge Road
Chevy Chase, MD 20815–6789
(301) 215–8500
http://www.hhmi.org

1349. (S)
HHMI-NIH Research Scholars Program

60 internships providing a grant of $16,800 to medical or dental students to conduct research in areas such as structural biology, cell biology, genetics, immunology, and neuroscience. Fellowships last from 9 months to 1 year. Must be attending an accredited U.S. medical or dental school. Deadline: early January.

1350. (S)
Hughes Doctoral Fellowships National Research Council

60 fellowships providing $10,700 toward tuition costs and $12,300 stipend to doctoral students in Ph.D. or Sc.D. programs in biological sciences. Fields of study are biochemistry, biophysics, cell biology, developmental biology, genetics, immunology, microbiology, molecular biology, neuroscience, pharmacology, physiology, structural biology, and virology. Deadline: varies.

1351. (S)
Research Training Fellowships for Medical Students

60 renewable fellowships of up to $21,200 to students enrolled in M.D. or D.O. degree programs in accredited U.S. institutions. International students attending a U.S. medical school are also eligible. Students conduct research in such areas as structural biology, cell biology, genetics, immunology, and neuroscience. Applicants may have prior research experience, but it isn't required. Request applications after September 15. Deadline: December 5.

1352. (A, H, S, SS)
Hualapai Tribal Council
Scholarship Program
P.O. Box 179
Peach Springs, AZ 86434
(928) 769–2216
http://www.itcaonline.com/tribes_hualapai.html

Varying numbers of scholarships of $700 to full-time students for graduate and undergraduate study in all fields of study. Must be members of the Hualapai Tribe. Must maintain passing grades. Deadline: 2 weeks before each semester.

1353. (SS)
Hudson Institute
Herman Kahn Fellowship
ATTN: Director of Programs
P.O. Box 26919
5395 Emerson Way
Indianapolis, IN 46226
(317) 545–1000
http://www.hudson.org

Up to 3 fellowships of $18,000, plus travel expenses, to doctoral candidates who have completed all their course work and are working on their dissertation on a policy-relevant issue. Open to the following areas of study: criminology, economic development and urban planning, education, national security, policy issues, social welfare policy and civil society, and international political economy and security. Award assists recipient in conducting a year of research and study in Indianapolis or Washington, DC. Based on high academic achievement, proposed research, and faculty recommendation. Must be U.S. citizens. Deadline: April 15.

1354. (Contest)
Humboldt State University
Raymond Carver Short Story Contest
Toyon Magazine
Humboldt State University
1 Harpst Street
Arcata, CA 95521–8299
(707) 826–3758
http://www.humboldt.edu/~carver

Awards of $500 and $1,000 for unpublished short stories of up to a maximum of 6,000 words. Must be U.S.

citizens. Visit web site for specific submission guidelines. There is a reading fee. Deadline: December 31.

(A, H, S)
Huntington Library and Art Gallery
ATTN: Head of Research
1151 Oxford Road
San Marino, CA 91108
(818) 405–2116
http://www.huntington.org

1355. (H)
Clark-Huntington Joint Bibliographical Fellowship

Fellowships of $4,000 for 2 months to postdoctoral fellows in descriptive bibliography and the history of the book. The Huntington and the Clark have complementary collections in the fields of British and American history and literature, the history of science, music, the history of the book, and fine printing. Visit web site for contact information at the Clark Library. Deadline: mid-December.

1356. (H)
Evelyn S. Nation Fellowship in the History of Medicine

Fellowships of $2,000 per month to doctoral students and postdoctoral scholars to conduct research in the area of the history of medicine. Doctoral candidates must have completed all course work and be at the dissertation stage. There is no application form, but applicants need to follow specific guidelines, including a curriculum vitae of not more than 3 pages, 3 letters of recommendation, and a description of proposed projects. Must be in residence at Huntington and participate in, and make a contribution to, its intellectual life. Deadline: mid-December.

1357. (H)
Francis Bacon Foundation Fellowships in Renaissance England

Fellowships of $2,000 per month to doctoral students and postdoctoral scholars to conduct research on Renaissance England. Doctoral candidates must have completed all course work and be at the dissertation stage. There is no application form, but applicants need to follow specific guidelines, including a curriculum vitae of not more than 3 pages, 3 letters

of recommendation, and a description of proposed projects. Must be in residence at Huntington and participate in, and make a contribution to, its intellectual life. Deadline: mid-December.

1358. (H)
Haynes Foundation Fellowships in Los Angeles Region History

Fellowships of $2,000 per month to doctoral students and postdoctoral scholars to conduct research on Los Angeles region history. Doctoral candidates must have completed all course work and be at the dissertation stage. There is no application form, but applicants need to follow specific guidelines, including a curriculum vitae of not more than 3 pages, 3 letters of recommendation, and a description of proposed projects. Must be in residence at Huntington and participate in, and make a contribution to, its intellectual life. Deadline: mid-December.

1359. (A, H)
Huntington-British Academy Fellowships for Study in Great Britain

Fellowships of varying amounts to doctoral scholars or equivalent to conduct research in Great Britain for 1 month. There is no application form, but applicants need to follow specific guidelines, including a curriculum vitae of not more than 3 pages, 3 letters of recommendation, and a description of proposed projects. In cooperation with the British Academy, the Huntington offers a limited number of exchange fellowships in any of the fields in which the Huntington collections are strong. Deadline: mid-December.

1360. (A, H)
Huntington Fellowships

Fellowships of $2,000 per month to doctoral students and postdoctoral scholars. There is no application form, but applicants need to follow specific guidelines, including a curriculum vitae of not more than 3 pages, 3 letters of recommendation, and a description of proposed projects. Doctoral candidates must have completed all course work and be at the dissertation stage. Must be in residence at Huntington and participate in, and make a contribution to, its intellectual life. Deadline: mid-December.

1361. (H)
Msgr. Francis J. Weber Research Fellowship in Roman Catholic History

Fellowships of $2,000 per month to doctoral students and postdoctoral scholars to conduct research in Roman Catholic history. Doctoral candidates must have completed all course work and be at the dissertation stage. There is no application form, but applicants need to follow specific guidelines, including a curriculum vitae of not more than 3 pages, 3 letters of recommendation, and a description of proposed projects. Must be in residence at Huntington and participate in, and make a contribution to, its intellectual life. Deadline: mid-December.

1362. (H)
Trent R. Dames Civil Engineering History Fellowship

Fellowships of $2,000 per month to doctoral students and postdoctoral scholars to conduct research on civil engineering history. There is no application form, but applicants need to follow specific guidelines, including a curriculum vitae of not more than 3 pages, 3 letters of recommendation, and a description of proposed projects. Must be in residence at Huntington, and participate in, and make a contribution to, its intellectual life. Deadline: mid-December.

1363. (H)
W.M. Keck Foundation Fellowship for Young Scholars

Fellowships of $2,300 per month to doctoral students and nontenured faculty to conduct research. There is no application form, but applicants need to follow specific guidelines, including a curriculum vitae of not more than 3 pages, 3 letters of recommendation, and a description of proposed projects. Must be in residence at Huntington for 1 to 5 months and participate in, and make a contribution to, its intellectual life. Deadline: mid-December.

1364. (S)
Idaho Society for Clinical Laboratory Science, Inc. Internships
c/o Magic Valley Memorial Hospital
Twin Falls, ID 83301
(208) 737–2000
http://www.idscls.org

3 medical technology internships per year to graduate students or fourth-year undergraduates. Must be recommended by a teaching supervisor in a clinical area, by supervising pathologists, and by 2 professors in science courses at the undergraduate level. Amount of funding varies. Must be Idaho residents. Deadline: varies.

(A, H)
Illinois Arts Council
100 West Randolph, Suite 10–500
Chicago, IL 60601
(312) 814–6750
(800) 237–6994
http://www.state.il.us/agency/iac
info@arts.state.il.us

1365. (A)
Artist Fellowship Program

Grants of $7,000 to artists who are Illinois residents. The grant is not for academic study but rather for completion or creation of new work in choreography, visual arts, literature, film, video, playwriting, or music composition. Selection based on quality of work submitted. Deadline: September 1.

1366. (A)
Ethnic and Fold Arts Master/Apprentice Program

A limited number of awards of $2,000 to teacher/master artist and $1,000 to apprentice to practice their art. The informal apprenticeships take place wherever the master artist and apprentice practice their art. Both master and apprentice must submit an application. Deadline: September 1.

1367. (A, H)
Literary Awards Program

Awards of $1,000 to writers and the magazines that publish their work. Writers must be must be Illinois residents. Magazines must be published in Illinois for at least once a year. Open to original works of fiction, poetry, and creative nonfiction. Deadline: December 31.

(S)
Illinois Environmental Protection Agency
P.O. Box 19276
Springfield, IL 62794–9276

(217) 524–4335
http://www.epa.state.il.us/p2/internships/
program-info.html

1368. (S)
Governor's Environmental Corps

Internships providing a monthly stipend of $1,225 to graduate and undergraduate students in biological sciences, physical sciences, chemistry, engineering, pre-law, personal computers, and communications. Interns work in a specific area of the Illinois EPA, such as air pollution control, land pollution control, water pollution control, laboratories, public information, legal counsel, or community relations. Deadline: March 28.

1369. (S)
Office of Pollution Prevention

Internships providing monthly stipends ranging from $2,100 to $2,700 to graduate and upper-level undergraduate students majoring in chemistry, engineering, environmental management, or occupational health and safety. Interns work as temporary full-time employees of that facility, focusing on an assigned P2 project. Deadline: January 31.

(SS)
Illinois State Government
Department of Central Management Services
503 William G. Stratton Building
Springfield, IL 62706
(217) 782–5213
http://www.state.il.us/gov/intopportunities.
cfm#curry

1370. (SS)
Dunne Fellowship Program

Fellowships providing $27,000 and state benefits to college graduates who are placed in different positions throughout the Governor's Office and agencies under the Governor's jurisdiction. Selection based on academic achievement, leadership ability, extracurricular activities, and community/public service involvement. Deadline: January 31.

1371. (SS)
Mazullo Internship Program

Fellowships providing $27,000 and state benefits to college graduates who are placed in different positions throughout the Governor's Office and agencies under the Governor's jurisdiction. Must be Illinois residents. Selection based on academic achievement, leadership ability, extracurricular activities, and community/public service involvement. Deadline: January 31.

(A, H, S, SS)
Illinois State Government
Office of the Governor
107 William G. Stratton Building
Springfield, IL 62706
(217) 782–5213
http://www.state.il.us/gov/intopportunities.
cfm#curry

1372. (A, H, S, SS)
Michael Curry Summer Internship Program

Summer internships providing $1,200 per month to graduate and upper-level undergraduate students to work in one of the agencies under the jurisdiction of the Governor. Must be pursuing a career in public service and Illinois residents. The 10-week full-time internships offer positions in Springfield and Chicago. Open to all majors (including law). Deadline: January 31.

1373. (SS)
Rod R. Blagojevich Governmental Internship

Internships providing academic credit open to graduate and undergraduate students interested in experiencing the day-to-day operations of the chief executive's office. Program provides students with the opportunity to become familiar with all aspects of the operation of the Governor's Office. Interns assist administratively, aid in media relations, and where appropriate, respond to correspondence from Illinois citizens. Must have at least a 3.2 GPA and be organized, self-motivated, and energetic. Deadline: rolling.

1374. (A, H, S)
Illuminating Engineering Society of North America
Robert Thunen Memorial Education Fund
Scholarships
120 Wall Street, Floor 17
New York, NY 10005
(212) 248–5000
http://www.iesna.org
iesna@iesna.org

2 scholarships of $2,500 to graduate students in architecture, architectural engineering, electrical engineering, interior design, or theater. Students must be enrolled in an accredited institution in northern CA, OR, WA, or northern NV. Students must have a specific lighting project as part of their course work. Visit web site for more information. Deadline: none given.

1375. (H, SS)
The Independent Institute
Olive W. Garvey Fellowship
100 Swan Way
Oakland, CA 94621–1428
(510) 632–1366
http://www.independent.org

Fellowships of $1,000, $1,500, and $2,500 to full- or part-time graduate and undergraduate students under the age of 35. Selection is based through a competitive essay contest on the meaning and significance of economic and personal liberty. Topic varies yearly. Visit web site for complete instructions. Deadline: May 1.

1376. (S)
Indiana Society of Professional Land Surveyors
55 Monument Circle, Suite 1222
Indianapolis, IN 46204
(317) 687–8859
http://www.ispls.org/grants_program.htm

Grants of varying amounts to graduate and undergraduate students who are pursuing careers in land surveying. Awarded to advance and promote the study of land surveying. Must be residents of Indiana and attend an accredited program in Indiana. Visit web site for more information. Deadline: none specified.

1377. (H, S, SS)
Institute for Advanced Study
Postdoctoral Fellowship Award
Einstein Drive
Princeton, NJ 08540
(609) 734–8000
http://www.ias.edu

170 fellowships of varying amounts to postdoctoral fellows. Although most fellows are appointed by faculty invitation, some are selected from among the many applicants who wish to spend a year or more in the schools of historical studies, mathematics, natural sciences, or social science. Half the members are supported by the Institute. Deadline: varies by school.

1378. (Contest)
Institute for Brand Leadership Essay Contest
http://www.instituteforbrandleadership.
org/IBL EssayContest-2002Rules.html
dblumenthal@instituteforbrandleadership.org

Awards of $500, $1,500, and $3,000 to graduate and undergraduate students in all fields of study as well as those who are not currently enrolled in school. Based on an essay between 1,500 and 2,500 words that answers the question "Why and under what circumstances are people more likely to buy brand names rather than their generic counterparts?" Essay must apply a theory or set of theories from a particular discipline or area of study. Submissions must be e-mailed. Deadline: October 15.

1379. (S)
Institute for College Research Development and Support
Project TAPS
8701 George Avenue, Suite 603
Silver Springs, MD 20910
(301) 585–7588
http://www.icrds.org

Assistance in the form of a stipend of $45,000, plus benefits and travel, to faculty of historically Black colleges and other minority institutions to participate in a 9-month administrative training program conducted during the academic year. An administrative infrastructure model developed by the Institute serves as the basis for the training. Deadline: none specified.

1380. (SS)
Institute for Educational Leadership
Education Policy Fellowship Program
1001 Connecticut Avenue, N.W.
Suite 310
Washington, DC 20036
(202) 822–8405
http://www.iel.org/programs/epfp.html

Fellowships of varying amounts to graduate students to learn about how public policies in education are designed and implemented in CA, CO, CT, IL, MI, NJ, NY, NC, OH, OR, and Washington, DC. Recipients must be identified and endorsed by their agencies. Women and minorities are encouraged to apply. Deadline: none specified.

(A, H, SS)
Institute for Humane Studies—George Mason University
3301 N. Fairfax Drive, Suite 440
Arlington, VA 22201–4432
(703) 993–4880
http://www.theihs.org

1381. (H, SS)
Felix Morley Journalism Competition

Cash awards of $250, $750, $1,000, or $2,500 to full-time graduate and undergraduate students and writers under the age of 25. Selection is based on a competition for the best published newspaper or magazine articles inspired by liberty. Judging based on writing ability, potential to succeed, and an appreciation of liberty. Deadline: December 1.

1382. (A, H)
Film & Fiction Scholarships

Scholarships of up to $10,000 in tuition and stipend to graduate students in filmmaking, fiction writing, or playwriting. Must have a demonstrated interest in classical liberal ideas and their application in contemporary society. Must demonstrate the desire, motivation, and creative ability to succeed in their chosen profession. Deadline: January 15.

1383. (H)
Hayek Fund for Scholars

Grants of up to $1,000 to graduate students and untenured faculty to participate in career-enhancing activities, such as presentations at academic or professional conferences, travel to academic job interviews, travel to and research at archives or libraries, participation in career development or -enhancing seminars, distribution of a published article to colleagues in your field, and submission of unpublished manuscripts to journals or book publishers. Deadline: open.

1384. (H)
Humane Studies Fellowship

Up to 90 fellowships of up to $12,000 to full-time graduate, professional, law, and undergraduate students interested in the classical liberal tradition. Awards are based on academic or professional performance, relevance of one's work to the advancement of a free society, and potential for success. Students are eligible to reapply in subsequent years. December 31.

1385. (H)
Summer Graduate Research Fellowships

Fellowships of a $3,000 stipend, and travel expenses to 2 IHS seminars, to graduate students interested in the classical liberal tradition to work on a thesis chapter or a paper of publishable quality and to participate in interdisciplinary seminars under the guidance of a faculty supervisor. Fellows spend most of the summer completing a journal article or thesis chapter. Deadline: February 15.

1386. (H)
Young Communicators Fellowships

Awards of up to $5,000 ($2,500 12-week housing stipend and a $2,500 travel allowance) to graduate and upper-level undergraduate students and recent graduates pursuing specified nonacademic careers. Must have clearly demonstrated an interest in the "classical liberal" tradition of individual rights and market economies, be intent on pursuing a career in journalism, film, writing (fiction or nonfiction), publishing, or market-oriented public policy, and have arranged or applied for an internship, training program, or other short-term opportunity related to applicant's intended career. Deadline: March 15 (summer), 10 weeks in advance (other positions).

1387. (SS)
Institute for Local Self-Reliance
Minnesotans for an Energy-Efficient Economy (ME³)
2425 18th Street, N.W.
Washington, DC 20009–2096
(202) 232–4108
http://www.ilsr.org/interns.html

Paid internships lasting 3 to 4 months and providing $280 per week to graduate and undergraduate students. Interns conduct independent research, analyze complex data sets, and analyze data. Must write well and demonstrate experience in working successfully in fast-paced environments. Deadline: rolling.

1388. (SS)

Institute for Public Representation
Graduate Fellow/Staff Attorney
Georgetown University Law Center
600 New Jersey Avenue, N.W.
Washington, DC 20001
(202) 662–9535
http://www.law.georgetown.edu/clinics/ipr

Fellowships providing a stipend of $36,370 to graduate/law students to work as staff attorneys. Award is meant to help them train for public service legal jobs. The program specializes in federal administrative law and clinical legal training. Fellowships are in the areas of civil rights law, communications law, and environmental law. Must be committed to public interest law, have strong writing and communication skills, and have an interest in clinical legal education. Deadline: December 1.

(S, SS)

Institute for Supply Management
P.O. Box 22160
Tempe, AZ 85285–2160
(480) 752–6276
(800) 888–6276
http://www.napm.org

1389. (SS)

Chapter Awards

State and regional chapters offer scholarships to graduate or undergraduate students who are members. Some awards are limited to specific institutions and geographic areas. Majors of interest: business, purchasing, procurement, materials management, inventory control, and business administration. Deadline: varies by chapter.

1390. (SS)

Doctoral Dissertation Grant

4 grants of $10,000 to graduate students in business, economics, industrial engineering, management, or purchasing logistics to conduct dissertation research on purchasing or materials management. Must be used while attending an accredited U.S. institution. Based on proposed research, with preference given to students pursuing careers in teaching or research at the college level. Deadline: January 31.

1391. (SS)

Eastern Purchasing and Supply Management
Group (EPSMG)

1 or more scholarships of varying amounts to graduate students. Must be member of EPSMG or an affiliate. Must be a resident within their geographic boundaries (eastern PA, NJ counties near Philadelphia, DE, MD, DC, VA, NC, SC). Must be used for professional education and development. Visit web site for contact information. Deadline: February 28.

1392. (S, SS)

NAPM-Lehigh Valley Chapter
Scholarships

5 scholarships of $1,000 to graduate or undergraduate students in business, engineering, or a business-related field. Must be attending an accredited college or university in the Allentown-Bethlehem-Easton area. Visit web site for more information and contact. Deadline: none specified.

1393. (SS)

Institute for the Study of World Politics
Dissertation Fellowships
1755 Massachusetts Avenue, N.W.
Washington, DC 20036
(202) 797–0882
written inquiries only
http://www.columbia.edu/cu/polisci/grad

20 to 25 fellowships of varying amounts to doctoral candidates working in environmental issues, international relations, population studies (social science aspects), human rights, arms control, or Third World development. Must have completed course work and be conducting dissertation research. Financial need is considered. Deadline: February 15.

1394. (S)

Institute of Electrical & Electronics Engineers
Charles Le Geyt Fortescue Fellowship
3 Park Avenue, 17th Floor
New York, NY 10016–5997
(212) 419–7900
http://www.ieee.org

Awards of $24,000 to first-year full-time graduate students pursuing careers in electrical engineering. May attend a recognized engineering school in the U.S. or Canada. Awarded every other year. Send a self-addressed, stamped envelope for an application. Deadline: January 31.

1395. (S)
Institute of Food Technologist (IFT)
Arthur T. Schramm Fellowship
525 West Van Buren, Suite 1000
Chicago, IL 60607
(312) 782–8424
http://www.ift.org

23 awards ranging from $1,000 to $10,000 to graduate students to support research in food science and technology at an accredited institute in the U.S. or Canada. Must be enrolled in an IFT-approved curriculum in food engineering, nutrition, food technology, or food science. Renewable. Obtain applications from school department heads or IFT. Applications must be submitted to the institution's department head. Deadline: February 1.

1396. (S)
Institute of Geophysics and Planetary Physics
Summer of Applied Geophysical Experience
Grants
GRA Program Coordinator
STB/EPO
P.O. Box 1663, MS M 709
Los Alamos National Laboratory
Los Alamos, NM 87545
http://www.ees.lanl.gov/jobs.shtml

Grants of varying amounts to graduate students in geophysics to introduce students to geophysical exploration and research. Program incorporates the use of geophysical data and geological information to derive integrated subsurface interpretations. Deadline: none specified.

1397. (S)
Institute of Industrial Engineers (IIE)
IIE Scholarships
3577 Parkway Lane, Suite 200
Northcross, GA 30092
(770) 449–0460
(800) 494–0460
http://www.iienet.org

Scholarships of varying amounts for graduate or undergraduate students who are industrial engineering majors. Must be active IIE members with at least 1 full year of study remaining at an accredited U.S. or Canadian institution. Must have at least a 3.4 GPA on a 4.0 scale. Applications mailed only to students who have been nominated by the department head. Deadline: November 1 (nomination) and February 15 (applications).

(SS)
Institute of Internal Auditors Research Foundation
247 Maitland Avenue
Altamonte Springs, FL 32701–4201
(407) 937–1356
http://www.theiia.org/ecm/iiarf.cfm?doc_id=234

1398. (SS)
Esther R. Sawyer Scholarship Award

Scholarships of $5,000 to graduate students in internal auditing. Must be enrolled or entering an IIA-endorsed school. Selection based on an original manuscript on a specific topic related to modern internal auditing. Award also includes registration and travel expenses for the recipient to attend the Annual International Conference and up to $3,000 to the IIA-endorsed school the student is attending. Topics vary yearly. Deadline: March 1.

1399. (SS)
Michael J. Barrett Doctoral Dissertation Award

Varying number of awards ranging from $1,000 to $10,000 to doctoral students pursuing a degree in business in the area of internal auditing. Must have completed all course requirements except for the dissertation and intend to teach internal auditing for at least 2 years. Award is for full-time dissertation research. Deadline: May 15 and October 31.

(A, H, S, SS)
Institute of International Education
U.S. Student Programs Division
1400 K Street, N.W.
Washington, DC 20005
(202) 898–0600
http://www.iie.org

1400. (A)
CINTAS Fellowship Program

10 to 15 fellowships of $7,500 to foster and encourage the professional development of and recognize talented creative artists in architecture; music composition; painting; printmaking; sculpture; and writing. For people of Cuban citizenship or Cuban ancestry (at least 1 Cuban parent). Deadline: none specified.

1401. (A, H)
Drama and Theatre in the Age of Shakespeare at the University of Birmingham

Varying number of grants of varying amounts for 6-week summer school session in Great Britain, to study Elizabethan-era drama, theater, or literature. Funding made available to B.S./B.A. holders. Recipients chosen on the basis of academic achievement, financial need, and potential contribution to summer school life. Must be U.S. citizens. For more information, write or visit web site. Deadline: October 31.

1402. (A, H)
English Theatre, Literature, and Culture Since 1940 at the University of London

Varying numbers of grants for 6-week summer school session in Great Britain to study English theater, literature, or culture after 1940. Funding made available to B.S./B.A. holders. Recipients chosen on the basis of academic achievement, financial need, and potential contribution to summer school life. Must be U.S. citizen. For more information, write or visit web site. Deadline: October 31.

1403. (A, H, S, SS)
Fellowships

1,600 grants ranging from $2,000 to $25,000 to graduate students for study in a foreign country. The award covers round-trip transportation, tuition, books, and health and accident insurance. Fellowship amounts vary depending on country. Students must be U.S. citizens and have a bachelor's degree. Must have proficiency in the language of the host country. Law applicants may hold J.D. Deadline: set by campus Fulbright Program advisors; October 31 (for at-large applicants).

1404. (H)
Finnish Government Reciprocal Scholarship Program

Varying number of scholarships providing a monthly stipend ranging from 200 euros to 300 euros, plus free tuition, to graduate students in Finnish language, literature, culture, history, archaeology, politics, and folklore. Award covers a period of study ranging from 3 to 9 months in Finland. 36 countries participate in this exchange program. Selection based on criteria set by home institution. Applicants must be fluent in Finnish, English, Swedish, or German. Recipients may not work full-time during the scholarship period. U.S. students should contact above address; all other applicants should write to: Department of International Relations, Vuorikatu 8A 7, SF–00100, Helsinki 10, Finland; telephone: 9-0-171-636. Deadline: March 31.

1405. (A, H, S, SS)
Fulbright and International Fellowships for U. S. Citizens

1,600 grants ranging from $2,000 to $25,000 to graduate students for study in a foreign country. The award covers round-trip transportation, tuition, books, and health and accident insurance. Fellowship amounts vary depending on country. Students must be U.S. citizens and have a bachelor's degree. Must have proficiency in the language of the host country. Law applicants may hold J.D. Deadline: set by campus Fulbright Program advisors; October 31 (for at-large applicants).

1406. (A, H, S, SS)
Fulbright Grants for Foreign Nations

Numerous fellowship grants of varying amounts to foreign graduate students for study and/or research in all fields of study in a country other than student's native country. Must be proficient in the language of the country in which student plans to undertake study. Fellowships must be applied for in the home country. The institute administers the program for a variety of sponsors. Deadline: May 1 and October 31.

1407. (H)
Fulbright-Hays Doctoral Dissertation Research Abroad Program

Grants are made to colleges and universities to fund doctoral students to conduct research in other countries in modern foreign languages and area studies for periods of 6 to 12 months. Must be a U.S. citizen or permanent resident. Must have adequate skills in the language necessary to carry out the dissertation project. Deadline: late October.

1408. (H)
Fulbright-Hays Group Projects Abroad Program

Grants of varying amounts to support overseas projects in training, research, and curriculum development in modern languages and area studies to graduate or undergraduate junior or senior students, elementary or secondary school teachers, or faculty members. Applicants must plan to teach or already be teaching a foreign language or area studies. Projects can be short-term (5 to 6 weeks in length) or up to 3 years. Must be U.S. citizens. Deadline: late October.

1409. (A, H, S, SS)
Levi Strauss Foundation International Scholarship Program

Scholarships ranging from $1,000 to $1,500 to graduate and undergraduate students in a variety of majors. Must be dependents of regular Levi Strauss employees. Selection based on financial need and academic achievement. Deadline: July 15.

1410. (A, H, S, SS)
Scholarships for Study in Switzerland

Scholarships ranging from 1,350 to 1,650 Swiss francs per month to non-Swiss students for postgraduate study in all fields of study at Swiss universities. Awards are made to assist individuals to further their studies and begin research. Non-U.S. citizens must contact above address. U.S. citizens must inquire with their graduate institutions. Deadline: May 1 and October 31.

1411. (S)
Institute of Paper Science and Technology Fellowship Program
500 10th Street, N.W.
Atlanta, GA 30318

(404) 894–5700
http://www.ipst.edu

35 fellowships providing full tuition, plus a stipend of $11,250, to graduate students who have B.S. degree with a major in chemistry, chemical engineering, physics, mechanical engineering, paper science, biology, or pulp and paper technology. Applicants must have a 3.0 GPA on a 4.0 scale and submit GRE scores. Open to U.S., Canadian, and Mexican citizens. Deadline: March 15.

(H, SS)
Institute of Turkish Studies
Intercultural Center
Box 571033
Room #305 R
Georgetown University
Washington, DC 20057–1033
(202) 687–0295
http://www.turkishstudies.org

1412. (H, SS)
Dissertation Writing Grants

Grants ranging from $5,000 to $10,000 to graduate students in any field of the social sciences and/or humanities for dissertation writing and not research. Applicants must certify that they will not be involved in teaching beyond the half-time level. Must be U.S. citizens or permanent residents and currently enrolled in an accredited U.S. institution. Deadline: March 14.

1413. (H, SS)
Summer Language Study Grants for Graduate Students

Grants ranging from $1,000 to $2,000 to graduate students in any field of the social sciences and/or humanities to spend at least 2 months in Turkey at an established Ottoman or Turkish language training facility. Must be U.S. citizens or permanent residents and currently enrolled in an accredited U.S. institution. Deadline: March 14.

1414. (H, SS)
Summer Research Grants for Graduate Students

Grants ranging from $1,000 to $2,000 to graduate students in any field of the social sciences and/or humanities for summer travel to Turkey to carry out projects. Must not be engaged in dissertation writing. Must be U.S. citizens or permanent residents and currently enrolled in an accredited U.S. institution. Deadline: March 14.

1415. (SS)
Institute of World Affairs
Hadden Fellows
1321 Pennsylvania Avenue, S.E.
Washington, DC 20003
(202) 544–4141
http://www.iwa.org
info@iwa.org

Fellowships to graduate students with an interest in the field of international peace building and a desire to work on focused projects in the field. Must be fluent in English and have strong writing and communication skills. Fellows gain experience in both the theory and practice of designing and administering conflict resolution programs in divided societies. Fellowship/internship is unpaid. There is no application. Visit web site for specific guidelines. Deadline: none specified.

1416. (A, H)
Institut Francais de Washington
Gilbert Chinard Fellowships
234 Dey Hall CB #3170
University of North Carolina
Chapel Hill, NC 27599–3170
(919) 962–0154
http://www.unc.edu/depts/institut/institutapp.htm

4 awards of $1,500 to graduate students in the final writing stage of their dissertation or who have held their doctorate no longer than 6 years before application submission in the areas of French history, literature, art, and music. To support scholars undertaking research in France. Support is for maintenance, not travel, for periods of at least 2 months. There is no application. Applicants submit curriculum vitae and a 2-page research proposal. Ph.D. candidates are required to submit a letter from their dissertation advisor. Deadline: January 15.

1417. (S, SS)
Intel Corporation
Staffing Department
FM4–145
P.O. Box 1141

Folsom, CA 95763–1141
(916) 356–8080
http://www.intel.com

750 to 800 summer, fall, and spring internships providing relocation allowance ranging from $500 to $700, round-trip travel, and salaries ranging from $750 to $1,000 per week for graduates and from $450 to $750 per week for undergraduates. Summer internships are from 8 to 15 weeks; fall and spring internships range from 4 to 8 months. Open to undergraduate, graduate, and doctoral students with at least a 3.0 GPA who are majoring in accounting, business, computer science, education, engineering (chemical, computer, electrical, and industrial), finance, human resources, materials science, mathematics, and physics. Deadline: rolling (majority filed by March 1).

1418. (SS)
Inter-American Bar Foundation
Law Fellowships
1819 H Street, N.W.
Washington, DC 20006
(202) 393–1217
http://users.erols.com/iaba

Fellowships of varying amounts to law students and law school graduates. The Foundation operates a fellowship program whose purpose is to strengthen legal relations in the Americas.

(S, SS)
Inter-American Foundation
901 North Stuart Street, 10th Floor
Arlington, VA 22203
(703) 306–4301
http://www.iaf.gov

1419. (S, SS)
Doctoral Dissertation Fellowships

15 fellowships ranging from $3,000 to $7,000 to doctoral candidates working in physical or social science fields concerning Latin American and Caribbean studies. Must have completed all their course work. Award assists recipient in traveling to the country of intended study. Research proposals must deal with development activities among the poor. Must speak and write in the language of the country in which study will be completed. Deadline: November 20.

1420. (S, SS)
Master's Research Fellowships

10 to 15 fellowships ranging from $1,000 to $3,000 to master's degree candidates working in the physical or social science fields concerning Latin American and Caribbean studies. Must have completed all their course work. Award assists recipient in traveling to the country of intended study. Must speak and write in the language of the country in which study will be completed. Deadline: November 20.

(SS)
Intercolligiate Studies Institute
3901 Centerville Road
P.O. Box 4431
Wilmington, DE 19807
(302) 652–4600
http://www.isi.org/programs/fellowships

1421. (SS)
Bache Renshaw Fellowship

1 to 2 fellowships providing full tuition and a stipend of $12,000 to doctoral students in education at Virginia's Curry School of Education. Awarded to individuals who appreciate the importance of our Western heritage and who are capable of preparing future teachers in the liberal arts. Selection based on application, personal statement (declaring intent to teach, why teaching was chosen, and need for fellowship), academic achievement, recommendation letters, and 3 essays. Deadline: January 15.

1422. (SS)
Richard M. Weaver Fellowship

Fellowships paying tuition and a stipend of $5,000 to graduate students who are pursuing careers as educators. Assists future teachers who are motivated by the need to integrate the idea of liberal education with their teaching efforts. Selection based on application, personal statement (declaring intent to teach, why teaching was chosen, and need for fellowship), academic achievement, recommendation letters, and 3 essays. Deadline: January 15.

1423. (SS)
Salvatori Fellowship

2 fellowships of $10,000 to graduate students in majors related to American founding. Award seeks to further an understanding and appreciation of both the principles of the Founding Fathers and the culture that formed their values and views. Selection based on application, personal statement (declaring intent to teach, why teaching was chosen, and need for fellowship), academic achievement, recommendation letters, and 3 essays. Deadline: January 15.

1424. (SS)
Western Civilization Fellowships

3 fellowships of $20,000 to graduate students in Western Civilization studies or related areas. Designed to address our culture's loss of memory by supporting graduate-level study of the institutions, values, and history of the West. Selection based on application, personal statement (declaring intent to teach, why teaching was chosen, and need for fellowship), academic achievement, recommendation letters, and 3 essays. Deadline: January 15.

1425. (S)
International Agricultural Centre (IAC)
P.O. Box 9101
6700 HB Wageningen
The Netherlands
+31 (0) 317 483 618
http://www.iac.wageningen-ur.nl

Fellowships providing room and board, a daily allowance of 7 euros, health insurance, study tours, and a book allowance, to master's and doctoral students in agriculture-related areas. Applicants should have some experience in their field of study. Must be at least 25 years of age. Deadline: 6 months before beginning study.

1426. (A)
International Art Contest
Art Department
P.O. Box 756
Bribie Island
4507 Australia
+617 3408 0266 (Fax)
http://www.artdept.com.au/contest/compapplicat.
html

Awards of varying amounts to artists in the following categories: Realism—includes paintings where the artist has made an attempt to portray the subject as seen; Modern—includes all paintings that are not considered realistic; Mixed—generally includes artworks that are not essentially paintings such as assemblage and sculpture; and Digital—art produced with the use of a computer. The majority of the composition must be created by the artist (entries predominantly photographic, or photo collages, will not be accepted). Winning entries are featured on the Art Department home page for the following year. Contest aim is to provide an introduction to active artists, create interaction between artists worldwide, and offer a window to what is going on in the world of popular and contemporary art. An important condition of entry is that the artwork nominated must be from a mature, preferably professional, artist and that it exhibit proficiency and provide career reference. Deadline: July 14.

1427. (S)
International Astronomical Union
Exchange of Astronomers Travel Grant
98bis, Bd Arago
F–75014 Paris
France
+33 1 4325 8358
http://www.iau.org

Varying numbers of travel grants to graduate students, postdoctoral fellows, and faculty-staff members. Students and fellows must be majoring in astronomy and faculty-staff must be employed in an astronomy department at any accredited educational research institution or observatory. The award is intended to assist individuals to visit institutions abroad. Proposed trip must last at least 3 months to allow time to interact with the host institution and for benefits to astronomy. Send a self-addressed, stamped envelope for information. Deadline: none specified.

1428. (SS)
International Business Machines Corporation (IBM)
ATTN: Manager, University and Scientific Relations
Thomas J. Watson Research Center
P.O. Box 218
Yorktown Heights, NY 10598
(914) 945–3000
http://www.ibm.com

Numerous scholarships of $10,000 to minority or female graduate students majoring in chemistry, computer science, engineering (electrical and mechanical), mathematics, information science, material science, physical science, or physics. Departments where students are studying receive $2,000. Selection of recipients is made in consultation with university graduate departments in each field. Request applications from departments. Deadline: varies by school.

(S)
International Chiropractors Association (ICA)
1110 North Glebe Road, Suite 1000
Arlington, VA 22201
(800) 423–4690
http://www.chiropractic.org

1429. (S)
Scholarships

Awards of varying amounts to graduate and undergraduate students who are student members of ICA and pursuing chiropractic medicine. Number and amount of award are determined on an individual basis. Based on academic achievement and service. Awards are good at schools with ICA chapters. Deadline: spring.

1430. (S)
Women's Auxiliary (WAICA) Scholarships

Scholarships of varying amounts to graduate and undergraduate students who are student members of ICA and pursuing chiropractic medicine. Number and amount of awards are determined on an individual basis. Based on academic achievement and service. Awards are good at schools with ICA chapters. Deadline: spring.

1431. (S)
International Desalination Association
IDA Scholarships
P.O. Box 387
Topsfield, MA 01983
(978) 887–0410
http://www.ida.bm

Scholarship of $6,000 for graduate students majoring in a desalination field. Must have been in the upper 5% of their undergraduate class. Award supports graduate study and research in desalination and water reuse. Based on academic record, career goals, and financial need. For information, contact above address or: Dr. Shigeki Toyama, Professor of Chemical Engineering, Nagoya University, Furo-Cho, Chikusa-ku, Nagoya 464–01, Japan. Deadline: varies.

1432. (SS)
International Federation of University Women
ATTN: Fellowships Committee
8 rue de l'Ancien-Port
CH-1201 Geneva, Switzerland
(41.22) 731–23–80
http://www.ifuw.org

20 to 30 fellowships and grants ranging from $2,500 to $10,000 (may be in the form of pounds sterling, Canadian dollars, or Swiss francs) to women graduates for advanced research, study, and training. The awards are intended to help finance short-term graduate and postgraduate study and research and training projects and to serve as complementary funds for longer programs. Applicants must be well started on the research program to which the application refers. Fellowships are intended to cover at least 8 months of work and should be taken up within 9 months of the date of award. They are not normally given for a master's or for the first year of a doctoral program. The competitions are held every 2 years. The next competition will offer fellowships and grants for the 2004–2005 academic year.

1433. (SS)
International Food Service Executives Association
Worthy Goal Scholarships
836 San Bruno Avenue
Henderson, NV 89015
(702) 564–0997
http://www.ifsea.com

Varying numbers of scholarships of $500 and a limited number of $1,000 to full-time graduate and undergraduate students pursuing a career in commercial food service training. Applicants must submit a transcript, letter of enrollment from the college, and 3 letters of recommendation (at least 1 from an employer). Based on financial need, academic achievement, and professional intentions. Visit their web site or write to get an application. Deadline: February 1.

1434. (S, SS)
International Foundation of Employee Benefit Plans
Graduate Research Grants
ATTN: Director of Research
18700 West Bluemound Road, Box 69
Brookfield, WI 53008-0069
(414) 786–6710
http://www.ifebp.org

5 to 7 awards of up to $10,000 to postdoctoral students to conduct research on issues within employee benefits or labor studies, such as health care, retirement, income security, and related areas. Students may have majored in health sciences, business, economics, finance, labor or industrial relations, law, or social sciences. Must be U.S. citizens and include a proposal of up to 20 pages on proposed research project, curriculum vitae, and 2 letters of recommendation (1 must be from thesis/dissertation advisor). Deadline: none.

1435. (A)
International Furnishings and Design Association—Editorial Foundation
IFDA Student Design Competition
World Headquarters
191 Clarksville Road
Princeton Junction, NJ 08550
(609) 799–3423
http://www.ifda.com
ifda@ifda.com

3 awards of $2,000 and 1 award of $3,500 to graduate or second-, third-, or fourth-year undergraduate design students. First-place winner's school receives a $2,000 grant and each runner-up's school receives $1,000. Design competition categories change each year. Based on storage/living space innovations, creativity of design, practicality, aesthetic value, and adherence to requirements. Deadline: March 1.

International In-flight Food Service Association Foundation
5775 Peachtree-Dunwoody Road
Building G, Suite 500
Atlanta, GA 30342
(404) 252–3663
http://www.ifsanet.com/ifsafoundation.html

1436. (SS)
Jenny Poole Scholarship Award

Up to 2 scholarships of $5,000 to graduate and undergraduate students pursuing careers in hospitality programs, specializing in onboard food service/catering. Selection is based on academic achievement and goals. Award can be used to cover tuition, books, living expenses, and associated costs. Must be employed by a company that holds current IFSA membership, be employed by an airline or catering company whose primary business is in onboard services, have at least 2 years experience in the onboard food service industry, provide 2 letters of recommendation, and be able to pursue study within the full calendar year following acceptance of award. For more information or an application, visit web site. Deadline: mid-February.

1437. (SS)
J.J. O'Neill Leadership Development Award

An award of up to $25,000 to individuals to either attend a graduate program to work on a master's degree in business administration or to attend the Executive Education Level course in Leadership Management. Must be employed by a company that holds current IFSA membership, be employed by an airline or catering company whose primary business is in onboard services, have at least 2 years' experience in the onboard food service industry, provide 2 letters of recommendation, and be able to pursue study within the full calendar year following acceptance of award. Award can be used to cover tuition, books, living expenses, and associated costs. For more information or an application, visit web site. Deadline: mid-February.

1438. (S)
International Lead Zinc Research Organization Inc.
Fellowship Program
P.O. Box 12036
2525 Meridian Parkway
Research Triangle Park, NC 27709–2036
(919) 361–4647
written inquiries only
http://www.ilzro.org

Varying number of fellowships, ranging from $15,000 to $25,000, to doctoral and postdoctoral fellows who are conducting research involving lead, zinc, and cadmium compounds in ceramics, chemistry, metallurgy, electrochemistry, and environmental health. Deadline: May.

1439. (S)
International Order of Alhambra
Scholarship Fund and Endowment Fund
Scholarship Committee Chairperson
4200 Leeds Avenue
Baltimore, MD 21229
(410) 242–0660
http://www.orderalhambra.org

1 grant of $400 per quarter (renewable up to 4 quarters, for a total of $1,600) to graduate or upper-level undergraduate students. Must be majoring in a field involving the handicapped and retarded. Applicants should send a short résumé, stating year in college and the courses they are pursuing. Must be U.S. citizen. Graduate scholarships are available for students in Canada, California, or Virginia. Deadline: none.

(H, S)
International Order of the King's Daughters/Sons
Health Careers Director
P.O. Box 1017
Chautauqua, NY 14722–1017
written contact only
http://www.iokds.org/index.html

1440. (S)
Health Careers Scholarships

20 to 30 scholarships ranging from $500 to $1,000 for graduate and upper-level undergraduate students.

Must be studying in a health field, such as medicine, dentistry, nursing, physical therapy, occupational therapy, and medical technologies. R.N. applicants must be in the second year of their program and B.A. candidates in at least the third year. Medical and dental students must be in the second year of medical and dental school respectively. Undergraduates who are pre-med majors are not eligible. Must be a U.S. or Canadian citizen and attending an accredited 4-year U.S. or Canadian institution. Must enclose a self-addressed, stamped envelope with application requests. Deadline: April 1.

1441. (H)
International Order of the King's Daughters/Sons
Students Ministry Scholarship Department
http://www.rts.edu/info/finance03.cfm#found2

Scholarships ranging up to $1,000 to full-time graduate students who are studying for a Master of Divinity degree, preferably with the purpose of becoming ministers of an organized congregation. Applicants must have a B average or better for all graduate and undergraduate work and must attend a school or seminary accredited by the Association of Theological Schools in the United States or Canada. Application requests are accepted January 1 through March 31 only, must be made by the applicant himself or herself, and must include the following: self-addressed, stamped business envelope, name of institution that has accepted you, anticipated graduation date, and how you found out about this scholarship. For more information, visit web site. Send requests to: Students Ministry Scholarship Department, Mrs. Thomas A. Rich, Jr., 3520 Wilmot Avenue, Columbia, SC 29205. Deadline: April 30.

1442. (A)
International Showcase II
Slowinski Gallery, SC
215 Mulberry Street
New York, NY 10012
http://users.aol.com/slowart/artist.htm
slowart@aol.com

A first prize of $1,000 in the Annual International Soho group exhibition held in September. Open to all media. For prospectus, print form from Internet at above web site or e-mail address or send a self-addressed, stamped envelope. Deadline: May 30.

1443. (S)
International Society for Optical Engineering (SPIE)
Scholarships and Grants
ATTN: Scholarship Committee Chair
P.O. Box 10
Bellingham, WA 98227–0010
(360) 676–3290
http://www.spie.org

Numerous scholarships ranging from $500 to $5,000 to graduate or undergraduate students who are pursuing careers in optical or optoelectronic applied science and engineering. May be attending a 2- or 4-year college or university. For more information, send a self-addressed, stamped envelope or visit the web site. Deadline: April 1.

1444. (S)
International Society of Arboriculture
Research Trust
P.O. Box 3129
Champaign, IL 61826–3129
(217) 355–9411
http://www.ag.uiuc.edu/~isa

Scholarships of $2,500 to graduate students in horticulture, botany, entomology, phytopathology, or physiology. Must be pursuing careers as horticulturists, plant pathologists, plant physiologists, entomologists, soil specialists, and others engaging in the scientific study of shade trees. Individuals must submit proposals for possible research study. Send a self-addressed, stamped envelope for guidelines. Deadline: November 1.

(S)
International Society of Women Airline Pilots
2250-E Tropicana Avenue
Suite 19–395
Las Vegas, NV 89119–6594
http://www.iswap.org

1445. (S)
Fiorenze De Bernardi Merit Award

Scholarships ranging from $500 to $1,500 to female students who are pursuing careers as airline pilots and have at least 350 hours of flight experience. Selection based on financial need, career goal, work experience, and recommendations. Interview is required. Deadline: April 1.

1446. (S)
International Aviation Career Scholarship

1 scholarship of $1,200 to a female pilot with a commercial license and at least 250 hours flight time who is pursuing a career as an airline pilot. Deadline: varies.

1447. (S)
International Union for Vacuum Science
Welch Foundation Research Scholarships
Secretary General
7 Mohawk Crescent
Nepean, Ontario K2H 7G7
Canada
(613) 829–5790
http://www.iuvsta.org

Scholarships of $12,500 (U.S.) to a graduate student pursuing a career in vacuum science. Award is for students proposing research in a foreign lab in which they haven't studied. Research should contribute to the study of vacuum science techniques or their application in any field. Deadline: April 15.

1448. (S)
International Women's Fishing Association
Graduate Scholarships
P.O. Box 3125
1295 North Lake Way
Palm Beach, FL 33480
http://www.iwfa.org

Scholarships of up to $3,000 to female graduate students majoring in marine science. Must be attending an accredited U.S. institution. Based on aptitude, ability, character, need, academic achievement, and recommendations. Write an introductory letter briefly detailing your goals and include a self-addressed, stamped envelope. Deadline: March 1.

1449. (S)
Iota Sigma Pi Award Program
Gladys Anderson Emerson Scholarship
4200 East University Boulevard
Middleton, OH 45042–3497
(513) 727–3372
http://chem-faculty.ucsd.edu

1 scholarship of $1,000 to a female graduate or upper-level undergraduate student majoring in chemistry or biochemistry. Can be used at any accredited college or university and student need not be a member of Iota Sigma Pi. Based on academic achievement. Visit web site for contact information. Deadline: January 1.

1450. (S)
Iowa Nurses Association
Executive Nurse Fellowships
1501 42nd Street, Suite 471
West Des Moines, IA 50266
(515) 225–0495
http://www.iowanurses.org
info@iowanurses.org

20 fellowships of $15,000 to nurses in senior executive rolls in health services, public health, and nursing education. The 3-year fellowships are designed for fellows to remain in their current positions. Award supports self-selected learning activities, independent study, and access to an electronic communications network. The program provides matching funds of up to $15,000 each year during the first 2 years to support the required comprehensive leadership project. Deadline: January 31.

1451. (A)
Islip Art Museum
50 Irish Lane
East Islip, NY 11730
(631) 224–5402
http://www.islipartmuseum.org

Artist fees ranging from $500 to $800 to artists to participate in the Museum's Project Space. Artists are invited to submit proposals for visual art projects, such as large-scale works, mixed media installations, performances, and electronic media installations (video, audio, projection). Proposals will be reviewed by a panel of artists and museum staff. A limited amount of funds is available for artists fees only. Artists fees may vary and will be determined by the panel, after a review of each proposal. Must be 18 years old or older and a New York State resident. Interested artists may call the Museum or write for further guidelines. The project is held during early spring and held during the summer months. Deadline: sometime in April.

1452. (S)

Jackson Laboratory
Summer Student Program
600 Main Street
Bar Harbor, ME 04609
(207) 288–6000
http://www.jax.org

Scholarships of up to $1,500 to cover the cost of room and board during the 9-week internships open to graduate, medical, veterinary, or undergraduate students, or high school juniors. Interns participate in an existing research program on mammalian genetics. Students must live at Highseas, located on the East Coast adjoining Acadia National Park. Selection is based on interest, written statement for applying, recommendations, scientific ability and curiosity, and academic achievement. Other than partial- to full-room and board scholarship, no compensation is provided. Deadline: February 28 (college level) and March 31 (high school juniors).

1453. (A, Contest)

Jacksonville University Biannual Playwriting Contest
ATTN: Director
College of Fine Arts
Department of Theatre Arts
Jacksonville, FL 32211
(904) 744–3950
http://www.ju.edu

Top cash award of $1,000 to playwrights for best original, unproduced, full-length or one-act play or musical. The award is presented at the premier production. This is a cash award and not a scholarship. Applications are only available in September of odd-numbered years. For rules send a self-addressed, stamped envelope after September 1 of odd-numbered years. Deadline: varies.

1454. (S)

James F. Lincoln Arc Welding Foundation Awards Program
ATTN: Secretary
P.O. Box 17188
Cleveland, OH 44117–1199
http://www.weldingawards.com

12 graduate scholarships and 17 undergraduate scholarships of up to $2,000 for students of engineering and technology who solve design engineering or fabrication problems involving the knowledge or application of arc welding. Send a self-addressed, stamped envelope for more information. Deadline: June 15.

1455. (A)

James Harrison Steedman Memorial Fellowship in Architecture
Steedman Governing Committee
Washington University in St. Louis
School of Architecture
One Brookings Drive
Campus Box 1079
St. Louis, MO 63130
(314) 935–6293
http://www.cooper.edu/admin/career_services/
fellowships/steed.html
steedman@arch.wustl.edu

Award of $20,000 to an individual who received a professional architectural degree within the last 8 years and who has at least 1 year of experience in an architect's office. Award is for travel and study abroad. Only awarded in even-numbered years. There is a $50 application fee. Deadline: late January.

1456. (A, H, SS, Contest)

Jane Austen Society of North America Essay Contest
Aurise Eaton
106 Barlow's Run
Williamsburg, VA 23188
(800) 836–3911
http://www.jasna.org
javaahe@aol.com

6 awards of at least $500 to high school, undergraduate, and graduate students. Applicants must write an essay of 1,200 to 2,000 words on one of the topics listed on the web site. Essay should contain personal, original insight into Jane Austen's artistry, ideas, and values. Deadline: May 1

1457. (S)

Jane Coffin Childs Memorial Fund for Medical Research
Postdoctoral Fellowships
Administrative Director
333 Cedar Street, LW 300-SHM

New Haven, CT 06510
(203) 785–4612
http://www.jccfund.org

20 to 25 fellowships providing from $22,000 to $24,000, plus allowances, to postdoctoral (M.D., Ph.D., or equivalent) fellows to conduct cancer research. U.S. citizens may use the fellowship in a U.S. or foreign institution. Foreign citizens must use the fellowship in U.S. only. Preference is given to individuals 30 years or younger. Renewable. Deadline: February 1.

(A, H, S, SS)
Japanese American Citizens League (JACL)
National Headquarters
1255 Post Street, Suite 727
San Francisco, CA 94109
(415) 345–1075
(415) 345–1077
http://www.jacl.org

1458. (A, H, S, SS)
Abe & Ester Hagiwara Student Aid Award

Scholarships of varying amounts to graduate and undergraduate students, or graduating high school seniors, for all areas of study. May be used at a trade school, business school, college, or university. Must be JACL members, their children, or any American citizen of Japanese ancestry. Request applications and additional information from local JACL Chapters or regional offices, or send self-addressed, stamped envelope to the above address. Must be U.S. citizen or legal resident. Must submit FAFSA form as proof of financial need. Deadline: March 1.

1459. (A, H, S, SS)
Graduate Scholarships

7 scholarships of varying amounts to graduate students accepted to or enrolled in an accredited graduate school. Open to all areas of study. Must be JACL members, their children, or any American citizen of Japanese ancestry. Must be U.S. citizen or legal resident. Send a self-addressed, stamped envelope for information. Deadline: April 1.

1460. (A, H, S, SS)
Japan Foundation
Doctoral Fellowships
152 West 57th Street, 39th Floor
New York, NY 10019
(212) 489–0299
http://www.cgp.org/jfny

Fellowships providing a stipend of approximately 210,000 yen per month plus 100,000 yen for housing to doctoral candidates to conduct dissertation research in Japan. For any area of study pertaining to Japan. Student must have completed all course work. Must be proficient in Japanese language. Fellowships range from 4 to 14 months. Must be a U.S. citizen or legal resident. Deadline: November 1.

1461. (A, H, S, SS)
Jesse Marvin Unruh Assembly
Fellowship Program
The Center for California Studies
California State University, Sacramento
6000 J Street
Sacramento, CA 95819–6081
(916) 278–6906
(800) 776–1761
http://www.csus.edu/calst/Programs/jesse_unruh.html

Fellowships providing a monthly stipend of at least $1,882, plus health, vision, and dental benefits, to graduate students in any field of study. Applicants must have completed either a B.S. or B.A. by the time the fellowship year begins in October. Recipients are awarded full-time employment with the California Assembly for 11 months. Must be California residents. Fellows earn a maximum of 12 graduate course credit hours. Deadline: February 26.

1462. (A, H)
Jewish Braille Institute of America
Scholarships
110 East 30th Street
New York, NY 10016
(212) 889–2525
(800) 433–1531
http://www.jewishbraille.org

Scholarships of varying amounts to graduate students who are legally blind and are pursuing a career in Jewish service, such as a cantor, rabbi, or Jewish communal worker. Deadline: none specified.

1463. (A, H, S, SS)
Jewish Family & Children Services
Stanley Olson Youth Scholarship Fund
1710 Scott Street
San Francisco, CA 94115
(415) 359–3494
http://www.jfs.org

Scholarships of up to $2,500 to graduate and undergraduate students accepted to, or enrolled in, a college or university for all areas of study, with preference given to liberal arts majors. Award may be used for studies personal, business, or professional purposes. Must be Jewish students, under 25 years of age, and residents of San Francisco, San Mateo, Santa Clara, Marin, or Sonoma County, California. Based on academic achievement and financial need. Must be a U.S. citizen. Write a letter briefly detailing your educational and financial situation and include a self-addressed, stamped envelope. Deadline: none.

(H, S, SS,)
Jewish Federation of Metropolitan Chicago
Jewish Vocational Service
Scholarship Secretary
1 South Franklin Street
Chicago, IL 60606–4694
(312) 346–6700
http://www.juf.org

1464. (S)
Academic Scholarship Program for Studies in the Sciences

Scholarships of varying amounts to graduate and upper-level undergraduate students studying mathematics, engineering, or science. Must be residents of Chicago, IL, and Cook County. Selection based on academic achievement and financial aid. Deadline: March 1.

1465. (S, SS)
Levie Educational Fund Scholarship

60 to 80 renewable scholarships from $1,000 to $5,000 per year to graduate, professional school, or undergraduate students. Must be Jewish students living in the metropolitan area of Chicago and be Cook County residents. Must be majoring in medicine, nursing, social work, dentistry, or other "helping professions" and enrolled in or planning to enroll in a vocational or occupational school or a 2- or 4-year institution. Request applications after December 1. Deadline: March 1.

1466. (H, S, SS)
Scholarship Fund
http://www.jvschicago.org/scholarship

Awards of varying amounts to graduate students and upper-level undergraduates. Must have been born and raised in either Cook County, the Chicago metropolitan area, or northwest Indiana or prior to entering school have worked full-time in Cook County or the Chicago metropolitan area. Must intend to remain in the Chicago metropolitan area after completing school. May be entering a helping profession: medicine, education, Jewish communal service, the rabbinate, social service, law, or communications at the University of Illinois, Champaign-Urbana. Deadline: March 1.

1467. (A, H, S, SS)
Jewish Foundation for Education of Women
Scholarship
ATTN: Executive Director
135 East 64th Street
New York, NY 10021
(212) 288–3931
(212) 288–5798
http://www.jfew.org

Numerous scholarships ranging from $500 to $3,500 to female, full-time, graduate or professional school or undergraduate students in all areas of study. Must live within 50 miles of New York City, including New Jersey and Long Island. Must have financial need. Include a self-addressed, stamped envelope with application requests. Awarded on a nonsectarian basis. Deadline: January 31.

(A, H, S, SS)
Jewish Social Service Agency of Metropolitan Washington
6123 Montrose Road
Rockville, MD 20852

(301) 816–2630

http://www.jssa.org

1468. (A, H, S, SS)
David Korn Scholarship Fund

2 to 3 grants ranging from $1,000 to $2,000 to graduate and undergraduate students in any area of study. Must be a Jewish resident of the Washington, DC, metropolitan area, a U.S. citizen or working toward citizenship, and under age 30. Selection based on financial need. In the event the recipient doesn't complete a full year of school, the award becomes a loan and must be repaid. Deadline: February 28.

1469. (SS)
Hyman P. Moldover Scholarship for Communal Service

Awards of $5,000 to full-time graduate students in a Jewish communal service graduate program. Selection based on academic achievement, leadership, potential, and financial need. Must be a Jewish resident studying in the Washington, DC, metropolitan area, a U.S. citizen or working toward citizenship, and intending to work professionally in the Jewish community upon graduation. In the event the recipient doesn't complete a full year of school, the award becomes a loan and must be repaid. Deadline: February 28.

1470. (A, H, S, SS)
Irene Stambler Vocational Opportunities Grant Program

Varying number of grants of up to $2,000 to female, Jewish graduate and undergraduate students for all fields of study. Must be residents of the Washington, DC, metropolitan area who are seeking to improve their earning potential because of divorce, separation, or death of their spouse. Award may be used to complete an educational or vocational program or to start or expand a small business. Based on financial need. Must be a U.S. citizen or permanent resident seeking citizenship. Deadline: none.

1471. (A, H, S, SS)
Vocational Opportunities Grant Program

Varying number of grants of up to $2,000 to female, Jewish graduate and undergraduate students for all fields of study. Must be residents of the Washington, DC, metropolitan area who are seeking to improve their earning potential because of divorce, separation, or death of their spouse. Award may be used to complete an educational or vocational program or to start or expand a small business. Based on financial need. Must be a U.S. citizen or permanent resident seeking citizenship. Deadline: none.

1472. (S)
John Frederick Steinman Fund
Psychiatry Fellowships
8 West King Street

Lancaster, PA 17603

written inquiries only

http://www.sshechan.edu/Eberly/millersville02.htm

Fellowships of $3,500 to osteopathic or allopathic physicians. Must have either an M.D. or D.O. degree and wish to study for 2 more years in psychiatry. Selection based on academic record, qualifications, performance, and future promise. Must want to pursue a career as a trained psychiatrist, or be a psychiatrist who wishes to obtain a subspecialty in child psychiatry or other areas. Preference given to physicians who commit to practice in the Lancaster, PA, area. Deadline: February 1.

1473. (A, H, S, SS)
John Gyles Education Scholarships
P.O. Box 4808

712 Riverside Drive

Fredericton, New Brunswick E3B 5G4

Canada

(506) 459–7460

Several scholarships of up to $3,000 to graduate or undergraduate students in any area of study. Must be attending a 2- or 4-year accredited institution in either the U.S. or Canada. Must maintain at least a 2.75 GPA. Must be a citizen of either the U.S. or Canada. Deadline: various dates.

1474. (S)
Johns Hopkins University School of Medicine
Minority Summer Internship Program (MSIP)
Graduate Student Affairs

725 N Wolfe Street

Hunterian G-1

Baltimore, MD 21205

(410) 614–3385
http://www.hopkinsmedicine.org/
graduateprograms/msip.cfm

10-week summer internships providing a $2,500 stipend and housing to underrepresented minority and economically disadvantaged students who will be applying to medical school. Program will provide a research experience similar to that of a first-year graduate student. Applicants should be prepared for long days and short weekends. Deadline: February 1.

1475. (A, H, S, SS)
John Simon Guggenheim Memorial Foundation
90 Park Avenue
New York, NY 10016
(212) 687–4470
http://www.gf.org
fellowships@gf.org

The Foundation offers fellowships (averaging $26,500) to further the development of scholars and artists by assisting them to engage in research in any field of knowledge and creation in any of the arts, under the freest possible conditions and irrespective of race, color, or creed. Fellowships are awarded to men and women who have already demonstrated exceptional capacity for productive scholarship and exceptional creative ability in the arts. This is a very competitive fellowship. In 2003, there were 3,282 applicants and only 184 fellowships. Applications must be requested in writing. Deadline: varies by country.

1476. (S)
Joseph Collins Foundation
Joseph Collins Grants
153 East 53rd Street
New York, NY 10022
written inquiries only

150 renewable grants of $3,000 to graduate students interested in specializing in general practice, neurology, or psychiatry. Students must live within 200 miles of the school they will attend. Applicants must be studying at a U.S.-accredited medical school. Applications must be submitted through the medical school. Deadline: March 1.

1477. (A)
Joseph H. Bearns Prize in Music
Department of Music
703 Dodge Hall
Columbia University
New York, NY 10027
(212) 854–3825
http://www.columbia.edu

Awards of $2,500 and $3,500 to composers who are between 18 and 25 years of age. 2 categories of competition: $3,500 for larger composition forms and $2,500 for smaller composition forms. Applicants may submit only 1 entry and be U.S. citizens. Deadline: February 1 of odd-numbered years.

1478. (A, H, S, SS)
Junior League of Northern Virginia
Scholarships
7921 Jones Branch Drive, #320
McLean, VA 22102
(703) 893–0258
http://www.jlnv.org

8 to 10 awards ranging from $500 to $2,000 to female graduate or undergraduate students who have been accepted to or enrolled in an accredited institution. Open to all fields of study. Must be over 23 years of age, residents of Northern Virginia, U.S. citizens, and have financial need. Deadline: December 1.

1479. (S)
Juvenile Diabetes Foundation International
Summer Student Program
ATTN: Grant Administrator
120 Wall Street
New York, NY 10005–4001
(212) 785–9500
(800) 533–CURE
http://www.jdf.org

Stipends of up to $2,500 to graduate, medical school, or undergraduate students for an 8-week summer research internship to do research work in diabetes at an accredited research institution. Funds are sent directly to the institution. Send a self-addressed, stamped envelope for information on which institutions you may apply to. Deadline: October 15.

1480. (A)
Kala Institute
Fellowship Awards
1060 Heinz Avenue
Berkeley, CA 94710
(510) 549–2978
http://www.kala.org

5 to 8 awards of $2,000 to artists who have produced innovative work in printmaking or digital, sound, or video arts and have a keen interest in expanding their technical repertoire through access to Kala's printmaking, photo-process, letterpress, computer, and video editing equipment. Artists with experience combining computer graphics with techniques such as lithography, intaglio, relief printing, and book arts are encouraged to apply. The fellowship does not include housing. Award does include 6 consecutive months of free residency at Kala Art Institute, 24/7 access to Kala's printmaking workshop and electronic media center, and exhibition of artwork created during the residency in a group show at the Kala Gallery. Applicants will be judged on conceptual creativity, originality, and artistic excellence as well as technical familiarity with traditional printmaking and/or digital media. Deadline: May 3 (postmark).

(A, H, S, SS)
Kappa Kappa Gamma
530 East Town Street
Columbus, OH 43216
(614) 228-6515
http://www.kappakappagamma.org
kkghq@kappa.org

1481. (A, H, S, SS)
Graduate Scholarships

Scholarships to any member pursuing a graduate degree on a full-time basis. Open to any field of study. For more information, contact local chapter or visit web site. Deadline: none specified.

1482. (A, H, S, SS)
Rose McGill Fund/Circle Key Grant

Grants of varying amounts to alumna members who wish to pursue part-time educational programs related to career opportunities. Open to any field of study. For more information, contact local chapter or visit web site. Deadline: none specified.

1483. (A, H, S, SS)
Kappa Kappa Gamma Foundation of Canada
Graduate Scholarship for Canadian Women
Attn: Scholarship Committee
615 Mt. Pleasant Road, Suite 142
Toronto, Ontario M4S 3C5
http://kappakappagamma.org/found.htm

Scholarship of $3,000 to a female student in a doctoral program. Must be a Canadian citizen. For specific information and an application, visit their web site. Deadline: January 31.

1484. (S)
Kathleen S. Anderson Award
Manomet Center for Conservation Sciences
P.O. Box 1770
Manomet, MA 02345
(508) 224–6521
http://www.nmnh.si.edu/BIRDNET/Grants/
anderson.html

1 or 2 research awards of $1,000 to graduate or veterinary students or undergraduate students majoring in animal science, biology, or veterinary science. Awards are made to assist research projects involving the ecological and behavioral activities of birds. Preference is given to projects relevant to bird conservation. Selection is based on application, essay, and recommendations. Must submit 2 copies of proposal with budget and references. Award is not renewable. Deadline: December 1.

1485. (A, H, S, SS)
Kathryn M. Whitten Trust
Farmers & Merchants Company of Long Beach
P.O. Box 891
Long Beach, CA 90801
(562) 437–0011

25 scholarships of varying amounts totaling $20,000 to graduate, professional school, or undergraduate students or graduating high school seniors for use in any area of study. No major strings attached. Must be residents of the Long Beach, CA, area. Write a letter briefly detailing your educational and financial situation and include a self-addressed, stamped envelope. Deadline: none specified.

1486. (A, H, S, SS)
Kellogg National Fellowship Program
W. K. Kellogg Foundation
One Michigan Avenue East
Battle Creek, MI 49017
(269) 968–1611
http://www.wkkf.org

50 grants of $30,000 to doctoral candidates in the early years of their careers. May be used for all fields, but preference is given to agriculture, business, education, health, and leadership. The purpose is to foster the development of effective and broad leadership skills and abilities in the U.S. Renewable for up to 3 years. Deadline: none specified.

1487. (A)
Kennedy Center for the Performing Arts
Alliance for Art Education Network
Internships
2700 F Street, N.W.
Washington, DC 20566
(202) 416–8000
http://www.kennedy-center.org

20 12- to 16-week internships (summer, fall, winter/spring) providing $800 per month to teachers of the arts, graduate students, recent college graduates, and undergraduates. Internships are open to students from all majors. Positions are available in Advertising, Alliance for Arts Education, Kennedy Center American College Theater Festival, Community Outreach, Cultural Diversity Affairs, Development, Education Administration, Events for Teachers, Government Liaison, Marketing, National Symphony Orchestra, Performance Plus, Press Office, Programming, Public Relations, Special Events, Subscriptions, and Theater for Young People. Internships in the American College Theatre Festival and the Press Office offer the unique ability to meet big-name festival judges (such as casting directors from Paramount Studios and heads of daytime casting for ABC). Deadline: March 1, June 1, and November 1.

(A)
Kennedy Center for the Performing Arts
American College Theatre Festival
2700 F Street, N.W.
Washington, DC 20566
(202) 416–8000
http://www.kcactf.org

1488. (A)
Barbizon Awards for Theatrical Design Excellence

Awards to graduate or undergraduate students based on the quality, effectiveness, originality, and excellence in rendering techniques. Any full-length production entered in KCACTF that has one or more of the visual elements designed by a bona fide student enrolled at the participating institution will be adjudicated for design excellence. Deadline: none specified.

1489. (A)
CSU Summer Arts Scholarships

4 full-tuition scholarships to talented graduate or undergraduate students selected through the SCETA Auditions and the KCACTF. Each scholarship recipient will be able to select their own classes from those being offered during Summer Arts Program at California State University. Deadline: none specified.

1490. (A)
David Mark Cohen National Playwriting Award

A cash award of $1,000 to a working playwright whose original script is produced by a college or university theater program. Award also includes possible publication by Dramatic Publishing, Inc., and up to $500 to defer travel and expenses to attend a script-in-hand reading at the annual August conference of the Association for Theatre in Higher Education. Presented in an effort to promote the writing and production of new plays while honoring and perpetuating the memory of David Mark Cohen. Deadline: none specified.

1491. (A)
Embassy Communications Playwriting Award

1 award of $10,940 to a graduate or undergraduate student who has written the best comedy play. The student must write a teleplay for one of Embassy Communications' television series. Write an introductory letter briefly detailing your educational and financial situation and professional goals. Deadline: December 20.

1492. (A)
Festival Acting Awards

Up to 6 graduate or undergraduate students who exemplify excellence in performance are selected from the productions presented at Festival of varying amounts. Deadline: none specified.

1493. (A)
Irene Ryan Acting Scholarships

16 scholarships of $250 and 2 scholarships of $2,500 to graduate and undergraduate students. Must be used for studying acting at any accredited U.S. institution. Selections are judged at the National Festival in Washington, DC. In addition, the student judged the Best Partner in the National Auditions is awarded a cash prize of $250. Deadline: none specified.

1494. (A)
Kate Drain Lawson Awards for Design Excellence

Awards of varying amounts to graduate or undergraduate students whose works have outstanding design merit as exhibited in the production when viewed at the original production. Adjudicators assess students' work on sight, removing the students' rendering and visual presentation abilities from the criteria. The Regional Awards take into consideration both excellence in production and the student's presentation quality. Eligibility may be for 1 or all awards in the following categories: Costume Design, Lighting Design, and Scene Design. A student may be eligible for one or both the KDL (Kate Drain Lawson) and the Regional award in the following categories: Audio Design, Makeup Design, and Property Design. Deadline: none specified.

1495. (A)
Mehron Make-Up Design Award

1 award of varying amount to an outstanding college student designer as well as national recognition and the opportunity to exhibit their work at the Kennedy Center. Mehron Inc. is a premier performance makeup company and emphasizes education theatre. Designs will be appraised on the basis of quality, effectiveness, originality, and creativity. Deadline: none specified.

1496. (A)
Michael Kanin Playwriting Awards Program

10 playwriting awards ranging from $500 to $10,940 to graduate and undergraduate students majoring in theater or drama. Awards go to student writers whose plays (drama, comedy, or musicals) are produced as part of the festival. Deadline: varies.

1497. (A)
National Critics Institute Scholarship

1 scholarship to an outstanding student to participate in the work-study program for professional theater critics and arts writers at the Eugene O'Neill Theatre Center in Waterford, CT, each summer. The national winner will attend the Eugene O'Neill Center during the national writing conference in July, working with leading professional newspaper and magazine critics from across the United States. All expenses will be paid. Deadline: none specified.

1498. (A)
National Ten-Minute Play Competition

1 award of varying amount for a student-written 10-minute script from Region VIII will be selected to participate in the National 10-Minute Play Festival, cast from the Ryan Finalists at the Kennedy Center during the KCACTF National Festival in April, and performed as a staged reading at that festival.

1499. (A)
Outstanding Ensemble

1 award of varying amount to a graduate or undergraduate theater major. 6 regional finalists are selected from KCACTF Region VIII Associate or Participating entries. Each regional finalist will be interviewed at the festival by a panel of regional judges, and one national finalist will be selected from each region. One of the national finalists will be selected to stage-manage the KCACTF National 10-Minute Play Festival in April.

1500. (A)
Outstanding Student Assistant Director

An award of varying amount to the winner of the regional competition. Student will be selected to represent Region VIII at the KCACTF National Festival in April. Deadline: none specified.

1501. (A)
Outstanding Student Director Award

An award of varying amount to the winner of the regional competition. Student director will be selected to represent Region VIII at the KCACTF National Festival in April to participate as an assistant director in the National 10-Minute Play Festival.

1502. (A)
Outstanding Student Stage Manager Award

1 award of varying amount to the winner of the regional competition. Student will be selected to represent Region VIII at the KCACTF National Festival in April. Deadline: none specified.

1503. (A)
Regional Festival Setup Award

1 award will be given to the college or university at the Regional Festival that displays the highest standards of theater professionalism in setup and strike of their production. Deadline: none specified.

1504. (A)
Short Play Publication Award

1 award for a 1 student-written short play. The play will be selected for publication in an annual collection of KCACTF short plays published by Dramatic Publishing, Inc. Write an introductory letter including professional goals. Deadline: varies.

1505. (A, SS)
Kennedy Center for the Performing Arts
Vilar Institute for Arts Management
Fellowships
Washington, DC 20566
(202) 872–0466
http://www.kennedy-center.org

Fellows receive a stipend of $18,000 (paid bimonthly) to graduate students and recent graduates. All courses, materials, health insurance, and attendance at selected performances and other educational events at the Kennedy Center are provided as part of the fellowship. Housing during the fellowship is the responsibility of the individual. The U.S. Department of State will provide transportation to and from Washington, DC, for international fellows only. A minimum of a bachelor's degree in the arts or a related discipline and at least 2 years of professional administration experience working with a performing arts organization, or more than 5 years experience performing with a professional arts company (theater, dance, music), is required. Deadline: April 1.

1506. (S)
Kinsey Institute for Research in Sex, Gender, & Reproduction
Dissertation Awards
Indiana University
Morrison 303
Bloomington, IN 47405
(812) 855–7686
http://www.kinseyinstitute.org

Awards of $1,000 to the best unpublished dissertation in the area of sex, gender, and reproduction, completed and submitted to an accredited institution between January 1 and December 31 of the year prior to deadline date. Winner will be invited to visit the Institute and discuss his/her work. Travel expenses will be provided. Deadline: March 1.

1507. (A, H, S, SS)
Knights of Vartan-Etchmiadzin Lodge
Scholarships
Scholarship Committee Chair
36 E. 31st Street, 9th Floor
New York, NY 10016
barsamrug@yahoo.com

Scholarships of $1,000 to graduate and undergraduate students in any field of study. Must be of Armenian descent, U.S. citizens, and a resident of Queens, Nassau, or Suffolk County. Students who are sons and daughters of members in good standing are eligible for an additional $1,000 award. Deadline: mid-May.

1508. (H)
Koahnic Broadcast Corporation Training Center
818 East 9th Avenue
Anchorage, AK 99501
(907) 258–8880
http://www.knba.org

4 year-long internships providing $24,960 and benefits to graduate and undergraduate students to work with KNBA and national radio programs in Anchorage. For specific information and deadline, visit web site.

(A, H, S, SS)
Korean American Scholarship Foundation
1952 Gallows Road, Suite 340 B
Vienna, VA 22182
(703) 748–5935
http://www.kasf.org
national@kasf.org

1509. (A, H, S, SS)
Chair Scholarships

Scholarships of $1,000 to full-time graduate or undergraduate students. Some scholarships are restricted to academic majors; others are not. Selection based on academic achievement, extracurricular activities, letters of recommendation, and essay. Visit web site to find more information and the region where to submit application. Deadline: June 5.

1510. (A, H, S, SS)
Designated Scholarships

Scholarships of $1,000 or more to full-time graduate or undergraduate students. Some scholarships are restricted to academic majors; others are not. Selection based on academic achievement, extracurricular activities, letters of recommendation, and essay. Visit web site to find more information and the region where to submit application. Deadline: June 5.

1511. (A, H, S, SS)
General Scholarships

Scholarships ranging from $1,000 to $2,000 to full-time graduate or undergraduate students. Some scholarships are restricted to academic majors; others are not. Selection based on academic achievement, extracurricular activities, letters of recommendation, and essay. Visit web site to find more information and the region where to submit application. Deadline: June 5.

1512. (A, H, S, SS)
Korean Heritage Scholarship Foundation Scholarship
William P. Min
Attorney at Law
3435 Wilshire Boulevard, Suite 2150
Los Angeles, CA 90010
(213) 386–0535
http://www.koreanheritage.org
info@koreanheritage.org

35 scholarships of $1,000 to full-time graduate or undergraduate students. Open to 1) a child of Korean-Americans who sustained property damage, personal injury, and/or monetary loss in the 1992 Los Angeles riot, 2) minority students, including Korean-Americans, in the greater Los Angeles area, 3) children of peace officers or firefighters in the Greater Los Angeles area, or 4) students from the Republic of Korea studying in the U.S. Visit web site for more information and an application. Deadline: February 28.

(A, H, S, SS)
Kosciusko County Community Foundation, Inc.
102 East Market Street
Warsaw, IN 46580
(574) 267–1901
http://www.kcfoundation.org

1513. (A, H, S, SS)
Ben Bibler Body for Life Memorial Scholarship Fund

Scholarships of varying amounts to graduate or undergraduate students or high school seniors. Must be a resident of Kosciusko County, IN, have graduated from a high school or have an equivalent of a high school diploma such as a GED, demonstrate a good work ethic, be currently employed and be of good character, and have participated in community service through church, service organizations, or youth group activities at least 2 hours per week. Selection is not based on financial need, but applicants should be willing to contribute to their education through employment. Deadline: April 1.

1514. (A, H, S, SS)
Chauncey L. Griffith Educational Fund

Scholarships of varying amounts to graduate or undergraduate students or graduating high school seniors for use in any field of study. Must be a resident of Kosciusko County, IN, have graduated from a high school located in Kosciusko County, IN, and be in the upper 25% of their high school or college class. Must be under 25 years of age. Deadline: April 1.

1515. (S)
Deborah M. Cooley Memorial Scholarship

Scholarships of varying amounts to graduate and undergraduate students pursuing careers in nursing, physical therapy, radiology, medical technology, or pharmacy. Must be a resident of Kosciusko County, IN, at the time of application for this scholarship. Must show financial need. Deadline: April 1.

1516. (A, H, S, SS)
Dorothy L. Mills "Living-Learning-Loving" Scholarship Fund

Scholarships of varying amounts to graduate and undergraduate students in any area of study. Must be a nontraditional student, typically a student who is over the age of 20 who has not followed a traditional educational path. Must be a resident of Kosciusko, Wabash, Miami, or Blackford County, IN. An essay on an assigned topic is required. Deadline: July 15.

1517. (H, S)
Dr. Harold Mason Memorial Scholarship

Scholarships of varying amounts to graduate and undergraduate students and graduating high school seniors pursuing a career in the medical field or foreign missionary service. Selection based on academic achievement, goals, essay, and financial need. Must be a resident of Kosciusko County, IN, and must have graduated from Lakeland Christian Academy. Deadline: April 1.

1518. (A, H, S, SS)
Edward B. and Mary Edith Funk Educational Endowment

Scholarships of varying amounts to graduate or undergraduate students or high school seniors pursuing any field of study. Must be a resident in Kosciusko County, IN. Selection will be based on academic achievement, participation in sports and community service, and financial need. Deadline: April 1.

1519. (A)
Elmer E. Ostrom Scholarship

Scholarships of varying amounts to graduate and undergraduate students and graduating high school seniors who are majoring in music and pursuing a career as a church organist. Preference is given to students studying 1) to be an organist in a Lutheran church, 2) to be a church organist, 3) to be an organist, 4) a course of study in music. Selection based on

academic achievement, recommendations, goals, and financial need. Deadline: April 1.

1520. (S)
Everett and Ethel Vandermark Scholarship Fund

Scholarships of varying amounts to graduate or undergraduate students or high school seniors pursuing a career in a medical profession. Open to residents of Kosciusko County, IN, who have graduated from a public high school which is physically located in Kosciusko County, IN. Selection based on academic achievement and financial need. Deadline: April 1.

1521. (SS)
Fleda C. Vandeveer Educational Endowment Scholarship

Scholarships of varying amounts to graduate or undergraduate students or high school seniors in any area of study. Order of preference is given to students who 1) were or are residents of Milford, IN, and intend to become a teacher in the educational system; 2) were or are residents of Milford, IN, and pursuing an education in areas or fields related to education; 3) were or are residents of Milford, IN, pursuing an education in areas or fields unrelated to education; 4) were or are residents of Kosciusko County, IN, and intend to become a teacher in the educational system; 5) were or are residents of Kosciusko County, IN, and pursuing an education in areas or fields related to education; and 6) were or are residents of Kosciusko County, IN, pursuing an education in areas or fields unrelated to education. Selection based on academic achievement and financial need. Deadline: April 1.

1522. (A, H, S, SS)
Gasaway Education Fund Scholarship

Scholarships of varying amounts to graduate or undergraduate students or high school seniors in any area of study. Must be a resident of Kosciusko County, IN, or have graduated from a high school located in Kosciusko County, IN. Selection based on academic achievement and financial need. Deadline: April 1.

1523. (A, H, S, SS)
George and Gertrude Schiff Charitable Endowment Scholarship Fund

Scholarships of varying amounts to graduate and undergraduate nontraditional students who have not attended a school of higher learning within the 2 years prior to application. Renewable with a B average. Deadline: July 15.

1524. (S)
June Reed Memorial-Kosciusko County Nurses Society Scholarship Fund

Scholarships of varying amounts to graduate and undergraduate students and graduating high school seniors pursuing a career in nursing. Selection based on academic achievement, goals, essay, and financial need. Must be a resident of Kosciusko County, IN. Deadline: April 1.

1525. (S)
The K21 Foundation Medical Scholarship Funds

Scholarships of varying amounts to graduate or undergraduate students or graduating high school seniors. Must be a resident of Kosciusko County, IN, or be employed in a health care field in Kosciusko County, IN. Must be a part-time or full-time student pursuing a degree in a health-related field. Selection based on career goals, financial need, and academic achievement. Renewable with a C average. Deadline: April 1.

1526. (A, H, S, SS)
Mary Elsbury Memorial Scholarship

Scholarships ranging from $16 to $300 to graduate and undergraduate students. Preference is given in the following order: 1) to nontraditional students who graduated from the Warsaw Community School system or its successor, who are over the age of 25, and who are seeking advanced education for the first time or to continue past advanced education that has been interrupted for more than 1 year; 2) to nontraditional students who graduated from a school other than the Warsaw Community School system or its successor, who are over the age of 25, and are seeking advanced education for the first time or to continue past advanced education that has been interrupted for more than 1 year; 3) to students who graduated from the Warsaw Community School system or its successor and who are under the age of 25; and 4) to students who graduated from a school other than the Warsaw Community School system or its successor and who are under the age of 25. Deadline: July 15.

1527. (A, H, S, SS)
Mary (Leedy) Hand Memorial Scholarship Endowment

Scholarships of up to $1,000 to graduate and undergraduate students in any field of study. Preference is given in the following order: 1) to students over 25 years of age who are seeking advanced education for the first time or to continue after 1 or more years' interruption and who are members of Winona Lake Free Methodist Church; 2) to students pursuing advanced education directly after high school who are members of a Kosciusko County church other than the Winona Lake Free Methodist Church; and 3) any Kosciusko County resident. Deadline: July 15.

1528. (A, H, S, SS)
Pete and Fay Thorn Education Fund Scholarship

Scholarships of varying amounts to graduate and undergraduate students for study in any field. Must be a resident of Kosciusko County, IN, and have graduated from a high school serving Kosciusko County, IN, be under 25 years of age with a financial need, and plan to attend an accredited college or university. Must show evidence of financial need and a scholastic record indicative of a successful college career. Deadline: April 1.

1529. (SS)
Priscilla and George Bowser Educational Endowment

Scholarships of varying amounts to graduate, professional, or undergraduate students who are pursuing a degree in higher education as a teacher or in the study of law through Harvard University, Indiana University, and/or Purdue University (and their satellite campuses). Must be a resident of Kosciusko County, IN, and have graduated from a high school providing education for Kosciusko County, IN, residents. Must be or have been a resident for 5 or more years, attending any combination of a grade school, middle school, and/or high school providing education for Kosciusko County, IN. Deadline: none specified.

1530. (A, H, S, SS)
Ralph and Lucetta Frantz Scholarship

Scholarships of varying amounts to graduate and undergraduate students for study in any field. Must be residents of, and have graduated from a high school serving, Kosciusko County, IN. Must show evidence of financial need and a scholastic record indicative of a successful college career. Deadline: April 1.

1531. (A, H, S, SS)
The Ringle Educational Trust Scholarship

Scholarships of varying amounts to graduate and undergraduate students for study in any field. Must have been a resident of Kosciusko County, IN, at the time of his or her graduation from high school. Must show evidence of financial need and a scholastic record indicative of a successful college career. Must be an active member of any religious faith who has been accepted at an accredited college or university. Selection based on academic achievement, involvement in school, church, and community, letters of recommendation, goals, and financial need. Deadline: April 1.

1532. (A, H, S, SS)
Robert and Lenny Nichols Scholarship

Scholarships of varying amounts to graduate and undergraduate students pursuing a career in music or pharmacy. Must be a resident of Kosciusko County, IN. Must have graduated from Warsaw Community High School and have attended Madison Elementary School a minimum of 2 years, excluding kindergarten. Selection based on academic achievement, involvement in school, church, and community, letters of recommendation, goals, and financial need. Deadline: April 1.

1533. (A, S)
Robert and Susan Brennan Scholarship

Scholarships of varying amounts to graduate and undergraduate students pursuing a career in music or pharmacy. Must be a resident of Kosciusko County, IN, and must have graduated from Warsaw Community High School. Applicant must have participated in school and/or community activities through high school career. Must maintain high academic standards. Renewable with reapplication. Deadline: April 1.

1534. (A, H, S, SS)
Robert T. and Emma Gilliam Memorial Fund Scholarship/Loan

Scholarships of varying amounts to graduate or undergraduate students or high school seniors pursuing

any field of study. Must have graduated from Warsaw Community High School and attend, or plan to enroll in, an Indiana college, university, or vocational or trade school. Selection based on financial need and recommendation letters. Deadline: April 1.

1535. (S)
Ruth Ladd Memorial Scholarship

Scholarships of varying amounts to graduate and undergraduate students and graduating high school seniors who are pursuing a career in health care services. Selection based on academic achievement, goals, essay, and financial need. Must be a resident of Kosciusko County, IN. Deadline: April 1.

1536. (S)
Seth V. Lewis Scholarship

Scholarships of varying amounts to graduate and undergraduate students and graduating high school seniors who are seeking training and education necessary to become licensed by the State of Indiana as nurses and in any other medical or medically related field. Selection based on academic achievement, goals, essay, and financial need. Must be a resident of Kosciusko County, IN. Deadline: April 1.

1537. (A, H, S, SS)
Thomas R. and Anne Marie Walter Educational Trust

Scholarships of varying amounts to graduate and undergraduate students and graduating high school seniors who are pursuing any area of study. Selection based on academic achievement, goals, essay, and financial need. Must be a resident of Kosciusko County, IN, at the time of high school graduation. Must be actively pursuing education in such a manner as to achieve a timely graduation. Deadline: April 1.

1538. (A, H, S, SS)
Wilson-Rhodes Memorial Scholarship Fund

Scholarships of varying amounts to graduate and undergraduate students and graduating high school seniors in any field of study and enrolled in, or attending, Indiana University at Bloomington. Order of preference is given to students who 1) are graduating high school seniors or graduates of Wawasee High School; 2) are graduating high school seniors or graduates of any other secondary school located in the Wawasee Community School District; 3) graduating high school seniors or graduates of any secondary school located in Kosciusko County, IN. Selection based on academic achievement, goals, essay, and financial need. Must be a resident of Kosciusko County, IN. Deadline: April 1.

(A, H, S, SS)
Kosciuszko Foundation
15 East 65th Street
New York, NY 10021
(212) 734–2130
http://www.kosciuszkofoundation.org

1539. (A, H)
General Fellowships, Scholarships, and Prizes

Various fellowships, scholarships, and prizes of varying amounts for research and study on matters related to Polish history, for study in Poland, and for performance of Polish music. Write an introductory letter briefly describing your educational and financial situation. Deadline: varies.

1540. (A, H, S, SS)
Grants to Polish Citizens for Study in the U.S.

Various grants providing stipends of varying amounts to graduate students for any area of study. Must be Polish citizens living in Poland and wish to study in the U.S. Must hold a master's degree and have an excellent command of English. Stipend covers housing, living costs, accident insurance, and if necessary, round-trip transportation. Write an introductory letter briefly describing your educational and financial situation. Contact New York or Warsaw office. Warsaw address: ul. Nowy Swiat 4, Room 118, 00–497 Warszawa. Deadline: October 15.

1541. (A)
Music Competitions

Scholarships from $1,000 to $2,500 to graduate and (2) undergraduate students. 2 scholarships for piano and for piano and violin are open to talented youth who have not yet reached advanced levels in college. Applicant must be prepared to perform in auditions at the Kosciuszko Foundation House in New York City in May or June. Deadline: March 31.

1542. (A, H, S, SS)
Tuition Scholarships

Numerous scholarships ranging from $500 to $1,000 to full-time graduate students of Polish descent to study in all fields of study. Also open to non-Polish U.S. citizens who are pursuing studies and/or research relating to Polish subjects. Must have at least a 3.0 GPA. Must be U.S. citizens or permanent residents. There is a nonrefundable $25 application fee for nonmembers of the Foundation. Deadline: January 15.

(SS)
KPMG Foundation
Three Chestnut Ridge Road
Montvale, NJ 07645–0435
(201) 307–7932
http://www.kpmgfoundation.org

1543. (SS)
Minority Doctoral Student Scholarships

Up to 15 scholarships of $10,000 to minority graduate doctoral students in accounting and information systems. Awarded to increase the completion rate among minority doctoral students. Awards are renewable for up to 5 years. Visit web site for more information. Deadline: May 1.

1544. (SS)
Ph.D. Project
http://www.phdproject.org

An information clearinghouse for minority graduate students interested in pursuing a doctoral degree in business in order to become a business school professor. The Project hosts an annual conference with invited attendees. Students must apply to be considered for inclusion in the Ph.D. Project. The Ph.D. Project pays all expenses for attendees from anywhere in the U.S. The aim is to match students with business school programs. Most programs will waive the student's tuition and fees and provide a stipend and/or research/teaching assistantships. This is not a scholarship program and does not offer any funding to doctoral students. Provides a network of peer support throughout the programs. Deadline: mid-September.

1545. (H, S, SS)
Kraft General Foods Corporate
University Relations
Three Lakes Drive
Northfield, IL 60093
(847) 646–2000
http://www.kraftfoods.com

100 to 150 12-week summer internships providing salaries ranging from $800 to $900 per week for graduate students and from $400 to $600 per week to undergraduates. Open to students with majors in engineering (chemical, mechanical, industrial, electrical, etc.), information systems, food science, biology, chemistry, microbiology, biochemistry, accounting, finance, human resources, or liberal arts (for business areas). Internships are conducted in Glenview, IL, Northfield, IL, White Plains, NY, and Tarrytown, NY. Interns at Kraft USA may work in beverages, desserts, dinners and enhancers, Post cereals, and Maxwell House Coffee; at Kraft General Foods USA may conduct research in any KGF product; and at Corporate Headquarters, as well as all other locations, in corporate affairs, sales, finance, and human resources. Deadline: March 31.

(A)
Kurt Weill Foundation for Music
7 East 20th Street
New York, NY 10003
(212) 505–5240
http://www.kwf.org

1546. (A)
Dissertation Fellowships

Fellowships and travel grants of varying amounts to doctoral candidates in music. Award supports dissertation research on Kurt Weill and his music and travel anywhere in the world to study primary documents. Grants are also available to fund productions and performances of Kurt Weill's music. Deadline: November 1.

1547. (A)
Research and Travel Grants

Awards of varying amounts to graduate students to support specific research expenses. Must be researching a topic related to Kurt Weill and/or Lotte Lenya and submit a detailed outline of the proposed project. Travel grants should be requested to reimburse reasonable travel expenses to locations of primary source material. Deadline: none specified.

1548. (A, S, SS)
Laban/Bartenieff Institute of Movement Studies
Work-Study Program
520 8th Avenue, Suite 304
New York, NY 10018
(212) 643–8888
http://www.limsoline.org

Work-study awards ranging from $500 to $1,500 to graduate students and professionals in areas of human movement studies (dance, education, health fields, behavioral sciences, fitness, athletic training, etc.). The award is only for work-study at the Laban/Bartenieff Institute in the Laban Movement studies certificate program. Deadline: May 1.

1549. (SS)
Lake County Public Defender's Office
Internships
15 S. County Street
Waukegan, IL 60085
(847) 377–3360
http://www.co.lake.il.us/pubdef/contact.asp

Internships for law, graduate, and undergraduate students to work in the Public Defender's Office. Senior law students who qualify for a license under Supreme Court Rule 711 may try cases under the supervision of a licensed attorney. Law student interns assist in case management, client relations, and courtroom work. Internships are also available in Investigations Division. Deadline: none specified.

1550. (S)
Lalor Foundation
Postdoctoral Grants
77 Summer Street, 8th Floor
Boston, MA 02110–1006
(617) 426–7172
http://www.lalorfound.org

10 to 15 grants of $20,000 to postdoctoral fellows to conduct research in mammalian reproductive physiology, childbearing, sterilization, and/or prevention or

termination of pregnancy. Renewable for 1 more year. Deadline: January 15.

1551. (SS)
Lambda Alpha International
Land Economics Foundation Graduate Scholarship
710 East Ogden Avenue, Suite 600
Naperville, IL 60563–8614
(630) 579–3284
http://www.lai.org
LAI@lai.org

1 scholarship of $3,000 to a graduate student majoring in land economics, architecture, law, geography, urban planning, landscape architecture, environmental planning, civil engineering, government, public administration, real estate, or urban studies. Must be enrolled in an accredited institution in a university in the United States, Canada, or Great Britain. For information, visit their web site. Deadline: February 28 (postmark).

1552. (A, S)
Landscape Architecture Foundation
Scholarships & Internships
818 18th Street, N.W.
Washington, DC 20006
(202) 331–7070
http://www.laprofession.org

Awards of $1,000, and internships providing scholarships of $2,000, to graduate and undergraduate students to recognize innovative horticultural research or design relating to landscape architecture. Selection based on ability and financial need. Send a self-addressed, stamped envelope for information. Deadline: early May.

1553. (SS)
La Raza Lawyers
P.O. Box 30
San Jose, CA 95103
http://www.larazalawyers-santaclara.com
larazalawyers@yahoo.com

Scholarships of $1,000 to Hispanic law students. Must attend law school in the Bay Area or be residents of Santa Clara County. Selection is based on academic achievement, recommendation letters, and financial aid. Visit web site for more information. Deadline: August 1.

1554. (S, SS)
The Leadership Alliance
Postbaccalaureate Research Education Program
15 Sayles
Box 1963
Providence, RI 02912
(401) 863–7994
http://www.theleadershipalliance.org

Grants providing a salary of $21,000 per year to participants with a bachelor's degree in a biomedical or behavioral science (received within prior 36 months). Participants work as apprentice scientists in a preceptor's laboratory to strengthen research skills and competitiveness when pursuing a graduate degree. Grants are made to domestic, private, and public universities or research institutions with graduate programs in the biomedical or behavioral sciences. Selected individuals must intend to apply for graduate school within 2 years of completing PREP. Visit web site for more information. Deadline: mid-December.

(SS)
Leakey Foundation
P.O. Box 29346
1002A O'Reilly Avenue
San Francisco, CA 94129–0346
(415) 561–4646
http://www.leakeyfoundation.org
grants@leakeyfoundation.org

1555. (SS)
Franklin Mosher Baldwin Fellowships

Fellowships of up to $12,000 to graduate students in an area of study related to human origins research. Must be a citizen of an African country and pursuing a master's, doctorate, or equivalent degree. Award may be used for tuition, travel, living expenses, fees, insurance, books, and other relevant expenditures. Deadline: February 15.

1556. (SS)
General Research Grants

Awards ranging from $3,000 to $12,000 (doctoral) and up to $20,000 to postdoctoral students and senior scientists for expenses directly related to research projects. Doctoral students must have completed all degree requirements other than their dissertation and postdoctoral and senior scientists must hold a doctorate or equivalent in anthropology or a related discipline. Visit web site for types of projects supported. Deadline: January 5 (spring) and August 15 (fall).

(A)
Leeway Foundation
123 South Broad Street, Suite 2040
Philadelphia, PA 19109
http://www.leeway.org

1557. (A)
Award for Achievement

1 award of $20,000 to an individual woman artist, arts program or arts organization, focusing on the Greater Philadelphia region, in order to help them achieve personal and community transformation. Visit web site for more information. Deadline: none specified.

1558. (A)
Award for Excellence

1 award of $30,000 to an individual woman artist, arts program or arts organization, focusing on the Greater Philadelphia region, in order to help them achieve personal and community transformation. Visit web site for more information. Deadline: none specified.

1559. (A)
Bessie Berman Award

An award of $35,000 to a woman artist age 50 years or older to recognize and assist in the advancement of mature, dedicated, outstanding women artists 50 years or older. The annual Bessie Berman Award is awarded in the same discipline as the other Leeway Foundation grants for that year. Artists at all stages of development are encouraged to apply. Deadline: none specified.

1560. (A)
Edna Andrade Award

An award of $15,000 to emerging women artists who are current residents of Bucks, Chester, Delaware, Montgomery, or Philadelphia County, PA; must be 20 years of age or older and have a commitment from a recognized institution, organization, or mentor for a specific date or dates. Open to all fields, including

the performing, literary, and visual arts, as well as mixed-media and community-based arts projects. Grants may support exceptional chances for advanced study with a significant mentor (not degree-related), travel associated with an imminent, concrete opportunity (book tour, artist's exhibition, commission, performance, residency, etc.), and rental of equipment, purchase of materials, or other expenses needed for an arts project (e.g., an exhibition or performance). Deadline: none specified.

1561. (A)
Inspiration Award

1 award of $7,500 to an emerging women artist who is a current resident of Bucks, Chester, Delaware, Montgomery, or Philadelphia County, PA; is 20 years of age or older and has a commitment from a recognized institution, organization, or mentor for a specific date or dates. Open to all fields, including the performing, literary, and visual arts, as well as mixed-media and community-based arts projects. Grants may support exceptional chances for advanced study with a significant mentor (not degree-related), travel associated with an imminent, concrete opportunity (book tour, artist's exhibition, commission, performance, residency, etc.), and rental of equipment, purchase of materials, or other expenses needed for an arts project (e.g., an exhibition or performance). Deadline: none specified.

1562. (A)
Seedling Award

1 award of $2,500 to an emerging woman artist who is a current resident of Bucks, Chester, Delaware, Montgomery, or Philadelphia County, PA; must be 20 years of age or older and have a commitment from a recognized institution, organization, or mentor for a specific date or dates. Open to all fields, including the performing, literary, and visual arts, as well as mixed-media and community-based arts projects. Grants may support exceptional chances for advanced study with a significant mentor (not degree-related), travel associated with an imminent, concrete opportunity (book tour, artist's exhibition, commission, performance, residency, etc.), and rental of equipment, purchase of materials, or other expenses needed for an arts project (e.g., an exhibition or performance). Deadline: none specified.

1563. (A)
Window of Opportunity Grants

Grants of up to $2,000 to women artists who are current residents of Bucks, Chester, Delaware, Montgomery, or Philadelphia County, PA; must be 20 years of age or older and have a commitment from a recognized institution, organization, or mentor for a specific date or dates. These grants are open to women artists in all fields, including the performing, literary, and visual arts, as well as mixed-media and community-based arts projects. Grants may support exceptional chances for advanced study with a significant mentor (not degree-related), travel associated with an imminent, concrete opportunity (book tour, artist's exhibition, commission, performance, residency, etc.), and rental of equipment, purchase of materials, or other expenses needed for an arts project (e.g., an exhibition or performance). Must not have been a recipient of a Leeway Emerging or Established Artist Award in the past 2 years. Deadline: January 28, April 8, June 24, and November 4.

1564. (A, H, S, SS)
Legacy Scholarship Committee

An Uncommon Legacy Foundation, Inc.
P.O. Box 33727
Washington, DC 20033
(202) 265–1926
http://www.uncommonlegacy.org
info@uncommonlegacy.org

Awards of at least $2,500 to lesbian graduate and undergraduate students enrolled full-time at an accredited U.S. college or university. Consideration will include: academic performance (at least a 3.0 GPA on a 4.0 scale), honors, personal/financial hardship and, especially, service to the lesbian/gay/bisexual/transgender community. A written personal statement (1,000 words or less) that offers insights into her achievements and goals, and how these goals illustrate her lesbian leadership is required. Deadline: July 1.

(A, H, S, SS)
Leopold Schepp Foundation

551 Fifth Avenue, Suite 3000
New York, NY 10176
(212) 986–3078

1565. (A, H, S, SS)
Graduate Awards

Graduate students between ages 17 and 30 may apply for assistance for all areas of study (except medicine). For full-time study only at any accredited college or university. Based on academic achievement, financial need, and interview in New York. Request applications after June 1. Deadline: December 31.

1566. (A, H, S, SS)
Postdoctoral Awards

Awards of varying amounts to postdoctoral fellows to support independent study and research that will improve the general welfare of mankind. Inquire about availability of grants in chosen field of study. Must be U.S. citizen or legal resident. Deadline: December 31.

1567. (A)
Leslie T. Posey and Frances U. Posey Foundation

c/o Southeast Foundation
1800 Second Street, Suite 750
Sarasota, FL 34236
(941) 957–0442
http://www.selbyfdn.org

6 scholarships ranging from $1,000 to $4,000 to graduate students whose bachelor's degrees were in art, painting, or sculpture of the traditional kind. Applicants must be full-time students and maintain satisfactory progress. Deadline: March 1.

1568. (S)
Leukemia & Lymphoma Society
Awards

1311 Mamaroneck Avenue
White Plains, NY 10605
(914) 949–5213
(800) 955–4572
http://www.leukemia.org

Awards ranging from $22,500 to $40,000 per year, for up to 5 years, to postdoctoral (M.D.s, Ph.D.s, or equivalent degrees) fellows to conduct research on leukemia or allied diseases. Amount, type, and length of award is based on experience and training. Deadline: October 1.

1569. (A, H)
Library of Congress
Junior Fellows Program Coordinate
Collections Services
LM642
101 Independence Avenue
Washington, DC 20540–4000
(202) 707–5325
http://www.loc.gov

18 to 20 summer internships, providing a monthly stipend of $1,200, to graduate students, recent graduates, and junior and senior undergraduates to introduce them to the art of librarianship. Interns are assigned to geography and map, manuscript, music, prints and photographs, rare book and special collections, African and Middle Eastern, Asian, European, Hispanic, serial and government publications, and motion picture, broadcasting, and recorded sound. Interns prepare material for display presentation or for researchers' use. Applicants may come from any major, but the majority of interns major in history, American studies, languages, geography, and cartography. Deadline: March 1.

1570. (A, H, S, SS)
Lloyd D. Sweet Scholarship Foundation
Scholarships
Box 217
Chinook, MT 59523
(406) 357–3374
http://www.chinookmontana.com/Sweetscholar

Approximately 100 scholarships of varying amounts to graduates of Chinook High School in Chinook, MT. May be used for graduate or undergraduate study at any U.S.-accredited institution. May be used for any field of study. Deadline: March 2.

1571. (A)
Loren L. Zachary Society for the Performing Arts
Annual Opera Awards National Vocal
Competition
2250 Gloaming Way
Beverly Hills, CA 90210–1717
(213) 276–2731
http://www.sfbacnats.org/auditions.htm

10 awards of up to $20,000, plus travel expenses, in an annual vocal competition open to young (females 21–33 years, males 21–35 years) opera singers. Competition is geared toward finding employment in European opera houses. Applications are available in December. Send self-addressed, stamped envelope for application. Deadline: March 15.

1572. (Contest)
Louisiana Literature Prize for Poetry
ATTN: Contest Director
Box 792
Southeastern Louisiana University
Hammond, LA 70402
http://www.selu.edu/orgs/lalit/poetryprize.html

Contest for unpublished poetry. Contact Contest Director. Send a self-addressed, stamped envelope for rules. Must deal with some aspect of Louisiana. Deadline: April 15.

1573. (S)
Louisiana Student Financial Assistance
Commission
Rockefeller Scholarship
Office of Student Financial Assistance
P.O. Box 91202
Baton Rouge, LA 70821–9202
(800) 259–5626, ext. 1012
http://www.osfa.state.la.us

30 scholarships of $1,000 to graduate or undergraduate students majoring in forestry, wildlife, fisheries, or marine sciences at either Nicholls University, Louisiana Tech, LSU in Baton Rouge, McNeese University, Northeast University, Northwestern University, Southwestern, or University of New Orleans. Student must have at least a B average. Based on academic record, extracurricular activities, and Louisiana residency. Deadline: June 1.

(Contest)
L. Ron Hubbard's Contests
P. O. Box 1630
Los Angeles, CA 90078
http://www.writersofthefuture.com

1574. (Contest)
Illustrators of the Future Contest

3 awards of $500 each quarter and 1 yearly award of $4,000 to artists in the areas of fantasy art and science

fiction. 1 entry is considered 3 black-and-white works illustrating a science fiction or fantasy story with no recurring theme. Your entry may not have been previously published. Entries may be sent anytime; however, only 1 entry per quarter. Send photocopies only. Individual artists retain copyrights. Deadline: September 30, December 31, March 31, and June 30.

1575. (Contest)
Writers of the Future Contest

Awards of $500, $750, and $1,000 every quarter and 1 yearly award of $4,000 to unpublished fiction writers submitting original works of science fiction, fantasy, and horror with fantastic elements. Entries must be works of prose, up to 17,000 words in length. Will not consider poetry or works intended for children. Professional publication is deemed to be payment and at least 5,000 copies or 5,000 hits. Entries must be typewritten or a computer printout in black ink on white paper, double-spaced, with numbered pages. All other formats will be disqualified. Each entry must have a cover page with the title of the work, the author's name, address, and telephone number, and an approximate word count. Every subsequent page must carry the title and a page number, but the author's name must be deleted to facilitate fair judging. Only 1 submitted manuscript per quarter. Deadline: October 1, January 1, April 1, and July 1.

1576. (A)
LucasFilm
Human Resources—Intern Department
P.O. Box 2009
San Rafael, CA 94912
(415) 662–1999
http://www.lucasfilm.com/internships_top.html

15 to 20 internships ranging from 9 to 12 weeks during the summer, fall, and spring. Compensation of minimum wage is only provided during the summer internships. Open to graduate students who will be returning to school after the internship ends and to undergraduate juniors and seniors. Open to all majors. Program looks for students with professionalism and maturity. Applicants for the fall and spring internships must obtain a letter from their college verifying they will receive academic credit for the internship. Deadline: April 30 (summer), August 30 (winter).

(S)
Lucent Technologies
600 Mountain Avenue
Murray Hill, NJ 07974
http://www.bell-labs.com/fellowships/#CRFP

1577. (S)
Cooperative Research Fellowship Program

Fellowships providing full tuition and fees, a living stipend of $17,000, and conference travel expenses to minority graduate students working toward doctoral degrees in chemistry, communications science, engineering (chemical, computer science, electrical, and mechanical), information science, materials science, mathematics, operations research, physics, and statistics. Internships are offered during the summer at Bell Laboratories, where they gain firsthand research and development experience. Renewable for 4 years with satisfactory academic progress. Must be U.S. citizens or permanent residents. Deadline: early January.

1578. (S)
Graduate Research Program for Women

Fellowships providing full tuition and fees, a living stipend of $17,000, and conference travel expenses to female undergraduate seniors planning to attend graduate school and first-year graduate students. Applicants must intend to work or be working toward doctoral degrees in chemistry, communications science, engineering (chemical, computer science, electrical, and mechanical), information science, materials science, mathematics, operations research, physics, and statistics. Recipients also receive a $2,000 grant to support aspects of the recipient's professional development not normally covered by other awards (child care, personal computing equipment, software, and visits to other university research labs). Internships are offered during the summer at Bell Laboratories, where they gain firsthand research and development experience. Renewable for 4 years with satisfactory academic progress. Must be U.S. citizens or permanent residents. Deadline: early January.

1579. (S)

Lupus Foundation of America
Summer Fellowships for Research
1300 Piccard Drive, Suite 200
Rockville, MD 20850–4303
(310) 670–9292
http://www.lupus.org

Varying numbers of fellowships of up to $2,000, research grants of up to $15,000 as seed research monies, to graduate or medical students to conduct a summer research project on lupus erythematosus. Project must be sponsored and supervised by an established investigator. Applicants must submit an application form, a 5-page narrative of the research project, a proposed budget, lay-language abstract, biographical sketch, evidence of compliance with government regulations, a state of concurrent support from other sources, and a statement of support by a sponsor. Deadline: February 1.

1580. (S)

M.A. Cartland Shackford Medical Fellowships
Wellesley College
Secretary Graduate Fellowships
Center for Work & Service
Wellesley, MA 02481–8200
(617) 283–3525
http://www.wellesley.edu

Fellowships providing a stipend of up to $7,000 to females who have been accepted to an accredited medical school. Must have obtained a bachelor's degree from a U.S. institution and be a U.S. citizen or legal resident. Must want to practice general medicine, not psychiatry. Deadline: December 1.

1581. (S)

Maine Community Foundation
Downeast Feline Fund
245 Main Street
Ellsworth, ME 04605
(207) 667–9735
http://www.maine.cf.org

Varying number of scholarships of varying amounts to third- or fourth-year veterinary school students. Must be residents of Maine and attending a veterinary school in CT, ME, MA, NH, RI, or VT. Not renewable. Deadline: varies.

(S)

Maine Society of Land Surveyors
126 Western Avenue, PMB 211
Augusta, ME 04330
(207) 882–5200
http://www.msls.org

1582. (S)

Merit-Based Awards

1 or more scholarships of varying amounts to graduate students majoring in land surveying. Selection will be based on academic achievement, extracurricular activities, leadership, and goals. Recipient(s) is required to attend the Society's Annual Banquet and Meeting. Visit web site for more information and an application. Deadline: November 31.

1583. (S)

Research-Based Awards

1 or more scholarships of varying amount to graduate students to conduct a research project associated in some way with the land surveying profession. Recipient(s) is required to attend the Society's Annual Banquet and Meeting. Visit web site for more information and an application. Deadline: November 31.

1584. (A, H, S, SS)

Maryland Higher Education Commission
House of Delegates Scholarships
State Scholarship Administration
839 Bestgate Road, Suite 400
Annapolis, MD 21401
(410) 260–4500
http://www.mhec.state.md.us

Scholarships ranging from at least $200 to $1,700, providing full tuition and fees to students chosen by their delegate. Student must be a full-time student at the University of Maryland at College Park or any out-of-state institution if the academic major is not available in Maryland. Students cannot be General State Award recipients. May be used for graduate, professional school, or undergraduate study but will only pay undergraduate rates. Contact your District Delegate to the State Legislature or above address. Deadline: established by individual delegates.

1585. (S)

Maryland Society of Surveyors
Educational Trust
P.O. Box 686
College Park, MD 20741–0686
(800) 303–6770
http://www.marylandsurveyor.org

5 scholarships of $500 to graduate or undergraduate students pursuing a career as land surveyors. Award may only be used for tuition. Selection is based on academic activities, extracurricular activities, goals essay, references, and financial need. Visit web site for more information and an application. Deadline: August 1.

1586. (A, H, S, SS)

Maryland State Department of Education
House of Delegates Scholarships
State Scholarship Administration
16 Francis Street
Annapolis, MD 21401–1781
(410) 974–5370
http://www.msde.state.md.us
ssama:@mhec.state.md.us

Scholarships ranging from at least $200 to $1,700 providing full tuition and fees to students chosen by their delegate. Student must be a full-time student at the University of Maryland at College Park or any out-of-state institution if the academic major is not available in Maryland. Students cannot be General State Award recipients. May be used for graduate, professional school, or undergraduate study but will only pay undergraduate rates. Contact your District Delegate to the State Legislature or above address. Deadline: established by individual delegates.

1587. (A)

Mary Roberts Rinehart Fund
English Department
MSN 3E4
George Mason University
Fairfax, VA 22030–4444
(703) 323–2220
http://www.gmu.edu/departments/writing/rinehart.htm

2 grants of $2,500 to writers who need financial assistance not otherwise available to complete work defi-

nitely projected. Grants are awarded in 2 of 4 categories: fiction and poetry; and drama and nonfiction on an alternate basis. Applicants must submit unpublished work. Send a self-addressed, stamped envelope for guidelines. Deadline: November 1.

1588. (S)

Massachusetts Association of Land Surveyors and Civil Engineers
Engineering Center
One Walnut Street
Boston, MA 02108–3616
(617) 227–5551
http://www.engineers.org/malsce/malsce_scholarship.html
malsce@engineers.org

1 or more scholarships of varying amounts to graduate and undergraduate students majoring in surveying, civil or environmental engineering. Must be a Massachusetts resident enrolled full-time in an accredited U.S. institution. Selection based on academic achievement, extracurricular activities, and goals. Visit web site for contact person and deadline.

1589. (S)

Maternity Center Association
Hazel Corbin Grant
281 Park Avenue South, 5th Floor
New York, NY 10010
(212) 777–5000
http://www.maternity.org/mca

Awards providing a monthly stipend of varying amounts to nurse-midwifery students enrolled in an accredited school of midwifery. Must already be nurses and plan to practice nurse-midwifery in the U.S. for at least 1 year upon certification. Deadline: varies.

1590. (SS)

Maurice Amado Foundation
Research Fund in Sephardic Studies
Research Fund Coordinator
Center for Jewish Studies
302 Royce Hall, UCLA
Box 951485
Los Angeles, CA 90095–1404
(310) 825–5387

http://www.cjs.ucla.edu/Fellow/Amado_Fellowships.
htm
CJS@humnet.ucla.edu

Grants of up to $5,000 to graduate students, junior (tenure) or senior faculty to support research and writing leading to publication in the field of Sephardic studies. Open to faculty and graduate students worldwide who become UCLA visiting scholars in residence. Deadline: December 31.

1591. (S)
McLean Hospital
Attn: Director, Volunteer Services
115 Mill Street
Belmont, MA 02478–9106
(617) 855–2000
http://www.mcleanhospital.org

Varying number of internships lasting 3 months, with openings year-round, are open to graduate or professional school students and upper-level undergraduate students. Applicants should have an interest in a medical career, mental health, or mental health research, and should have strong interpersonal skills. Interns talk with patients and assist with activities in inpatient units, group residencies, or day treatment programs. Interns may also assist children and adolescent patients with schoolwork or assist staff in clinical or basic research. No monetary compensation is provided. Submit a letter detailing interests, an application form, résumé, and references. An interview is required. Deadline: open.

1592. (Contest)
Memphis State University
River City Writing Awards in Fiction
ATTN: Editor
Department of English
Memphis State University
Memphis, TN 38152
(901) 678–4591
http://www.people.memphis.edu/~rivercity/contests.
html

1 first prize of $2,000 and 1 second prize of $500 for unpublished short stories. Send a self-addressed, stamped envelope for rules and information. Deadline: early December.

1593. (A, H, SS)
Metro-Goldwyn-Mayer Studios, Inc.
Internship Coordinator
2500 Broadway Street
Santa Monica, CA 90404
(310) 449–3000
http://www.mgm.com/corp_career_internships.do

30 internships (no salary) in Santa Monica and New York are open to U.S. and Canadian graduate and undergraduate students. Internships in Canada provide a salary of $125 and are open to graduate students, college graduates, undergraduates, and high school graduates. Must have an interest in advertising, communications, film, journalism, or related fields. Interns work in Story & Development (New York and Los Angeles) and Publicity/Promotions. Internships range from 3 to 6 months and are conducted during the summer, fall, and spring. Deadline: rolling.

(A, H, SS)
Metropolitan Museum of Art
Secretary of Grants Committee
Office of Academic Programs
1000 Fifth Avenue off 82nd Street
New York, NY 10028
(212) 535–7710
http://www.metmuseum.org/education/studyander_
research.asp

1594. (A)
Andrew W. Mellon Art History Fellowships

Awards of $26,000 for senior fellows and $18,000 for predoctoral fellows, with an additional $2,500 for travel. Fellowships for senior scholars are also available for as short a term as 1 month. Must have received their doctorate or have completed substantial work toward it. Awards are provided to promising young scholars with research projects in art history related to the Museum's collections, as well as for visiting scholars from this country and abroad who can serve as advisors and make their expertise available to catalog and refine the collections. Deadline: November 9.

1595. (A, H)
Andrew W. Mellon Fellowships in Conservation

Stipends of $26,000 for 1 year for senior scholars, with an additional $3,000 for travel. Applicants should have reached an advanced level of experience or training. To provide training in one or more of the following departments: paintings, objects, paper, textile, and Asian art conservation, musical instruments, arms and armor, and The Costume Institute. Deadline: January 5.

1596. (A)
Chester Dale Fellowships

Predoctoral fellowships providing $15,000, plus $2,500 for travel expenses, and postdoctoral fellowships of $25,000 plus $2,500 for travel expenses to graduate, professional, and postdoctoral individuals in a field related to fine arts of the Western world. Preference given to U.S. citizens under 40 years of age. Award is for independent study at the Metropolitan Museum and ranges from 3 months to 1 year. Deadline: November 15.

1597. (A)
Classical Fellowship

A fellowship providing an $18,000 stipend, with an additional $3,000 for travel, to an outstanding graduate student who has been admitted to the doctoral program of a U.S. university and who has submitted an outline of a thesis dealing with either Greek or Roman art. The thesis outline must already have been accepted by the applicant's advisor at the time of application for the fellowship. Deadline: November 9.

1598. (A, H)
Internship in Educational Media

A 12-month internship providing an honorarium of $20,000 to graduate students in museum studies, design, instructional technology, or related fields who are interested in planning, creating, and producing publications for families, teachers, students, and the general museum public. The intern will acquire important skills in preparing materials for print, electronic, and video production. Strong computer skills are required. Interns work full-time from mid-June to late May and participate in the Summer Internship Program orientation. Deadline: January 25.

1599. (A, H)
Internship Program—Education Department

10 graduate and 22 undergraduate internships providing compensation of $2,500 for Met graduate students, $2,200 for Met undergraduates, and $2,000 for Cloister undergraduates in a summer internship program lasting from 9 to 10 weeks. Interns are assigned to administration, conservation, library, and curatorial departments (Arts of Africa, Oceania, and the Americas; American Art; Ancient Near Eastern Art; Arms and Armor; Asian Art; the Costume Institute; European Paintings; Greek and Roman Art; Islamic Art; Musical Instruments; Photographs; Prints and Illustrated Books; and 20th Century Art). The Cloisters is the Medieval Arts branch of the Met and offers a formal 9-week internship in European art of the Middle Ages. Applicants can contact The Cloisters at: Fort Tryon Park, New York, NY 10040, (212) 923–3700. Deadline: January 21 (Met undergraduates), January 28 (Met graduate students), and February 4 (Cloisters).

1600. (A)
Jane and Morgan Whitney Fellowships

Varying number of scholarships of $25,000 and $15,000, plus $2,500 travel allowance, to graduate students in fine arts. Awards are for study and research using the Museum's collections. Selected based on academic achievement and proposed research. Deadline: mid-November.

1601. (A, H)
J. Clawson Mills Scholarships

Varying numbers of scholarships of $25,000 and $15,000, plus $2,500 travel allowance to graduate students in fine arts. Awards are for study and research using the Museum's collections. Selection based on academic achievement and allows students the opportunity to undertake study and research related to their work in art history, archaeology, and art conservation, either at the Museum or abroad. Proposed projects should relate to the Museum's collection. Possible fields of research for art history candidates include Western art; Asian art; the arts of Africa, Oceania, and the Americas; antiquities; arms and armor; costumes; drawings; illuminated manuscripts; paintings; photographs; sculpture; and textiles. Some fellowships for travel abroad are also available for students whose projects involve firsthand examination of paintings in major European collections. Conservation fellows may work with paintings, textiles, musical instruments, costumes, paper (including photographs), or objects (including sculpture, metalwork, glass, ceramics, furniture, and archaeological objects). Applicants for the conservation fellowship should have reached an advanced level of experience or training. Deadline: November 2.

1602. (A, H)
Lifchez/Stronach Curatorial Internship

An internship providing an honorarium of $15,000 to a recent college graduate or a graduate student enrolled in an art history master's program who plans to pursue a career in this field. Applicant should have financial need or another disadvantage that might jeopardize such a career without this support. The intern is assigned to a curatorial department to work on projects appropriate to his or her academic background, professional skills, and career goals. Interns work full-time from mid-September to early June and may participate in the Summer Orientation Program. Deadline: January 25.

1603. (A, H, SS)
Norbert Schimmel Fellowship for Mediterranean Art and Archaeology

Awards of $18,000 in stipend, with an additional $3,000 for travel, for predoctoral fellows in the areas of history of art, classics, and archaeology. Preference will be given to a candidate who, in the opinion of the Grants Committee, would profit most from utilizing the resources of the Ancient Near Eastern Art or Greek and Roman Art Departments. Awarded to an outstanding graduate student who has been admitted to the doctoral program of a university in the United States and who has submitted an outline of a thesis dealing with ancient Near Eastern art and archaeology or with Greek or Roman art. Deadline: none specified.

1604. (A, H)
Polaire Weissman Fund Fellowships

Varying numbers of scholarships of $25,000 and $15,000, plus $2,500 travel allowance, to graduate students in fine arts and costume history. Awards

provide experience with costume history and conservation at the Metropolitan Museum. Preference given to students interested in museum careers and teaching careers. Deadline: November 15.

1605. (A, H)
Roswell L. Gilpatric Internship

10-week internships are awarded each summer to graduate students, recent college graduates, and current undergraduate juniors and seniors. Graduate students must have completed at least 1 year of graduate work in art history or an allied field. Graduate interns work on projects related to the Museum's collection or to a special exhibition, as well as in administrative areas; specific duties depend upon the needs of the departments to which interns are assigned. Undergraduate interns work on departmental projects throughout the Museum, give gallery talks, and work at the Information Desk in the Great Hall. Applicants for college internships should have a broad background in art history. Deadline: none specified.

1606. (A, H)
Six-Month Internships

6-month-long internships providing an honorarium of $10,000. Graduating college seniors, recent graduates, and graduate students in art history or allied fields are eligible for this program. Interns are placed in one of the Museum's departments, where they work on projects that suit their academic background, professional skills, and career goals. This program is intended to promote greater diversity in the national pool of future museum professionals. Your application essay should include some discussion of how you could further this goal. Interns work full-time from early June to early December and participate in the Summer Orientation Program. Deadline: January 25.

1607. (A)
Starr Fellowships in Asian Paintings Conservation

Fellowships provide training in the conservation and mounting of Asian paintings. This is not a tuition or financial aid program. Stipend amounts will vary depending on the availability of funds and circumstances. The duration of the grant is determined by annual review. No prior experience is expected or required. However, this intensive and comprehensive program is intended for a person who might pursue this field as a lifetime career. The department is concerned with the complete mounting, remounting, and conservation of hanging scrolls, handscrolls, folding screens, prints, albums, books, etc., in the Museum's collection. Deadline: none specified.

1608. (A)
Summer Graduate Internships

Varying numbers of 9-week summer internships providing $2,500 to graduate students in museum studies to obtain practical experience in various museum departments. Selected on basis of academic achievement and future career goals. Must have at least 1 year of museum studies and have a strong art history background. Deadline: late January.

1609. (A)
Theodore Rousseau Fellowships

Varying number of scholarships of $25,000 and $15,000, plus $2,500 travel allowance, to graduate students in fine arts for study in Europe. Awards are for firsthand examination of paintings in major European collections. Selected based on goal of becoming museum curators of painting. Deadline: mid-November.

1610. (A)
William Kelly Simpson Internship for Egyptian Art

Summer internships providing honorariums of $3,250 for graduate students and $3,000 for undergraduates. Internships are full-time from early June to mid-August, including 1 week of orientation for graduate interns and 2 weeks for college interns. Interns meet with museum professionals and take field trips to other institutions. Graduate students must have completed the course work for an M.A. degree in Egyptology or in art history with a main emphasis on ancient Egyptian art. The intern will work with the curatorial staff on projects related to the Museum's Egyptian collection or a special exhibition. Deadline: mid-January.

(A)
Metropolitan Opera
Lincoln Center
New York, NY 10023

(212) 870–4515
http://www.metopera.org

1611. (A)
Central Opera Service

Awards ranging from $100 to partial tuition of several thousand dollars to students with superior musical talent and potential. Students should order the *Career Guide for the Young American Singer* ($8 plus $1.75 for shipping and handling) to obtain a list of national and international competitions, special grants, apprentice programs, and hiring policies of various American opera companies. The Service only publishes the *Guide*. Deadline: varies by program.

1612. (A)
Lindemann Young Artist Development Program

Stipends of varying amounts to train and nurture graduate students and individuals with bachelor's or master's degrees through training and performance opportunities. Program also provides private voice lessons with approved teachers outside of the Met's staff. Must audition in the spring. Each singer must prepare 5 arias in their original language and key but will perform only 2—one chosen by the singer, and the other by the judges. Deadline: none specified.

1613. (A)
National Council Regional Award

1 to 5 awards ranging from $200 to $5,000 to graduate and undergraduate students majoring in music or vocal music. Applications must be requested at the District level. Call for contact person. Age limitation: 19–33 years. Applicants must audition. Renewable. Deadline: varies.

1614. (S)
Mexican American Physicians Association
9901 IH 10 West, Suite 800
San Antonio, TX 78230
(210) 558–2862
http://www.mapa-sa.org/scholarship.htm

Scholarships providing a set of new medical instruments (stethoscope, blood pressure cuff, etc.) to minority first-year medical students. Visit web site for more information. Deadline: none specified.

1615. (A, H, S, SS)
Michigan Commission on Indian Affairs
Michigan Department of Civil Rights
Tuition Waivers Program
741 N. Cedar Street, Suite 102
Lansing, MI 48909
(517) 373–0654
http://www.state.mi.us

Tuition waivers to graduate and undergraduate students who are Native North American Indians to attend state-supported public 2- or 4-year colleges or universities in any area of study. Must be a Michigan resident for at least 12 consecutive months and at least ¼ Native American Indian certified by the Michigan Commission on Indian Affairs. Deadline: 2 months prior to class registration.

1616. (A, H, S, SS)
Michigan Department of Education
Michigan Tuition Grants
608 West Allegan Street
Lansing, MI 48933
(517) 373–0760
(800) MGA–LOAN
http://www.mde.state.mi.us/money

Numerous renewable grants ranging from $100 to $1,900 to full-time undergraduate and graduate students in all fields of study. Must be Michigan residents and attending an independent nonprofit Michigan institution. Based on financial need. Renewable. Deadline: varies.

(S)
Michigan Dietetic Association Institute
4990 Northwind Drive, Suite 140
East Lansing, MI 48823–5031
(517) 351–8335
http://www.eatrightmich.org/home.asp

1617. (S)
Bernice Hagelshaw Scholarship

Scholarships of varying amounts to graduate and upper-level undergraduate students enrolled in an American Dietetic Association-accredited program in Michigan. Selection is based on academic achievement, leadership, and community activities. Must be planning to become an active member of the ADA and state dietetic association and a registered dietitian. Visit web site for additional eligibility criteria. Deadline: late March.

1618. (S)
Delphine Rutkowski Memorial Scholarship

Scholarships of varying amounts to graduate and upper-level undergraduate students enrolled in an American Dietetic Association-accredited program in Michigan. Must be enrolled in an ADA-approved didactic program. Must have demonstrated leadership in student dietetic association. Deadline: late March.

1619. (S)
Evelyn Mallison Scholarship

Scholarships of varying amounts to graduate and upper-level undergraduate students enrolled in, or admitted to, a Greater Detroit area Dietetic Internship, AP4, or Coordinated Program. Selection based on financial need. Visit web site for additional eligibility criteria. Deadline: late March.

1620. (S)
MDA Institute Advanced Degree Scholarship

Scholarships of varying amounts to graduate and upper-level undergraduate students enrolled in an American Dietetic Association-accredited program in Michigan. Selection is based on academic achievement, leadership, and community activities. Must be planning to become an active member of the ADA and state dietetic association and a registered dietitian. Visit web site for additional eligibility criteria. Deadline: late March.

1621. (S)
MDA Memorial Scholarship

Scholarships of varying amounts to graduate and upper-level undergraduate students enrolled in an American Dietetic Association-accredited program in Michigan. Selection is based on academic achievement, leadership, and community activities. Must be planning to become an active member of the ADA and state dietetic association and a registered dietitian. Visit web site for additional eligibility criteria. Deadline: late March.

1622. (S)

MDA Past Presidents' Scholarship

Scholarships of varying amounts to graduate and upper-level undergraduate students enrolled in an American Dietetic Association-accredited supervised practice program. Selection is based on academic achievement, leadership, and community activities. Visit web site for additional eligibility criteria. Deadline: late March.

1623. (S)

MI Dietetic Educators Practice Group Scholarship

Scholarships of varying amounts to graduate and upper-level undergraduate students enrolled in, or graduated from, an ADA-accredited/approved didactic program in Michigan. Must have been accepted to an ADA-accredited/approved supervised practice program (DI, CUP, AP4). Selection based on academic achievement and financial need. Scholarships of varying amounts to graduate and upper-level undergraduate students enrolled in an American Dietetic Association-accredited supervised practice program. Visit web site for additional eligibility criteria. Deadline: late March.

1624. (S)

Suzanne J. Bosserd Memorial Scholarship

Scholarships of varying amounts to graduate and upper-level undergraduate students majoring in dietetics and enrolled in an American Dietetic Association-accredited program in Michigan. Selection is based on academic achievement, leadership, and community activities. Must plan to enroll in an American Dietetic Association-accredited/approved Dietetic Internship, AP4, or Coordinated Program in Michigan. Deadline: late March.

1625. (S)

Tri-City Council for Dietetic Education Scholarship

Scholarships of varying amounts to graduate and upper-level undergraduate students enrolled in an American Dietetic Association-accredited program in Michigan. Must be currently enrolled in the Central Michigan University Dietetic Internship and reside in the Tri-City area and demonstrate financial need. Deadline: late March.

1626. (S)

Microsoft
ATTN: Scholarships
One Microsoft Way
Redmond, WA 98052–6399
(206) 882–8080
http://www.microsoft.com

Some scholarships of varying amounts to graduate and undergraduate students who are computer science majors. Scholarships are only at certain colleges and universities. Student must contact their school's financial aid or scholarship office and inquire whether their school participates in the Microsoft Scholarship Program. If Microsoft scholarships are offered, the student may inquire further. Those students whose schools don't participate should not contact Microsoft. Deadline: none specified.

(A, H, S, SS)

Midland Foundation
109 E. Main Street
P.O. Box 289
Midland, MI 48640–0289
(989) 839–9661
http://www.midlandfoundation.com
info@midlandfoundation.com

1627. (A, H, S, SS)

American Association of University Women, Midland Chapter

2 scholarships of up to $2,000 to female graduate and undergraduate students who have had a delay or interruption (at least 1 semester) in their education. Selection based on academic achievement, potential contribution to society, essay, and financial need. Must be a Midland County resident. Deadline: July 15.

1628. (S)

Crystal Graham Memorial Scholarship

1 scholarship of $1,000 to a graduate or undergraduate student pursuing a career in a health profession field. Preference will be given to students pursuing physical therapy, occupational therapy, speech therapy, physician's assistant, nursing, and medicine, in

that order. Selection based on academic achievement, personal and career goals, essay, and financial need. Must be a Midland County resident. Deadline: July 15.

1629. (S, SS)
Deborah Lynn Hawkins Special Educator Endowed Scholarship

1 award of $1,000 to a graduate or upper-level undergraduate pursuing a career in special education or occupational, physical, or speech therapy, but only if primary interest is working with special education students. Grade point average and financial need are not major considerations. The most important criterion is a strong desire to have a public school career working with severe special needs students. Must be a Midland County resident. Deadline: July 15.

1630. (S)
George E. Olson Memorial Scholarship

1 scholarship of $1,000 to a graduate or upper-level undergraduate student majoring in an earth science-related field (meteorology, geology, hydrology, ecology, forestry, etc.). Selection based on academic achievement, personal and career goals, essay, and financial need. Must be a Midland County resident. Deadline: July 15.

1631. (SS)
Jim Ayre Memorial Scholarship

1 or more scholarships of $500 to graduate or undergraduate students pursuing a degree in business or real estate. Must attend Delta College, Central Michigan University, Northwood University, or Western Michigan University. Selection based on academic achievement, personal and career goals, essay, and financial need. Must be a Midland County resident. Deadline: July 15.

1632. (A, SS)
Sarah Keishian Dergazarian Vocal Music Education Scholarship

1 scholarship of $500 to a graduate or upper-level undergraduate music education major. Selection based on academic achievement, personal and career goals, essay, and financial need. Must be a Midland County resident. Deadline: July 15.

1633. (S)
Stephen D. Redman, M.D., Memorial Scholarship

1 scholarship of $1,500 to a graduate, medical, or upper level undergraduate student majoring in a human health field. Must be attending or planning to attend medical school with the intention to practice primary care. Selection based on academic achievement (3.5 GPA or better on a 4.0 scale), personal and career goals, essay, and financial need. Must be a Midland County resident. Deadline: July 15.

1634. (S)
Turner Alfrey Jr. Memorial Scholarship

1 scholarship of $1,500 to a graduate or undergraduate sophomore, junior, or senior student pursuing a career in teaching or research in the fields of science or engineering. Preference will be given to the following fields: polymers, mechanical, or chemical engineering, mathematics, chemistry, or physics. Selection will be based on academic achievement and an essay. Must be a Midland County resident. Renewable with satisfactory academic progress. Deadline: July 15.

1635. (A)
Virginia A. (Nicholson) Dent Endowed Scholarship

1 scholarship of $1,500 to a graduate or undergraduate student who is a violin student. Selection based on academic achievement, goals, and financial need. Renewable with maintained academic progress. Must be a Midland County resident. Deadline: July 15.

1636. (H)
Military Chaplain Association
P.O. Box 7056
Arlington, VA 22207–7056
http://www.mca-usa.org/scholarshipapplication.pdf

Scholarships of varying amounts to seminary students intending to pursue a career as a military chaplain. Must be full-time students in an accredited seminary, currently approved and serving as a chaplain candidate in one of the armed forces. Deadline: none specified.

1637. (A, H)

Millay Colony for the Arts, Inc.

Residencies

454 East Hill Road

P.O. Box 3

Austerlitz, NY 12017

(518) 392–3103

http://www.millaycolony.org

The colony provides 60 residencies every year to writers, composers, and visual artists. The Pollock-Krasner Foundation reviews applications in terms of talent and financial need. Acceptance by either a colony or for financial support from the Foundation does not imply acceptance by the other. No cash award is made by the Colony. The award is the residency fee. Support from the Pollock, and Krasner Foundation includes costs beyond colony residency, including materials, shipping, and loss of income. Residencies are for 1 month, usually running from the first through the twenty-eighth of each month. Deadline: February 1 (for residencies in June through September), May 1 (for residencies in October through January), and September 1 (for residencies in February through May).

1638. (SS)

Miller Center of Public Affairs

Fellowship Program

2201 Old Ivy Road

P.O. Box 400406

Charlottesville, VA 22904–4406

(434) 924–4694

http://www.millercenter.virginia.edu/programs/apd/fellowship.html

Fellowships of up to $15,000 to graduate students to support 1 year of research and writing that focuses on important public policy questions, 20th-century politics, and governance in the U.S. May include areas in a broad range of disciplines, including research in history, political science, policy studies, law, political economy, and sociology. Selection based on scholarly quality and on potential to shed new light on important public policy questions. Deadline: February 1.

(S)

Minerology Society of America

1015 Eighteenth Street, N.W., Suite 601

Washington, DC 20036–5275

(202) 775–4344

http://www.minsocam.org

1639. (S)

MSA Grant for Research in Crystallography

1 award of $5,000 to a graduate student for research in crystallography. Selection is based on qualifications, quality, innovativeness, and scientific significance of research and the likelihood of success of the project. There are no restrictions on how the grant funds are used, as long as they are spent in research. The only restrictions are that the applicant be between 25 and 36 and cannot be an MSA Counsellor. Visit web site for more information. Deadline: June 1.

1640. (S)

MSA Grant for Research in Minerology and Petrology

1 award of $5,000 to a graduate student for research in minerology and petrology. Selection is based on qualifications, quality, innovativeness, and scientific significance of research and the likelihood of success of the project. There are no restrictions on how the grant funds are used, as long as they are spent in research. The only restriction is that the applicant be between 25 and 36. Visit web site for more information. Deadline: June 1.

1641. (A, H, S, SS)

Minnesota Chippewa Tribe

Scholarship Fund

Education Division

P.O. Box 217

Cass Lake, MN 56633

(218) 335–8581

http://www.mnchippewatribe.org

Approximately 850 scholarships of up to $3,000 to graduate or undergraduate students who are ¼ Native American Indian and enrolled members of the Minnesota Chippewa Tribe or eligible for enrollment. Open for any area of study. Student must have been accepted to college and applied for all available financial aid through the college. Based on financial need. Must be U.S. citizens. Deadline: June 1.

1642. (S)

Minnesota Society of Professional Surveyors

5301 South Park Drive

Savage, MN 55378

(800) 890–LAND

http://www.mnsurveyor.com

Scholarships of varying amounts to full-time graduate and undergraduate students in a surveying or mapping program. Must be Minnesota residents and enrolled in an MSPS-approved institution. Selection based on application, academic achievement, recommendation letters, and essay. Deadline: October 31 (postmark).

1643. (A)

Minnesota State Arts Board

Grants Program

400 Sibley Street, Suite 200

St. Paul, MN 55101–1928

(800) 8MN–ARTS

(651) 215–1600

http://www.arts.state.mn.us

Grants ranging from $1,000 to $10,000 or a special residency stipend to artists who are Minnesota residents. Awards are not for academic work but rather for career advancement. Artists may work in the fields of literature, music, theater, dance, or visual arts. Project assistance and fellowships are also available. Visual artists are eligible for a special residency in New York City. Deadline: September (visual arts), November (music and dance), February (literature and theater).

1644. (S)

Minority Medical Faculty Development Program

Robert Wood Johnson Foundation Fellowships

8601 Georgia Avenue, Suite 411

Silver Spring, MD 20910

(301) 565–4080

http://www.mmfdp.org

Up to 12 fellowships providing a stipend of $65,000 per year and $26,000 for research support to minority physicians. Must have completed, or be completing, formal clinical training and want to pursue an academic career. Must be U.S. citizens. Write for more information. Deadline: March 31.

(S)

Mississippi Dietetic Association

330 North Mart Plaza, Suite 2

Jackson, MS 39206

(601) 981–0740

http://www.eatrightmississippi.org

1645. (S)

Colgate-Palmolive Fellowship in Nutrition and Oral Heal/Dental Education

1 fellowship of $15,000 to a graduate student to support doctoral research in nutrition and oral health or dental education. Recipient must have a career in nutrition and dental/health professions education as short- and long-term goals. Deadline: April 30.

1646. (S)

International Awards

Awards of varying amounts to a professional foreign dietitian/nutritionist, preferably from a developing country, to enable him/her to attend a workshop or seminar or to participate in a continuing education or orientation project in the U.S. Priority is given to a qualified nutritionist/dietitian who had high financial need and a goal of applying the U.S. experience in his/her country. Deadline: May 30.

1647. (S)

Leadership Development Fund

1 award of varying amount to recognize an emerging leader among current, recent graduates of supervised practice programs and encourage his/her participation in Association activities. Visit web site for eligibility criteria. Deadline: February 28.

1648. (S)

Marie and August LoPresti Sr. Endowment Fund

Awards of varying amounts to graduate and upper-level undergraduate students. Must be U.S. citizens residing in northeast Ohio, meet defined academic qualifications, show evidence of professional potential, and demonstrate financial need. This award also funds faculty development. Visit web site for specific eligibility criteria. Deadline: February 28.

1649. (S)
Susan T. Borra Fellowship in Nutrition Communication

1 award of $5,000 to help deserving individuals enhance their capabilities in the area of nutrition communications as fellows in leading universities, health organizations, professional societies, and industry. Award can fund an internship at a corporation, association, or university. Deadline: February 28.

1650. (S)
Missouri League for Nursing, Inc.
Meinecke Scholarship
P.O. Box 104476
Jefferson City, MO 65110
(573) 635–5355
http://www.moleaguenursing.org

Scholarships ranging from $100 to $5,000 to students pursuing an M.S.N., B.S.N., R.N., or L.P.N. degree. Must be enrolled in a nursing education program in Missouri that has current accreditation from the National League for Nursing. Students must be Missouri residents. Each school may submit only 1 candidate. Based on academic record, extracurricular activities, and financial need. Apply through the director of nursing at student's school. Deadline: September 30.

1651. (Contest)
Missouri Review
Editors' Prize In Poetry
1507 Hillcrest Hall, UMC
Columbia, MO 65211
http://www.missourireview.org

1 first prize of $2,000 plus publication for short fiction, nonfiction essays, and poetry (up to 10 pages). Fiction and nonfiction entries must not be longer than 25 pages. Entries must be unpublished and will not be returned. Charges a $15 entry fee. Individuals may enter more than one category but each entry in each category must be mailed in a separate envelope. Send a self-addressed, stamped envelope for rules or visit web site. Deadline: October 15.

(A, H, SS)
Modern Language Association
Office of Special Projects
26 Broadway, 3rd Floor
New York, NY 10004–1789
(646) 576–5141
http://www.mla.org

1652. (A, H)
Aldo and Jeanne Scaglione Prize for Comparative Literary Studies

An award of $2,000 and a certificate for an outstanding scholarly work in French or francophone linguistic or literary studies. Authors must be members of the MLA. Deadline: May 1.

1653. (A, H)
Aldo and Jeanne Scaglione Publication Award for a Manuscript in Italian Literary Studies

1 award of a $10,000 subvention to the press, for the publication of the manuscript, and a certificate, for an outstanding manuscript dealing with any aspect of the languages and literatures of Italy. Manuscripts approved for publication before award deadline; authors must be current members of the MLA. The prize is awarded each year to an author of an outstanding manuscript dealing with any aspect of the languages and literatures of Italy, including medieval Latin and comparative studies or intellectual history if the work's main thrust is clearly related to the humanities. Materials from ancient Rome are eligible if related to postclassical developments. Also eligible are translations of classical works of prose and poetry produced in Italy prior to 1900 in any language (e.g., neo-Latin, Greek) or in a dialect of Italian (e.g., Neapolitan, Roman, Sicilian). A manuscript may be in English or Italian but is eligible only if a not-for-profit press that is a member of the Association of American University Presses has favorably evaluated it. Deadline: August 1.

1654. (A, H)
James Russell Lowell Prize

1 award of $1,000 for an outstanding literary or linguistic study, a critical edition of an important work, or a critical biography. Open to studies dealing with

literary theory, media, cultural history, or interdisciplinary topics. Authors must be current members of the MLA. Deadline: March 1.

1655. (A, H, SS)
Katherine Singer Kovacs Prize

An award of $1,000 and a certificate for an outstanding book published in English in the field of Latin American and Spanish literatures and cultures. Competing books should be broadly interpretive works that enhance understanding of the interrelations among literature, the other arts, and society. Deadline: May 1.

1656. (A, H)
Kenneth W. Mildenberger Prize

An award of $1,000 for a winning book and an award of $500 for a winning article. Winners also receive a certificate and a 1-year membership in the MLA. For a work in the field of teaching foreign languages and literatures. The competition alternates between books, in even-numbered years, and articles published in refereed journals, in odd-numbered years. Authors need not be members of the MLA. Books must have been published up to 2 years prior to the competition year. Deadline: May 1.

1657. (A, H)
Mina P. Shaughnessy Prize

1 award of $1,000, a certificate, and a 1-year membership in the MLA, for a research publication in the field of teaching English language, literature, rhetoric, and composition. Authors need not be members of the MLA. Selection committee will look for evidence of fresh and effective approaches to teaching and for works likely to be widely useful. Deadline: May 1.

1658. (A, H)
MLA Prize for a First Book

1 award of $1,000, a certificate, and a 1-year membership in the association for a scholarly book in the field of English or other modern languages and literatures. At the time of publication of the book, author must not be enrolled in a program leading to an academic degree or hold a tenured, tenure-accruing, or tenure-track position in postsecondary education.

Authors or publishers must request an application form from the MLA. Authors need not be members of the MLA. Deadline: May 1.

1659. (A, H, SS)
William Sanders Scarborough Prize

1 prize of $1,000 and a certificate for an outstanding scholarly study of Black American literature or culture published the previous year. Books that are primarily translations will not be considered. Deadline: May 1.

1660. (A)
Money For Women
Barbara Deming Memorial Artist Grants
P.O. Box 630125
Bronx, NY 10463
written inquiries only
http://www.womenarts.org/fund/
sourcesforIndividualartists.htm

20 grants of up to $1,000 for feminists active in the arts. Awards support and recognize artistic work that speaks for peace, social justice, the condition of women, and self-realization. Write for complete details. Deadline: none specified.

1661. (S)
Montreal Neurological Institute
Izaak Walton Killam Fellowships & Jeanne Timmins Fellowships
ATTN: Institute Director
3801 University
Montreal, Quebec H3A 2B4
Canada
(514) 398–6644
http://www.mni.mcgill.ca

Fellowships of $25,000 Canadian to neurologists, neurosurgeons, and Ph.D.s to conduct research and study in clinical and basic neurosciences. Open to all nationalities. Deadline: October 15.

(S, SS)
Morris K. Udall Fellowships
130 South Scott Avenue
Tucson, AZ 85701–1922
(520) 670–5529
http://www.udall.gov

1662. (SS)

Conflict Resolution Fellowships

2 fellowships of $24,000 to students whose work is in the areas of environmental public policy or environmental conflict resolution. Must be in the final, writing year of doctoral work. Visit web site for more information and application. Deadline: February 3.

1663. (S, SS)

Environmental Public Policy & Conflict Resolution Fellowships

2 fellowships of $24,000 to doctoral students in the area of environmental public policy or environmental conflict resolution. Must have completed all course work and be in the final, writing year of their doctoral work. Deadline: February 3.

1664. (SS)

Native American Congressional Internships

10-week internships providing airfare to and from Washington, DC, dormitory lodging, allowance for food, transportation, and incidentals, and a stipend of $1,200, paid at the end of the program, to Native American graduate or law students, undergraduate juniors or seniors, or students graduating from a tribal college. Must be enrolled as a member of a recognized tribe, have at least a B average, and have an interest in tribal government and policy. Selection is based on academic achievement, essay, letters of recommendation, and professional resume. Visit web site for more information and an application. Deadline: February 3.

1665. (A, H, S, SS)

Mortar Board National Foundation Fellowships

1200 Chambers Road, #201
Columbus, OH 43212
(800) 989–6266
(614) 488–4094
http://www.mortarboard.org/4fellowship_application.pdf

1 fellowships of $5,000 and several of $2,000 to graduate or professional students for any field of study. Must be Mortar Board members and alumni in good standing. Deadline: January 31.

1666. (S)

Mote Marine Laboratory

Internship Coordinator
Mote Marine Library
1600 Ken Thompson Parkway
Sarasota, FL 34236
(941) 388–4441
http://www.mote.org

55 internships lasting from 8 to 16 weeks providing no compensation. Open to graduate students, recent college graduates, undergraduate students. Interns work in research (biomedical, chemical fate & effects, coastal resources, environmental assessment & enhancement, fisheries & aquaculture, marine mammals, sea turtles, Southwest Florida Coast research and shark biology, as well as support programs in aquarium, education, communications, graphics, and business. Deadline: rolling.

1667. (S)

Mount Desert Island Biological Lab

Graduate Student Fellowships

P.O. Box 35
Old Bar Harbor Road
Salisbury Cove, ME 04672
(207) 288–9880, ext. 102
http://www.mdibl.org/edu/graduate.shtml

A limited number of fellowships ranging from $500 to $1,000 to graduate students to work at the laboratory. Must submit an application, graduate school transcript, a letter of recommendation from the MDIBL principal investigator you plan to work with, and a 1-page statement describing the proposed research. Deadline: March 31.

1668. (A, H, SS)

MTV: Music Television

Intern Coordinator
1515 Broadway, 22nd Floor
New York, NY 11036
(212) 258–8000
http://www.mtv.com

150 10- to 13-week summer, fall, or spring internships providing no compensation. Open to graduate, undergraduate, and high school students. Students must receive academic credit for internship. Internships are in advertising, art promotions, graphics, international programming, marketing, on-air talent, press and public

relations, programming, talent relations, video library, or a particular MTV program. Deadline: rolling.

1669. (H, SS)
Muktabodha Indological Research Institute
Graduate Student Research Fellowships in Hindu Studies
P.O. Box 85857
Emeryville, CA 94662
http://www.muktabodha.org
info@muktabodha.org

Fellowships of $10,000 to graduate students undertaking dissertation research in Hinduism. Must have completed their doctoral course work in religion, South Asian studies, or related program and who are now undertaking their dissertation research. Normally used to support research in India. Preference given to the study of textile sources of the Hindu Tantric tradition, though other fields of Hindu studies are welcome. Deadline: March 1.

1670. (S)
Muscular Dystrophy Association
Postdoctoral Fellowship Program
3300 East Sunrise Drive
Tucson, AZ 85718
(800) 572–1717
http://www.mdusa.org

60 fellowships of $25,000 and $28,000 to postdoctoral students in medicine, biological sciences, and life sciences. Fellows must be conducting postdoctoral research into the causes, diagnosis, and treatment of neuromuscular diseases. Preferences are given to individuals who received an M.D., Ph.D., or D.Sc. or an equivalent degree within 3 years of the starting date of fellowship support. Write for complete information. Deadline: July 10 and January 10.

(S)
Myasthenia Gravis Foundation of America
5841 Cedar Lake Road, Suite 204
Minneapolis, MN 55416
(952) 545–9438
http://www.myasthenia.org

1671. (S)
Henry R. Viets Fellowship

4 to 8 fellowships of $2,000 to medical and pre-med students who are pursuing either basic or clinical research related to myasthenia gravis under the supervision of specified preceptor. Award may be used in own medical school or in another near place of residence. Renewable. Deadline: March 15.

1672. (S)
Dr. Kermit E. Osserman Postdoctoral Research Fellowship
Blanche McClure Postdoctoral Research Fellowships

Fellowships of $30,000 to postdoctoral fellows to conduct full-time research on myasthenia gravis or related conditions under supervision of a specified preceptor. Deadline: November 1.

1673. (S)
Mycological Society of America
Graduate Fellowships
P.O. Box 7065
Lawrence, KS 66044–7065
(785) 843–1235
(785) 843–1274 (Fax)
http:www.msafungi.org
krose@allenpress.com
hardwick@allenpress.com

3 fellowships of $2,000 and 1 of $500 to graduate or doctoral students majoring in mycology (study of fungus). Graduate students must be members of Mycological Society of America. May be enrolled at any U.S. or Canadian university. Previous recipients are not eligible. Write or visit the web site for more information. Deadline: April 1.

(S, SS)
National Aeronautics and Space Administration
NASA Headquarters
Office of Human Resources and Education
Mail Code FE
Washington, DC 20546
(202) 358–0402
http://www.nasa.gov

1674. (S)
Graduate Student Researchers Program

Up to 300 awards providing stipends of $24,000 to students enrolled in, or accepted to, a graduate program and planning to major in engineering, mathematics, or science. Selection based on academic achievement, quality of proposed research program, and its relevance to NASA interests and utilization of research facilities. Must be U.S. citizens. Renewable up to 3 years. Deadline: February 1.

1675. (S, SS)
Internships

1,000 6-week or 4-month summer internships providing salaries ranging from $400 to $700 per week for graduates and from $100 to $400 per week for undergraduates. Internship sites are in AL, CA, FL, MD, MS, OH, TX, and VA. Open to high school students (at least 16 years old), undergraduates, graduate or professional school students. Internships are in accounting, budgeting, engineering, mathematics, procurement, and science. There are some internships that are specifically for minorities, while others have no restrictions. Deadline: ranges from December 31 to April 1, depending on program.

1676. (S)
Summer School for High-Performance Computational Earth and Space Sciences
http://esdcd.gsfc.nasa.gov/ESS/summer_school.html

15 3-week summer programs providing stipends of $1,440, plus reimbursement for domestic travel to and from Greenbelt, MD, and housing. Open to graduate students in disciplines that affect earth and space science. Must be U.S. citizens and enrolled in an accredited U.S. institution. Students are given hands-on parallel computer training and small group interaction experience. Visit web site, for more information, application, and contact person. Deadline: February 24.

(A, H, S, SS)
National Art Materials Trade Association
15806 Brookway Drive, Suite 300
Huntersville, NC 28078
(704) 892–6244
http://www.namta.org
info@namta.org

1677. (A, H, S, SS)
Academic Scholarship

2 scholarships of $1,500 to graduate or undergraduate students in any field of study. Must be employees, employee dependents or relatives, or individuals in an organization related to art or the art materials industry. Selection based on academic achievement, extracurricular activities, interests, career goals, and financial need. Deadline: March 15.

1678. (A)
NAMTA Art Major Scholarship Program

1 scholarship of $2,500 to a graduate or undergraduate student who is majoring in the field of art. Must be an employee, employee dependent or relative, or an individual in an organization related to art or the art materials industry. Selection based on academic achievement, extracurricular activities, interests, career goals, and financial need. Deadline: March 15.

(SS)
National Asian Pacific American Bar Association
1341 G Street, N.W., 5th Floor
Washington, DC 20005
(202) 626–7693
http://www.napaba.org
foundation@napaba.org

1679. (SS)
Law Foundation Scholarships

Varying number of scholarships of approximately $1,500 to Asian-American law students enrolled in an accredited law school in the U.S. Selection will be based on an essay, commitment to, and interest in, pro bono public interest and/or public service legal work, financial need, leadership potential, maturity and responsibility, and commitment to serving the needs of the Asian-Pacific-American community. Visit web site for more information and an application. Deadline: mid-September.

1680. (SS)
Presidential Anheuser-Busch Scholarships

2 scholarships of $5,000 to Asian-American law students. Must demonstrate outstanding leadership potential to serve the Asian-Pacific-American community. Selection will be based on an essay, commitment to

and interest in pro bono public interest and/or public service legal work, financial need, leadership potential, maturity and responsibility, and commitment to serving the needs of the Asian Pacific American community. Visit web site for more information and an application. Deadline: mid-September.

1681. (SS)
National Association for Armenian Studies and Research, Inc.
Fund Award
Board of Directors
395 Concord Avenue
Belmont, MA 02178
(617) 489–1610
http://www.naasr.org

Scholarships of varying amounts to graduate and postgraduate students majoring in Armenian studies. Must be of Armenian descent and U.S. citizens or permanent residents. Award is only for conducting research in Armenian studies and may be used for travel, research materials, or similar expenses. Deadline: 3–6 months before grant request date.

(A, H, S, SS)
National Association for the Advancement of Colored People (NAACP)
4805 Mt. Hope Drive
Baltimore, MD 21215–3297
(301) 358–8900
http://www.naacp.org

1682. (A, H, S, SS)
Agnes Jones Jackson Scholarship

Scholarships of $2,500 for graduate students to help minority students finance college study in all areas of study. Students must be NAACP member for at least 1 year or fully paid life members, under the age of 25 by April 30, and have a minimum 3.0 GPA. Send legal-size self-addressed, stamped envelope. Deadline: April 30.

1683. (S)
Willems Scholarship

Scholarships of $3,000 for graduate students and $2,000 for undergraduate students. Must be majoring in chemistry, computer science, engineering, mathematical sciences, or physics. Students must have been NAACP members for 1 year or more and have at least a 3.0 GPA. Apply between January 1 and April 15. Deadline: April 30.

(SS)
National Association for the Advancement of Colored People (NAACP) Legal Defense & Educational Fund, Inc.
99 Hudson Street
New York, NY 10013
(212) 965–2202
http://www.naacpldf.org

1684. (SS)
Earl Warren Legal Training Scholarships

15 to 20 scholarships of $3,000 to law students, with preference given to entering first-year students. Selection is based on academic achievements, community involvement, and leadership qualities. Applications must be requested in writing between November 30 and February 15. Visit web site for specific guidelines for requesting an application. Deadline: July 31.

1685. (SS)
Earl Warren Shearman & Sterling Scholarships

2 scholarships of $15,000 ($13,500 for school costs and $1,500 to attend the LDF's Civil Rights Institute) to African-American undergraduates who are applying to law school. Selection is based on academic achievement and career plans. Awards are not disbursed until law school enrollment is verified. Renewable for second and third years of law school, with continued academic progress. Applications must be requested in writing between November 30 and February 15. Visit web site for specific guidelines for requesting an application. Deadline: July 31.

1686. (A, S, SS)
National Association of American Business Clubs (AMBUCS)
Scholarships
Box 5127
High Point, NC 27262
(336) 869–2166
http://www.ambucs.com

400 to 500 scholarships ranging from $500 to $1,500 for college juniors and seniors and graduate students majoring in music therapy, physical therapy, occupational therapy, rehabilitation, speech-language pathology, hearing-audiology, special education, and related areas. Based on academic achievement, financial need, and eligibility requirements. Renewable. Deadline: April 15.

1687. (S)
National Association of Black Geologists and Geophysicists
NABGG Scholarship Program
4212 San Felipe, Suite 420
Houston, TX 77027–2902
http://www.nabgg.org

Scholarships of varying amounts are available to minority graduate and undergraduate students in geoscience programs. 3 nominations from each of 10 target schools are accepted for consideration for this scholarship. Minority students who don't attend one of the target schools but who are in geoscience programs may also apply directly to the organization. Visit web site for more information. Deadline: none specified.

(H)
National Association of Black Journalists
University of Maryland
8701-A Adelphi Road
Adelphi, MD 20783–1716
(301) 445–7100
http://www.nabj.org

1688. (H)
Allison Fisher Scholarship
http://www.allisonfisherfund.org

1 scholarship of $2,500 to an African-American graduate or undergraduate student majoring in print journalism. Must be attending an accredited 4-year institution, be a student member of NABJ, and maintain at least a 3.0 GPA. Selection based on interest in journalism, academic achievement, and financial need. Recipient will be supported to attend the NABJ National Convention for formal recognition and be assigned to participate in the student convention projects. Visit web site for more information. Deadline: April 12.

1689. (H)
Carole Simpson Scholarship

1 scholarship of $2,500 to an African-American graduate or undergraduate student majoring in broadcast journalism. Must be attending an accredited 4-year institution, be a student member of NABJ, and maintain at least a 2.5 GPA. Selection based on interest in journalism, academic achievement, and financial need. For more information, visit web site. Deadline: April 12.

1690. (H)
Gerald Boyd/Robin Stone Scholarship

1 scholarship of $2,500 to an African-American graduate or undergraduate student majoring in print journalism. Must be attending an accredited 4-year institution, be a student member of NABJ, and maintain at least a 2.5 GPA. Selection based on interest in journalism, academic achievement, and financial need. For more information, visit web site. Deadline: April 12.

1691. (H)
Merck Company Foundation Sustaining Scholarship

1 scholarship of $5,000 to an African-American graduate or undergraduate student majoring in medical or business journalism, with an interest in print, radio, or television. Must be attending an accredited 4-year institution, be a student member of NABJ, and maintain at least a 2.5 GPA. Selection based on interest in journalism, academic achievement, and financial need. For more information, visit web site. Deadline: April 12.

1692. (H)
NABJ Scholarships

10 scholarships of $2,500 to African-American graduate or undergraduate students majoring in journalism—print, photography, or radio, and television. Must be attending an accredited 4-year institution, be a student member of NABJ, and maintain at least a 2.5 GPA. Selection based on interest in journalism, academic achievement, and financial need. For more information, visit web site. Deadline: April 12.

1693. (H)
Washington Post Scholarship

1 scholarship of $2,500 to an African-American graduate or undergraduate student majoring in print journalism. Must be attending an accredited 4-year institution, be a student member of NABJ, and maintain at least a 3.0 GPA. Selection based on interest in journalism, academic achievement, and financial need. Visit web site for more information. Deadline: April 12.

1694. (A, H, S, SS)
National Association of Colored Women's Clubs
Center for African-American History & Culture
Temple University
Weiss Hall, Suite B-18
Cecil B Moore & 13th Street
Philadelphia, PA 19122
http://www.temple.edu/caach/new_page.17.htm

Varying numbers of scholarships of $1,000 to graduate female African-American, Hispanic-American, or Native American students. Open to all majors. Write an introductory letter briefly explaining your educational and financial situation. Student must be recommended by a member of the organization. The organization does not disseminate member information. Applicant must contact a local chapter and ask for an introduction in order to obtain a recommendation letter. Students should look in their local phone books for chapters and initiate the procedure. Deadline: April of even-numbered years.

1695. (S)
National Association of Pediatric Nurse Associates & Practitioners
NAPNAP—McNeil Scholarships
20 Brace Road, Suite 200
Cherry Hill, NJ 08034–2633
(856) 857–9700
http://www.napnap.org

Scholarships of $2,000 to students in graduate pediatric nurse practitioner program. Financial need is a major consideration. Must be a U.S. citizen. For more information, visit web site. Deadline: May 30 and September 30.

1696. (S)
National Association of Retail Druggists Foundation
NARD Presidential Scholarship
205 Daingerfield Road
Alexandria, VA 22314
(703) 683–8200
http://www.healthy.net

1 scholarship of $2,000 to a full-time pharmacy student who is a student member of NARD. Selection is based on academic achievement and demonstrated leadership qualities. Must be attending an accredited U.S. pharmacy school.

1697. (A)
National Association of Teachers of Singing Foundation
Artists Awards Competition
4745 Sutton Place Court, Suite 201
Jacksonville, FL 32224
(904) 992–9101
http://www.nats.org/welcome.html

6 awards ranging from $2,500 to $5,000 to singers between the ages of 21 and 35 who have studied with a NATS teacher for at least 1 year. Award is used to assist young singers who are ready for professional careers. 6 awards every 18 months. Deadline: varies.

1698. (A, H, S, SS)
National Association of University Women (NAUW)
NAUW Fellowship Award
1001 E Street, S.E.
Washington, DC 20003
(202) 547–3967
written inquiries only
http://www.crcwd.com/test/Default.htm

1 fellowship of $2,500 to a female doctoral candidate with a master's degree to continue her graduate work in any field of study. Priority is given to African-American females. Applications may be requested between January 1 and April 30. Deadline: April 30.

1699. (H, S, SS)
National Association of Water Companies
Scholarships
725 K Street, N.W., Suite 1212

Washington, DC 20006
(202) 833–8383
http://www.nawc.org

2 scholarships of $2,500 to graduate or undergraduate students majoring in biology, computer science/data processing, earth science, engineering/technology, natural resources, physical sciences, math, trade/technical specialties, some social sciences, or communications. Must be attending an accredited 2- or 4-year college or university and pursuing a career in the investor-owned water utility industry. Must have a 3.0 GPA or better. Selection based on application, academic achievement, career goals, essay, transcript, and recommendation letters. Deadline: April 1.

(S)

National Audubon Society
700 Broadway
New York, NY 10003
(212) 979–3000
http://www.audubon.org

1700. (S)
Government Affairs Internship Program

15 12-week summer internships and 3 to 8 12- to 20-week fall and winter internships providing no compensation. Open to graduate students, recent college graduates, or upper-level undergraduate students. Internships may be in Washington, DC, Milwaukee, WI, Sante Fe, NM, Elgin, AZ, Trabuco Canyon, CA, Sharon, CT, Naples, FL, Frankfort, KY, Monson, ME, Garrison, NY, Ithaca, NY, and Harleyville, SC. No environmental experience is necessary, but applicant must have interest in environment. Finalists are interviewed by phone. Interns build displays, lead nature walks, and collect field data. Deadline: April 1 (summer); August 1 (fall); and January 1 (winter).

1701. (S)
Wildlife Management Internships

15 12-week summer internships and 3 to 8 12- to 20-week fall and winter internships providing no compensation. Open to graduate students, recent college graduates, or upper-level undergraduate students. Internships may be in Washington, DC, Milwaukee, WI, Sante Fe, NM, Elgin, AZ, Trabuco Canyon, CA, Sharon, CT, Naples, FL, Frankfort, KY, Monson, ME, Garrison, NY, Ithaca, NY, and Harleyville, SC. No environmental experience is necessary. Finalists are interviewed by phone. Deadline: varies.

1702. (SS)
National Bar Institute
One Woodward Avenue, Suite 2400
Detroit, MI 48221
(313) 961–8380
http://www.nationalbar.org/nbi/index.html

Up to 3 fellowships ranging from $1,000 to $10,000 (though normally about $2,500) to full-time law students. Must be U.S. citizens or legal residents, be enrolled in an accredited U.S. law school, have at least 2 consecutive years of full-time law student experience, and intend to return to the Black community to practice law. Selection is based on academic achievement, potential for significant contributions, commitment to the Black community, and financial need. The NBI is the philanthropic arm of the National Bar Association. Visit web site for more information and an application. Deadline: May 15.

(SS)

National Black Law Students Association
1225 11th Street, N.W.
Washington, DC 20001–4217
(202) 842–3900
http://www.nblsa.org

1703. (SS)
Nelson Mandela Scholarship

6 scholarships of $1,000 to African-American college students/graduates who plan to enter law school during the year of the award. Must submit a proposal, between 500 and 1,000 words in length, geared toward an area of law as it reflects NBLSA's convention theme. The proposal will be judged on purpose, content, grammar, and style. Visit web site for current topic and submission guidelines. Deadline: February 3.

1704. (SS)
Sandy Brown Memorial Scholarship

2 scholarships of not less than $500 to rising second- or third-year law students. Must submit an essay on the current NBLSA convention theme. Essays will be

judged on content, grammar, and style. Visit web site for current topic and submission guidelines. Deadline: February 3.

(S)

National Black Nurses Association
8630 Fenton Street, Suite 330
Silver Spring, MD 20910–3803
(301) 589–3200
http://www.nbna.org

1705. (S)
BET Emerge Publications Scholarship

1 scholarship ranging from $500 to $2,000 to a licensed person pursuing an advanced or bachelor's degree. Selection based on academics, recommendations, participation in student nurses activities, involvement in the African-American community, and an essay. Must be a member of NBNA and a member of a local chapter (if one exists). Deadline: April 15.

1706. (S)
Dr. Hilda Richards Scholarship

1 scholarship ranging from $500 to $2,000 to a licensed person pursuing an advanced or bachelor's degree. Selection based on academics, recommendations, participation in student nurses activities, involvement in the African-American community, and an essay. Must be a member of NBNA and a member of a local chapter (if one exists). Deadline: April 15.

1707. (S)
Kaiser Permanent Scholarship

1 scholarship ranging from $500 to $2,000 to a licensed person pursuing an advanced or bachelor's degree. Selection based on academics, recommendations, participation in student nurses activities, involvement in the African-American community, and an essay. Must be a member of NBNA and a member of a local chapter (if one exists). Deadline: April 15.

1708. (S)
Dr. Lauranne Sams Scholarship

1 scholarship ranging from $500 to $2,000 to a licensed person pursuing an advanced or bachelor's degree. Selection based on academics, recommendations, participation in student nurses activities, involvement in the African-American community, and

an essay. Must be a member of NBNA and a member of a local chapter (if one exists). Deadline: April 15.

1709. (S)
Mayo Foundation Scholarship

1 scholarship ranging from $500 to $2,000 to a licensed person pursuing an advanced or bachelor's degree. Selection based on academics, recommendations, participation in student nurses activities, involvement in the African-American community, and an essay. Must be a member of NBNA and a member of a local chapter (if one exists). Deadline: April 15.

1710. (S)
NBNA Board of Directors Scholarship

1 scholarship ranging from $500 to $2,000 to a licensed person pursuing an advanced or bachelor's degree. Selection based on academics, recommendations, participation in student nurses activities, involvement in the African-American community, and an essay. Must be a member of NBNA and a member of a local chapter (if one exists). Deadline: April 15.

1711. (S)
Nurse of the Year Award

1 award ranging from $500 to $2,000 to a licensed person pursuing an advanced or bachelor's degree. Selection based on academics, recommendations, participation in student nurses activities, involvement in the African-American community, and an essay. Must be a member of NBNA and a member of a local chapter (if one exists). Deadline: April 15.

1712. (S)
Penn State Scholarship

1 scholarship ranging from $500 to $2,000 to a licensed person pursuing an advanced or bachelor's degree. Selection based on academics, recommendations, participation in student nurses activities, involvement in the African-American community, and an essay. Must be a member of NBNA and a member of a local chapter (if one exists). Deadline: April 15.

(SS)

National Business Aircraft Association
1200 18th Street, N.W., Suite 400
Washington, DC 20036–2527

(202) 783–9000

http://www.nbaa.org

1713. (SS)
Concordia International Aviation MBA Scholarship

1 scholarship providing 50% of tuition and fees to graduate students pursuing an M.B.A. through a distance learning program at Concordia University in Canada. Must be a full-time employee of an NBAA company, have been in a middle- or senior-level management position for at least 3 years, and have a satisfactory GMAT score. Deadline: July 31.

1714. (SS)
Indiana Business Aviation Association (IBAA) PDP Scholarship

4 scholarships of $1,000 to full-time graduate or undergraduate sophomore, junior, or senior students in a college or university offering an NBAA Professional Development Program (PDP). Must have at least a 3.0 GPA on a 4.0 scale. Selection based on academic achievement, extracurricular activities, recommendation letter, and essay. Deadline: late August.

1715. (SS)
UAA Janice K. Barden Aviation Scholarship

5 scholarships of $1,000 to graduate or undergraduate junior or senior students in an aviation-related program at an NBAA and University Aviation Association (UAA) member institution who will be attending the following academic year. Must have at least a 3.0 GPA on a 4.0 scale and be a U.S. citizen. Selection is based on academic achievement, recommendation letters, extracurricular activities, and 250-word essay on aviation goals. Deadline: November 1.

1716. (SS)
USAIG PDP Scholarship

3 scholarships of $1,000 to full-time graduate or undergraduate sophomore, junior, or senior students in a college or university offering an NBAA Professional Development Program (PDP). Must have at least a 3.0 GPA on a 4.0 scale. Selection based on academic achievement, extracurricular activities, recommendation letter, and essay. Scholarship is sponsored by U.S. Aircraft Insurance Group. Deadline: late August.

(S)

National Center for Atmospheric Research (NCAR)
ATTN: Administrator
P.O. Box 3000
Boulder, CO 80307
(303) 497–1250
http://www.ncsa.uiuc.edu/General/GIBN/ncar.2.html

1717. (S)
NCAR Graduate Research Assistantships

Approximately 10 research assistantships of $12,400, or $11,500 if comprehensive exam is not yet passed, to graduate students working on their Ph.D. thesis. Must be in a graduate program with interests complimentary to NCAR. Awards are based on proposals submitted. Deadline: January 1, April 1, July 1, and October 1.

1718. (S)
NCAR Postdoctoral Appointments

Approximately 10 fellowships of $29,400 and a stipend of $30,600, plus insurance and travel, to postdoctoral fellows with 1 year experience who have just received their Ph.D. or have obtained their Ph.D. within 4 years and have been working. Research objectives are decided by each fellow. Selection is based on scientific capability, potential, originality, and independence, and ability to undertake research. Deadline: early January.

(S)

National Center for Infectious Diseases/Association of Public Health Laboratories
Emerging Infectious Diseases (EID) Laboratory Fellowship Program
2025 M Street, N.W., Suite 550
Washington, DC 20036
(202) 822–5227
http://www.cdc.gov/ncidod/feedback.htm
fellowships@aphl.org

1719. (S)
EID Advanced Laboratory Training Fellowship

Fellowships of $24,952 (bachelor's) and $27,813 (master's) to candidates with bachelor's and master's degrees to support public health initiatives and provide doctoral-level scientists opportunities to conduct high-priority infectious disease research in public health laboratories. Fellows are placed within local, state, or federal (CDC) public health laboratories and receive advanced infectious disease laboratory-related training. Deadline: late February.

1720. (S)
EID Postdoctoral Laboratory Research Fellowship Program

Fellowships of at least $34,229 to doctoral students (Ph.D., M.D., or D.V.M.) with an emphasis on research or development in infectious diseases. Fellows conduct applied research or development in areas relevant to public health. Must be U.S. citizens. Deadline: late February.

(A, H, S, SS)
National Collegiate Athletic Association (NCAA)
6201 College Boulevard
Overland Park, KS 66211–2422
(913) 339–1906
http://www.ncaa.org

1721. (A, H, S, SS)
Graduate Scholarship Program

Scholarship grants of $5,000 to graduate students in any area of study. Must be a student athlete attending an NCAA member institution. Must be nominated by their faculty athletic representative or Director of Athletics and have at least a 3.0 GPA. Selection is made in the academic year in which the student completes his/her final season of eligibility in intercollegiate athletics. Contact Athletic Director or above address. Not renewable. Deadline: varying according to sport.

1722. (A, H, S, SS)
Postgraduate Scholarship Program

125 scholarships of varying amounts to graduate students who excelled academically and athletically while undergraduates. Applicants must be college seniors. Scholarships are awarded as follows: 29 football; 28 basketball (14 women, 14 men); and 68 for sports other than football or basketball (34 women; 34 men). Deadline: February 22 (basketball); April 22 (other sports); and October 25 (football).

1723. (A, H, S, SS)
Walter Byers Postgraduate Scholarship

2 scholarships of $7,500 (1 male, 1 female) to graduate or professional students who are or were varsity student athletes. May be used for any area of study. Must have at least a 3.5 GPA. Deadline: February 5.

1724. (S)
National Consortium for Graduate Degrees for Minorities in Engineering, Inc. (GEM)
ATTN: Executive Director
P.O. Box 537
Notre Dame, IN 46556
(219) 239–7183
http://www.nd.edu/~gem

125 portable fellowships of full tuition and fees plus a $5,000 stipend that can be used at member universities to pursue the M.S. degree in engineering. Open to Native Americans, African-Americans, Mexican-Americans, and Puerto Ricans. Applicants must at least be undergraduate juniors. Award includes paid summer research work experience. Deadline: December 1.

1725. (S)
National Council of State Garden Clubs, Inc. Scholarships
ATTN: Scholarship Chair
4401 Magnolia Avenue
St. Louis, MO 63110–3492
http://www.gardenclub.org

30 to 35 scholarships of $3,500 to graduate and upper-level undergraduate students pursuing a career in agriculture, biology, botany, floriculture, forestry, horticulture, natural resources, or related areas. Must have at least a 3.0 GPA and be nominated by their home state's Garden Club. Selection based on academic achievement, financial need, and recommendation letters. Deadline: March 1.

1726. (SS)
National Defense Council Foundation
1220 King Street, Suite #1
Alexandria, VA 22314
(703) 836–3443
http://www.ndcf.org/Interns/Intern.html

Internships providing a daily travel stipend to graduate and undergraduate students. Internships provide real-world experience in foreign policy and defense studies. Interns research and write about issues such as low-intensity conflict, counternarcotics, analysis of future threats, energy as it relates to national security, and other current topics of national interest. Deadline: 45 days prior to desired start date.

(A, H)

National Endowment for the Arts
Nancy Hanks Center
1100 Pennsylvania Avenue, N.W.
Room 720
Washington, DC 20506–0001
(202) 682–5428
http://arts.endow.gov/guide/Heritage02.html

1727. (A)
American Jazz Masters Fellowships

Fellowships of $20,000 to living artists on the basis of nominations from the public, including the jazz community. The recipients must be citizens or permanent residents of the United States. Nominations may be made by submitting a 1-page letter that details the reasons that the nominated artist should receive an American Jazz Masters Fellowship. Describe the nominee's contributions and explain why this individual deserves national recognition. Include with your nomination letter a resume or a short biography that outlines the career of the nominated artist. Deadline: January 24.

1728. (A, H)
Fellowships for Creative Writers

Fellowships of $20,000 to published creative writers of exceptional talent. Fellowships enable recipients to set aside time for writing, research, travel, and general career advancement. Applicants in fiction must have published at least 5 different short stories, works of short fiction, or excerpts from novels in 2 or more literary journals, anthologies, or publications that regularly include fiction as a portion of their format; or a volume of short fiction or a collection of short stories; or a novel or novella. Applicants in creative nonfiction must have published at least 5 different creative essays (such as personal essays or memoirs); or a volume of creative nonfiction. Applicants in poetry must have published a volume of 48 or more pages of poetry or 20 or more different poems or pages of poetry in 5 or more literary journals, anthologies, or publications that regularly include poetry as a portion of their format. Up to 16 poems may be in a single volume of poetry of fewer than 48 pages. This volume, however, may count as only one of the required 5 places of publication. Applications should not be sent before January 1. Deadline: mid-March.

1729. (A)
Literature Fellowships

Grants are for $10,000 or $20,000, depending upon the length and scope of the project, to published creative writers and translators of exceptional talent in the areas of prose and poetry. The Arts Endowment advances its goal of expanding the opportunities for artists to interpret, explore, and create work. This program operates on a 2-year cycle, with fellowships in prose available 1 year and fellowships in poetry available the next. Deadline: none specified.

1730. (A)
National Heritage Fellowships

12 one-time fellowships of $10,000 to master folk and traditional artists. These fellowships are intended to recognize the recipients' artistic excellence and support their continuing contributions to our nation's traditional arts heritage. Selection criteria are authenticity, excellence, and significance within the particular artistic tradition. The individuals who are nominated should be worthy of national recognition; they should have a record of continuing artistic accomplishment and must be actively participating in their art form, either as practitioners or as teachers. The recipients must be citizens or permanent residents of the United States. Deadline: October 1.

1731. (A, H)
Translation Projects

Grants of $10,000 and $20,000, depending upon the length and scope of the project, to published translators of literature for projects that involve the specific translation of prose (fiction, creative nonfiction, and drama) or poetry (including verse drama) from other languages into English. Applications should not be sent before January 1. Deadline: mid-March.

1732. (A)
Visual Artists Fellowships

Fellowships ranging from $15,000 to $20,000 to professional artists in the visual arts. Awards assist creative development and are not for academic study. This is not a scholarship program. Must be a U.S. citizen or legal resident. Students are ineligible. Deadline: January, February, and March.

(A)
National Federation of Music Clubs
Chairman, Scholarship Department
NFMC Headquarters
1336 North Delaware Street
Indianapolis, IN 46202–2481
(317) 638–4003
http://www.nfmc-music.org

1733. (A)
Hinda Honigman Scholarship for the Blind

1 scholarship of $250 and 1 scholarship of $500 to students between 16 and 26 years old. Must be legally blind. Include a self-addressed, stamped envelope to obtain an application and information. Deadline: March 15.

1734. (A)
NFMC Music for the Blind

1 scholarship of $200 to a student between age 19 and 31, in the area of musical composition. Must be legally blind. Include a self-addressed, stamped envelope for application and information. Deadline: March 30.

1735. (A)
Scholarships and Awards

About $138,000 annually is awarded in music scholarships ranging from $100 to $5,000 by affiliated music clubs. Latest information can be obtained through subscription to appropriate publications. The following bulletins may be ordered from above address: YAI—Young Artist Auditions Bulletins ($1.75 each); SAI—Student Auditions Bulletin ($1.75 each). Awards based on musical talent and promise. Deadline: varies by competition.

1736. (A)
Young Artist Auditions

8 awards ranging from $500 to $5,000 for instrumentalists. Must be between the ages of 18 and 29 by March 1 of the year of auditions; vocalists must be between the ages of 23 and 34. Awarded in odd-numbered years. Visit web site to find current contact address for this competition. Deadline: varies.

(A, H, S, SS)
National Federation of the Blind (NFB)
Scholarships
ATTN: Chairperson
1800 Johnson Street
Baltimore, MD 21230
(301) 659–9314
http://www.nfb.org

1737. (A, H, S, SS)
American Brotherhood for the Blind Scholarship

1 scholarship of $6,000 to assist a blind graduate or undergraduate student. This is open to both male and female students entering any field of study. Based on academic achievements, service to the community, and financial need. Request application after July 1 and enclose a self-addressed, stamped envelope. Deadline: March 31.

1738. (A, S, SS)
Howard Brown Rickard Scholarship

1 scholarship of $2,500 for a blind graduate or undergraduate student majoring in architecture or a specific social or natural science. Based on academic achievements, service to the community, and financial need. Request application after July 1 and enclose a self-addressed, stamped envelope. Deadline: March 31.

1739. (A, H, S, SS)
Merit Scholarships

3 scholarships of $4,000, 7 scholarships of $2,500, and 9 scholarships of $1,800 for male and female graduate and undergraduate students. Must be legally blind. May be used for any field of study at an accredited college or university. Based on academic achievements, service to the community, and financial need. Request applications after July 1. Deadline: March 31.

1740. (A, H, S, SS)

Stokoe Scholarship

1 scholarship of varying amount to assist a blind graduate student. This is open to both male and female students entering any field of study. Based on academic achievements, service to the community, and financial need. Request application after July 1 and enclose a self-addressed, stamped envelope. Deadline: March 31.

1741. (S)

National Fund for Medical Education Corporation Medical Perspectives Fellowship Program
333 California Street, Suite 410
San Francisco, CA 94118
(415) 476–8181
http://futurehealth.ucsf.edu/nfme.html

Fellowship program providing $250 per week stipend, plus project-related expenses, to medical students to carry out projects that will give them learning experiences not usually encountered. Contact Dean of Student Affairs at any accredited medical school. Deadline: March 1.

(A)

National Gallery of Art
Center for Advanced Study in the Visual Arts
Washington, DC 20565
(202) 842–6482
http://www.nga.gov

1742. (A)

Andrew W. Mellon Predoctoral Fellowship

1 fellowship of $20,000 per year (plus a stipend of $16,000, a $4,000 housing subsidy, and a per diem allowance for photography and travel, depending on the terms of each fellowship) to a doctoral candidate who has completed all course work and is working on dissertation in a field other than Western art. Award supports advancement and completion of a doctoral dissertation in a field other than Western art. Fellow must spend 1 year of the fellowship period on dissertation research abroad and 1 year at the Center to complete the dissertation. Deadline: November 15.

1743. (A)

Chester Dale Predoctoral Fellowships

Up to 2 fellowships of $20,000 per year (plus a stipend of $16,000, a $4,000 housing subsidy, and a per diem allowance for photography and travel, depending on the terms of each fellowship) to a doctoral candidate who has completed all course work and is working on dissertation in Western art. The Dale Fellow may use the fellowship to study in the United States or abroad; there are no residence requirements at the Center. Deadline: November 15.

1744. (A, H)

David E. Finley Predoctoral Fellowship Program

1 fellowship to a doctoral candidate who has completed all course work and is working on dissertation. Duration of the fellowship is for 36 months. The first 2 years are for research and travel in Europe to visit collections, museums, monuments, and sites related to a well-advanced dissertation in Western art. During this 2-year period, residency abroad is expected, for which travel funds are available. The third year is to be spent in residence at the Center to complete the dissertation and to perform curatorial work. Half of the year in residence will be devoted to a research project, designed to complement the subject of the dissertation, at the Gallery or other Washington-area collections. Applicants should be interested in pursuing a career as a museum curator. Must be U.S. citizens or enrolled in a U.S. university, with all predissertation requirements fulfilled before the date of application. Candidates must know 2 foreign languages related to dissertation topic. Deadline: November 15.

1745. (A, H)

Graduate Lecturing Fellowships

2 fellowships providing stipends of $4,000 to graduate students in art history. Must have completed at least 1 year of course work before beginning their fellowships. Awarded to provide experience presenting original works of art to the public. Fellows give approximately 3 talks per month, October through May, on both weekdays and weekends, and prepare a monthly topic chosen in consultation with Gallery staff. Graduate lecturing fellows are invited to participate in the intern orientation program, a series of

weekly sessions designed to introduce all functions, programs, and departments of the Gallery. Fellows are also provided with working space. Candidates must have taken appropriate course work in European or American art, which constitutes the core of the Gallery's collections. Students specializing in other areas of art history or in studio art may apply, but must have a strong background in European or American art history. Send all application materials to: Department of Academic Programs, National Gallery of Art, 2000B South Club Drive, Landover, MD 20785. Deadline: April 1.

1746. (A)
Ittleson Predoctoral Fellowship

1 fellowship of $20,000 per year (plus a stipend of $16,000, a $4,000 housing subsidy, and a per diem allowance for photography and travel, depending on the terms of each fellowship) to a doctoral candidate who has completed all course work and is working on dissertation in a field other than Western art. Fellow must spend 1 year of the fellowship period on dissertation research abroad and 1 year at the Center to complete the dissertation. Deadline: November 15.

1747. (A, H, SS)
J. Paul Getty Trust Paired Fellowships for Research in Conservation and the History of Art and Archaeology

1 fellowship of $12,000, in addition to an allowance of up to $5,500 for project-related research and travel expenses, to candidates who with the appropriate terminal degree for 5 years or more. An equivalent record of professional accomplishment, in exceptional cases, may fulfill this requirement. Award supports research teams working in any field of art history, archaeology, or architecture. Each team may apply for a supplemental allowance of up to $5,000 for expenses related to photography for publication, the creation of drawings, maps, or charts, or other expenditures directly related to the publication of the study. If relocation to Washington, DC, is necessary, up to $1,500 for round-trip travel to Washington, DC, is available for the residency period. It is expected that one copy of all photographs made for the project will be given to the National Gallery photographic archives. Timely publication of results is expected. Deadline: March 21.

1748. (A, H)
Paul Mellon Predoctoral Fellowship

1 fellowship of $20,000 per year (plus a stipend of $16,000, a $4,000 housing subsidy, and a per diem allowance for photography and travel, depending on the terms of each fellowship), to a doctoral candidate who has completed all course work and is working on dissertation. Award supports completion of doctoral dissertation in Western art and enables a candidate to reside abroad for 2 years to develop expertise in a specific city, locality, or region related to the dissertation. The third year is to be spent in residency at the Center to complete the dissertation. Deadline: November 15.

1749. (A, H)
Predoctoral Fellowship Program for Travel Abroad for Historians of American Art

Up to 10 fellowships of up to $3,000 to doctoral students in art history who study aspects of art and architecture of the United States, including native and pre-Revolutionary America. The travel fellowship is for a period of 6 to 8 weeks of continuous travel abroad in areas such as Africa, Asia, Europe, or South America, to sites of historical and cultural interest including museums, exhibitions, collections, monuments, and historic sites. Awarded to support a breadth of art-historical experience beyond the candidate's major field, not for the advancement of a dissertation. Preference given to those who have had little opportunity for professional travel abroad. Amount of award dependent on the travel plan. A narrative report at the conclusion of the travel period is required. Deadline: February 15.

1750. (A)
Robert H. and Clarice Smith Fellowship

1 fellowship of $20,000 per year (plus a stipend of $16,000, a $4,000 housing subsidy, and a per diem allowance for photography and travel, depending on the terms of each fellowship) to a doctoral candidate who has completed all course work and is working on dissertation on 17th-century Dutch or Flemish art. Award supports advancement or completion of either a doctoral dissertation or a resulting publication. For those preparing a publication based on the dissertation, candidates may have graduated two

years prior to award. The Smith Fellow may use the fellowship to study either in the United States or abroad; there are no residence requirements at the Center. Deadline: November 15.

1751. (A)
Samuel H. Kress and Mary Davis Predoctoral Fellowships

1 Kress and 1 Davis Fellowship of $20,000 per year (plus a stipend of $16,000, a $4,000 housing subsidy, and a per diem allowance for photography and travel, depending on the terms of each fellowship) to doctoral candidates who have completed all course work and are working on dissertation. Awards support the advancement and completion of a doctoral dissertation in European art on a topic prior to the early 19th century. Fellows are expected to spend 1 year of the fellowship period on dissertation research abroad and 1 year at the Center to complete the dissertation, devoting half-time to Gallery research projects designed to complement the subject of the dissertation and to provide curatorial experience. Deadline: November 15.

1752. (A)
Samuel H. Kress Foundation Paired Fellowships for Research in Conservation and the History of Art and Archaeology

1 fellowship of $12,000, in addition to an allowance of up to $5,500, for project-related research and travel expenses to candidates with the appropriate terminal degree for 5 years or more. An equivalent record of professional accomplishment, in exceptional cases, may fulfill this requirement. Award supports research teams working on European visual arts prior to the early 19th century. Each team may apply for a supplemental allowance of up to $5,000 for expenses related to photography for publication, the creation of drawings, maps, or charts, or other expenditures directly related to the publication of the study. If relocation to Washington, DC, is necessary, up to $1,500 for round-trip travel to Washington is available for the residency period. Paired Research Fellows spend 2 to 3 months conducting field, collections, and/or laboratory research, followed by 2 months in residency at the Center for discussion, research, and writing. The first segment of the fellowship may involve activities such as travel to visit collections or sites and/or consulta-

tion with other scholars. It is expected that 1 copy of all photographs made for the project will be given to the National Gallery photographic archives. Timely publication of results is expected. Deadline: March 21.

1753. (A)
Senior Fellowship Program

1 Paul Mellon, 1 Frese, and from 4 to 6 Ailsa Mellon Bruce and Samuel H. Kress Fellowships of up to $40,000 plus an allowance for photography and for travel to a professional meeting to scholars who possess a record of professional accomplishment at the time of application or who have had a doctorate for 5 years or more. Awards are to be used to support research in the history, theory, and criticism of the visual arts (painting, sculpture, architecture, landscape architecture, urbanism, prints and drawings, film, photography, decorative arts, industrial design, and other arts) of any geographical area and of any period. The Samuel H. Kress Senior Fellowships support research on European art prior to the early 19th century. The Frese Senior Fellowship is for study in the history, theory, and criticism of sculpture, prints and drawings, and the decorative arts of any geographical area and of any period. Applications are also solicited from scholars in other disciplines whose work examines artifacts or has implications for the analysis and criticism of physical form. Deadline: October 1.

1754. (A)
Wyeth Predoctoral Fellowship

1 fellowship of $20,000 per year (plus a stipend of $16,000, a $4,000 housing subsidy, and a per diem allowance for photography and travel, depending on the terms of each fellowship) to a doctoral student in American art. Award supports advancement and completion of a doctoral dissertation that concerns the visual arts (preferably painting or sculpture) of the United States before 1945. The Wyeth Fellow is expected to spend 1 year of the fellowship period on dissertation research in the United States or abroad and 1 year at the Center to complete the dissertation. Selection based on academic achievement and proposed research. Must be proficient in 2 foreign languages. Must be a U.S. citizen and be in enrolled in a U.S. university. Deadline: November 15.

1755. (S, SS)

National Geographic Society Scholarship Research Grants

P.O. Box 98199

Washington, DC 20090–8199

(202) 828–5466

http://www.nationalgeographic.com

Numerous grants ranging from $1,200 to $75,000 to conduct field research in anthropology, archeology, astronomy, biology, botany, ecology, glaciology, mineralogy, oceanography, paleontology, physical and human geography, zoology, and other sciences relevant to geography. Preference given to postdoctoral researchers. Based on proposed research. Open to all nationalities. Deadline: none.

1756. (S)

National Ground Water Association API/NGWA Scholarship

601 Dempsey Road

Westerville, OH 43081

(800) 551–7379

http://www.ngwa.org/about/schship_api-ngwa.html

ngwa@ngwa.org

4 scholarships of $3,000 to graduate (master's and doctoral) students in subsurface environmental science or a related program. Award can be used for tuition or to purchase materials, supplies, and/or laboratory analytical services directly related to student's research. Visit web site for more information. Deadline: July 1.

1757. (S)

National Heart, Lung, and Blood Institute Minority Graduate Research Awards

Health Information Center

ATTN: Web Site

P.O. Box 30105

Bethesda, MD 20824–0105

(301) 592–8573

http://www.nhlbi.nih.gov

Awards of varying amounts to graduate and undergraduate students in biomedical research, behavioral science, laboratory and clinical medicine. Provides an opportunity for underrepresented minority students to receive training in fundamental biomedical sciences and clinical research disciplines. Visit web site for more information. Deadline: none specified.

1758. (S)

National Hemophilia Foundation Judith Graham Pool Postdoctoral Research Fellowships

116 West 32nd Street, 11th Floor

New York, NY 10001

(212) 328–3700

http://www.hemophila.org

Awards of $35,000 to postdoctoral (M.D.s and Ph.D.s) fellowships to conduct hemophilia-related research. Awarded through professional and graduate schools or research institutions. Established investigators and faculty members are ineligible. Renewable depending on progress. Deadline: December 1.

(S)

National Housing Endowment

1201 15th Street, N.W.

Washington, DC 20005

http://www.nationalhousingendowment.com

nhe@nahb.com

1759. (S)

Centex Homes/NHE/Build Your Future Scholarship

1 award of up to $2,500 to full-time graduate or undergraduate students in a housing-related program such as construction management, residential building, construction technology, civil engineering, architecture, or related trade specialties. Must have at least a 2.5 GPA on a 4.0 scale for all courses and a 3.0 GPA on a 4.0 scale on core curriculum courses. Visit web site for guidelines and application. Deadline: April 2.

1760. (S)

Herman J. Smith Scholarship

Awards of $2,000 to full-time graduate and undergraduate students in construction management, mortgage finance, or construction-related fields. Renewable based on academic achievement and financial need. For more information or application, visit web site. Deadline: May 1.

1761. (S)
Lee S. Evans Scholarship

Up to 8 awards of up to $5,000 to full-time graduate and undergraduate students entering the field of residential construction management. Recipients must have at least 1 full year of academic course work after scholarship is received. Preference is given to current members and students enrolled in a program emphasizing construction management. For specific guidelines and application, visit web site. Deadline: December 2.

1762. (S)
National Institute for Nursing Research
NRSA Research Fellowships
31 Center Drive, Room 5B–10
Bethesda, MD 20892–2179
written inquiries only
http://mentalhealth.about.com

Fellowships of $8,800 to predoctoral and $32,300 to postdoctoral students to conduct nursing research. Must be professional registered nurses and hold a bachelor's, master's, or doctoral degree in nursing. Must be U.S. citizen or legal resident. Predoctoral awards are renewable for up to 5 years, and postdoctoral degrees are renewable for up to 3 years. Deadline: December 5, April 5, and August 5.

(S)
National Institute of Arthritis & Musculoskeletal & Skin Diseases
National Institutes of Health
1 AMS Circle
Building 45, Room 5AS–49E
Bethesda, MD 20892–6500
(301) 594–5128
http://www.niams.nih.gov

1763. (S)
Arthritis/Bone & Skin Diseases Research Grants

40 fellowships and 185 institutional trainees providing varying amounts of assistance to doctoral and postdoctoral fellows in the areas of arthritis, osteopathic, or dermatology research. Award is for laboratory and clinical research on arthritis and rheumatic diseases, bone and musculoskeletal diseases, and cutaneous diseases. Must be U.S. citizens. Deadline: varies.

1764. (S)
Predoctoral Fellowship Awards for Minority Students

Fellowships providing a stipend of $16,500, an institutional allowance of $2,500, tuition, fees, and health insurance to minority doctoral students to conduct full-time research in arthritis, muscle, bone, musculoskeletal, and/or skin disease. Must be a U.S. citizen or permanent resident. Renewable up to 5 years. Deadline: November 1 and May 1.

1765. (S)
Predoctoral Fellowship Awards for Students with Disabilities

Fellowships providing a stipend of $16,500, an institutional allowance of $2,500, tuition, fees, and health insurance to disabled doctoral students to conduct full-time research in arthritis, muscle, bone, musculoskeletal, and/or skin disease. Must be a U.S. citizen or permanent resident. Renewable up to 5 years. Deadline: November 1 and May 1.

1766. (S)
Short-Term Predoctoral Research Training
Health Professional Students

Fellowships providing a stipend of $1,255 per month, tuition, and fees to medical school students. Recipients must conduct research for periods of 2 to 3 months. Deadline: none specified.

(S)
National Institute of Dental and Craniofacial Research
Special Assistant for Manpower Development
Extramural Program
Westwood Building, Room 510
Bethesda, MD 20892
(301) 402–0799
http://www.nidr.nih.gov

1767. (S)
Dentist Scientist Award

Unspecified number of fellowships providing a salary of up to $50,000 and $25,000 for research expenses for individuals with a dental degree for postdoctoral work. Amount of award depends on the institution's salary scale. Maximum of $75,000 total over a 5-year period. Applicants must be citizens or noncitizen nationals of the U.S. Must be nominated by a U.S. university dental school. Deadline: none specified.

1768. (S)
Individual Fellows

Fellowships ranging from $18,600 to $32,300 to postdoctoral health scientists to conduct full-time research in areas reflecting the national need for biomedical and behavioral research. Must hold a D.D.S., D.M.D., or Ph.D. Must arrange to work with a sponsor who is affiliated with, and has the staff and facilities needed for, the proposed training. Must be U.S. citizen or legal resident. Deadline: January 10, May 10, and September 10.

1769. (S)
Short-Term Training for Dental Research

Awards providing at least $834 to students enrolled at an accredited U.S. dental school. Award is designed encourage students in pursuing a career in biomedical/dental research. Must be U.S. citizen. Application is through individual institution. For additional information about the program, contact above address. Deadline: none.

1770. (S)
National Institute of Diabetes and Digestive and Kidney Diseases (NIDDK)
6707 Democracy Boulevard, Rm. 609
Bethesda, MD 20892–5460
(301) 594–7692
http://www.niddk.nih.gov

Awards of varying amounts to graduate and undergraduate students and postdoctoral fellows to conduct NIDDK-related research. Individuals from underrepresented racial and ethnic groups, as well as individuals with disabilities, are always encouraged to apply for NIH programs. Deadline: none specified.

(S)
National Institute of Environmental Health Sciences
Division of Extramural Research and Training
P.O. Box 12233
Research Triangle Park, NC 27709–2233
http://www.niehs.nih.gov/dert/contact.htm

1771. (S)
Individual Predoctoral Fellowships for Minorities

Fellowships providing an annual stipend, an annual institutional allowance, and tuition, fees, and health insurance to minority graduate students in a doctoral or equivalent research program, a combined M.D./Ph.D. program, or another combined professional doctorate/research Ph.D. graduate program. Must be a U.S. citizen or permanent resident. Must be in a biomedical, behavioral sciences, or health services research program. Deadline: May 1 and November 1.

1772. (S)
Individual Predoctoral Fellowships for Students with Disabilities

Fellowships providing an annual stipend, an annual institutional allowance, and tuition, fees, and health insurance to disabled graduate students in a doctoral or equivalent research program, a combined M.D./Ph.D. program, or another combined professional doctorate/research Ph.D. graduate program. Must be a U.S. citizen or permanent resident. Must be in a biomedical, behavioral sciences, or health services research program. Deadline: May 1 and November 1.

(S)
National Institute of General Medical Sciences (NIGMS)
45 Center Drive MSC 6200
Room 1AS–25
Bethesda, MD 20892–6200
(301) 496–7301
http://www.nigms.nih.gov

1773. (S)
Fellowship Awards for Minority Students

Fellowships providing an annual stipend of $19,968, a tuition and fee allowance, and an annual institutional allowance of $2,750 that can be used for travel to scientific meetings and for laboratory and other training expenses. Awarded to minority graduate students seeking doctoral degrees in biomedical and behavioral sciences. Up to 5 years of support for research training leading to a Ph.D., M.D./Ph.D., or another combined professional doctorate-research doctoral degree. Must be U.S. citizens or permanent residents. Deadline: February 24.

1774. (S)
Fellowship Awards for Students with Disabilities

Fellowships providing an annual stipend of $19,968, a tuition and fee allowance, and an annual institutional allowance of $2,750 that can be used for travel to scientific meetings and for laboratory and other training expenses. Awarded to minority graduate students to seek doctoral degrees in biomedical and behavioral sciences. Up to 5 years of support for research training leading to a Ph.D., M.D./Ph.D., or another combined professional doctorate-research doctoral degree. Must be U.S. citizens or permanent residents. Deadline: February 24.

1775. (S)
Medical Scientist Training Program

Awards of varying amounts to students to pursue a combined M.D./Ph.D. degree. Provides for investigators who can bridge the gap between basic and clinical research by supporting research training. In addition to biomedical sciences, program also supports computer sciences, social and behavioral sciences, economics, epidemiology, public health, bioengineering, biostatistics, and bioethics. Must be a U.S. citizen or permanent resident. Deadline: not specified.

1776. (S)
Pharmacology Research Associate Program
http://www.nigms.nih.gov/about_nagms/prat.html

Awards of varying amounts to postdoctoral scientists to receive training in pharmacology in NIH and FDA laboratories and clinics. Must have received a Ph.D. or a professional degree (M.D., D.D.S., D.O., D.V.M., or Pharm.D.) within the last 5 years. Must be U.S. citizens or permanent residents. Deadline: January 2.

(S)

National Institutes of Health
Graduate Partnership Program
10 Center Drive
Building 10/Room IC129
Bethesda, MD 20892–1153

(301) 594–9605
http://gpp.nih.gov
appinfo@nih.gov

1777. (S)
Ruth L. Kirschstein National Research Service Award
Dual Degree Predoctoral Fellowship for Training Clinical Scientists

Fellowships providing support for up to 5 years to students enrolled in an M.D./Ph.D. or M.D./M.P.H. program. Award funds research to investigate problems of environmentally relevant disease in humans. Must be U.S. citizens, noncitizen nationals, or permanent residents and identify a research sponsor. Visit web site for more information. Deadline: none specified.

1778. (S)
Ruth L. Kirschstein National Research Service Award
Predoctoral Awards for Students with Disabilities

Fellowships providing a stipend, tuition, fees, and institutional allowance to students identified as disabled through the ADA criteria who are enrolled in or accepted to a doctoral program. Must be U.S. citizens, noncitizen nationals, or permanent residents and identify a research sponsor. Visit web site for more information. Deadline: none specified.

1779. (S)
Ruth L. Kirschstein National Research Service Award
Predoctoral Fellowship for Minority Students

Fellowships providing a stipend, tuition, fees, and institutional allowance to minority students enrolled in or accepted to a doctoral program. Must be U.S. citizens, noncitizen nationals, or permanent residents and identify a research sponsor. Visit web site for more information. Deadline: none specified.

1780. (S, SS)
National Institutes of Health
John E. Fogarty JSPS Short-Term Fellowships for Biomedical and Behavioral Research in Japan
Division of International Training and Research
ATTN: JSPS Fellowship Program

Fogarty International Center
NIH Building 31, Room B2C39
31 Center Drive–MSC 2220
Bethesda, MD 20892–2220
http://www.nih.gov/fic/programs/jspsshort.html
hsps@hih.gov

Up to 20 short-term fellowships of 16,000 yen per day, domestic travel of 150,000 yen, and round-trip airfare to doctoral candidates and qualified scientists engaged in biomedical or behavioral science research (Ph.D., M.D., or other doctoral degree and can demonstrate that their collaboration with Japanese colleagues holds exceptional professional promise). Must be U.S. citizens or permanent residents. Award supports American researchers in pursuing collaborative research in Japan for periods ranging from 7 to 60 days. Deadline: April 28.

(S)
National Institutes of Health
(866) 849–4047
http://www.lrp.nih.gov
lrp@nih.gov

1781. (S)
National Institutes of Health
Predoctoral Fellowship Awards for Minority
Students

Awards providing tuition, fees, health insurance, plus a stipend to minority graduate students to support research training leading to a Ph.D., M.D./Ph.D., or other combined professional degree and research doctoral degree in biomedical, behavioral, or health services research. Must be U.S. citizens or permanent residents and admitted to an accredited graduate program. An institutional allowance of $2,500 per 12-month period is awarded to the non-federal, non-profit sponsoring institution. Renewable up to 5 years. Deadline: May 1 and November 15.

1782. (S)
Office of Loan Repayment & Scholarship

The NIH Loan Repayment Program (LRP) is a competitive program that offers repayment of up to $35,000 per year of educational loan debt for health professionals pursuing careers in clinical, pediatric, contraception and fertility, or health disparities research. Recipients must commit to at least 50% research effort

for 2 years. Open to M.D., Ph.D., Pharm.D., D.O., D.D.S., D.M.D., D.P.M., D.C., N.D., or equivalent (D.V.M. qualify for Pediatric Research LRP). Must be U.S. citizen or permanent resident. Visit web site for more information. Deadline: January 31.

(S)
National Institutes of Health
Research and Training Opportunities
2 Center Drive
Building 2, Room 2E06
Bethesda, MD 20892–0240
(301) 496–2427
http://www.training.nih.gov/student/Pre-IRTA

1783. (S)
Clinical Electives Program

Awards providing a subsidy of $300 to third- and fourth-year medical and dental students to participate in rotations that offer students in-depth exposure in certain subspecialties. Students are given firsthand experience in the design, conduct, and management of clinical trials. Students are introduced to translational medicine—the first step research takes from bench to bedside. Participation is at NIH in Bethesda, MD. Deadline: rolling.

1784. (S)
Clinical Research Training Program
http://www.training.nih.gov/crtp

15 fellowships providing a living stipend of $25,300, a computer allowance of $1,200, a book allowance of $250, and a conference travel allowance of up to $1,300 to medical and dental students who have completed or are in the process of completing 1 year of clinical rotations (generally third year). Candidates in M.D./Ph.D. programs are also eligible to apply. Must be U.S. citizens or permanent residents. Deadline: January 15.

1785. (S)
HHMI-NIH Research Scholars Program

42 fellowships providing a salary of $17,800, subsidized housing, round-trip moving expenses, and up to $250 book allowance to medical and dental students to spend 9 months to a year on the NIH campus conducting translational or applied medical research. 12 to 14 students in the program are selected to receive

continued support of an annual stipend of $21,000 and cost-of-education allowance of $16,000 to pay for tuition and other education-related expenses. Students participate after their second or third year in medical or dental school. Students enrolled in M.D./Ph.D. programs or who already have an M.D., D.D.S., or Ph.D. are not eligible. Deadline: mid-January.

1786. (S)
Interim or Year-Off IRTA Fellowship Program

Fellowships providing stipends ranging from $21,300 to $26,300 to graduate and medical students. Program augments the educational preparation and development of future scientists. Fellows work in laboratories at NIH or other locations in Baltimore and Frederick, MD; Research Triangle Park, NC; Phoenix, AZ; or Hamilton, MT. Must be U.S. citizens accepted to or enrolled in accredited graduate, doctoral, or medical school in the U.S. Deadline: rolling.

1787. (S)
NIH Academy Fellowship Program

Fellowships of $23,800 to recent college graduates to spend a year engaged in biomedical investigation at NIH in Bethesda, MD. Must be U.S. citizens or permanent residents and have graduated from an accredited U.S. institution within the last year. Must apply online. Deadline: March 15.

1788. (S)
Postbaccalaureate IRTA Fellowship Program

Fellowships providing stipends of up to $20,500 to recent (within 2 years) college graduates to spend a year engaged in biomedical investigation at NIH in Bethesda or a selected off-campus location. Must be U.S. citizens or permanent residents who graduated from an accredited U.S. institution. Deadline: none.

1789. (S)
Technical IRTA Fellowship Program

Fellowships providing a stipend ranging from $17,500 to $24,000 to students with a bachelor's or master's degree to participate in developmental experiences in NIH and other locations in Baltimore and Frederick, MD, Research Triangle Park, NC, Phoenix, AZ, or Hamilton, MT. Fellowships are for 2 years and can be extended to a maximum of 3 years. Deadline: rolling.

1790. (S)
National Institutes of Health
Warren Grant Magnuson Clinical Center
Predoctoral Fellowships
Department of Clinical Bioethics
Building 10, Room 1C118
10 Center Drive
Bethesda, MD 20892–1156
(301) 496–2429
http://bioethics.nih.gov/opportunities/pre-doc.html

Fellowships of varying amounts to students with an undergraduate degree who are planning postgraduate work. Selection based on academic achievement, commitment to scholarship, and the contribution they are likely to make in the field of bioethics. Awards are for 2 years. Deadline: March 15.

(A, H, S, SS)
National Italian American Foundation (NIAF)
ATTN: Education Director
1860 19th Street, N.W.
Washington, DC 20009–5599
(202) 387–0600
http://www.niaf.org

1791. (A, H)
Aracri Scholarship

1 scholarship of $1,000 to a graduate or undergraduate student majoring in Italian art, literature, or theater. Award allows student to conduct research on Calabrese art, music, literature, and/or theater. Based on academic achievement, Italian descent, and financial need. Please send a self-addressed, stamped envelope for an application. Deadline: May 31.

1792. (S)
Carmela Gagliardi Foundation Health Sciences Scholarship

Scholarships of $5,000 to students who are enrolled in or have been accepted to an accredited medical school. Applicants must be of Italian descent and have been in the top 25% of their class. Selection based on academic achievement and financial need, which is verified by school's Financial Aid Office. Renewable. Deadline: March 1.

1793. (S)

Piancone Family Agriculture Scholarship

1 scholarship of $2,000 to an Italian-American graduate or undergraduate student pursuing an agriculture major. Must be a resident of DE, MD, MA, NJ, NY, PA, VA, or Washington, DC. Please include a self-addressed, stamped envelope with request. Selection based on application, academic achievement, recommendation letters, and financial need. Deadline: May 31.

1794. (A, H, S, SS)

Robert J. DiPietro Scholarships

2 scholarships of $1,000 to Italian-American graduate or undergraduate students. Must not be over 25 years of age. Based on an essay ranging from 400 to 600 words on how the applicant intends to preserve and use his/her ethnicity throughout life. Must submit 4 copies of the essay, with applicant's name and title of essay on each copy. Enclose a self-addressed, stamped envelope for information. Deadline: May 31.

1795. (A, H, S, SS)

Sarina Grande Scholarship

1 scholarship of $1,000 to an Italian-American graduate or undergraduate student. May have any major. Enclose a self-addressed, stamped envelope. Deadline: May 31.

1796. (Contest)

National Juried Competition
Phoenix Gallery
568 Broadway, Suite 607
New York, NY 10012
(212) 226–8711
http://www.phoenix-gallery.com

A national competition with varying awards. Competition runs through July. Juror: Eleanor Heartney, Critic, Curator. Contributing Editor: Art in America, New Art Examiner. Award: Solo/Group Show. Minimum entry fee is $20 for up to 2 entries. Additional entries are $5 each. Entries are nonrefundable. Send self-addressed, stamped envelope for prospectus to: Phoenix Gallery.

(A, H, Contest)

National League of American Pen Women, Inc.
Scholarship Grants for Women
1300 Seventeenth Street, N.W.

Washington, DC 20036
(202) 785–1997
http://www.americanpenwomen.org/

1797. (Contest)

Alabama, Montgomery Branch
Spring Poetry Contest

Cash awards of varying amounts for poetry. Each poem has a 50-line limit, but there are no limits on number of entries. Open to anyone. A small entry fee is required. Visit web site for submission guidelines and contact address. Deadline: April 1.

1798. (Contest)

Arkansas, Pioneer Branch
Arkansas Writers' Conference Letters Contest

Cash awards of varying amounts in a writing competition. Visit web site for entry fee and to locate address, contact person from whom to request contest brochure. Deadline: April 30.

1799. (Contest)

California, Nob Hill Branch
Soul-Making Literary Competition

Cash awards of $100, $50, and $25 for entries in poetry, short-short stories, short stories, essays, creative nonfiction, novel excerpt, and song/lyrics. Contest is open to anyone, but entry fees must be submitted in U.S. funds. Visit web site for submission guidelines and contact person. Deadline: November 30.

1800. (Contest)

California, Palm Springs Branch
DeAnn Lubell Professional Writers' Competition

Cash awards of $50, $75, and $100 for poetry, short stories, essays and editorials, and web-based articles. Entries must have been published within the past 5 years. Visit web site for entry fees, submission guidelines, and contact person. Deadline: March 15.

1801. (Contest)

California, Palomar Branch
International Haiku Contest

Cash awards of $20, $40, and $100 for haiku poetry. All proceeds from this contest provide a scholarship for graduating high school seniors. Visit web site for submission guidelines and contact person for contest brochure. Deadline: March 1.

1802. (Contest)
California, Santa Clara Branch
Limerick Contest

Cash awards for original limericks. Winning entries may appear in *The Pen Woman*. Visit web site for entry fees, submission guidelines, and contact person. Deadline: March 17.

1803. (Contest)
California, Simi Valley Branch
Dorothy Daniels Honorary Writing Award

Awards for entries in fiction (2,000-word limit), nonfiction, and poetry. Essays and journals are ineligible. Visit web site for entry fees, submission guidelines, and contact person. Deadline: July 31.

1804. (Contest)
Colorado, Pikes Peak Branch
Flash Fiction Contest

Cash awards of $15, $25, and $60 for all fiction genres: contemporary, historical, romance, mystery, sci-fi, horror, western, adventure, inspirational, etc. All entries will receive constructive critiquing. Visit web site for entry fees, submission guidelines, and contact person. Deadline: May 7.

1805. (A, H)
Scholarships

3 scholarships of $1,000 to women age 35 or over who are not members of NLAPW in the areas of fine art, creative writing, and music. Applicants must submit slides; manuscripts; or musical compositions suited to that year's competition. Must submit a letter stating the person's age, background, and creative purpose for the money. Criteria varies. Send a self-addressed, stamped envelope after August 1 of odd-numbered years for guidelines. Deadline: January 15 of even-numbered years.

1806. (S)
National League of Nurses Foundation
Promise of Nursing Graduate Nursing Education
Scholarship Program
61 Broadway, 33rd Floor
New York, NY 10006
http://www.nln.org

Up to 50 awards of up to $15,000 for tuition, books, and fees to graduate students in or admitted to a graduate nursing program. Must live in a specified area in certain states. Must have at least a 3.25 GPA on a 4.0 scale. Award may be used for courses yet to be completed, for dissertation research, or for scholarly project support. Deadline: April 7.

(S)
National Medical Fellowships, Inc.
5 Hanover Square, 15th Floor
New York, NY 10004
(212) 483–8880
http://www.nmf-online.org

1807. (S)
Aura E. Severinghaus Scholarships

1 scholarship of $2,000 to a minority senior medical student attending Columbia University College of Physicians and Surgeons. Selection is based on academic achievement, leadership, and community service. Visit web site for more information and deadline.

1808. (S)
Bay Area Community Service Scholarships

Scholarships of $7,500 (6-week rotation) and $15,000 (12-week rotation) to rising third- and fourth-year medical students enrolled in medical schools in the Bay Area (UC Davis School of Medicine, U of SF School of Medicine, or Stanford Medical School). Students may choose to complete basic science or clinical science research projects or a clinical rotation. Selection is based on demonstrated commitment to practice in California, interest in community-based primary care or research, satisfactory academic performance, financial need, and leadership. Visit web site for more information and deadline.

1809. (S)
Bristol-Myers Squibb Fellowship Program in
Academic Medicine for Minority Students

35 scholarships of $6,000 to minority medical students to encourage them to pursue a career in biomedical research and academic medicine. Must be attending an accredited allopathic or osteopathic medical school in the U.S. Recipients spend 8 to 12 weeks working in a research laboratory. Priority is

given to second- and third-year students. Fellowships are not renewable. Visit web site for more information and deadline.

1810. (S)
California Community Service Program

Scholarships of $7,500 to rising third- and fourth-year medical students attending an accredited medical school in California. The program includes a 6-week rotation in a community health center dedicated to medically underserved populations. Selection is based on demonstrated commitment to practice in California, interest in community-based primary care or research, satisfactory academic performance, financial need, and leadership. Visit web site for more information and deadline.

1811. (S)
Fellowship Program in AIDS Care

8 scholarships of $7,000 to minority medical students to participate in a 4-week, multidisciplinary training program in HIV/AIDS clinical care and research. Must be attending an accredited allopathic or osteopathic medical school in the U.S. Visit web site for more information and deadline.

1812. (S)
Franklin C. McLean Award

1 award of $3,000 to a senior student in recognition of outstanding academic achievement, leadership, and community service. The McLean Award, NMF's oldest and most prestigious honor, was established in 1968 in memory of the noted Chicago bone physiologist who established the organization. Visit web site for more information and deadline.

1813. (S)
Gerber Foundation Fellowship in Pediatric Nutrition

1 scholarship of $3,000 to a minority medical student. Must be attending an accredited allopathic or osteopathic medical school in the U.S. Award provides supplemental support for a student or resident doing ongoing research in the area of pediatric nutrition. Visit web site for more information and deadline.

1814. (S)
Henry G. Halladay Awards

5 awards of $760 each to African-American men enrolled in the first year of medical school who have overcome significant obstacles to obtain a medical education. These awards were made possible through an endowment established by the late Mrs. Henry G. Halladay to honor the memory of her husband. Visit web site for more information and deadline.

1815. (S)
Hugh J. Anderson Memorial Scholarship

Up to 5 scholarships of $2,500 to medical students. Student must either be a Minnesota resident attending any U.S.-accredited medical school or a student attending an accredited Minnesota medical school. Visit web site for more information and deadline.

1816. (S)
Irving Graef Memorial Scholarship

1 2-year scholarships of $2,000 to a third-year student recognizing outstanding academic achievement, leadership, and community service. The scholarship is renewable in the fourth year if the award winner continues in good academic standing. This scholarship program was established by NMF's board in 1978 and permanently endowed by the Irving Graef Medical Fund in 1980 to honor the memory of one of NMF's most active board members. Visit web site for more information and deadline.

1817. (S)
James H. Robinson Memorial Prize

1 award of $500 to a minority medical student. This award was established by the NMF board in 1986 to honor the memory of James H. Robinson, M.D., who was clinical professor of surgery and associate dean of student affairs at Jefferson Medical College of Thomas Jefferson University in Philadelphia, PA. Dr. Robinson served as vice-chairman of NMF's board of directors and chairman of the board's planning and development committee. Visit web site for more information and deadline.

1818. (S)
Metropolitan Life Foundation Awards

17 awards of $4,000 to minority second-, third-, and fourth-year medical students attending an accredited allopathic or osteopathic U.S. medical school. Selection is based on academic excellence, leadership, and financial need. Limited to schools in certain cities. Must be U.S. citizens. Visit web site for more information. Deadline: February 28.

1819. (S)
Need-Based Scholarship Program

Scholarships ranging from $500 to $10,000 to first- and second-year medical students. Selection based on financial need as determined by the student's total resources, cost of education, and receipt of other scholarships and grants. Some awards are available to third-year students. Visit web site for more information and deadline.

1820. (S)
Ralph W. Ellison Memorial Prize

1 fellowship of $500 to a second- through fourth-year underrepresented medical student in recognition of outstanding academic achievement, leadership, and financial need. Visit web site for more information and deadline.

1821. (S)
Special Awards Program

Awards of varying amounts to African-American medical students for extraordinary accomplishments, academic excellence, leadership, and potential for outstanding contributions to medicine. Visit web site for more information and deadline.

1822. (S)
William and Charlotte Cadbury Award

1 award of $2,000 to a senior medical student in recognition of outstanding academic achievement, leadership and community service. The Cadbury Award was established in 1977 by Irving Graef, M.D., and the NMF board of directors to honor the organization's former executive director and staff associate. Visit web site for more information and deadline.

1823. (S)
W. K. Kellogg Foundation Fellowship in Health Policy Research

1 scholarship providing tuition, fees, and a partial living stipend for up to 5 years to a minority medical student to complete advanced research training. Visit web site for more information and deadline.

1824. (S)
Wyeth-Ayerst Prizes in Women's Health

2 awards of $5,000 to graduating female students who will practice or conduct research in the field of women's health. Wyeth-Ayerst Laboratories, a leading developer and marketer of pharmaceutical products for women, established these graduation prizes for female minority medical students. These awards recognize the outstanding talents and future potential of graduating female students. Visit web site for more information and deadline.

1825. (S)
National Multiple Sclerosis Society Fellowships & Grants
733 Third Avenue
New York, NY 10017
(800) FIGHT MS
http://www.nmss.org

Fellowships and grants of varying amounts to advanced doctorates (M.D./Ph.D.), recent M.D./Ph.D.s, and senior investigators to stimulate, coordinate, and support research into the cause, prevention, alleviation, and cure of MS. No scholarship or predoctoral support is available. Deadline: varies.

1826. (S)
National Oceanic and Atmospheric Administration National Sea Grant College Program
14th Street & Constitution Avenue, N.W.
Room 6013
Washington, DC 20230
(202) 482–6090
written inquiry only
http://www.noaa.gov

1 fellowship of $30,000 to cover salary and living expenses to a graduate student in marine science or marine-related field. Students are paired with an individual in the

executive or legislative branch of government or a DC-based association. Must be enrolled in an accredited graduate or professional school program in a marine-related field. Fellowship generally begins between January 15 and February 1 and runs for 1 year. Send a self-addressed, stamped envelope for information. Deadline: spring/summer.

1827. (S)
National Physical Science Consortium
Graduate Fellowships for Minorities and Women in the Physical Sciences
University Village
Suite E 200
3375 South Hoover Street
Los Angeles, CA 90007
(800) 854–NPSC
http://www.npsc.org

Fellowships of $12,400 for years 1 through 4 and $15,000 for years 5 and 6 to graduate minority (Hispanic-American, African-American, or Native American) or female students majoring in astronomy, chemistry, computer science, geology, materials science, mathematical science, physics, or other subdisciplines. Must have at least a 3.0 GPA. Renewable up to 6 years. Deadline: November 15.

1828. (Contest)
National Poetry Competition
The Chester H. Jones Foundation
P.O. Box 498
Chardon, OH 44024
(216) 286–6310
http://www.pw.org/mag/ga9901.htm

1 first prize of $1,000, 1 second prize of $500, 1 third prize of $250, 1 fourth prize of $100, 1 honorable mention of $50, and commendation awards of $10 and publication of all winners. For information and entry form send a self-addressed, stamped envelope. Deadline: March 31.

1829. (H)
National Press Club
Feldman Scholarship
General Manager's Office
529 14th Street, N.W.

Washington, DC 20045
(202) 662–7500
http://npc.press.org/programs/aboutscholarship.cfm#feldman

1 scholarship of $5,000 to a graduate student pursuing a master's degree in journalism. Must have applied to, or be enrolled in, an accredited graduate journalism program. Selection is based on 3 recommendation letters, financial aid information, a goals essay, and biographical sketch. Deadline: May 1.

(A, H)
National Press Photographers Foundation
3200 Croasdaile, Suite 306
Durham, NC 27705
(919) 383–7246
http://www.nppa.org/contests/default.htm

1830. (A, H)
Bob East Scholarship

1 scholarship grant of $1,500 to a graduate or undergraduate student who plans to attend graduate school. Must be pursuing a career in newspaper photojournalism. Must submit a portfolio that includes at least 5 single images in addition to a picture story. This award will be chosen primarily on quality of the portfolio. Visit web site for specific guidelines and submission address. Deadline: February 14.

1831. (A, H)
College Photographer of the Year Competition

1 Colonel William Lookadoo Scholarship grant of $1,000 and 1 Milton Freier Award of $500 to graduate and undergraduate students. Award recognizes outstanding work of students currently working toward a degree and provides a forum for student photographers to gauge their skills against those of their peers. Visit web site for specific guidelines and submission address. Deadline: March 31.

1832. (A, H)
Kit C. King Graduate Scholarship Fund

1 scholarship of $500 to a graduate student in journalism with an emphasis in photojournalism. The applicant must have some indication of acceptance to such an accredited graduate program in photojournalism. The applicant must present a portfolio that

demonstrates talent and initiative in documentary photojournalism. The portfolio should be accompanied by a statement of goals and philosophy relating to documentary photojournalism. Visit web site for specific guidelines and submission address. Deadline: March 1.

1833. (A, H)
NPPF Media Photojournalism Scholarship

1 scholarship of $1,000 to a graduate or undergraduate student pursuing a career in photojournalism. Based on aptitude and potential for success in use of photography as a communications tool. Request information before February 1. Visit web site for specific guidelines and submission address. Deadline: March 1.

1834. (A, H)
Television News Scholarship

1 scholarship of $1,000 to a graduate student or upper-level undergraduate enrolled in a recognized 4-year college or university having courses in TV news photojournalism. Applicants must complete the entry form and submit it along with a videotape containing examples of their work. The tape should contain no more than 3 complete stories (total time for all stories: 6 minutes) with voice narration and natural sound. Applicants must also include a letter from their professor/advisor. Applicants must include a 1-page biographical sketch including a personal statement addressing their professional goals. Visit web site for specific guidelines and submission address. Deadline: March 1.

1835. (A, H, SS)
National Public Radio
Human Resources Department
635 Massachusetts Avenue, N.W.
Washington, DC 20001
(202) 513–3047 (Fax)
http://www.npr.org/about/jobs/intern/index.html
internship@npr.org

30 internships to graduate or undergraduate students or those who have graduated from college within 6 months of beginning the internship. Interns work between 20 and 40 hours per week during the 8- to 10-week internship period. Internships are offered during the summer, fall, and winter/spring semesters. Interns may receive academic credit if arranged between NPR and student's institution. For specific internship descriptions, application, and more information, visit web site. Deadline: February 15 (summer), July 30 (fall), and November 15 (winter/spring).

1836. (S)
National Radio Astronomy Observatory
Summer Research Assistantships
520 Edgemont Road
Charlottesville, VA 22903
(804) 296–0211
http://www.nrao.edu

20 scholarships from $1,000 to $1,300 per month, plus travel expenses, to graduate students who have completed no more than 2 years of study and undergraduate students with at least 3 years of study. Students must be majoring in astronomy, physics, computer science, or electrical engineering. Deadline: February 1.

(S)
National Research Council (NRC)
Fellowship Office
2101 Constitution Avenue, N.W.
Washington, DC 20418
(202) 334–2872
http://www.nationalacademies.org/directories/nrc_p.htm

1837. (S)
Graduate Fellowships

Varying number of fellowships providing up to $7,000 for tuition and fees and a stipend of $14,000 to graduate students who are pursuing master's or doctoral degrees in engineering, mathematics, computer science, chemistry, earth science, life sciences, psychology, or the social sciences. Must be U.S. citizens or legal residents. May be used at any accredited institution offering graduate degrees in these fields. Must not have completed more than 1 year of graduate study. Some awards are for minorities. Renewable up to 3 years. Deadline: November 10.

1838. (S)
Postdoctoral Awards for Research in Federal Laboratories

Stipends of at least $27,750 and up to $44,000, plus benefits, to postdoctoral fellows in the areas of aeronautics, chemistry, computer science, environmental studies, meteorology, engineering, nutrition, mathematics, physics, or psychology. Research must be conducted at participating federal laboratories. Applicants must be U.S. citizens or legal residents. Deadline: January 15, April 15, or August 15.

1839. (S)
Predoctoral and Dissertation Fellowships

Approximately 60 awards of up to $14,000, plus cost of education allowance, to full-time graduate students and 20 dissertation awards of $18,000 to graduate students who are Native Alaskan, Native American, African-American, Mexican-American, Pacific Islanders, or Puerto Rican. Students must be at or near the beginning of graduate study in the areas of behavioral sciences, biological sciences, computer sciences, engineering, physical sciences, mathematics, economics, government, political sciences, or the humanities. Must have completed less than 1 year of graduate studies toward an M.S., Ph.D., or Sc.D degree in a biological science. Students who are pursuing, or who hold, degrees from allopathic or osteopathic medical schools, veterinary schools, or dental schools are also eligible to apply if they are pursuing either a Ph.D. or Sc.D. Awards are for 3 years and may possibly be extended for an additional 2 years. Application period: early September to early November. Deadline: early November.

(S)
National Renewable Energy Laboratory
1617 Cole Boulevard
Golden, CO 80401–3393
(303) 275–3000
http://www.nrel.gov/education/teacher.html

1840. (S)
DOE Preservice Teacher Training Internship Program
http://www.scied.science.doe.gov/scied/sci_ed.htm

10-week research internships to students who have completed their undergraduate degree but have not yet begun to teach K–12 science, math, or technology. Students conduct research under the guidance of a mentor scientist, develop transfer strategies of the laboratory experience to the classroom, and introduce the preservice teacher to research, science methodology, and technologies. Participants are required to produce a research paper and abstract, produce an inquiry-based education module related to the research and aligned with national standards, and prepare and deliver an oral presentation of the research and the educational module. Visit web site for an application and deadline.

1841. (S)
Laboratory Science Teacher Professional Development (LSTPD) Program

A summer research program providing paid stipend and travel and living expenses open to science, math, or technology teachers to work as a research team in a renewable energy or energy efficiency area of interest. The program runs from mid-June through early-August. Deadline: February 28.

(S, SS)
National Restaurant Association Educational Foundation
175 West Jackson Boulevard, Suite 1500
Chicago, IL 60604–2814
(800) 765–2112
(312) 715–1010
http://www.nraef.org

1842. (S, SS)
HJ Heinz Graduate Scholarships

Graduate fellowships ranging from $1,000 to $2,000 for teachers and administrators enrolled in a master's or doctoral program to improve their teaching skills in food service courses or administering food service career education. Deadline: February 15.

1843. (SS)
Teacher Work-Study Grants

Up to 8 scholarships of $2,000 for teachers and administrators for graduate study or who wish to update their knowledge in the food service industry by participating in an 8-week "hands on" experience in the industry. Deadline: February 15.

1844. (SS)

Thad and Alice Eure Memorial Scholarship

2 scholarships of $1,000 to graduate and undergraduate students pursuing a career in the restaurant and food service industry. Only student honor delegates confirmed to participate in Salute to Excellence are eligible to apply. Deadline: February 15.

1845. (A, S)

National Roofing Foundation
Scholarship Awards Program
10255 West Higgins Road, Suite 600
Rosemont, IL 60018–5607
(708) 299–9070
(800) 323–9545
http://www.nrca.net/nrf/Default.asp

Awards of $1,000 to graduate students, undergraduate students, and high school seniors in architecture or construction as related to the roofing industry. Must be U.S. citizens. Must be used for full-time study at an accredited 4-year college or university. Send a self-addressed, stamped envelope to receive an application. Deadline: January 31.

1846. (A)

National School Orchestra Association
Merle J. Composition Contest
4153 Chainbridge Rd.
Fairfax, VA 22030
(703) 279–2113
http://www.astaweb.com/grants.html

Awards of $1,500, publicity, and aid in publishing, to composers for original unpublished compositions suitable for the average elementary, middle school, or senior high school string orchestra in the U.S. Length of composition not to exceed 5 minutes. Please send self-addressed, stamped envelope for guidelines or visit web site. Deadline: April 1.

(H, S, SS)

National Science Foundation
4201 Wilson Boulevard
Arlington, VA 22230
(703) 306–1234

(800) 877–8339
http://www.nsf.gov

1847. (S)

Bioengineering and Bioinformatics Summer Institutes Program

From 5 to 8 grants of varying amounts to graduate and undergraduate students who are pursuing degrees in biology, computer science, engineering, math, and physical science. Deadline: late June.

1848. (S)

Graduate Student Travel Awards

7 travel awards of up to $4,000 to graduate students who are within 18 months of earning their doctoral degrees. Award assists student in selecting a postdoctoral mentor and may be used to cover airfare and per diem expenses while visiting the host scientist's institution. May apply for travel funds to cover a maximum of 3 visits. Deadline: 3 months prior to travel.

1849. (S, SS)

Minority Postdoctoral Research Fellowships

12 fellowships providing a research allowance of $9,000, an institutional allowance of $5,000, and a monthly stipend of $3,000 to minority doctoral students or a minority postdoctoral fellow who earned a doctoral degree within 4 years of the application date. Degrees must be in the areas of biology and social, behavioral, and economic sciences. Research may be conducted at any appropriate U.S. or foreign host institution. Must be a U.S. citizen, national, or permanent resident alien. Must not have completed more than 2 years of postdoctoral support prior to submitting application. Awards are for 2 years but may be extended for a third. Deadline: early December.

1850. (H, S, SS)

Postdoctoral Research Fellowships

Fellowships of up to $40,000 for postdoctoral students in biology, chemistry, engineering, history, mathematics, medicine, physics, social sciences, the philosophy of science, and other related areas. Must have their doctoral degree or equivalent research training. Some awards provide support for programs in a country that is a NATO member. Deadline: none specified.

1851. (S, SS)
Research Starter Grants

Starter grants of up to $50,000 to fellows who pursue an academic career and accept a tenure-track position at a U.S. institution eligible to receive NSF funding. This 1-year, nonrenewable starter grant is meant to assist in establishing an independent research program. Award must be matched by institution funds. Deadline: early December.

1852. (H, S, SS)
Scholarships

Scholarships of varying amounts to graduate and undergraduate students in biology, chemistry, computer science, engineering, history, mathematics, medicine, physics, social sciences, the philosophy of science, and other related areas. Deadline: none specified.

(A)
National Sculpture Society
237 Park Avenue, Ground Floor
New York, NY 10017
(212) 764–5645
http://www.nationalsculpture.org/scholarships.asp

1853. (A)
Alex J. Ettl Grant

1 award of up to $4,000 to a figurative or realist sculptor who isn't a professional member of the Society. Submit at least 10 photographs (8 × 10 inches) of at least 8 different works and a brief biographical sketch. For more information on how to submit entries, send a self-addressed, stamped envelope to above address. Deadline: October 31.

1854. (A)
Emerging Artists Awards

Awards of $250, $500, $750, and $1,000 in a competition open to young artists (under age 36) or artists in the early stages of their career. Must be U.S. residents. Selections are based on 5 to 10 black-and-white photos (8 × 10 inches preferred) of each applicant's work. Deadline: April 30.

1855. (A)
Scholarships

Scholarships of at least $1,000 are awarded on a competitive basis to students showing talent in figurative or representational sculpture. You must be enrolled in a college or art school but may be majoring in subjects other than art. Photos of your work (8 × 10 black-and-white preferred), a brief biography, and letters of recommendation are also required. This award is based completely on the quality of sculpture submitted. You must also demonstrate financial need. Figurative, realist, or representational sculpture is preferred. Deadline: April 30.

1856. (H, SS)
National Security Education Program
David L. Boren Graduate Fellowships
1825 Connecticut Avenue, N.W.
Washington, DC 20009
(800) 498–9360
http://nsep.aed.org

Overseas awards of $10,000 per semester for 2 semesters, or domestic study awards of up to $12,000 total, to graduate students, to pursue specialization in area and language study or add an international dimension to their education. Fellowships support the study of languages, cultures, and world regions (other than Western Europe, Canada, Australia, and New Zealand) that are critical to U.S. national security but are less frequently studied by U.S. graduate students. Must be enrolled or accepted to an accredited U.S. institution and be in a graduate degree program. Visit web site for specific guidelines. Deadline: January 31.

1857. (SS)
National Society of Hispanic MBAs
NSHMBA/HSF Scholarship Program
1303 Walnut Hill Lane, Suite 300
Irving, TX 75031
(877) 467–4622
http://www.nshmba.org/hsf.asp

15 scholarships of $10,000, 3 scholarships of $15,000, and varying numbers of scholarships of $2,500, $5,000, and $7,500 to Latino graduate full-time or part-time students pursuing a master's degree in management/business. Awarded on a competitive basis based on academic

achievement, community service, financial need, essay, and letters of recommendation. Must be a U.S. citizen or legal resident. Students must submit scholarships to the Hispanic Scholarship Fund; contact and application information is available on web site. Deadline: none specified.

1858. (S)
National Society of the Daughters of the American Revolution
Irene and Daisy MacGregor Memorial Scholarship
NSDAR Administration Building
1776 D Street, N.W.
Washington, DC 20006–53303
(202) 628–1776
no phone calls
http://www.dar.org

Scholarships of $5,000 to students enrolled in an accredited school of medicine. Awards are renewable for up to 4 years with annual transcript review required for renewal. Deadline: April 15.

1859. (S)
National Space Club
Dr. Robert H. Goddard Historical Essay Award
655 15th Street, N.W., #300
Washington, DC 20005
(202) 639–4210

1 award of $500 for essays dealing with any significant aspect of the historical development of rocketry and astronautics. Essays should not exceed 5,000 words and should be fully documented. Must be U.S. citizens. Deadline: November 1.

(S)
National Speleological Society (NSS)
2813 Cave Avenue
Huntsville, AL 35810–4413
(205) 852–1300
http://www.caves.org

1860. (S)
International Exploration Committee Grants

Grants of varying amounts to graduate students or individuals who will be conducting Society-sponsored speleological expeditions. Recipients must provide an article on the expedition for publication in the *NSS*

News or an audiovisual program for distribution for the NSS A/V Library within 1 year from receiving the grant. Deadline: none specified.

1861. (S)
Ralph W. Stone Research Grant

Research grants of $500 to graduate students conducting care-related research. Must be members of NSS and conducting graduate thesis research in the biological sciences, earth sciences, or social sciences that is cave-related. Visit web site for more information or write to above address. Deadline: May 1.

1862. (S)
Sara Corrie Memorial Fund

Up to 6 grants of up to $250 to graduate students or organizations to conduct cave research in the United States. Recipients must submit a brief report of how the money will be used within 6 months of receipt. Deadline: none specified.

(S, SS)
National Strength & Conditioning Association
Challenge Scholarships
P.O. Box 9908
Colorado Springs, CO 80932–0908
(719) 632–6367 (Fax)
http://www.nsca-lift.org

1863. (S, SS)
GNC Nutritional Research Grant

1 award of up to $2,500 to a graduate student in strength and conditioning to conduct research. Must submit a research proposal, application, transcript, abstract, proposed time schedule, itemized budget, references, proof of IRB approval, and information about the faculty co-investigator. Must be an NSCA member for at least 1 year prior to application deadline and pursuing a career in strength and conditioning. Deadline: March 15.

1864. (S, SS)
Graduate Research Grant

1 award of up to $2,500 to a graduate student in strength and conditioning to conduct research. Must submit a research proposal, application, transcript, abstract, proposed time schedule, itemized budget,

references, proof of IRB approval, and information about the faculty co-investigator. Must be an NSCA member for at least 1 year prior to application deadline and pursuing a career in strength and conditioning. Deadline: March 15.

1865. (S, SS)
Power Systems Professional Scholarship

1 scholarship of $1,000 to graduate or undergraduate students working under a strength and conditioning coach in the school's athletic department (student assistant, volunteer, or graduate student). Must submit an application, resume, transcript, 3 letters of recommendation, and an essay of 500 words or less describing course of study, career goals, and financial need. Must be an NSCA member for at least 1 year prior to application deadline and pursuing a career in strength and conditioning. Deadline: March 15.

1866. (S, SS)
Women and Minority Scholarship

2 scholarships of $1,000 to women and minority graduate and undergraduate students to enter into the field of strength and conditioning. Must submit an application, resume, transcript, 3 letters of recommendation, and an essay of 500 words or less describing course of study, career goals, and financial need. Must be NSCA members for at least 1 year prior to application deadline and pursuing careers in strength and conditioning. Deadline: March 15.

(S)

National Student Nurses' Association Scholarships
45 Main Street, Suite 606
Brooklyn, NY 11201
(718) 210–0705
http://www.nsna.org

1867. (S)
Alice Robinson Memorial Scholarship

1 scholarship ranging from $1,000 to $2,500 to a student in a generic master's or doctoral program or nursing undergraduate program. Funds are not available for a graduate student unless it is for a first degree in nursing. Selection is based on academic achievement, financial need, and involvement in nursing student organizations, and community activ-

ities related to health care. There is a $10 processing fee. Deadline: January 30.

1868. (S)
Cleo Doster Memorial Scholarship

1 scholarship ranging from $1,000 to $2,500 to a student in a generic master's or doctoral program or nursing undergraduate program. Funds are not available for a graduate student unless it is for a first degree in nursing. Selection is based on academic achievement, financial need, and involvement in nursing student organizations, and community activities related to health care. There is a $10 processing fee. Deadline: January 30.

1869. (S)
Frances Tompkins Memorial Scholarship

1 scholarship ranging from $1,000 to $2,500 to a student in a generic master's or doctoral program or nursing undergraduate program. Funds are not available for a graduate student unless it is for a first degree in nursing. Selection is based on academic achievement, financial need, and involvement in nursing student organizations, and community activities related to health care. Graduating high school seniors are not eligible. There is a $10 processing fee. Deadline: January 30.

1870. (S)
Jeanette Collins Memorial Scholarship

1 scholarship ranging from $1,000 to $2,500 to a student in a generic master's or doctoral program or nursing undergraduate program. Funds are not available for a graduate student unless it is for a first degree in nursing. Selection is based on academic achievement, financial need, and involvement in nursing student organizations, and community activities related to health care. There is a $10 processing fee. Deadline: January 30.

1871. (S)
Mary Ann Tuft Scholarship

2 scholarships ranging from $1,000 to $2,500 to students in generic master's or doctoral programs or nursing undergraduate programs. Funds are not available for a graduate student unless it is for a first degree in nursing. Selection is based on academic

achievement, financial need, and involvement in nursing student organizations, and community activities related to health care. There is a $10 processing fee. Deadline: January 30.

1872. (S, SS)
National Tropical Botanical Garden Internship Program
3530 Papalina Road
Kalaheo, HI 96741
(808) 332–7324
http://www.ntbg.org

6 internships providing $240 per week to graduate students, recent college graduates, or upper-level undergraduate students of any age. Internships last from 10 to 18 weeks during the summer, fall, and spring in Kauai, HI. Interns work in a different department each week at Lawai Gardens and will work in Living Collections, Research, Administration, the Visitor's Center, and the Hawaii Plant Conservation Center. Though many interns have a background in botany and horticulture, there are no academic requirements for selection, but should have a serious interest in plants. Deadline: March 1.

(S)
National Wildlife Federation
Fellowship Coordinator Organization
Campus Ecology
11100 Wildlife Center Drive
Reston, VA 20190–5362
(703) 438–6318
http://www.nwf.org

1873. (S)
Doctoral Awards

Awards of varying amounts to graduate students, early doctoral students, doctoral dissertation students who are pursuing careers in biology, chemistry, evolutionary biology, zoology, plant biology, ecology, environmental sciences, ethics, geology, and natural history. The program is an opportunity for students to pursue their vision of an ecologically sustainable future through projects to green their campuses and communities. Fellows gain practical experience in the conservation field and firsthand knowledge of the challenges and opportunities inherent in successful conservation efforts. Deadline: none specified.

1874. (S)
Environmental Fellowships

Varying number of fellowships ranging from $4,000 to $10,000 to graduate or law school students. Fields supported are: environmental education, wildlife habitat management, land use planning, general topics relating to natural resource conservation, and environmental law. Must be principally engaged in research rather than course work. Deadline: varies.

1875. (S)
Resources Conservation Internship Program

12 24-week internships running from January to June and July to December that provide salaries of $270 per week plus health insurance. Open to recent college graduates and graduate students. Open to students with extensive course work or experience in biology, chemistry, civil engineering, ecology, energy, environmental biology, environmental science, fisheries science, forestry, geology, hydrology, toxicology, water resources, wildlife biology, international environmental issues, economics, political science, journalism, natural resource management, or land management. Deadline: October 1 (January internships) and April 1 (July internships).

1876. (S)
National Women's Health Network
Internship Coordinator
514 10th Street, N.W., Suite 400
Washington, DC 20004
(202) 347–1140
http://www.womenshealthnetwork.org

5 12-week internships open to graduates, college graduates, or undergraduate students to work in the only public-interest organization devoted to women and health. Interns work on federal health care projects, such as writing testimony for FDA hearings, and conduct research in response to written and telephone requests for information. Internships offer no compensation and take place in summer, fall, or spring. Deadline: April 15 (summer), May 15 (fall), and November 15 (spring).

1877. (A)

National Writers Union
Internship Program
113 University Place
New York, NY 10003
(212) 254–0279
http://www.nwu.org

Unpaid full-time internships to graduate and undergraduate students available each school session for college and university students or recent graduates. Internships are generally located in the New York and Oakland, California offices. Interns are responsible for their own housing, living expenses, and any other costs. Interns will gain experience working in a national organization dedicated to improving the working lives of freelance writers. Interns will be exposed to national issues and events and participate in staff meetings where strategy is determined and plans are made. Interns are given a high amount of responsibility and work side-by-side with staff members working on important issues and projects. Deadline: none.

(A, H, S, SS)

National Zoological Park
3001 Connecticut Avenue, N.W.
Washington, DC 20008
(202) 673–4950
http://natzoo.si.edu

1878. (A, H, S, SS)
Minority Traineeships

12-week summer or fall internships providing a stipend of at least $2,400 to minority graduate, undergraduates, and recent college graduates. Interns work in one of the following programs: facilities design; landscaping; zoo photography; as well as various areas in the science and social sciences. Intern responsibilities may include working on ongoing and special projects, animal observation and handling, data recording, laboratory analysis, data processing, and report writing. Selection is based on statement of interest, academic achievement, relevant experience, and letters of reference. Interns must make their own lodging arrangements. Send a self-addressed, stamped envelope for specific application requirements. Deadline: February 1.

1879. (A, S)
Traineeship in Facilities Design

Varying number of 12-week summer or fall traineeships, providing a stipend of up to $2,400 to graduate students, recent college graduates, and undergraduates in the areas of architectural or engineering programs and who have an interest in zoo/museum facilities. Trainees work in facilities design, about zoo facilities planning and construction. Trainees spend time on field observation, literature research, and data entry. Selection is based on statement of interest, academic achievement, relevant experience, and letters of reference. Trainees must make their own lodging arrangements. Send a self-addressed, stamped envelope for specific application requirements. Deadline: mid-February, varies.

1880. (A, S)
Traineeship in Landscaping

Varying number of 12-week summer or fall traineeships, providing a stipend of up to $2,400, to graduate students, recent college graduates, and undergraduate students in the area of landscaping. Trainees assist with the zoo's landscaping program, educational plant exhibits, plant-animal interactions, and exhibit landscaping. Selection is based on statement of interest, academic achievement, relevant experience, and letters of reference. Trainees must make their own lodging arrangements. Send a self-addressed, stamped envelope for specific application requirements. Deadline: mid-February, varies.

1881. (A, H)
Traineeship in Zoo Photography

Varying number of 12-week summer or fall traineeships providing a stipend of up to $2,400, to graduate students, recent college graduates, or undergraduate students. Trainees assist in zoo photography. Selection is based on statement of interest, academic achievement, relevant experience, and letters of reference. Trainees must make their own lodging arrangements. Send a self-addressed, stamped envelope for specific application requirements. Deadline: mid-February, varies.

(SS)
Native Law Center
University of Saskatchewan
101 Diefenbaker Place
Saskatoon, SK S7N 5B8
http://www.usask.ca/nativelaw/programs/
scholarships.html

1882. (SS)
Harvey Bell Memorial Prize

1 or more awards of up to $1,000 to students about to complete their LL.B. degree in Canada. Selection is based academic achievement and on the probable contribution as a lawyer in establishing the rights of Native people in Canada and toward the solution of problems faced by Native people and their communities within the Canadian legal student. Deadline: July 31.

1883. (SS)
Roger Carter Scholarship Awards

4 awards of $250 to Native Canadian second- or third-year law students. Must attend law school in Canada. Selection based on academic achievement and the student's past and expected contribution to furthering the needs, concerns, and aspirations of Native people and their communities in Canada. Deadline: July 31.

1884. (S)
Natural Sciences and Engineering Research Council of Canada
Science and Engineering Scholarships
350 Albert Street
Ottawa, Ontario K1A 1H5
Canada
(613) 995–5992
http://www.nserc.ca

60 scholarships of $17,500 to graduate students majoring in agriculture, biology, chemistry, computer science, engineering, food science, forestry, or geography. Awards assist students with outstanding academics and research ability in going into graduate studies and research that will lead to a Ph.D. Award is only good at Canadian institutions. Deadline: December 8.

1885. (S)
Nature Conservancy
Internship Coordinator
4245 North Fairfax Drive, Suite 100
Arlington, VA 22203–1606
(800) 628–6860
http://www.tnc.org

130 to 150 internships providing from minimum wage to $6 per hour, plus free housing, for most positions on preserves to graduate students, recent college graduates, undergraduates, and high school graduates majoring in communications, fundraising, legal, or botany to work at an environmental internship. Interns can work at headquarters in botany, fundraising, communications, or legal and in field offices in stewardship or as natural or environmental scientists on any of TNC's preserves. Locations available are at Arlington, VA (HQ), or at 50 field and 8 regional offices in all 50 states, or preserves in AZ, CA, CO, FL, GA, IL, ME, MN, NC, NY, or SD. Internships last from 8 weeks to 6 months during the summer or on an ongoing basis. Deadline: rolling.

1886. (S)
Nebraska Space Grant Scholarships and Fellowships
Nebraska Space Grant Consortium
UNO Aviation Institute
Allwine Hall 422
University of Nebraska at Omaha
Omaha, NE 68182–0508
(402) 554–3772
http://www.unomaha.edu
nasa@cwis.unomaha.edu

Academic year fellowships of $7,500 and summer awards of $2,500 to graduate and undergraduate students working on a degree in an aerospace-related area. Must be attending one of the following schools: University of Nebraska at Omaha, University of Nebraska at Lincoln, University of Nebraska at Kearney, University of Nebraska Medical Center, Creighton University, Western Nebraska Community College, Chadron State College, and Nebraska Indian Community College. Applicants must be U.S. citizens. Special attention is given to applications submitted by women, underrepresented minorities, and individuals with disabilities. Contact via e-mail for more information. Deadline: none specified.

1887. (A, H, S, SS)
Nevada State Board of Education
Student Incentive Grant Program
1850 East Sahara, Suite 200
Las Vegas, NV 89104
(702) 486–6455
http://www.nsn.k12.nv.us./nvdoe

Grants of up to $5,000 to graduate or undergraduate students in all areas of study. Must be Nevada residents and enroll in an eligible, accredited Nevada institution. Apply through the financial aid office at school student is attending. Deadline: none specified.

1888. (A, H, SS)
Newberry Library
American Society for 18th-Century Studies
Fellowships
Committee on Awards
60 West Walton Street
Chicago, IL 60610–7324
(312) 943–9090
http://www.newberry.org

Various fellowships of approximately $800 per month to postdoctoral scholars who are members of the American Society for 18th-Century Studies at the time they apply. Scholars may be working in the fields of art history, history, law, literature, or philosophy. Deadline: March 1 and October 1.

(S)
New England Board of Higher Education
45 Temple Place
Boston, MA 02111
(617) 357–9620
http://www.nebhe.org

1889. (S)
Excellence Through Diversity Program

Grants providing a stipend of $12,000, plus $5,000 toward tuition and fees, to minority doctoral students in the arts, business, engineering, or science. Education is not area of emphasis, with the exception of mathematics education and science education. Must not already be enrolled in a doctoral program. Must be residents of New England or planning to attend a doctoral program in New England. Deadline: none specified.

1890. (S)
Minority Doctoral Scholars Program

Grants providing a stipend of $12,000, plus $5,000 toward tuition and fees, to minority doctoral students in the arts, business, engineering, or science. Education is not area of emphasis, with the exception of mathematics education and science education. Must not already be enrolled in a doctoral program. Must be residents of New England or planning to attend a doctoral program in New England. Deadline: none specified.

1891. (A, H, S, SS)
New Hampshire Charitable Fund
37 Pleasant Street
P.O. Box 1335
Concord, NH 03301
(603) 225–6641
(800) 464–6641
http://www.nhcf.org

Grants averaging $1,100 (totaling $460,805) to graduate and undergraduate students who are residents of New Hampshire. May be used for all areas of study. Write an introductory letter detailing briefly the educational and financial situation, and include a self-addressed, stamped envelope. Deadline: varies.

1892. (A, H)
New Hampshire State Council on the Arts (Grants)
40 N. Main Street
Phoenix Hall
Concord, NH 03301–4974
(603) 271–2789
http://www.state.nh.us/nharts

Grants of up to $2,000 to artists who are New Hampshire residents. Grants are not for academic study but rather for career advancement in the areas of the arts, performing arts, or literature. Deadline: April 1.

1893. (A, H, S, SS)
New Jersey Department of Higher Education
Educational Opportunity Fund (EOF) Grants
Office of Student Assistance
4 Quakerbridge Plaza CN 540
Trenton, NJ 08625
(609) 984–2709

(800) 792–8670 (in NJ)
http://www.state.nj.us/treasury/osa

Grants of up to $4,000 to graduate students who have been New Jersey residents for at least 1 year. Must be full-time students at a New Jersey institution. Students must be inadmissable by regular admissions standards. Must be economically and educationally disadvantaged. Deadline: March 1 and October 1.

1894. (S)
New Jersey Osteopathic Education Foundation Scholarships and Loans
One Distribution Way, Suite 201
Monmouth Junction, NJ 08852
(732) 940–9000
http://www.njosteo.com

5 to 8 scholarship/loans of up to $3,500 to students about to begin their first year of study at an osteopathic medical school. Must be New Jersey residents and agree to practice in New Jersey for 2 years following their internship or residency. Must be a U.S. citizen. Deadline: April 30.

1895. (A)
New Jersey Society of Architects
NJSA Scholarship Program
196 W. State Street
Trenton, NJ 08608
(609) 393–5690
http://www.aia–nj.org/njsf.htm

25 scholarships ranging from $1,000 to $2,500 to graduate and undergraduate students enrolled in or accepted to an accredited school of architecture. Must be a U.S. citizen and a New Jersey resident. Deadline: May 20.

1896. (A, H, S, SS)
New Jersey State Federation of Women's Clubs
Margaret Yardley Fellowship Program
55 Labor Center Way
New Brunswick, NJ 08901
(732) 249–5474
(800) 465–7392
http://www.njsfwc.org

Fellowships of $1,000 to female full-time graduate students in all areas of study. Preference given to New Jer-

sey residents. Based on financial need. Must be enrolled in an approved graduate program. Deadline: varies.

1897. (A)
New Jersey State Opera
Cash Awards
50 Park Place, 10th Floor
Newark, NJ 07102
(201) 623–5757
http://www.newjerseystateopera.org

A cash award of $2,500 in a competition for professional singers (between 22 and 34 years of age) in the field of opera. Singers who are under contract with an artist's management team are ineligible. Deadline: varies.

(Contest, A, H)
New Letters Literary Awards
UMKC
University House, 5101 Rockhill Road
Kansas City, MO 64110–2499
(816) 235–1168
http://iml.umkc.edu/newletters

1898. (Contest)
Alexander Patterson Cappon Fiction Prize

1 award of $750 is given to the best short story. Awards were established to discover and reward new writers, to give them a chance to compete with more established writers, and to encourage the more established writers to try new genres or new work in competition. There is a $15 entry fee for the first submission and $10 for each subsequent submission (made to: New Letters Literary Awards). Individuals may enter more than one category, but each entry in each category must be mailed in a separate envelope. Send a self-addressed, stamped postcard for notification of receipt and entry number. All entries must be unpublished work. For more information write to the above address or visit web site. Deadline: May 20— postmark (date varies slightly each year).

1899. (Contest)
Dorothy Churchill Cappon Creative Nonfiction Prize

1 award of $1,000 is given to the best expository nonfiction. Awards were established to discover and reward new writers, to give them a chance to compete

with more established writers, and to encourage the more established writers to try new genres or new work in competition. There is a $15 entry fee for the first submission and $10 for each subsequent submission (made to: New Letters Literary Awards). Individuals may enter more than one category, but each entry in each category must be mailed in a separate envelope. Send a self-addressed, stamped postcard for notification of receipt and entry number. All entries must be unpublished work. For more information write to the above address or visit the web site. Deadline: May 20—postmark (date varies slightly each year).

1900. (Contest)
New Letters Poetry Prize

1 award of $750 to the best group of 3 to 6 poems. Awards were established to discover and reward new writers, to give them a chance to compete with more established writers, and to encourage the more established writers to try new genres or new work. There is a $15 entry fee for the first submission and $10 for each subsequent submission (made to: New Letters Literary Awards). Individuals may enter more than one category, but each entry in each category must be mailed in a separate envelope. Send a self-addressed, stamped postcard for notification of receipt and entry number. All entries must be unpublished work. For more information write to the above address or visit the web site. Deadline: May 20—postmark (date varies slightly each year).

1901. (A, H)
New Letters Weekend Writers Conference Scholarships

Some limited scholarship aid to students wishing to attend The New Letters Weekend Writers Conference and the Mark Twain Creative Writing Workshop. For more information, contact the Director of the Professional Writing Program, James McKinley, by phone (816–235–1120) or fax (816–235–2611) or e-mail (mckinleyj@UMKC.edu).

1902. (A)
New Orleans International Piano Competition
P.O. Box 19599–0599
New Orleans, LA 70179–0599
(504) 895–0700
http://www.noipc.org/Data/Home

Awards of (1 each) $12,000, $6,000, $3,000, 3 of $750, and 6 of $500 to pianists of any age and nationality. Applicants must submit 3 copies of an audio cassette tape recording (or 3 CDs) consisting of any solo piano repertoire selected by the competitor, recording not to exceed 45 minutes in length. Deadline: March 15.

(A, H, S, SS)
New York Bureau of Higher Education Opportunity Programs
Scholarship Unit
Cultural Center, Room 5A 55
Albany, NY 12230
(518) 474–5642
http://www.higher.nysed.gov
HEOPI1@higher.nysed.gov

1903. (A, H, S, SS)
Awards, Scholarships & Fellowships

Varying number of awards, scholarships, and fellowships of varying amounts to graduate or undergraduate students through state and federal programs administered by the New York State Education Department. Must be residents of New York State. 1 year's New York residency immediately preceding effective date of award. Open to all areas of study. Deadline: varies.

1904. (A, S, SS)
New York State Professional Opportunity Scholarships

Scholarships ranging from $1,000 to $5,000 to minority or economically disadvantaged graduate students enrolled or about to enroll in an approved professional field. Must be a New York State resident, U.S. citizen, permanent resident, or refugee. Must not have defaulted on a student loan. Students may be entering or enrolled in architecture, landscape architecture, and other professional areas. Deadline: mid-January.

1905. (A)
New York City Opera
Julius Rudel Award
New York State Theater
20 Lincoln Center
New York, NY 10023
(212) 870–5600
http://operabase.com/level1/nanyc.html

Award of $12,000 to artists in opera and music management. Must present evidence of artistic accomplishments, résumé, letters of recommendation, and a statement outlining how affiliation with NYC Opera will assist and further individual's artistic and career goals. Recipient performs administrative tasks for NYC Opera but is also encouraged to continue outside artistic work. Deadline: none.

1906. (A)
New York Life Foundation for the Arts
Artist's Fellowships & Services
155 Avenue of the Americas, 14th Floor
New York, NY 10013–1507
(212) 366–6900
http://www.nyfa.org
nyfaweb@nyfa.org

Over 200 fellowships and services of varying amounts to artists who are New York State residents. Award assists the artist in creating new work and to bring that work to the attention of the public; it isn't for academic study. Award may be used in any of the following areas: arts, performing arts, literature, or architecture. Deadline: none.

1907. (A, SS)
Nike
Internship Program
One Bowerman Drive
Beaverton, OR 97005
(503) 671–6453
(800) 890–6453
http://www.info.nike.com

15 10-week summer internships to minority graduate students and undergraduate seniors. Interns can work in marketing, finance/accounting, records management, international division, customer service, retail resources, human resources, research design and development, and film/video. Students should be willing to ask for additional work, be flexible, have a passion to be the best, and have an appreciation for sports and fitness. Deadline: March 1.

(S)
Ninety-Nines
4300 Amelia Earhart Road
Oklahoma City, OK 73159–0965

(800) 994–1929
(405) 685–7969
http://www.ninety-nines.org

1908. (S)
Amelia Earhart Memorial Research Grant

1 research grant of varying amount to individuals wanting to conduct research on women's issues in aviation. Must have private license to join organization. Must be a member of The Ninety-Nines for 2 years prior to application. Must be residents of Oklahoma City, OK. Deadline: December 31.

1909. (S)
Majorie Van Vliet Aviation Memorial
Scholarship

Scholarships of $2,000 to graduate or undergraduate students, and even high school seniors, to use for tuition and/or flight training. May be majoring in, or planning to major in, aeronautics, aviation maintenance, or flight training. Must live in one of the New England states, be planning a career in aviation, and have applied to an aviation-related education or training program. Must have financial need. Visit web site for Eastern New England Ninety-Nines for more information. Deadline: January 31.

1910. (S)
San Fernando Valley Chapter
Career Scholarship

3 scholarships of $3,000 to graduate and undergraduate students and individuals to further their aviation education. Selection based on academic achievement, letters of recommendation, extracurricular activities, and goals. Must be at least 21 years of age and a U.S. citizen and reside in the Greater Los Angeles area. Visit web site for more information. Deadline: April 18.

1911. (S)
Scholarship Committee

Varying number of scholarships of varying amounts to females working on an additional rating. 1 scholarship is also available to an individual wanting to work on a Flight Engineer rating. Must have private license to join organization. Must be members of The Ninety-Nines for 2 years prior to application. Other chapters also offer scholarships. Some scholarships have residency requirements. Deadline: December 31, may vary by chapter.

1912. (SS)

Nixon Center
1615 L Street, N.W., Suite 1250
Washington, DC 20036
(202) 887–1000
http://www.nixoncenter.org/internsh.htm

Internships to graduate and undergraduate students interested in international affairs. Internship positions are in Washington, DC. Interns learn about international affairs, meet influential people in government, think tanks, and academic and media circles. Interns are being recruited in Chinese studies, immigration policy, regional strategic programs, strategic studies, and U.S.-Russian relations. Deadline: May 1.

1913. (A, H, S, SS)

Non-Commissioned Officers Association
NCOA Scholarships
P.O. Box 33610
San Antonio, TX 78265
(210) 653–6161
(800) 662–2620
http://www.ncoausa.org

9 academic scholarships of $900 to graduate or undergraduate students who are sons or daughters of members, and 4 academic scholarships to spouses of members, with $1,000 awards for 3 of the applicants. Awards are for any area of study at accredited colleges or universities. Applicant must be under the age of 25 (with the exception of spouses) at the time of the initial award. Renewable by reapplication; must carry minimum of 15 credit hours per semester, and must maintain a B average. Based on recommendation, academic record, patriotism, and essay on "Americanism." Deadline: March 31.

1914. (S)

North American Die Casting Association
David Laine Memorial Scholarships
Scholarship Committee
9701 West Higgins Road, Suite 880
Rosemont, IL 60018
(847) 292–3600
http://www.diecasting.org

Scholarships of varying amounts to graduate and undergraduate students who are enrolled in the Foundry Educational Foundation at an engineering college that participates in the FEF program. Students must have been employed with a company producing die castings or with a die casting equipment manufacturer or supplier or be willing to co-op (temporary or summer employment). There are other criteria that the student must fulfill. Contact above address for all information. Deadline: none specified.

(A, S)

North American Nature Photography Association
10200 West 44th Avenue, Suite 304
Wheat Ridge, CO 80033–2840
(303) 422–8527
http://www.nanpainfinityfoundation.org

1915. (A, S)

Janie Moore Green Grant

1 grant of $1,000 to a graduate or undergraduate student in the study of photography. Applicants must send 3–5 duplicate transparencies or prints demonstrating their photographic abilities and write an essay explaining what inspired them to pursue a course of study in photography. Deadline: August 31.

1916. (A, S)

Philip Hyde Grant

1 grant of $1,000 to a graduate or undergraduate student or individual who is working on an existing project designed to improve, protect, or preserve the condition of the environment. Must be an NANPA member. Visit web site for specific guidelines. Deadline: August 31.

1917. (S)

North American Society of Pacing and Electrophysiology
NASPE Traveling Fellowship
6 Strathmore Road
Natick, MA 01670
(508) 647–0100
http://www.naspe.org

2 fellowships of $6,000 for 1–3 months to postdoctoral students to conduct traveling research. Must be citizens or permanent residents of North America who have a

doctoral degree in medicine, philosophy, osteopathy, or science. These awards are also open to registered nurses and those with a degree in engineering. One is also available to a Canadian resident or non-Canadian who will use the fellowship in Canada. Deadline: November 1.

1918. (A, H, S, SS)
North Carolina State Education Assistance Authority
Student Financial Aid for North Carolinians
P.O. Box 2688
Chapel Hill, NC 27515–2688
(919) 549–8614
http://www.dpi.state.nc.us
ncseaa@ga.upc.edu

Scholarships, grants, work study, and loans funded by the state of North Carolina, private North Carolina organizations, and the federal government to graduate and undergraduate students for any field of study. Must be North Carolina residents. Deadline: varies by program.

1919. (A)
North Carolina Symphony
Bryan Young Artists Competition
2 E. South Street
Raleigh, NC 27601
(919) 733–2750
written inquiries only
http://www.ncsymphony.org/index.cfm?flash=yes

Awards of up to $3,000 to music performers (piano, vocal, or strings). Must be under 30 years of age (time will deducted for any applicant who has served in the military), North Carolina residents, and attending a U.S. institution. For more information, send a self-addressed, stamped envelope. Deadline: November 2.

(A)

North Carolina Writers' Network
3501 Highway 54 West, Studio C
Chapel Hill, NC 27516
http://www.ncwriters.org/litcomps.htm

1920. (A)
Blumenthal Writers & Readers Series

20 awards of $200 to any writer who is a legal resident of North Carolina and who has not published a full-length book of poems (48 pages or more). Manu-

scripts should be between 20 and 24 pages. Manuscripts will not be returned. Include an self-addressed, stamped envelope for a list of winners. Multiple submissions are accepted. 1 manuscript per entry fee. Applicants must include a 1-page synopsis if submitting only a portion of your work. Deadline: October 1.

1921. (A)
Doris Betts Fiction Competition

Awards of $50, $100, and $150 to any writer who is a legal resident of North Carolina or a member of NCWN. Entrants should submit 2 copies of a typed, original, and unpublished story, not to exceed 6 double-spaced pages (1,500 words or less). Entries will not be returned; enclose a self-addressed, stamped envelope for a list of winners. Visit web site for specific guidelines. Deadline: March 1.

1922. (A)
Mary Belle Campbell Poetry Book Publication Award

Awards of publication, 100 copies of a limited letterpress edition chapbook, and a reading and reception to poets who are residents of or teach in NC, GA, SC, TN, or VA. Poetry manuscripts must be nominated by creative writing professors or literary editors. Manuscripts by teaching poets and poetry workshop leaders active in the field of poetry who have published no more than 1 book or chapbook are accepted. Submit 2 copies of a typed manuscript, stapled in the upper left-hand corner. Clear, readable copies of poems are acceptable. Manuscripts should be no more than 32 pages. Title page, dedication page (optional), preface, contents, acknowledgments, and section title pages (optional) count as part of manuscript length. A letter of nomination and curriculum vitae or résumé must be enclosed. Names should not appear on manuscript. Entries will not be returned; enclose a self-addressed, stamped envelope for a list of the winners and finalists. The winners will be announced in November. There is no entry fee, because only poets who are nominated are eligible. Deadline: August 1.

1923. (A)
Randall Jarrell/Harperprints Poetry Chapbook Competition

1 award of publication, $200, and a reading and reception to any writer who is a legal resident of North

Carolina and who has not published a full-length book of poems (48 pages or more). Multiple submissions are accepted. 1 manuscript per entry fee. Deadline: January 31.

1924. (A)
Rose Post Creative Nonfiction Competition

Awards of $100, $200, and $400 to any writer who is a legal resident of North Carolina or is a member of NCWN. Awarded to encourage the creation of lasting nonfiction work that is outside the realm of conventional journalism and that has relevance to North Carolinians. Subjects may include traditional categories such as reviews, travel articles, profiles or interviews, place/history pieces, or culture criticism. Winning entries will be published in the *Independent Weekly* (pending editor's approval). Deadline: November 1.

1925. (S)
North Dakota Society of Professional Land Surveyors
P.O. Box 475
Steele, ND 58482
(701) 475–0279
http://www.ndspls.org

1 scholarship of $500 to a graduate or upper-level undergraduate student pursuing a career in land surveying. Selection will be based on academic achievement, interest in land surveying, probability of success, and financial need. Visit web site for more information and an application. Deadline: May 1.

1926. (S)
Nyanza Project
204 Heroy Geology Lab
Department of Earth Sciences
Syracuse University
Syracuse, NY 13244–1070
(315) 443–4925
http://www.geo.arizona.edu/nyanza

A research training program providing all expenses (airfare, room and board, and research costs) to graduate and undergraduate (sophomores to seniors) students and secondary school teachers. Graduate students and secondary school teachers may be at any stage of their program/career and submit the same application materials as undergraduates. Preference is given to graduate students with demonstrable research interest in tropical lake systems. Only 9 undergraduates are admitted into the program. U.S.-based undergraduates must be attending an accredited U.S. college or university. Applicants may be of any nationality, and members of underrepresented minorities are strongly encouraged to apply. Applications may only be sent by mail, though guidelines and application are available on their web site. Deadline: December 24.

(S, SS)
Oak Ridge Institute for Science and Education
Oak Ridge Associated Universities
230 Warehouse Road
Building 1916–T2
Oak Ridge, TN 37830
(865) 241–5947
(615) 576–9558
http://www.orau.gov/orise.htm

1927. (S)
Civilian Radioactive Waste Management Fellowship

Varying number of fellowships providing a $14,400 stipend, $300 per month during practicum, some travel expenses, and tuition and fees of up to $8,000 per year to graduate students (master's and doctoral) in earth sciences, engineering, materials science, and radiation sciences. Recipients must attend a university designated as a participating university in this program. Visit web site for list of participating schools and for an application. Deadline: last Monday in January.

1928. (S)
Fusion Energy Sciences Fellowship

Varying number of fellowships providing a $19,800 stipend, tuition, fees, some travel expenses, and $200 per month during the practicum, to first- and second-year graduate students in physical sciences, engineering, mathematics, or a related discipline. Applicants must not have progressed beyond the end of the second year when the fellowship begins. Award provides opportunities for study and research in the area of fusion energy sciences and technology related to the development of fusion energy. Renewable for 2 years. Deadline: late January.

1929. (S)
Global Change Education Program
http://www.atmos.anl.gov/GCEP/gref.html

10 to 15 awards of tuition, support stipend for a year of research, and transportation and housing at the SURE activities to graduate students. Renewable with progress reports. Must have completed the first year of graduate work. Deadline: February 1.

1930. (SS)
Higher Education Research Experience for Law Students

3-month summer opportunity providing a weekly stipend of $400 and round-trip travel reimbursement allowance to law students who have completed their first year and who are interested in environmental and patent law. Allows students to participate in research on legal aspects of energy-related techniques and procedures, national energy-related problems, and efforts related to their solutions. Deadline: first Monday in February.

1931. (S)
NRC Graduate Fellowship Program

Varying number of fellowships providing a monthly stipend of $2,400, books, and related expenses, and full tuition and fees to graduate students in engineering, health physics, and other related scientific disciplines. Must be U.S. citizens, and naturalized citizens must fulfill certain criteria to be eligible to apply. Deadline: December 1.

1932. (S)
NSF Graduate Research Fellowships

800 fellowships providing $21,500 stipend for 12-month tenures, $10,500 cost-of-education allowance, and $1,000 international research travel allowance to graduate students majoring in science, math, or engineering. Must be enrolled in an accredited, nonprofit U.S. institution or appropriate international institution. Award is for 3 years, but it may be used over a 5-year period. Deadline: November 7.

1933. (SS)
Savannah River Site Law Internship Program

Varying numbers of internships providing a weekly stipend and limited travel reimbursement to law

students who have completed their first year and are interested in environmental or patent law. Internship allows students to participate in research on legal aspects of energy-related techniques and procedures, national energy-related problems, and efforts related to their solutions. Internships are 3 months long in the summer, but longer appointments are available during the academic year. Deadline: February 15.

1934. (S)
Ocean Conservancy
Internship Coordinator
1725 DeSales Street, N.W., Suite 600
Washington, DC 20036
(202) 429–5609
http://www.oceanconservancy.org

15 3-month internships providing a stipend ranging from $200 to $1,000, plus reimbursement for daily travel expenses, to graduate students, though no compensation is provided for undergraduates. Students respond to public requests for information, make local presentations, research and write educational material, and summarize legislation. The CMC is dedicated to protecting marine life, especially marine mammals, sea turtles, fishes, and their habitats. The internships are conducted in Hampton, VA, Marathon and St. Petersburg, FL, San Francisco, CA, and Washington, DC. Deadline: May 17 (summer), August 2 (fall), December 7 (winter), and March 8 (spring).

1935. (S)
Office of Rural Community Affairs
Outstanding Rural Scholar Recognition and
Forgiveness Loan Program
Program Administrator
P.O. Box 12877
Austin, TX 78711
(800) 544–2042
(512) 936–6730
http://www.orca.state.tx.us

Scholarship/loans of varying amounts to graduate and undergraduate students in dental health/services, health administration, health and medical sciences, health information management/technology, nursing, or therapy/rehab. Applicant must be nominated by a rural community, with the sponsor applying for the student. Must work 1 year for each year of financial assistance or award reverts to loan status. Must attend an accredited Texas institution and be a resident of Texas. Selection based on application, academic achievement, transcript, test scores, essay, financial need, and recommendation letters. Deadline: May 1.

1936. (S)
Ohio League for Nursing Scholarships
Student Aid Committee
20545 Center Ridge Road
Cleveland, OH 44116
(440) 331–2721
http://www.ohioleaguefornursing.org

20 to 25 scholarships of varying amounts to graduate or undergraduate students in accredited nursing programs. Must be residents of Greater Cleveland area (Cuyahoga, Geauga, Lake, and Lorain Counties. Must agree to work in a health care facility in that area for at least a year after graduation. Must be U.S. citizen or legal resident. Deadline: May 15.

1937. (SS)
Olin Instiute for Strategic Studies
1737 Cambridge Street
Cambridge, MA 02138
(617) 495–2280
http://www.isop.ucla.edu/eas/fellowships/olin.htm

Up to 10 fellowships of $20,000 (dissertation) and $35,000 (postdoctoral) to graduate students to conduct basic research in the area of security and strategic affairs. Of particular interest is research into the causes and conduct of war, military strategy and history, defense policy and institutes, civil-military relations, and the ways in which the U.S. and other societies can provide for their security. Preference is given to graduate students who have made progress on their dissertation and are likely to complete it during their fellowship and recent doctoral recipients. Deadline: January 15.

1938. (A)
Omaha Symphony Guild New Music Competition
ATTN: Donna Rausch
904 South 86th Street
Omaha, NE 68114
http://www.omahasymphony.org/newmusiccomp

1 award of $2,000 and a performance with the Omaha Symphony Chamber Orchestra. This competition is open to all composers (no age limit). The composition must be scored for chamber orchestra and shouldn't be longer than 18 minutes. It must be unpublished and not have been performed by a professional orchestra. For other qualifying criteria, send a self-addressed, stamped envelope. Deadline: May 15.

1939. (A, H, S, SS)
Omega Psi Phi Fraternity, Inc.
Charles Drew Memorial Scholarship
3951 Snapfinger Parkway
Decatur, GA 30025
(404) 284–5533
http://www.oppf.org/about/programs.asp

Numerous scholarships of $300 to graduate students and undergraduate sophomores, juniors, or seniors who are members of Omega Psi Phi. Must be used at a 4-year college or university. Must have at least a B average. Open to all areas of study. Deadline: March 31.

(S)
Oncology Nursing Society
125 Enterprise Drive
Pittsburgh, PA 15275–1214
(412) 859–6298
http://www.ons.org
research@ons.org

1940. (S)
Cancer Nursing Pain Research

1 award of $8,500 to a graduate student in nursing. Awarded to encourage cancer nursing pain research. Visit web site for more information. Deadline: February 1.

1941. (S)
Community Health Research

1 award of $5,000 to graduate students in nursing to encourage nursing research in community-based health agencies (community hospitals, physician's offices, and nursing homes). Submission of quantitative and qualitative research projects (descriptive studies, surveys, experimental and quasi-experimental studies)

is encouraged. Visit web site for more information and deadline date.

1942. (S)
Congress Scholarships

27 scholarships of $1,000 toward registration, travel, and per diem Congress expenses to professional staff registered nurses involved in oncology nursing. Must have creatively responded to extraordinary challenges in practice. Must have demonstrated innovativeness in responding to challenges in practice. Must be able to attend the ONS Congress. Visit web site for more information. Deadline: December 1.

1943. (S)
Doctoral Scholarships

Scholarships of $3,000 to registered nurses in doctoral nursing degree or related programs. Awarded to improve oncology nursing by assisting registered nurses in fulfilling their education. Must have a current license to practice as a registered nurse and demonstrate an interest in, and commitment to, oncology nursing. Visit web site for more information. Deadline: February 1.

1944. (S)
Ethnic Minority Researcher and Mentorship Grants

1 grant of $8,500 ($7,500 for research and $1,000 to mentor/consultant) to minority graduate students to encourage oncology nursing research. Must be a licensed registered nurse and be master's prepared. Those early in research career are strongly encouraged to find a doctorally prepared oncology nurse scientist who is an expert in your content area to work as a consultant or co-investigator. ONS Research Team can assist in finding a mentor/consultant. Visit web site for more information. Deadline: November 1.

1945. (S)
Master's Scholarships

Scholarships of $3,000 to minority full- or part-time students enrolled in, or accepted to, a graduate nursing degree program in an accredited U.S. institution. Must have a current license to practice as a registered nurse. Must demonstrate interest in, and commitment to, oncology nursing. Visit web site for more information. Deadline: February 1.

1946. (S)
Neuro-oncology Nursing Research

1 award of $10,000 to a graduate student in nursing. Awarded to stimulate quality research in oncology nursing education. Visit web site for more information. Deadline: February 1.

1947. (S)
New Investigator Research Grants

2 awards of $5,000 to master's and doctoral graduate students who have no prior research funding. Students may apply for thesis and dissertation research funding. Awarded to encourage new researchers in the exploration of oncology nursing. Visit web site for more information. Deadline: February 1.

1948. (S)
Novice Researcher and Mentorship Grants

2 grants of $7,500 to master's graduate and undergraduate students with no previous research funding. Doctoral students are not eligible. Awarded to encourage oncology nursing research by new or novice principal investigators. Visit web site for more information. Deadline: February 1.

1949. (S)
Oncology Nursing Education Research

1 award of $7,500 to graduate students in nursing. Awarded to stimulate quality research in oncology nursing education. Visit web site for more information. Deadline: February 1.

1950. (S)
Oncology Nursing Research

2 awards of $7,500, 3 awards of $8,500, and 3 awards of $10,000 to graduate students in nursing. Awarded to stimulate quality research in oncology nursing education. Visit web site for more information. Deadline: February 1.

1951. (S)
ONS Chapter Research

1 award of $5,000 to graduate students to encourage oncology nursing research by ONS chapters. Awarded to stimulate quality research in oncology nursing education. Visit web site for more information. Deadline: February 1.

1952. (S)
ONS/Foundation Nursing Outcomes Grants

1 grant of $5,000 to a graduate student examining the relationship between or among organizational variables, performance variables, and patient variables. Preference is given to studies that examine nurses' contributions to cancer care and the outcomes of nursing actions, interventions, or therapeutics. Visit web site for more information. Deadline: February 1.

1953. (S)
ONS/Sigma Theta Tau International Grant

1 grant of $10,000 to a licensed registered nurse. Must be master's-prepared. Recipients are encouraged to publish results in the ONS Foundation or STT International publication. Awarded to stimulate quality research in oncology nursing research. Visit web site for more information. Deadline: February 1.

1954. (S)
Pain Assessment & Management Research

1 award of $6,000 to a graduate student in nursing. Awarded to promote oncology nursing research in area of pain assessment and pain management. Visit web site for more information. Deadline: February 1.

1955. (S)
Post-Master's Certificate Scholarships

2 scholarships of $3,000 to students enrolled in, or applying to, a post-master's nurse practitioner certificate academic credit-bearing program in an accredited school of nursing. Must have a previous master's degree in nursing, a current license to practice as an RN, and demonstrated interest in, and commitment to, oncology nursing. Visit web site for more information. Deadline: February 1.

1956. (S)
Research Fellowships

2 awards of up to $10,000 to cover transportation, lodging, tuition, and other expenses to doctoral fellows who are registered nurses to support short-term oncology research training. Recipient will also receive up to $1,700 to attend ONS Congress the year following receipt of the award. Mentor and/or mentor's institution receives $2,000 to cover mentor's

consultative or research-related expenses and/or other institutional costs. Membership in ONS is preferred but not required. Doctoral students are not eligible for this award. Visit web site for more information. Deadline: June 1.

1957. (S)
Symptom Assessment and Management

2 awards of $9,000 to graduate students in nursing. Awarded to promote oncology nursing research in area of pain assessment and pain management. Visit web site for more information. Deadline: February 1.

1958. (S)
Thesis and Dissertation Projects

Awards of varying amounts to graduate students in nursing. Award supports work that is considered preliminary in nature or related to thesis or dissertation. Related work may include a study to pilot the data gathering procedures, a feasibility study that is required prior to a subsequent revision of the thesis or dissertation proposal, a study to test experimental manipulation, or preliminary work to develop and pretest a new instrument. Visit web site for more information. Deadline: November 1.

1959. (A, H, S, SS)
Open Society Institute
Community Fellowships Program
Program Officer
400 West 59th Street, 3rd Floor
New York, NY 10019
(212) 548–0152
http://www.soros.org

Up to 10 fellowships providing a $48,750 stipend over 18 months, a start-up grant in the amount of $2,000 for project support, a travel grant to cover expenses to 2 OSI-sponsored conferences during the fellowship period, and financial contributions toward graduate school debt payments. Award may be used to support the project and/or fellow. Fellows are strongly encouraged to seek other contributions to support their work during the fellowship. Applicants may come from any field, such as education, law, the arts, public service, and health; may choose to create a public interest project in any social issue area; need not be from New York

City to apply but must perform their fellowship project in New York City; and must be legally able to work in the United States in order to accept the fellowship offer. Visit web site for more information. Deadline: mid-April.

1960. (Contest)
OP Loftbed Scholarship
OP Loftbed Company
210 E. Lakeview Drive
Thomasville, NC 27360
http://www.oploftbed.com

1 scholarship of $500 to a graduate or undergraduate student in any field of study. Award is based on responses to a list of questions designed to make applicants think, evaluate themselves, and show who they really are. Must be U.S. citizens who are attending an accredited college or university in the U.S. Applicants must apply on-line. Deadline: July 31.

(S)
Oral Health America
Director of Programs
410 North Michigan Avenue, Suite 352
Chicago, IL 60611
(312) 836–9900
http://www.oralhealthamerica.org

1961. (S)
Dental Faculty Development Fellowships

Numerous fellowship awards of up to $20,000 to postdoctoral students with a D.D.S. or D.M.D. degree to work at the postdoctoral level. Applicants must agree to teach for 2 consecutive years upon completion of the fellowship. Must be U.S. citizens. Deadline: September 1.

1962. (S)
Dental Scholarships for Minority Students

Scholarships of up to $2,000 to African-Americans, Mexican-Americans, or Native Americans who are U.S. citizens. Award is only for the first year of dental school at an accredited dental school. Student must provide 2 letters of recommendation and show a minimum need of $2,000. Send a self-addressed, stamped envelope for information and an application. Deadline: May 1.

1963. (S)
Grants for Dental Research and Special Projects

Varying number of grants of $35,000 to individuals employed by nonprofit, tax-exempt organizations, or nonprofit organizations, and institutions in the U.S. or its protectorate. The awards are for research projects with national scope. Will not fund multiyear grants, but will allow initial funding of a project that spans 2 years. Award cannot be used to purchase major equipment or pay principal investigator's salary. Proposals to increase patient access to, and utilization of, dental care, to enhance quality of care available, to accelerate transfer of knowledge from research lab to practice, or to assist dental education quality are given preference. For information on application criteria contact above address. Deadline: varies.

1964. (S)
Hillenbrand Fellowship

Fellowships providing a $40,000 stipend, plus travel expenses, to dental school graduates for education in dental administration. Selected on the basis of academic records, qualifications, potential for dental administration, and personal attributes. Must have attended an accredited U.S. dental school and be a U.S. citizen. Awarded every other year. Send a self-addressed, stamped envelope for information. Deadline: December 1 (odd-numbered years).

1965. (H)
Oregon Public Broadcasting
Jon R. Minority Internship
7140 S.W. Macadam Avenue
Portland, OR 97219–3099
(503) 293–1972
http://www.opb.org

Internships providing a $3,000 stipend to minority graduate or undergraduate students enrolled in an accredited college or university and majoring in broadcasting or telecommunications. Selection is based on goals essay, recommendation letters, academic achievement, declaration of interest, and interview. Internships runs from mid-June through August. Deadline: March 1.

(A, H, S, SS)

Oregon State Scholarship Commission
1500 Valley River Drive, Suite 100
Eugene, OR 97401–2130
(541) 687–7400
http://www.ossc.state.or.us

1966. (A, H, S, SS)
Flora M. Von Der Ahe Scholarship

Scholarships of varying amounts to full-time graduate or undergraduate students in any field of study. Must be residents of Umatilla County, Oregon. Must attend an accredited two- or four-year college, university, or vocational/technical school in Oregon. Must have at least a 2.5 GPA or meet the school's admission standard. Based on financial need. Deadline: December.

1967. (A, H, S, SS)
Ida M. Crawford Scholarship Fund

Scholarships of varying amounts to graduate or undergraduate students or graduating high school seniors. Must attend a 2- or 4-year college or university or vocational or technical school anywhere in the U.S. Cannot be used for study in medicine (acupuncture, chiropractic, and naturopathic studies), law, theology, teaching, or music. If in high school, must have at least a 3.5 GPA. If an undergraduate or graduate student, must have at least a 3.5 GPA. Deadline: December.

1968. (A, H, S, SS)
Jenkins Scholarship Fund

Scholarships of varying amounts to full-time graduate or undergraduate students or graduating high school seniors for any area of study. Must have graduated from a high school in Portland Public School District #1. Must attend an accredited college or university in the U.S. If a graduating high school senior, must have at least a 3.5 GPA. If in college, must have at least a 3.0 GPA. Write an introductory letter detailing the financial and educational situation. Deadline: December.

1969. (A, H, S, SS)
John Lamar Cooper Scholarship Fund

Scholarships of varying amounts to graduate students. Must be Hood River residents who are Oregon

high school graduates or students who obtained a GED. May be used for full-time graduate or undergraduate study in any major at an accredited Oregon college or university. If in college, must have at least a 2.5 GPA. Write an introductory letter detailing financial and educational situation. Deadline: December.

1970. (A, H, S, SS)
Privately Funded Awards—Bowerman Foundation Scholarships

Varying number of scholarships of varying amounts to Oregon students in final year of graduate or undergraduate school in any area of study. Specify whether graduate or undergraduate student. Send a self-addressed, stamped envelope for an application. Deadline: none specified.

1971. (A, H, S, SS)
W.C. and Pearl Campbell Non-Linfield Scholarship Fund

Scholarships of varying amounts to graduate or undergraduate students or graduating high school seniors for any area of study. Must attend a college or university (other than Linfield College) in the state of Oregon. If a graduate or undergraduate, must have at least a 3.75 GPA. If in high school, must have at least a 3.75 GPA and an 1100 SAT. Deadline: December.

1972. (S)
Orentreich Foundation for the Advancement of Science (OFAS)
Biomedical Research Station
RD 2 Box 375
Cold Spring-on-Hudson, NY 10516
(845) 265–4200
http://www.orentreich.org

Grants of varying amounts to postgraduate fellows in science or medicine at accredited universities and institutions in the U.S. Preference is given to research focused in dermatology, aging, endocrinology, or serum markers for human disease. Deadline: none specified.

(H, SS)

Organization of American Historians
112 N. Bryan Avenue
Bloomington, IN 47408–7311

(812) 855–7311
http://www.oah.org

1973. (SS)
Huggins-Quarles Award

2 awards of $1,000 to minority graduate students at the dissertation research stage of their doctoral program. Must submit a brief 2-page abstract of their dissertation project, along with a 1-page budget explaining travel and research plans. Visit web site for more information. Deadline: December 1.

1974. (H, SS)
Jamestown Scholars: Dissertation Fellowships

Fellowships of $5,000 to graduate students pursuing a doctoral degree in history, American studies, and related fields. Research should contribute to our understanding of the development and legacy of 17th-century Jamestown. Visit web site for more information. Deadline: June 30.

1975. (H)
La Pietra Dissertation Travel Fellowship in Transnational History

1 fellowship of $1,250 to a graduate student whose dissertation topic deals with aspects of American history that extend beyond U.S. borders. Award may be used for international travel to collections vital to dissertation research. Must be enrolled in an accredited U.S. institution. Visit web site for more information. Deadline: December 1.

1976. (H)
Lerner-Scott Dissertation Prize

1 prize of $1,000 to a graduate student for the best doctoral dissertation in U.S. women's history. Application must contain a letter of support from a faculty member at the degree-granting institution, along with an abstract, table of contents, and sample chapter from dissertation. Visit web site for more information. Deadline: December 1.

1977. (H)
Louis Pelzer Memorial Award

1 award of $500 to graduate students for essays dealing with any period or topic in the history of the United States. Selection is based on the significance of the subject matter, literary craftsmanship, and competence in the handling of evidence. Visit web site for submission guidelines. Deadline: December 1.

1978. (H, SS)
Mary K. Bonsteel Tachau Precollegiate Teaching Awards

Awards of $750, a 1-year member to OAH, and a 1-year subscription to the OAH *Magazine of History* to precollegiate teachers engaged at least half-time in teaching history or social studies. Awarded to enhance the intellectual development of other history teachers and/or students. Visit web site for specific areas in which candidates should demonstrate exceptional ability. Deadline: December 1.

1979. (SS)
White House Historical Association Fellowships

Fellowships providing $2,000 per month and a travel stipend to doctoral students, postdoctoral fellows, and precollegiate teachers to conduct projects shedding light on the role of the White House as home, workplace, museum, structure, and symbol. Applicant's work should enhance the understanding of how the White House functions in its capacities and of life and work at all levels within the walls of the President's house. Visit web site for more information. Deadline: December 1.

(H, S, SS)
Organization of American States Dept. of Fellowships & Training
17th Street & Constitution Avenue, N.W.
Washington, DC 20006
(202) 458–3000
http://www.oas.org

1980. (H, S, SS)
Graduate Fellowships (Agency-Placed)

Fellowships providing international round-trip travel, health insurance, monthly allowance, and a modest once-a-year book allowance to graduate students for study and research in education, environment and sustainable development, governance, science and technology, and poverty alleviation and social development. Cannot be used for introductory language studies or medical sciences and related areas. Must be citizens or permanent residents of OAS member states and use the award to study in a country other than the country of origin. Awards are for the duration of the program of studies or up to 2 years, whichever is less. Must have clear academic goals, a focused area of study, and career objectives contributing to the development of the country. Visit web site for submission guidelines. Deadline: varies by country.

1981. (H, S, SS)
Graduate Fellowships (Self-Placed)

Fellowships providing tuition, fees, international travel, health insurance, living expenses, and books or other study materials to graduate students in education, environment and sustainable development, governance, science and technology, and poverty alleviation and social development. Cannot be used for introductory language studies or medical sciences and related areas. Must be citizens or permanent residents of OAS member states and use the award to study in a country other than the country of origin. Visit web site for submission guidelines. Deadline: varies by country.

1982. (H, S, SS)
OAS PRA Fellowships for U.S. Residents

Fellowships providing tuition, fees, travel expenses, and stipend to graduate students in all areas of study (except medicine and foreign languages). Must be U.S. citizens or legal residents. Fellowships are for study abroad in an OAS member country. Must have a bachelor's degree and demonstrate the ability to pursue advanced studies. Applicants must be fluent in the language of country of intended study. Deadline: March 1.

1983. (A, H, S, SS)
Organization of Istanbul Armenians Scholarship
Scholarship Committee
P.O. Box 55153
Sherman Oaks, CA 91413
http://www.oia.net/scholarship

Up to 6 scholarships of $1,250, 3 of $1,000, and 2 at $750 to full-time graduate and undergraduate students in any field of study. Must be of Armenian descent enrolled in an accredited institution. Selection based on academic achievement and involvement in the Armenian community. Deadline: November 5.

(S)
Our World-Underwater Scholarship Society
200 E. Chicago Avenue, Suite 40
Chicago, IL 60559–1756
(630) 986–6990
http://www.owuscholarship.org

1984. (S)
Divers Alert Network Internship

1 3-month internship providing $3,000 in funding to a graduate or undergraduate student or individual with a background in science or medicine with an interest in research methodology and data collection. Internship is meant to explore data collection and to provide experience that may motivate individuals toward careers in diving or diving-related fields. Intern must be a certified scuba diver with diving physiology knowledge, a science major, strong people and organizational skills, and computer knowledge. Housing is not provided. Internship takes place in Durham, NC, and other field locations. Deadline: none specified.

1985. (S)
European Rolex Scholarships

2 scholarships of £15,000 to graduate students who are about to complete their master's but have not been awarded the degree. Must be a citizen of a European nation, speak fluent English, be between the ages of 21 and 24 by the deadline date, and be a qualified scuba diver to CMAS 3 star or equivalent. Applicants must have high academic achievement and interest in the underwater world. The award is used to cover the cost of spending 1 year investigating career possibilities in underwater and water-related fields. Request applications in the fall. Visit web site for more information. Deadline: November 30.

1986. (S)
Lake Michigan Biological Station

1 10- to 12-week summer internship providing $5,000 to a graduate or undergraduate student to receive the type of experience he/she is looking for

while also providing contributions to research goals. Internship takes place in Zion, IL, and housing is not provided. Should be a certified scuba diver with recent diving experience; a bachelor's degree in some sort of biological science is preferred; experience with freshwater diving, research diving, and boat diving is preferred. Deadline: none specified.

1987. (S)
National Geographic Society Internship

1 internship providing $5,000 to a graduate or undergraduate student to work as an experienced underwater photographer. There are no age limits to this internship. Intern must have extensive experience as an underwater photographer and own basic underwater photographic equipment and basic diving gear. Highly specialized equipment will be provided by National Geographic. National Geographic will have first right of refusal to all photographs made, but the copyright remains with the photographer. Intern will spend time at the NGS's Washington, DC, headquarters. Funding must be used to pay for transportation to and from field sights and expenses in the field. Some additional funding may be available, depending on the scope and nature of the field projects. Deadline: rolling.

1988. (S)
North American Rolex Scholarship

1 scholarship of $20,000 to a graduate student who is about to complete a master's but has not been awarded the degree. Must be between the ages of 21 and 24 by deadline date and be a qualified scuba diver to CMAS 3 star or equivalent. Applicants must have high academic achievement and interest in the underwater world. The award is used to cover the cost of spending 1 year investigating career possibilities in underwater and water-related fields. The award covers travel and per diem expenses for the period, which usually lasts 35 to 40 weeks. Request applications in the fall. Deadline: November 30.

1989. (S)
REEF Internship

1 8- to 12-week internship providing $3,000 to a graduate or undergraduate student to expose them to the entire range of environmental nonprofit activities. There are opportunities for creative projects to be de-

signed and implemented by the intern. Interns should be certified scuba divers with recent diving experience, experience with ocean and boat diving is required, and interns must have the ability to work long days interacting with the public. For more specific information, visit web site. Deadline: none specified.

1990. (S)
University of Maine Darling Center Marine Lab Internship

1 internship providing $3,000 to a graduate or undergraduate student to focus on research on the ecology of the American lobster and the green sea urchin. Internship may run from 23 weeks to 6 months, with dormitory-style housing and meals prepared by the interns in the kitchen. Internship takes place in Walpole, ME. Interns must be certified scuba divers, with advanced certification preferred, small boat handling experience preferred, as well as cold-water diving experience, should have an enthusiasm for field marine research, and ability to work well in a team. For more information, visit web site. Deadline: none specified.

1991. (S)
Ove Arup & Partners, California
Arup Fellowship
2440 South Sepulveda Boulevard, Suite 180
Los Angeles, CA 90064
(310) 312–5040
http://www.arup.com

70 to 100 internships (2 to 5 are for U.S. citizens) providing a salary ranging from $450 to $500 per week, round-trip travel, 2-week interim dorm housing, and end-of-fellowship bonus of $800. The internships last 24 months and are open to recent college graduates with either a bachelor's or master's of science in architectural, civil, electrical, mechanical, or structural engineering. U.S. interns are in London and return to full-time jobs at one of the U.S. offices (Los Angeles, San Francisco, or New York City). Deadline: December 31.

(S)
Paleontological Research Institution
1259 Trumansburg Road
Ithaca, NY 14850
(607) 273–6623
http://www.priweb.org

1992. (S)

Katherine Palmer Award

1 award recognizes an individual who is not a professional paleontologist for the excellence of his/her contribution to the field of paleontology. Visit web site for more information and deadline.

1993. (S)

Student Award in Systematic Paleontology

1 award of $500 to a graduate student in systematic paleontology. Student must be nominated in a 500-word description of proposed research project with a letter of recommendation from his/her primary advisor. Visit web site for more information and deadline.

1994. (S)

The Paleontological Society

Grants

P.O. Box 1897

Lawrence, KS 66044–8897

http://paleosoc.org

Limited number of $500 grants to graduate, postdoctoral, and undergraduate students. Graduate and undergraduate students must be in research programs involving any aspect of paleontology. Postdoctoral student members must have appointments and primary involvement in a program of paleontological research. Applicants must be members of the Society. Deadline: March 1.

1995. (A)

Paramount Pictures

Internships in Film & Television

5555 Melrose Avenue

Hollywood, CA 90038

(323) 956–5000

http://www.paramount.com/studio/jobs.htm

Varying numbers of paid internships in producing, directing, and film and TV writing at Paramount Pictures providing approximately $25,000 to graduates of the graduate film programs at New York University, Columbia University, University of California at Los Angeles, University of Southern California, or the American Film Institute. Students must apply through their universities and not apply directly to Paramount. Awards are renewable. Deadline: February 1.

1996. (S)

Parkinson's Disease Foundation

Summer Fellowship

William Black Medical Research Building

Columbia-Presbyterian Medical Center

710 West 168th

New York, NY 10032–9982

(800) 457–6676

http://www.parkinsonsfoundation.org

Fellowships providing stipends to medical and undergraduate students to conduct 10-week summer research projects on Parkinson's disease. Project must be under the supervision of a research investigator. Deadline: April 1.

(A)

PEN American Center

568 Broadway

New York, NY 10012

(212) 334–1660

http://www.pen.org

1997. (A)

Ernest Hemingway Foundation Award

1 award of $7,500 for a distinguished first novel or collection of fiction published by a U.S. writer in the preceding year. Send a self-addressed, stamped envelope for guidelines and deadline.

1998. (A)

PEN/Faulkner Award for Fiction

Prizes of $7,500 and $2,500 to the most distinguished work of fiction published by a U.S. writer in the previous calendar year. Authors or publishers must submit 4 copies of a published book. Send a self-addressed, stamped envelope for guidelines. Deadline: December 31.

1999. (A)

PEN/Revson Foundation Fellowship

1 fellowship of $12,750 is given in alternating years to a poet or fiction writer age 35 or under whose body of work to date shows exceptional promise and deserves recognition from a wider readership. Send a self-addressed, stamped envelope for guidelines. Deadline: January 15.

2000. (A)
Renato Poggioli Translation Award

1 award of $3,000 to assist a translator of Italian whose work-in-progress is especially outstanding. Applicants must send a letter of application and curriculum vitae, statement of purpose, and a sample of the translation with the original Italian text. Deadline: January 15.

2001. (A)
Translation Prize

1 prize of $3,000 for a superior book-length translation from any language into English published in the preceding year. Send a self-addressed, stamped envelope for guidelines.

(S, SS)
Pfizer
Attn: Internship Coordinator
Corporate Personnel
235 East 42nd Street
New York, NY 10017
(212) 573–2880
http://www.pfizer.com

2002. (S, SS)
Internships

80 to 100 summer internships providing a salary ranging from $910 to $1,070 per week to graduate students in pharmaceuticals and health care. Internships last from 12 to 15 weeks at Boulder, CO, Groton, CT, Terre Haute, IN, Lee's Summit, MO, Parsippany, Rutherford, or Clifton, NJ, or New York, NY. Interns work in research, legal, medical devices, quality control, marketing, personnel, tax, licensing and development, sales, public affairs, strategic planning, medical affairs, finance, controllers, engineering, CIT (Corporate Information Technology), and treasury. The Strategic Development Group (part of the Medical Devices Department) offers a special research internship open to graduate students, highly qualified undergraduate seniors, and recent college graduates. Applicants must have at least a 3.8 GPA and a background in science, engineering, or medicine. Deadline: rolling.

2003. (S)
Pfizer AGS Postdoctoral Fellowship Program

Varying number of fellowships of $40,000 per year for 2 years to postdoctoral fellows in geriatric medicine. Open to recent M.D.s and D.O.s who will complete their residency training by July 1 of year following the deadline date. Deadline: December 2.

2004. (A, SS)
PGA Tour
Minority Internship Program
112 TPC Boulevard
Ponte Vedra Beach, FL 32082
(904) 285–3700
http://www.pga.com

15 to 20 9-week summer internships providing $250 per week, round-trip travel, and a housing stipend to undergraduate and graduate minority students. Internships are available in Los Angeles, CA, Trumbull, CT, Jacksonville, FL, Ponte Vedra Beach, FL (HQ), or Atlanta, GA. Depending on placement, interns assist with architectural design of golf courses, arrange banquets at the TPC club, conduct research for upcoming tournaments, contact corporate sponsors, teach golf lessons, manage the TPC driving range, collect Nielsen ratings data, or write for *Golf Digest*. 10 unpaid internships year-round for nonminority and minority graduates, undergraduates, and recent college graduates in creative services, productions, corporate marketing, and business development. Must submit résumé and cover letter when requesting an application. Deadline: February 15.

2005. (S)
Pharmaceutical Research and Manufacturers Association Foundation
Fellowships in Pharmaceuticals
1100 15th Street, N.W.
Washington, DC 20005
(202) 835–3400
http://www.phrma.org

Fellowships ranging from $10,000 to $12,000, plus $500 for expense money, to doctoral candidates, medical and dental students, physicians, dentists, or veterinarians, postdoctoral instructors, assistant professors, or investigators in the areas of pharmacology, toxicology, morphology, or pharmaceutics. Some of the awards are for thesis preparation; others are for clinical training or are research starter grants. Awards are for a maximum of 2 years. Applicants must have received a bachelor's degree or Pharm.D. degree in pharmacy, chemistry, biology, or a related area from an accredited school in the U.S. Deadline: October 1.

2006. (H)
Phi Beta Kappa Society
Mary Isabel Sibley Fellowship
1785 Massachusetts Avenue, N.W., Fourth Floor
Washington, DC 20036
(202) 265–3808
http://www.pbk.org

1 fellowship of $6,000 to postdoctoral students in archaeology; Greek language, history, or literature; or the study of French language and literature. Open to females between the ages of 25 and 30 who have demonstrated ability to conduct original research and who have attained their doctorate or have completed all course work and only need to complete their dissertation. Recipients must conduct full-time research during the fellowship duration. Award may be used at any accredited institution. Deadline: none specified.

(A, H, S, SS)
Phi Eta Sigma Founders Fund Scholarships
Dr. John W. Sagabiel
525 Grise Hall
Western Kentucky University
1 Big Red Way
Bowling Green, KY 42101–3576
(270) 745–6540
http://www.phietasigma.org

2007. (A, H, S, SS)
Charles M. Thompson Scholarship

1 scholarship of $2,000 to a first-year graduate (master's or doctoral) student or professional school student in any field of study. Must be Phi Eta Sigma members entering their first year of study. Awarded in honor of Dean Thompson, a founder of Phi Eta Sigma, Grand President from 1939 until 1963, and Dean of the College of Business at the University of Illinois. Deadline: March 1.

2008. (A, H, S, SS)
Fred H. Turner Scholarship

1 scholarship of $2,000 to a first-year graduate (master's or doctoral) student or professional school student in any field of study. Must be Phi Eta Sigma members entering their first year of study. Awarded in honor of Dean Turner, member of the Executive Committee from 1938 until 1976, who served as editor of the *Forum* and Grand Historian. He was Dean of Students at the University of Illinois. Deadline: March 1.

2009. (A, H, S, SS)
Kendrick C. Babcock Scholasrhip

1 scholarship of $2,000 to a first-year graduate (master's or doctoral) student or professional school student in any field of study. Must be Phi Eta Sigma members entering their first year of study. Awarded in honor of Dean Babcock, one of the 3 founders of Phi Eta Sigma, who was Dean of the College of Arts and Sciences at the University of Illinois. Deadline: March 1.

2010. (A, H, S, SS)
Scott Goodnight Scholarship

1 scholarship of $2,000 to a first-year graduate (master's or doctoral) student or professional school student in any field of study. Must be Phi Eta Sigma members entering their first year of study. Awarded in honor of Dean Goodnight, Grand President of Phi Eta Sigma from 1933 until 1939 and Dean of Men at the University of Wisconsin. Deadline: March 1.

2011. (A, H, S, SS)
Thomas Arkle Clark Scholarship

1 scholarship of $2,000 to a first-year graduate (master's or doctoral) student or professional school student in any field of study. Must be Phi Eta Sigma members entering their first year of study. Awarded in honor of Dean Clark, dean at the University of Illinois and one of the 3 founders of Phi Eta Sigma, who was the first Grand President, serving from 1927 to 1933. Deadline: March 1.

2012. (A, H, S, SS)

Phi Kappa Phi Honor Society
Phi Kappa Phi Graduate Fellowships
Chapter Secretary
P.O. Box 16000
Baton Rouge, LA 70893
(504) 388–4917
http://www.phikappaphi.org

50 fellowships of $7,000 to members who will be entering their first year of graduate or professional school or undergraduate seniors. Must be a member, or about to become a member, of a PKP chapter. Must have begun applying to a graduate or professional school, preferably in the U.S. Preference is given to students planning on working toward a Ph.D. Applicants must plan on being full-time students. Apply through local chapters only. Visit web site for more information. Applications available after November 1. Deadline: March 1.

2013. (A, H, S, SS)

Philanthropic Educational Organization (PEO)
Sisterhood
Executive Offices
3700 Grand Avenue
Des Moines, IA 50312–2899
(515) 255–3153
http://www.peointernational.org

75 scholarships of $5,000 to female graduate students to résumé or continue their graduate education in any field of study. Grants and educational loans to women who are within 2 years of completing their graduate or undergraduate degrees. There is also an International Peace Scholarship available to women from other countries to complete their studies. Must apply and receive recommendation letters through local chapters. Applicants must locate PEO chapters because the national PEO will not give out names and addresses. Apply between September 1 and December 31. Deadline: January.

(A)

Phi Mu Alpha—Sinfonia Foundation
ATTN: Grant Committee
10600 Old State Road
Evansville, IN 47711
(812) 867–2433
http://www.sinfoniafoundation.org

2014. (A)

Delta Iota Alumni Scholarship

1 scholarship of $500 to a graduate or undergraduate member. Selection based on at least a 3.3 GPA on a 4.0 scale, references, essay, and student membership for at least 2 semesters. Deadline: May 1.

2015. (A)

Research Assistance Grants

Grants of up to $1,000 to graduate students to conduct research related to American music or music in America. Must provide evidence of previous successful writing and research or unusual knowledge or competence in the field to be researched. Deadline: March 1.

2016. (A)

Sinfonia Foundation Scholarships

4 scholarships of $500 to graduate or undergraduate members. Selection based on at least a 3.3 GPA on a 4.0 scale, references, essay, and student membership for at least 2 semesters. Deadline: May 1.

2017. (S)

Phi Rho Sigma Medical Society
Elliott Dollar Student Loan Fund
P.O. Box 90264
Indianapolis, IN 46290
(317) 255–4379
http://www.phirhosigma.org
central_office@phirhosigma.org

Awards of varying amount to medical students who are Phi Rho Sigma members. Must be recommended by chapter president, chapter counselor, and the dean or other administrative officer at the medical school student is attending. Students are eligible to borrow up to the amount of the student's annual tuition. Deadline: none.

2018. (S)

Phi Sigma Kappa
Terrill Graduate Fellowship
2925 East 96th Street
Indianapolis, IN 46240
(317) 573–5420
http://www.phisigmakappa.org/events_programs/
scholarships.asp

1 scholarship of $2,000 to an undergraduate member, alumnus, or present graduate student who will be a full-time student in a graduate or professional school the following year. Must have at least a B average. Deadline: January 31.

2019. (S)
Physician Assistant Foundation of the American Academy of Physician Assistants Educational Program
950 North Washington Street
Alexandria, VA 22314
(703) 519–5686
http://www.aapa.org/paf

Numerous scholarships of $1,000, $2,000, and $5,000 to graduate and undergraduate students in a physician assistants program. Based on academic record, extracurricular school activities, community involvement, and financial need. Deadline: January 15.

2020. (A, H, S, SS)
Pilot International Foundation PIF/Lifeline Scholarship Program
P.O. Box 4844
Macon, GA 31208–4844
(478) 743–7403
http://www.pilotinternational.org/html/home.shtml

Scholarships of varying amount to any applicant seeking retraining for a second career working directly with persons with disabilities or training those who will, or are seeking to, improve his/her professional skills in their current occupation of working with persons with disabilities or training those who will. May be used for graduate or undergraduate study. Renewable for up to 3 years. Send a self-addressed, stamped envelope to above address to find the location of the nearest Pilot Club. Deadline: April 1.

2021. (SS)
Pitt Rivers Museum James A. Swan Fund
ATTN: Director
University of Oxford South Parks Road
Oxford OX1 3PP UK
0865–270927
http://www.prm.ox.ac.uk/research.html

Approximately 10 awards ranging from 1,000 to 2,000 pounds to graduate students to support research in Africa relating to the small people, such as Bushmen, Pygmies, and other hunter-gatherers. Awards are renewable. Deadline: none.

2022. (A, Contest)
Pittsburgh New Music Ensemble Harvey Gaul Composition Contest
P.O. Box 99476
Pittsburgh, PA 15233
(412) 889–7231
http://www.pnme.org

Awards of $3,000 to graduate or undergraduate students or professionals for an original music competition. Awards are for new works scored for 5 to 15 instruments. There is an entry fee, which must accompany submissions. Applicants may enter more than 1 competition. Must be a U.S. citizen. Deadline: April 15.

(A)
Playwright's Center
2301 Franklin Avenue East
Minneapolis, MN 55406–1099
(612) 332–7481
http://www.pwcenter.org

2023. (A)
McKnight Advancement Grant

Grants of $8,500 to playwrights to assist in production or creative work. Applicants must demonstrate exceptional artistic merit and potential and must submit 2 works that have been fully produced by a professional theater. Recipients must spend 2 months of the grant year participating in center programs. Applications available after November 2. Deadline: early January.

2024. (A)
Midwest Playlabs

4 to 6 playwrights receive honoraria, travel expenses, and room and board to attend a 2-week workshop. Playwrights must submit unpublished and unproduced full-length plays. Each play receives a public reading followed by an audience discussion of the work. Selection based on an open script competition. Applications available after October 1. Must be U.S. citizens. Deadline: December 1.

2025. (A)
Playwright-in-Residence Fellowship

Fellowships of $5,000 to playwrights who have not had more than 2 of their productions of their work fully staged by professional theaters. Fellows must spend 12 months as core members of the Center. Funds are made to assist in creation and development of their craft. Applications available after November 15; send a self-addressed, stamped envelope. Must be U.S. citizen or legal permanent resident. Deadline: March 1.

(A, Contest)
Poetry Society of America
15 Gramercy Park
New York, NY 10003
(212) 254–9628
http://www.poetrysociety.org/psa-awards.html

2026. (Contest)
Cash Awards

Cash awards of $100 in an annual competition aimed at advancing excellence in poetry, and encouraging skill in traditional forms, as well as experimentation in contemporary forms. These are cash awards, not scholarships. Please send a self-addressed, stamped envelope for contest rules brochure. Deadline: December 31.

2027. (Contest)
Contests Open to PSA Members

Various contests with varying amounts of awards to PSA members. Only 1 submission per contest. Entries must be unpublished on date of entry and not scheduled for publication by the date of the PSA awards ceremony held in the spring. These are cash awards, not scholarships. Send self-addressed, stamped envelope for contest rules. Deadline: December 31.

2028. (A, Contest)
National Chapbook Fellowships

An award of $1,000 and an invitation to read at The PSA Festival of New American Poets to a winning poet who has not published a full-length poetry collection. Send a self-addressed, stamped postcard for confirmation of receipt and a self-addressed stamped envelope for announcement of the winners. Payment of a $12 nonrefundable entry fee (check or money order payable in U.S. dollars to Poetry Society of America). This fee is not waived for PSA members. Entries will be accepted after October 1. Poets may apply to 1 contest only and must be a U.S. resident. Deadline: December 21.

2029. (A)
New York Chapbook Fellowships

An award of $1,000 and an invitation to read at The PSA Festival of New American Poets to a winning poet who has not published a full-length poetry collection. This contest is open to any New York City resident (in the 5 boroughs) who is 30 or under and has not published a full-length poetry collection. This contest is open to any U.S. resident who has not published a full-length poetry collection. Send a self-addressed, stamped postcard for confirmation of receipt and a self-addressed, stamped envelope for announcement of the winners. Payment of a $12 nonrefundable entry fee (check or money order payable in U.S. dollars to Poetry Society of America). This fee is not waived for PSA members. Entries will be accepted after October 1. Poets may apply to 1 contest only. Deadline: December 21.

2030. (Contest)
Poets and Patrons, Inc.
2630 Longview Drive
Lisle, IL 60532
http://www.poetsandpatrons.org

Prizes of $75 and $25 awarded for original, unpublished poems of up to 40 lines. There is no entry fee. These are cash awards, not scholarships. Send self-addressed, stamped envelope for rules. Deadline: September 1.

2031. (A, H, S, SS)
Point Foundation Scholarship
P.O. Box 261111
Lakewood, CO 80226
(866) 33–POINT
http://www.thepointfoundation.org
info@thepointfoundation.org

Awards of varying amounts to full-time graduate and undergraduate students attending, or planning to attend, an institute of higher education and who are underprivileged and/or have been socially marginalized principally by reason of sexual orientation. Selection based on demonstrated evidence of both community involvement and financial need a minimum 3.0 GPA; must submit 2 to 3 letters of recommendation, a copy of current transcript, and 3 1-page essays answering questions listed on the web site to be eligible for this award. Deadline: August 1.

2032. (A)
Polish Music Center
Stefan and Wanda Wilk Prizes for Research in Polish Music
Thornton School of Music
University of Southern California
840 West 34th Street
Los Angeles, CA 90089–0851
(213) 740–9369
http://www.usc.edu/go/polish_music
polmusic@email.usc.edu

1 award each of $500 and $1,000 to graduate students and scholars for research on Polish music. Selection is based on the best papers reflecting original research on some aspect of music in Poland. Students must declare that their paper was written while registered as a student at an accredited institution. Submissions must be previously unpublished. Polish scholars and students in Poland are ineligible. Deadline: September 30.

2033. (SS)
Population Fellows Program
University of Michigan
1214 South University, 2nd Floor
Ann Arbor, MI 48104–2548
(734) 763–9456
http://www.sph.umich.edu/pfps

Fellowships providing a modest stipend, health insurance, paid vacation and sick leave, travel funds to and from placement site, housing assistance, and professional development budget to graduate (master's and doctoral) students pursuing a degree in population-related areas. Must be a U.S. citizen or legal resident and committed to a career in international population and family planning. Students apply for inclusion in a pool of fellows, and then the program contacts prospective host agencies. Students matching the requirements are offered the positions. Visit web site for more information and application. Deadline: April 1 and November 1.

(A, H)
Prairie Schooner
201 Andrews
University of Nebraska
Lincoln, NE 68588–0334
(402) 472–4636
http://www.unl.edu/schooner/psmain.htm

2034. (A, H)
Bernice Slote Awards

An award of $500 for best work by a beginning writer published in *Prairie Schooner*. No entry or reading fee. These are cash awards, not scholarships. Winners announced in the spring issue of the following year. Send a self-addressed, stamped envelope for rules. Deadline: none specified.

2035. (A, H)
Lawrence Foundation Awards

An award of $500 for best short story published in *Prairie Schooner*. No entry or reading fee. These are cash awards, not scholarships. Winners are announced in the spring issue of the following year. Send a self-addressed, stamped envelope for rules. Deadline: none specified.

2036. (A, H)
Virginia Faulkner Award for Excellence in Writing

1 award of $1,000 for best short story, poetry, or nonfiction article published in *Prairie Schooner*. All genres eligible. No entry or reading fee. These are cash awards, not scholarships. Winners are announced in the spring issue of the following year. Send a self-addressed, stamped envelope for rules. Deadline: none specified.

2037. (A, H)
Writing Awards

Awards ranging from $250 to $1,000 for best work published in *Prairie Schooner*. No entry or reading fee. These are cash awards, not scholarships. Winners are announced in the spring issue of the following year. Send a self-addressed, stamped envelope for rules. Deadline: varies.

Presbyterian Church (USA)
Financial Aid for Studies
100 Witherspoon Street
Louisville, KY 40202–1396
(502) 472–4636
http://www.pcusa.org/pcusa/pcusa.htm

2038. (S)
Grant Program for Medical Studies

Varying number of scholarships ranging from $500 to $1,500 to full-time students enrolled in an accredited dental, medical, or nursing school. Must be a member of Presbyterian Church (USA). Must be recommended by academic advisor and by pastor. Must be U.S. citizen or permanent resident. Selection based on application, academic achievement, transcript, recommendation letters, and financial need. Deadline: rolling.

2039. (A, H, S, SS)
Native American Education Grant

40 to 45 awards ranging from $200 to $1,500 to graduate and undergraduate students in all fields of study. Must be Native Americans, Aleuts, or Eskimos who have completed at least 1 semester of work at an accredited institution. Preference given to Presbyterian undergraduate students. Renewal is based on continued financial need and satisfactory academic progress. Must be U.S. citizens or permanent residents. Renewable with continued satisfactory academic progress and financial need. Deadline: June 1.

2040. (H, S, SS)
Presidential Management Intern Program
William J. Green Jr. Federal Building
600 Arch Street, Room 3400
Philadelphia, PA 19106
(215) 861–3066
http://www.pmi.opm.gov

2-year internship open to graduate (master's and doctoral) students from a wide variety of academic disciplines interested in a career in the analysis and management of public policies and programs. Through the federal government internship, interns may receive assignments involving domestic or international issues, technology, science, criminal justice, health, financial management, and other fields in support of public service programs. Candidates must be nominated by their schools. Deadline: none specified.

2041. (S)
Prevent Blindness America
Grants and Fellowships
ATTN: School Administrator
500 East Remington Road
Schaumburg, IL 60173
(708) 843–2020
http://www.preventblindness.org/about/rsrch_
grants.html

Grants and fellowships ranging from $1,000 to $12,000 to graduate or medical students, postdoctoral students, or research individuals to conduct medical research that may lead to advances in preventing blindness, treatment and cures of visual disorders, restoring vision, and preserving sight. Research grants may be used to help defray costs of personnel, equipment, and supplies. Deadline: March 1.

(A)
Princess Grace Foundation—USA
ATTN: Executive Director
150 East 58th Street, 21st Floor
New York, NY 10155
(212) 317–1470
http://www.pgfusa.com

2042. (A)
Film Awards

Nominations for film grants are submitted by deans and department chairmen, in conjunction with the faculty of established colleges and universities located within the United States, by invitation only. All nominees must have already completed 1 film. Film grants are made as scholarships for undergraduate and graduate thesis film productions. A candidate must apply in their second to last year of study. Deadline: June 1.

2043. (A)
Student Awards

The Princess Grace Film Award is available to undergraduate and graduate students in their second-to-last year of study in film. Must be a U.S. citizen and have completed at least 1 film to qualify for this award. Student must be nominated by a dean or department chairman. Eligible applicants will be invited to apply. Deadline: March 31 (playwriting and theater), April 30 (dance), and June 1 (film).

2044. (S, SS)
Proctor & Gamble
Internships
P.O. Box 599
Cincinnati, OH 45201
(513) 983–1100
http://www.pg.com

300 summer internships providing salaries ranging from $700 to $1,150 to graduate students and from $450 to $675 for undergraduate sophomores, juniors, and seniors, plus relocation and round-trip travel expenses. Internships last from 9 to 14 weeks. Interns are assigned to Brand Management, Product Supply, Financial Management, Market Research, Management Systems, Cosmetics and Fragrances, Pharmaceuticals, Product Supply/Manufacturing, Engineering, and Research and Product Development in Baltimore, MD, Cincinnati, OH, or in any one of 49 different sites across the country. Deadline: February 1.

(S)
Professional Land Surveyors of Colorado
Colorado Surveyors Education Foundation Inc.
P.O. Box 2276
Arvada, CO 80001
http://www.plsc.net

2045. (S)
American Congress on Surveying and Mapping

1 or more scholarships of up to $1,000 open to graduate and undergraduate students enrolled in a Colorado accredited institution. Must be majoring in surveying, geography, remote sensing, geomatics, cartography, photogrammetry, geodesy, or GIS. Preference is given to full-time students and ACSM members. Must have at least a 2.5 GPA on a 4.0 scale. Visit Colorado state chapter web site for more information, contact person, and application. Deadline: December 1 (spring) and June 1 (fall).

2046. (S)
Central Colorado Professional Land Surveyors

1 or more scholarships of at least $500 to graduate or undergraduate students majoring in surveying, GIS, or

a mapping-related program. Must have an emphasis on surveying or mapping and have completed at least 6 semester hours in surveying. Must have at least a 3.0 GPA on a 4.0 scale. Open to full- or part-time students. Deadline: December 1 (spring) and June 1 (fall).

2047. (S)
PLSC Scholarship

1 or more scholarships of at least $1,000 to students majoring in surveying. Must be enrolled at the Metropolitan State College of Denver, have completed at least 6 hours in surveying course work, and have at least a 2.5 GPA on a 4.0 scale. Open to both full- and part-time students. Visit Colorado state chapter web site for more information and application. Deadline: December 1 (spring) and June 1 (fall).

2048. (Contest)
Quincy Writer's Guild Annual Creative Writing Contest
Michael Barrett
P.O. Box 433
Quincy, IL 62306–0433
http://www.artsqcy.org/quincywritersguild.htm

Awards for unpublished poetry, short story, and nonfiction. Entry fee: $2 per poem and $4 for short stories and articles. This is a cash award, not a scholarship competition. Send self-addressed, stamped envelope for guidelines. Deadline: April 15.

2049. (S)
Radio Technical Commission for Aeronautics
William E. Jackson Award
1828 L Street, N.W., Suite 805
Washington, DC 20036
(202) 833–9339
http://www.rtca.org/wejaward/wej.asp

1 scholarship of $2,000 through a competition open to graduate and undergraduate students in aviation electronics, aviation, and telecommunications. Based on a written report, which may be in the form of an essay, thesis, or paper that has been completed within the last 3 years. Student must also submit a 1- to 2-page summary, biographical information, and an endorsement letter by student's instructor, professor, or department head to the Commission. Deadline: June 30.

Radio-Television News Directors Foundation
1600 K Street, N.W., Suite 700
Washington, DC 20006–2838
(202) 659–6510
http://www.rtnda.org

2050. (H)
Abe Schechter Graduate Scholarship

1 scholarship of $1,000 to an incoming or full-time graduate student attending an accredited institution. Open to any major as long as career intent is television or radio news. Selection is based on academic achievement and a 1-page essay detailing accomplishments and goals, recommendation letter, and resume. Deadline: May 5.

2051. (H)
Fellowships

Up to 10 fellowships of $1,000 to $2,500 to minority journalists working in television or radio to develop or strengthen their management skills. For specific guidelines, visit web site. Deadline: May 5.

(A, H)
Ragdale Foundation
1260 North Green Bay Road
Lake Forest, IL 60045
(847) 234–1063
http://www.ragdale.org/fellowships.asp

2052. (A, H)
Frances Shaw Fellowship/Internship

1 fellowship of varying amount to a woman who began writing seriously after the age of 55. Fellows are flown to Ragdale from anywhere in the continental U.S. and receive a free 2-month residency. Deadline: February 1.

2053. (A, H)
Goberville Memorial Fellowship

1 fellowship covering all fees, and a $250 stipend for travel and materials, to a Wisconsin visual artist who is accepted for a residency. Wisconsin applicants will automatically be considered for this award upon acceptance to Ragdale's residency program. Wisconsin artists are encouraged to apply by submit-

ting materials according to the regular Ragdale application guidelines. Deadline: none specified.

(H, SS)
Rand
RAND M-12
12700 Main Street
Santa Monica, CA 90407–2138
(310) 393–0411
http://www.rand.org

2054. (H, SS)
Fellows in Population Studies and the Study of Aging

Fellowships ranging from $38,250 to $50,000 to doctoral fellows in the field of demographic and aging research. Must be U.S. citizens or permanent residents and have completed a doctoral degree or its equivalent in a relevant discipline. Program enables junior researchers to sharpen their analytic skills, learn to communicate research results effectively, and advance their research agenda. Renewable for a second year. Visit web site for more information. Deadline: February 1.

2055. (H, SS)
Graduate Student Summer Associate Program

25 fellowships, providing stipends of varying amounts, to graduate students to conduct independent research that can be completed during the 3-month stay. Students in a wide range of disciplines are generally within a year or two of completing their doctorates. Undergraduates and postdoctoral fellows are ineligible to apply. Visit web site for more information. Deadline: February 1.

2056. (S)
Reach for the Education of Adults in the Chicago Area
REACh Scholarship Committee Chair
c/o Fifth Third Bank
1209 N. Milwaukee Avenue
Chicago, IL 60622
(773) 227–5296
http://www.reach-chicago.org/scholarships/2003_scholarship.htm

3 to 5 scholarships of $1,000 to students who are graduate or undergraduate students and residents of the

Chicago area. Must be at least 25 years of age. Must be enrolled in, or admitted to, a degree or certificate program at an accredited college or university that is a member of the REACh organization. Must have at least a 3.0 GPA on a 4.0 scale. For more information and application, visit web site. Deadline: February 15.

2057. (SS)
Reason Foundation
Gray Internship
3415 S. Sepulveda Boulevard, Suite 400
Los Angeles, CA 90034
(310) 391–2245
http://www.reason.com/intern.shtml

10-week internship providing a stipend of $2,000, up to $400 in travel expenses, and housing to a graduate or undergraduate student to help with research, proofreading, and other tasks. Deadline: March 21.

2058. (A, H, S, SS)
Recording for the Blind
Mary P. Oenslager Scholastic Achievement Award
20 Rozelle Road
Princeton, NY 08540
(866) RFBD–585
(866) 732–3585
http://www.rfbd.org

3 scholarships of $5,000, 3 scholarships of $1,500, and 3 scholarships of $750 for blind graduate or undergraduate college seniors majoring in any field of study. Students must have at least a 3.0 GPA or better on a 4.0 scale and be registered with Recording for the Blind. Based on scholastic achievement, extracurricular activities, essay, and recommendation letters. Deadline: February 15.

2059. (A, H, S, SS)
The Reserve Officers Association of the United States
Henry J. Reilly Memorial Scholarship—Graduate Program
1 Constitution Avenue, N.E.
Washington, DC 20002–5624
(202) 479–2200
http://www.troa.org

Numerous scholarships of up to $500 to students who are active, or associate, ROA or ROAL members accepted

into a graduate program at a regionally accredited 4-year institution in the U.S in any area of study. If unemployed, must be enrolled in 2 graduate courses. If employed, must be enrolled in 1 graduate course. Must maintain a 3.3 GPA on a 4.0 scale. Based on recommendations, academic record, and curriculum vitae. Deadline: April 30.

2060. (S)
Resources for the Future
Gilbert F. White Fellowship Program
ATTN: Fellowship Director
1616 'P' Street, N.W.
Washington, DC 20036–1400
(202) 328–5000
http://www.rff.org/about_rff/white.htm

Varying number of fellowships of varying amounts to postdoctoral fellows to devote a year to scholarly work in energy, the environment, natural resources, or social sciences. Faculty members on sabbatical are encouraged to apply. Fellowships range from 9 months to 12 months. Deadline: February 28.

2061. (S)
Rhode Island Society of Professional Land Surveyors
Pierre H. Guillermette Scholarship
280 Drybridge Road
North Kingstown, RI 02852
(401) 294–1262
http://www.rispls.org/rispls.htm

1 or more scholarships of varying amounts to graduate or undergraduate students pursuing a program or degree in land surveying. Must be a Rhode Island resident. Selection is based on academic achievement, extracurricular activities, and goals. Renewable with reapplication. Deadline: October 30.

2062. (A)
Rhode Island State Council on the Arts
Individual Professional Artists Fellowships
83 Park Street, 6th Floor
Providence, RI 02903
(401) 222–3880
http://www.risca.state.ri.us

Awards of $3,000 to professional artists for the creation of works in the following areas: literary arts, music composition, choreography, media, crafts, or visual arts. Must be residents of Rhode Island. Send a self-addressed, stamped envelope for specific guidelines. Deadline: March 15.

2063. (A, H, S, SS)
The Rhodes Scholarship
Office of the American Secretary
8229 Boone Boulevard, Suite 240
Vienna, Virginia 22182
http://www.rhodesscholar.org
amsec@rhodesscholar.org

Scholarships covering all approved college fees to select talented graduate students for study at the University of Oxford. Candidate must be unmarried, be between 18 and 23 on October 1 of the year of application, and have sufficient standing to assure completion of a graduate degree. Based on scholarship, character, leadership, and physical vigor. Candidate can apply in either state of legal residence or state where minimum of 2 years of college training was received. Contact above address or applicant's own college. Deadline: none specified.

2064. (S)
Robert Mondavi Winery
Internship Program
P.O. Box 106
Oakville, CA 94562
(707) 963–9611
http://www.robertmondavi.com

13 internships providing a salary ranging from $10 to $12 per hour to graduate and upper-level undergraduate students and recent graduates who have a science background and are at least 21 years of age. Internships last from 3 to 6 months from July to December, with some part-time work available. Interns must have an interest in the winemaking industry. Deadline: rolling.

2065. (S)
Rocky Mountain Biological Laboratory
Lee R. G. Snyder Memorial Fund
P.O. Box 519
Crested Butte, CO 81224
(970) 349–7231
http://www.rmbl.org/apps/snyder.html

Varying number of grants of $500 to graduate students who are enrolled in accredited biology programs or related fields to conduct research at RMBL. Allowable expenses that are covered include supplies, field travel while at RMBL, station fees, housing, and lab rental. Food costs, salaries, and permanent equipment costs are not covered. Visit web site for more details and application. Deadline: February 15.

2066. (A, SS)
Rolling Stone Internships
Editorial Department
1290 Avenue of the Americas
New York, NY 10104
(212) 484–1616
http://www.rollingstone.com

4 to 6 12-week summer, fall, and spring internships providing no compensation, 2 scholarships of $3,000 for minority students during the summer session only. Open to graduate and undergraduate students from any major. Interns must be outgoing, self-motivated, and have an interest in rock and roll. The best interns want to learn every aspect of magazine publishing and are inquisitive and enthusiastic. Interns are placed in a variety of departments, such as advertising, editorial, and publicity. Applicants must send in a résumé, transcript, a letter of recommendation from a professor or professional, and a cover letter stating why the student is applying for the internship and wants to work at *Rolling Stone*. Finalists are interviewed in person or by phone. Deadline: rolling.

2067. (A, H, S, SS)
Roothbert Fund
Scholarships
3475 Riverside Drive, Room 252
New York, NY 10115
(212) 870–3116
http://www.roothbertfund.org
mail@roothbertfund.org

Scholarships ranging from $2,000 to $3,000 to graduate and undergraduate students in any field of study and for a wide range of careers. Applicants must send in an application, essay, transcript, and recommendation letters. Finalists must be interviewed in New York, New Haven, Philadelphia, or Washington, DC. Applicants must cover their own traveling costs. Recipients must attend at least 1 weekend fellowship conference during the first year of the grant. Applications may be requested in writing or on-line between December 1 and January 25. Deadline: February 1.

(S)

Roswell Park Cancer Institute
Carlton and Elm Streets
Buffalo, NY 14263
(716) 845–2339
http://www.roswellpark.org

2068. (S)
Graduate Fellowships

Up to 25 fellowships providing competitive stipends and room and board to master's and doctoral graduate students. All research revolves around the cancer program, with emphasis placed on multidisciplinary and translational research. Visit web site for detailed information and application. Deadline: February 14.

2069. (S)
Summer Oncology Research Program

Research programs providing $280 per week to medical and dental students to engage in clinical and/or basic research for an 8-week period. Some funding is available to defray room/board costs. Deadline: February 14.

2070. (A, H, S, SS)
Rotary Foundation Scholarships for International Understanding
Graduate Scholarships
1600 Ridge Avenue
Evanston, IL 60201
http://www.rotary.org

Graduate scholarships of up to $18,000 to students with a bachelor's degree to study in a country where there are Rotary Clubs. Applicants must be between the ages of 18 and 30, married or single. Must not be a member of the Rotary. Open to citizens of all countries with Rotary Clubs. Applicants may be studying any area of interest. Deadline: July 15.

2071. (S)
Royal Society
Rosenhein Research Fellowships
Executive Secretary
6 Carlton House Terrace
London SW1Y 5AG UK
http://www.royalsoc.ac.uk

Fellowships of 10,670 British pounds to graduate or undergraduate students majoring in biochemistry of plants and simpler forms of animal life. Open to students of all nationalities who have demonstrated ability to do independent scientific research. Preference given to students under age 30. Deadline: none specified.

2072. (A, H, S, SS)
Ruder-Finn
Intern Coordinator
301 East 57th Street
New York, NY 10022
(212) 593–6423
http://www.ruderfinn.com

8 internships providing $300 per week to college graduates of any age to work in this public relations firm, which represents foreign governments, corporate communications, and health-based campaigns. Internships last from 12 to 16 weeks during the summer, fall/winter, and winter/spring in New York City. Interns are assigned to arts, marketing communications, investor relations, health care, lifestyle, public affairs, high-tech, research, visual technology, media, Japan desk, and financial services. Interns create and update media lists, write pitch letters, conduct on-the-street interviews, and help in whatever needs to be done. Deadline: April 15 (summer), April 15 (fall/winter), and November 15 (winter/spring).

2073. (A, H, S, SS)
Ruritan National Foundation Educational
Grant Program
P.O. Box 487
Ruritan Road
Dublin, VA 24084
(703) 674–5431
(877) 787–8727
http://www.ruritan.org/foundation/scholarships.htm

Limited grants of $750 to graduate, professional school, or undergraduate students, with preference given to undergraduate freshmen and sophomores. Based on financial need, character, scholarship, and academic promise. Must have 2 letters of recommendation from Ruritan members. Applicants should live in or near a community with a Ruritan chapter. Deadline: April 1.

2074. (A, H, S, SS)
Ruth Eleanor and John Bamberger Memorial Foundation
136 S. Main, Suite 418
Salt Lake City, UT 84101
(801) 364–2045
http://intensivephonics.com/grants/Utah

66 scholarship grants ranging from $75 to $1,877 to graduate and undergraduate students and high school seniors. Must be Utah residents. Open to all majors, though preference is given to students majoring in nursing. Write an introductory letter briefly detailing your educational and financial situation. Deadline: none specified.

2075. (SS)
Rutherford Institute
Summer Internship Program
P.O. Box 7482
Charlottesville, VA 22906–7482
(434) 987–3888
http://www.rutherford.org/join/internship.asp

Internships for law students interested in receiving a grounding in critical areas of law affecting civil liberties and religious freedom. Interns analyze and discuss a broad range of constitutional and cultural issues under the instruction of attorneys who have practical and theoretical knowledge of their fields. Deadline: none specified.

(A, H, S, SS)
Sachs Foundation
90 South Cascade Avenue, Suite 1410
Colorado Springs, CO 80903
(719) 633–2353
http://www.frii.com/~sachs/back.htm
sachs@frii.com

2076. (A, H, S, SS)
Graduate Grant

Unspecified number of grants of $4,000 to graduate students in any field of study. Must attend an accredited U.S. institution. Must be African-American residents of Colorado who have graduated from college. Renewable up to 4 years. Write an introductory letter detailing financial and educational situation. Deadline: March 15.

2077. (A, H, S, SS)
Professional Award

Approximately 40 scholarships of $3,000 to graduate and professional school students. Must be African-American residents of Colorado and have at least a 3.4 GPA. Applications available after January 1. Write an introductory letter detailing financial and educational situation. Deadline: March 1.

2078. (A, H)
St. John's College
Harper-Wood Studentship
The Master
Cambridge CB2 1TP
UK
written inquiries only

1 studentship of up to 4,125 pounds sterling for a graduate student to conduct 1 year of study in any country in the area of creative writing in English poetry and literature. Student may be a graduate of any university in the United Kingdom, the Commonwealth, or the U.S. and is sponsored by St. John's. Must not be more than 30 years of age. Deadline: May 31.

(A, H, S, SS)
San Antonio Women's Celebration and Hall of Fame
ATTN: Scholarship Chairperson
P.O. Box 461104
San Antonio, TX 78246

2079. (A, H, S, SS)
General Scholarship

From 1 to 10 scholarships of $500 to female students who are residents of Bexar County. Open to graduate, professional school, undergraduate, nontraditional students returning to school and graduating high school seniors. Awards are good for any major at any accredited college or university. Either obtain an application from the school's scholarship office or, in January, send a self-addressed, stamped envelope with 52¢ in postage. Deadline: April 15.

2080. (A, H, S, SS)
June Meyer Memorial Scholarship

1 scholarship of $1,000 to a female, nontraditional student who is a resident of Bexar County. Open to

graduate, professional school, and undergraduate students in any major. Award is good for any major at any accredited college or university. Either obtain an application from the school's scholarship office or, in January, send a self-addressed, stamped envelope with 52¢ in postage. Deadline: April 15.

(A, H, S)
San Francisco Foundation
225 Bush Street, Suite 500
San Francisco, CA 94104
(415) 733–8500
415) 477–2783 (Fax)
http://www.sff.org/awards/arts.html

2081. (A, H)
Joseph Henry Jackson Literary Award

1 award of $2,000 to writers who are residents of either Northern California or Nevada (for 3 consecutive years immediately prior to closing date of the competition). May submit unpublished work-in-progress (fiction, nonfiction, or poetry). Applicants must be between 20 and 35 years of age. Writers of nonfiction are also eligible for the $1,000 Joseph Henry Jackson Honorable Mention Award. Deadline: January 15.

2082. (A)
Murphy and Cadogan Fine Arts Fellowships

Varying number of awards of $2,500 to graduate students pursuing fine arts study. Prospective applicants must be nominated by instructors at their college, must have completed at least 1 semester of graduate study, and must have at least 2 semesters remaining before graduation. Artwork submitted must have been completed within the past 2 years. Must be attending one of the following 8 Bay Area colleges and universities: Academy of Art College, California College of Arts and Crafts, John F. Kennedy University, Mills College, San Francisco Art Institute, San Francisco State University, Stanford University, or the University of California at Berkeley. Please contact Department Chair or the Foundation in January for application information. Deadline: varies.

2083. (A, H)
Phelan Art Award in Filmmaking
http://www.filmarts.org

6 awards of $2,500 to California-born artists in film and video. Awards are given in even-numbered years. Must be U.S. citizen. Begin submissions on November 15. Visit web site for more information. Deadline: January 15.

2084. (A)
Phelan Art Award in Video
http://www.bavc.org

Awards range from $2,500 to $7,500 to California-born artists in film and video. Awards are given in even-numbered years. Must be U.S. citizen. Begin submissions on November 15. Visit web site for more information. Deadline: varies.

2085. (A, H)
Phelan Award in Photography
http://www.sfcamerawork.org

3 awards of $2,500 to California-born artists in print making, photography, or film and video. Awards are given in odd-numbered years. Must be U.S. citizen. Begin submissions on November 15. Winners participate in a group exhibition at the SF Camerawork gallery. Visit web site for more information. Deadline: none specified.

2086. (A)
Phelan Award in Printmaking
http://www.kala.org

3 awards of $2,500 to California-born artists in print-making. Awards are given in odd-numbered years. Must be U.S. citizen. Begin submissions on November 15. Winners participate in a group exhibition in the Kala Institute's gallery. Visit web site for more information. Deadline: none specified.

2087. (S)
Switzer Environmental Fellowships
switzer@sff.org

10 fellowships of $13,000 to graduate students pursuing careers in the environmental arena. Applicants must be nominated by a professor or environmental professional, be a U.S. citizen, be enrolled in an accredited graduate institution in California, and have strong academic qualifications. Upon receipt of a satisfactory letter of nomination, the Foundation will mail an application to the candidate.

Deadline: December 6 (nominations) and January 31 (applications).

(A, H, S)

Santa Barbara Foundation
15 E. Carrillo Street
Santa Barbara, CA 93101
(805) 963–1873
http://www.sbfoundation.org

2088. (A)
Mary K. and Edith Pillsbury and Joyce H. Fahlman Music Scholarships
http://www.sbfoundation.org/Student_Aid/Arts/arts.html

28 to 35 scholarships ranging from $400 to $2,500 to graduate and undergraduate students of all ages in the area of music performance and music composition. Applicants must be Santa Barbara County residents or have strong ties to the county. Awards may be used for music lessons, camps, or college tuition. Selection based on recommendations, financial need, interviews, and auditions. Renewable. Visit web site for more information. Deadline: May 15.

2089. (A, H)
Mary K. and Edith Pillsbury Creative Writing Scholarships
http://www.sbfoundation.org/Student_Aid/Arts/arts.html

Scholarships of varying amounts to graduate and undergraduate students demonstrating unusual aptitude or potential in the field of writing. Financial need is a criterion. Must be planning to study writing at an approved college or university or the Music and Arts Conservatory of Santa Barbara. Must be residing in and have resided in Santa Barbara County for 2 years prior to the application deadline if attending a college or university in the county or have resided long-term in the county if attending a college or university outside the county. Deadline: October 15.

2090. (S)
Medical Student Program

Awards of varying amounts to students accepted to or enrolled in medical school. Must have attended Santa Barbara County schools since seventh grade,

be a Santa Barbara County high school graduate, and be either a U.S. citizen or legal resident. Financial need is considered. Applications are accepted beginning October 1. Deadline: January 15.

2091. (S)
Ruth and Walter Klass Scholarship
http://www.sbfoundation.org/Student_Aid/Graduate/graduate.html

Varying number of scholarships to graduate and undergraduate students pursuing careers in natural sciences or health and medicine, including fields such as engineering, physics, biology, chemistry, nursing, and medical studies, with priority going to those students focusing on acute illnesses. Must have attended Lompoc Valley schools for middle school or high school. Students must be citizens or permanent residents of the United States. Recipients will be selected through use of the general student loan application. Academic performance and financial need are primary criteria for awards. Contact: Student Aid Director, P.O. Box 1403, Santa Barbara, CA 93102, (805) 965–7212. Deadline: January 31.

2092. (S)
Schwalenberg Medical School Loan
http://www.sbfoundation.org/Student_Aid/medical/medical.html

Loans of varying amounts to medical school students for up to 14 quarters; can be received in addition to a maximum of 3 years of undergraduate loans. Loans are interest-free, and repayment begins 18 months after the student receives an M.D. or otherwise leaves school. For students who enter family practice or internal medicine, when 50% of the medical school loan has been repaid in a timely manner, the loan is considered paid in full. For more information, contact: Scholarship Foundation of Santa Barbara, P.O. Box 3620, Santa Barbara, CA 93130, (805) 965–7212. Deadline: none.

(S, SS)

Schering-Plough
2000 Galloping Hill Road
Kenilworth, NJ 07033–0530
(908) 298–4000
http://whatdrivesyou.com/spri-intern

2093. (SS)
MBA Summer Intern Program

Paid internships lasting 10 to 12 weeks, to graduate students in M.B.A. programs. Interns work on significant projects and attend seminars, meetings, briefings, and workshops designed to provide an overview of individual businesses and management development opportunities. Visit web site for specific information. Deadline: none specified.

2094. (S)
Summer Internships

Paid internships open to graduate and undergraduate students in life sciences, engineering, or computer sciences. Provides a salary and housing. Visit web site for contact information and other details. Deadline: none specified.

2095. (A, H, S, SS)
Scholarship Foundation of St. Louis
8215 Clayton Road
St. Louis, MO 63117
(314) 725–7990
http://www.sfstl.org
info@sfstl.org

680 scholarships of up to $3,000 to students at all levels of education (graduate, professional, postdoctoral, undergraduate, and vocational/technical students and graduating high school seniors) in any major (except ministry). Students must be residents of St. Louis City, St. Louis County, Franklin County, Jefferson County, Lincoln County, St. Charles County, or Warren County in Missouri or Clinton, Jersey, Madison, Monroe, or St. Clair County in Illinois for at least 2 years prior to the date of application and have at least a 2.0 GPA. Request applications after January 1; include a self-addressed, stamped envelope. Deadline: April 15.

2096. (A, H, S, SS)
Scholarship Fund of Game Wardens of Vietnam Association, Inc.
ATTN: John W. Woody, President
P.O. Box 701786
San Antonio, TX 78270
(866) 220–7477
http://www.tf116.org
president@tf116.org

1 scholarship of $400, 1 scholarship of $500, and 1 scholarship of $600 to graduate, professional, or undergraduate students or graduating high school seniors who are children of veterans from the River Patrol Force (also known as the Brown Water Navy). May be used for any field of study. No restrictions on age or marital status of student. Based on academic record and financial need. Visit web site for current contact information. Deadline: April 15.

(A, H, S, SS)
Screen Actors Guild Foundation
Scholarship and Awards Program
5757 Wilshire Boulevard
Los Angeles, CA 90036–3635
(323) 549–6708
http://www.sagfoundation.org

2097. (A, H, S, SS)
Ann Doran Scholarship

Varying number and amounts of scholarships to graduate or undergraduate students in any field of study. Must be members of the Screen Actors Guild, or children of members, who are accepted for admittance or already enrolled for at least 12 credit hours at an accredited university, college, or junior college in the U.S. Student must have been a member of the Guild for 5 years, or parent must have been a member for 10 years. Applicant must submit an essay to be eligible for this award. Applications are available after November 2. Deadline: March 15.

2098. (A, H, S, SS)
John L. Dales Scholarship Fund

Scholarships of $2,000 to graduate, postgraduate, or undergraduate students in any field of study. Must be SAG members for at least 5 years or dependents of members of at least 8 years. Financial need is a consideration. Renewable with reapplication. Deadline: April 30.

2099. (A, H, S, SS)
Transitional Scholarships

Varying number and amounts of scholarships to graduate or undergraduate students who are accepted for admittance or already enrolled for at least 12 credit hours at an accredited university, college, or junior college in the U.S. Must have been members of the Screen Actors Guild for at least 10 years. Applicant must submit an essay to be eligible for this award. Applications are available after November 2. Deadline: March 15.

2100. (A, H)
Scripps Howard Foundation Scholarship
Charles M. Schulz Award
312 Walnut Street, 28th Floor
P.O. Box 5380
Cincinnati, OH 45201–5380
(513) 977–3000
(513) 977–3035
http://www.scripps.com/foundation

Scholarships of $500 to $3,000 per year to full-time graduate and undergraduate students majoring in graphic art, allied art, and other journalism-related majors. Preference is given to full-time graduate students and upper-level undergraduate students or previous recipients who are preparing to work in any print or broadcast medium. Request application before December 20. Include a self-addressed mailing label with the words "Scholarship Application." Please indicate your major and your career goals. Deadline: February 25.

(S)
Semi-Conductor Research Corporation
P.O. Box 12053
79 Alexander Drive
Building 4401 #300
Research Triangle Park, NC 27709
(919) 541–9400
http://www.src.org/Default.asp?bhcp=1

2101. (S)
Robert M. Burger Fellowship

Fellowships providing tuition, fees, and a monthly stipend of $1,800 to doctoral program students in disciplines relevant to microelectronics. The fellowship supports research in microelectronics-related public policy, economic policy, and/or management issues. Selection based on quality, relevance, and timeliness of the proposed research, academic achievement, leadership abilities, and the appropriateness of the institutional environment for the research. Must be a U.S. citizen or permanent resident, have a master's degree, and plan to undertake a doctoral program

in economics, business, or other related area. Deadline: April 30.

2102. (S)
SRC Doctoral Fellowship

7 to 10 fellowships providing tuition, fees, and a stipend of $1,400 per month to doctoral students majoring in areas of microelectronics. Must be U.S. citizens. Research will be performed under the guidance of an SRC-designated faculty member. Renewable for up to 4 years. Deadline: February 1.

2103. (S)
SRC Master's Scholarship for Women and Minorities

Scholarships of tuition, fees, and a monthly stipend of $1,800 to female or minority graduate students pursuing a master's degree with research relevant to microelectronics. Renewable for up to 2 years. Deadline: February 3.

2104. (S)
SRC SiGe Design Challenge

Awards ranging from $3,000 to $25,000 to graduate and undergraduate students in electrical engineering. Through a contest that creates novel circuit designs that demonstrate the value of using SiGe technology for IC design. Students must enter as a team of 4, with a faculty advisor. Deadline: none specified.

2105. (A, H, S, SS)
Seminole Tribe of Florida
Higher Education Awards
6073 Stirling Road
Hollywood, FL 33024
(305) 584–0400, ext. 154
http://www.seminoletribe.com

Awards of varying amounts to graduate and undergraduate students in all fields of study at any U.S.-accredited institution. Must be an enrolled member of the Seminole Tribe of Florida or eligible to become a member. Renewable. Deadline: April 15, July 15, and November 15.

2106. (A, H, S, SS)
Seneca Nation Higher Education
Education Grants
Box 231
Salamanca, NY 14779

(716) 945–1790

http://www.sni.org/#120

Awards of up to $5,000 to graduate, doctoral, and undergraduate students in all fields of study. Must be used at accredited U.S. institutions. Must be enrolled members of the Seneca Nation of Indians. Based on financial need. Deadline: July 15, December 15, and May 20.

2107. (A, S, SS)

Sense of Smell Institute

Tova Fellowship

145 East 32nd Street

New York, NY 10016–6002

(212) 725–2755

http://www.senseofsmell.org/home.asp

Fellowships of $10,000 to graduate students in the thesis or dissertation stage of their master's or doctoral program in the fields of architecture, marketing, medicine, nutrition, psychology, or sociology. Must be looking to expand their studies to include the areas of olfaction and aromachology. Applicants should be able to take a multidisciplinary approach to deepen the understanding of human odor perception. Application should include: a 1- or 2-page proposal outlining involvement with, and interest in, the study of olfaction and aromachology (including what you hope to gain from the knowledge), a letter of recommendation from a faculty advisor and a transcript or other evidence of enrollment in an accredited course of study in a field related to the topic. Award is intended to defray education-related costs such as tuition, fees, books, and research expenses. Deadline: May 25.

2108. (S)

Service Employees International Union Fund

Peggy Browning Fund Internship

1818 Market Street, Suite 2300

Philadelphia, PA 19103

(215) 665–6815

http://www.peggybrowningfund.org/intern.html

10-week internships providing a stipend of $4,000 for law students. Interns work directly with attorneys in the legal department and professional staff at the national headquarters. Assignments focus primarily on research and writing. Deadline: January 15.

2109. (A, H, S, SS)

Sigma Nu Educational Foundation, Inc.

Emergency Aid Grants/Academic Encouragement Awards

P.O. Box 1869

9 Lewis Street

Lexington, VA 24450

(703) 463–2164

http://www.sigmanu.com/foundation

22 scholarship grants from $50 to $1,000 to graduate and undergraduate students with any major. Must be members of Sigma Nu. Emergency Aid Grants are based on financial need, and Academic Encouragement Awards are based on academic achievement. Deadline: varies by chapter.

2110. (S)

Sigma Theta Tau International

Research Grants

550 West North Street

Indianapolis, IN 46202

(317) 634–8171

http://www.nursingsociety.org

Grants of $6,000 to registered nurses who have a master's degree in nursing to conduct a well-defined research project relevant to nursing. Must have completed all course work. Preference given to Sigma Theta Tau members. Funds may be used to support dissertation research, but the dissertation is not acceptable as the final report. Deadline: March 1.

(S)

Sigma XI—The Scientific Research Society

Research Grants

P.O. Box 13975

99 Alexandria Drive

Research Triangle Park, NC 27709

(919) 549–4691

(800) 243–6534

http://www.sigmaxi.org

2111. (S)

Grants-in-Aid Research Program (GIAR)

Awards of up to $1,000 to graduate and undergraduate students in science and engineering. Award must be used to conduct research. Preference is given to scientists in the early stages of their careers. 75% of awards are for student members. Contact for more information. Deadline: March 15 and October 15.

2112. (S)
National Academy of Science Grants

Grants of up to $2,500 to graduate and undergraduate students in astronomy or eye/vision research. Award must be used to conduct research. Preference is given to scientists in the early stages of their careers. Contact for more information. Deadline: March 15 and October 15.

(A, S)
Skidmore Owings & Merrill Foundation
224 South Michigan Avenue, Suite 1000
Chicago, IL 60604
(312) 554–9090
(312) 360–4545 (Fax)
http://www.som.com/opener.cfm

2113. (A)
Architecture Traveling Fellowship Program

2 fellowships of $15,000 to graduate and undergraduate students majoring in architecture. Must be U.S. citizens. Awarded to broaden their education and provide an enlightened view of society's need to improve the built and natural environments. For information or an application, send a self-addressed, stamped envelope or visit web site. Deadline: mid-April.

2114. (A)
Interior Architecture Traveling Fellowship

1 fellowship of $7,500 to a graduate student or recent graduate in interior design or architecture. Award reflects the Foundation's interest in interior design as part of a comprehensive architectural vision. Its aim is to encourage young designers to explore the relationship between architecture and interiors—with particular emphasis on the 3-dimensional modeling of space and the integration of interior spaces and elements with building architecture and systems. The work submitted should display awareness and skillful handling of the full range of elements that support a designed interior space, including furniture and finishes, lighting and artwork. Award allows fellow to visit buildings and settings that are central to his or her area of interest and study. Must be U.S. citizen. Deadline: mid-April.

2115. (S)
Mechanical/Building Systems Traveling Fellowship

1 grant of $7,500 to a graduate mechanical engineering student. Award recognizes research on such topics as energy-efficient design, the application of new technologies, the appropriate use or reuse of natural resources and the integration of building systems as components of a work of architecture. The relevance of the research proposed by the candidate is a consideration for awarding the grant and is made solely for the support of 1 student. Typical expenditures include living expenses, travel to research project sites, experimental equipment, and supplies. The Foundation's intention is to enhance the professional life of students who, in the school's judgment, show intellectual and professional promise and are, therefore, deserving of recognition. Must be U.S. citizen. Deadline: none specified.

2116. (S)
Structural Engineering Traveling Fellowship

1 fellowship of $7,500 to a graduate student who has recently completed a program in structural engineering. By enabling the fellow to experience buildings, bridges, and other structures firsthand, the Foundation's hope is that the fellowship will help the student to gain a critical appreciation of the aesthetics of structure, thus influencing the teaching and practice of structural engineering in the future. Must be U.S. citizen. Deadline: November 15.

2117. (A)
Urban Design Traveling Fellowship

1 fellowship of $7,500 to a graduate student or recent graduate of an urban design program. Awarded to encourage young architects with an interest in urban design to broaden their knowledge of the design of modern, high-density cities. It recognizes the nominee's ability to deal with pertinent urban design issues such as appropriate development character, sense of place, preservation and adaptive reuse, wayfinding and ease of access and movement, and sustainable patterns of densification and growth. Must be U.S. citizen. Deadline: mid-April.

2118. (S)

Slocum-Lunz Foundation, Inc.

South Carolina Wildlife & Marine

P.O. Box 12559

217 Fort Johnson Road

Charleston, SC 29422–2559

written inquiries only

Scholarships of up to $2,000 to graduate, doctoral, and upper-level undergraduate students. The award supports research in the natural sciences and marine science. The academic work doesn't have to be performed in South Carolina. Deadline: April 1.

2119. (A, H, S, SS)

Slovene National Benefit Society Scholarship Awards

Scholarship Chairperson

247 West Allegheny Road

Imperial, PA 15126–9774

http://www.snpj.com

Renewable scholarships of $500 to graduate and undergraduate students for any field of study. Must have been members for at least 2 years of the Slovene Benefit Society. Award is good at any accredited 2- or 4-year college or university. Based on academic record, financial need, and recommendations. Deadline: August 1.

(A, H)

Smithsonian American Art Museum and Renwick Gallery

Office of Fellowships and Grants

750 9th Street, Suite 9300

MRC 902

P.O. Box 37012

Washington, DC 20013–7012

(202) 287–3271

http://www.si.edu/organize/office/musstud/intern.htm

2120. (A)

Douglass Foundation Fellowship in American Art

1 fellowship of $17,000, plus research and travel, to a predoctoral student and $30,000, plus research and travel allowances, to a 1-year senior or postdoctoral student. Awarded to conduct scholarship research in American art. Subjects matching the interests of the museum and its research staff are supported. Visit web site for an application. Deadline: January 15.

2121. (A)

James Renwick Fellowship in American Craft

1 fellowship of $17,000, plus research and travel, for a predoctoral student and $30,000, plus research and travel allowances, for a 1-year senior or postdoctoral student. Awarded for research in American studio crafts or decorative arts from the 19th century to the present. Visit web site for an application. Deadline: January 15.

2122. (A)

Patricia and Phillip Frost Fellowship

1 fellowship of $17,000, plus research and travel, for a predoctoral student and $30,000, plus research and travel allowances, for a 1-year senior or postdoctoral student. Awarded to support research in American art and visual culture. Areas of American art history corresponding with the museum's collection and the interests of research staff are encouraged. Visit web site for an application. Deadline: January 15.

2123. (A)

Predoctoral Fellowships

Fellowships of $17,000, plus research and travel allowance, to graduate students who have completed all their course work. Residencies range from 3 to 12 months and support independent and dissertation research. Areas of research include art history corresponding with the museum's collection, American realism, American art, studio crafts, and decorative arts from the 19th century to the present. Deadline: January 15.

2124. (A)

Sara Roby Fellowship in Twentieth-Century American Realism

1 fellowship of $17,000, plus research and travel, for a predoctoral student and $30,000, plus research and travel allowances, for a 1-year senior or postdoctoral student. Awarded to a scholar whose research topic matches the Sara Roby Foundation's interest in American realism. Visit web site for an application. Deadline: January 15.

2125. (S)
Smithsonian Astrophysical Observatory Predoctoral Fellowships
60 Garden Street, Mail Stop 47
Cambridge, MA 02138
http://www.si.edu/ofg/fell.htm
predoc@cfa.harvard.edu

Fellowships of varying amounts to graduate students from institutions throughout the world (except Harvard) to do their thesis research at SAO. Open to students in astronomy, astrophysics, and planetary sciences, including theory, observation, instrument development (especially detectors and interferometers) and laboratory experiments. Visit web site for more information. Deadline: April 15.

(H, SS)
Smithsonian Center for Latino Initiatives (SCLI)
A&I 1465
Washington, DC 20560–0448
(202) 357–1600
http://www.latino.si.edu

2126. (H, SS)
Graduate Student Fellowships in Latino Studies

Awards of varying amounts to Hispanic graduate students to conduct research in the social sciences. The goal of the program is to support the scholarly development and research interests of Latino graduate students and to expose them to the resources available at the Smithsonian and to museum work. Deadline: none specified.

2127. (H, SS)
Interpreting Latino Cultures: Research and Museums

A group of 15 Hispanic/Latino/a doctoral candidates and faculty from several U.S. institutions and the Smithsonian Institution to discuss issues of Hispanic cultural representation. A 2-week program introduces graduate students to qualitative research methods, literature, and issues, methods for researching, interpreting, and reinterpreting museum collections relating to Latino history and culture, access to community of Latino scholars, curators, and archivists, and establishing a network among students and faculty. Deadline: none specified.

(H, S, SS)
Smithsonian Center for Materials Research and Education (SCMRE)
Archeological Conservation Training Program
Museum Support Center
4210 Silver Hill Road
Suitland, MD 20746–2863
(301) 238–3700
http://www.si.edu

2128. (H)
Conservation Postgraduate Fellowships

3 fellowships of $22,000, plus $2,000 travel and research funds, plus access to SCMRE courses, to recent graduates in conservation or those with equivalent experience. Fellows combine work with a research project. Visit web site for specific application guidelines. Deadline: February 28.

2129. (H, S, SS)
Conservation Science Fellowships

Fellowships of varying amounts to graduate students. Applications will also be accepted from anyone with a degree or certificate of advanced training in the conservation of artifacts or art objects. Award is for research relevant to the care, preservation, and conservation of museum collections. Areas of interest typically include the composition of museum objects as they relate to their deterioration and the study of materials and deterioration mechanisms as they relate to methods of preservation. Open to all areas of study, but proposals from the perspectives of materials science, engineering, and chemistry will be especially considered. Deadline: rolling.

2130. (SS)
Graduate Internship

Internships for graduate students in a graduate library and information science program or the equivalent. This is an unpaid internship lasting 1 semester. Applicants must submit a cover letter, statement of expectations, and a curriculum vitae including references. Deadline: July 1.

2131. (S)
Postdoctoral Fellowship in Molecular Evolution

1 fellowship of $30,000 and health insurance to a postdoctoral fellow to conduct research at the Smithsonian's molecular research facilities. Must have completed or be near completion of doctoral degree. Fellowships last from 12 to 24 months. Fellowship involves research concerning preservation of natural history specimens and collections. A degree in organic, bio-organic, or biochemistry is preferred. Visit web site for more information. Deadline: March 1.

2132. (H)
Postgraduate Fellowship

1 fellowship providing a stipend of $22,000, plus a travel and research allowance of $2,000, to postgraduate fellows in conservation training programs or persons of comparable training and experience. Must submit a letter specifying interest and intent in applying, a curriculum vitae with references, copies of publications, transcripts, and 2 supporting letters. Deadline: March 1.

2133. (SS)
Postgraduate Fellowships in Archaeological Conservation

Fellowships to postgraduate fellows in archaeological conservation. Fellowships are to be spent at a number of archaeological fieldwork sites and at SCMRE for a period of 1 year, usually starting in the fall. Deadline: February 1.

2134. (SS)
Pregraduate Internships in Archeological Conservation

Numerous internships to graduate students in their final year of study and recent graduates. Fellowships are to be spent at a number of archaeological fieldwork sites or at SCMRE for a period of 1 year, usually starting in the fall. Deadline: February 1.

2135. (SS)
Technical Information/Special Library Internship

1 internship to a graduate student in library science. The internship provides training in a specialized library setting. Intern will be in the Technical Information Office but could undertake special projects within the SCMRE Paper Laboratory and RELACT program. Deadline: July 1.

2136. (SS)
Third-Year Internship

Internships paying $14,000, plus a $2,000 travel and research allowance, to graduate students in a conservation training program or the equivalent. The application package must include a cover letter specifying the internship applied for, a statement of expectations, and a curriculum vitae, including references. Deadline: none specified.

2137. (S)
Smithsonian Environmental Research Center
Work/Learn Program
P.O. Box 28
647 Contees Wharf Road
Edgewater, MD 21037
(443) 482–2200
http://www.serc.si.edu

A 12-week summer research program providing $90 per week to graduate students and $75 per week to undergraduates. Living accommodations are provided. Students are provided the opportunity to work on specific projects involving long-range studies of the local watershed and its estuary. Meals are not supplied. Based on academic achievements, professional promise, relevant training and experience, and letters of recommendation. Deadline: July 1 (fall), December 1 (spring), and April 1 (summer).

(H, S)
Smithsonian Institute
National Air and Space Museum (NASM)
Fellowship Coordinator
Rm. 3313
Washington, DC 20560–0312
http://www.nasm.edu/nasm/joinnasm/fellow/fellow.htm

2138. (H, S)
A. Verville Fellowship

1 fellowship of $45,000, plus limited additional funds for travel and miscellaneous expenses, for a

12-month in-residence to graduate students who want to do research on the analysis of major trends, developments, and accomplishments in the history of aviation or space studies. Open to all interested candidates with demonstrated skills in research and writing. Graduate predoctoral students will normally not be considered. Deadline: January 15.

2139. (H, S)
Guggenheim Fellowship

Fellowships of $20,000 to predoctoral and $30,000 to postdoctoral candidates, with limited additional funds for travel and miscellaneous expenses, for 3- to 12-month in-residence research fellowships in aviation and space history. Predoctoral applicants must have completed all preliminary work and examinations and be conducting dissertation research. Deadline: January 15.

2140. (H)
Ramsey Fellowship in Naval Aviation History

A fellowship providing a $45,000 stipend for a competitive 9- to 12-month, in-residence fellowship focused on the history of aviation at sea and in naval service, particularly in the U.S. Navy. The fellowship is open to all interested candidates with demonstrated skills in research and writing. Visit web site for more information. Deadline: January 15.

2141. (H)
Smithsonian Institute
National Museum of American History
Lemelson Center Fellowships
Lemelson Center
Room 1016
Washington, DC 20560–0604
(202) 357–2096
http://www.si.edu/lemelson/lemelson/
seniorfellowships.html

Awards of varying amounts to pre- and postdoctoral students to support projects that present creative approaches to the study of invention and innovation in American society. Fellowships are for a maximum of 10 weeks and carry a prorated stipend. Deadline: January 15.

(H, S, SS)
Smithsonian Institute
National Museum of Natural History (NMNH)
Department of Anthropology
Washington, DC 20560–0112
(202) 357–4760
http://www.si.edu/ofg/fell.htm

2142. (H, SS)
American Indian Research Program

Awards providing a stipend to Native American graduate students of Native American history and culture. Aware is to encourage participation of Native Americans in Smithsonian activities and to support collection research, exhibitions, and public programming as they relate to Native peoples. Deadline: none.

2143. (H, S)
Conservation Department Program

4 awards providing a stipend to Native American graduate and postgraduate students in conservation training programs or those entering the internship year of the training program. Graduate areas of study may be in organic and inorganic materials, archaeology, and ethnographic collections. Visit web site for contact information. Deadline: none specified.

2144. (S)
National Capitol Shell Club
Alaskan Scholarship Award

Awards ranging from $500 to $1,000 for graduate students at an institution in the Eastern Seaboard states. Based on financial need, education, plans for the future, interests, samples of work, and proposed program. Open to marine biology, specifically malacology (study of mollusks). If no applicant in the field of malacology is chosen, related fields in marine biology will be considered. Obtain application from the Institute in early February. Deadline: April 15.

2145. (H)
Smithsonian Institute
National Museum of the American Indian (NMAI)
NMAI Cultural Resources Center
4220 Silver Hill Road
Suitland, MD 20746
(301) 238–6624, ext. 6322
http://www.si.edu/ofg/fell.htm

Fellowships of varying amounts to graduate and post-graduate students in conservation. Fellowships provide experience relevant to the care, preservation, and conservation of the Museum's collection. Open to areas of study that include organic and inorganic materials, archaeology, and ethnographic collections. Fellowship lasts for 1 year. Deadline: none specified.

(A, H, S, SS)
Smithsonian Institute
Office of Fellowships and Grants
750 9th Street, N.W., Suite 9300
Washington, DC 20560–0902
(202) 275–0655
http://www.si.edu

2146. (A, H, S, SS)
Graduate Student 10-Week Fellowships

Fellowships provide stipends of $300 per week for 10 weeks to graduate students who have completed at least 1 full-time semester or its equivalent before the appointment period and have not yet been advanced to candidacy if enrolled in a doctoral program. Available for study in art and in some humanities, sciences, and social sciences. Students are expected to be able to write and converse fluently in English. Award is given to allow students to study and conduct independent research under the guidance of Smithsonian staff members for 10 weeks. Travel and research allowances are not offered. Deadline: mid-January.

2147. (A, H, S, SS)
Internships

700 internships providing no compensation, though a few positions may offer stipends, to graduate students, recent college graduates, undergraduate students, and graduating high school seniors. Some positions have specific requirements. Request "Internships and Fellowships," a free brochure listing museum addresses and position descriptions, or send a $5 check and request "Internship Opportunities at the Smithsonian Institution." Internships last from 2 months to 1 year, and students work at least 20 hours per week during the summer, fall, or spring. Deadline: February 15 (summer), June 15 (fall), and October 15 (spring).

2148. (SS)
James E. Webb Internship Program

Fellowships providing stipends of $400 per week to graduate students and undergraduate seniors in business and/or public administration. Must have at least a 3.0 GPA and demonstrate relevance of the internship to the student's academic and career goals. Deadline: February 1.

2149. (A, H)
Minority Graduate Fellowships

Fellowships providing $250 per week plus travel to minority graduates to fund research and study at the Smithsonian or the Cooper-Hewitt Museum of Design in New York City. Students must be studying architecture, art, design, or museum studies. Deadline: March 1, July 1, and October 15.

2150. (A, H, S, SS)
Minority Student Internship Program

10-week internships providing $350 per week to graduate or undergraduate students in disciplines of research conducted at the Institution. Selection is based on academic achievement, essay, references, and relevance of research. Deadline: February 1 (summer), June 15 (fall), and October 15 (spring).

2151. (S)
Molecular Evolution Fellowship

Fellowships of varying amounts to doctoral students who complete their degree before the fellowship begins. Fellowship is conducted at the NMNH or STRI. Visit web site for specific guidelines. Deadline: March 1.

2152. (A. SS)
National Museum of African Art Internships

Internships for the academic year and for the summer to graduate and upper-level undergraduate students majoring in African studies, Afro-American studies, art history, or museum studies. Interns work for 10 weeks in one of several museums. Internships don't always include financial aid. Request financial aid information at initial inquiry. Deadline: December 15 and April 1.

2153. (A, H, S, SS)
Native American Internship Awards

Internships providing stipends of $350 per week for 10 weeks, plus a travel allowance, to graduate and undergraduate students. Interns pursue directed research projects supervised by Smithsonian staff members. Must submit an application, essay, transcript, and recommendation letters. Deadline: February 1 (summer), June 1 (fall), and October 1 (winter/spring).

2154. (A, H, S, SS)
Native American Visiting Student Awards

Awards providing a stipend of $100 per day for up to 21 days and $350 per week for 3 to 10 weeks, plus a travel and research allowance, to advanced graduate students. Students pursue independently designed research projects. Must submit an application, proposed research project statement, resume, transcripts, and recommendation letters. Deadline: February 1 (summer), June 1 (fall), and October 1 (winter/spring).

2155. (A, H, S)
Postdoctoral Fellowships

Fellowships providing stipends of $25,000 for 12 months, prorated for shorter periods; a travel/relocation and research allowance is also available. Open to postdoctoral scholars up to 7 years beyond the degree in the areas of art history, some humanities, or select sciences. Awards are given to provide postdoctoral scholars an opportunity to conduct research at the Smithsonian Institution for a period of 3 to 12 months. Deadline: January 16.

2156. (A, H, S, SS)
Predoctoral Fellowships

Fellowships of $14,000 per year (prorated for shorter periods) plus relocation and research allowances to Ph.D. students. Candidates must have completed all course work and predissertation requirements at the time of appointment. Open to the areas of art history, select humanities, certain sciences, and social sciences. Awards are given to provide students an opportunity to conduct dissertation research at the Smithsonian Institution for a period of 3 to 12 months. Deadline: mid-January (postmark).

2157. (H, S, SS)
Senior Postdoctoral Fellowships

Fellowships of up to $25,000 per year, plus allowances, to postdoctoral scholars who received their degree over 7 years prior to application in the areas of art history, some humanities, certain sciences, and select social sciences. Awards are given to provide postdoctoral scholars an opportunity to conduct research at the Smithsonian Institution for a period of 3 to 12 months. Senior postdoctoral scholars must apply 2 years in advance. Deadline: mid-January.

(A, H, S, SS)
Smithsonian Institution
Cooper-Hewitt Museum
2 East 90th Street
New York, NY 10128
(212) 860–6868
http://www.si.edu/organize/office/musstud/intern.htm

2158. (A, H)
Academic Year Internships

Full academic year internships at the Cooper-Hewitt Museum to graduate and undergraduate students who are enrolled in an accredited institution and majoring in art, design, museum studies, or architecture. 1-month minimum term. Deadline: none.

2159. (A, H, SS)
Kell Muñoz Fellowship

1 fellowship providing a stipend of $25,000 to Hispanic/Latino graduate students to work in the museum's education department. Candidates with experience or training in arts administration, art history, education, communications, design, or architecture are eligible. Computer skills are essential. Fellows work 25 hours a week. Housing and transportation are not provided. Deadline: March 1.

2160. (A, H)
Peter Krueger Summer Internship Program

10-week summer internships at the Cooper-Hewitt Museum open to graduate or undergraduate students who are enrolled in an accredited institution and majoring in art history, design, or architectural history. Internship commences in June and ends in August. Housing is not provided. Deadline: March 31.

2161. (A, H)
Summer Internships

Fellowships of varying amounts to cover 10-week summer internships at the Cooper-Hewitt Museum. Undergraduate students who have completed at least 2 years of study in art, design, architecture, or museum studies at an accredited institution are eligible for the fellowships. Deadline: March 31.

2162. (S)
Transportation Research Board Graduate Research Award Program VIII
Attn: Transportation Research Board

Research awards providing a stipend of $6,000 to graduate students to conduct research. Award is paid in progress payments of 25% installments during the research, with final payment on completion and acceptance of the paper.

(A, H, S)
Smithsonian Institution
Horticulture Services Division
P.O. Box 37012
A&I Building, Room 2282, MRC 420
Washington, DC 20013–7012
(202) 357–1926
http://www.gardens.si.edu/horticulture/res_ed/
res_ed.htm

2163. (A, S)
Enid A. Haupt Fellowship in Horticulture

1 award of varying amount to a graduate student in horticulture, botany, landscape architecture, or a related field. Fellowship is full-time, in-residence for 12 to 24 months. Recipient is eligible for a stipend and research allowance. Deadline: March 1.

2164. (A, H, S)
Internships

Internships with limited stipends of $360 or $420 to graduate and undergraduate students in horticulture. Internships are usually 16 weeks in length. Internship provides a practical learning experience in the activities and practices of a major horticulture program and offers exposure to the day-to-day activ-

ities of an office within the largest museum complex in the world. Deadline: February 1.

(S, SS)
Smithsonian Tropical Research Institute
Office of Education
P.O. Box 2072
Balboa, Republic of Panama
(507) 212–8026
http://www.stri.org
fellows@tivoli.se.edu

2165. (S)
A. W. Mellon Research Exploration Awards in Tropical Biology

Awards of $3,000 for graduate students and $6,000 for senior investigators (postdoctoral). Must conduct a research project on a comparative issue between The Organization for Tropical Studies and STRI sites. Funding may include travel to and from either/both sites, station fees at either/both sites, and minor equipment needs to carry out the project. Visit web site for more information. Deadline: rolling.

2166. (S)
Predoctoral Fellowships

Fellowships of varying amounts to doctoral students who have completed all course work and examinations and are engaged in dissertation research. Award is to assist applicants to conduct a research project of 3 to 12 months under the guidance of a Smithsonian staff member. Deadline: January 15.

2167. (S)
Short-Term Fellowships

Fellowships of varying amounts providing a stipend, modest research allowance, and airfare to graduate students and occasionally to undergraduates and postdoctoral candidates. Proposed projects may be exploratory or complete in themselves, with the usual duration being 3 months. Deadline: February 15, May 15, August 15, and November 15.

2168. (S, SS)
Three-Year Postdoctoral Fellowships in Tropical Biology

Awards of varying amounts to postdoctoral fellows in anthropology, behavior and physiology of tropical plants or animals, ecology, evolution, or paleontology. Research should be based at one of the STRI facilities, but proposals that include comparative research on other tropical countries will be considered. Deadline: January 15.

(A, H, SS)
Social Science Research Council
810 Seventh Avenue
New York, NY 10019
(212) 377–2700
http://www.ssrc.org

2169. (H, SS)
Berlin Program for Advanced German and European Studies Fellowships

Awards of $30,000 for living and research expenses to doctoral candidates and postdoctoral recipients (within last 2 years) to stay in Berlin for a period ranging from 10 to 12 months. Additional travel funds may also be awarded. Must be U.S. or Canadian citizens or permanent residents. Doctoral students must have completed all course work except for the dissertation. Visit web site for more information. Deadline: December 1.

2170. (H, SS)
Central Asia, Louis Dupree Prize for Research

1 prize of $2,000 for the most promising dissertation involving field research in Central Asia, a region broadly defined to include Afghanistan, Azerbaijan, Kyrgyzstan, Mongolia, Turkmenistan, Tajikistan, Uzbekistan and culturally related contiguous areas of Iran, Pakistan, Kazakhstan, and China. Candidates who receive a dissertation research fellowship from an SSRC/ACLS program are eligible to apply. Visit web site for more information and deadline.

2171. (SS)
Corporation as a Social Institution Fellowships

Fellowships to graduate students working on projects that focus on corporations or firms. Provides some funding for dissertation research but primarily convenes a series of workshops and conferences bringing students and scholars working in the areas of sociology, economics, law, and business. Program supports innovative research on the social, cultural, and economic aspects of the corporation. Visit web site for a list of suggested projects. Deadline: January 1.

2172. (H, SS)
Eurasia Fellowships

Fellowships of varying amounts to doctoral students and postdoctoral fellows to conduct research on the Russian Empire, the Soviet Union, and the New Independent States. Research related to the non-Russian states, regions, and people is particularly encouraged. Fellowships awarded under this program are contingent upon the receipt of funding from the U.S. Department of State. Must be U.S. citizens or permanent residents. Visit web site for more detailed information. Deadline: November 1.

2173. (SS)
Fellowships in Applied Economics

Fellowships of varying amounts to graduate students in economics. As this is a fairly new program, interested individuals need to visit the web site for more information, and subscription to the SSRC mailing list is encouraged. All questions about the program must be sent to pae@ssrc.org.

2174. (H, SS)
International Dissertation Field Research Fellowship Program

Awards of up to $17,000 to full-time graduate students in the humanities and social sciences, regardless of citizenship. Must be enrolled in a doctoral program in an accredited U.S. institution and have completed all doctoral requirements except the fieldwork component. Award supports 9 to 12 months in the field. Proposals may be for field research on all areas or regions of the world, as well as for research that is comparative, cross-regional, cross-cultural, and for all periods in history, but must address topics that have relevance to contemporary issues and debates. Visit web site for more information and guidelines. Deadline: mid-November.

2175. (SS)
International Migration Summer Institute and Fellowships

Awards of varying amounts to advanced doctoral candidates involved in research or writing for their dissertations and recent doctoral recipients revising their dissertations for publications or initiating new research. Award covers plane fares, meals, and lodging necessary for participation in the Institute. Selectees are comprised of roughly equal numbers of advanced graduate students, recent doctoral recipients, and senior scholars. Visit web site for more information. Deadline: none specified.

2176. (SS)
Japan Programs Fellowships

Fellowships of varying amounts to fund 3 separate research programs. The JSPS Postdoctoral Fellowship is for postdoctoral fellows and recent doctoral recipients to conduct short- and long-term research in Japan. The SSRC Japan Studies Dissertation Workshop is open to graduate students and faculty to give and receive critical feedback on dissertation progress. The Abe Fellowship is open to scholars and nonacademic research professionals in the social sciences and the humanities to support research projects addressing one or more of 3 themes. Visit web site for more information. Deadline: December 1.

2177. (SS)
Minority Summer Dissertation Research

Awards of varying amounts to minority graduate students to participate in a 3-week training workshop in preparing dissertation and funding proposals to carry out research on immigration. Students meet with senior scholars in the field to consider theoretical perspectives and methodological approaches to their research projects and develop and critique one another's proposals. Visit web site for more information. Deadline: none specified.

2178. (SS)
Philanthropy and the Nonprofit Sector Annual Dissertation Fellowship

Up to 7 fellowships of $18,000 to full-time graduate students in the social sciences and humanities, regardless of citizenship. Must be enrolled in an accredited U.S. institution and conducting research on this country; proposals that identify countries outside the U.S. as cases for comparative inquiry are welcome. Visit web site for more information. Deadline: early December.

2179. (SS)
Research Fellowships on African Youth in a Global Age

12 fellowships of up to $10,000 to graduate students to support field research and participation in fieldwork workshops. Must hold at least a master's degree. Also open to doctoral students and individuals who are no more than 5 years beyond their doctoral degrees. The principal purpose of this program is to support researchers and practitioners in an African institution. A few fellowships are also available to doctoral candidates based in other regions who seek field research funding for their dissertations. Visit web site for more information. Deadline: May 2.

2180. (SS)
Sexuality Research Fellowships

Approximately 10 fellowships of up to $28,000 to graduate students in a social, health, or behavioral science department in an accredited U.S. institution. Award supports 12 continuous months of research and covers direct research costs, matriculation fees, and living expenses. Must have completed all requirements for the doctoral degree except for the dissertation. Visit web site for more information. Deadline: mid-December.

(S)

Society for Exploration Geophysicists
SEG Education Foundation
8801 S. Yale Avenue
Tulsa, OK 74137
(918) 497–5500
http://www.seg.org/business/foundation

2181. (S)
General Scholarships

Varying number of scholarships of varying amounts to graduate and undergraduate students, as well as some for graduating high school seniors pursuing a career in exploration geophysics. Selection is based on academic achievement, career goals, and financial need. Visit web site for more information and an application. Deadline: March 1.

2182. (S)
G. W. Hohmann Scholarships

Scholarships of varying amounts to graduate and undergraduate students in geophysics, with an emphasis on mining or electrical methods. Selection is based on academic achievement, career goals, and financial need. Visit web site for more information and an application. Deadline: March 1.

2183. (S)
Lucien LaCoste Scholarships

Scholarships of $10,000 to graduate students in geophysics with a special emphasis on gravity exploration. Selection is based on academic achievement, career goals, and financial need. Visit web site for more information and an application. Deadline: March 1.

2184. (S)
Margaret S. Sheriff Award

Scholarships of $6,000 to graduate students in geophysics. Must be non-U.S. residents. Selection is based on academic achievement, career goals, and financial need. Visit web site for more information and an application. Deadline: March 1.

2185. (S)
Robert E. Sheriff Award

Scholarships of $12,000 to graduate students in geophysics. Must be non-U.S. residents. Selection is based on academic achievement, career goals, and financial need. Visit web site for more information and an application. Deadline: March 1.

2186. (S)
Society for Imaging Science and Technology
Raymond Davis Scholarship
7003 Kilworth Lane
Springfield, VA 22151
(703) 642–9090
http://www.imaging.org

1 or more scholarships of $1,000 or more to full-time graduate students and upper-level undergraduate students majoring in photographic science or engineering. Award is meant to assist in continuing studies in the theory or practice of photographic science, including any type of image formation initiated by radiant energy. Deadline: December 15.

(S)
Society for Neuroscience
Education Department
11 Dupont Circle, N.W., Suite 500
Washington, DC 20036
(202) 462–6688
http://web.sfn.org

2187. (S)
Donald B. Lindsley Prize in Behavioral Neuroscience

An award of $1,000 to the most outstanding doctoral thesis in the general area of biological neuroscience submitted and approved during the previous calendar year. Visit web site for submission guidelines. Deadline: March 25.

2188. (S)
IBRO/MBL Summer Course Fellowships

Fellowships to highly qualified and motivated researchers from developing countries to take summer neuroscience courses at the Marine Biological Laboratory at Woods Hole, MA. Visit web site for specific guidelines. Deadline: February 1.

2189. (S)
Minority Conference Fellowship Program

Fellowships providing travel assistance to SfN's Annual Meeting, supplemental funds to participate in enrichment activities outside fellow's home, and a complimentary SfN membership to minority predoctoral and postdoctoral students in neuroscience. Selection based on academic achievement, professional goals, research interests, and experience. Must be U.S. citizens or permanent residents. Deadline: January 2.

2190. (S)
Minority Neuroscience Fellowship Program

Fellowships providing training stipends, travel assistance and registration for the SfN Annual Meeting, enrichment program, mentoring, and complimentary SfN membership to minority predoctoral and postdoctoral graduate students. Visit web site for information. Deadline: September 3.

2191. (S)

SfN-IBRO International Travel Fellowships

A limited number of fellowships of up to $1,500 to defray travel costs to attend the Annual Meeting, plus complimentary meeting registration, to promising young scientists from less developed and less-well-funded countries to attend the Annual Meeting. Visit web site for submission guidelines. Deadline: April 1.

2192. (S)

Society for Neuroscience Chapters/Eli Lilly Graduate Student Travel Awards

Awards of $500 to cover travel expenses and meeting registration fees to outstanding graduate students. Visit web site for submission guidelines. Deadline: March 25.

2193. (S)

Society for Neuroscience Chapters Postdoctoral Trainee Travel Awards

Awards of $1,250 for travel expenses and meeting registration fees to postdoctoral fellows. Visit web site for submission guidelines. Deadline: June 2.

2194. (S)

Society for Neuroscience Travel Awards for the 6th International Brain Research Organization (IBRO) World Conference

Awards of up to $1,500 to graduate students from the U.S., Canada, and Mexico to attend the IBRO World Conference. Visit web site for submission guidelines. Deadline: February 28.

2195. (S)

Society for Organic Petrology
TSOP Student Grants
Peter D. Warwick
U.S. Geological Survey
956 National Center
12201 Sunrise Valley Drive
Reston, VA 20192
http://www.tsop.org/grants.htm

2 grants of $1,000 to graduate students for thesis research in organic petrology. Research must demonstrate the utility and significance of organic petrology in solving the thesis problem. Open to full-time students working on a master's, but doctoral candidates and part-time graduate students may apply. Visit web site for more information. Deadline: May 1.

(SS)

Society for Research in Child Development
University of Michigan
3131 South State Street, Suite 302
Ann Arbor, MI 48108–1623
(734) 998–6578
http://www.srcd.org

2196. (SS)

Congressional Science Fellowships in Child Development

1 to 5 fellowships of at least $25,000 to postdoctoral scientists and professionals to work in the area of child development for 1 year in Washington, DC, with staffs of senators, representatives, and congressional committees. The purpose of the program is to establish an effective liaison between science and Congress. Fellows are placed in relevant federal agencies, such as NIH, ACF, and the Department of Education. This fellowship is designed to provide greater interaction between the developmental research community and Congress. Fellows spend a year working as a legislative assistant on the staff of a congressional committee, for a member of Congress, or in a congressional support agency that works directly for members of committees of Congress. Visit web site for specific information and an application. Deadline: mid-December.

2197. (SS)

Executive Branch Fellowships

Fellowships ranging from $45,000 to $65,000 (depending on experience) to doctoral fellows (Ph.D., M.D., Ed.D., and D.S.W.) to use their research skills in child development outside of the academic setting to inform and influence public policy. Fellowships are for 1 year in a relevant federal agency that sponsors developmental research, providing advice and guidance to programs and working in partnership with research teams within the federal government. Deadline: mid-December.

2198. (SS)

Millennium Fellows

20 or more awards to minority upper-level undergraduate students to encourage them to pursue graduate

school in the areas of child development and other related disciplines. Students attend SRCD Biennial Meeting, preconference activities, and field trips. Each new fellow is assigned a Junior Mentor, doctoral students who serve as role models and provide information and guidance about graduate school experience. Visit web site for information. Deadline: January 15.

2199. (S)
Society for Technical Communication Graduate Scholarships
901 North Stuart Street, Suite 904
Arlington, VA 22203–1822
(703) 522–4114
http://www.stc.org

2 scholarships of $1,000 to full-time graduate students and 2 scholarships to undergraduate students planning to enroll in an accredited master's or doctoral degree program who are pursuing a career in any area of technical communication (broadcast engineering and related areas). Awards are good at any accredited college or university in the U.S. or Canada. Deadline: February 15.

2200. (A, H)
Society for the Protection of Ancient Buildings Memorial Trusts Scholarships
37 Spital Square
London E1 6DY
UK
http://www.spab.org.uk

2 to 3 scholarships of 3,200 British pounds to graduate and undergraduate students to travel for 9 months to research conservation architecture to be used in the United Kingdom. Emphasis on practical training, traditional building, modern and traditional repairs. Open to students of all nationalities attending accredited institutions. Deadline: December 31.

2201. (S)
Society for the Scientific Study of Sexuality
P.O. Box 416
Allentown, PA 18105
http://www.ssc.wisc.edu/ssss/awards_grants.htm

Scholarship grants of $1,000 to graduate and doctoral students, dissertation students, medical students, and

M.D./Ph.D. students to conduct research in anatomy, behavior, biochemistry, biology, chemistry, clinical research, developmental biology, evolutionary biology, genetics, or pharmacology. Deadline: September 1.

(SS)
Society of Actuaries
475 N. Martingale Road, Suite 800
Schaumburg, IL 60173–2226
(847) 706–3500
http://www.beanactuary.com

2202. (SS)
Actuarial Scholarships for Minority Students

Scholarships of varying amounts to minority graduate and undergraduate students who are interested in pursuing actuarial careers. Selection is based on academic achievement, extracurricular activities, goals, and financial need. Must be admitted or enrolled in an accredited U.S. institution that offers either a program in actuarial sciences or courses that will serve to prepare the student for an actuarial career. Must demonstrate mathematical ability and an understanding of and an interest in an actuarial career. Students receive an additional $500 for each actuarial exam passed. Visit web site for more information and an application. Deadline: May 1.

2203. (SS)
Casualty Actuaries of the Southeast (CASE) Scholarship

1 or more scholarships of at least $1,000 to graduate or undergraduate students in southeastern states. Award is to encourage pursuit of the CAS designations. Must demonstrate high scholastic achievement and a strong interest in mathematics or a mathematics-related field. Must be admitted or enrolled in an accredited U.S. institution that offers either a program in actuarial sciences or courses that will serve to prepare the student for an actuarial career. Open to U.S. citizens or permanent residents. Preference given to applicants who have passed an actuarial exam and who have not yet won either this scholarship or another Society of Actuary or Casualty Actuary Society scholarship. Visit web site for more information and an application. Deadline: May 25.

(A, H)
Society of Architectural Historians (SAH)
ATTN: Executive Director
1365 North Astor Street
Chicago, IL 60610
(312) 573–1365
http://www.sah.org

2204. (A, H)
Annual Domestic Tours & Annual Meeting Awards

2 awards of varying amounts to graduate and undergraduate students to participate in an architectural study tour conducted by regional experts or attend annual SAH meeting. Must be student members of SAH. Deadline: none specified.

2205. (A, H)
Edilia and François-Auguste de Montêquin Fellowship

1 fellowship of $2,000 open to graduate students and junior scholars and $6,000 to senior scholars. The research to be supported must focus on Spanish, Portuguese, or Ibero-American architecture, including colonial architecture produced by the Spaniards in the Philippines and the United States. Deadline: November 15.

2206. (A, H)
Rosann S. Berry Annual Meeting Fellowship

1 fellowship of a $500 stipend and meeting registration fee to an advanced graduate student. Award offsets cost of travel, lodging, and meals directly related to the meeting. Applicants must have been a member of the Society of Architectural Historians for at least 1 year before applying for this award and must currently be engaged in advanced graduate study (normally beyond the master's level) that involves some aspect of the history of architecture or of one of the fields closely allied to it (e.g., city planning, landscape architecture, decorative arts, or historic preservation). Graduate students presenting papers at the meeting are strongly encouraged to apply. Deadline: November 15.

2207. (A, H)
Sally Kress Tompkins Fellowship

1 fellowship of $9,200 to a graduate student in architectural history or other related fields. Permits an architectural historian to work on a 12-week HABS project during the summer. Fellow will either conduct research on a nationally significant building or site and prepare a written history to become part of the permanent HABS collection or conduct research on a particular topic relating to architectural history in support of future HABS projects. The fellow will be stationed in the field, working in conjunction with a HABS measured drawings team, or in the HABS Washington, DC, office. Contact: Coordinator, Sally Kress Tompkins Fellowship, HABS/HAER/HALS Division National Park Service, 1849 C Street, N.W., 2270, Washington, DC 20240, (202) 354–2185, (202) 371–6473 (Fax). Deadline: February 7.

2208. (S)
Society of Biological Psychiatry Fellowship and Research Awards
Elliott Richelson, M.D.
Mayo Clinic Jacksonville
Research—Birdsall 310
4500 San Pablo Road
Jacksonville, FL 32224
(904) 953–2842
http://www.sobp.org/contacts.asp

Awards of up to $1,500 to medical school graduates in their third, fourth, or fifth year of residency or fellowship training and young investigators under age 35 to conduct basic science and clinical science research in biological psychiatry, and awards of up to $2,500 to senior investigators over age 35. Must be actively involved in the area of research described in submission. Studies and data cannot have been published. Selection based on past academic excellence and potential for professional growth in biological psychiatry or clinical neuroscience. Must receive nomination by department of psychiatry. Deadline: December–January.

2209. (A, H, S, SS)
Society of Daughters of the United States Army Scholarships
P.O. Box 78
West Point, NY 10096
(800) 890–8253
(914) 446–0566
http://www.pojonews.com/enjoy/locnums

8 scholarships of $750 to daughters, stepdaughters, adopted daughters, or granddaughters of career U.S. Army commissioned or warrant officers on active duty, retired, or deceased. May be used for graduate or undergraduate study in any field of study. Good at any accredited 2- or 4-year college, university, professional school or vocational/technical school. Renewable. Based on academic record and financial need. Deadline: March 31.

(S)
Society of Economic Geologists
7811 Shaffer Parkway
Littleton, CO 80127
(720) 981–7882
http://www.segweb.org
seg@segweb.org

2210. (S)
BHP Exploration Funds

Grants ranging from $500 to $3,000 to graduate students for economic geology research that focuses on new descriptions of are deposits and mining districts outside of North America, as well as research on topical subjects. Must describe what the project is, why the research is important, how it will be done, and a budget summary. Visit web site for more information. Deadline: February 1.

2211. (S)
Hickok-Radford Award

Grants ranging from $500 to $3,000 to graduate students for field projects in challenging arctic or subarctic regions. Must describe what the project is, why the research is important, how it will be done, and a budget summary. Visit web site for more information. Deadline: February 1.

2212. (S)
Hugh McKinsty Fund

Grants ranging from $500 to $3,000 to graduate students for research with a substantial field component. Must describe what the project is, why the research is important, how it will be done, and a budget summary. Visit web site for more information. Deadline: February 1.

2213. (S)
Thesis Research Grants

Grants ranging from $500 to $3,000 to graduate students for research with a substantial field component. Must describe what the project is, why the research is important, how it will be done, and a budget summary. Visit web site for more information. Deadline: February 1.

2214. (A)
Society of Environmental Graphic Design
Student Scholarship Award
1000 Vermont Avenue, Suite 400
Washington, DC 20005
(202) 638–5555
http://www.segd.org
segd@segd.org

Scholarships ranging from $1,000 to $3,000 to graduate and undergraduate students who are majoring in graphic design (preference is given to this major), environmental design, landscape architecture, architecture, interior design, or industrial design. Award is good at any accredited institution. The award is given to encourage students in these areas to pursue a career in environmental graphic design. Deadline: mid-March.

2215. (S)
Society of Hispanic Professional Engineers
Foundation
Educational Grants
5400 East Olympic Boulevard, Suite 210
Los Angeles, CA 90022
(323) 725–3970
http://www.shpefoundation.org

90 awards ranging from $500 to $3,000 to Hispanic full-time graduate and undergraduate students majoring in engineering and science. Students must have completed algebra, geometry, trigonometry, chemistry, and physics. Recipient must submit application for renewal. Selection based on academic achievement, career goals, and financial need. Deadline: April 15.

2216. (A)
Society of Illustrators Scholarships
Annual Student Scholarship Show
Director
128 East 63rd Street
New York, NY 10021–7303
(212) 838–2560
written inquiries only
http://www.societyillustrators.org

30 cash awards ranging from $500 to $2,500 to graduate and undergraduate students attending an art school, college, or university and pursuing a career in illustration. Based on artistic ability. The Society relies on college instructors to make the preliminary evaluations and then submit nominations. This is not a scholarship. Deadline: February 1.

2217. (S)
Society of Manufacturing Engineering Education Foundation Scholarships
One SME Drive
P.O. Box 930
Dearborn, MI 48121
(313) 271–1500
http://www.sme.org

Varying number of awards scholarships ranging from $2,000 to $5,000 to master's or doctoral students in engineering, business, work measurement, and productivity improvement. Selection based on either the quality of a submitted paper or academic achievement, leadership abilities, and character. Must be attending an SME-approved institution and be student members of SME. Deadline: February 1.

2218. (S)
Society of Mining, Metallurgy, and Exploration Industrial Minerals Division Scholarship
8307 Shaffer Parkway
Littleton, CO 80162
(303) 973–9550
http://www.smenet.org/contact.cfm
sme@smenet.org

Scholarships of up to $2,000 to graduate students or upper-level undergraduate students majoring in mining engineering, geology, or minerals economics who want an emphasis on industrial minerals. Awards are good at any U.S. ABET-accredited institution offering a bachelor's, master's, or doctorate degree program. Must be student members of SME. Deadline: November 30.

(A, S)
Society of Motion Picture and Television Engineers
595 West Hartsdale Avenue
White Plains, NY 10607
(914) 761–1100
http://www.smpte.org/students/scholarship.crm

2219. (A, H)
Lou Wolff Scholarship

Scholarships of varying amounts to graduate and undergraduate students and graduating high school seniors who are pursuing studies in motion pictures and television, with emphasis on technology. Selection is based on academic achievement, goals, recommendation letters, and financial need. For more information and deadline date, visit web site.

2220. (A, S)
Student Paper Award

1 award of varying amount to a graduate or undergraduate student member who submits a paper dealing with some technical phase of motion pictures, photographic instrumentation, or closely allied arts and sciences. Selection based on technical merit, originality, and presentation. For specific guidelines and deadline date, visit web site.

2221. (S)
Society of Naval Architects and Marine Engineers Graduate Scholarships
Executive Director
601 Pavonia Avenue, Suite 400
Jersey City, NJ 07306
(201) 798–4800
(800) 798–2188
http://www.sname.org

5 to 8 scholarships of up to $12,000 to graduate students pursuing careers in naval architecture, marine engineering, and ocean engineering, but students aren't limited to these areas. Applicants must be U.S. or Canadian citizens. Awards are good at the University of California (Berkeley), Florida Atlantic Univ.

(Boca Raton), Massachusetts Institute of Technology (Cambridge), University of Michigan (Ann Arbor), University of Newfoundland (St. John's), and the State University of New York Maritime College (Fort Schuyler). Students must contact the college they are interested in and not the society. Based on academic achievement, professional promise, and leadership. Deadline: February 1.

(S)
Society of Nuclear Medicine
Education and Research Foundation
1060 Arbor Lane
Northfield, IL 60093
http://www.snmerf.org/student/student_req.htm

2222. (S)
Cassen Postdoctoral Fellowship Award

Awards of $25,000 to postdoctoral fellows to provide an opportunity for recent doctoral degree recipients who have demonstrated exceptional ability, to broaden their experience by participating in research activities at an institution other than their degree-granting institution. Renewable for a second year. Visit web site for specific submission guidelines. Deadline: November 1.

2223. (S)
Pilot Research Grants

Grants of up to $8,000 to young investigators to support deserving projects that are pilot in nature. This program allows investigators to apply for limited research funding for initial clinical and basic research while other major grant support is being sought. Awards may not be used for salaries, equipment purchase, institutional overhead, or travel but are designed to provide essential materials so that innovative ideas can be quickly tested. Visit web site for submission guidelines. Deadline: November 15.

2224. (S)
Student Fellowships

10 to 15 fellowships of up to $3,000 to graduate, medical, and pharmacy school students, as well as undergraduate pre-med students. Award allows students the opportunity to spend funded elective time with leaders in the field. For specific guidelines and application, visit web site. Deadline: November 15.

(S)
Society of Sedimentary Geology
6128 E. 38th Street, Suite 308
Tulsa, OK 74135–5814
(800) 865–9765
(918) 610–3361
http://www.sepm.org
foundation@sepm.org

2225. (S)
Gerald M. Friedman Student Fund

1 award of at least $500 to a graduate student in any area of sedimentary geology. Award funds research projects and travel to professional meetings, or field trips. Must submit a statement summarizing project objectives, budget, letters of support from advisor that also confirm that the student is in good academic standing. Students must acknowledge support in master's thesis, doctoral dissertation, and other publications. Deadline: December 31.

2226. (S)
Gulf Coast Section of SEPM Foundation
Ed Picon Fellowship

4 scholarships of $2,500 to graduate students majoring in an earth science. Thesis or dissertation must be related to stratigraphy or a related field. Preference is given to research pertaining to the Gulf Coast Basin. Must submit a statement about the research topic, and advisor must write a letter of support. Deadline: July 31.

2227. (S)
John Sanders Endowment Fund

1 award of at least $500 to graduate students to support research in the areas of coastal or environmental geology. Must submit a statement summarizing project objectives, budget, letters of support from advisor that confirm that the student is in good academic standing. Students must acknowledge support in master's thesis, doctoral dissertation, and other publications. Deadline: December 31.

2228. (S)
Ken Hsu Endowment

Provides travel support to students participating in SEPM activities. Visit web site for more information. Deadline: none specified.

2229. (S)

Mobile Student Participation Grant

1 to 2 grants providing all travel costs and meeting expenses, plus a 1-year SEPM membership, to graduate students to travel to the SEPM Annual meeting to present a paper. Each SEPM section selects 1 to 2 recipients for travel expenses. Deadline: none specified.

2230. (S)

North American Micropaleontology Section (NAMS) Fund

Provides support of varying amounts to graduate students conducting research in micropaleontology. Only awarded when endowment fund is over the minimum.

2231. (S)

Pacific Section SEPM

Martin Van Couvering Scholarship Fund

7 or 8 awards ranging from $100 to $125, free registration voucher good at any conference exhibitor's book, conference luncheon, and participation in field trips. Students do not apply directly but must be selected by members of the Executive Committee. Visit web site for more information and deadline.

2232. (S)

Pacific Section SEPM

Texaco/PS-AAPG Scholarship

Scholarships of $1,000 to graduate and undergraduate students in geology or geophysics. Must attend an accredited school associated with sister society PS-AAPG. Obtain an application from schools in September. Visit web site for information, contact, and deadline.

2233. (S)

Permian Basin Section SEPM

Wendell J. Stewart Scholarships

Up to 2 scholarships of $500 to graduate and undergraduate students and graduating high school seniors who are enrolled or plan to enroll as earth science majors or a related field. Visit web site for information, contact, and deadline.

2234. (S)

Robert J. & Ruth A. Weimer Student Grant

Awards of varying amounts to graduate students. Must submit a statement summarizing project objec-

tives, budget, letters of support from advisor that confirm that the student is in good academic standing. Students must acknowledge support in master's thesis, doctoral dissertation, and other publications. Deadline: December 31.

2235. (S)

Robert J. Weimer Fund

1 grant of at least $500 to a graduate student conducting research in areas of sedimentary geology. Must submit a statement summarizing project objectives, budget, letters of support from advisor that also confirm that the student is in good academic standing. Students must acknowledge support in master's thesis, doctoral dissertation, and other publications. Deadline: December 31.

2236. (S)

Rocky Mountain SEPM

Donald L. Smith Research Grant

http://www.rms-sepm.org/NewFiles/scholarmain.html

1 scholarship of $1,000 to a graduate student working toward a doctorate degree in geology. Research should be directly applicable to better understand the geology of the Rocky Mountain region. Visit web site for specific submission guidelines. Deadline: April 1.

2237. (S)

Rocky Mountain SEPM

Edwin D. McKee Grant

http://www.rms-sepm.org/NewFiles/scholarmain.html

1 scholarship of $1,000 to a graduate (master's) or undergraduate senior student in geology. Award must be used for thesis-related research in sedimentology and/or the application of sedimentology to better understand the geology of the Rocky Mountain region. Visit web site for specific submission guidelines. Deadline: April 1.

2238. (S)

Rocky Mountain SEPM

Fluvial Sedimentology Award

http://www.rms-sepm.org/NewFiles/scholarmain.html

1 scholarship of $1,000 to a graduate student to support master's- or doctoral-level student research in

modern or ancient fluvial sedimentology. Visit web site for specific submission guidelines. Deadline: April 1.

2239. (S)
Student Tuition Grants

2 grants of tuition to any SEPM Short Course to full-time graduate students majoring in some area of sedimentary geology. Awarded on a first-come, first-serve basis.

2240. (A, H, S, SS)
Society of the First Infantry Division Foundation Scholarship
1933 Morris Road
Blue Bell, PA 19422–1422
(215) 661–1969
http://www.bigredone.org/foundation/index.cfm

2 scholarships of $1,000 to graduate and undergraduate students who are children or grandchildren of a First Division veteran. May be used for any field of study. Must attend a 2- or 4-year institution. For more information, contact above address or visit web site. Deadline: August 1.

(S)
Society of Toxicology
1767 Business Center Drive, Suite 302
Reston, VA 20190
(703) 438–3115
http://www.toxicology.org

2241. (S)
Biological Modeling Student Award

1 Aegis Award of $500, plus ACSLTOX software license for a year and a plaque, and 1 Taylor and Francis Prize of $500, a book certificate, and a plaque, to a graduate or postdoctoral student whose abstract has been accepted by the SOT for presentation at the Annual Meeting. Research must be on biologically based modeling; issues of interest may include biological insights gained through model development, model validation, and mathematical/statistical/computational approaches to modeling. Deadline: January 15.

2242. (S)
Burdock Group Travel Awards

Cash awards of $500 to cover travel expenses not met by other funding to full-time graduate students with an interest in toxicology of food and food ingredients to attend the annual SOT meeting. Students who have not attended an annual meeting are encouraged to apply. Students may have the following areas of interest: food-borne natural and xenobiotic agents, food safety, toxicology, risk assessment of foods, and food ingredients. Visit web site for specific application guidelines. Deadline: January 31.

2243. (S)
Carcinogenesis Student Award

1 cash award each of $100, $300, and $500 to a graduate student, based on a poster presentation at the annual SOT meeting. Poster must present research in the areas of animals systems and models, comparative and clinical toxicology, nutrition, organ level or molecular toxicology, metabolism, or other related areas. Deadline: January 31.

2244. (S)
Carl C. Smith Mechanisms Graduate Student Award

Cash awards of $100, $300, and $500, plus a plaque, to graduate students for an abstract submitted to the Annual Meeting, with the student at the presenting author. Visit web site for specific submission guidelines. Deadline: October 7.

2245. (S)
Colgate-Palmolive-SOT Awards for Student Research Training in Alternative Methods

Awards of $2,500 to defray travel, per diem, and training expenses to graduate students proposing training involving in vitro methods or alternative techniques to reduce, replace, or refine the use of animals in toxicological research. Must be student members of SOT. Applicants must provide a proposed itinerary, budget, and rationale. Visit web site for specific guidelines and application. Deadline: until funds are committed.

2246. (S)
Comparative and Veterinary Student Award

1 award each of $300 and $500 to a current or recent graduate student or residency trainee for the best manuscript submitted to a refereed journal during the award year. Areas of research may include animals systems and models, comparative and clinical toxicology, nutrition, organ level or molecular toxicology,

metabolism, or other related areas. Must submit manuscript and letter from mentor/sponsor who is an SOT member. Deadline: January 31.

2247. (S)
Dermal Toxicology Student Award

2 awards of varying amounts and certificates to graduate students for skin-related research for contribution to advancing the understanding of skin toxicology and pharmacology. Selection is based on abstracts submitted prior to the SOT Annual Meeting. Deadline: February 1.

2248. (S)
Frank C. Lu Food Safety Award

1 cash award of $500 and a plaque to a graduate student for an abstract presented at the Annual Meeting. Selection based on methodology/approach, uniqueness/creativity inherent in the project, thoroughness of investigation, hypothesis, soundness of judgment used in interpreting results, and relevance to food safety. Abstract may deal with research on food-borne natural and xenobiotic agents, food safety, toxicology, risk assessment of foods, and food ingredients. Visit web site for specific guidelines for submission of abstract. Deadline: January 31.

2249. (S)
Graduate Student Fellowship Awards

Awards of $16,000 to graduate students in doctoral programs in toxicology who are student members of SOT. Selection will be based on original dissertation research, research productivity, importance and relevance of toxicology, scholastic achievement, and letters of recommendation. Deadline: October 9.

2250. (S)
Immunotoxicology Best Presentation Award

1 cash award of varying amount and a plaque to both a graduate student and a postdoctoral fellow, based on a submission of a written presentation to be made at the Annual Meeting. Presentation must be accompanied by a letter of recommendation from the student's or postdoctoral fellow's advisor. Electronic submissions are strongly encouraged, and no manuscripts will be accepted. Deadline: February 7.

2251. (S)
Inhalation Student Award

1 cash stipend of $500 and a plaque to a graduate student for the best abstract presented in the field of respiratory toxicology. Nomination should include a copy of the abstract, a letter of nomination from the sponsor, and a short student-written synopsis that includes the rationale for the study, the significance of the results, and the student's role in the work. Deadline: none specified.

2252. (S)
In Vitro Student Award

First-, second-, and third-place cash awards to graduate students and postdoctoral fellows on submitted abstracts. Abstracts must be accompanied by a letter of support from advisor. Deadline: October 15.

2253. (S)
Mary O. Amdur Student Award

1 cash stipend of varying amount to a graduate student based on submitted abstract. A copy of the abstract should be accompanied by a letter of nomination from the advisor and a student-written short synopsis. Synopsis should include the rationale for the study, the significance of the results, and the student's role in the work. Deadline: none specified.

2254. (S)
Metals Student Awards

Cash awards of $100 and $250 to pre- and postdoctoral students for a submitted abstract, introduction, results, and conclusion of no more than 5 pages. Advisor must also submit a letter. Visit web site for specific submission guidelines. Deadline: January 30.

2255. (S)
Midwest Victor A. Drill Award

1 cash award of $1,500 in expenses to a graduate student presenting a poster at the Spring Midwest Regional Chapter Meeting. Visit web site for contact person for more information. Deadline: none specified.

2256. (S)
Molecular Biology Student Award

Cash awards of $100, $300, and $500 to full-time graduate students for abstracts submitted to the annual meeting. Include a 2-page summary of significance and a letter of recommendation. Abstract must deal with molecular biology and any aspect of molecular biology research. Deadline: November 1.

2257. (S)
Mountain West Student Award

1 cash award each of $50 and $100 to a predoctoral graduate student working in a research laboratory of a member of the Mountain West Regional Chapter. Student may be conducting research in any area related to toxicology. Deadline: August 15.

2258. (S)
National Capital Area Chapter Student Award

4 awards of $700 each to 2 predoctoral and 2 postdoctoral graduate students. Must be enrolled full-time in a program within NCAC-SOT region. Selection based on abstract dealing with research in toxicology or a related field submitted for presentation at the Annual Meeting. Must not be receiving a concurrent travel award from national SOT or any of the specialty sections. Deadline: January 21.

2259. (S)
Neurotoxicology Student Awards

Awards of $150, $300, and $500 to predoctoral students and 1 of $500 to a postdoctoral fellow for an abstract dealing with neurotoxicological research. Abstract must be submitted to the Annual Meeting and be no longer than 1 page in length. Abstract must be accompanied by a letter of support from the advisor outlining the student's role in the research. Deadline: November 2.

2260. (S)
North Carolina Research Merit Award

Cash awards of $500 to graduate (master's and doctoral) candidates (not postdoctoral fellows) for submitted abstracts to be presented at the SOT Annual Meeting. Student must prepare and present a poster at the Spring SOT Meeting and be present for the judging of posters. Student must also prepare a short write-up of their research for the NC SOT newsletter. Deadline: none specified.

2261. (S)
North Carolina Student Travel Award

1 cash award of varying amount to a graduate student for an abstract submitted for presentation at the NCSOT Annual Meeting. Abstract must deal with research in toxicology. Deadline: January 15.

2262. (S)
Northland Student Award

Cash awards of $50, $75, and $100 to graduate students in training. Selection based on submitted abstract and an oral or poster presentation at the SOT annual meeting. Visit web site for information and contact person. Deadline: none specified.

2263. (S)
Regulatory and Safety Evaluation Student Award

Up to 4 cash awards of up to $500 toward travel expenses to graduate students for an abstract submitted for presentation at the Annual Meeting. Abstract must be accompanied by a letter of sponsorship from their advisor, a synopsis, and significance of research involving regulated chemicals, drugs, foods, medical devices, etc. Students applying for this award should be conducting research in safety or hazard assessment, essay development, models, regulatory and/or scientific policy, method validation, or other areas involving regulations or safety evaluations. Deadline: February 1.

2264. (S)
Reproductive & Development Student Award

1 award of cash and a plaque to a graduate student for a submission of a full presentation, letter of support, and a cover letter outlining significance of work to field of reproductive toxicology. Electronic submissions are strongly encouraged. Deadline: January 6.

2265. (S)
Risk Assessment Best Student Abstract Award

1 cash award of $500 to a graduate student or postdoctoral fellow for an abstract with "risk assessment" as a key word. Within 2 weeks of acceptance of the abstract, a copy of the abstract, a brief synopsis (less than 5 pages), and a letter of support from the advisor must be submitted. Deadline: within 2 weeks of acceptance of abstract.

2266. (S)

Robert L. Dixon International Travel Award

1 award of $2,000 to a graduate doctoral student to attend the International Congress of Toxicology meeting. Student must be study an area of reproductive toxicology and be a student member of SOT. Selection is based on perceived benefit to applicant, originality of dissertation research, importance of research to reproductive toxicology, scholastic achievement, and letter of recommendation. Deadline: October 9.

2267. (S)

Taylor and Francis Food Safety Award

1 award of $500 plus a $100 gift certificate for Taylor and Francis publications and a plaque to a graduate student for an abstract presented at the Annual Meeting. Selection based on methodology/approach, uniqueness/creativity inherent in the project, thoroughness of investigation, hypothesis, soundness of judgment used in interpreting results, and relevance to food safety. Abstract may deal with research on food-borne natural and xenobiotic agents, food safety, toxicology, risk assessment of foods, and food ingredients. Visit web site for specific guidelines for submission of abstract. Deadline: January 31.

2268. (S)

Toxicologic and Exploratory Pathology

1 cash award of $500 toward travel expenses and a plaque to a graduate student based on an abstract submitted for presentation at the Annual Meeting. Abstract should deal with basic or applied research dealing with pathogenisis of a toxic response. Abstract must be accompanied by a letter of recommendation from an academic advisor who is an SOT member. Nominee must be the senior author on the submitted abstract. Visit web site for more information. Deadline: January 10.

(S, SS)

Society of Vacuum Coaters Foundation
1451 Juliana Place
Alexandria, VA 22304–1516
(703) 751–8203
http://www.svc.org
svcfoundation@svc.org

2269. (S)

Scholarship Fund

1 or more awards of $5,000 to graduate or undergraduate students in vacuum coating technology. Must submit an application, transcript, and 2 letters of recommendation. Selection will be based on relevance of applicant's field of study to vacuum coating technology, academic achievement, motivation, social values, goals, and financial need. Deadline: January 15.

2270. (S)

Student Sponsorship

Sponsorships providing full travel support and conference registration fees to graduate and undergraduate students to attend the Annual SVC Technical Conference. Students are required to make a technical presentation at an SVC TechCon and prepare a manuscript for the Technical Conference Proceedings. Deadline: none specified.

(S)

Society of Vertebrate Paleontology
60 Revere Drive, Suite 500
Northbrook, IL 60062
http://www.vertpaleo.org
svp@vertpaleo.org

2271. (S)

Alfred Sherwood Romer Prize

1 award of varying amount to a graduate student in either a master's or doctoral program with a substantive portion of their research completed. Applicants who have completed their degree should be no more than 2 years past terminal degree. Selection will be based on the breadth and significance of the results, general relevance to the field, and innovative use of techniques, as well as effectiveness of presentation. For more information, visit web site. Deadline: mid-April.

2272. (S)

Bryan Patterson Award

2 grants of $1,000 or 1 grant of $2,000 to graduate and undergraduate students to conduct vertebrate paleontology research. Proposals must be for fieldwork and should be innovative rather than routine, venture-

some rather than predictable, and unusual rather than run-of-the-mill. Must be members of the Society of Vertebrate Paleontology. Visit web site for more information and an application. Deadline: mid-April.

2273. (S)
John L. Lazendorf Paleoart Prize

1 award of $500 in each of 3 categories to graduate or undergraduate students to recognize achievements of scientific illustrations and naturalistic art in paleontology. Paleoart is defined as the scientific or naturalistic rendering of paleontological subject matter pertaining to vertebrate fossils. The 3 categories are: two-dimensional art, three-dimensional art, and technical illustration. The award is not limited to any particular vertebrate group, and entrant does not need to be an SVP member. For submission guidelines, visit web site. Deadline: mid-April.

2274. (S)
Predoctoral Fellowship Grant

1 fellowship of $2,500 to a graduate student in the final stages of the doctoral program to pursue research. Must be within 18 months of doctoral completion. Selection will be based on scholarly contributions to the field, including the dissertation project, professional activity within the field, and promise of a productive and important professional role in vertebrate paleontology. Deadline: mid-April.

2275. (S)
Preparator's Grant

1 grant of $5,000 to a graduate or undergraduate student for a proposal for training apprenticeships and workshops—primarily travel expenses to learn or teach preparation. The committee will consider any proposal that furthers the field of vertebrate paleontology through the advancement of preparation. Visit web site for application and contact information. Deadline: mid-April.

2276. (S)
Richard Estes Memorial Grant

1 award of $1,000 to a graduate student toward research in nonmammalian vertebrate paleontology, with emphasis on systematics, morphology, biogeography, and paleoecology. For specific guidelines, please visit web site. Deadline: mid-April.

2277. (S)
Student Poster Prize

1 award of $400 to a graduate or undergraduate student for a poster that is single-authored and submitted for the competition during the annual SVC meeting. Entry should be accompanied by a brief abstract. Selection will be based on knowledge of the material and creativity of the presentation. For specific guidelines, visit web site. Deadline: mid-April.

(S)
Society of Women Engineers
ATTN: Executive Assistant
230 E. Ohio Street, Suite 400
Chicago, IL 60611–3265
(800) 666–ISWE
(312) 596–5223
http://www.swe.org

2278. (S)
Electronics for Imaging Scholarships

4 scholarships of $4,000 to female graduate or undergraduate students pursuing a degree in any area of engineering. Must have at least a 3.0 GPA on a 4.0 scale. Preference is given to students attending select schools in the San Francisco Bay area.

2279. (S)
General Scholarships

Scholarships of $1,000 to female graduate students majoring in engineering (auto, chemical, electrical, industrial, manufacturing, materials, mechanical, or technology). Selection based on academic achievement, discipline, leadership abilities, and career interest. Must be attending a 4-year ABET-accredited or SWE-approved U.S. institution. Must be active contributors and supporters of SWE. Selection based on application, academic achievement, transcript, test scores, career goals, and essay. Must be U.S. citizens. Please send self-addressed, stamped envelope with information request. Nonrenewable. Deadline: February 1.

2280. (S)
Microsoft Corporation Scholarships

2 scholarships of $2,500 to female first-year graduate students majoring in computer engineering or computer science. Must have at least a 3.5 GPA on a 4.0 scale. Visit web site for more information.

2281. (S)
Olive Lynn Salembler Scholarship

1 scholarship of $2,000 to a female graduate or undergraduate student who has been out of the engineering job market for a minimum of 2 years, to aid in obtaining the credentials necessary to reenter the job market as an engineer. Must have employment experience in an engineering career field. Must be attending a 4-year ABET-accredited or SWE-approved U.S. institution. Selection based on application, academic achievement, transcript, test scores, career goals, and essay. Must be U.S. citizens. Please send self-addressed, stamped envelope with information request. Nonrenewable. Deadline: May 15.

2282. (S)
Past Presidents Scholarships

2 scholarships of $1,500 to female graduate students in an engineering degree program at an accredited U.S. institution. Must have at least a 3.0 GPA on a 4.0 scale and be a U.S. citizen.

2283. (S)
Rocky Mountain Section Scholarships

3 scholarships of $500 to female graduate or undergraduate students who are pursuing engineering or computer science degrees in Colorado or Wyoming. Must not be receiving full funding from another organization. Selection is based on academic performance, interest in technical organizations, leadership, and engineering goals. Deadline: March 1.

2284. (S)
Santa Clara Valley Section Scholarships
http://swe-goldenwest.org/scvs/www/index.htm

Approximately 20 scholarships of $1,000 to female full-time graduate and undergraduate students, including entering freshmen, who are pursuing engineering degrees. Selection is based on academic achievement. Must be attending or planning to attend an accredited 4-year institution, must be a resident of or attend a school in the South San Francisco area. If you qualify to apply, contact the Santa Clara Valley Section directly at the web site provided. Deadline: none specified.

2285. (S)
Soil and Water Conservation Society of America
Scholarships
945 SW Ankeny Road
Ankeny, IA 50021–9764
(800) THE–SOIL
(515) 289–2331
http://www.swcs.org

Scholarships ranging from $1,000 to $1,400 to graduate or undergraduate students who have completed at least 2 years of study at an accredited college or university, have at least a 2.5 GPA, and are enrolled in an agricultural or natural resource-related curriculum. Open to the following majors: agronomy, soil science, range management, forestry, geography journalism, agribusiness, agricultural education, wildlife management, and other related fields. Deadline: April 1.

(S)
Soil Science Society of America
677 South Segoe Road
Madison, WI 53711
(608) 273–8080
http://www.soils.org

2286. (S)
Emil Truog Soil Science Award

1 award of $500 to a recent doctoral recipient for outstanding contribution to soil science as evidenced in dissertation. Visit web site for more information and deadline.

2287. (S)
Francis & Evelyn Clark Soil Biology
Scholarship

1 award of $2,000 to a graduate student in the field of soil biology, biochemistry, or microbial ecology. Selection based on academic achievement, recommendations, essay, and financial need. Visit web site for more information and deadline.

(A, H)
Solomon R. Guggenheim Foundation
1071 Fifth Avenue
New York, NY 10128
(212) 360–3540
(212) 423–3781
http://www.guggenheim.org

2288. (A, H)
Hilla Rebay Foundation Research Award

2 grants of $500 to graduate-level summer interns for travel, research, and scholarship related to Hilla Rebay, her circle of associates, and abstract art. Interested applicants who have been accepted into the summer program are invited to apply. Contact for more information or visit web site. Deadline: December 1.

2289. (A, H)
Hilla Rebay Graduate Interns

Up to 15 summer internships providing stipends of $1,000 to graduate students who are interested in pursuing museum careers. Awarded in honor of the Guggenheim Museum's first Director. Indicate on your application if you wish to apply for this stipend. Stipends are for 9 weeks. Contact for more information or visit web site. Deadline: December 1.

2290. (A, H)
Hilla Rebay International Internships

2 9-month internships providing stipends of $15,000 to graduate students, 1 curatorial and 1 education student (doctoral candidates preferred), to train in the Curatorial Departments of the Solomon R. Guggenheim Museum in New York; the Guggenheim Museum Bilbao, Spain; and the Peggy Guggenheim Collection, Venice. Interns spend a maximum of 3 months at each site: January 15–April 15 (SRGM), May 15–August 15 (PGC), September 15–November 15 (GMB). Candidates must demonstrate fluency in English, Spanish, and Italian (spoken and written). Deadline: September 30.

2291. (A, H)
Summer Internship Program

35 10-week summer unpaid internships for graduate students, undergraduate juniors and seniors, and recent graduates. Applicants must be studying arts administration, art history, conservation, education, film and media studies, museum studies, and other related fields. Selection based on academic achievement, skills, and interests. 2 students demonstrating a commitment to museum careers are selected to receive a $2,500 stipend. The internship is open to U.S. citizens only, and the program encourages applications from African-American, Alaskan, Native American, Asian-American, Hispanic, and Pacific Islander candidates. Preference given to New York City residents. Deadline: November 1 (spring), February 15 (summer), and May 1 (fall).

(A, H, S, SS)
Sons of Italy Foundation
219 E Street, N.E.
Washington, DC 20002
(202) 547–2900
http://www.osia.org/public/foundation.htm

2292. (A, H, S, SS)
Henry Salvatori Scholarship

1 scholarship ranging from $4,000 to $25,000 to graduate and undergraduate students in any area of study. Must be U.S. citizens of Italian descent (at least one Italian or Italian-American grandparent) and be enrolled in, or planning to enroll in, a 4-year, accredited academic institution. Selection is merit based. Previous SIF scholarship recipients are not eligible. A nonrefundable $25 processing fee must accompany each application. For more information, visit web site. Deadline: February 28 (postmark).

2293. (A, H, S, SS)
National Leadership Grants

10 to 13 merit-based grants ranging from $2,000 to $5,000 to full-time graduate and undergraduate students in any area of study. Must be U.S. citizens of Italian descent (at least one Italian or Italian-American grandparent) and be enrolled in, or planning to enroll in, a 4-year, accredited academic institution. Selection is merit based. Previous SIF scholarship recipients are not eligible. A nonrefundable $25 processing fee must accompany each application. For more information, visit web site. Deadline: February 28 (postmark).

(A, SS)
Sony Music Entertainment, Inc.
550 Madison Avenue, 2nd Floor
New York, NY 10022–3211
(212) 833–8000
http://www.sony.com

2294. (A, SS)
Credited Internship

70 to 80 10-week summer, fall, and spring internships providing no compensation to graduate and undergraduate students who will be returning to

school after the internship and must receive academic credit for the internship. All majors are accepted, but an interest in the music business is an asset. Interns are placed in promotions, publicity, retail marketing, artists and repertoire (A&R), A&R administration, and business affairs. Applicants must submit a cover letter and résumé. Finalists are interviewed in person or by phone. Deadline: rolling.

2295. (A, SS)
Minority Internship

45 10-week summer, fall, and spring internships, with compensation varying with the position. Open to minority (African-American, Hispanic-American, Asian-American, and Native American) graduate and undergraduate students who will be returning to school after the internship, must receive academic credit for the internship, and have at least a 3.0 GPA. All majors are accepted, but an interest in the music business is an asset. Interns are placed in promotions, publicity, retail marketing, artists and repertoire (A&R), A&R administration, and business affairs. Applicants must submit a cover letter and resume. Finalists are interviewed in person or by phone. Deadline: April 1.

2296. (S)
Sordoni Foundation
Fellowships
R.R. 5, Box 148
Elmcrest Drive
Dallas, PA 18612
written inquiries only

19 fellowships of varying amounts totaling $17,000 to graduate or undergraduate students, high school graduates, and graduating high school seniors who are pursuing any field of study. Must be a resident of the Dallas, PA, area. No major strings attached. Write an introductory letter briefly detailing your educational and financial situation. Deadline: none specified.

(A, H, S, SS)
Soroptimist International of the Americas
The Soroptimist Foundation, Inc.
Two Penn Center Plaza, Suite 1000
Philadelphia, PA 19102–1883
(215) 732–0512
http://www.soroptimist.org

2297. (A, H, S, SS)
Venture Student Aid Award

Varying number of awards of varying amounts to students with physical disabilities. You must be between the ages of 15 and 40 and demonstrate financial need. Send a self-addressed, stamped envelope or visit web site for more information. Deadline: December 31.

2298. (A, H, S, SS)
Women's Opportunity Awards

1 award of $5,000 and 2 awards of $3,000 in each of 29 geographic areas to graduate and undergraduate women to use for any expenses related to their educational pursuits. These include tuition and books, housing, child care, and transportation. These awards are not scholarships. May be used for any field of study. Awards made to promote upward mobility in women and to assist in their efforts toward training and entry or reentry into the labor market. Applicants must be over 30 years of age. Selection is based on financial need as well as a statement of clear career goals. Deadline: December 1.

2299. (A, H)
Sotheby's
Internship Program
1334 York Avenue at 72nd Street
New York, NY 10021
(212) 606–7000
http://www.sothebys.com

40 to 50 8-week summer internships in New York providing no compensation. Open to recent college graduates and undergraduate juniors and seniors. Interns are assigned to a Client-Service Department, such as the Press Office, Graphics, or Marketing, or in one of 33 expert departments, such as American Paintings or Chinese Works of Art. Interns may be from any major but have an interest in the auction business. Deadline: March 15.

2300. (S)
South Dakota State Department of Military and Veteran Affairs
National Guard Educational Benefits
Director of Personnel
425 East Capitol Avenue
Pierre, SD 575

(605) 773–4981
http://www.state.sd.us/military/VetAffairs/sdmva.htm

Scholarships providing up to 50% of tuition costs to graduate or undergraduate students in any field of study. Must be members of the South Dakota Army or Air Force National Guard. May be used at any accredited South Dakota institution. Must be South Dakota residents and U.S. citizens. Deadline: rolling.

(A, H)
Southwest Review Awards
Southern Methodist University
P.O. Box 750374
Dallas, TX 75275–0374
(214) 768–1036
http://www.southwestreview.org

2301. (A, H)
Elizabeth Matchett Stover Award

1 prize of $250 to the best poem or group of poems published in the magazine during the preceding year. Poetry is not submitted directly for the award but simply for publication in the magazine. Winners selected from among those published in each 2-year period. This is not a scholarship competition. For specific guidelines, please visit web site. Deadline: none.

2302. (A, H)
McGinnis-Ritchie Memorial Award

2 awards of $500 to the best works of fiction and nonfiction that appeared in the magazine in the previous year. Please note that manuscripts are submitted for publication, not for the prizes themselves. Winners are selected from among those published in each 2-year period. This is not a scholarship competition. The preferred length for articles and fiction is 3,500 to 7,000 words. For specific guidelines, please visit web site. Deadline: none.

2303. (A, H)
Morton Marr Poetry Prize

1 award of $1,000 to a poem by a writer who has not yet published a first book. May submit no more than 6 poems in a "traditional" form (e.g., sonnet, sestina, villanelle, rhymed stanzas, blank verse). A cover letter with name, address, and other relevant information may accompany the pieces, which must be printed without any identifying information. Include a self-addressed, stamped envelope for a reply or return of poem(s). Entry fee is $5 per poem. For specific guidelines, please visit web site. Deadline: November 30 (postmark).

2304. (Contest)
The Sow's Ear Poetry Review
245 McDowell Street
Bristol, TN 37620–2450
(703) 628–2651
http://www.abingdonartsdepot.org/sow.htm

1 prize of $500, publication is given in poetry and 50 copies, plus two prizes of $100. Entries may consist of 1 to 5 unpublished poems. No multiple submissions. Reading fee of $10 must be included. Manuscripts accepted March 1 through April 30. For specific rules, send a self-addressed, stamped envelope. Deadline: April 30.

2305. (S)
Space Foundation
Space Industrialization Fellowships
ATTN: Educational Grant Program Chairperson
310 S. 14th Street
Colorado Springs, CO 80904
(719) 576–8000
http://www.spacefoundation.org

Varying number of fellowships of $4,000 to graduate students in the sciences, engineering, environmental studies, business, law, economics, social sciences, or the humanities. Must intend to devote their careers to practical space research, engineering, business, or other application ventures. Deadline: October 1.

2306. (A, H)
Stanley Drama Award
Playwriting/Musical Awards Competition
c/o Wagner College, Drama Department
631 Howard Avenue
Staten Island, NY 10301
(718) 390–3100
http://www.wagner.edu/stanleydrama.html

An annual award of $2,000 for an original full-length play or musical, or a series of 2 or 3 thematically related one-act plays, that have not been professionally produced or received tradebook publication. The script must be unpublished and unproduced and be recommended by a theater professional. Application must accompany script. Previous winners are ineligible. Send a self-addressed, stamped envelope for application information. Deadline: September 1.

2307. (SS)
State Farm Insurance
Doctoral Dissertation Awards
One State Farm Plaza
Bloomington, IL 61710
(877) 734–2265
http://www.statefarm.com

2 awards of $10,000 to graduate doctoral students in insurance or business. Awarded to increase the number of qualified teachers of insurance and business in colleges and universities. Must have completed a major portion of their course work, have an approved proposal, and not completed their dissertation. Must be U.S. citizens. Awarded in business and insurance/risk management. Recipient's school receives $3,000. Obtain applications from dean or director of doctoral program. Visit web site for more information. Deadline: March 31.

2308. (SS)
Stimson Center
Fellowships in China
11 Dupont Circle, N.W., Ninth Floor
Washington, DC 20036
(202) 223–5956
http://www.stimson.org

Awards of varying amounts to graduate students or individuals with at least 5 years professional experience in a field related to foreign policy and international relations. Must be a U.S. citizen and passport holder and have a bachelor's degree or above from an accredited institution. Chinese language ability is preferred but not required. Must propose an appropriate research topic, subject to Stimson Center approval. Visit web site for more information. Deadline: June 1.

(A, H)
Story Line Press
Three Oaks Farm
P.O. Box 1240
Ashland, OR 97520–0055

(541) 512–8792
http://www.storylinepress.com

2309. (A, H)
Nicholas Roerich Competition

1 prize of $1,000 and publication to a full-length poetry manuscript. Entries must be at least 48 pages in length. Writers who have published chapbooks of under 32 pages are eligible to submit. Each submission must include a 1-paragraph biographical statement, $20 entry fee, and a self-addressed, stamped envelope for manuscript return. Deadline: October 15.

2310. (A, H)
Three Oaks Prize for Fiction

1 prize of $1,500 for the best unpublished novel, novella, or collection of short stories in English by any writer. There is no specific length requirement, but must be reasonable. Each submission must include a 1-paragraph biographical statement, $25 entry fee, and a self-addressed, stamped envelope for manuscript return. Deadline: April 30 (postmark).

2311. (S)
Sudden Infant Death Syndrome Alliance
Student Research Fellowship Program
1314 Bedford Avenue, Suite 210
Baltimore, MD 21208
(410) 653–8226
http://www.sidsalliance.org/index/default.asp

Fellowships of $2,000 to graduate students in medicine or related professional fields. Must be enrolled in an accredited U.S. institution. Must have completed at least 2 years of study and be able to spend from 8 to 12 weeks to conduct research related to SIDS. Deadline: March 15.

2312. (S, SS)
Surfrider Foundation
Internship Program
P.O. Box 6010
San Clemente, CA 92674–6010
(949) 492–8170
(800) 743–SURF
http://www.surfrider.org

12 internships providing no compensation to graduate students, recent college graduates, undergraduate students, and high school students to work in environmen-

tal activism projects. Internship can last from 8 weeks to 1 year and are conducted year-round in San Clemente. Deadline: rolling (at least 3 weeks before starting date).

2313. (A)
Swann Foundation
Fellowship for the Study of Caricature and Cartoon
Prints & Photographs Division
Library of Congress
101 Independence Avenue, S.E.
Washington, DC 20540–4730
(202) 707–9115
http://www.loc.gov/rr/print/swann/swannhome.html

1 dissertation fellowship of $15,000 to a graduate student working toward the completion of a dissertation or thesis for that degree or engaged in postgraduate research within 3 years of receiving a masters or doctoral degree. Award must be used in the school year following the award. Although research must be in the field of caricature and cartoon, there is no limitation regarding the place or time period covered. Must be enrolled an institution in the U.S., Mexico, or Canada. Nonrenewable. Deadline: mid-February.

(A, H)
Synod of the Trinity
3040 Market Street
Camp Hill, PA 17011
(800) 242–0534
(717) 737–0421
http://www.syntrin.org/program/funding.htm

2314. (H)
Mary L. Clark Ministry Study Grant

Scholarships of up to $1,000 to graduate students preparing to become a minister of Word and Sacrament in the Presbyterian ministry. Must be residents of Pennsylvania, West Virginia, or parts of Ohio or attend Synod-related schools (Beaver, Davis and Elkins, Grove City College, Lafayette, Waynesburg, Westminister, or Wilson). Must be Presbyterian. Must be a U.S. citizen or legal resident. Deadline: March 1.

2315. (A, H)
Mary Meade Maxwell Fund

Scholarships of up to $1,000 to graduate students who are preparing for full-time church-related voca-

tions. Must be residents of Pennsylvania, West Virginia, or parts of Ohio or attend Synod-related schools (Beaver, Davis and Elkins, Grove City College, Lafayette, Waynesburg, Westminister, or Wilson). Must be Presbyterian. Must be a U.S. citizen or legal resident. Deadline: March 1.

2316. (S)
Tailhook Association Educational Foundation
Scholarship Awards
9696 Businesspark Avenue
San Diego, CA 02131
(858) 689–9223
(800) 322–4665
http://www.tailhook.org/Foundation.htm

4 scholarships of $1,000 to graduate or undergraduate students who are members, dependents, or individuals sponsored by members. Must be majoring in aerospace education. Must have been accepted to or enrolled at an accredited 4-year program. Based on academic achievement and citizenship. Deadline: July 15.

2317. (A, H, S, SS)
Talbots Women's Scholarship Fund
One Talbots Drive
Hingham, MA 02043
(781) 749–7600
(781) 741–4369
http://www.talbots.com/about/scholar

50 scholarships of $1,000 and 5 scholarships of $10,000 to female graduate and undergraduate students who are seeking a degree from an accredited 4-year or 2-year college, university, or vocational-technical school. Applicants must have earned a high school diploma or GED at least 10 years prior to this application year. The award requires an essay and transcript with the application. Scholarship selection is based on a number of criteria, including financial need, academic record, scholarship essay, potential to succeed, leadership and participation in community activities, honors, work experience, a statement of educational and career goals, and an outside appraisal. Request information after October 1. Deadline: varies.

2318. (S)
Tanglewood Music Center
Fellowship Program
301 Massachusetts Avenue
Boston, MA 02115

(617) 638–9230
http://www.bso.org
tmc@bso.org

Designed to meet the needs of young instrumental-ists, singers, composers, and conductors who have completed most of their formal training and who are active performers—focusing on performance in chamber music, orchestral music, and contemporary music. Tuition costs for an entire summer session at Tanglewood are available. Depending on financial need, some members are also provided room and board in the Center's dormitories. Those who can will be asked to pay their own dorm fees. In addition, students may qualify (upon special application) for one of a limited number of stipends available in cases of extreme financial need. All receiving a fellowship must pay the $60 registration fee, and if residing in the dorms, the $55 room reservation fee. Must be a competent musician who has completed most of his/her formal training and is an active performer. Applicant must be at least 18 years of age. (If you are less than 18 years old, you are directed to the Young Instrumental and Vocal Programs of the Boston University Tanglewood Institute, 855 Commonwealth Avenue, Boston, MA 02215.) Inquiries may be made in October. Visit the web site for audition deadlines.

2319. (A)
Tennessee Arts Commission
Individual Artist's Fellowships
401 Charlotte Avenue
Nashville, TN 37243–0780
(615) 741–1701
http://www.arts.state.tn.us

1 grant of $5,000 open to working artists in each of the following categories: crafts, dance (performance), literary (prose), media (film and video), music (instrumental performance), theater (acting), and visual arts (two-dimensional work only). Students are ineligible, since grant is not for academic study but to assist in the creation of work. This award provides fellowships to outstanding artists who live and work in Tennessee. No matching funds are required, and no specific project has to be carried out with the funds. Award is for 1 year. Deadline: January 21.

2320. (S)
Tennessee Space Grant Consortium Graduate
Fellowship Program
Program Coordinator
Vanderbilt University
Box 1592, Station B
Nashville, TN 37235
(615) 343–1148
http://vuse.vanderbilt.edu/~tnsg/homepage.html

Varying numbers of awards of varying amounts to graduate students. Must be used for research, and student must be a U.S. citizen. Visit web site for more information. Deadline: varies.

2321. (S)
Teratology Society
Student Travel Grants
9650 Rockville Pike
Bethesda, MD 20814
(301) 571–1841
http://www.teratology.org

35 to 40 travel grants to assist graduate students and postdoctoral fellows in presenting abstracts at the Teratology Society's Annual Meeting. The award is given to promote interest in, and advance study of, biological abnormalities. Send a self-addressed, stamped envelope for more information. Deadline: May 1.

(H)
Texas Association of Broadcasters
Texas Broadcast Education Foundation
502 East 11th Street, Suite 200
Austin, TX 78701
(512) 322–9944
http://www.tab.org/scholarships.php

2322. (H)
BELO Corporation Scholarship

1 scholarship of $2,000 to an undergraduate senior planning to attend a graduate program or to an undergraduate junior. Must be student members and/or attending a fully accredited program that emphasizes radio or television broadcasting or communications at a 4-year college or university in Texas that holds membership in TABE. Selection based on academic achievement, recommendation letters, financial need, extracurricular activities, and commit-

ment to broadcasting. For more information, visit web site. Deadline: May 9.

2323. (H)
Bonner McLane Scholarship

1 scholarship of $2,000 to an undergraduate senior planning to attend a graduate program or to an undergraduate junior. Must be student members and/or attending a fully accredited program that emphasizes radio or television broadcasting or communications at a 4-year college or university in Texas that holds membership in TABE. Selection based on academic achievement, recommendation letters, financial need, extracurricular activities, and commitment to broadcasting. For more information, visit web site. Deadline: May 9.

2324. (H)
Lady Bird Johnson Scholarship

1 scholarship of $2,000 to a graduate or undergraduate student at the University of Texas at Austin in a program with emphasis on communications. Selection based on academic achievement, recommendation letters, financial need, extracurricular activities, and commitment to broadcasting. Recipient will be eligle to apply for an internship at the Lady Bird Johnson Wildflower Center. For more information, visit web site. Deadline: May 9.

2325. (H)
Scholarships

2 or more scholarships of $2,000 to graduate or undergraduate students. Must be student members and/or attending a fully accredited program that emphasizes radio or television broadcasting or communications at a 4-year college or university in Texas that holds membership in TABE. Selection based on academic achievement, recommendation letters, financial need, extracurricular activities, and commitment to broadcasting. For more information, visit web site. Deadline: May 9.

2326. (H)
Tom Reiff

1 scholarship of $2,000 to a rising undergraduate senior planning to attend a graduate program or a rising undergraduate junior. Must be student members

and/or attending a fully accredited program that emphasizes radio or television broadcasting or communications at a 4-year college or university in Texas that holds membership in TABE. Selection based on academic achievement, recommendation letters, financial need, extracurricular activities, and commitment to broadcasting. For more information, visit web site. Deadline: May 9.

2327. (H)
Vann Kennedy

1 scholarship of $2,000 to a graduate or undergraduate student. Must be student members and/or attending a fully accredited program that emphasizes radio or television broadcasting or communications at a 4-year college or university in Texas that holds membership in TABE. Selection based on academic achievement, recommendation letters, financial need, extracurricular activities, and commitment to broadcasting. For more information, visit web site. Deadline: May 9.

2328. (H)
Wendell Mayes Jr.

1 scholarship of $2,000 to a graduate or undergraduate student. Must be student members and/or attending a fully accredited program that emphasizes radio or television broadcasting or communications at a 4-year college or university in Texas that holds membership in TABE. Selection based on academic achievement, recommendation letters, financial need, extracurricular activities, and commitment to broadcasting. For more information, visit web site. Deadline: May 9.

2329. (S)
Texas Floral Endowment
Scholarships
P.O. Box 140255
Austin, TX 78714
(512) 834–0361
http://www.tsfa.org/scholarship.html

Scholarships ranging from $500 to $1,000 to graduate or undergraduate students or any individual who is pursuing a floral career, such as horticulture or floriculture. The award may be used at any accredited floral design school, state association-credentialed class, community college, or 4-year university. Award must be used within 2 years. Deadline: June 1.

2330. (S)
Texas Osteopathic Medical Association Scholarship Awards
1415 Lavaca Street
Austin, TX 78701–1634
(512) 708–8662
http://www.txosteo.org

Scholarships ranging from $750 to $1,750 to first-, second-, and third-year students enrolled in an accredited college of osteopathic medicine. Must be Texas residents. Deadline: May 1.

2331. (S)
Texas Surveyors Foundation, Inc. Scholarship Information
2525 Wallingwood Drive, #300
Austin, TX 78746–6922
(512) 327–7871
http://www.tsps.org

Scholarships of varying amounts to graduate and undergraduate students pursuing a surveying-related course of study. Must be enrolled in or accepted for enrollment in an accredited college or university and be a Texas resident. Selection based on academic achievement, extracurricular activities, goals essay, recommendation letters, and financial need. Deadline: September 15 (fall), January 15 (spring), and May 1 (summer).

2332. (Contest)
TextbookX.com Scholarship
Akademos, Inc.
25 Van Zant Street, Suite 1A-2
Norwalk, CT 06855-1727
(800) 887–6459
http://www.textbookx.com/service/contact.php

5 scholarships ranging from $250 to $1,000 to graduate and undergraduate students in any field of study. Must be enrolled in good standing at an accredited U.S. college or university. Must be a legal resident of the U.S. or an international student with a valid visa to be eligible. Must write a 250- to 750-word essay on the following topics: Does science leave room for faith? Does faith leave room for science? In responding to these questions, you must make reference to 1 book that has had a significant influence on your thoughts. Must apply online. Deadline: December 15.

2333. (A, H, S, SS)
Theta Delta Chi Educational Foundation Scholarship
215 Lewis Wharf
Boston, MA 02110
(617) 742–8886
http://www.tdx.org/about.html
written inquiries only

Scholarships of $1,000 to graduate and undergraduate students in all areas of study. Must be active members of TDC and attend a 2- or 4-year accredited U.S. institution. Based on academic achievement (45%), service to the fraternity (35%), and financial need (20%). Deadline: May 15.

2334. (A, H, S, SS)
Thomas J. Watson Foundation Watson Fellows Program
293 South Main Street
Providence, RI 02903
(401) 274–1952
http://www.watsonfellowship.org

Grants of $22,000 to graduating undergraduate seniors to spend 1 year abroad to explore a particular interest, test their aspirations and abilities, to view their lives and American society in greater perspective, and develop a more informed sense of international concern. The fellowship is intended to allow students to immerse themselves in other cultures for an entire year. Applicants must submit a detailed proposal for their project. Visit web site for more information. Deadline: first Tuesday in November.

2335. (Contest)
Thomas Wolfe Society Thomas Wolfe Student Essay Prize
Dr. James Clark
809 Gardner Street
Raleigh, NC 27607
http://www.ncsu.edu/chass/extension/wolfe

1 prize of $500 to a graduate or undergraduate student for an essay written on a topic related to Thomas Wolfe

or his works. Selection based on originality, style, clarity, documentation, and contribution to knowledge or understanding of Thomas Wolfe. Visit web site for specific submission guidelines. Deadline: January 15.

2336. (S, SS)
3M
Staffing & College Relations
224 1W-02
3M Center
St. Paul, MN 55144–1000
(800) 328–1343
http://www.mmm.com

200 14-week summer internships providing a stipend ranging from $550 to $650 for graduate students and from $425 to $500 per week for undergraduate students. Students can work in St. Paul, MN, Austin, TX, or in one of 80 plants throughout the country (one is located in North Carolina). Majors accepted: biology, chemistry, computer science, engineering (chemical, electrical, mechanical, industrial, and ceramic), materials science, and physics. For finance positions, applicants must be seniors in accounting or business, though a few sophomores, juniors, or MBA candidates have been accepted. For marketing positions, applicants must be seniors pursuing marketing-related degrees, including communications, journalism, or advertising; MBA candidates are also eligible. All students must have at least a 3.0 GPA. Deadline: December 1.

2337. (SS)
Thurgood Marshall Scholarship Fund
Sidney B. Williams Jr. Intellectual Property Law Scholarship
60 East 42nd Street, Suite 833
New York, NY 10165
(212) 537–8888
http://www.thurgoodmarshallfund.org

Up to 9 scholarships of $10,000 to minority law students who are pursuing a career in intellectual property law. Selection is based on outstanding academic undergraduate and school performance and financial need. Must hold a past or present full- or part-time position in an area related to intellectual property law. Visit web site for more information and an application. Deadline: February 28.

2338. (S)
Tower Hill Botanic Garden
Scholarship Program
11 French Drive
P.O. Box 598
Boylston, MA 01505
(508) 869–6111
http://www.towerhillbg.org

Scholarships ranging from $500 to $2,000 to graduate students or upper-level undergraduate students majoring in horticulture or horticulture-related areas. Must reside in New England or attend a college or university in New England. Selection based on interest in horticulture, purpose, academic achievement, and financial need. Send a self-addressed, stamped envelope for information. Deadline: May 1.

2339. (S, SS)
Ty Cobb Educational Foundation
P. O. Box 725
Forest Park, GA 30298
written inquiries only
http://www.tycobbfoundation.com

223 scholarships ranging from $400 to $1,000 to graduate and undergraduate students and scholarships of up to $3,000 to graduate medical and dental school students. Must be Georgia residents who have completed 45 quarter hours or 30 semester hours with at least a B average. Various fields are acceptable, including medicine, dentistry, veterinary medicine, and law. Students may attend any U.S. institution. Selection based on academic achievement and financial need. Write a letter describing your financial and educational situation and enclose a self-addressed, stamped envelope for an application. Deadline: June 15.

(A, H, S, SS)
Tylenol Scholarship
http://www.tylenol.com

2340. (A, H, S, SS)
Cash for College Sweepstakes

4 scholarships of $1,000 to graduate and undergraduate students who are enrolled in or plan to enroll in an accredited program the following fall semester. Must attend an accredited college or university in the U.S, be at least 17 years old, and a

U.S. citizen or legal resident. Apply on-line. Deadline: April 30.

2341. (S)
Tylenol Scholarship

10 scholarships of $10,000 and 150 scholarships of $1,000 to graduate or undergraduate students who are pursuing a major that will lead to a health-related field. Must attend an accredited U.S. institution and have 1 or more years of postsecondary education remaining. Applications are available on-line. Deadline: April 30.

2342. (A, H, S, SS)
Union of Marash Fund
Student Fund
1 Sussex Road
Great Neck, NJ 11020–1828

Scholarships ranging from $500 to $1,000 to full-time graduate and undergraduate students in accredited institutions. Must be descendants of a Marashtsi (a part of Armenia/Asia Minor). U.S. citizenship is not required. Selection is based on academic achievement, moral character, financial need, and community involvement. Renewable. Deadline: July 1.

(S)
Unitarian Universalist Association
25 Beacon Street
Boston, MA 02108
written inquiries only
(617) 742–2100
http://www.uua.org/info/scholarships.html

2343. (H)
Barbara Marshman and Ann B. Fields Scholarship

1 award of $500 to a graduate student who is a religious educator. Must serve a UU congregation. Visit web site for more information. Deadline: May 1.

2344. (H)
David Eaton Scholarship

Awards of $2,500 to an African-American graduate student enrolled full-time in a Master's of Divinity degree program leading to an ordination as a UU minister. Applicants must be dedicated to creating an antiracist, multicultural religious organization and country. Deadline: April 15.

2345. (H)
David Pohl Scholarship

1 award of $2,250 to a graduate student enrolled full-time in a Master's of Divinity degree program leading to an ordination as a UU minister. Awarded to promising ministerial candidates. Deadline: April 15.

2346. (H)
John Haynes Holmes Memorial Fellowships

Awards of varying amounts to seminarians who intend to serve as parish ministers, ministers of religious education, directors of religious education, or professors. For more information and contact person, visit web site. Deadline: April 1.

2347. (H)
Olympia Brown and Max Kapp Awards

Awards of $2,250 each to 1 woman and 1 man who are graduate students enrolled full-time in a Master's of Divinity degree program leading to an ordination as a UU minister. In addition to meeting the requirements for general financial aid, choose to submit as part of their general financial application a paper, sermon, or other special project on some aspect of Universalism. Deadline: April 1.

2348. (H)
Reverend Chuck Thomas Scholarship

1 award of $2,500 to an applicant who has shown outstanding commitment to Universal Unitarism as a lay leader and who has not yet entered seminary. Should be planning to enroll full-time in a Master's of Divinity degree program leading to an ordination as a UU minister. Deadline: April 1.

2349. (H)
Robert and Martha Atherton Scholarship

2 awards of $2,500 each to students in the second or third year of seminary. Must have proven ability and dedication to the UU faith and to helping mankind and recognize that sound family orientation is the foundation of a healthy and strong society. Student must be patriotic and have an attitude of friendship and caring for mankind.

2350. (H)
Stanfield and D'Orlando Scholarship

15 scholarships of varying amounts to graduate or undergraduate UU students preparing for a career in fine arts. Must be in the area of painting, drawing, photography, and/or sculpture. Performing arts majors are not eligible. Must be an active UU, demonstrate financial need, and enroll in an accredited institution.

2351. (H)
Stanfield Legal Scholarship

Awards of varying amounts to students entering, or already enrolled in, law school. Selections are based on intellectual attainment, potential, character, and spiritual philosophy. Pre-law and political science majors are not eligible. Deadline: February 15.

2352. (S, SS)
United Agribusiness League
UAL Scholarship Program
54 Corporate Park
Irvine, CA 92714
(714) 975–1424
http://www.ual.org

Varying numbers of scholarships ranging from $2,000 to $3,500 to graduate or undergraduate students majoring in agriculture or agribusiness. Must be UAL member employees or their dependent children. Must be enrolled in an accredited college or university. Renewable. Send a self-addressed, stamped envelope for information. Deadline: March 31.

(H)
United Church of Christ
700 Prospect Avenue East
Cleveland, OH 44115
(216) 736–3839
http://www.ucc.org

2353. (H)
Adrienne M. and Charles Shelby Rooks
Fellowship for Minority Theological Students

Scholarships ranging from $500 to $5,000 to minority graduate students pursuing a teaching vocation in the field of religion. Must be a member of a UCC congregation for at least 1 year prior to receiving a scholarship, enrolled in an ATC-accredited seminary working toward becoming an ordained minister, have at least a B average, and demonstrate leadership ability through local church, Association, Conference, or academic environment. Renewable. Visit web site for more information. Deadline: March 1.

2354. (H)
Cannon Endowment Scholarship

Scholarships of approximately $2,500 to graduate seminarian students planning to become military chaplains. Must be a member of a UCC or other faith congregation for at least 1 year prior to receiving a scholarship, enrolled in an accredited seminary working toward becoming an ordained minister, have at least a B average, and demonstrate leadership ability through their local church or academic environment. Visit web site for more information. Deadline: March 1.

2355. (H)
Doctoral Student Awards

Awards of varying amounts to minority doctoral students in a program leading toward a Ph.D., Th.D., or Ed.D. within a field related to religious studies. Preference given to students with outstanding academic achievement, teaching effectiveness, and commitment to UCC who intend to become professors in colleges, seminaries, or graduate schools. Visit web site for more information. Deadline: March 1.

2356. (H)
Garrett Trust Fund Scholarships

Scholarships ranging from $300 to $1,000 to graduate students in a Master of Divinity program in an accredited seminary. Must be a member of a UCC congregation for at least 1 year prior to receiving a scholarship, be enrolled in an ATC-accredited seminary working toward becoming an ordained minister, have at least a B average, and demonstrate leadership ability through local church, Association, Conference, or academic environment. Visit web site for more information. Deadline: March 1.

2357. (H)
Global Partner Church Awards

2 awards ranging from $1,000 to $2,000 to graduate students. 1 is for a student of an overseas/global partner church, and 1 is for an international student

studying at a UCC seminary. Continuing education funds for a clergy person of an overseas/partner church are also awarded. Awarded upon nomination by the Area Offices of the common Global Ministries/Wider Church Ministries. Visit web site for more information. Deadline: March 1.

2358. (H)
Make a Difference! Doctoral Studies Awards

Awards of $2,500 to doctoral students who are considering teaching at a seminary of the UCC. Must be a member of a UCC congregation for at least 1 year prior to receiving a scholarship, enrolled in an ATC-accredited seminary working toward becoming an ordained minister, have at least a B average, and demonstrate leadership ability through local church, Association, Conference, or academic environment. Visit web site for more information. Deadline: March 1.

2359. (H)
Make a Difference! Educational Support Awards

Awards of $500 to graduate seminarian students at one of the 7 UCC seminaries. Must be a member of a UCC congregation for at least 1 year prior to receiving a scholarship, enrolled in an ATC-accredited seminary working toward becoming an ordained minister, have at least a B average, and demonstrate leadership ability through local church, Association, Conference, or academic environment. Visit web site for more information. Deadline: March 1.

2360. (H)
Make a Difference! Seminarian Scholarships

Awards ranging from $1,500 to $2,500 to graduate seminarian students at 1 of the 7 UCC seminaries. Must be a member of a UCC congregation for at least 1 year prior to receiving a scholarship, enrolled in an ATC-accredited seminary working toward becoming an ordained minister, have at least a B average, and demonstrate leadership ability through local church, Association, Conference, or academic environment. Visit web site for more information. Deadline: March 1.

2361. (H)
Master of Divinity Student Awards

Awards of varying amounts to minority full- and part-time students enrolled in an accredited school of theology. Must have at least a B average. Preference is given to students who have demonstrated leadership through service to the church exceptional academic performance and intend to become pastors and teachers within the UCC. Visit web site for more information. Deadline: March 1.

2362. (H)
Richard and Helen Brown Pastoral Scholarships

Scholarships of up to $10,000 to minority seminarians who belong to the UCC. Must be a member of a UCC congregation for at least 1 year prior to receiving a scholarship, enrolled in an ATC-accredited seminary working toward becoming an ordained minister, have at least a B average, and demonstrate leadership ability through local church, Association, Conference, or academic environment. Visit web site for more information. Deadline: March 1.

2363. (H)
William R. Johnson Scholarship

Scholarships of approximately $2,500 to second- and third-year seminary students who are gay, lesbian, bisexual, or transgender. Must be open about their sexual orientation and enrolled in an ATC-accredited seminary. Must be a member of a UCC congregation for at least 1 year prior to receiving a scholarship and have proof of In Care status, working toward becoming an ordained minister, have at least a 3.0 GPA on a 4.0 scale, and demonstrate leadership ability through local church, Association, Conference, or academic environment. Renewable. Visit web site for more information. Deadline: March 1.

2364. (A, H, S, SS)
United Federation of Teachers Graduate Scholarships
260 Park Avenue, South
New York, NY 10010
(212) 777–7500
http://www.uft.org/?fid=103&tf=636

6 scholarships of $2,000 over 2 semesters for students in a master's program in any field of study, 1 scholarship of $8,000 over 4 years to a medical student, 1 scholarship of $6,000 over 3 years to a law student, and 1 scholarship of $6,000 over 3 years to a graduate

student in education. Must have been a graduate of the New York City public school system. Applicants must have been winners of a UFT undergraduate college scholarship. Must attend accredited institution. Must be New York residents and U.S. citizens. Nonrenewable.

2365. (H)
United Methodist Communications
Stoody-West Scholarship
P.O. Box 320
Nashville, TN 37202–0230
(888) 278–4862
http://www.umcom.org
scholarships@umcom.org

2 scholarships of $6,000 to graduate students in religious journalism. Religious journalism includes newswriting for secular press, church press, and for church institutions, including electronic, broadcast, and print media. Visit web site for more information. Deadline: none specified.

(A, H, S, SS)
United Negro College Fund
8260 Willow Oaks Corporate Drive
P.O. Box 10444
Fairfax, VA 22031–4511
(800) 331–2244
http://www.uncf.org

2366. (A, H, S, SS)
General Scholarships

Numerous scholarships of varying amounts to graduate and undergraduate students. Must attend an UNCF college or university and have at least a 2.5 GPA on a 4.0 scale. Some scholarships require a higher GPA or specific major. Visit web site for more specific information. Deadline: varies.

2367. (S)
Merck Graduate Science Research Dissertation Fellowships

12 fellowships providing a stipend of $30,000 and a department grant of $10,000 to African-American doctoral students in the life or physical sciences. Must be engaged in, or within 1 to 3 years of completing, dissertation research. Must be a U.S. citizen or permanent resident. Deadline: mid-December.

2368. (S)
Merck Postdoctoral Science Research Fellowship
uncfmerck@uncf.org

10 fellowships providing a stipend of $55,000 and a department grant of $15,000 to African-American postdoctoral fellows to conduct biomedical science research. Must be a U.S. citizen or permanent resident. Deadline: mid-December.

2369. (S)
Pfizer Biomedical Research Initiative

4 postdoctoral fellowships providing up to $53,500 (stipend of $44,500, fringe benefits of $4,000, and travel allowance of $5,000) to minority postdoctoral fellows to conduct biomedical science research. Selection is based on academic achievement, demonstrated ability, and proposed research project. Must be U.S. citizens. Deadline: April 15.

2370. (S, SS)
United States Agency for International Development
Intern Program
USAID Information Center
Ronald Reagan Building
Washington, DC 20523–1000
(202) 712–4810
http://www.info.usaid.gov

Provides a 2-year program to individuals with a graduate degree in agriculture, agricultural economics, business administration, human geography or non-Western area studies, nutrition or public health, rural sociology, social/applied anthropology, or urban development. Individuals are sent to a development country in Asia, Africa, Latin America, the Near East, or the Caribbean. Deadline: none specified.

2371. (S)
United States Arms Control and Disarmament Agency
Hubert H. Humphrey Doctoral Fellowships
Intelligence, Technology and Analysis Division, Room 4930
320 21st Street, N.W.
Washington, DC 20451

(202) 647–4153

http://dosfan.lib.uic.edu/acda/aboutacd/hh1.htm

Fellowships providing a stipend of $8,000, plus tuition grants of up to $6,000, to doctoral candidates in biology, chemistry, engineering, physics, psychology, or some social sciences. Doctoral candidates must have completed all their course work except for their dissertation. Candidates for a J.D. degree are also eligible during their third year of study. All applicants must attend accredited U.S. institutions. Fellowships are generally awarded for a 12-month period to encourage specialized training and research in arms control, nonproliferation, and disarmament. Deadline: March 31.

2372. (S)

United States Department of Agriculture
Saul T. Wilson Jr. Scholarship
APHIS, Human Resources/Employment
4700 River Road, Unit 21
Riverdale, MD 20737–1230
(800) 762–2738
(301) 734–6466
http://www.usda.gov

Scholarships of $10,000 to graduate and $5,000 to undergraduate students working toward a veterinary degree. Recipients are employed during the summers and school breaks as Veterinary Student Trainees and receive a salary, Federal Employees Retirement System coverage, participate in a 401(k), and paid vacation and sick leave. Recipients are provided with a job with APHIS after completing their D.V.M., where recipient may become a full-time agency employee for at least 1 calendar year for each year of scholarship support. Must be a U.S. citizen enrolled in an accredited U.S. institution. Graduate students must not have completed more than 1 year of study. Deadline: March 1.

2373. (S)

United States Department of Agriculture
USDA/Woodrow Wilson Fellowship Program
ATTN: Program Manager
STOP 5474
5601 Sunnyside Avenue
Beltsville, MD 20705
(301) 504–2223
http://www.usda.gov/da/employ/99InternWeb3.htm#WWF

8 to 10 fellowships providing 1 year of financial assistance for 1 year of USDA service to graduate students in a course of study consistent with the agency's areas of interest. Must maintain a 3.0 GPA on a 4.0 scale. Deadline: none specified.

2374. (S, SS)

United States Department of Commerce
Internships
Administration Building
Room A-123
Gaithersburg, MD 20899
(301) 975–3026
http://www.commerce.gov

Varying number of internships in volunteer programs and Co-op and Student Employment (SE) Programs that pay from $275 to $500 per week and last from 2 weeks to 4 months. Open to graduate and undergraduate students. Students might be assigned to one of the following agencies: National Technical Information Service, National Telecommunications and Information Administration, Technology Administration, Patent and Trademark, Bureau of Economic Analysis, Bureau of Export Administration, Economics and Statistics Administration, Economic Development Administration, Minority Business Development Agency, or the U.S. Travel and Tourism Administration. Students must be able to receive academic credit. The program is conducted in Washington, DC. Deadline: rolling.

2375. (S)

United States Department of Commerce
National Oceanic and Atmospheric Administration (NOAA)
Dr. Nancy Foster Scholarship
1305 East-West Highway
1252 Murphy Hall
Silver Spring, MD 20910
http://fosterscholars.noaa.gov/welcome.html

5 scholarships providing a 12-month stipend of $20,000, and an annual cost-of-education allowance of up to $12,000, to full-time graduate students pursuing a master's- or doctoral-level degree in oceanography, marine biology, or maritime archaeology, including the curation, preservation, and display of maritime artifacts. The stipend is not intended to be used as a research grant. Must be a U.S. citizen attending an accredited

U.S. institution. Selection is based on financial need (40%), academic achievement (20%), recommendations (18%), organizational, analytical, and written communication skills based on statement of intent (10%), and research and career goals and objectives (7%). Women and minority students are encouraged to apply. Deadline: mid-May.

(S, SS)
United States Department of Defense
(410) 854–6206
http://www.dod.mil/c3i/iasp

2376. (S)
Defense Acquisition Scholarship Program—NCEE

Awards ranging from $13,000 to $15,000 for graduate students pursuing master's degrees. Must be majoring in engineering, mathematics, physical sciences, or business. Applicants must be U.S. citizens and have a 3.0 GPA or better. Recipients must agree to serve the government 1 calendar year for each year they were provided a scholarship. Deadline: March 20.

2377. (S, SS)
Information Assurance Scholarship Program

Scholarships providing full cost of tuition, books, expenses, supplies, and equipment, and stipend ($15,000 graduate and $10,000 undergraduate) to graduate or upper-level undergraduate students enrolled in information assurance fields. Recipients must agree to work for the DoD as a civilian employee or to complete a service obligation with the armed forces or the National Guard or Reserves after completing course of study. Must be U.S. citizens. Program is administered by the National Security Agency. Deadline: April 8.

(S, SS)
United States Department of Education
Higher Education Programs
1990 K Street, N.W., 6th Floor
Washington, DC 20006–8521
(202) 502–7700
http://www.ed.gov/offices/OPE/HEP/iegps/flasf.html

2378. (SS)
Christa McAuliffe Fellowships

Varying number of fellowships of $25,000 to graduate and undergraduate students. Must attend an accredited institution. Contact state student loan office. Deadline: January.

2379. (H)
Foreign Language and Area Studies Fellowships Program

Fellowships of approximately $26,435 to graduate students enrolled in a program of modern foreign language training in a language for which the institution has developed or is developing performance-based instruction. Must be a U.S. citizen, national, or permanent resident. Selection based on high academic achievement. Awarded to assist in the development of knowledge, resources, and trained personnel for modern foreign language and area/international studies, to stimulate the attainment of foreign language acquisition and fluency, and to develop a pool of experts to meet national needs. Deadline: mid-November.

2380. (S)
Graduate Assistance in Areas of National Need

Fellowships providing a stipend of up to $18,060 and a tuition allowance of up to $10,857 through academic departments and programs of institutions of education to assist graduate students in a field designated as a national need: biology, chemistry, computer and information science, engineering, geological science, mathematics, and physics. Students are not eligible to apply directly to this program. Students must contact academic department to apply for this fellowship. Deadline: late November.

2381. (S)
Indian Business, Engineering, Natural Resources Fellowships

35 new scholarships and 90 continuation scholarships ranging from $600 to $34,000 to graduate and undergraduate students majoring in engineering, natural resources, related areas, and business. Must be Native American or Alaskan and U.S. citizens. Renewable for up to 4 years. Deadline: early February.

2382. (A, H, SS)
Jacob K. Javits Fellows Program

Varying number of fellowships providing up to $11,000 for tuition and fees, plus a stipend of up to $21,500, to students who are entering graduate school for the first time in the next academic year, who have not yet completed their first full year of a master's degree program (terminal degree for the field of study) or a doctoral program in selected fields of study of the arts, humanities, and social sciences. The fellowship is awarded annually for the lesser of up to 48 months or the completion of their degree. Deadline: mid-December.

(S)

United States Department of Energy—Office of Energy Research
1000 Independence Avenue, S.W.
Room 3H-087
Washington, DC 20585
(800) 342–5363
http://www.energy.gov

2383. (S)
Albert Einstein Distinguished Educator Fellowships

Fellowships lasting 10 months to elementary and secondary school math and science teachers to spend time in a congressional office or a federal agency. Fellows provide their educational expertise, years of experience, and personal insights to these offices. Past fellows have drafted legislation and influenced policy that seek to improve K–16 education in the U.S., initiated collaborations and established partnerships between federal agencies, designed and implemented national science, math, and technology education programs, and created web-based science education programs. Visit web site for additional information and deadline.

2384. (S)
DOE Student Research Participation

200 graduate and 200 faculty Summer Research Awards of varying amounts to graduate students and faculty. The program may last from 10 weeks up to 1 year. The amount of stipend depends on the level of the appointment. Students and faculty must be ma-joring, or teaching, in the fields of science and/or engineering. Applicants must be U.S. citizens or permanent residents. Deadline: December–January.

2385. (S)
Global Change Education Project
http://gonzalo.er.anl.gov/GCEP or http://www.finucar.edu/soars

Fellowships providing tuition, fees, transportation and housing for SURE activities, and a stipend to graduate students enrolled in doctoral programs in atmospheric sciences, ecology, global carbon cycles, climatology, paleoclimatolgy, terrestrial processes, integrated assessment and prediction, computer modeling, or earth system processes. Renewable up to 5 years. Must have at least a 3.0 GPA, plan a career in the global change sciences, be a U.S. citizen or permanent resident, and have completed at least 1 year of the graduate program. Deadline: February 1.

2386. (S)
Mickey Leland Energy Fellowship Program
Hispanic Internship Program (HIP)
(202) 586–5095

7 internships providing a stipend ranging from $500 to $650, plus travel expenses, to Hispanic first-year graduate or undergraduate sophomore, junior, or senior students in geology, engineering, math, and science. Internship provides either airfare or standard government relocation rates (for students who choose to drive) for 1 round trip to the internship site and to Washington, DC, for the technical forum. Must be U.S. citizens and have at least a 2.8 GPA on a 4.0 scale. Deadline: January 31.

2387. (S)
Mickey Leland Energy Fellowship Program
Historically Black College and Universities (HBCU) Program
(202) 586–7421

Internships providing a stipend ranging from $500 to $650, plus travel expenses, to African-American first-year graduate or undergraduate sophomore, junior, or senior students in geology, engineering, math, and science. Internship provides either airfare or standard government relocation rates (for students who choose to drive) for 1 round trip to the internship site and to Washington, DC, for the technical forum.

Must be U.S. citizens and have at least a 2.8 GPA on a 4.0 scale. Deadline: January 31.

2388. (S)
Mickey Leland Energy Fellowship Program
Tribal Colleges and Universities (TCU) Program
(202) 586–5095

Internships providing a stipend ranging from $500 to $650 plus travel expenses to Native American, first-year graduate or undergraduate sophomore, junior, or senior students in geology, engineering, math, and science. TCU is also open to disabled students. Internship provides either airfare or standard government relocation rates (for students who choose to drive) for 1 round trip to the internship site and to Washington, DC, for the technical forum. Must be U.S. citizens and have at least a 2.8 GPA on a 4.0 scale. Deadline: January 31.

2389. (S)
United States Department of Health & Human Services—AHCPR
Doctoral Dissertation Research Grant
Agency for Health Care Policy and Research
2101 East Jefferson Street, Suite 602
Rockville, MD 20852
(301) 594–1449
(301) 433–3091
http://www.ahrq.gov/fund/minortrg.htm

15 dissertation research grants of up to $20,000 to doctoral students to conduct research on any aspect of health care services (organization, delivery, financing, quality, etc.). Must have completed all course work and be about to begin dissertation research. Open to health or medical sciences, management, or social services. Deadline: late January, varies.

2390. (S)
United States Department of Health & Human Services
Indian Health Service Scholarships
The Reyes Building
801 Thompson Avenue, Suite 120
Rockville, MD 20852–1627
(301) 443–6197
http://www.ihs.gov/JobsCareerDevelop/DHPS/
Scholarships/Scholarship_index.asp

Financial assistance to federally recognized Native American and Native Alaska (federally recognized only) graduate students and undergraduate juniors and seniors enrolled in health professions and allied health professions programs. Recipients incur service obligations and payback requirements upon acceptance of the scholarship funding. Priority health career categories: allopathic and osteopathic medicine, nursing, pharmacy, dietetics, public health nutrition, medical technologist, dentistry, health education, medical social work, chemical dependency counseling, physician assistant, public health, clinical psychology, optometry, physical therapy, radiologic technology, respiratory therapist, ultrasonographer/x-ray, health records administration, paraoptometrics, podiatry, civil engineering, coding specialist, environmental engineering, injury prevention specialist, x-ray dental hygiene, counseling psychology, and health care administration. Applicants who are more than 4 years away from securing a degree are not eligible to apply. Each scholarship is awarded for a 1-year period, with reapplication for each continuation. For more information, visit web site. Deadline: February 28.

2391. (S)
United States Department of Health & Human Services
National Health Services Corp. Scholarship Program
1010 Wayne Avenue, Suite 1200
Silver Spring, MD 20910
(800) 638–0824
http://search.dcp.psc.gov/os/1145.html

Scholarships providing tuition, fees, educational expenses, and a monthly stipend to students accepted to or enrolled in an allopathic or osteopathic medical school, physician assistant or nursing (master's) program. Students must be pursuing careers in family and general internal medicine, pediatrics, psychiatry, obstetrics/gynecology, advanced nurse practitioner, physician assistant, or certified nurse-midwife. Must be U.S. citizens. Recipients agree to service obligation for each year of assistance received, with a minimum of 2 years service. Deadline: last Friday in March.

2392. (SS)

United States Department of Health & Human Services
National Institute of Health Associate Fellowship Program
U.S. National Library of Medicine
Project Manager
8600 Rockville Pike
Bethesda, MD 20894
(865) 241–3319
http://www.nlm.nih.gov/about/training/associate/applicinfo.html

Up to 8 fellowships providing a monthly stipend of approximately $3,000 plus a monthly health insurance stipend to graduate students and U.S. and Canadian library/information professionals. Must have earned or be completing a master's degree in an ALA-approved library/information science program, earned by August of the year of appointment, and be either a U.S. or Canadian citizen. Experience is desirable but not essential. Deadline: mid-February.

2393. (S)

United States Department of Health & Human Services
NIH Summer Fellowship Program for Medical/Dental Students
Coordinator
Office of Education
Building 2, Room 2E06
2 Center Drive, MSC 0240
Bethesda, MD 20892–0240
(301) 496–2427
http://www.training.nih.gov/student/srfp/index.asp

125 internships lasting at least 8 weeks providing salaries ranging from $1,900 to $2,700 per month to medical and dental school students. Interns attend lectures and conduct research. Must be attending accredited medical or dental schools. For more information, visit web site. Applications must be submitted on-line. Deadline: February 1.

2394. (S)

United States Department of Health & Human Services
NIH Summer Internship Program
Coordinator
Office of Education
Building 2, Room 2E06
2 Center Drive, MSC 0240
Bethesda, MD 20892–0240
(301) 496–2427
http://www.training.nih.gov/student/srfp/index.asp

200 internships providing stipends ranging from $1,900 to $2,700 per month to graduate and professional school students. Internships are 8 weeks long during the summer. Acceptable majors are biology, biochemistry, chemistry, computer science, engineering, mathematics, psychology, physics, and liberal arts. Must be U.S. citizens or legal residents. For more information, visit web site. Applications must be submitted on-line. Deadline: February 1.

2395. (A, H, SS)

United States Department of State
Office of Academic Exchange Programs, European Programs Branch
Internships
SA-44
301 4th Street, S.W.
Washington, DC 20547
(202) 205–0525
(202) 619–4420
http://exchanges.state.gov/education/nonfulb/index2.htm#Graduate

Numerous unpaid and limited-pay internships for graduate students and undergraduate juniors and seniors. Students may be majoring in a wide variety of fields, including architecture, some humanities, certain sciences, and select social sciences. Interns gain firsthand knowledge of how U.S. diplomacy works and develop relationships with professionals in the field. Both domestic and overseas internships are available. Apply early. Deadline: November 1.

(H, SS)

United States Department of State
Office of Academic Exchange Programs, European Programs Branch
SA-44
301 4th Street, S.W.
Washington, DC 20547
(202) 205–0525
(202) 619–4420

2396. (H, SS)

**Edmund S. Muskie Freedom Support Act
Graduate Fellowship Program**

Approximately 340 fellowships including university tuition, fees, room, board, health insurance, monthly stipend, book allowance, and international and domestic travel to students under 40 years of age pursuing a master's degree. Selection is based on academic achievement and leadership potential. Award is for study in business administration, economics, education, environmental policy/management, international affairs, journalism and mass communications, law, library or information science, public administration, public health, or public policy (M.P.A./M.P.P.). Must attend an accredited U.S. institution. Administered by American Councils for International Education. Deadline: late October.

2397. (SS)

Edmund S. Muskie Ph.D. Fellowship Program

24 fellowships to graduate students from Georgia, the Russian Federation, and Ukraine to study on the doctoral level in the U.S. in business administration, economics, public administration, and public policy. Fellows must perform 1 year of public service in their home country for every year of supported study. Deadline: none specified.

2398. (H, SS)

Ron Brown Fellowship Program

Approximately 52 fellowships to graduate students and professionals from Albania, Bosnia and Herzegovina, Bulgaria, Croatia, the Federal Republic of Yugoslavia (Serbia and Montenegro), Macedonia, Romania, and Slovenia. Awarded for study at the master's degree level in an accredited U.S. institution. Award is for study in business administration (M.B.A.), economics (M.A.), educational administration (M.A.) Environmental policy/management (M.A.), journalism/communications (M.A.), law (LL.M.), or public administration/public policy (M.P.A./M.P.P.). Must be a citizen of a participating country, under the age of 49 at time of application, have an undergraduate degree or equivalent, taken

the TOEFL (minimum of 550 written or 213 computer based), GRE, or GMAT depending on field. 2 years of relevant professional work experience is preferred. This fellowship is funded by Support for Eastern European Democracy Act (SEED), sponsored by the Department of State and Bureau of Educational and Cultural Affairs and administered by Institute of International Education. Deadline: none specified.

(S, SS)

United States Department of Transportation
Director, Universities & Grants Programs
National Highway Institute, HHI-20
Federal Highway Administration
4600 N. Fairfax Drive, Suite 800
Arlington, VA 22203
(703) 235–0538
http://www.nhi.fhwa.dot.gov

2399. (S, SS)

Eisenhower Grants for Research Fellowships

Fellowships providing a tuition allowance, plus a monthly stipend of $1,700 (master's), $2,000 (doctoral), or $1,450 (undergraduate seniors), to graduate (master's and doctoral) students as well as graduating undergraduate seniors who are in a field of study that is directly related to transportation and who plan to enter the transportation profession. Recipients select 1 or more projects to conduct research on at one of the DOT facilities in the Washington, DC, metro area. Deadline: February 15.

2400. (S, SS)

Eisenhower Transportation Fellowship Program

Fellowships providing a tuition allowance of up to $10,000, plus a monthly stipend of $1,700 (master's) or $2,000 (doctoral), to graduate (master's and doctoral) students as well as graduating undergraduate seniors who are in a field of study that is directly related to transportation and who plan to enter the transportation profession. Deadline: February 15.

2401. (S)

**United States Information Agency
Fulbright Program**
M/PDP Room 518
301 4th Street, S.W., Room 602
Washington, DC 20547

Financial assistance to U.S. graduate students, teachers, and scholars to study, teach, lecture, and conduct research abroad in any area of study. It also assists foreign nationals to study, teach, lecture, and conduct research in the United States. Selection based on academic achievement, professional qualities, potential for success, ability and willingness to share ideas and experiences with people of diverse cultures.

(SS)

United States Institute of Peace

1200 17th Street, N.W., Suite 200
Washington, DC 20036–3011
(202) 429–1700
http://www.usip.org/fellows.html

2402. (SS)
Jennings Randolph Program for International Peace

10-month senior fellowships to outstanding scholars, policymakers, journalists, and other professionals to work on important issues concerning international conflict and peace. Fellowship provides a stipend of up to $80,000 (dependent on previous year's salary and professional standing), plus an office, voice mail, and a part-time research assistant. Visit web site for more information. Deadline: mid-September.

2403. (SS)
Peace Scholar Dissertation Fellowship

Fellowships of $17,000 to graduate students to support doctoral dissertations that explore the sources and nature of international conflict and strategies to prevent or end conflict and to sustain peace. Open to citizens of all countries who are enrolled in accredited U.S. colleges or universities. Must have completed all degree requirements except for dissertation. Visit web site for more information and an application. Deadline: November 1.

(Contest)

United States Naval Institute
Naval Institute Essay & Photo Contests

291 Wood Road
Annapolis, MD 21402–5034

(410) 295–1058
http://www.usni.org/Membership/CONTESTS.htm

2404. (Contest)
Arleigh Burke Essay Contest

1 first prize of $3,000, plus a Naval Institute gold medal and life membership in the Naval Institute; 1 second prize of $2,000 and a silver medal; and 1 third prize of $1,000 and a bronze medal, for a 3,500-word essay on any subject relating to the mission of the Naval Institute: "The advancement of professional, literary, and scientific knowledge in the naval and maritime services, and the advancement of the knowledge of sea power." Open to anyone. Deadline: December 1.

2405. (Contest)
Armed Forces Joint Warfighting Essay Contest

1 award each of $2,500, $2,000, and $1,000 for a 3,000-word essay on any subject relating to combat issues in a joint context. Essays may be heavy in uniservice detail but must have joint application. Open to anyone. Deadline: May 1.

2406. (Contest)
Enlisted Essay Contest

1 first prize award of $1,500, 1 second prize of $1,000, and 1 third prize of $500 for a 2,500-word essay on any subject relevant to military service. Open to active, reserve, and retired enlisted personnel of all service branches and countries. Deadline: September 1.

2407. (Contest)
International Navies Photo Contest

1 award each of $200, $100, and $50 for best photos of images of international naval and maritime subjects (from countries other than the United States). Amateur and professional photographers are eligible to enter up to 5 entries. For specific guidelines, rules, and updates send a self-addressed, stamped envelope to above address. Winning photos are published in the March International Navies issue of *Proceedings*. Deadline: August 1.

2408. (Contest)
Naval and Maritime Photo Contest

1 award each of $500, $350, $250, and 15 awards of $100 for best photos of naval or maritime subjects.

Amateur and professional photographers are eligible to enter up to 5 entries. For specific guidelines, rules, and updates send a self-addressed, stamped envelope to above address. Winning photos are published in the April issue of *Proceedings*. Deadline: December 31.

2409. (Contest)
Naval Intelligence Essay Contest

1 award of $1,000, plus a 5-year membership in the Naval Intelligence Professionals and 1–3 Naval Institute Press books for a 3,500-word essay on any subject pertaining to naval intelligence or intelligence support to naval or maritime forces. Open to military and civilian writers. Entries must be sent to: Naval Intelligence Essay Contest, Naval Intelligence Professionals, P.O. Box 9324, McLean, VA 22102–0324. Visit web site above for specific guidelines. Deadline: July 1.

2410. (Contest)
Tom Bartlett Marine Corps Photo Contest

1 first prize of $500, 2 second prizes of $200, and 3 third prizes of $100 for photos of any Marine Corps subject, not limited to the calendar year of the contest. Open to all amateur and professional photographers. Limit of 5 black-and-white prints, color prints, or color transparencies per person. Visit web site for contest guidelines. Deadline: February 15.

2411. (Contest)
Vincent Astor Memorial Leadership Essay Contest

1 first prize award of $1,500 plus a Naval Institute gold medal and life membership in the Naval Institute; 1 second prize of $1,000 and a silver medal; and 2 third prizes of $500 and bronze medals, for a 3,500-word essay on any subject relating to leadership in the sea services. Open to U.S. Navy, Marine Corps, and Coast Guard officers, regular and reserve, in pay grades O–1, O–2, and O–3, and officer trainees within 1 year of receiving their commissions. Deadline: February 15.

2412. (H, S, SS)
United States Olympic Committee
Intern Coordinator
One Olympic Plaza
Colorado Springs, CO 80909–5760
(719) 632–5551
http://www.usoc.org

25 to 30 internships during the summer, fall, and spring open to graduate students, recent college graduates, and upper-level undergraduate students. Internship pays $45 per week plus room and board. Interns are assigned to positions in Colorado Springs, CO; Lake Placid, NY; or Marquette, MI. Internships are in computer science, broadcasting, journalism, accounting, sports administration, public relations, marketing, fundraising, and athlete performance. Previous interns have written for *Olympic Coach,* arranged job interviews and employment for athletes, studied athletes' job training and job transition, and designed exercise programs for high school and college volleyball players. Students must submit a résumé, transcript, completed application form, and 3 faculty references. Students may also enclose up to 3 letters of recommendation and other relevant information (but not in page protectors or binders). Applicants to the journalism program must submit 6 recent writing samples photocopied onto $8\frac{1}{2}" \times 11"$ paper. Deadline: June 1 (fall); February 15 (summer); and October 1 (winter/spring).

(A, SS)
University Film and Video Association
Cheryl Justis
University of Illinois Press
1325 South Oak Street
Champaign, Il 61820–6903
(866) 244–0626
(217) 244–0626
(217) 244–9910 (Fax)

2413. (SS)
American Pavilion/Bon Appétit Culinary Program
http://www.ampav.com/ampav.html

A 12-day program open to culinary students, apprentices, and young professionals to work with a 15- to 20-person culinary team during the Cannes Film Festival. Individuals enjoy pre-Festival tours of wineries, restaurants, and outdoor markets in the south of France and meet such noted chefs as France's Roger Verge (Moulin de Mougins). The culinary crew is responsible for up to 1,000 meals per day—for lunches, dinners, receptions, parties, and other special events. Must submit a completed application form and at least 1 written recommendation from a teacher or employer. Students must also submit a copy of latest transcript with a $65 application fee payable to The American Pavilion and 2 passport-size photos for Festival accreditation. Participants are responsible for their round-trip transportation to Cannes. The Pavilion provides housing at a French residence apartment and 2 meals a day. For more information, call (310) 209–1200, e-mail culinary@ampav.com, or visit web site for an application. Applications are sent to: The American Pavilion, 1107½ Glendon Avenue, Los Angeles, CA 90024. Deadline: February 15.

2414. (A)
Carole Fielding Student Grants

Production grants of $4,000 and research grants of $1,000 to students enrolled in an accredited institution for projects. Application must include: a 1-page description of the project consisting of a statement of purpose, an indication of the resources available to complete the work, and a summary of the proposed production or research project; a 1-page resume of the applicant, including information on past film/video/ multimedia work and/or publications; a statement by the sponsoring UFVA member assessing the feasibility of the project and indicating his or her willingness to serve as faculty supervisor or consultant (not a "recommendation"); a 1-page budget indicating what portion of the total project will be supported by this grant. Award may be used for: (1) narrative: a copy of the script (limit: 30 minutes); (2) documentary: a short treatment (limit: 60 minutes); (3) experimental/animation/multi-media: a treatment or script, and/or storyboards no larger than 8½ × 11 inches; or (4) for research: a description of the methodology to be employed and a statement indicating the relationship of the proposed study to previous research in the field. Visit web site for application and address to send the application. Deadline: January 1.

2415. (A)
Eastman Student Scholarship Program

Scholarships of up to $5,000 to graduate and undergraduate students majoring in film, film production, or cinematography. Students must be nominated by a faculty member. The award is funded through the Kodak Student Filmmaker Program and administered by the University Film and Video Foundation. Visit web site for deadline date.

2416. (A)
L.A. Intensive

A limited number of scholarships for a weeklong program providing shared housing (2 people per room) at UCLA with 2 meals per day to film students, recent film graduates, and professionals interested in learning about the entertainment industry. Provides a one-on-one approach to the "Hollywood" terrain. Scholarship applicants are considered after all other candidates are considered and accepted. Cost for the program ranges from $1,215 to $1,850, depending on package and application date. For more information, please contact The American Pavilion at (310) 209–1300 or e-mail laintensive@ampav.com. Deadline: April 11 (early application), June 13 (general applications), and June 20 (scholarship applications).

2417. (A)
NextFrame Film Festival

First- and second-place prizes of varying amounts, as well as honorable mentions in each category. Additional awards are given for Cinematography, Editing, Screenwriting, and Director's Choice. Every finalist receives a prize. All entries must have been created while student is enrolled in an accredited college, university, or conservatory. Entries must be in any of 4 categories: animation, documentary, experimental, and narrative. Following a premiere showing at the Festival, a yearlong tour begins. Finalists are screened at university campuses, museums, media arts centers, and other venues around the world. Deadline: May 31.

2418. (A)
Scholarships

Scholarships ranging from $1,000 to $4,000 to undergraduate and graduate students working in film, video, or multimedia production or research projects in historical, critical, theoretical, or experimental studies of film or video. Must be sponsored by a faculty person who is an active member of the University Film and Video Association to be considered for this award. Deadline: January 1.

2419. (A)
Student Intern Program
Director, Kodak Student Filmmaker Program
(323) 468–4228

Internships to film students to attend and participate in the Cannes Film Festival. The program includes housing in a European-style residence apartment, 2 meals a day, an official Festival accreditation badge and the opportunity to attend Festival screenings (per ticket availability). Additionally, students can network with, and learn from, many of the entertainment industry's highest-ranking executives. Other program-related access includes prefestival workshops, Pavilion seminars, pitch sessions, and roundtables. There is an $1,850 nonrefundable program fee, and student is responsible for travel arrangements to and from France. Must submit all application documentation, a $50 nonrefundable application fee, and complete a phone interview. Deadline: November 22 (early application), January 24 (general applications), and February 24 (applications with scholarships).

2420. (A, H)
University of Alabama at Birmingham
Ruby Lloyd Apsey Play Search
Department of Theatre
Bell 101
700 13th Street South
Birmingham, AL 35294
(205) 934–3236
http://theatre.hum.uab.edu

Playwriting competition for talented, new playwrights. Entries must be original, unproduced, unpublished, and full-length. UAB reserves the rights for the premier production of the winning play without royalties. Especially interested in scripts by non-Americans. Deadline: January 1.

2421. (A)
University of Maryland
International Piano Festival & William Kapell Competition
College of Summer & Special Programs
College Park, MD 20742
(301) 454–5276
http://www.claricesmithcenter.umd.edu

15 awards ranging from $5,000 to $20,000 through a piano competition. Contestants must be between 18 and 33 years of age. Award is in the form of cash and recital engagements. Interested applicants must submit a taped audition. Deadline: April 1.

2422. (H)
University of Virginia
Batten Media Fellowship
P.O. Box 6550
Charlottesville, VA 22906–6500
(804) 924–7739
http://www.darden.edu/financialaid/meritsch.htm

Up to 3 fellowships providing full tuition and a partial living stipend to professionals in all aspects of the media to pursue a master's of business administration at the Darden Graduate School of Business. Must be U.S. citizens, have at least 3 years of full-time employment in the news media, and be offered admission through the standard admission process. Visit web site for more information. Deadline: March 29.

2423. (S)
Vanderbilt Minority Summer Research Program
Vanderbilt University
VU Station B 351820
Nashville, TN 37235–1820
http://medschool.mc.vanderbilt.edu/
minority_summer_research/html/eligibility.html

Internships providing $1,500 per month to minority medical students and undergraduate juniors to conduct research. Internships last from 8 to 13 weeks in the summer. Deadline: February 15.

2424. (A)
Vermont Council on the Arts Fellowships
136 State Street—Drawer 33
Montpelier, VT 05633–6001
(802) 828–3291
http://www.vermontartscouncil.org/grants/artists.
html

Varying number of fellowships of $2,000 to artists who are Vermont residents. Awards are not for academic study but rather to support career advancement in the area of art and performing art. Proposed project should be in the same genre as submitted work. Deadline: March 1.

2425. (S)
Vertical Flight Foundation
Undergraduate/Graduate Scholarships
217 North Washington Street
Alexandria, VA 22314–2520

(703) 684–6777

http://www.vtol.org/vff.html

9 scholarships of up to $2,000 to graduate and undergraduate students who are majoring in aerospace engineering, electrical engineering, or mechanical engineering and interested in helicopter or vertical flight. Scholarships are good at any accredited U.S. college or university. Deadline: February 1.

2426. (Contest)

Veterans of the Abraham Lincoln Brigade
George Watt Award Committee Chair
799 Broadway
New York, NY 10003
http://www.alba-valb.org
eunicelipton2@aol.com

At least 2 awards of $500 to a graduate and an undergraduate student who create a work about the Spanish Civil War, the antifascist political or cultural struggles of the 1920s and 1930s, or the lifetime histories and contributions of the Americans who served beside the Spanish Republic from 1937 to 1938. Entry may take the form of an essay, visual art, video or film, a dance, theatrical work, or a musical composition. Essays must be at least 5,000 words, and creative art forms should reflect at least 1 semester's worth of work. Work will be judged on the basis of originality and effectiveness of argument or presentation. The work must have been created to fulfill an undergraduate or graduate course or degree requirement. Deadline: April 1.

2427. (H)

Viacom Boston Internship Program
1170 Soldiers Field Road
Boston, MA 02134
http://www.wbz4.com

Unpaid internships open to graduate and undergraduate seniors, juniors, and sophomores who are able to receive credit for the internship. Internships run in 3 quarters, and interns work at least 15 hours per week. Most interns are journalism or communication majors, but internships may be of interest to students majoring in English, history, political science, fine arts, marketing, computer science, and other related studies. For more information, visit web site. Deadline: rolling.

2428. (A)

Virginia Center for the Creative Arts
Goldfarb Family Fellowship for Nonfiction Writers
Mt. San Angelo, Box VCCA
Sweet Briar, VA 24595
(804) 946–7236
http://www.vcca.com/newdir.html

1 fellowship providing a fully funded 2-week residency where a nonfiction writer may concentrate solely on his or her creative work. As with all residencies at the VCCA, writers will be provided a private bedroom, separate studio, and 3 prepared meals a day in a community of 20 other artists. Offered each year to 1 nonfiction writer during the fall scheduling period. The application process will be the same as the regular VCCA application process. You may not submit a reapp. You must submit work samples. Obtain an application by calling the VCCA office or from the web site. Deadline: May 15

2429. (A, H)

Virginia Museum of Fine Arts
Graduate & Professional Fellowships
Virginia Museum Boulevard & Grove Avenue
2800 Grove Avenue
Richmond, VA 23221–2466
(804) 340–1400
http://www.vmfa.state.va.us

12 to 18 awards of up to $5,000 to graduate students majoring in art, fine art, art history, architecture, photography, film, or video. Professional Artist Fellowships are also available. Applicants must be Virginia residents (for at least 5 of the last 10 years) and U.S. citizens or legal residents. Deadline: March 1.

2430. (A)

Virgin Islands Board of Education
Music Scholarships
No. 44–46 Kongens Gade,
Charlotte Amalie, VI 00802
(340) 774–0100
http://www.usvi.org/education
education@usvi.org

1 scholarship of $2,000 to graduate or undergraduate students. Must be Virgin Island residents enrolled in an accredited music program at a postsecondary institu-

tion. The scholarship is renewable if recipient maintains at least a C average. Deadline: March 31.

2431. (S)
Virgin Islands Board of Education
Nursing & Other Health Scholarships
P.O. Box 11900
St. Thomas, VI 00801
(809) 774–4546
http://www.usvi.org/education

Scholarships of up to $1,800 to graduate or undergraduate students accepted to, or enrolled in, an accredited school of nursing or medicine or an accredited institution offering courses in a health-related area. Must be residents of the Virgin Islands. Renewable with reapplication. Must have at least a C average. Deadline: March 31.

2432. (A)
WAMSO Young Artist Competition
1111 Nicollet Mall
Minneapolis, MN 55403
(612) 371–5654
http://www.wamso.org/about/contactus.html

Numerous prizes and scholarships ranging from $500 to $5,250 (first prize) plus performance to graduate and undergraduate students (performing on the piano or orchestral instruments) in schools in IA, MN, MO, NE, ND, SD, WI, Manitoba, or Ontario. Contestants must not be older than 26 years old as of December 1 of application year. Please indicate instrument when requesting a list of repertoires and information. Deadline: November 1.

(H, S, SS)
Washington Center for Internships and Academic Seminars
2301 M Street, N.W., Fifth Floor
Washington, DC 20037
(202) 336–7600
(800) 486–8921
http://www.twc.edu
info@twc.edu

2433. (SS)
Asian Pacific Internship Program

Internships to Asian graduate or undergraduate students to build their knowledge of U.S.-Asia and Pacific Rim relations by working in a challenging environment, interacting with key government, business, and association leaders, and developing leadership and professional skills. Interns gain firsthand experience with the policy-making process and have the opportunity to explore Asia-related career options. Must have at least a 2.75 GPA or above. Deadline: none specified.

2434. (SS)
Cordova Congressional Internship Program

20 internships to Puerto Rican graduate and undergraduate students to intern in a congressional office. The program enables students to explore issues of leadership and diversity, develop professional skills, and investigate various practical and theoretical aspects of governance and citizenship. Deadline: none specified.

2435. (SS)
Diversity Leadership Programs

Internships providing an assistance award of $2,000 to minority graduate and undergraduate students to experience the challenge and responsibility of being an element of society's public voice. Selection is based on academic achievement and goals. Must be a U.S. citizen or permanent resident. Deadline: none specified.

2436. (S, SS)
Environment Internship Program

Internships for graduate or undergraduate students to prepare future leaders to recognize and manage complex environmental issues and programs. The internship emphasizes leadership development based on hard choices new generations of environmental advocates will face in an uncertain future. Must have at least a 3.0 GPA, good written and verbal communication skills, a command of the English language, and an active interest in the environment. Deadline: none specified.

2437. (H, SS)
Mass Communications Internship Program

Internships providing $250 toward housing to graduate and undergraduate students in mass communications, such as journalism, broadcasting, production, advertising, public relations, photography, electronic communication, and graphic design. Interns attend White House press conferences, write stories for national and international publications, assist in production of television news shows, develop strategic marketing campaigns, conduct interviews, and draft press releases and media advisories. Deadline: none specified.

2438. (SS)
Nonprofits Leaders Program

Internships providing $1,000 toward housing, open to graduate and undergraduate students, that provides a unique opportunity to learn about career opportunities in the nonprofit sector. The program seeks to develop future leadership for the nonprofit community. Students work 4 days per week at their internship and 1 day taking part in a variety of programs designed to increase students' knowledge of the nonprofit sector and their leadership abilities. Deadline: none specified.

2439. (SS)
North American Leadership Programs and the Americas Internship Program

Internships for graduate and undergraduate students from the United States, Canada, Mexico, and Central and South America to explore public policy and international trade as upcoming leaders of the Western Hemisphere. This program is subdivided to include the Governors Leadership Program (El Programa de los Gobernadores) for students from Mexico and the Americas Internship Program for students from Central and South America. Deadline: none specified.

2440. (SS)
Women in Public Policy (WIPP)

Internships providing $1,000 toward housing costs open to female graduate and undergraduate students to prepare for careers in public policy by providing professional work experience and improving personal, professional, and academic well-being. Interns conduct research, write briefings and press releases on women's issues, write grant proposals, fundraise, coordinate events for political campaigns, serve as advocates for battered women in judicial proceedings, and write and produce marketing communications materials for women-owned businesses. Deadline: none specified.

2441. (A, H)
The Washington Prize
The Word Works
P.O. Box 42164
Washington, DC 20015
(202) 543–1868
http://www.writer.org/wordwork/washington_prize.html

1 first prize of $1,500 for an unpublished poetry manuscript ranging from 48 to 64 pages. Send a self-addressed, stamped envelope for guidelines or visit web site. Charges $20 fee. This is a cash award, not a scholarship competition. Deadline: March 1.

2442. (S)
Water Environment Federation
Student Paper Competition
601 Wythe Street
Alexandria, VA 22314–1994
(800) 666–0206
(703) 684–2452
http://www.wef.org

Awards of $250, $500, and $1,000 in each of 4 categories for papers written by graduate and undergraduate students on water pollution. Must submit 500- to 1,000-word abstracts on papers dealing with water pollution control, water quality problems, water-related concerns, or hazardous wastes. Individuals who have graduated within 1 calendar year are also eligible. Send a self-addressed, stamped envelope for guidelines. Deadline: January 1.

2443. (A)
Waverly Community House, Inc.
F. Lammont Belin Arts Scholarships
Scholarships Selection Committee
P.O. Box 142
1115 N. Abington Road
Waverly, PA 18471
(570) 586–8191
http://www.waverlycomm.com/belinarts.htm

Awards of up to $10,000 to artists in the following areas: painting, sculpture, music, drama, dance, literature, architecture, photography, printmaking, or film. Must live or have lived in the Abington or Pocono Northeastern

Region of Pennsylvania (Bradford, Carbon, Lackawanna, Luzerne, Monroe, Montour, Pike, Schuylkill, Sullivan, Susquehanna, and Wayne Counties). Applicants do not need to be a graduate student who is formally trained in any academic or professional program. Must furnish proof of ability. Deadline: December 15.

2444. (A, H, S, SS)
W.E.D. Educational Fund
William E. Doctor Scholarship
St. Mary's Armenian Apostolic Church
P.O. Box 39224
Washington, DC 20016
http://members.aol.com/wedfund/application.html

1 scholarship of up to $5,000 to a graduate, undergraduate, vocational, and/or special training student in any area of study. Must be of Armenian descent, a U.S. citizen, and enrolled in an accredited U.S. or Canadian institution. Selection based on academic achievement and financial need. Deadline: varies.

2445. (S)
Welder Wildlife Foundation
Scholarship Program
P.O. Drawer 1400
Sinton, TX 78387
(512) 364–2643
http://hometown.aol.com/welderwf/welderweb.html

10 to 15 scholarships of up to $850 to master's candidates and up to $900 to doctoral candidates who are majoring in wildlife ecology and management. Priority is given to proposals involving research conducted on the Foundation's refuge area or other areas located near Sinton, TX. Must be approved candidates at accredited institutions in the U.S. Renewable. Send a self-addressed, stamped envelope for an application. Deadline: October 1.

2446. (Contest)
Wellspring's Short Fiction Contest
Costalia Bookmakers, Inc.
P.O. Box 29527
Brooklyn Center, MN 55429
(612) 471–9259
http://www.hellskitchen.com/inkcon1.htm

Awards of $25, $75, and $100 twice a year for previously unpublished short fiction. Send a self-addressed,

stamped envelope for guidelines. Charges $10 entry fee. This is a cash award, not a scholarship competition. Deadline: January 1.

2447. (S)
Western Growers Association Scholarship Fund
P.O. Box 2130
Newport Beach, CA 92658
(949) 863–1000
http://www.wga.com

Scholarships of $1,000 for graduate and undergraduate study in agriculture. Must be enrolled in a 2- or 4-year accredited institution. There may be other restrictions. Write an introductory letter and include a self-addressed, stamped envelope. Deadline: May 1.

2448. (A, S, SS)
Western Interstate Commission for Higher Education (WICHE)
Minority Doctoral Scholars Program
P.O. Box 9752
Boulder, CO 80301–9752
(303) 541–0200
http://www.wiche.edu/home.htm

Grants providing a stipend of $12,000, plus $5,000 toward tuition and fees, to minority doctoral students in the arts, business, engineering, or science. Education is not area of emphasis, with the exception of mathematics education and science education. Must not already be enrolled in a doctoral program. Must be Colorado residents or planning to attend a doctoral program in Colorado. Deadline: none specified.

2449. (SS)
West Virginia Association of Land Surveyors
LSAW Auxiliary Scholarship
603 E. Iowa Street
Gassaway, WV 26624
(304) 364–5621
http://www.wvals.org

1 or more scholarships of varying amounts to graduate and undergraduate students pursuing a career in land surveying. Must be planning to practice in the state of West Virginia. Selection is based on academic achievement, references, extracurricular activities, goals essay, and personal interview. Visit web site for more

information, contact person, and application. Deadline: December 31.

(S, SS)

Weyerhaeuser
P.O. Box 9777
Federal Way, WA 98063–9777
(253) 924–2345
(800) 525–5440
http://www.weyerhaeuser.com

2450. (S, SS)
Internships

35 to 40 6-month summer/fall and winter/spring internships providing round-trip travel and a salary ranging from $440 to $560 per week for graduate students and from $280 to $400 per week for undergraduates. Open to graduate students and upper-level undergraduate students majoring in computer science, management information systems, computer information systems, industrial engineering, electrical engineering, or physics. Internships are at the Tacoma, WA, office and at 250 offices and plants nationwide. Deadline: January 10 (summer/fall) and October 1 (winter/spring).

2451. (S)
Science Internships

210 3-month summer internships providing round-trip travel and a salary ranging from $440 to $560 per week for graduate students and from $280 to $400 per week for undergraduates majoring in engineering (mechanical, chemical, electrical, or industrial), pulp and paper science, forestry, environmental science, accounting, or communications. Internships are at the Tacoma, WA, office and at 250 offices and plants nationwide. Graduate students are eligible for internships in Human Resources. Deadline: rolling.

2452. (A, H, S, SS)
White House Fellows Program
1600 Pennsylvania Avenue, N.W.
Washington, DC 20500
(202) 395–4522
http://www.whitehouse.gov/fellows/about/faq.html

Fellowships providing a salary of approximately $83,000 to individuals who have at least completed their undergraduate education and are working in their chosen professions. Fellows spend a year working full-time as paid special assistants to senior White House staff, the Vice-President, Cabinet Secretaries, and other top-ranking government officials. Deadline: February 1.

2453. (A, SS)
Whitney Museum of American Art
Internship Program
Personnel Office
945 Madison Avenue
New York, NY 10021
(212) 570–3600
http://www.whitney.org/information/employment.shtml
hr@whitney.org

20 internships providing no compensation to graduate students and undergraduate juniors and seniors interested in art museums. Interns are assigned to curatorial, development, education, film and video, library, operations, public relations, publications, and registrar in New York City or Stamford, CT. Internships last for 8 weeks full-time during the summer and from 10 to 16 weeks part-time during the fall and spring. Deadline: March 1 (summer) and rolling (fall and spring). Many departments at the Whitney Museum welcome student interns year-round to work on a variety of projects and gain valuable in-depth museum experience. There is also a formalized summer internship program, primarily for college juniors and seniors, with an application deadline of March 1. If interested in any positions, please send résumé, cover letter, and salary requirements by mail or e-mail. Deadline: none specified.

2454. (A)
Wichita State University Playwriting Contest
Wichita State University Theatre
WSU, Box 31
Wichita, KS 67208
http://finearts.wichita.edu/performing/contest.asp

2 or 3 awards for short or full-length plays by graduate or undergraduate U.S. college students. Any subject or style except musicals or children's plays may be submitted, but must be original, unpublished, and unproduced. Send a self-addressed, stamped envelope for

rules or visit web site. This is a cash award, not a scholarship competition. Deadline: February 15 (postmark).

2455. (S)
The Wildlife Society
Internship Coordinator
5410 Grosvenor Lane, Suite 200
Bethesda, MD 20814
(301) 897–9770
http://www.wildlife.org

2 internships providing $250 per week to graduate students, recent college graduates, and undergraduate students to work in Bethesda. The Wildlife Society is a nonprofit organization dedicated to enhancing the scientific, technical, managerial, and educational capability of wildlife professionals. Interns work in the Society's policy department, where they research conservation issues, prepare background information for use in testimony or comments, and assist with the preparation of Society publications. Internships last for 24 weeks and are conducted from January to June or July to December. Deadline: December 5 (January–June) and June 5 (July–December).

2456. (Contest)
Wildwood Prize in Poetry
ATTN: Director
Rose Lehrman Arts Center 213-E
Harrisburg Area Community College
One HACC Drive
Harrisburg, PA 17110–2999
(717) 780–2487
(800) 222–4222
http://www.hacc.edu

1 prize of $500 and publication is given each year for the best poem under 100 lines. Submit 1 to 3 poems in duplicate (1 copy should state author's name, address and telephone number). A $5 reading fee is required. Send self-addressed, stamped envelope for guidelines. Submit after September 30. This is a cash award, not a scholarship competition. Deadline: November 30.

2457. (S)
William T. Grant Foundation
Faculty Scholars Program—Research on Children, Adolescents, & Youth
570 Lexington Avenue, 18th Floor
New York, NY 10022–6837
(212) 752–0071
written inquiries only
http://www.wtgrantfoundation.org

Fellowships of up to $35,000 per year for 4 years to beginning investigators who are faculty members at universities or nonprofit institutions, national or international. Must be interested in the sociological and/or medical causes and consequences of factors that compromise the health development of children. Deadline: July 1.

2458. (S)
Wilson Ornithological Society
Research Grants
c/o Museum of Zoology
University of Michigan
Ann Arbor, MI 48109–1079
http://www.ummz.lsa.umich.edu/birds/wos.html

1 or 2 awards of up to $600 to graduate students, young professionals, and ornithologists to perform any kind of avian research. Award is only for research on birds, not for academic tuition. Interested individuals must submit a research proposal. Deadline: January 15.

2459. (A, H, S, SS)
Winchester Foundation
P.O. Box 1005
Winchester, IN 47394
(781) 756–8020
http://www.wfee.org/about.html

4 scholarship grants ranging from $190 to $6,000 to graduate, professional school, and undergraduate students in any field of study. Must attend accredited U.S. institutions and be residents of Indiana. Must be U.S. citizens or permanent residents. Write an introductory letter briefly detailing your educational and financial situation. Deadline: none specified.

2460. (S)

Wisconsin League for Nursing Inc.
Scholarships
P.O. Box 107
Long Lake, WI 54542
(414) 332–6271
http://www.cuw.edu/wln/ed_programs.htm

Scholarships of $500 to registered nurses pursuing a diploma or degree (B.S.N.-R.N. seeking M.S.N., R.N. seeking B.S.N., or A.D.N. diploma) in an accredited program in Wisconsin. Must be halfway through academic program. Must have at least a 3.0 GPA and demonstrate financial need. Must be recommended by dean or director at NLN-accredited school. Contact financial aid office or nursing department for an application. Must be Wisconsin residents and U.S. citizens. Deadline: February 28.

2461. (A)

Wolf Trap Foundation for the Performing Arts
Intern Coordinator
1624 Trap Road
Vienna, VA 22182
(703) 255–1900
http://www.wolf-trap.org

20 12-week internships during the summer (full-time), fall (part-time), and spring (part-time) providing $150 per week compensation open to graduate students, recent graduates, and undergraduate sophomores, juniors, seniors. Though open to all majors, 2 departments have some prerequisites. Interns gain valuable theater operations experience and a taste of the footlights. Deadline: March 10 (summer); rolling (fall and spring).

(H, S, SS)

Women in Aviation International
P.O. Box 11287
Daytona Beach, FL 32120–1287
(386) 226–7996
http://www.wiai.org

2462. (H, S, SS)
Adela R. Scharr Memorial Scholarship

1 scholarship of at least $500 to a female graduate or undergraduate student in engineering, sciences, liberal arts, business, or flight/maintenance training. If an undergraduate, must be a sophomore or above, have at least a C average. Visit web site for more information and deadline.

2463. (S, SS)
Alaska Chapter 99s

1 scholarship each of $500 and $1,000 to female graduate or undergraduate students. Must be residents of Alaska. The $1,000 scholarship is to a licensed woman pilot pursuing an advanced rating or certificate or pursuing a career in aviation. The $500 award is for private pilot training. Recipients must complete the goal for which the scholarship will be used within 12 months of receiving the award. They must also attend a Ninety-Nines meeting to report on their progress. Visit web site for more information and an application. Deadline: June 30.

2464. (S)
Career Scholarships

Awards of varying amounts to cover the cost of training to complete an advanced pilot or aviation training course, such as multiengine rating or jet-type rating, a flight instructor or airline transport pilot certificate, or college course. Applicants must be 2-year members of the Ninety-Nines. Visit web site for more information. Deadline: January 5.

2465. (SS)
Future Woman Pilot Scholarships

Scholarships of up to $1,000 to female graduate and undergraduate students and individuals to help them complete their Private Pilot certificate. Must be a Future Woman Pilot member of the Ninety-Nines. Must hold a current medical certificate, have logged at least 20 hours of flight time, have soloed, passed the Private Pilot Written Test, and a have financial need. Deadline: January 5.

2466. (H, SS)
Research Scholar Grants

Grants of varying amounts to graduate students, established scholars, and scientists work to add to the world's knowledge of women in aviation and aerospace. May be used to document and foster the leadership role of women in all facets of aviation, including social, economic, engineering, historical, political. Visit web site for more information and deadline.

2467. (S, SS)
Scholarships

Varying numbers of scholarships of varying amounts to female graduate and undergraduate students in dispatching, engineering, flight training (private pilot, type ratings), maintenance, aviation management. Selection based on academic achievement, attitude toward self and others, commitment to success, dedication to career, motivation, reliability, responsibility and teamwork, and financial need. Visit web site for more information. Deadline: early December.

2468. (SS)
Women in Corporate Aviation Career Scholarships

2 scholarships of $1,000 to female graduate or undergraduate students or individuals pursuing a career in corporate/business aviation. Award can be used toward the NBAA Professional Development Program courses, flight training, dispatcher training, or upgrades in aviation education, but it cannot be used for general business course work. If in college, must have a 3.25 GPA on a 4.0 scale. Deadline: none specified.

2469. (S)
Women in Defense
Horizons Foundation Scholarship Program
2111 Wilson Boulevard, Suite 400
Arlington, VA 22201–3061
(703) 247–2552
http://wid.ndia.org/horizon/index.htm

Scholarships of varying amounts to female graduate and undergraduate (juniors or seniors) students pursuing a career related to national security and/or national defense. Fields of preferred study include security studies, military history, government relations, engineering, computer science, physics, mathematics, business (as it relates to national security), law (as it relates to national security), international relations, political science, and economics. Other fields may be considered if relevance to national security or defense can be demonstrated. Selection based on academic achievement, participation in defense and national security activities, field of study, work experience, statement of objectives, recommendations, and financial need. Deadline: November 1 (spring) and July 1 (fall).

(H, S, SS)
Women of the Evangelical Lutheran Church of America (ELCA)
8765 W. Higgins Road
Chicago, IL 60631–4189
(800) 638–3522, ext. 2736
http://www.elca.org

2470. (H)
Amelia Kemp Scholarship

1 scholarship of approximately $1,200 to a minority graduate, professional school, undergraduate, or vocational student for a career other than the ordained ministry. Must be at least 21 years of age, a U.S. citizen, and a member of the ELCA. Should have had at least a 2-year interruption in education since high school. Selection based on academic achievement, goals, and involvement with Women of the ELCA. Visit web site for more information. Deadline: February 15.

2471. (SS)
Arne Administrative Scholarship

1 scholarship ranging from $450 to $1,000 to a graduate or professional school student interested in advancing in their field as an administrator. Must be a U.S. citizen and a member of the ELCA. Selection based on evidence of being a decision maker, of having the ability and willingness to study, and involvement in Women of the ELCA. Visit web site for more information. Deadline: February 15.

2472. (H, SS)
Belmer Scholarship

1 scholarship of approximately $1,200 to a graduate, professional school, undergraduate, or vocational student studying for service abroad. Must be at least 21 years of age, a U.S. citizen, and a member of the ELCA. Should have had at least a 2-year interruption in education since high school. Selection based on academic achievement, goals, and involvement with Women of the ELCA. Visit web site for more information. Deadline: February 15.

2473. (S)
Cronk Memorial Scholarship

1 scholarship of approximately $1,200 to a graduate, professional school, undergraduate, or vocational

student studying for service in health professions associated with ELCA projects abroad. Must be at least 21 years of age, a U.S. citizen, and a member of the ELCA. Should have had at least a 2-year interruption in education since high school. Selection based on academic achievement, goals, and involvement with Women of the ELCA. Visit web site for more information. Deadline: February 15.

2474. (S)
Edna Robeck Scholarship

1 scholarship of approximately $1,200 to a graduate, professional school, undergraduate, or vocational student studying for service in health professions associated with ELCA projects abroad. Must be at least 21 years of age, a U.S. citizen, and a member of the ELCA. Should have had at least a 2-year interruption in education since high school. Selection based on academic achievement, goals, and involvement with Women of the ELCA. Visit web site for more information. Deadline: February 15.

2475. (H, SS)
Emma Weinstein Scholarship

1 scholarship of approximately $1,200 to a graduate, professional school, undergraduate, or vocational student studying for service abroad. Must be at least 21 years of age, a U.S. citizen, and a member of the ELCA. Should have had at least a 2-year interruption in education since high school. Selection based on academic achievement, goals, and involvement with Women of the ELCA. Visit web site for more information. Deadline: February 15.

2476. (S)
First Triennium Board Scholarship

1 scholarship of approximately $1,200 to a graduate, professional school, undergraduate, or vocational student studying for service in health professions associated with ELCA projects abroad. Must be at least 21 years of age, a U.S. citizen, and a member of the ELCA. Should have had at least a 2-year interruption in education since high school. Selection based on academic achievement, goals, and involvement with Women of the ELCA. Visit web site for more information. Deadline: February 15.

2477. (H, SS)
Flora Prince Scholarships

1 scholarship of approximately $1,200 to a graduate, professional school, undergraduate, or vocational student studying for service abroad. Must be at least 21 years of age, a U.S. citizen, and a member of the ELCA. Should have had at least a 2-year interruption in education since high school. Selection based on academic achievement, goals, and involvement with Women of the ELCA. Visit web site for more information. Deadline: February 15.

2478. (S)
General Scholarship

1 scholarship of approximately $1,200 to a graduate, professional school, undergraduate, or vocational student studying for service in health professions associated with ELCA projects abroad. Must be at least 21 years of age, a U.S. citizen, and a member of the ELCA. Should have had at least a 2-year interruption in education since high school. Selection based on academic achievement, goals, and involvement with Women of the ELCA. Visit web site for more information. Deadline: February 15.

2479. (H)
Herbert W. & Corinne Chilstrom Scholarship
Arne Administrative Scholarship

1 scholarship ranging from $450 to $1,000 to a graduate or professional school student who is a second-career woman in the final year at an ELCA seminary. Must be a U.S. citizen and a member of the ELCA. Selection based on evidence of being a decision maker, of having the ability and willingness to study, and involvement in Women of the ELCA. Visit web site for more information. Deadline: February 15.

2480. (H, SS)
Kahler Scholarship

1 scholarship of approximately $1,200 to a graduate, professional school, undergraduate, or vocational student studying for service abroad. Must be at least 21 years of age, a U.S. citizen, and a member of the ELCA. Should have had at least a 2-year interruption in education since high school. Selection based on academic achievement, goals, and involvement with

Women of the ELCA. Visit web site for more information. Deadline: February 15.

2481. (S)
Mehring Scholarship

1 scholarship of approximately $1,200 to a graduate, professional school, undergraduate, or vocational student studying for service in health professions association with ELCA projects abroad. Must be at least 21 years of age, a U.S. citizen, and a member of the ELCA. Should have had at least a 2-year interruption in education since high school. Selection based on academic achievement, goals, and involvement with Women of the ELCA. Visit web site for more information. Deadline: February 15.

2482. (S)
Paepke Scholarship

1 scholarship of approximately $1,200 to a graduate, professional school, undergraduate, or vocational student studying for service in health professions associated with ELCA projects abroad. Must be at least 21 years of age, a U.S. citizen, and a member of the ELCA. Should have had at least a 2-year interruption in education since high school. Selection based on academic achievement, goals, and involvement with Women of the ELCA. Visit web site for more information. Deadline: February 15.

2483. (S)
Piero/Wade/Wade Scholarship

1 scholarship of approximately $1,200 to a graduate, professional school, undergraduate, or vocational student studying for service in health professions associated with ELCA projects abroad. Must be at least 21 years of age, a U.S. citizen, and a member of the ELCA. Should have had at least a 2-year interruption in education since high school. Selection based on academic achievement, goals, and involvement with Women of the ELCA. Visit web site for more information. Deadline: February 15.

2484. (H, SS)
Vickers/Raup Scholarship

1 scholarship of approximately $1,200 to a graduate, professional school, undergraduate, or vocational student studying for service abroad. Must be at least

21 years of age, a U.S. citizen, and a member of the ELCA. Should have had at least a 2-year interruption in education since high school. Selection based on academic achievement, goals, and involvement with Women of the ELCA. Visit web site for more information. Deadline: February 15.

2485. (S, SS)
Women's International Network of Utility Professionals
Fellowship Program
ATTN: Fellowships Administrator
P.O. Box 335
Whites Creek, TN 37189
(615) 876–5444
http://www.winup.org

1 fellowship each of $1,000 and $2,000 to female graduate students electrical industry (such as in advertising, business administration, communications, home economics, energy, electrical engineering, or science teacher) to conduct research. Selection based on academic achievement, financial need, and proposed research. Must be U.S. citizens or legal residents. Deadline: March 1.

(SS)
Women's Law and Public Policy Program
600 New Jersey Avenue, N.W., Suite 334
Washington, DC 20001
(202) 662–9650
http://wlppfp.org

2486. (SS)
Harriet Bung Fellowship

Fellowships of $35,000 to recent law school graduates and practicing attorneys to spend 1 year in Washington, DC. Fellows work on women's issues, primarily focusing on issues affecting women with disabilities. Visit web site for more information and application. Deadline: October 11.

2487. (SS)
Leadership & Advocacy for Women in Africa Program

Fellows in this program study for and receive a master's of law degree with emphasis on gender from Georgetown University Law Center. Deadline: none specified.

2488. (SS)
Rita Charmatz Davidson Fellowship

Fellowships of $35,000 to recent law school graduates and practicing attorneys to spend 1 year in Washington, DC. Fellows work on women's issues, primarily focusing on issues affecting poor women. Fellows are placed in Maryland. Visit web site for more information and application. Deadline: October 11.

2489. (SS)
Women's Law & Public Policy Fellowship Program

6 to 8 fellowships providing $35,000 and standard benefits to recent law school graduates and practicing attorneys to spend 1 year in Washington, DC. Fellows are placed in the offices of different entities to women's issues, primarily focusing on issues affecting women. Those students placed at the Georgetown University Law Center Domestic Violence Clinic for 2 years and leads to an LL.M. Visit web site for more information and application. Deadline: October 11.

2490. (S)
Women's National Farm and Garden Association Sarah Tyson Memorial Fellowships
Pam Henry
710 Watershed Drive
Ann Arbor, MI 48105
(734) 663–1788
http://community.mlive.com/cc/FarmandGarden

Varying numbers of fellowships of $500 to female graduate students conducting research in agriculture, horticulture, or allied subject areas. Must be enrolled in an accredited college or university in the U.S. Selection is based on research, academic achievement, and financial need. Send a self-addressed, stamped envelope for information. Deadline: April 1.

2491. (H, S, SS)
Women's Research and Education Institute Congressional Fellowships on Women and Public Policy
ATTN: Fellowship Director
1750 New York Avenue, N.W., Suite 350
Washington, D.C. 20006

(202) 628–0444
http://www.wrei.org

8 to 15 fellowships providing a $9,500 stipend, $500 for health insurance, and up to $1,500 toward 6 hours of tuition. Program trains women as potential public policy leaders. Program runs from September through April. Fellow works in a U.S. Congress office as a legislative aide on policy issues affecting women. Open to master's and doctoral students in the areas of allied health professions, biology and biomedical sciences, biomedical engineering, engineering and applied sciences, medicine, nursing, public and community health, technology management and policy, some humanities, and certain social sciences. Selection based on political and civic activity and interest in women's issues. Request applications after November 1. Deadline: February 14.

(A)
Women's Studio Workshop
Attn: Development Director
P.O. Box 489
Rosendale, NY 12472
(845) 658–9133
http://www.wsworkshop.org/
handsonart%20project.htm

2492. (A)
Clay Program

Grants of varying amounts to artists seeking a block of uninterrupted work time in our low-tech clay studio within a supportive environment. 2- to 6-week sessions are available each year from September through June. Award includes on-site housing and unlimited access to the studio. Artists are given a studio orientation but should be able to work independently. WSW offers a limited number of special scholarships to potters who agree to make bowls for the annual WSW Chili Bowl Fiesta fundraiser. Potters who will make 50 glazed bowls or 100 bisqued bowls will receive a half-cost fellowship, so the pots plus $200 will cover a 2-week residency. Please be sure to indicate on application interest in this opportunity. Deadline: March 15 postmark (fall residency) and November 1 postmark (spring residency).

2493. (A)
Hands-On-Art Visiting Artist Project

2 8-week residencies to emerging artists in the creation of an artist's book. Each award includes a $3,200 stipend, a $450 materials budget, housing, and unlimited studio access. The visiting artist lives in WSW's on-site apartment. Residents interact with students in WSW's studio-based art-in education program. Residencies will take place in September–October and March–April 2004 and provide opportunities to emerging artists who come from different regions of the country and/or diverse cultural backgrounds. Detailed information is provided on their web site. Deadline: July 1.

2494. (A)
WSW Fellowship Grants

Grants of varying amounts to emerging and established artists to provide concentrated work time and the ability to explore new ideas in a dynamic and supportive community of women artists. The facilities feature complete studios in intaglio, silkscreen, hand papermaking, photography, letterpress, and clay (a new addition to the WSW Fellowship Program). The award includes on-site housing and unlimited access to the studios. Artists are given a studio orientation but should be able to work independently. Technical assistance is available for an additional fee. Deadlines: March 15 postmark (for fall residency) and November 1 postmark (for spring residency).

(H, S, SS)
Woodrow Wilson National Fellowship Foundation
CN 5281
Princeton, NJ 08543–5281
(609) 452–7007
http://www.woodrow.org

2495. (H)
Andrew W. Mellon Fellowships in Humanistic Studies

Fellowships providing tuition, fees, and a stipend of $15,000 to graduating undergraduate seniors or recent graduates who are applying to a doctoral program. Applicants must be majoring in the traditional humanities and plan to teach at the college level. Visit web site for more information. Deadline: November 12.

2496. (SS)
Dissertation Grants in Women's Studies

15 grants of $3,000 to graduate students in any field of study that contributes to research about women that crosses disciplinary, regional, or cultural boundaries. Must have completed all predissertation requirements. May be used for expenses connected with the dissertation, including travel, books, microfilming, taping, and computer services. Deadline: none specified.

2497. (H)
Humanities at Work

20 practicum grants of up to $2,000 to doctoral students who have created summer internships for themselves outside of college teaching and research. The grants address 3 challenges: to expand the student's career horizons in the humanities, bring the insight of the humanities to all aspects of American life, and to bring the life of the larger community into the academy. Visit web site for more information. Deadline: mid-March.

2498. (H, SS)
Newcombe Dissertation Fellowships

Fellowships of $15,000 to doctoral candidates to conduct original and significant study of ethical or religious values in all fields of the humanities and/or social sciences. Must be attending an accredited U.S. institution and in the process of writing their dissertations. Visit web site for more information. Deadline: December 31.

2499. (SS)
Ronald H. Brown Commercial Service Fellowship Program

Fellowships providing tuition, room/board, travel, and mandatory fees to students pursuing an international and domestic public service education. Graduate students wanting to participate must begin the program as undergraduate juniors. Students work for the Department of Commerce during the summer. Must have at least a 3.0 GPA on a 4.0 scale and be U.S. citizens. Visit web site for specific guidelines and deadline.

2500. (H)
Thomas Pickering Graduate Foreign Affairs Fellowship

Fellowships providing tuition, room and board, mandatory fees, reimbursement for books, and 1 round-trip travel to first- and second-year graduate students in public policy and international affairs. Graduate fellows receive stipends during participation in 1 overseas and 1 domestic internship within the U.S. Department of State. May be majoring in public policy, international affairs, public administration, business, economics, political science, sociology, or foreign languages. Must have at least a 3.2 GPA on a 4.0 scale. Visit web site for more information and deadline.

2501. (S, SS)
U.S. Department of Commerce and Agriculture

Program prepares minority graduate and undergraduate students for careers in the areas of commerce and agriculture. Program begins after the sophomore undergraduate year and continues through graduate studies. State Department Fellowship includes an internship with the State Department and a graduate fellowship leading to a master's degree in international affairs. Visit web site for more information and deadline.

2502. (H)
WW Johnson & Johnson Dissertation in Women and Children's Health

Up to 15 grants of $3,000 to doctoral students in nursing, public health, anthropology, history, sociology, psychology, and social work. Must have completed all predissertation requirements and be enrolled in an accredited U.S. institution. Award encourages original and significant research about women that crosses disciplinary, regional, or cultural boundaries. Deadline: late October.

2503. (S)
Woods Hole Oceanographic Institute GFD Fellowship Program
Academic Programs Office
360 Woods Hole Road
Woods Hole, MA 02543
(508) 289–2950
http://www.whoi.edu
gfd@whoi.edu

Fellowships of $4,400 plus a travel allowance to graduate students in any field with an interest in nonlinear dynamics of rotating stratified fluids. Acceptable fields of study: classical fluid dynamics, physical oceanography, meteorology, a strophysics, planetary atmospheres, geological fluid dynamics, hydromagnetics, physics, and applied mathematics. Recipients complete a research project and present a lecture and a written report. Applications from women and underrepresented minorities are encouraged. For an application, visit web site. Deadline: February 15.

2504. (A, S)
Worcester County Horticultural Society Scholarship
Tower Hill Botanic Garden
11 French Drive
P.O. Box 598
Boylston, MA 01505–0598
(508) 869–6111
http://www.towerhillbg.org

2 scholarships ranging from $500 to $2,000 to graduate and upper-level undergraduate students majoring in landscape architecture, agriculture, floriculture, horticulture, or a related field. Must be a U.S. citizen or permanent resident and be attending an accredited 4-year college or university. Selection based on academic achievement, application, recommendation letters, and financial need. Deadline: May 1.

2505. (H, SS)
World Federalist Association (WFA) Internship Program
418 7th Street, S.E.
Washington, DC 20003
(202) 546–3950
http://www.wfa.org

10 to 15 internships lasting 3 months providing $25 per week to graduate and undergraduate students who are majoring in environmental studies, international law, political science, communications, philosophy, or related areas. Internships take place in Washington, DC, nationwide, or Amsterdam, Netherlands. Interns con-

duct research on world order and U.N. reform issues. They assist with writing, editing, and layout for newsletters and publications. They also assist with lobbying activities, coordinate college campus programs, organize conferences, write news releases, promote WFA ideas and events to the media, and work with grassroots activists. Applicants must have strong written and oral communication skills, be extremely self-motivated and directed, and be able to work on a number of projects simultaneously. Submit a letter detailing interests, a résumé, writing samples, and have an interview in person or by phone. Deadline: open.

2506. (A)
World Piano Competition
Ralf Ehrhardt, Membership Director
441 Vine St., Suite 1030
Cincinnati, OH 45202
(513) 421–5342
http://amsa-wpc.org

Awards ranging from $100 to $3,000 to pianists of all nationalities between the ages of 18 and 30 as of June 1, 2002. It is not open to previous winners of the Gold Prize in the Artist Division. Visit their web site for specific rules and guidelines. Deadline: February 15.

2507. (A)
Worldstudio Foundation Scholarships
220 Varick Street, Suite 507
New York, NY 10014
(212) 366–13137, ext. 18
http://www.worldstudio.org

Scholarships of $1,000, $1,500, and $2,000, plus 1 or 2 awards ranging from $3,000 to $5,000 (at the jury's discretion) to minority or economically disadvantaged graduate and undergraduate students and graduating high school seniors. Students must be pursuing a degree in the fine or commercial arts, design, architecture, or in 1 or more of the design/art disciplines listed on the brochure and on their web site. Selection is based on academic achievement, talent, financial need, and by their demonstrated commitment to giving back to the larger community through their work. Visit their web site for detailed information and an application. Deadline: February 14.

2508. (A)
Writers' Conferences & Centers (WC&C)
WC&C Scholarship Program
P.O. Box 386
Amherst, MA 01004
ATTN: Michael Pettit
http://awpwriter.org/contests/wccscholarship.htm

2 scholarships of $500 to writers who would like to attend a member conference of WC&C. The scholarships will be applied to fees to attend any of the member conferences of WC&C, an association of outstanding conferences, colonies, and festivals for writers. Submissions in fiction, nonfiction, and poetry will be considered. Separate submissions in different genres are permitted. A $10 reading fee, either check or money order in U.S. dollars made payable to Associated Writing Programs, must accompany all submissions. All submissions should include a self-addressed, stamped envelope for notification of results. Manuscripts cannot be returned. Deadline: March 30.

2509. (Contest)
Writer's Digest Writing Competition
ATTN: Contest Director
Writer's Digest Magazine
1507 Dana Avenue
Cincinnati, OH 45207
http://www.writersdigest.com/contests

Cash awards are available in a variety of contests: Annual *Writer's Digest* Writing Competition, Short Short Story Competition, International Self-Published Book Awards, International Screenplay Competition, *Personal Journaling's* Joy of Writing Contest, and Chronicle. Send a self-addressed, stamped envelope or visit web site for rules. This is a cash award, not a scholarship competition. Deadline: May 31.

2510. (Contest)
Writers' Journal Annual Short Story Contest
P.O. Box 394
Perham, MN 56573
(218) 346–7921
http://www.writersjournal.com
writersjournal@lakesplus.com

Contest for unpublished short stories. Send a self-addressed, stamped envelope for guidelines or contact by e-mail. Charges entry fee. This is a cash award, not a scholarship competition. Deadline: May 31.

2511. (A, H, S, SS)
Yakima Indian Nation
Scholarship Program
P.O. Box 151
Toppenish, WA 98948
(509) 865–2800
(509) 865–5528
http://www.ohwy.com/wa/y/yakamana.htm

Scholarships of $1,000 to graduate and undergraduate students in all fields of study. Must be enrolled members of the Yakima Indian Nation. May be used at any accredited institution. Deadline: July 1.

2512. (S)
Yosemite Association
Internship
P.O. Box 230
El Portal, CA 95318
(209) 379–2646
http://www.yosemite.org

25 to 30 internships providing $35 per week, $1,000 bonus at end of program, free housing, and round-trip travel to graduate students and undergraduate sophomores, juniors, and seniors. International students may apply. Interns work in 2 sections, Natural/Cultural Resources Interpretation and Wilderness Management. Interns in Interpretation prepare nature walks, talks and campfire programs in the areas of geology, plants, forest ecology, astronomy, and pioneer history. Interns in Management issue backcountry permits and discuss weather conditions, equipment, and trail conditions with hikers. Internships last from 10 to 12 weeks and are conducted during the summer, fall, or spring. Deadline: February 15.

2513. (A, H, S, SS)
Youth Foundation, Inc.
Alexander & Maude Hadden Scholarships
36 West 44th Street
New York, NY 10036
(212) 840–6291

90 renewable scholarships of $1,000 to graduate, undergraduate, and professional school students or gradu-

ating high school seniors for any field of study. Contact this Foundation in early fall. Send a self-addressed, stamped envelope. Student should write a letter briefly explaining their educational plans and financial situation. DO NOT SEND A POSTCARD! Interview is required. Selection is based on outstanding academic achievement, extracurricular activities, essay, recommendation letters, and interview. Deadline: April 15.

2514. (A, H, S, SS)
Zeta Phi Beta Sorority
Deborah Partridge Wolfe International Fellowship
National Educational Foundation
1734 New Hampshire Avenue, N.W.
Washington, DC 20009
(202) 387–3103
http://www.zphib1920.org
IHQ@ZPhiB1920.org

1 scholarship ranging from $500 to $1,000 to a female graduate or undergraduate student in any area of study. Must either be a U.S. citizen wanting to conduct full-time undergraduate or graduate study abroad or an undergraduate foreign student wanting to study full-time within the U.S. Must submit an application, transcript, and letters of recommendation. Deadline: February 1.

2515. (S)
Zonta International
Amelia Earhart Fellowship Awards
557 West Randolph Street
Chicago, IL 60661–2209
(312) 930–5848
http://www.zonta.org

35 awards of $6,000 to female graduate and postdoctoral students majoring in aerospace-related science or engineering. Award is made to recognize excellence, to encourage and support women in science and engineering, and to improve the status of women. Deadline: November 1.

SCHOLARSHIP INDEX

Crop Science Society of America 1097–1098

Crow Canyon Archeological Center 1099

Cushman Foundation for Foraminiferal Research, Inc.
  1100–1101

Cuyahoga County Medical Foundation 1102

Cyprus American Archaeological Research Institute
  1103–1104

Cystic Fibrosis Foundation 1105

Dafoe Fellowships 1106

Danforth Foundation 1107–1108

Danish Sisterhood of America Scholarships 1109–1112

Datatel Scholars Foundation 1113

Davis & Company, Inc. 1114

Defenders of Property Rights 1115

Defense Intelligence Agency 1116

Delaware State Dental Society 1117

Deloitte & Touche Foundation 1118

Delta Gamma Foundation 1119

Delta Kappa Gamma Society 1120

Delta Omicron International Music Fraternity 1121

Delta Sigma Theta Sorority 1122–1123

Demolay 1124

Deo B. Colburn Educational Foundation 1125

Dermatology Foundation 1126

Diabetes Education and Research Center 1127

Directors Guild of America 1128–1129

Dirksen Congressional Center 1130–1131

District of Columbia Commission on the Arts &
  Humanities 1132–1134

Dog Writers' Educational Trust Scholarship 1135

Drue Heinz Literature Prize 1136

Dublin Institute for Advanced Studies 1137

Dumbarton Oaks 1138–1141

Dupage Medical Society Foundation 1142

e7 Fellowship/Scholarship for Sustainable Energy
  Development 1143

The Earl Warren Legal Training Program, Inc. 1144

Earthwatch Institute 1145

Eastman Kodak Co. 1146–1148

East-West Center 1149–1150

Eaton Literary Agency 1151

Edelman Worldwide Public Relations 1152

Edmund Niles Huyck Preserve 1153

Educational Communications, Inc. 1154

Educational Foundation for Women in Accounting 1155

Educational Testing Service 1156

Education Writers Association 1157

Edward Arthur Mellinger Educational Foundation, Inc.
  1158

Edward Bangs and Elza Kelley Foundation 1159

Eighth Mountain Press 1160

Eleanor Brackenridge Scholarship Committee 1161

Electrochemical Society 1162

ELF: Eclectic Literary Forum 1163

Elmer O. and Ida Preston Educational Trust 1164

Emily Clark Balch Award 1165

Endowment Fund of Phi Kappa Psi Fraternity, Inc. 1166

Engineering Foundation 1167

Engineering Geology Foundation 1168–1169

Enrico Mattei Institute 1170

The Environmental Careers Organization (ECO) 1171–
  1173

Environmental Protection Agency 1174–1176

Epilepsy Foundation of America 1179–1182

Eppley Foundation for Research 1183

Ethel Louise Armstrong Foundation, Inc. 1184

Evrytanian Association of America 1185

Experimental Aircraft Association (EAA) Foundation,
  Inc. 1186–1188

Family Research Council 1189

Fannie and John Hertz Foundation 1190

Federal Bureau of Investigation (FBI) 1191

Federal Employee Education and Assistance Fund 1192

The Feminist Majority 1193

Fight for Sight, Inc. 1194

Fine Arts Work Center in Provincetown 1195

First Catholic Slovak Ladies Association 1196

The Flannery O'Connor Award for Short Fiction 1197

Florida Arts Council 1198

Florida Department of Education 1199–2000

Florida Department of Health & Rehabilitative Services
  1201

Florida Endowment Fund for Higher Education 1202

Florida House of Representatives 1203

Florida State Board of Administration 1204

Food and Drug Law Institute 1205–1206

Food Distribution Research Society, Inc. 1207–1208

The Ford Foundation 1209–1210

Foster City Annual Writers Contest 1211

Foundation for Biblical Archaeology 1212

Foundation for Chiropractic Education and Research
  1213–1214

Fox Inc. 1215

Fraser Institute 1216–1217

Freedoms Foundation 1218

Friedrich Ebert Foundation 1219–1220

Friends of the Library of Hawaii 1221

Friends of the National Zoo 1222–1223

Frito-Lay, Inc. 1224

Frontier Nursing Service (FNS), Inc. 1225

Fulbright Association 1226

Fulbright Teacher and Administrator Exchange 1227

Laban/Bartenieff Institute of Movement Studies 1548
Lake County Public Defender's Office 1549
Lalor Foundation 1550
Lambda Alpha International 1551
Landscape Architecture Foundation 1552
La Raza Lawyers 1553
Leakey Foundation 1554–1555
Leeway Foundation 1556–1562
The Leadership Alliance 1563
Legacy Scholarship Committee 1564
Leopold Schepp Foundation 1565–1566
Leslie T. Posey and Frances U. Posey Foundation 1567
Leukemia & Lymphoma Society 1568
Library of Congress 1569
Lloyd D. Sweet Scholarship Foundation 1570
Loren L. Zachary Society for the Performing Arts 1571
Louisiana Literature Prize for Poetry 1572
Louisiana Student Financial Assistance Commission 1573
L. Ron Hubbard's Contests 1574–1575
LucasFilm 1576
Lucent Technologies 1577–1578
Lupus Foundation of America 1579
M.A. Cartland Shackford Medical Fellowships 1580
Maine Community Foundation 1581
Maine Society of Land Surveyors 1582–1583
Maryland Higher Education Commission 1584
Maryland Society of Surveyors 1585
Maryland State Department of Education 1586
Mary Roberts Rinehart Fund 1587
Massachusetts Association of Land Surveyors and Civil Engineers 1588
Maternity Center Association 1589
Maurice Amado Foundation 1590
McLean Hospital 1591
Memphis State University 1592
Metro-Goldwyn-Mayer Studios, Inc. 1593
Metropolitan Museum of Art 1594–1610
Metropolitan Opera 1611–1613
Mexican American Physicians Association 1614
Michigan Commission on Indian Affairs 1615
Michigan Department of Education 1616
Michigan Dietetic Association Institute 1616–1625
Microsoft 1626
Midland Foundation 1627–1635
Military Chaplain Association 1637
Millay Colony for the Arts, Inc. 1636
Miller Center of Public Affairs 1638
Minerology Society of America 1639–1640
Minnesota Chippewa Tribe 1641
Minnesota Society of Professional Surveyors 1642

Minnesota State Arts Board 1643
Minority Medical Faculty Development Program 1644
Mississippi Dietetic Association 1645–1649
Missouri League for Nursing, Inc. 1650
Missouri Review 1651
Modern Language Association 1652–1659
Money for Women 1660
Montreal Neurological Institute 1661
Morris K. Udall Fellowships 1662–1664
Mortar Board National Foundation 1665
Mote Marine Laboratory 1666
Mount Desert Island Biological Lab 1667
MTV: Music Television 1668
Muktabodha Indological Research Institute 1669
Muscular Dystrophy Association 1670
Myasthenia Gravis Foundation of America 1671–1672
Mycological Society of America 1673
National Aeronautics and Space Administration 1674–1676
National Art Materials Trade Association 1677–1678
National Asian Pacific American Bar Association 1679–1680
National Association for Armenian Studies and Research, Inc. 1681
National Association for the Advancement of Colored People (NAACP) 1682–1683
National Association for the Advancement of Colored People (NAACP) Legal Defense & Educational Fund, Inc. 1684–1685
National Association of American Business Clubs (AMBUCS) 1686
National Association of Black Geologists and Geophysicists 1687
National Association of Black Journalists 1688–1693
National Association of Colored Women's Clubs 1694
National Association of Pediatric Nurse Associates & Practitioners 1695
National Association of Retail Druggists Foundation 1696
National Association of Teachers of Singing Foundation 1697
National Association of University Women (NAUW) 1698
National Association of Water Companies 1699
National Audubon Society 1700–1701
National Bar Institute 1702
National Black Law Students Association 1703–1704
National Black Nurses Association 1705–1712
National Business Aircraft Association 1713–1716
National Center for Atmospheric Research (NCAR) 1717–1718

National Center for Infectious Diseases/Association of
Public Health Laboratories 1719–1720
National Collegiate Athletic Association (NCAA) 1721–
1723
National Consortium for Graduate Degrees for
Minorities in Engineering, Inc. (GEM) 1724
National Council of State Garden Clubs, Inc. 1725
National Defense Council Foundation 1726
National Endowment for the Arts 1727–1732
National Federation of Music Clubs 1733–1736
National Federation of the Blind (NFB) Scholarships
1737–1740
National Fund for Medical Education 1741
National Gallery of Art 1742–1754
National Geographic Society Scholarship 1755
National Ground Water Association 1756
National Heart, Lung, and Blood Institute 1757
National Hemophilia Foundation 1758
National Housing Endowment 1759–1761
National Institute for Nursing Research 1762
National Institute of Arthritis & Musculoskeletal &
Skin Diseases 1763–1766
National Institute of Dental and Craniofacial Research
1767–1779
National Institute of Diabetes and Digestive and
Kidney Diseases (NIDDK) 1770
National Institute of Environmental Health Sciences
1771–1772
National Institute of General Medical Sciences
(NIGMS) 1773–1776
National Institutes of Health 1777–1779
National Institutes of Health, John E. Fogarty JSPS
Short–Term Fellowships for Biomedical and
Behavioral Research in Japan 1780
National Institutes of Health 1781–1782
National Institutes of Health, Research and Training
Opportunities 1783–1789
National Institutes of Health, Warren Grant Magnuson
Clinical Center 1790
National Italian American Foundation (NIAF) 1791–
1795
National Juried Competition 1796
National League of American Pen Women, Inc. 1797–
1805
National League of Nurses Foundation 1806
National Medical Fellowships, Inc. 1807–1824
National Multiple Sclerosis Society 1825
National Oceanic and Atmospheric Administration 1826
National Physical Science Consortium 1827
National Poetry Competition 1828
National Press Club 1829

National Press Photographers Foundation 1830–1834
National Public Radio 1835
National Radio Astronomy Observatory 1836
National Research Council (NRC) 1837–1839
National Renewable Energy Laboratory 1840–1841
National Restaurant Association Educational
Foundation 1842–1844
National Roofing Foundation 1845
National School Orchestra Association 1846
National Science Foundation 1847–1852
National Sculpture Society 1853–1855
National Security Education Program 1856
National Society of Hispanic MBAs 1857
National Society of the Daughters of the American
Revolution 1858
National Space Club 1859
National Speleological Society (NSS) 1860–1862
National Strength & Conditioning Association 1863–
1866
National Student Nurses' Association 1867–1871
National Tropical Botanical Garden 1872
National Wildlife Federation 1873–1875
National Women's Health Network 1876
National Writers Union 1877
National Zoological Park 1878–1881
Native Law Center 1882–1883
Natural Sciences and Engineering Research Council of
Canada 1884
Nature Conservancy 1885
Nebraska Space Grant Scholarships and Fellowships
1886
Nevada State Board of Education 1887
Newberry Library 1906
New England Board of Higher Education 1888–1889
New Hampshire Charitable Fund 1890
New Hampshire State Council on the Arts (Grants)
1891
New Jersey Department of Higher Education 1892
New Jersey Osteopathic Education Foundation 1893
New Jersey Society of Architects 1894
New Jersey State Federation of Women's Clubs 1895
New Jersey State Opera 1896
New Letters Literary Awards 1897–1900
New Orleans International Piano Competition 1901
New York Bureau of Higher Education Opportunity
Programs 1902–1903
New York City Opera 1904
New York Life Foundation for the Arts 1905
Nike 1907
Ninety-Nines 1908–1911
Nixon Center 1912

Non-Commissioned Officers Association 1913

North American Die Casting Association 1914

North American Nature Photography Association 1915–1916

North American Society of Pacing and Electrophysiology 1917

North Carolina State Education Assistance Authority 1918

North Carolina Symphony 1919

North Carolina Writers' Network 1920–1924

North Dakota Society of Professional Land Surveyors 1925

Nyanza Project 1926

Oak Ridge Institute for Science and Education 1927–1933

Ocean Conservancy 1934

Office of Rural Community Affairs 1935

Ohio League for Nursing 1936

Olin Instiute for Strategic Studies 1937g

Omaha Symphony Guild New Music Competition 1938

Omega Psi Phi Fraternity, Inc. 1939

Oncology Nursing Society 1940–1958

Open Society Institute 1959

OP Loftbed Scholarship 1960

Oral Health America 1961–1964

Oregon Public Broadcasting 1965

Oregon State Scholarship Commission 1966–1971

Orentreich Foundation for the Advancement of Science (OFAS) 1972

Organization of American Historians 1973–1979

Organization of American States Dept. of Fellowships & Training 1980–1982

Organization of Istanbul Armenians 1983

Our World-Underwater Scholarship Society 1984–1990

Ove Arup & Partners, California 1991

Paleontological Research Institution 1992–1993

The Paleontological Society 1994

Paramount Pictures 1995

Parkinson's Disease Foundation 1996

PEN American Center 1997–2001

Pfizer 2002–2003

PGA Tour 2004

Pharmaceutical Research and Manufacturers Association Foundation 2005

Phi Beta Kappa Society 2006

Phi Eta Sigma Founders Fund Scholarships 2007–2011

Phi Kappa Phi Honor Society 2012

Philanthropic Educational Organization (PEO) Sisterhood 2013

Phi Mu Alpha—Sinfonia Foundation 2014–2016

Phi Rho Sigma Medical Society 2017

Phi Sigma Kappa 2018

Physician Assistant Foundation of the American Academy of Physician Assistants 2019

Pilot International Foundation 2020

Pitt Rivers Museum 2021

Pittsburgh New Music Ensemble 2022

Playwright's Center 2023–2025

Poetry Society of America 2026–2029

Poets and Patrons, Inc. 2030

Point Foundation Scholarship 2031

Polish Music Center 2032

Population Fellows Program 2033

Prairie Schooner 2034–2037

Presbyterian Church (USA) 2038–2039

Presidential Management Intern Program 2040

Prevent Blindness America 2041

Princess Grace Foundation—USA 2042–2043

Proctor & Gamble 2044

Professional Land Surveyors of Colorado 2045–2047

Quincy Writer's Guild Annual Creative Writing Contest 2048

Radio Technical Commission for Aeronautics 2049

Radio-Television News Directors Foundation 2050–2051

Ragdale Foundation 2052–2053

Rand 2054–2055

Reach for the Education of Adults in the Chicago Area 2056

Reason Foundation 2057

Recording for the Blind 2058

The Reserve Officers Association of the United States 2059

Resources for the Future 2060

Rhode Island Society of Professional Land Surveyors 2061

Rhode Island State Council on the Arts 2062

The Rhodes Scholarship 2063

Robert Mondavi Winery 2064

Rocky Mountain Laboratory 2065

Rolling Stone Internships 2066

Roothbert Fund 2067

Roswell Park Cancer Institute 2068–2069

Rotary Foundation Scholarships for International Understanding 2070

Royal Society 2071

Ruder-Finn 2072

Ruritan National Foundation 2073

Ruth Eleanor and John Bamberger Memorial Foundation 2074

Rutherford Institute 2075

Sachs Foundation 2076–2077

St. John's College 2078

San Antonio Women's Celebration and Hall of Fame 2079–2080

San Francisco Foundation 2081–2087

Santa Barbara Foundation 2088–2092

Schering-Plough 2093–2094

Scholarship Foundation of St. Louis 2095

Scholarship Fund of Game Wardens of Vietnam Association, Inc. 2096

Screen Actors Guild Foundation 2097–2099

Scripps Howard Foundation Scholarship 2100

Semi-Conductor Research Corporation 2101–2104

Seminole Tribe of Florida 2105

Seneca Nation Higher Education 2106

Sense of Smell Institute 2107

Service Employees International Union Fund 2108

Sigma Nu Educational Foundation, Inc. 2109

Sigma Theta Tau International 2110

Sigma XI—The Scientific Research Society 2111–2112

Skidmore Owings & Merrill Foundation, Inc. 2113–2117

Slocum-Lunz Foundation, Inc. 2118

Slovene National Benefit Society Scholarship Awards 2119

Smithsonian American Art Museum and Renwick Gallery 2120–2124

Smithsonian Astrophysical Observatory 2125

Smithsonian Center for Latino Initiatives (SCLI) 2126–2127

Smithsonian Center for Materials Research and Education (SCMRE) 2128–2136

Smithsonian Environmental Research Center 2137

Smithsonian Institution, Cooper-Hewitt Museum 2138–2142

Smithsonian Institution, Horticulture Services Division 2143–2144

Smithsonian Institute, National Air and Space Museum (NASM) 2145–2147

Smithsonian Institute, National Museum of American History 2148

Smithsonian Institute, National Museum of the American Indian (NMAI) 2149

Smithsonian Institute, National Museum of Natural History (NMNH) 2150–2152

Smithsonian Institute, Office of Fellowships and Grants 2153–2164

Smithsonian Tropical Research Institute 2165–2168

Social Science Research Council 2169–2180

Society for Exploration Geophysicists 2181–2185

Society for Imaging Science and Technology 2186

Society for Neuroscience 2187–2194

Society for Organic Petrology 2195

Society for Research in Child Development 2196–2198

Society for Technical Communication 2214

Society for the Protection of Ancient Buildings 2215

Society for the Scientific Study of Sexuality 2216

Society of Actuaries 2217–2218

Society of Architectural Historians (SAH) 2219–2222

Society of Biological Psychiatry 2223

Society of Daughters of the United States Army Scholarships 2224

Society of Economic Geologists 2225–2228

Society of Environmental Graphic Design 2229

Society of Hispanic Professional Engineers Foundation 2230

Society of Illustrators Scholarships 2231

Society of Manufacturing Engineering Education Foundation 2232

Society of Mining, Metallurgy, and Exploration 2233

Society of Motion Picture and Television Engineers 2234–2235

Society of Naval Architects and Marine Engineers 2236

Society of Nuclear Medicine 2237–2239

Society of Sedimentary Geology 2199–2213

Society of the First Infantry Division Foundation Scholarship 2240

Society of Toxicology 2241–2268

Society of Vacuum Coaters Foundation 2269–2270

Society of Vertebrate Paleontology 2271–2277

Society of Women Engineers 2278–2284

Soil and Water Conservation Society of America 2285

Soil Science Society of America 2286–2287

Solomon R. Guggenheim Foundation 2288–2291

Sons of Italy Foundation 2292–2293

Sony Music Entertainment, Inc. 2294–2295

Sordoni Foundation 2296

Soroptimist International of the Americas 2297–2298

Sotheby's 2299

South Dakota State Department of Military and Veteran Affairs 2300

Southwest Review Awards 2301–2303

The Sow's Ear Poetry Review 2304

Space Foundation 2305

Stanley Drama Award 2306

State Farm Insurance 2307

Stimson Center 2308

Story Line Press 2309–2310

Sudden Infant Death Syndrome Alliance 2311

Surfrider Foundation 2312

Swann Foundation 2313

Synod of the Trinity 2314–2315

Tailhook Association Educational Foundation 2316

Talbots Women's Scholarship Fund 2317

APPENDICES

APPENDIX A
Graduate and Professional School Timetable for Scholarship and Admission Preparation

APPENDIX B
Scholarship & Application List Form

APPENDIX C
Scholarship & Program Application Tracking Chart

APPENDIX D
Financial Assistance Analysis Chart

APPENDIX E
Résumés for Graduate and Professional School Applicants
1. Current Undergraduate
2. Current Graduate or Professional School Student
3. Nonstudent Applicant

APPENDIX F
Query Letters
A. Current Undergraduate
B. Nonstudent Applicant
C. Current Graduate or Professional School Student

APPENDIX G
Request Postcards
A. Current Undergraduate
B. Nonstudent Applicant
C. Current Graduate or Professional School Student
D. Return Receipt Postcard

APPENDIX H
Recommendation Letters
A. Sample Form
B. Current Undergraduate
C. Current Graduate or Professional School Student
D. Nonstudent Applicant
E. Recommendation Letter Tracker

GRADUATE AND PROFESSIONAL SCHOOL TIMETABLE FOR SCHOLARSHIP AND ADMISSION PREPARATION

WHEN AND WHAT TO DO
Two Years Before Starting a Program
- Request information about graduate/professional school programs.
- Evaluate current course load and/or transcript of completed undergraduate years.
- Evaluate financial situation and whether you can attend school full- or part-time.
- Determine if there are any courses that you must take for admission.
- Sign up to take required admissions tests.
- Research for graduate/professional school scholarship opportunities, apply to as many as possible.
- Enter writing competitions that are not scholarship awards but rather cash awards.
- Work in a volunteer position in your community, if not doing so already.
- Update your résumé of all the activities you participate in, both in and out of school.
- Start working on personal statement concerning goals.

One Year Before Starting, During Summer
- Some graduate and medical school applications must be submitted.
- Take admissions tests.
- Personal statement should be in a finished form.

September
- Update your course plan.
- Retake admissions tests, if necessary.
- Take required achievement tests.
- Request graduate/professional school applications.
- Begin application procedure.
- Request required recommendation letters.
- Request and apply to any scholarships for which you qualify.
- Update your résumé.

Fall
- Some graduate and professional school applications due.
- Continuing applying to scholarships.

December
- Some graduate and professional schools begin interviewing students.
- Continue applying to scholarships.

January & February
- Begin submitting graduate/professional school applications.
- Continue applying to scholarships.
- Some graduate and professional schools interview and/or recruit students.
- Submit Free Application for Federal Student Aid (FAFSA) and any other required forms.

March & April
- Graduate and professional schools send out acceptances.
- Schools send out financial aid packages.
- Begin receiving scholarship award notifications.

Summer
- Submit copies of outside scholarship award letters to Financial Aid Office of the school you will be attending.
- Some professional schools begin classes in the summer.
- Possibly receive some scholarship award notification.
- Continue applying for scholarships during graduate/professional school years.

SCHOLARSHIP &
APPLICATION LIST FORM

SCHOLARSHIP/PROGRAM LIST FORM

Schlorship/Grant/Program and Addresses	Date Info. Requested	Date Info. Received	Date Applied	Comments

SCHOLARSHIP & PROGRAM
APPLICATION TRACKING CHART

SCHOLARSHIP / PROGRAM APPLICATION TRACKING CHART

Name & Address of Scholarship	Date Application Requested	Application Received & Opened	Required Materials				Recommendation Letters				Transcript				Application			Results & Comments
			Essay	Letters Rec.	Transcript	Essay Written	Written by	Date Sent	Date Ackn.		Date Req.	Date Sent	Date Ackn.		Date Sent	Date Ackn.		

FINANCIAL ASSISTANCE
ANALYSIS CHART

FINANCIAL ASSISTANCE ANALYSIS CHART

NAME OF SCHOOL			
ESTIMATED COSTS:			
Tuition & Fees			
Room & Board/Apt.			
Books & Supplies			
Travel			
Personal Expenses			
1. TOTAL BUDGET			
Family's Contribution			
Student's Contribution			
Student's Assets			
2. PERSONAL RESOURCES			
TYPES OF ASSISTANCE			
School Grants			
School Scholarships			
School Fellowships			
State Assistance			
Outside Awards			
3. TOTAL GIFT AID			
4. ASSISTANTSHIPS			
5. TOTAL FREE AID			
(No Loans = 3 + 4)			
Subsidized Stafford			
Unsubsidized Stafford			
Perkins Loans			
Other Loans			
6. TOTAL LOAN PACKAGE			
7. TOTAL FINANCIAL PKGE.			
(Add Lines 5 + 6)			

Note: If after reviewing your financial aid award package you realize that you cannot afford what has been determined to be your contribution, contact your school's financial aid office to see if additional funds can be found. Circumstances change and so can financial aid packages.

RÉSUMÉS FOR GRADUATE AND PROFESSIONAL SCHOOL APPLICANTS

SAMPLE UNDERGRADUATE RÉSUMÉ

JANE SMITH

Attending: Trinity University
Classification: Senior

Major: Journalism
Age: 21

MAILING ADDRESSES

PERMANENT	SCHOOL	SCHOOL'S ADDRESS
1234 Indian Valley	P.O. Box 5678	Trinity University
Portsmouth, VA 23702	Trinity Station	715 Stadium Drive
(804) 555–1111	San Antonio, TX 78284	San Antonio, TX 78212
SS# 123-45-6789	(210) 555–9876	(210) 736–7011
jsmith1234@yahoo.com	jsmith5678@trinity.edu	http://www.trinity.edu

LEADERSHIP POSITIONS AND OFFICES HELD

ACTIVITY	OFFICE	CLASSIFICATION	HOURS/MONTH
Langley Elementary Tutoring Prog.	Tutor	Freshman	4 hrs/month
Univ. Med. Center Hosp.	Volunteer Coordinator	Freshman	5 hrs/month
Student Newspaper	Photographer	Sophomore	10 hrs/month
Women in Communication (WIC)	Parliamentarian	Sophomore	4 hrs/month
WIC Food Drive	Creator/Coordinator	Junior	4 hrs/6 wks
Student Government	Class President	Senior	4 hrs/month

MEMBERSHIPS AND OTHER ACTIVITIES

ACTIVITY	CLASSIFICATION	HOURS/MONTH
Rape Crisis Center Volunteer	Freshman	3 hrs/month
Library Volunteer	Sophomore	3 hrs/month
Adult Literacy Program Volunteer	Junior	2 hrs/month
Habitat for Humanity Volunteer	Senior	10 hrs/day/1 week

WORK/STUDY EMPLOYMENT

EMPLOYMENT	CLASSIFICATION	HOURS/WEEK
Campus Tour Guide	Freshman	10 hrs/week
Student Assistant	Sophomore	12 hrs/week
Library Clerk	Junior	12 hrs/week
Typing Clerk	Senior	15 hrs/week

HONORS AND AWARDS

ENTITY/ACTIVITY/HONOR	TYPE OF AWARD	YEAR
Hampton Roads Memorial Foundation	Scholarship	Freshman
National Merit Scholarship	Academic	Freshman
National Writing Award	Essay	Sophomore
Faraday Memorial Foundation	Scholarship	Sophomore
Women in Communications	Scholarship/Academic Achievement	Junior
McNair Scholar	Academic Achievement	Senior

DAVID SANCHEZ

North Carolina State University
2nd Year Graduate Student

MAILING ADDRESSES

PERMANENT	SCHOOL	SCHOOL'S ADDRESS
1234 Indian Valley	P.O. Box 12345	NC State University
San Antonio, TX 78240	Raleigh, NC 27690	Box 7001
(756) 555–1111	(919) 555–4680	Raleigh, NC 27695
SS# 789-56-4321	dsanchez2@ncsu.edu	http://www.ncsu.edu

LEADERSHIP POSITIONS AND OFFICES HELD

ACTIVITY	OFFICE	CLASSIFICATION	HOURS/MONTH
Graduate Student Government	Representative	1st Year	2 hrs/month
Physiology Journal Club	Refreshment Comm Chair	2nd Year	1 hr/month

MEMBERSHIPS AND OTHER ACTIVITIES

CLUB/ACTIVITY	CLASSIFICATION	HOURS/MONTH
Big Brother/Big Sister	1st & 2nd Year	4 hrs/month
NCSU Ambassador	1st Year	2 hrs/month
Physiology Department Journal Club	1st & 2nd Year	4 hrs/month

EMPLOYMENT

EMPLOYMENT	CLASSIFICATION	HOURS/MONTH
Dorm Resident	1st & 2nd Year	40 hrs/month
Laboratory Instructor	1st Year	20 hrs/month
Research Assistant	2nd Year	48 hrs/month

HONORS AND AWARDS

AWARD	TYPE	YEAR
American MENSA Education & Research Foundation	Essay Competition	1st Year
National Science Foundation	Academic Fellowship	1st & 2nd Year
Philanthropic Foundation Scholarship	Merit/Financial Need	2nd Year

SAMPLE NONSTUDENT RÉSUMÉ

JANICE WASHINGTON
1234 Indian Valley
San Antonio, TX 78240
(756) 555–1111
SS# 789-56-4321

EDUCATION

University of Texas, Austin, 1978–1982, BBA, business major, marketing minor.

EMPLOYMENT

Citicorp, Advertising Account Manager, 1992–2002.
Southwest Airlines, Advertising Department, 1987–1992.
Via Metropolitan Transit, Advertising Department, 1984–1987.
Mendelsohn, Advertising, International Accounts Intern, 1983–1984.
Income Tax Processor, H & R Block, 1982–1983.

LEADERSHIP POSITIONS AND OFFICES HELD

Oakland First Baptist Church, Sunday School Teacher, 1996–1999, 4 hrs/month.
PeeWee League Baseball, Transportation Coordinator, 1998–2000, 12 hrs/month.
PeeWee League Baseball, Coach, 2001–2002, 16 hrs/month.
Stoffer Elementary School, Recreation Coordinator, 1996–1997, 1 hr/month.

MEMBERSHIPS AND OTHER ACTIVITIES

Adult Literacy Instructor, Morrow Public Library, 1996–1998, 4 hrs/month.
Habitat for Humanity Volunteer, 1998–1999, 8 hrs/6 days only.
Homeless Shelter Volunteer, 1999, 3 hrs/month.
Oakland First Baptist Church Choir, 1988–present, 8 hrs/month.
Toastmasters, 1997–present, 2 hrs/month.

HONORS AND AWARDS

Children's Story Hour Contest Winner, Short Story, 1998.
City-Wide Writer's Contest Winner, Essay, 1997.
National Writing Award, Essay, 1996.
Oakland First Baptist Church, Deacon of the Year, 1998.

PERSONAL STATEMENT

"Never, never, never quit." Winston Churchill. That quote sums up my entire life. Whatever situation I've faced, I take an aggressive, optimistic, and focused stance. I'm a forty-five year old female who's an obsessive, workaholic, chocoholic, insomniac who tries to relax by reading and who tries to counter my sweet tooth by using Equal. Not one to take the easy way out of any predicament, I've chosen a more difficult, meandering path to follow. Life has occasionally provided me with lemons, and I chose to make a lemon meringue pie. Lemonade might have been easier to make, but the pie is tastier and more filling. I'll savor life to it's fullest and never, never, never take no for an answer.

QUERY LETTERS

Ms. Jane Smith
P.O. Box 5678, Trinity Station
San Antonio, TX 78294

Date

Scholarship Foundation Name
Street Address
City, State   Zip Code

Dear Committee Member:

I am currently an undergraduate senior at Trinity University in San Antonio, TX. (If a specific age, sex, or ethnicity is required, state it). I am majoring in journalism and communication and would like to work in an area of print journalism. I have a 3.2 GPA (on a 4.0 scale) overall and a 3.85 GPA in my major.

I would like to request an application and more information about your program (or scholarship). Thank you for your assistance.

Sincerely,

(Signature)

Jane Smith

Ms. Janice Washington
905 Meadow Lane
Oakland, IN 47660

Date

College/Foundation/Company Name
Street Address
City, State   Zip Code

Dear Committee Member:

I am not currently in school but graduated from the University of Texas in Austin in 1982. I earned a B.B.A., with a major in business and a minor in marketing.

I am currently working at Citicorp, but am planning to return to work on an M.B.A. I have worked in various areas of marketing and advertising and would like to slightly change my emphasis in business. I would one day like to own my own advertising firm.

I would like to request an application and more information about your program (or scholarship). Thank you for your assistance.

Sincerely,

(Signature)

Janice Washington

Mr. David Sanchez
P.O. Box 12345
Raleigh, NC 27690

Date

College/Foundation/Company Name
Street Address
City, State   Zip Code

Dear Committee Member:

I am currently a second-year graduate student. I attend North Carolina State University in Raleigh, NC. I am majoring in physiology and would like to work in medical research. I have a 3.5 GPA (on a 4.0 scale) overall and a 3.85 GPA in my major.

I would like to request an application and more information about your scholarship. Thank you for your assistance.

Sincerely,

(Signature)

David Sanchez

REQUEST POSTCARDS

Dear Sir/Madam:

I'm currently an undergraduate and am applying to a graduate/professional school program. I'm interested in receiving:

_____ **Grad/Professional School Brochure**

_____ **Grad/Professional School Application**

_____ **Financial Aid Information**

_____ **Financial Aid Application**

_____ **Internship Information**

_____ **Internship Application**

_____ **Scholarship Information**

_____ **Scholarship Application**

Thank you for your assistance.

Sincerely,

Dear Sir/Madam:

I'm currently an undergraduate and am applying to a graduate/professional school program. I'm interested in receiving:

_____ **Grad/Professional School Brochure**

_____ **Grad/Professional School Application**

_____ **Financial Aid Information**

_____ **Financial Aid Application**

_____ **Internship Information**

_____ **Internship Application**

_____ **Scholarship Information**

_____ **Scholarship Application**

Thank you for your assistance.

Sincerely,

Dear Sir/Madam:

I'm currently an undergraduate and am applying to a graduate/professional school program. I'm interested in receiving:

_____ **Grad/Professional School Brochure**

_____ **Grad/Professional School Application**

_____ **Financial Aid Information**

_____ **Financial Aid Application**

_____ **Internship Information**

_____ **Internship Application**

_____ **Scholarship Information**

_____ **Scholarship Application**

Thank you for your assistance.

Sincerely,

Dear Sir/Madam:

I'm currently an undergraduate and am applying to a graduate/professional school program. I'm interested in receiving:

_____ **Grad/Professional School Brochure**

_____ **Grad/Professional School Application**

_____ **Financial Aid Information**

_____ **Financial Aid Application**

_____ **Internship Information**

_____ **Internship Application**

_____ **Scholarship Information**

_____ **Scholarship Application**

Thank you for your assistance.

Sincerely,

To whom it may concern:

I'm not currently in college but am applying to a graduate/professional school. Please send the following:

___ **College Brochure**
___ **College Application**
___ **Financial Aid Information**
___ **Financial Aid Application**
___ **Internship Information**
___ **Internship Application**
___ **Scholarship Information**
___ **Scholarship Application**
___ **Competition Guidelines**

Thank you for your assistance.
Sincerely,

To whom it may concern:

I'm not currently in college but am applying to a graduate/professional school. Please send the following:

___ **College Brochure**
___ **College Application**
___ **Financial Aid Information**
___ **Financial Aid Application**
___ **Internship Information**
___ **Internship Application**
___ **Scholarship Information**
___ **Scholarship Application**
___ **Competition Guidelines**

Thank you for your assistance.
Sincerely,

To whom it may concern:

I'm not currently in college but am applying to a graduate/professional school. Please send the following:

___ **College Brochure**
___ **College Application**
___ **Financial Aid Information**
___ **Financial Aid Application**
___ **Internship Information**
___ **Internship Application**
___ **Scholarship Information**
___ **Scholarship Application**
___ **Competition Guidelines**

Thank you for your assistance.
Sincerely,

To whom it may concern:

I'm not currently in college but am applying to a graduate/professional school. Please send the following:

___ **College Brochure**
___ **College Application**
___ **Financial Aid Information**
___ **Financial Aid Application**
___ **Internship Information**
___ **Internship Application**
___ **Scholarship Information**
___ **Scholarship Application**
___ **Competition Guidelines**

Thank you for your assistance.
Sincerely,

Dear Sir/Madam:

I'm a _____ year graduate student at _____

Please send me the following information:

_____ **Grad/Professional School Brochure**

_____ **Grad/Professional School Application**

_____ **Financial Aid Information**

_____ **Financial Aid Application**

_____ **Internship Information**

_____ **Internship Application**

_____ **Scholarship Information**

_____ **Scholarship Application**

Thank you for your assistance.
Sincerely,

Dear Sir/Madam:

I'm a _____ year graduate student at _____

Please send me the following information:

_____ **Grad/Professional School Brochure**

_____ **Grad/Professional School Application**

_____ **Financial Aid Information**

_____ **Financial Aid Application**

_____ **Internship Information**

_____ **Internship Application**

_____ **Scholarship Information**

_____ **Scholarship Application**

Thank you for your assistance.
Sincerely,

Dear Sir/Madam:

I'm a _____ year graduate student at _____

Please send me the following information:

_____ **Grad/Professional School Brochure**

_____ **Grad/Professional School Application**

_____ **Financial Aid Information**

_____ **Financial Aid Application**

_____ **Internship Information**

_____ **Internship Application**

_____ **Scholarship Information**

_____ **Scholarship Application**

Thank you for your assistance.
Sincerely,

Dear Sir/Madam:

I'm a _____ year graduate student at _____

Please send me the following information:

_____ **Grad/Professional School Brochure**

_____ **Grad/Professional School Application**

_____ **Financial Aid Information**

_____ **Financial Aid Application**

_____ **Internship Information**

_____ **Internship Application**

_____ **Scholarship Information**

_____ **Scholarship Application**

Thank you for your assistance.
Sincerely,

The material you submitted:

   Competition Entry

   Scholarship/Internship Application

   Application

   Transcript

   Other Form

   Financial Aid Information

   Recommendation Letter

   from _____

arrived safely in our office on _____

Sincerely,

The material you submitted:

   Competition Entry

   Scholarship/Internship Application

   Application

   Transcript

   Other Form

   Financial Aid Information

   Recommendation Letter

   from _____

arrived safely in our office on _____

Sincerely,

The material you submitted:

   Competition Entry

   Scholarship/Internship Application

   Application

   Transcript

   Other Form

   Financial Aid Information

   Recommendation Letter

   from _____

arrived safely in our office on _____

Sincerely,

The material you submitted:

   Competition Entry

   Scholarship/Internship Application

   Application

   Transcript

   Other Form

   Financial Aid Information

   Recommendation Letter

   from _____

arrived safely in our office on _____

Sincerely,

RECOMMENDATION LETTERS

RECOMMENDATION LETTER SAMPLE FORM

Name of Applicant _____

               (LAST)   (FIRST)   (MIDDLE)

Home Address _____

_____

_____

School now attending _____

School Address _____

_____

Student's SS #: ____ - ____ - _____   **How long have you known the applicant?** _____

In what capacity have you known the applicant? _____

_____

> **Please comment on any of the following characteristics: motivation, responsibility, integrity, honesty, diligence, per-severance, cooperation, leadership, emotional stability, common sense, judgment, appearance, and/or academic ability. Specific examples are helpful. Please use only one side of each page. Additional pages may be added.**

Name: _____

Address: _____

_____

Signature: _____   **Date:** _____

Name of Applicant   Smith   Jane

(LAST)   (FIRST)   (MIDDLE)

Home Address   1234 Indian Valley

Portsmouth, VA   23702

School now attending   Trinity University   715 Stadium Drive   San Antonio, TX 78212

School Address   P.O. Box 5678, Trinity Station, San Antonio, TX   78784   (210) 555–9876

Student's SS #:   123-45-6789   **How long have you known the applicant?** 2 years

In what capacity have you known the applicant?   Neighbor and friend

---

Please comment on any of the following characteristics: motivation, responsibility, integrity, honesty, diligence, per-severance, cooperation, leadership, emotional stability, common sense, judgment, appearance, and/or academic ability. Specific examples are helpful. Please use only one side of each page. Additional pages may be added.

Dear Selection Committee:

I am writing on behalf of Jane Smith, who is applying for your scholarship which she will use for educational purposes. I worked with Jane as her supervisor in the local Adult Literacy Program. She was always prepared and willing to stay long after the class was over whenever a student needed extra attention.

Jane is an extraordinarily talented and caring young woman. She has always worked during her years in college and every summer between terms. As the fourth of six children, she is concerned about helping her parents cope with her expenses.

Jane has been working very hard at her classes and has been getting good grades for her efforts. I believe her hope is to further her education and obtain a master's degree, teach for a few years, then return to obtain a doctorate in educational leadership.

I hope you will consider Jane for this scholarship. I know that she will accomplish her goals and go on to serve as a role model for other up-and-coming teachers.

Name:

Address:

Signature: **Date:**

Name of Applicant   Sanchez   David   T.
                         _____   _____   _____
                              (LAST)   **(FIRST)**   **(MIDDLE)**

Home Address   5869 Marble Falls
_____

                    Anywhere, VA 23712
_____

_____

School now attending   North Carolina State University
_____

School Address   Box 7001, NCSU Station   Raleigh, NC 27695   (919) 555–9876
_____

_____

Student's SS #:   987-65-5432   **How long have you known the applicant?** 1 year

In what capacity have you known the applicant?   Dean of Minority Student Affairs
_____

_____

> **Please comment on any of the following characteristics: motivation, responsibility, integrity, honesty, diligence, per-**
> **severance, cooperation, leadership, emotional stability, common sense, judgment, appearance, and/or academic**
> **ability. Specific examples are helpful. Please use only one side of each page. Additional pages may be added.**

Dear Selection Committee:

I am writing to enthusiastically support David Sanchez's application to your scholarship program. I have come to know David well this year through the various activities in which the students participate, activities that, for the most part, I supervise. I find him to be personable, mature, bright, and full of energy. I believe David has lots of leadership potential and would benefit immeasurably from your support.

David recently returned to his home town during spring break to recruit qualified minority students for the university. He officially represented the school's Admissions Office in this capacity and did a fine job. He scheduled and organized the visits to numerous junior high and high schools in his home town and surrounding communities and talked about his experiences at NC State. His interpersonal skills enabled him to work effectively with all the various individuals involved in this demanding process.

All in all, David Sanchez is an outstanding individual. His organizational and analytical skills are excellent. His interpersonal skills are highly developed, and his ability to conduct himself in difficult situations is admirable. I hope you will assist in his development and training by helping him with a scholarship. He will repay you many times over with his contributions to the community.

Name: _____

Address: _____

_____

Signature: _____   **Date:** _____

Name of Applicant   Washington   Janice   LaManda

(LAST)   (FIRST)   (MIDDLE)

Home Address   905 Meadow Lane

Oakland City, IN 47660

School now attending   none

School Address

Student's SS #:   456-12-7893   **How long have you known the applicant?** 3 years

In what capacity have you known the applicant?   Employment Supervisor

> **Please comment on any of the following characteristics: motivation, responsibility, integrity, honesty, diligence, perseverance, cooperation, leadership, emotional stability, common sense, judgment, appearance, and/or academic ability. Specific examples are helpful. Please use only one side of each page. Additional pages may be added.**

I am writing to recommend Janice LaManda Washington to your MBA program. I have come to know Janice well these past three years as her supervisor at Citicorp. We have worked together on several large accounts. She always demonstrated insight and vision when posed with a challenge.

I remember when she convinced me to join her in building a house for Habitat for Humanity. She not only was there every day but also was able to convince a caterer to feed every one of the volunteers. She then worked to find a way to help the new homeowners in financing new furniture for the additional rooms. Her enthusiasm was contagious. We couldn't wait until the next project.

I have always been impressed with her unflinching desire to learn and implement what she's learned. I know that Janice will be a welcome addition in your program and will add a new dimension to the class.

Janice will be a wonderful example to the younger students. Though she might be there to learn, she will also be the teacher. The school will never regret accepting Janice into the next class. She will grow to be a great alumni who will never hesitate to repay all that she receives from your program.

Name:

Address:

Signature: **Date:**

RECOMMENDATION LETTER TRACKER

Use one Tracker for each person writing recommendation letters for you.

Name: _____

Address: _____

_____

Phone number: (___ **)** _____

Scholarship letter was written for	Date Requested	Type of Form Supplied	Résumé Supplied	Envelope Supplied	Postcard Supplied	Postcard Received